Clinical Interpretation
of the WAIS–III
and WMS–III

PHOTO 1. David Wechsler circa 1942. Photo courtesy of the New York University Library Archives. Used with Permission.

Clinical Interpretation
of the WAIS–III
and WMS–III

Edited by

David S. Tulsky

Kessler Medical Rehabilitation Research
and Educational Corporation
West Orange, New Jersey, USA

Donald H. Saklofske

University of Saskatchewan
Saskatoon, Canada

Gordon J. Chelune

The Cleveland Clinic Foundation
Cleveland, Ohio, USA

Robert K. Heaton

University of California, San Diego
La Jolla, California, USA

Robert J. Ivnik

Mayo Clinic
Rochester, Minnesota, USA

Robert Bornstein

The Ohio State University
Columbus, Ohio, USA

Aurelio Prifitera

The Psychological Corporation
San Antonio, Texas, USA

Mark F. Ledbetter

Trinity Clinical Associates
San Antonio, Texas, USA

ACADEMIC PRESS

An imprint of Elsevier Science

Amsterdam   Boston   London   New York   Oxford   Paris
San Diego   San Francisco   Singapore   Sydney   Tokyo

Requests for permission to make copies of any part of the work should be mailed to:
Permissions Department, Academic Press, 6277 Sea Harbor Drive,
Orlando, Florida 32887–6777

Academic Press
An imprint of Elsevier Science.
525 B Street, Suite 1900, San Diego, California 92101–4495, USA
http://www.academicpress.com

Academic Press
84 Theobalds Road, London WC1X 8RR, UK
http://www.academicpress.com

Library of Congress Catalog Card Number: 2002109947

International Standard Book Number: 0–12–703570–2

PRINTED IN THE UNITED STATES OF AMERICA
03 04 05 06 07 MM 9 8 7 6 5 4 3 2 1

Contents

Introduction xvii

Preface xxi

Contributors xxvii

PART 1

The Evolution of the Wechsler Scales

1 *Historical Overview of Intelligence and Memory:*
Factors Influencing the Wechsler Scales

David S. Tulsky, Donald H. Saklofske, and Joseph H. Ricker

Introduction 7

The early 1800s 8

Galton and Cattell 10

Spearman's Two-Factor Theory and Thorndike's
  Multifactorial Theory 16

Binet and Simon: The Measurement of
  Intelligence in Children 17

Yerkes and intelligence tests in the Military 20

The Wechsler Scales of Intelligence   23
History of Memory Assessment   29
    The Concept of Memory   30
    Clinical Assessment of Memory   31

Discussion   34
References   36

2   *Revising a Standard: An Evaluation of the Origin and Development of the WAIS-III*

David S. Tulsky, Donald H. Saklofske, and Jianjun Zhu

Why a Revision Was Necessary   44
Changing Test Scores and Norms   45
Revised Test Structure   46
Goals for the WAIS-III Revision   46
Deciding What to Change   47
Changes and Reactions   49
Emphasis on the Factor Scores   51
Events Leading up to the WAIS-III   54
Wechsler's Unrealized Goal: Measurement
    of Nonintellective Factors   56
Description of Subtests   58
    Vocabulary   58
    Information   61
    Similarities   62
    Comprehension   62
    Block Design   65
    Picture Completion   67
    Matrix Reasoning   68
    Picture Arrangement   70
    Object Assembly   72
    Letter Number Sequencing   75
    Digit Span   76
    Arithmetic   81
    Digit Symbol   82
    Symbol Search   84

Summary   84
References   85

3 *The Wechsler Memory Scale, Third Edition:*
A New Perspective

David S. Tulsky, Nancy D. Chiaravalloti,
Barton W. Palmer, and Gordon J. Chelune

Historical Factors Leading to the Development of
    the Wechsler Memory Scale   95
The Wechsler Memory Scale   97
The Publication of the WMS-R   101
Development of the WMS-III   104
Description of WMS-III   107
Structure of WMS-III Index and Subtests Scores   108
    The Auditory Immediate and Delayed Index Scores   108
    Verbal Paired Associates   112
    The Visual Immediate and Visual Delayed Indexes   114
    Working Memory Index   122
    The Auditory Recognition Delayed Index   126
    General and Immediate Memory   130

Support for the WMS-III Structure   131
Conclusions   132
References   133

PART 2

Reducing Variance When Interpreting
WAIS-III and WMS-III Scores: Introduction
to Chapters 4–8

4 *Assessment of Cognitive Functioning with the*
WAIS-III and WMS-III: Development
of a Six-Factor Model

David S. Tulsky, Robert J. Ivnik, Larry R. Price, and Charles Wilkins

Contemporary Models of Cognitive Functioning   149
Factor-Analytic Studies of the Wechsler Scales   150
Joint WAIS-III/WMS-III Factor-Analytic Studies   153
The Development of New Norms for a Six-Factor
    Model of Cognitive Functioning   155
Development of New Index Scores   161
    Psychometric Properties   161
    Reliability Coefficients   172

Conclusion   176
References   176

5   *Demographic Effects and Use of Demographically Corrected Norms with the WAIS-III and WMS-III*

Robert K. Heaton, Michael J. Taylor, and Jennifer Manly

Demographic Influences and Normative Corrections   183
Sensitivity of Demographically Corrected WAIS/WMS
    Factor Scores to Neurocognitive Impairment   185
Subject Samples   186
Developing Demographically Corrected T-Scores   187
Age Effects   190
Education Effects   190
    Sex Effects   196
    Ethnicity Effects   198

Sensitivity of WAIS–WMS-Corrected Scores to
    Neuropsychiatric Disorders   198
Conclusions   207
References   209

6   *WAIS-III WMS-III Discrepancy Analysis: Six-Factor Model Index Discrepancy Base Rates, Implications, and a Preliminary Consideration of Utility*

Keith A. Hawkins and David S. Tulsky

Introduction   211
Understanding Difference Scores:
    The Logic of Discrepancy Analysis   212

Clinical Meaning versus Statistical Significance 212
Psychometric Foundations 213
Descriptive versus Inferential Uses of
     Discrepancy Data 213

Discrepancy Data Provided in This Chapter 215
WAIS-III WMS-III Discrepancy Data Provided
     with the Tests 215
Generating Six-Factor Model Index Score
     Discrepancy Base-Rates 216
How Do These Base Rate Differ from Those
     Already Available? 217
Unidirectional (1-Tail) versus Bidirectional (2-Tail)
     Discrepancy Base Rates 218

Understanding Discrepancy Base Rates:
     Clinically Informative Trends 219
The Rarity of a Discrepancy Varies across Comparison Pairs 219
Discrepancies Vary in Size across Intellectual Levels 220
The Direction of Discrepancies Varies with Intelligence Level 225

Which Index Contrasts Are Most Likely to
     Be Clinically Useful? 229
Sensitivity to Brain Dysfunction *per se* 230

Conventional Contrasts: Within-WAIS-III 235
Conventional Contrasts: Within WMS-III 236
Working Memory versus Memory Indexes 236
Auditory versus Visual Index 237

WAIS-III–WMS-III Contrasts 237
Traditional IQ-Memory Comparisons 237
VCI as "Best Estimate" of Premorbid Status 238
Discrepancies between the POI and WMS-III Scores 238
Index-to-Index Discrepancies 239

Does Discrepancy Analysis Work? 240
Challenge 1: Brain Impairment 240
Challenge 2: Subtest Variability 247
Challenge 3: Reliability 249
Challenge 4: False Negatives for Co-occuring
     Intellectual–Memory Declines 249
Challenge 5: Sensitivity 250
Challenge 6: False Positives with High-IQ Subjects 252
Challenge 7: False Negatives with Low-IQ Subjects 252
Challenge 8: Demographics 254

Concluding Comments 256
References 271

7 Diagnostic Validity

Glenn E. Smith, Jane H. Cerhan, and Robert J. Ivnik

Overview 273
Group versus Individual Statistics 274
Asking the Right Question 279
Diagnostic Validity Indices 280
    Odds Ratios 280
Diagnostic Validity Indices and the WAIS-III and WMS-III 283
From Diagnostic Validity to Clinical Utility 285
Understanding Base Rates 287
    Likelihood Ratios 290

Likelihood Ratios and WAIS-III and WMS-III Indices 293
Clinical Application 298
References 300

8 Use of the WAIS-III and WMS-III in the Context of Serial Assessments: Interpreting Reliable and Meaningful Change

Tara T. Lineweaver and Gordon J. Chelune

Serial Assessment and Evidence-Based Health Care 304
Case Examples 306
Factors Affecting Test–Retest Performances 307
    Bias 308
    Error 312

Methods for Assessing Reliable Change 314
    Reliable Change Indices 315
    Standardized Regression-Based Change Scores 317

Meaningful and Reliable Test–Retest Change on the WAIS-III and WMS-III 318
Application of the SRB Approach 323
Using Demographically Corrected Scores in the Context of Serial Assessments 326
Impact of Serial Assessments on Base Rates of Discrepancy Scores 327

Summary and Conclusions 332
References 334

PART 3

Dealing with "curveballs" when using the WAIS-III and WMS-III: The interpretation of an unstandardized administration

9 *Assessment of the Non-Native English Speaker: Assimilating History and Research Findings to Guide Clinical Practice*

Josette G. Harris, David S. Tulsky, and Maria T. Schultheis

Introduction 343
Ellis Island and the Assessment of the Immigrant 345
Assessment of Military Recruits During World War 1 362
Advances, Current Approaches and Opinions 365
The Relationship between Acculturation
  and Cognitive Functioning 369
The Relation between Acculturation
  and WAIS-III and WMS-III Scores 370
Discussion 378
References 387

10 *Accuracy of WAIS-III—WMS-III Joint Factor Scores When One or More Subtests Is Omitted or an Alternate Subtest Is Employed*

Barton W. Palmer, Michael J. Taylor, and Robert K. Heaton

Background 392
Method 396
  Sample 396
  Conversion of Scores to a Common Metric 397
  Evaluation of Estimation Accuracy 397

Determining the Accuracy of Prorated Estimates
of Full Scale IQ and General Memory Index   399
Determining the Accuracy of Subtest Substitution-Based
Estimates of the Factor Scores   400
Impact of Subject Characteristics on The Accuracy
of Estimates: 400
Examining Sensitivity and Specificity   401

Results   402
Organization of the Results Tables and Text   402
Summary of Results by Factor Score   403
Predicting Full Scale IQ and General Memory Index
from the Subtests within the WAIS-III and
WMS-III Factor Scores   413
Sensitivity and Specificity: Selected Examples   415

Discussion   416
Verbal Comprehension   419
Perceptual Organization   419
Processing Speed   420
Working Memory   420
Auditory Memory factor   420
Visual Memory factor   421
Full Scale IQ and General Memory Index   422
Caveats and Limitations   422

Conclusions   424
References   425

11 *Accommodating Clients with Disabilities on the WAIS-III and WMS*

Jeffery P. Braden

The Challenge of Clients with Disabilities   451
Decision-Making Framework for Accommodations   455
Construct-Irrelevant Variance   455
Construct Underrepresentation   456
Representing the Construct of Intelligence   457
Deleting Subtests When Estimating Intelligence   458
A Model for Accommodation Decision
Making in Assessment   459
Legal Issues in Accommodations   459
How Should Accommodations Affect Test Scores?   461
Summary   465

Research on Accommodations	466
Deafness	466
Visual Disabilities	467
Motor Impairments	471
Learning Disabilities	472
Neuropsychological Assessment and Accommodations	476
Research on Clinicians with Disabilities	478
Conclusions	479
Practices to Promote	481
Practices to Avoid	482
References	483

PART 4

Training Others to Administer the WAIS-III and WMS-III: A Guide to Practical Issues

12 The WAIS-III and WMS-III: Practical Issues and Frequently Asked Questions

Laura H. Lacritz and C. M. Cullum

Introduction	491
Why Use the WAIS-III and WMS-III If You Already Have the WAIS-R and WMS-R?	492
Administration	495
Teaching the Basics	495
Introduction of Tests and Establishing and Maintaining Rapport	496
Testing the Impaired Patient	498
Repeating Instructions/Items	499
When and How to Query	502
Testing the Limits	503

Practical Issues with WAIS-III Subtests   505
    Vocabulary   505
    Similarities   506
    Arithmetic   507
    Information   508
    Comprehension   508
    Digit Span and Letter–Number Sequencing   509
    Picture Completion   510
    Digit-Symbol and Coding   511
    Block Design   511
    Matrix Reasoning   512
    Picture Arrangement   513
    Symbol Search   513
    Object Assembly (optional)   514

Practical Issues with the WMS-III   514
    Logical Memory I and II   514
    Verbal Paired Associates I and II   516
    Faces I and II   516
    Family Pictures I and II   516
    Spatial Span   517
    Word List I and II (optional)   518
    Visual Reproduction I and II (optional)   518
    Information and Orientation (optional)   519
    Mental Control (optional)   519

Frequently Asked Questions   519
    FAQ Regarding WAIS-III/WMS-III Administration   519
    FAQ Regarding WAIS-III and WMS-III Scoring   521
    FAQs Regarding WAIS-III and WMS-III Interpretation   522

Conclusions   530
Acknowledgements   530
References   530

Appendix 1:   Pioneer's in the Assessment of Intelligence and Memory   533
              David S. Tulsky and Nancy D. Chiaravalloti

Appendix 2:   Reviews and Promotional Material for the
            Wechsler–Bellevue and Wechsler Memory Scale   579
              David S. Tulsky

Index   603

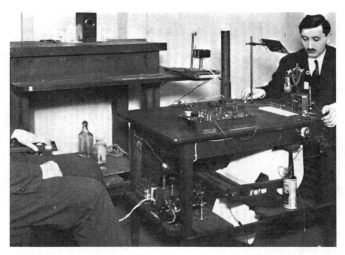

PHOTO 2.   David Wechsler in his late 20's. This photo shows David Wechsler at work on an apparatus that recorded galvanometric excursions for his dissertation research. This photo was obtained from Wechsler, D. (1974). *The Selected Papers of David Wechsler.* A. Edwards (Eds). New York: Academic Press. The article was originally published in American Journal of Psychology, 1928, 40, 600–606.

PHOTO 3.   David Wechsler using a "home made" polygraph apparatus. Dr. Wechsler interest in the measurement of galvanometric skin response lasted throughout his career. Photo courtesy of New York University School of Medicine

PHOTO 4.   David Wechsler circa 1960. Photo courtesy of the Bellevue Hospital Center. Used with Permission.

Introduction

In 1992 The Psychological Corporation formed an external advisory board, under the leadership of Nelson Butters, to consult with their WMS-III project development team. The role of this panel was later expanded to embrace the WAIS—III project as well. The members of this external panel came together because we hoped to have the opportunity to share our experience as clinicians and to improve the utility of the WAIS–III and WMS–III that would be used by the next generation of psychologists. For the four of us who remained on the advisory panel until the release of the WAIS—III and WMS—III in 1997, it quickly became apparent that changing widely accepted standards such as the WAIS-R and WMS-R to better reflect current scientific knowledge was complex and no easy matter.

The Wechsler tests are part of a lengthy tradition of psychological testing that can trace its roots back to the beginnings of modern psychology and are used by the majority of clinicians. However, over time, there have been advances in our knowledge about constructs like cognition, intelligence, memory, as well as our knowledge about clinical conditions, neurocognitive dysfunction and psychoeducational deficits. In view of such advances, it is unclear whether the same approaches to testing can continue to meet demands in the field. Today, psychologists expect and need more from their assessment instruments than was available at the time the WAIS–III and WMS–III revisions were being planned. We all would like to better use our test data in a time efficient manner for differential diagnosis, prediction and prognosis, and development of rehabilitation strategies in a variety of educational, neuropsychological, and rehabilitation settings. Those of us who joined the advisory panel did so with the hope of bringing issues that we believed are clinically important to the forefront of assessment practice.

While consulting on the advisory board, several of our suggestions were adopted. For instance, the WAIS–III and WMS–III were co-normed and the projects were linked; new visual memory subtests were created with an emphasis on those that appeared ecologically valid. The WAIS–III subtest scaled scores were age corrected rather than allowing this correction to occur at the more global index score level (as had been done with WAIS–R), and greater emphasis was placed on base rate data. Other suggestions such as incorporating demographic normative information, aggregating the best parts of the WAIS–III and WMS–III into a single battery to measure cognitive functioning, and development of normative information for use in serial testing were not adopted or included in the Technical Manual. While the final revisions of the time-honored Wechsler tests were an improvement over their predecessors, we nonetheless felt that there were questions left unanswered and clinical needs that were not yet addressed. Indeed, it was our persisting curiosity and lack of a sense of closure that sparked the post-publication research that forms much of the basis of this volume

As members of the advisory panel, we came to believe that there was a need to reformulate some of our original views to better improve the practice of assessment. In a planning meeting shortly after the official publication of the WAIS—III and WMS—III, we discussed a variety of ideas—looking a the joint factor structure of the WAIS—III and WMS—III, demographically adjusted norms, clinical utility of base rate data and discrepancy scores, use of tests in the context of serial assessments, etc. Unifying these individual ideas and interests was a common theme or desire in our clinical use of the WAIS–III and WMS–III – how can we better understand and account for sources of individual variation in cognitive performance? What follows is our attempt to address the lingering questions and concerns we had about the latest revisions of the Wechsler tests. To be sure, the latest Wechsler tests are not perfect instruments. However, tests are merely tools, and it is incumbent on the test user to employ these tools wisely and in an informed manner.

From the beginning, it was our desire that this book have broad clinical appeal and applicability to users of the Wechsler scales. While at times this volume may have a neuropsychological tone to its content, we believe that the issues examined are relevant to all clinicians practicing assessment and diagnosis. The material that follows goes beyond what was published in the WAIS–III and WMS–III Technical Manual and presents a view of how these two tests can be used in clinical practice. It is our hope that the material and procedures delineated in the following pages will foster more focused, efficient, and accurate uses of these instruments.

Gordon J. Chelune
Robert K. Heaton
Robert J. Ivnik
Robert Bornstein
October, 2002

PHOTO 5   David Wechsler giving a lecture at Hebrew University entitled: "Intelligence in a Changing World." Photo by David Harris and provided courtesy of Hebrew University. Used with Permission.

Preface

The genesis of this book can be traced back to 1995 when the standard-ization studies for the newest editions of the Wechsler Adult Intelligence Scale (WAIS-III) and Wechlser Memory Scale (WMS-III) were just getting underway. The WAIS–III/WMS–III scientific advisory board had raised questions around the general issue of how much change could be introduced into the new revisions of these tests. One specific question posed by the board members asked if the two tests could or should be published as a single battery, combining select subtests across the scales, rather than the two traditionally separate intelligence and memory tests. This raised the related question of whether such merging would allow the WAIS–III and WMS–III to continue to be recognized as the separate instruments that Wechsler had originally designed. Thus, the issue became one of how much weight should be given to preserving history versus how "radical" could the revision efforts afford to be? These questions weighed in heavily on the development team and, as will be described by Tulsky, Saklofske, & Zhu (Chapter 2), these questions were often difficult to answer. Frequently, compromises needed to be found.

At the same time, the advisory board was developing a view of assessment that would push the bounds of traditional diagnostic practices that had become commonplace in the field. Could new scores, norms, and methods help the clinician to reduce some previously unexplained variance when testing with the WAIS–III and WMS–III? What began to evolve was a model of assessment that placed emphasis on the index scores within a more comprehensive model of cognitive functioning that also included variables across both tests, demographically adjusted test scores, a more systematic and informed use of base rate data, and reliable change index scores when conducting serial testing. Furthermore, the team believed that these scores should be interpreted within the tenets of evidence-based psychological science and practice. Applying these new scores and methods would result in more informed practice and improve the diagnostic capabilities of the clinician.

It is from these discussions that the core idea for the book formed. Could new procedures in testing be introduced with the Wechsler scales that offered methods and procedures that differed from those offered in the separately published WAIS–III and WMS–III? Could additional normative information help reduce the variance in making clinical decisions? Our answer to these questions was a resounding *YES* and the second section of this book presents this new information.

The advisory team was also sensitive to the unusual conditions that frequently present to the clinician and wanted to provide additional empirical data to guide decisions or, at the very least, discuss what is commonly done in practice. Unusual circumstances, such as testing an individual whose first language isn't English or who has a disability, tend to increase the unexplained variance in a testing session and are thus, very pertinent to clinical practice. At other times, a subtest may be spoiled or can not be administered and the examiner may then substitute another subtest or prorate a score. Decision rules or at least guidelines are needed to assist the clinician in deciding what should be done in these situations. Before this publication, there had not been a systematically conducted study testing the impact on score variance when an optional subtest is used as a substitute score or the total score is based upon a prorating method. Another purpose of the book was to answer such relevant clinical questions. Additionally, we sought to provide practical suggestions for the most "frequently asked questions" and offer some essential tips for professionals who are in the position of training new examiners.

In preparing this book to address the above needs, it became increasingly important that clinicians understand and appreciate the rich history of the Wechsler scales, which is heavily derived from the earliest efforts of testing. These historical vignettes are fascinating, in their own right, and serve as critical background information against which to evaluate the new information that is presented in the remainder of the book. Though the themes and stimuli used in the original Wechsler scales were commonplace and mainly were derived from other tests and sources, the modifications that Wechsler made in the creation of his tests were truly "revolutionary". Wechsler's tests had the impact of changing the way practitioners would measure intellectual functioning and memory to this very day. For example, co-norming tasks and other tests into a single battery using a large and representative adult standardization sample had a profound effect on psychological testing practices, and may well be the most important factor that resulted in the ultimate success of the Wechsler scales. In order to appreciate the true value of co-norming the WAIS–III and WMS–III, it is important to remember how valuable it had been for David Wechsler to "co-norm" the common verbal and performance tests of the era.

The final decision to pursue this book was reinforced when it became apparent that the WAIS–III and WMS–III would not include these new ideas about testing and approaches to assessment discussed by the advisory team. In fact, we are convinced that this follow-up book to the WAIS–III—WMS–III Technical Manual is absolutely necessary to fulfill the goals and objectives of the advisory board. Active planning for the book began in the spring of 1999 when David Tulsky met with members of the advisory board in Chicago, IL to map out the content and identify potential contributors to this project. Shortly, thereafter, the project was officially launched and Don Saklofske was invited to play a pivotal role in writing and editing chapters. From its initial stages, a peer review process was established. Members of the editorial team served as reviewers, and each chapter was reviewed by a minimum of 2 members from the team. In practice, however, the peer review process was even more rigorous. Several outside reviewers were also solicited to assist us in the process because of their particular expertise in a specific content area. Hence, the majority of the chapters were read by 3 or 4 expert reviewers.

This book should serve the reader in several ways. It will provide a rich historical and contemporary perspective on the assessment of intelligence and memory with the WAIS-III and WMS-III. It will address the issues raised by the advisory panel members during the development of these tests and which have been further supported by the research literature and practice needs. The book is grounded in the scientist-practitioner model where empirically supported findings are then placed in the context of clinical practice but also informed by such practices. For example while the joint factor model describes 6 core factors made up of the WAIS-III and WMS-III subtests, secondary factors made up of immediate and delayed memory were also retained because of their diagnostic value in the assessment of clinical populations. We strove to ensure that good practice has been balanced with empirical evidence in presenting the new normative information in section two of this book. We trust that both researchers and practicing psychologists who employ the WAIS-III and WMS-III in their work will find this book of value.

David S. Tulsky, Ph.D.
Donald H. Saklofske, Ph.D.
October, 2002

PHOTO 6.   David Wechsler participating in one of the plenary sessions of the Board of Governors at Hebrew University in Jerusalem. Dr. Wechsler was an active member of the American Friends of the Hebrew University. Photo by David Harris and provided courtesy of Hebrew University. Used with Permission.

PHOTO 7.   David Wechsler is pictured at the right of this photo at an unveiling of a plaque at the Center for Human Development, Hebrew University, which was funded by the American Friends of the Hebrew University. The photo is by "Photo Emka" and provided courtesy of Hebrew University. Used with Permission.

Contributors

Numbers in parenthesis indicate page numbers on which authors contributions begin.

Jeffrey Braden (447), University of Wisconsin, Department of Educational Psychology, Madison, Wisconsin.

Jane H. Cerhan (271), The Mayo Clinic, Department of Psychiatry and Psychology, Rochester, Minnesota.

Gordon J. Chelune (93, 301), Cleveland Clinic Foundation, the Mellen Center, Cleveland, Ohio.

Nancy D. Chiaravalloti (93, 577), Kessler Medical Rehabilitation Research and Education Corporation, Neuroscience Laboratory, West Orange, New Jersey; and the University of Medicine and Dentistry of New Jersey–The New Jersey Medical School, Department of Physical Medicine and Rehabilitation, Newark, New Jersey.

C. Munro Cullum (487), University of Texas, Southwestern Medical Center at Dallas, Dallas, Texas.

Josette G. Harris (341), University of Colorado School of Medicine, Department of Psychiatry and Neurology, Denver, Colorado.

Keith A. Hawkins (209), Yale University School of Medicine, Department of Psychiatry, CMHC, New Haven, Connecticut.

Robert K. Heaton (179, 389), University of California San Diego, Department of Psychiatry, San Diego, California.

Robert J. Ivnik (145, 271), The Mayo Clinic, Department of Psychiatry and Psychology, Rochester, Minnesota.

Laura H. Lacritz (487), University of Texas Southwestern Medical Center at Dallas, Neuropsychology, Dallas, Texas.

Tara T. Linweaver (301), The Cleveland Clinic Foundation, Department of Psychiatry and Psychology, Cleveland, Ohio.

Jennifer Manly (179), GH Sergievsky Center, Columbia University, New York, New York.

Barton W. Palmer (93, 389), University of California San Diego, Department of Psychiatry, San Diego, California.

Larry R. Price (145), Southwest Texas State University, College of Education, San Marcos, Texas.

Joseph H. Ricker (7), University of Pittsburgh, Department of Physical Medicine and Rehabilitation, Pittsburgh, Pennsylavania.

Donald H. Saklofske (7, 43), University of Saskatchewan, Department of Educational Psychology and Special Education, Saskatoon, Saskatchewan, Canada.

Maria Schultheis (341), Kessler Medical Rehabilitation Research and Education Corporation, Rehabilitation Engineering, West Orange, New Jersey; and the University of Medicine and Dentistry of New Jersey – The New Jersey Medical School, Department of Physical Medicine and Rehabilitation, Newark, New Jersey.

Glenn E. Smith (271), The Mayo Clinic, Department of Psychiatry and Psychology, Rochester, Minnesota.

Michael J. Taylor (179, 389), University of California San Diego, San Diego, California.

David S. Tulsky (7, 43, 145, 209, 341, 577), Kessler Medical Rehabilitation Research and Education Corporation, Spinal Cord Injury Research Laboratory, West Orange, New Jersey; and the University of Medicine and Dentistry of New Jersey– the New Jersey Medical School, Department of Physical Medicine and Rehabilitation, West Orange, New Jersey.

Charles Wilkins (145), The Psychological Corporation, San Antonio, Texas.

Jianjun Zhu (43), The Psychological Corporation, San Antonio, Texas.

Dedication

This book is dedicated to:

Sindy, for her unwavering love, support, patience, and loyalty.
This book could not have been prepared without her encouragement.
D.S.T.

and

Vicki, my beautiful wife and colleague, and inspiration
D.H.S.

Acknowledgements

This book represents the contributions of many individuals. On behalf of the editorial team, we extend our profound appreciation to the following individuals and organizations.

First, and foremost, we thank the contributors for their hard work and significant contributions. Our goal was to attract talented and dedicated authors who would prepare a definitive chapter in their respective topic area. No better group could have assisted us in achieving this goal.

Second, we acknowledge The Psychological Corporation (TPC) for providing unrestricted access to the WAIS–III and WMS–III data sets. This allowed us to develop new normative information, perform new analyses, and reprint outdated items–important work that could not have been accomplished without the assistance of TPC. Larry Weiss, Ph.D. (Director of the Psychological Measurement Group) was particularly helpful with many aspects of this project.

Each chapter underwent rigorous peer-review and we often called upon individuals outside of our editorial team. Reviewers whose time and expertise helped ensure a quality text included Corwin Boake, Bruce Caplan, Nancy D. Chiaravalloti, Brigida Hernandez, Jennifer Manly, Scott R. Millis, Barton W. Palmer, Glenn Smith, and Susana Urbina. Other individuals who provided invaluable feedback, suggestions, and other assistance in key aspects of this project included John DeLuca, Glenn Larrabee, Carolann Murphy, Joseph Ricker, John Richardson, Maria Schultheis, John Wasserman, and Gary Zerbe.

Certain support personnel at Kessler Medical Rehabilitation Research and Education Corporation (KMRREC) also deserve recognition. Special thanks to Robb Mackes and Marita Delmonico at the KMRREC library, who spent many hours acquiring much needed, but often quite obscure, reference material, and Michael Platt, media specialist, for his professional assistance with photographs and images. Senior management at KMRREC provided vital support for this project. In particular, we thank Mitchell Rosenthal for his guidance and advice and Joel DeLisa for authorizing the space and support required to complete this project.

Libraries throughout the country assisted us in this project. Particularly helpful were the library staff and archivists at the following institutions who performed photographic research services and provided reproductions:

- *Ellis Island Immigration Museum.* George Tselos, Eric Byron, Janet Levine, Jeffrey Dosik, and Barry Moreno graciously let us search through their archives and reproduced important photographs of antique psychological tests.
- *Archives of the History of American Psychology.* David Baker, Dianna Ford, and other staff searched their archives for photographs.
- And *National Archivists, Stanford University Archives, New York University Archives, New York University School of Medicine, Teachers' College – Columbia University Archives, Hebrew University, University of Minnesota Archives, the City College of the City University of New York,* the *Judge Baker Foundation, Harvard University Archives, The University of Illinois at Chicago, Bellevue Hospital, Yale University Library,* and the *British Psychological Society.*
- Several publications allowed us to reprint material including the *Buros Institute of Mental Measurement, Cambridge University Press,* the *American Psychological Association, Scientific American, Clark University Press, Lippincott, Williams, & Wilkins, Pacific* Books, and the *New Yorker Magazine – cartoonbank.com.* Finally, two photo archive companies, Brown Brothers and Culver Photos, granted permission for us to reprint important pictures taken at Ellis Island in the early days of the 20th century.

Finally, we extend our appreciation to Brad Bielawski, Barbara Makinster, Trevor Dahl, Nikki Levy, and the rest of the staff at Academic Press for working so diligently on this project. Their expertise and dedication helped make this a reality. Mr. Bielawski deserves special mention because he never backed away from a challenge and persevered to ensure that we achieved our mutual goal—a state-of-the-art text on psychological testing.

David S. Tulsky, PhD
West Orange, NJ
February, 2003

PART 1

The Evolution of the
Wechsler Scales

This book provides new research on the WAIS-III and WMS-III that will enhance the clinical utility of these commonly used tests. Toward that end, new data, research, and models that inform the assessment of cognitive functioning with the WAIS-III and WMS-III will be provided. As a way to reach these goals, Chapters 1–3 in this section are devoted to an examination of the historical and foundational factors that impact on the measurement of intelligence and memory. Changes to the Wechsler scales have been incremental over the years and these historical factors should serve to create the framework from which the new advances proposed in this book can be made.

The emphasis on history evolved as this book was being prepared. One simple reason for its inclusion is that it is a fascinating story, and one that is on the verge of being forgotten. To tell this story, we have used pictures mixed with words whenever possible. We have attempted to give proper credit to some of these early pioneers in assessment who are well known but also those who may have been overlooked by history. Early psychometric practices had a profound influence on David Wechsler. Through an understanding of the history of intelligence testing, it becomes more evident how Wechsler advanced the field by integrating clinical assessment and test construction practices. Another rationale for these chapters, and perhaps the most important one, is based upon the realization that change in psychological tests and testing practices during the 20th century was fairly slow and incremental in nature. Psychometric testing developed rapidly during the first couple of decades of the 20th century, but there has not been a significant paradigm shift to force a major re-examination of psychological testing practices. Testing is similar in many ways to the techniques that were developed in the formative years of the last century. Thus, it is both striking how similar the Wechsler approach is to these early assessment methods and, how little has changed in the actual instruments and subtests.

At the same time, there have been some significant changes and improvements in testing practices over the years. Wechsler possessed the analytical skills and practical experience needed to recognize the utility of various tasks for assessing intelligence and for addressing the needs of practitioners. He applied an innovative approach to the assessment of intelligence and memory and this work lead to significant advances in the field. The resulting advances made by Wechsler include: 1) collecting new normative data thereby co-norming a variety of well know clinical tasks, 2) targeting the standardization efforts on adults instead of children, 3) creating the first extensively normed clinically relevant memory battery, 4) restructuring the concept of intelligence by aggregating performance and verbal tasks, and 5) introducing a deviation IQ methodology (instead of mental ages). Soon after the Wechsler Bellevue Intelligence Scale was published, it was becoming evident that Wechsler had indeed transformed psychology and psychological assessment practices.

Chapter 1 provides the reader with an understanding of the forces that impacted on David Wechsler, prior to and during the development of the original Wechsler tests. The focus of Chapters 2 and 3 is on the WAIS-III and WMS-III, respectively. In both of these chapters, we present insights into the test development projects, describe new areas of research on the tests, and present a detailed account of the origins of the tasks that comprise the scales. The reader will become aware of just how strong a resemblance our current practice of assessment is to the earliest mental tests that were developed in the beginning of the 20th century. It was the Wechsler Bellevue I and Wechsler Memory Scales that grouped together currently available tests and procedures and, most importantly, provided a cohesive and comprehensive 'state of the art' normative data base. At the time, these changes were monumental.

Looking at the modifications made in the last 25 years, the Wechsler scales have retained the majority of the original subtests. However, there has been some important and meaningful changes. Scores are now computed differently (e.g., a 4-factor model of score interpretation on the WAIS-III), new procedures have been added (e.g., procedures for delayed and recognition memory), and base rates of discrepancy scores have been included in the manuals. None of these changes, by themselves, are especially "revolutionary," but they are significant when taken together. The sum of these incremental advancements provided new ways to use the scales that David Wechsler had originally developed and which have gone through several transformations over the decades (i.e, WB-I, WAIS, WAIS-R, WAIS-III; WMS, WMS-R, WMS-III).

In many ways, Wechsler conducted one of the first and most important "co-norming projects" in which he gathered together tests for the WB I. Verbal and performance tasks had never been integrated into a single scale and Wechsler's model of assessment incorporated both domains of functioning. In the next section of the book, we will present our own modifications and changes to the current WAIS-III and WMS-III which include a joint six-factor model of cognitive functioning, the use of demographic normative information, the use of change scores, and a more informed use of base rates). The history provided here will provide a contextual backdrop for the second and third sections of this book.

As a final note, there are some important events in psychological testing that have been omitted or not emphasized. Information that seemed beyond the scope of the Wechsler scales was not presented here even though it may be of relevance to the history of intelligence testing. Additionally, major historical accounts that are presented later in the book were not included in these opening chapters so as to not risk redundancy. For instance, even though Howard A. Knox and his team of Public Health Service Officers at Ellis Island had a major influence on the development of several Performance-based tests in use today, this information is not provided in Chapter 1. Rather, the discussion of the Ellis Island program was placed in Chapter 9 where it could be presented along with the complex problem of testing the non-English speaker.

David S. Tulsky

Donald H. Saklofske

Historical Overview of Intelligence and Memory: Factors Influencing the Wechsler Scales

David S. Tulsky
*Kessler Medical Rehabilitation Research and Education Corporation
University of Medicine and Dentistry of New Jersey*

Donald H. Saklofske
*University of Saskatchewan
and*

Joseph Ricker
University of Pittsburgh

INTRODUCTION

Despite some evidence to suggest that "ability-like" differences were considered important in the selection criteria of civil service programs in China as early as 2200 B.C., the measurement and study of intelligence is a relatively recent event, one that began in that latter part of the 1800s. The scientific study of individual differences was initiated by Wilhelm Wundt, who formed the initial psychological laboratory in Germany, and Sir Frances Galton who established the anthropomorphic laboratory in London. Though in its infancy, several novel ideas about test development and measurement can be attributed to this period, which then stimulated an incredibly productive period in test development in the early 1900s. In fact, almost all the templates for modern-day assessment procedures originated during an incredibly short period (between 1905 and 1925). Details of the "explosion" in the testing movement will be described throughout this book in the context of how these pioneering efforts set the stage for modern-day assessment. For instance, the origins of the specific Wechsler subtests

　　　7

are reviewed in Chapter 2 (Tulsky, Saklofske, & Zhu, this volume) and Chapter 3 (Tulsky, Charavalloti, Palmer, & Chelune, this volume), and this information will not be repeated here. Additionally, the testing of immigrant and nonnative English speakers is reported in depth in Chapter 9 (Harris, Tulsky, & Schultheis, this volume), so descriptions of the pioneering programs at Ellis Island are saved for that chapter. This chapter describes some of the earliest work in testing and its profound and fascinating influence on David Wechsler.

THE EARLY 1800S

Though the foundation of Wilhelm Wundt's laboratory is the recognized milestone in the birth of psychological science, several prior events layed the foundations for the description and the measurement of intelligence in the Western world. Educators were struggling with notions akin to intelligence prior to the middle of the 1800s. In France in the early 1800s, for example, Itard developed educational programs (including the use of one of the first form boards) for the Wild Boy of Aveyron (Itard, 1801/1962). Séguin, who had studied with Itard, established experimental classrooms and developed puzzle "form boards" in his *methode medico-pedagogique* for the treatment and education of children with mental retardation (see Séguin, 1866; Sylvester, 1913; see Figure 1). These efforts mark some of the initial

FIGURE 1.   (A) The Seguin Form Board as modified by H. H. Goddard. (Courtesy of the Archives of the History of American Psychology). This form board was modeled after those used by Séguin (1866) in his treatment of individuals with mental retardation. (B) (Reprinted from Baldwin, B.T. (1911). The psychology of mental deficiency. *Popular Science Monthly, 79,* 82–93). The original caption of the latter picture reads:

approaches to the education of children and adults with mental retardation and are further suggestive of the increasing awareness of educators about individual differences in intelligence. This also marked a point where the distinction between the person with mental retardation (who was then referred to as a *sot* or *idiot*) was distinguished in a practical sense from the person with mental illness (who was referred to as *demented* or a *lunatic*). Though this distinction had been previously described by Esquirol in 1845 and Fitz-Herbert in 1534 (see Esquirol, 1845/1938; Fitz-Herbert, 1534/1793; Pintner, 1923), Séguin (1866) introduced new methods to classify individuals. The form board devices that were developed in the mid-to late 1800s purportedly allowed examiners to determine how quickly individuals could assemble the puzzle. Norsworthy (1906) was one of the first to use these devices in a battery of tests that she developed to assist in classifying and diagnosing children with mental retardation (Norsworthy, 1906; Pichot, 1948; Sylvester, 1913). Taken together, this work from the 19th and early 20th centuries offers a clear indication of the importance accorded to early descriptions of intelligence as a key individual-differences variable.

Another important event that provided the impetus for the scientific study of individual differences (and ultimately the formation of psychology as a discipline) came from the field of astronomy. Astronomer Friedrich Wilhelm Bessel observed that his colleagues and assistants in his observatory recorded different measurements of the same stimuli (i.e., the measurement of the distance from the earth to a star). Bessel's documentation of these differences in perception and judgment mark the first modern-day account of individual differences. Though the initial interpretation was to treat the differences as error, from an educational and applied

---

With this form board, another type of test used in America, the child is required to place the ten blocks as rapidly as possible in their respective places. The experimenter observes and notes superfluous and jerky movements, the adoption of a method or system. i.e., hunting the block to fit the space and vice versa, the ability to profit by experience when the test is repeated, the ability to increase a set pace of procedure, the degree of sustained attention, the span of motor control, and many other phases of mental expression. One bright boy of ten recently placed the blocks in their respective places in twelve seconds and a defective of nineteen required, after much urging and many vacillating and uncoordinated movements, seven minutes and eighteen seconds. Dr. Healy, psychopathologist for the Chicago Juvenile Court, has modified this type of form board by having the geometric forms a part of a puzzle picture which covers the face of the board. This test alone throws much light on the mind of a child and may be used as a diagnostic test for children of varying grades of arrested mental ability.

perspective, these key events led to the study of human intelligence and cognitive abilities. Though such efforts to describe and understand individual differences occurred well before the founding of psychology in the latter part of the 19th century, the concept of intelligence was not systematically advanced as a scientific tenet of individual differences prior to the creation of Wilhelm Wundt's psychological laboratory in Leipzig, Germany.

GALTON AND CATTELL

The 19th century witnessed some remarkable and creative attempts to capture the essence of human mentality through the use of various tests. In the 1870s, the earliest psychological laboratories were founded by Sir Francis Galton in London, England, and Wilhelm Wundt in Leipzig, Germany. It was also in Galton and Wundt's research that the origins of today's psychometric science and the study of intelligence can be found. However, it was Galton's influence on James McKeen Cattell (Sokal, 1987) also ensured that the mental testing movement was firmly established in North America.

FIGURE 2.   Sir Frances Galton (right) with his colleague, the famed statistician, Karl Pearson (left). Karl Pearson wrote Galton's biography, and this picture was originally taken for the biography. (Photo originally printed in K. Pearson (Ed.). *The Life, Letters and Labours of Frances Galton*, Volume 3, Cambridge University Press. Plate XXXVI. Used with permission.)

Many recognize Sir Frances Galton as the founding force behind contemporary intelligence testing. A cousin of Charles Darwin, Galton was influenced by his theory of evolution. Galton first discussed intelligence within an evolutionary model in his book *Hereditary Genius* (Galton, 1869). He proposed that individual differences in intelligence not only existed, but were "derived by inheritance, under exactly the same limitations as are the form and physical features of the whole organic world" (Galton, 1869, p. 1). While arguing that intelligence was inherited, Galton also "alluded to the presence in each individual of both a general ability and special abilities" (Matarazzo, 1972, p. 25). By using a series of tests, or "psychometric experiments" as he called them, one could measure an individuals' cognitive strengths and weaknesses (Galton, 1883). His views about intelligence and its causes were described in several key publications including *Hereditary Genius* (Galton, 1869), *an Inquiry into Human Faculty and Its Development* (Galton, 1883), and *Natural Inheritance* (Galton, 1889). The public also had the opportunity to see and experience these tests, first introduced at the International Exhibition held in London in 1884 (see Figure 3).

The tests developed by Galton reflected the influence of Wundt's psychophysical procedures, which were further adapted to measure various sensory and motor processes. As historians point out, these new instruments were used to define the growing new scientific discipline of psychology (see Sokal, Davis, & Merzbach, 1975, 1976) and to separate it from philosophy (Davis, 1970). The Brass Instrument era became the conventional name for the late 1800s because scores of laboratories had "an array of apparatus glinting with the brass fitting" (Davis, 1970, p. 604). Of great significance was the development and acceptance of a scientific methodology that could be applied to the systematic study of human behavior. Tests that were believed to tap intelligence, albeit mainly sensorimotor abilities, were used to objectively measure and quantify both physical and hypothesized mental variables.

Galton later met James McKeen Cattell, who was beginning to study individual differences in reaction time based upon psychomotor tasks he learned while studying for his doctorate with Wundt. Cattell has said that Galton was one of his primary influences, and credited him with instilling the scientific goal to measure the psychological differences between people (see Sokal, 1987). Cattell (1890) coined the term *mental test* and developed ten tasks (primarily dealing with psychophysics, reaction time, and sensory sensitivity) to measure the construct of intelligence. With Cattell's (1890) paper, psychometric science was established as the first attempt to systematically measure intelligence (see Figures 4 and 5).

FIGURE 3.   The Anthropometric Laboratory at the International Exhibition in London. (Photo courtesy of the Archives of the History of American Psychology. Photo was originally printed in K. Pearson (Ed.). *The Life, Letters and Labours of Frances Galton*, Volume 2, Cambridge University Press. Plate L. Used with permission.)

I.	Dynamometer Pressure
II.	Rate of movement
III.	Sensation-areas
IV.	Pressure causing pain
V.	Least noticeable difference in weight
VI.	Reaction-time for sound
VII.	Time for naming colours
VIII.	Bi-section of a 50 cm. Line
IX.	Judgment of 10 seconds time
X.	Number of letters remembered on once hearing.

Cattell, J.M. (1890) . Mental Tests and Measurements.

FIGURE 4.   Cattell's ten "mental" tests. (Cattell, J. M. (1890). Mental tests and measures).

Laboratory of Psychology of Columbia College,

PHYSICAL AND MENTAL TESTS.

Name..Date of Birth...

Birthplace..of father........................of mother..........................

Class..Profession of father...

Color of eyes.. of hair...

Perception of size...Memory for size......................................

Height...Weight...

Breathing capacity $\begin{cases} 1................................ \\ 2......................... \end{cases}$ Size of head......................Right handed?............

Strength of hand, right $\begin{cases} 1.............................. \\ 2................................. \end{cases}$ Left $\begin{cases} 1............................. \\ 2.............................. \end{cases}$

Keenness of sight, right eye..Left...

Keenness of hearing, right ear...............................Left ....

Reaction-time $\begin{cases} \quad 1 \qquad 2 \qquad 3 \qquad 4 \qquad 5 \qquad \text{Av.} \\ .... \\ .... \end{cases}$

After-images...

Color vision...Perception of pitch.....................................

Perception of weight 1.........2........3....... Sensation areas 1........2......3......4......5......

Sensitiveness to pain $\begin{cases} \text{right hand}........................ \\ \text{left hand}........................ \end{cases}$ Preference for color......................

  1   2   3

Perception of time...

Accuracy of movement.......................Rate of perception and movement......................

Memory..

Imagery...

Are you willing to repeat these tests at the end of the Sophomore and Senior

years?......................Do you wish to have a copy of these tests sent you?......................

Date of measurement...Recorded by..

FIGURE 5.   Original record form used at Columbia University (College). (Reprinted from Cattell & Farrand, 1896.)

Initially, the field responded positively to Cattell's new test, and in accepting a new faculty position at Columbia College, Cattell negotiated the implementation of his new test. By 1894, Cattell and his colleague, Livingston Farrand, were testing all of the students who were entering Columbia College and the Columbia School for the Mines (see Figure 5; Cattell & Farrand, 1896; Sokal, 1987). Cattell's tests were based upon the premise that intelligence would develop based upon how quickly an individual could process information. Those with faster ability to process information would ultimately learn more quickly and retain more knowledge. Cattell viewed processing speed as the central element of intelligence and believed that, by studying this variable, a person's intelligence could also be estimated. His views were widely accepted by the leaders of psychology at the time, as evidenced by the recommendations made by an American Psychological Association committee in 1895 (composed of James McKeen Cattell, Lightner Witmer, Joseph Jastrow, Edmund C. Sanford, and James Mark Baldwin) (Cattell & Farrand, 1896). Only James Mark Baldwin objected to Cattell's approach to testing, as the committee recommended Cattell's mental "anthropometry" as the preferred method of assessing abilities by a vast majority opinion (see Sokal, 1987).

Within a few years of this recommendation, however, questions were posed about the use of such testing practices. In 1899, Stella Sharp's dissertation questioned whether Cattell's original 10 tasks could measure complex cognitive functioning. She advocated for the French school of measurement advanced by Binet and Henri (1895) which was "of the complex type" (Sharp, 1899, p. 339). About this time, Jastrow had abandoned his anthropometric testing program and decided not to publish the results that he had obtained (see Sokal, 1987). Most important to the demise of anthopometric testing was the dissertation of Clark Wissler at Columbia. Wissler computed the correlations between the various tests in the Cattell–Farrand assessment scales and demonstrated, fairly conclusively, that the 10 tasks were neither correlated with one another, nor were they correlated with the academic grades of the students of Columbia University (Wissler, 1901). Rather, the largest correlations were observed between various measures of academic achievement (e.g., Latin and mathematics achievement correlated .55 versus strength of hand, and achievement, which correlated −.08). With the publication of this dissertation, strong evidence was provided that the Cattell measures lacked validity, as the data Cattell and Farrand had obtained did not yield empirical support for Cattell's theory. Sokal (1987) noted that Wissler's analysis "struck most psychologists as definitive, and with it, anthropometric testing, as a movement, died" (p. 38). Thus, as Sharp had written in 1899, the German and American experimental psychologists had mistaken simple sensory processes for intelligence, where more complex tasks were required.

Though these data would seem to be powerful evidence in convincing Cattell to give up his experiments testing intelligence (Sokal, 1987), there is some evidence that he brought this technology with him when he founded the Psychological Corporation in 1921 (Sokal, 1981). Figure 6 shows a test used for job selection in the early 1920s, at a later point of Cattell's career. The photo was a promotional piece for the Psychological Corporation, and the instrument was mostly used to assess driving and other occupational skills. A caption attributed to the photo reads:

> A corporation of scientists will test you before you get that position. For instance, you will be shown this color perimeter to ascertain your field of vision and the color zones of the retina of your eyes. This is one of the score of psychological tests that will be used by the group of twenty leading scientists now incorporated as the Psychological Corporation with offices in the Grand Central Terminal Building, New York City. Among the directors of the company are many college professors. The plan is to serve the employers in a matter of selection of people adapted to special positions. The work has grown out of the tests made by the Army and the set of psychological tests perfected and used at Columbia College.

FIGURE 6.   Early testing at the Psychological Corporation. This photo was likely a promotional piece used to generate business at The Psychological Corporation in the 1920s. From the caption that came with the photo, it appears that this apparatus was used to test individuals for employment as well as being part of a driving assessment battery that was used to test individuals requesting a drivers license. It is not known if this was used in Wechsler's test battery for individuals applying to become a taxi driver. (Wechsler, 1926).

Though Cattell's methodology and tests for measuring intelligence have proven to be a failure, contemporary research has shown that more complex measures of reaction time are positively associated with IQ (Deary, 2000; Deary & Stough, 1996). Even current measures like the WAIS-III and WISC-III have incorporated measures of information-processing speed in the batteries as integral measures. Wickett (1998) points out that we have "come full circle" (p. 251) as psychologists are paying more attention to reaction time (which was captured in Galton and Cattell's work more than 100 years ago). Whether or not some credit is owed to Cattell's founding work in reaction time, it is largely through his initial efforts that interest in testing and particularly intelligence testing found a foothold in both scientific and applied psychology.

SPEARMAN'S TWO-FACTOR THEORY AND THORNDIKE'S MULTIFACTORIAL THEORY

A short time after Cattell and Galton's pioneering work on the measurement of intelligence, debates about the definition and makeup of the construct were beginning to emerge. The first, and perhaps one of the greatest, of all the debates about the structure of intelligence ensued between Charles Spearman (a student of Wundt) and E. L. Thorndike (a student of Cattell). The initial data from the Cattell and Farrand (1896), Sharp, (1899) and Wissler (1901) studies, that specifically showed the lack of relationship between various simple "ability" tasks, were central to this debate.

Spearman argued for a general factor of intelligence, or g, that causes or determines one's ability on any specific intellectual task. Thus, general mental ability represents what is common to all of the tests that ostensibly tap intelligence. Based upon this hypothesis, it follows that if g exists, then a high correlation would be expected between all of the ability tasks, as well as a high correlation between these tasks and other external indicators of intelligence, such as academic performance.

Rather then viewing the data from studies by Cattell and others as a blow to his original hypothesis, Spearman (1904) advanced the idea that intelligence is best represented as two factors, a *general* factor, common to every ability, and an *specific* factor, unique or specific to one particular ability. He proposed that the general factor was representative of overall intellect. Specific factors reflected more narrow and specialized abilities, but still shared some variance with the general ability factor. He explained the results obtained by Sharp (1899) and Wissler (1901) as an artifact of examining specific abilities that are not necessarily correlated. Without stating it formally, he was suggesting that Cattell's tests measured specific abilities and not general intelligence.

E. L. Thorndike argued for quite a different theory, contending that abilities must be sorted into different classes or types of operations. He posited three major types of intelligence: (a) abstract or verbal intelligence, involving facility in the use of symbols; (b) practical or mechanical intelligence, involving facility in manipulating objects; and (c) social intelligence, involving facility in dealing with human beings. E. Thorndike, Lay, and Dean (1909) interpreted the research data as indicating that intelligence could not be combined as a "general" ability factor and further argued that Spearman's interpretation was so extravagant "that one is almost tempted to replace Spearman's statement by the equally extravagant one that there is 'nothing whatever common' to all mental functions, or to any half of them" (1909, p. 368).

This debate between Spearman and Thorndike continued for years with both proclaiming victory for their respective sides of the argument in each article (for an extensive review, see R. Thorndike, 1990). The "catchy" journal titles, such as "A friendly challenge to Professor Thorndike" (Spearman, 1922), "Measurement of Intelligence: I. The Present Status" (Thorndike, 1924), and "Agreement on Cooperation" (Spearman, 1925) were superceded by the strong statements contained within each paper. Interestingly, while many other developments have occurred in the cognitive sciences, this debate is just as relevant today as it was years ago. Recent journals and book chapters are filled with contemporary writings debating the relative importance of general and specific factors (Lezak, 1988; Neisser et al., 1996), the kinds of abilities that make up or best describe intelligence (e.g., Das & Naglieri, 2001; Horn & Cattell, 1966; Horn & Noll, 1997; Naglieri & Das, 1997; Sternberg et al, 2000), and the number of factors that make up intellectual functioning (see Carroll, 1993; Gardner, 1998; Guilford, 1967; Kaufman, 1994; Sattler, 2001; Wechsler, 1991).

BINET AND SIMON: THE MEASUREMENT OF INTELLIGENCE IN CHILDREN

Binet was interested in selecting tasks that could help the French school system identify children for special education instruction (Binet & Simon, 1905/1916a, 1908/1916b, 1911/1916c). Binet rejected Cattell's methodology

FIGURE 7.   Alfred Binet with his wife, Laure Balbiani Binet, and their two daughters, Madeleine and Alice (Courtesy of the Archives of the History of American Psychology, Theta Wolf Papers.)

for measuring intelligence exclusively with sensorimotor tasks (Matarazzo, 1972). Rather, he sought a different set of tasks that would require more complex mental reasoning, which he was also convinced was a global property of performance (see review by Thorndike, 1990). His keen observations of his own daughters, Madeleine and Alice, and the tasks that they were able to do, were instrumental in helping him develop his method of measuring intelligence (Binet, 1903). With the introduction of the 1905 and subsequent 1908 and 1911 Binet–Simon scales, the field of intelligence testing began its rapid ascent. The 1905 scale contained 30 tests that were hierarchically ordered for difficulty, ranging from sensory (following a moving object with one's eyes) and motor (grasping a small object which is touched) items to much more cognitively complex and demanding items, such as telling how two common objects are different or alike, defining abstract terms. The 1911 version extended the number of tests or "stunts."

Again, the tests varied in difficulty so that the easiest task would be correctly completed by most of the youngest children (e.g., normal 3-year-olds) and the hardest would be difficult for most normal adults. Kite was one of the first to translate the majority of Binet's work to English and H. H. Goddard was one of the first to use the scale in work with "feeble-minded" individuals at the Vineland Training School (Binet & Simon, 1916d; Zenderland, 1987; 1998).

The concept of mental age was introduced with the expanded 1908 scale. As Matarazzo (1972, p. 40) states, "thus was mankind introduced to the first objective and highly practical measure of intellectual functioning." But Binet also described this test as one part of a more comprehensive assessment and as a standardized method for obtaining a sample of a child's current intellectual functioning.

The scales were designed to ascertain "the general level of intelligence" while essentially dismissing the functional views that focused on separate facilities such as memory, attention, sense discrimination, and so on (see Terman, 1916, pp. 42–43). The scales provided a single score following Binet and Simon's break from the contemporary view that one should measure each domain separately and then sum the results. Instead, they tried to "triangulate the height of his tower without first getting the dimensions of the individual stones which made it up," based upon the assumption that the parts of cognitive functioning are interwoven and intertwined (Terman, 1916, p. 43). Binet and Simon were the first to publish mental age scores. They utilized the idea of age standards by determining empirically what average skills could be performed by a child in a certain age group and publishing these as "age norms" (Terman, 1916). In his Stanford Revision, Terman both extended the scale to assess adult intelligence and presented a new total score called the 'Intelligence Quotient (IQ)' This composite IQ score was determined by dividing mental age by chronological age (MA/CA) and was now thought to represent a child's score in relation to all children.

Although many people were involved in translating, adapting, and providing user manuals for the Binet-Simon scales (see Binet & Simon, 1916d; Herring, 1922; Kuhlmann, 1922; Melville, 1917; Yerkes, Bridges, & Hardwick, 1915; Terman, 1916), the Stanford adaptation (Stanford-Binet; Terman, 1916) became the standard. Even as this new test was starting to revolutionize methodology for performing cognitive assessments, another equally significant event in the history of intelligence testing was already occurring. Yerkes was mobilizing American psychologists to assist the U.S.

effort during World War I by performing intellectual assessments of all military recruits.

YERKES AND INTELLIGENCE TESTS IN THE MILITARY

On April 6, 1917, a group of experimental psychologists met in Cambridge, Massachusetts, to discuss how the new field of psychology could assist the armed forces. Immediately following the Cambridge meeting, Yerkes asked the American Psychological Association council to form a committee to determine how psychologist could develop psychological assessment measures for military selection (Yerkes, 1918, 1921). The heads of the various psychological committees included G. Stanley Hall, E. L. Thorndike, Raymond Dodge, S. I. Franz, G. M. Whipple, Carl E. Seashore, John B. Watson, and Robert M. Yerkes.[1] The more influential force was the subcommittee of psychologists who had expertise in testing, especially with the so-called feeble-minded individual, and included Walter V. Bingham, Henry H. Goddard, Thomas H.Haines, Lewis M. Terman, Frederick L. Wells, Guy M.Whipple, and Robert M. Yerkes (see Figure 12). This committee made great advances in the field of intelligence testing.

Another meeting of psychologists at the Training School in Vineland, New Jersey, in May, 1917, resulted in the recommendation to test all recruits entering the army. Goals included developing procedures to screen "intellectually incompetent" individuals (to exempt them from military service) and to identify those capable of performing "special tasks" (to give them more responsibility and greater duties) (Yerkes, 1921, p. 299). The committee sought to develop a group-administered intelligence test, and they relied heavily on the work of Arthur S. Otis, who had devised a system of group testing (Otis, 1918). Several tests, adaptations of the Binet tasks, had been modified for group administration (e.g., *Practical Judgment*, which was an adaptation of the Binet *Comprehension Question*, where the examinee checks the best of four answers to a comprehension question).

This general form, Exam Alpha, was heavily dependent upon the comprehension of verbal instructions, so the individual taking the exam had to be able to read. The committee also developed alternate forms of the test to

[1]James McKeen Cattell was initially appointed to the committee but resigned in October, 1917. Walter D. Scott and James R. Angell were added to the committee to take his place.

reduce the probability of coaching and other forms of cheating. These initial tests were first pilot tested on approximately 1000 individuals (by members of the committee), then further developed and recommended as a test that could be used for all military recruits who were literate. The Secretary General provided funding to pilot test the measures on some 4000 soldiers. The results of this initial testing phase provided some validity (e.g., the correlation was approximately 0.5 between the scores on the intellectual examination and their officer's ratings of the men), and helped the committee demonstrate their value to the armed services (Yerkes, 1921).

The acceptance of the testing was established and advanced at an astounding pace. By August 1917, the Surgeon General had appointed 24 psychologists as civilian examiners, 16 men as first lieutenants in the Sanitary Corps, and Robert M. Yerkes was appointed the leader of the team. Figure 8 shows recruits taking the test in a group setting, and Figure 9 depicts the scoring of the test protocols.

In addition to the general "Form Alpha" (which was the test that all literate recruits would take), the testing program included a "Form Beta" which, Yerkes explained, could be administered satisfactorily to men who were unfamiliar with English and/or who were illiterate (Yerkes, 1921). This test was, "in effect Alpha translated into pictorial form" (Yerkes, 1919a, p. 224). These subtests were administered without the verbal instructions and, it was generally believed that, non-English speakers could take Form Beta because the examiner demonstrated the task through pantomime and other nonverbal means.[2] Form Beta included such subtests as Picture Completion, where the examinee looked at a set of pictures, each with a critical part missing, and then drew the missing part and Digit Symbol, where the examinee associated a symbol with a number. These tasks are very similar to subtests on the current WAIS-III.

The army also developed an individual examination protocol, which was administered when the recruits failed the initial group examinations. These individualized scales were administered by selected examiners trained to test with the Yerkes–Bridges point scale, the Stanford–Binet, and the Pintner–Paterson scales. The final form of testing was an individually administered Performance Scale that could be used when individuals were not fluent in English. This performance scale included several tasks that served as early versions of subtests that remain popular today. For instance, the Performance

---

[2]The precursors to many of these procedures were developed by Howard Knox for testing immigrants at Ellis Island in the early 1900s. See chapter 9 (Harris, Tulsky, & Schultheis, this volume) for a description of testing the nonnative English speaker.

FIGURE 8.   Photo depicting the group administration of test Alpha during the World War I testing program. (From Yerkes, 1921. Photo courtesy of the National Archives. In the public domain.)

FIGURE 9.   The testing program generated nearly 2 million records that had to be scored. Here is the scene of scoring protocols at Camp Lee. October, 1917. (From Yerkes, 1921. Photo courtesy of the National Archives. In the public domain.)

Scale included the Manikin and Profile subtests (which are identical to items on the WAIS); a Cube Construction test (similar to Block Design on the WAIS); a Picture Arrangement test using the, then popular, "Foxy Grampa" cartoons to develop the stories, that required examinees to put the cards in sequential order (similar to the Picture Arrangment on the Wechsler Scales, see Figure 10); and a Memory for Designs (from the Binet tests and identical to Visual Reproduction used in the Wechsler Memory Scale). Photos of recruits being administered the Manikin test and shown in Figure 11 and a recruit being administered Cube Construction is shown in Figure 12.

The extent of the army testing program was staggering. From the initial test administered in September 1917 through the close of the program in January 1919, the U.S. Army had employed 115 psychologists, trained 255 enlisted personnel in the military school of psychologists, organized the testing effort in 35 training camps, and had tested 1,726,966 men (Yerkes, 1919b, 1921). This included 42,000 commissioned officers and 83,500 men who required individual examination in addition to the group examination. Though several historians have been critical of the ultimate success of the testing program (see Gould, 1981; Kevles, 1968; Samelson, 1977), and some interpretations of the data have been labeled racist, or at the very least, misguided (e.g., Brigham, 1923; Yerkes, 1923, 1921, 1941), this work clearly established psychology as a profession and a discipline. It also demonstrated the importance of intelligence and its measurement in describing human behavior and individual differences.

Yerkes later claimed that testing these 1.7 million recruits was an experience that was said to have "transformed him" (see Reed, 1987). In fact, the whole field of psychology was 'transformed' as a result of this effort. More relevant to this book, however, is that David Wechsler was one of the enlisted psychologists who had been assigned to perform individual examinations of the recruits who had failed the group testing. The influence of the military testing experience is evident in Wechsler's work.

THE WECHSLER SCALES OF INTELLIGENCE

David Wechsler was well trained in the issues and measurement of intellectual functioning. Both his formal training and clinical experiences in the army created the necessary basis for merging and integrating what would appear to be a set of diverse ideas about intelligence testing. At Columbia University, Wechsler studied with James McKeen Cattell, E. L. Thorndike, and R. S. Woodworth. Wechsler also valued the several months he spent

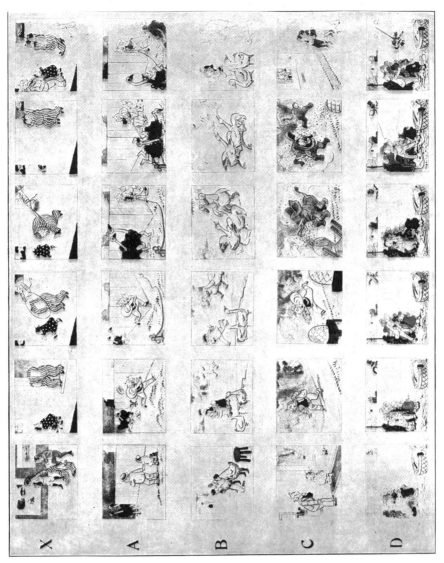

FIGURE 10.   The Foxy Grandpa Picture Arrangement test items that were part of the Army Performance Battery. This test is a precursor to the Picture Arrangement subtest. (From Yerkes, 1921. Photo courtesy of the National Archives. In the public domain.)

studying with Charles Spearman and Karl Pearson in London, and he took pride in being trained, first and foremost, as a psychometrician (Shackelford, 1976). Several of his mentors (Cattell, Thorndike, and Spearman) had strong beliefs about intelligence and intellectual testing. Wechsler believed that

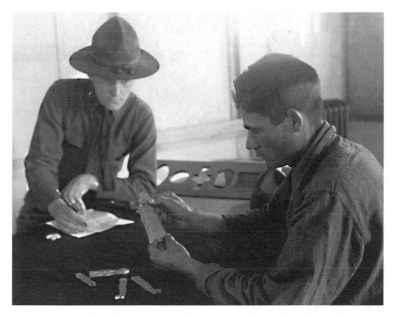

FIGURE 11.   Individual administration of the Army Performance Battery. The recruit in this photo is completing the Manikin test from the Pitner–Patterson Scale of Performance Tests (Pintner & Paterson, 1917). (Photo From Yerkes, 1921. Photo courtesy of the National Archives. In the public domain.)

FIGURE 12.   Individual administration of the Army Performance Battery. The recruit in this photo is completing the Cube Construction test (a precursor to the Block Design subtest). (From Yerkes, 1921. Photo courtesy of the National Archives. In the public domain.)

"they were all right" and that he should merge these different viewpoints together into a theory and framework that everyone could accept (Shackelford, 1976).

This goal was more difficult than it might sound, as Thorndike and Spearman were locked in one of the great debates in psychology about intelligence and its measurement. Spearman (1904, 1927) argued that intelligence was mediated by a general or *g* factor that was responsible for how one would perform on a variety of tasks. Thorndike interpreted the data differently, contending that intellect consisted of several distinct abilities (see E. Thorndike, Lay, Dean, 1909). Wechsler had the difficult task of bridging the gap between the perspectives of these two key figures of that era. Wechsler's earlier writing (1939) graciously paid tribute to the contributions of both of these great psychologists while not appearing to take "sides" in the debate. It should also be mentioned that Wechsler had very close ties with Cattell, who was his primary mentor as he completed his graduate degree. He was also one of Cattell's first employees at the Psychological Corporation. It is unclear just what influence Cattell had on Wechsler, as he is seldom referenced in his many papers and books, and his tests on reaction time were bypassed when Wechsler was developing his scale. Instead, Wechsler was more keen to pursue the kinds of tests that he had used when conducting individual examinations in the military. This included both the Performance measures as well as the tasks from the Stanford–Binet scales.

It was, in fact, from Wechsler's experience in the military that he began to determine which tasks could be used to measure intelligence and used them in his testing sessions. Drawing from his observations of the strengths, limitations, and even failures of previous efforts to assess intelligence, he further realized that intelligence could and should be measured by a diverse set of tasks, some verbal and some nonverbal or perceptual. Wechsler determined that a new adult intelligence test for adults should emphasize both verbal and nonverbal intelligence.

Wechsler began with a definition of intelligence as "the capacity of the individual to act purposefully, to think rationally, and to deal more effectively with his environment" (Wechsler, 1944, p. 3). In this definition of intelligence, he tried to include elements from other leading theorists and researchers of the time (e.g., Thorndike, Spearman, Thurstone cited in Henmon et al., 1921). Wechsler believed that a definition had to be accepted by one's peers first and foremost in order to gain more widespread acceptance (Shackelford, 1976).

Congruent with Spearman's ideas, Wechsler contended that global intelligence was important and meaningful as it measured the individual's overall behavior. Wechsler (1939) wrote that "Professor Spearman's generalized proof of the two factor theory of human abilities constitutes one of the greatest discoveries of psychology" (Wechsler, 1944, p. 6). At the same time, he was beginning to ally himself with the views of Thorndike. He believed intelligence was made up of specific abilities, each of which was important and different from the another. Hence, he emphasized the importance of sampling a variety of intellectual tasks:

> To the extent that tests are particular modes of communication, they may be regarded as different *languages*. These languages may be easier or harder for different subjects, but it cannot be assumed that one language is necessarily more valid than another. Intelligence can manifest itself in many forms, and an intelligence scale, to be effective as well as fair, must utilize as many different languages (tests) as possible. (Wechsler, 1974, p. 5).

Bridging the ideas of Spearman and Thorndike, Wechsler (1939) developed the Wechsler Bellevue Form I. This test provided a score reflecting general intelligence (Full-Scale IQ or FSIQ). However, it was at this point that Wechsler openly discussed the limitations of a reliance on only a general measure. In his 1939 book, he wrote that

> We may say that "g" is a psychomathematical quantity which measures the mind's capacity to do intellectual work . . . . Everybody will agree that the capacity to do intellectual work is an necessary and important sign of general intelligence. The question is whether it is the only important or paramount factor. In this writer's opinion it is not. (p. 8).

> It thus appears that the entity or quantity which we are able to measure by intelligence tests is not a simple quantity. Certainly it is not something which can be expressed by one single factor alone, say "g", whether you define it in its most general terms as mental energy, the ability to educe relations or merely as the intellectual factor. Intelligence is this and yet something more. (p. 11)

Hence, Wechsler placed an increasing emphasis on the measurement of two broad types of abilities, verbal and performance, that should be analyzed separately to make inferences about an individual's intellectual functioning. The FSIQ captured Spearman's idea about a general intelligence, which was characterized as a dominant *g* or general factor, showing Wechsler's agreement with parts of Spearman's theory that there was an overall intelligence. Contrary to Spearman's view, however, Wechsler placed more emphasis upon the importance of the specific factors and even printed tables so that examiners could review the differences between various types of abilities (e.g., Verbal–Performance discrepancies; Wechsler, 1944). Supporting this notion, Matarazzo (1972) points out that in Wechsler's fourth revision of his book (Wechsler, 1958), his beliefs had shifted away from Spearman's perspective, and he was giving more credence to interacting abilities.

This idea of measuring both verbal and performance intelligence as well as global intelligence revolutionized the field of cognitive testing. Wechsler (1944) wrote:

> The most obviously useful feature of the Wechsler–Bellevue scales is their division into a Verbal and Performance part. Its a priori value is that it makes a possible comparison between a subject's facility in using words and symbols and his ability to manipulate objects, and to perceive visual patterns. In practice this division is substantiated by differences between posited abilities and various occupational aptitudes. Clerical workers and teachers, in general, do much better on verbal tests, whereas manual workers and mechanics do better on performance. The correlations are sufficiently high to be of value in vocational guidance, particularly with adolescents of high school age. Apart from their possible relation to vocational aptitudes, differences between verbal and performance test scores, particularly when large, have a special interest for the clinician because such discrepancies are frequently associated with certain types of mental pathology. (p. 146)

Thorndike's influence can be seen in Wechsler's writing as he discusses the importance of each subtest and the ability of the examiner to perform profile analyses (e.g., examining differences between subtests). The Wechsler–Bellevue (and all of the derivatives) contained subtests designed to tap qualitatively different types of cognitive abilities, such as abstract and verbal reasoning (e.g., Similarities, Vocabulary), nonverbal reasoning (e.g., Block Design, Object Assembly), and practical intelligence (e.g., Picture Arrangement, Comprehension). Building a scale that was composed of multiple subtests, each of which could be grouped into different types of intelligence, would allow the scale to match Thorndike's ideas, while at the same time these abilities (which were correlated) could be aggregated into a single "global" score, which would allow the scale to coincide with Spearman's perspective. Through the structure of the Wechsler–Bellevue, David Wechsler found a way to "walk the fine line" between a global and a multifactorial model of intellectual functioning.

Although the Wechsler scales tap a number of different abilities, David Wechsler also believed that his scale was not a complete measure of intelligence and that there were some elements missing in his definition of intelligence. He reviewed correlational and factor analytic studies on the Wechsler scales and concluded that they did not account for the total percentage of overall variance of intelligence. From these data, he thought that there must be something else: a group of attributes that contributed to this unexplained variance. Wechsler believed that these attributes, or nonintellective factors as he called them, were not so much skills as they were traits and included such factors as planning and goal awareness, field dependence, persistence, and enthusiasm (Wechsler, 1950, 1975). He was quite convinced that these factors contribute to intelligent behavior and to a more complete understanding and measurement of the complexities of human behavior. Although he made several attempts at developing subtests to tap into these conative abilities, none of them reached such psychometric integrity that they could be included on any of the revised Wechsler scales. However, Wechsler again anticipated current research that is seeking to further explore the interface between personality and intelligence (e.g., Collis & Messick, 2001; Saklofske & Zeidner, 1995).

Chapter 2 (Tulsky, Saklofske, & Zhu, this volume) will more specifically describe the Wechsler tests (e.g., WAIS-R, WAIS-III) for assessing adult intelligence. We now turn our attention to some of the main historical antecedents related to the development of the Wechsler Memory Scales (WMS). This will be elaborated upon in Chapter 3 (Tulsky, Chiaravalloti, Palmer, & Chelune, this volume who provide a more detailed examination of the WMS-R and WMS-III).

HISTORY OF MEMORY ASSESSMENT

Concurrent with the efforts to define and measure intelligence were studies related to the conceptualization and assessment of human memory. Like the counterpart term *intelligence*, the term *memory* is quite broad, defined by different researchers and clinicians in different ways. In conventional use, the term memory often encompasses many aspects of cognition. The origins of the scientific study of memory are often attributed to the work of Hermann Ebbinghaus who (as described by Robert Wozniak, 1999) "not only brought learning and memory into the laboratory, he set a standard for careful scientific work in psychology that has rarely been surpassed" (p. 1).

Ebbinghaus (1885/1964) believed that one could study the phenomenon of memory by controlling for the degree of learning and then measuring retention rates. His work was innovative on many levels. He measured constructs that had barely been studied before and identified complex relationships between learning and memory. He employed a scientific and systematic approach and developed new methods of studying the phenomenon (e.g., learning to criterion). Finally, he developed new tasks (memory for nonsense stimuli) to be used as part of his methodology, and these tasks were used for years to come in experimental research. Most important, this seminal study set the experimental study of memory in motion. As Goodenough (1949) reported: "the success of Ebbinghaus's method led quickly to the devising of other 'memory tests'... [which] included tests for measuring the span of visual apprehension, memory for digits, for lists of words, for sentences, and so on" (p. 45). Before discussing the clinical applications of these methods, it is important to review some of the terms and concepts of memory.

The Concept of Memory

The concept of memory is difficult to summarize as there are so many components of the construct. Koriat and Goldsmith (1996) have described memory with two metaphors: *storehouse* memory and *correspondence* memory. These classifications represent two somewhat divergent ways of conceptualizing and evaluating memory. The storehouse metaphor, compares memory to a receptacle of inputs and requires a quantitative assessment of the items stored. The correspondence metaphor, however, treats memory as a perception of the past that emphasizes accuracy (over quantity) of the recollection.

The storehouse metaphor has been the focus of the experimental approach, most notably in the tradition begun by Ebbinghaus, and continues through to this day in cognitive psychology and cognitive neuroscience research. It has been criticized as focusing chiefly on explicit (i.e., episodic) recall of items from lists or narratives (Neisser, 1991). Assessment within this domain focuses on immediate and delayed recall (sometimes referred to as primary and secondary memory), retention, material-specific memory, and (more recently), cognitive concepts such as working memory, encoding, storage, and retrieval.

The correspondence metaphor essentially emphasizes so-called everyday memory, but this also is a poorly defined construct (Klatzky, 1991). Everyday memory research has been characterized by its attempt to understand "the sorts of things people do every day" (Neisser, 1991, p. 35), by its choice of topics having "obvious relevance to daily life" (Klatzky, 1991, p. 43), and in particular, by its emphasis on practical aspects of memory assessment. The types of memory emphasized by this framework include autobiographical memory, eyewitness recall testimony, memory for procedural actions, memory for familiar faces, and memory for places (see, Cohen, 1989; Davies & Logie, 1993; Gruneberg, Morris, & Sykes, 1991; Harris & Morris, 1984; Neisser & Winograd, 1988; Rubin, 1986; Winograd & Neisser, 1992).

Proponents of the experimental laboratory approach have emphasized experimental design and external validity of results. In general, every-day memory researchers recognize the contributions of controlled experiments, but also assert that rigid adherence to such methodology would neglect many meaningful (and clinically relevant) memory phenomena (Conway, 1991; Gruneberg & Morris, 1992). The current assessment of memory derives primarily from the storehouse approach to the study of memory. Such studies allowed for the quantification of operationally specified abilities gauged by overt task performance (Koriat & Goldsmith, 1996). The storehouse analogy of memory has received greater attention in clinical syndromes and diagnostic assessment, and will be the focus of this discussion.

Clinical Assessment of Memory

Memory has historically been an important focus of clinical neurology's examination of mental status (Davis & Forcyt, 1975), and much of the clinical assessment of memory follows from the European psychometric assessment and behavioral neurology traditions. Although the original intent of intelligence testing was to differentiate individuals with "inferior intelligence" from those of "normal intelligence," Binet recognized that there were different types of memory aptitude. For example, Binet and Simon (1905/1916a) noted that individuals have "certain aptitudes" for memory. They suggested that "some have a good auditory or musical memory, and a whole repertoire of songs; others have mechanical ability. If all were carefully examined, many examples of these partial aptitudes would probably be found" (Binet & Simon, 1905/1916a, p. 38–39). Binet and Simon (1905/1916a) also wrote that memory was distinct from intelligence, stating that

> at first glance, memory being a psychological phenomenon of capital import-ance, one would be tempted to give it a very conspicuous part in an examin-ation of intelligence. But memory is distinct from and independent of judgment. One may have good sense and lack memory. The reverse is also common. (p. 43)

Tests from the original Binet–Simon battery that specifically assessed memory functions included the Repetition of Three Figures, Repetition of Sentences of Fifteen Words, Exercise of Memory on Pictures, Drawing a Design from Memory, and Immediate Repetition of Figures. Shortly after, the Swiss neurologist Edouard Claparède published a list of 15 words (Claparède, 1919) designed to be a one-trial recall test. The words recalled from the list were also originally intended to be written down by patients. This word list was later adapted by Claparède's doctoral student, André Rey, and was the basis of the Rey Auditory Verbal Learning Test (Rey, 1964), which continues to enjoy widespread clinical and research use with a variety of clinical populations.

Historically (at least up until the early 1980s), U.S. neuropsychological assessment often has minimized the formal assessment of memory (Erickson & Scott, 1977). For example, the Halstead Reitan Neuropsychological Test Battery (Reitan & Wolfson, 1993), arguably one of the most widely used batteries of neuropsychometric tests, has only one memory index (Tactile Performance Test), and that is a measure of incidental learning (a cognitive function that is generally well preserved in most neurologic conditions).

The first published memory assessment battery was most likely that of Wells and Martin (1923). This battery was actually a collection of 26 items of verbal and visual immediate recall. No delayed recall conditions were offered. The battery did, however, offer normative data based on 50 healthy individuals (and clinical data based on 111 psychiatric patients). Questions have been raised as to the test's unique assessment of memory per se (see Erickson & Scott, 1977), as it was highly correlated with the IQ from the Stanford-Binet.

The Babcock Test of Mental Efficiency (Babcock & Levy, 1940) was introduced as a broad assessment of cognitive efficiency, but with particular attention paid to those cognitive functions known to decline with dementia and aging. This collection of tests did offer some advances (such as a paired associate learning paradigm), but it was quite time-consuming to administer, and was ultimately quite highly correlated with the overall IQ.

In a 1945 study (which predated the publication of the WMS later in that same year), Eysenck and Halstead (1945) demonstrated that existing clinical measures of memory were highly correlated with standardized IQ test scores. In what was, at the time, a comprehensive study of extant psychometric measures of memory, univariate intercorrelations were derived among the Raven's Progressive Matrices (Raven, 1938) and 15 memory tests (including 10 auditory memory tests and 5 visual memory tests). All of the memory tests were highly correlated with the Raven's Progressive Matrices ranging from 0.63 to 0.96. Factor analysis of all of the existing tests resulted in only one factor emerging that accounted for 74% of the variance in the model. This factor was labeled 'intelligence.'

Wechsler had been treating his memory scale separately from the Wechsler Bellevue Scale though there was probably some overlap in developing the scales. Wechsler had experience with memory tasks as he had used a verbal associative memory task that had been created by Woodworth and Wells (see Woodworth, 1932) for his masters' thesis on Korsakoff's patients (Wechsler, 1917). He was also familiar with the other memory test that were currently available (e.g., Binet subtests, Wells, Whipple, Babcock), and he writes that he officially began development some time around 1935. In fact, the overlap in development cycles have caused some to question whether the original plans would have linked the memory and IQ tasks (see Boake, 2002), but it is more likely that he treated them as separate as had Binet.

The Wechsler Memory Scale was published in 1945 and it was designed to provide a "rapid, simple, and practical memory examination (Wechsler, 1945, p. 3). Similar to his work on the Wechsler Bellevue Scale, the WMS also included several tasks with which Wechsler was familiar (this will be reviewed in Tulsky, Chiaravalotti, Palmer, & Chelune, Chapter 3, this volume). The WMS represented an approach that is somewhat comparable to that of IQ testing, namely the development of the 'memory quotient.' The WMS certainly represented an important advance in clinical assessment in that it provided for the assessment of information presented through multiple paradigms (i.e., narrative, paired associate learning, and graphic reproduction). However, WMS was not free from criticism. First, it assessed primarily immediate episodic recall. Second, the clinical reliance on the memory quotient most likely overportrayed the importance of cutoff scores, and downplayed (or ignored) the relevance of impairment within different domains of learning.

Cronholm and Mollander published a memory assessment battery also designed for clinical use (Cronholm & Mollander, 1957). The primary focus of the battery was to assess memory functioning in several research studies of individuals with cerebral palsy, brain injury, or who had undergone electroconvulsive therapy. This battery included three memory subtests: a 30-item verbal paired associate learning test, a 20-item visual recognition memory test, and a visual–verbal paired associate test in which six fictitious individuals were presented to the subject, and the subject was required to learn five pieces of information about each. This battery had both immediate and several-hour delayed recall conditions. Parallel forms were also available. In spite of its comprehensiveness for the time, this battery never experienced widespread use beyond the research studies for which it had been designed.

In order to address the shortcomings of the WMS, and to provide a test to be used outside of research studies, the Williams Scale for the Measurement of Memory (Williams, 1968) was developed. The Williams scale evaluated learning and retention in both verbal and nonverbal domains. It also had three parallel forms. The test–retest reliability of the battery was poor, however (White, Merrick, & Harbison, 1969), and many of the subtests were highly intercorrelated.

In 1987, the WMS was finally revised (WMS-R). Among other things, the revision featured an improved normative database and added delayed recall conditions. WMS-R added the differentiation of verbal and visual memory, but this distinction has been debated (see Smith, Malec, & Irnik, 1992).

Additional individual tests have been developed for the detailed assessment of specific forms of memory in their own right. For example, Buschke (Buschke, 1973; Buschke & Fuld, 1974) developed the selective reminding test in order to examine storage, retention, and other variables derived from the experimental verbal learning and cognitive neuropsychological literature. The California Verbal Learning Test (Delis, Kramer, Kaplan, & Ober, 1987), which is administered in a format similar to the Rey Auditory Verbal Learning Test, was also introduced as a memory task that evaluated multiple process components of learning, recall, and recognition. The Benton Visual Retention Test (Benton & Spreen, 1964) has seen wide use as a measure of recall for visual information. It has been suggested, however, that this test (as well as many tests of visual recall) tap into numerous other cognitive functions such as visuospatial abilities and graphomotor skills. Drawing from this rich historical tradition and the earlier publication of Wechsler's earlier tests of memory, the WMS-III was published in 1997. (This will be discussed in Chapter 3, this volume).

DISCUSSION

While the authors of this chapter have not intended it to be a comprehensive review of all of the historical developments of intelligence testing, it has been designed to provide some background to the factors that influenced David Wechsler as he was thinking about developing the his intelligence and memory tests. Interested readers should refer to insightful review papers that have been prepared by Peterson (1925), R. Thorndike (1990), Sokal (1987), and Boake (2002). The latter author, during his presentation of the historical events, has paid special tribute to the number of innovative professionals who have long been forgotten. Boake emphasizes that those pictured in a photo taken on the steps of the Vineland Institute in 1917 at a committee meeting to develop the psychological examination of recruits (see Figure 13) should be recognized by all psychologists. Toward that end, we have reproduced the picture here and have gone a step further and included a text box (see Appendix I) with brief biographical sketches and recommendations for further reading on some of the key figures in the early movement of psychology (e.g., William Healy, Rudolph Pintner, Lewis L. Thurstone, etc.) who have not been discussed in the current text. Their omission from the current chapter does not downplay their role in the history of testing. Students of psychology and testing should read and follow-up the stories of the key figures of early psychological testing as they were important contributors to the current measures of assessment used today. Finally, several stories have been saved for future sections where they are woven together with new research and advances so that readers can be aware of the historical antecedents when examining new data and changes guiding assessment practices.

FIGURE 13.   Committee on Psychological Examination of Recruits on the steps of the Vineland School in Vineland, New Jersey, on May 28, 1917. Front row (Left to right): Edgar A. Doll, Henry H. Goddard, Thomas H. Haines. Second Row: Frederick L. Wells, Guy M. Whipple, Robert M. Yerkes, Walter V. Bingham, Lewis M. Terman. From Robert Yerkes Papers, Manuscripts and Archives, Yale University Library.)

REFERENCES

Babcock, H., & Levy, L. (1940). *Test manual and directions: The revised examination for the measurement of efficiency of mental functioning.* Chicago: Stoetling Publishing.

Benton, A., & Spreen, O. (1964). Visual Memory Test performance in mentally deficient and brain damaged patients. *American Journal of Mental Deficiency, 68,* 630–633.

Binet, A. (1903). *L'étude expérimentale de l'intelligence* [Experimental study of intelligence]. Paris: C. Reinwald & Schleicher, 1903.

Binet, A., & Henri, V. (1895). La psychologie individuelle. *L'Annee psychologique, 2,* 411–465.

Binet, A., & Simon, T. (1916a). New methods for the diagnosis of the intellectual level of subnormals. In *The development of intelligence in children.* (E. S. Kite, Trans.). Baltimore: Williams & Wilkins Company. (Original work published 1905)

Binet, A., & Simon, T. (1916b). The development of intelligence in the child. In *The development of intelligence in children* (E. S. Kite, Trans.). Baltimore: Williams & Wilkins Company. (Original Work published 1908)

Binet, A., & Simon, T. (1916c). New investigation upon the measure of the intellectual level among school children. In *The development of intelligence in children.* (E. S. Kite, Trans.). Baltimore: Williams & Wilkins Company. (Original Work published 1911)

Binet, A., & Simon, T. (1916d). *The development of intelligence in children.* (E. S. Kite, Trans.). Baltimore: Williams & Wilkins Company.

Boake, C. (2002). From the Binet-Simon to the Wechsler-Bellevue: Tracing the history of intelligence testing. *Journal of Clinical and Experimental Neuropsychology, 24*(3), 383–405.

Brigham, C. C. (1923). *A study of American intelligence.* Princeton, NJ: Princeton University Press.

Bushcke, H. (1973). Selective reminding for analysis of memory and learning. *Journal of Verbal Learning and Verbal Behavior, 12,* 543–550.

Buschke, H., & Fuld, P. A. (1974). Evaluating storage, retention, and retrieval in disordered memory and learning. *Neurology, 24,* 1019–1025.

Carroll, J. B. (1993). *Human cognitive abilities: A survey of factor analytic studies.* Cambridge, MA: Cambridge University Press.

Cattell, J. M. (1890). Mental tests and measurements. *Mind, 15,* 373–381.

Cattell, J. M., & Farrand, L. (1896). Physical and mental measurements of the students of Columbia University. *Psychological Review, 3,* 618–648.

Claparède, E. (1919). Percentilage de quelques tests d'aptitude [Percentages of several aptitude tests]. *Archives de Psychologie, 17,* 313–324.

Cohen, G. (1989). *Memory in the real world.* Hillsdale, NJ: Erlbaum.

Collis, J. M., & Messick, S. (Eds.) (2001). *Intelligence and personality: Bridging the gap in theory and measurement.* Hillsdale, NJ: Lawrence Erlbaum.

Conway, M. A. (1991). In defense of everyday memory. *American Psychologist, 46,* 19–27.

Cronholm, B., & Mollander, L. (1957). Memory disturbances after electroconvulsive therapy. *Acta Psychiatrica Scandinavica, 32,* 280–306.

Das, J. P., & Naglieri, J. A. (2001) The Das-Naglieri Cognitive Assessment System in theory and practice. In J. W. Andrews, D. H. Saklofske, & H. Janzen (Eds.), *Handbook of psychoeducational assessment* (pp. 34–63). San Diego: Academic Press.

Davies, G. M., & Logie, R. H. (Eds.) (1993). *Memory in everyday life.* Amsterdam: Elsevier Science Publishers.

Davis, J. C., & Foreyt, J. P. (Eds.). (1975). *Mental examiner's sourcebook.* Springfield, IL: Charles C. Thomas Publishing.

Davis, R. C. (1970). *The Brass Age in psychology Technology and Culture, 11,* 604–611.

Deary, I. J. (2000). *Looking down on human intelligence: From psychometrics to the brain.* Oxford: Oxford University Press.

Deary, I. J., & Stough, C. (1996). Intelligence and inspection time: Achievements, prospects, and problems. *American Psychologist, 51,* 599–608.

Delis, D. C., Kramer, J., Kaplan, E., & Ober, B. A. (1987). *The California Verbal Learning Test.* San Antonio, TX: The Psychological Corporation.

Ebbinghaus, H. E. (1964). *Memory: A contribution to experimental psychology.* New York: Dover. (Original Work published 1895)

Erickson, R. C., & Scott, M. L. (1977). Clinical memory testing: A review. *Psychological Bulletin, 84*(6), 1130–1149.

Esquirol, J. E. D. (1845/1938). Mental maladies: A treatise on insanity. (E. K. Hunt, Trans.) Philadelphia: Lea & Blanchard.

Eysenck, H., & Halstead, H. (1945). The memory function. *American Journal of Psychiatry, 102,* 174–180.

Fitz-Herbert, A. (1534/1793). *The New Natura Bevium.* Dublin.

Galton, F. (1869). *Heredity genius: An inquiry into its laws and consequences.* London: Macmillan and Co.

Galton, F. (1883). *An inquiry into human faculty and its development.* London: Macmillan and Co.

Galton, F. (1889). *Natural Inheritance.* London: Macmillan.

Gardner, H. (1998). Are there additional intelligences? The case for naturalist, spiritual, and existential intelligences. In J. Kane (Ed.), *Education, information, and transformation* (pp. 111–131). Englewood Cliffs, NJ: Prentice-Hall.

Goodenough, F. L. (1949). *Mental testing: Its history, principles, and application.* New York: Rinehart & Company, Inc.

Gould, S. J. (1981). *The mismeasure of man.* New York: W. W. Norton & Company.

Gruneberg, M. M., & Morris, P. E. (1992). Applying memory research. In M. Gruneberg & P. Morris (Eds.), *Aspects of memory* (2nd ed., pp. 1–17). London: Routledge.

Gruneberg, M. M., Morris, P. E., & Sykes, R. N. (1991). The obituary on everyday memory and its practical applications is premature. *American Psychologist, 46,* 74–76.

Guilford, J. P. (1967). *The nature of human intelligence.* New York: McGraw-Hill.

Harris, J. E., & Morris, P. E. (Eds.) (1984). *Everyday memory, actions, and absent-mindedness.* London: Academic Press.

Harris, J. G., Tulsky, D. S. & Schultheis, M. T. (2003). Assessment of the non-native english speaker: Assimilating history and research findings to guide clinical practice. In: D. S. Tulsky et al. (Eds.) *Clinical Interpretation of the WAIS-III and WMS-III.* (pp. 343–390). San Diego: Academic Press.

Henmon, V. A. C., Peterson, J., Thurstone, L. L., Woodrow, H., Dearborn, W. F., & Haggerty, M. E. (1921). Intelligence and its measurement: A symposium. *Journal of Educational Psychology, 12*(4), 195–216.

Herring, J. P. (1922). *Herring revision of the Binet-Simon Tests. Examination manual form A.* Yonkers-on-Hudson, NY: World Book Company.

Horn, J. L., & Cattell, R.B (1966) Refinement and test of the theory of fluid and crystallized general intelligences. *Journal of Educational Psychology, 57*(5), 253–270.

Horn, J. L., & Noll, J. (1997). Human cognitive capabilities: $G_f - G_c$ Theory. In D.P. Flanagan, J. L. Genshaft, & P. L. Harrison (Eds.), *Contemporary intellectual assessment: Theories, tests, & issues.* New York: The Guilford Press.

Itard, J. M. G. (1801/1962). *The wild boy of Aveyron,* (Trans. G. Humphrey & M. Humphrey) New York: Meredith Publishing.

Kaufman, A. S. (1994). *Intelligent testing with the WISC-III.* New York: John Wiley & Sons.

Kevles, D. J. (1968). Testing the Army's intelligence: Psychologists and the military in World War I. *Journal of American History, 55,* 565–581.

Klatzky, R. L. (1991). Let's be friends. *American Psychologist, 46,* 43–46.

Koriat, A., & Goldsmith, M. (1996). Memory metaphors and the real-life/laboratory controversy: Correspondence versus storehouse conceptions of memory. *Behavioral and Brain Sciences, 19*(2), 167–228.

Kuhlman, F. (1922). *Handbook of mental tests: A further revision and extension of the Binet-Simon scale.* Baltimore: Warwick & York, Inc.

Lezak, M. D. (1988). IQ: R. I. P. *Journal of Clinical & Experimental Neuropsychology, 10(3),* 351–361.

Matarazzo, J. D. (1972). *Wechsler's measurement and appraisal of adult intelligence* (5th ed.). Baltimore: Williams & Wilkins.

Melville, N. J. (1917). *Standard method of testing juvenile mentality by the Binet-Simon Scale with the original questions, pictures, and drawings.* Philadelphia: J. B. Lippincott Company.

Naglieri, J. A., & Das, J. P. (1997). *Cognitive Assessment System,* Itasca, IL: Riverside Publishing.

Neisser, U. (1991). A case of misplaced nostalgia. *American Psychologist, 46,* 34–37.

Neisser, U., Boodoo, G., Bouchard, T. J., Boykin, A.W., Brody, N., Ceci, S. J., Halpern, D. F., Loehlin, J. C., Perloff, R., Sternberg, R. J., & Urbina, S. (1996). Intelligence: knowns and unknowns. *American Psychologist, 51*(2), 77–101.

Neisser, U., & Winograd, E. (Eds.) (1988). *Remembering reconsidered: Ecological and traditional approaches to the study of memory.* New York: Cambridge University Press.

Norsworthy, N. (1906). *The psychology of mentally deficient children.* New York: The Science Press.

Otis, A. S. (1918). An absolute point scale for the group measurement of intelligence. Part I. *Journal of Educational Psychology, 9,* 239–260.

Peterson, J. (1925). *Early conceptions and tests of intelligence.* Yonkers-on-Hudson, NY: World Book Company.

Pichot, P. (1948). French pioneers in the field of mental deficiency. *American Journal of Mental Deficiency, 53,* 128–137.

Pintner, R. (1923). *Intelligence testing: Methods and results.* New York: Henry Holt and Co.

Raven, J. C. (1938). Standardization of progressive matrices. *British Journal of Medical Psychology, 19,* 137–150.

Reed, J. (1987). Robert M. Yerkes and the mental testing movement. In M. M. Sokal (Ed.), *Psychological testing and american society: 1890–1930* (pp. 75–94). New Brunswick, NJ: Rutgers University Press.

Reitan, R. M., & Wolfson, D. (1993). *Halstead-Reitan Neuropsychological Test Battery.* Tucson: Neuropsychology Press.

Rey, A. (1964). *L'examen clinique en psychologie* [Clinical exams in psychology]. Paris: Presses Universitaires de France.

Rubin, D. C. (1986). *Autobiographical memory.* Cambridge, UK: Cambridge University Press.

Saklofske, D. H., & Zeidner M. (Eds.) (1995). *International handbook of personality and intelligence.* New York: Plenum Press.

Samelson, F. (1977). World War I intelligence testing and the development of psychology. *Journal of the History of the Behavioral Sciences, 13,* 274–282.

Sattler, J. M. (2001). *Assessment of children: Cognitive applications (4th ed.).* San Diego, CA: Jerome M. Sattler, Inc.

Séguin E (1866). *Idiocy and its treatment by the physiological method.* New York: William Wood & Co.

Shackelford, W. (Producer). (1976). *A conversation with David Wechsler* (Videotape). (Available from Jeffrey Norton Publishers. On The Green, Guilford, CT 06437–2612).

Sharp, S. E. (1899). Individual psychology: A study in psychological method. *The American Journal of Psychology, 10(3),* 329–391.

Sokal, M. M., Davis, A. B., & Merzbach, U. C. (1975). A national inventory of historic psychological apparatus. *Journal of the History of the Behavioral Sciences, 11,* 284–286.

Sokal, M. M., Davis, A. B., & Merzbach, U. C. (1976). Laboratory instruments in the history of psychology. *Journal of the History of the Behavioral Sciences, 12,* 59–64.

Sokal, M. M. (1981). The origins of the Psychological Corporation. *Journal of the History of the Behavioral Sciences, 17,* 54–67.

Sokal, M. M. (1987). James McKeen Cattell and mental anthropometry: Nineteenth-century science and reform and the origins of psychological testing. In M. M. Sokal (Ed.), *Psychological testing and American society: 1890–1930* (pp. 21–45). New Brunswick, NJ: Rutgers University Press.

Smith, G. E., Malec, JF., & Ivnik, R. J. (1992). Validity of the construct of nonverbal memory: A factor-analytic study in a normal elderly sample. *Journal of Clinical and Experimental Neuropsychology, 14(2),* 211–221.

Spearman, C. (1904). "General intelligence," objectively determined and measured. *American Journal of Psychology, 15,* 201–293.

Spearman, C. (1922). A friendly challenge to Professor Thorndike. *Psychological Review, 29,* 406–407.

Spearman, C. (1925). Agreement on cooperation. *Journal of Educational Psychology, 22,* 401–410.

Spearman, C. E. (1927). *The abilities of man.* New York: Macmillian.

Sternberg, R. J., Forsythe, G. B., Hedlund, J., Horvath, J., Snook, S., Williams, W. M., Wagner, R.K., & Grigorenko, E. L. (2000). *Practical intelligence in everyday life.* New York: Cambridge University Press.

Sylvester, R. H. (1913).The form board test [Special Issue] *Psychological Monographs, 15 (4),* No. 65.

Terman, L. M. (1916). *The measurement of intelligence.* Boston: Houghton Mifflin.

Thorndike, E. L., Lay, W., & Dean, P. R. (1909). The relation of accuracy in sensory discrimination to general intelligence. *American Journal of Psychology, 20,* 364–369.

Thorndike, E. L. (1924). Measurement of intelligence: 1. The present status. *Psychological Review, 31,* 219.

Thorndike, R. M. (with Lohman, D. F.) (1990). *A century of ability testing.* Chicago: Riverside Publishing Company.

Tulsky, D. S., Chiaravalloti, N. D., Palmer, B. W., & Chelune, G. J. (2003). The Wechsler Memory Scale, third edition: A new perspective. In D. S. Tulsky et al. (Eds). *Clinical Interpretation of the WAIS-III and WMS-III*. (pp. 93–139). San Diego: Academic Press.

Tulsky, D. S., Saklofske, D. H., & Zhu, J. (2003). Revising a standard: An evaluation of the origin and development of the WAIS-III. In D. S. Tulsky et al. (Eds). *Clinical Interpretation of the WAIS-III and WMS-III*. (pp. 43–92). San Diego: Academic Press.

Wechsler, D. (1917). A study of retention in Korsakoff psychosis. *Psychological Bulletin, 2*, 403–45.

Wechsler, D. (1926). Tests for taxicab drivers. *Journal of Personnel Research, 5*, 24–30.

Wechsler, D. (1939). *Wechsler–Bellevue Intelligence Scale*. New York: The Psychological Corporation.

Wechsler, D. (1944). *The measurement of adult intelligence* (3rd ed.). Baltimore: Williams & Wilkins.

Wechsler, D. A. (1945). A standardized memory scale for clinical use. *Journal of Psychology, 19*, 87–95.

Wechsler, D. (1950). Cognitive, conative, and non–intellective intelligence. *American Psychologist, 5*, 78–83.

Wechsler, D. (1958). *The measurement and appraisal of adult intelligence* (4th ed.). Baltimore: The Williams & Wilkins Company.

Wechsler, D. (1974). Wechsler Intelligence Scale for Children-Revised. New York: The Psychological Corporation.

Wechsler, D. (1975). Intelligence defined and undefined: A relativistic appraisal. *American Psychologist, 30*, 135–139.

Wechsler, D. (1991). *Wechsler Intelligence Scale for Children* (3rd ed.). San Antonio, TX: The Psychological Corporation.

Wells, F. L., & Martin, H. A. A. (1923). A method of memory evaluation suitable for psychotic cases. *American Journal of Psychiatry, 3*, 243–258.

Wicket, J. C. (1998). Hans J. Eysenck's influence on intelligence research. *Psihologija, 3*, 249–256.

White, J. G., Merrick, M., & Harbison, J. J. (1969). Williams Scale for the Measurement of Memory: Test reliability and validity in a psychiatric population. *British Journal of Social and Clinical Psychology, 8*, 141–151.

Williams, M. (1968). The measurement of memory in clinical practice. *British Journal of Social and Clinical Psychology, 7*, 19–34.

Winograd, E., & Neisser, U. (Eds.) (1992). *Affect and accuracy in recall: Studies of "flashbulb memories."* New York: Cambridge University Press.

Wissler, C. (1901) The correlation of mental and physical tests. *Psychological Review*, 3 (16).

Woodworth, R. S. (1932). Autobiography. In C. Murchison (Ed.), *History of psychology in autobiography (Vol 2*, pp. 359–380) Worcester, MA: Clark University Press.

Wozniak, R. H. (1999). Introduction to memory: Hermann Ebbinghous (1885/1913). In R. H. Wozniak (Ed.), *Classics in psychology, 1855–1914: Historical essays*. Bristol, UK: Thoemmes Press.

Yerkes, R. M. (1918). Psychology in relation to the war. *Psychological Review, 25*, 85–115.

Yerkes, R. M. (1919a). The measurement and utilization of brain power in the army. *Science*, 44, 221–226; 251–259.

Yerkes, R. M. (1919b). Report of the Psychology Committee of the National Research Council. *Psychological Review, 26*, 83–149.

Yerkes, R. M. (1921). *Psychological examining in the United States Army: Memoirs of the National Academy of Science, Vol 15*. Washington: Government Printing Office.

Yerkes, R. M. (1923). Eugenic bearing of measurements of intelligence in the US Army. *Eugenics Review, 14*, 223–245.

Yerkes, R. M. (1924). The work of committee on scientific problems of human migration, National Research Council. *The Journal of Personnel Research, III*, 189–196.

Yerkes, R. M. (1941). Man-power and military effectiveness: The case for human engineering. *Journal of Consulting Psychology, 5*, 205–209.

Yerkes, R. M., Bridges, J. W., & Hardwick, R. S. (1915). *A point scale for measuring mental ability*. Baltimore: Warwick & York, Inc.

Zenderland, L. (1987). The debate over diagnosis: Henry Herbert Goddard and the medical acceptance of intelligence testing. In M. M. Sokal (Ed.): *Psychological Testing and American Society 1890–1930*. New Brunswic: Rutgers University Press.

Zenderland, L. (1998). *Measuring Minds: Henry Herbert Goddard and the Origins of American Intelligence Testing*. Cambridge, UK: Cambridge University Press.

CHAPTER 2

Revising a Standard: An Evaluation of the Origin and Development of the WAIS-III

David S. Tulsky
Kessler Medical Rehabilitation Research and Education Corporation
University of Medicine and Dentistry of New Jersey

Donald H. Saklofske
University of Saskatchewan
and

Jianjun Zhu
The Psychological Corporation

The Wechsler Bellevue Intelligence Scale was published in 1939, and since the initial publication, the test has been revised three times: Wechser Adult Intelligence Scale (WAIS, Wechsler, 1955), The Wechsler Adult Intelligence Scale—Revised (WAIS-R; Wechsler, 1981a), and the Wechsler Adult Intelligence Scale, Third Edition (WAIS-III, Wechsler, 1997a). This chapter focuses mainly on the most recent revision, although at the end of the chapter a review of each subtest and its origins is presented.

The development of the WAIS-III began officially in November, 1992, and marked the first revision of the adult test to be undertaken following David Wechsler's death in 1981. A project team was formed by the publisher, The Psychological Corporation, that included the authors of this chapter. Specifically, Tulsky and Zhu were the project directors who led the revision process. Saklofske interfaced with the revision team through his work as project director of WAIS-III Canadian standardization project. These experiences made the authors intimately familiar with the WAIS-III and the revision process leading to its publication.

Clinical Interpretation of the WAIS-III and WMS-III   **43**

WHY A REVISION WAS NECESSARY

The WAIS-R was among the most frequently used tests for assessing the cognitive abilities of adults (see Archer, Maruish, Imhof, & Piotrowski, 1991; Butler, Retzlaff, & Vanderploeg, 1991; Camara, Nathan, & Puente, 2000; Harrison, Kaufman, Hickman, & Kaufman, 1988; Lees-Haley, Smith, Williams, & Dunn, 1996; Piotrowski & Keller, 1989; Watkins, Campbell, & McGregor, 1988). Though still an extremely popular and widely used test when development of the WAIS-III began, a 5-year development plan would allow the WAIS-III to be released just when the normative information was becoming outdated. Cognitive tests appear to require new normative data every 15–20 years (see Flynn, 1984, 1987; Matarazzo, 1972), and based on these estimates, the norms of the WAIS-R would be in danger of becoming obsolete by the late 1990s. The revision not only afforded an opportunity to update the normative information but presented an opportunity to make other larger or smaller changes, based upon research findings and clinical usage.

The question confronting the research team was how many other changes should be made. Given that the test was so widely used in the field, it would have been possible to either make no changes and only renorm the WAIS-R or, similarly, make a few "cosmetic" changes that would not impact upon the structure of the test or interpretation of the test results. On the surface, this would have been the simplest and easiest solution. It would not pose a threat to the Wechsler test tradition and, based upon the popularity of the WAIS-R, simply updating the norms would have been accepted by many in practice.

At the same time, given the advances in theory, research, and assessment practices related to intelligence, the research team engaged in a critical examination of how many changes could or should be made. For instance, should factor-based index scores, as had been done for the WISC-III, be developed for the WAIS-III, should new subtests be created and added to the scale, and should some traditional subtests be eliminated? More importantly, had the IQ structure that had defined the Wechsler scales since their inception outlived its usefulness or was it still an appropriate measure of cognitive functioning? This latter question represented one of the most significant changes that the research team could have made. Moreover, such a revision would be in line with several contemporary publications. Several theorists and researchers were advancing models identifying multiple factors of cognitive functioning (e.g., Carroll, 1993), and the recent literature on the WISC-III had demonstrated the clinical utility of a four-factor structure (see Prifitera & Saklofske, 1998).

The initial portion of this chapter reviews the changes that were made to the WAIS-III and the process that had occurred when making the changes. The second part of the chapter reviews the origins and historical antecedents of the WAIS-III subtests, and how they have changed over the years in subsequent revisions of the Wechsler Bellevue Intelligence Scale.

CHANGING TEST SCORES AND NORMS

Over the last three decades, it has been shown that the norms on standardized cognitive tests can become outdated over relatively short periods (see Flynn, 1984, 1987, Matarazzo, 1972). Flynn demonstrated that IQ scores from tests such as the Wechsler and Stanford-Binet tend to increase by approximately one third to two thirds of a point a year for various reasons (e.g., improved education). Following from these estimates and assuming that all else remained constant (e.g., test items and content remained relevant), the life span of the norms of a cognitive test would be only 15–20 years depending upon how much score inflation could be tolerated in research and clinical test practices.

The WAIS-R was published in 1981, and according to these projections, would need to have been renormed before the turn of the millennium. If, at the minimum, periodic renorming was not performed, the test's mean scores (i.e., IQ and subtest scores), and possibly other psychometric characteristics (e.g., reliability, SE_M), would likely begin to show increasing differences from the published norms. This inflationary or upward shift in mean scores, even if consistent across scales and ages, could result in interpretation errors if the actual amount of increase was unknown, or not factored into test scores as a kind of 'reliable inflation' constant or correction factor. Hence, at the very least, new normative data should be collected periodically, and, if necessary, other changes could also then be made to the test before data are collected on a new standardization sample. Since the WAIS-R standardization sample had been collected during 1979–1980, new normative information would certainly have been needed by the targeted 1997 publication date set for the WAIS-III. However, of importance to the development of the WAIS-III was the recognition that many improvements to the test could be made that would assure its continuing and contemporary value in both research and clinical practice.

REVISED TEST STRUCTURE

Many of the changes made to the children's version, the WISC-III, helped to establish the goals for the WAIS-III revision process. The WISC-III was published in 1991, and although it clearly continued the Wechsler tradition for assessing intelligence, some significant changes were introduced. Possibly the greatest change occurred because of the introduction of a new optional subtest, Symbol Search, which was initially intended to assist in strengthening and more clearly defining the third "freedom from distractability" factor (see Cohen, 1952a, 1952b, 1957, 1959; Kaufman, 1979; Wielkiewicz, 1990). The subtest design was drawn from experimental research on cognition and attention conducted by Shiffrin and Schneider (1977). It had been anticipated that this subtest would correlate with the Arithmetic, Digit Span, and Coding subtests, and therefore all would load collectively on a third factor in exploratory factor analyses. However, the empirical findings suggested a different pattern. Symbol Search was most highly correlated with the Coding subtest, and not with Digit Span nor Arithmetic, which clustered together. This new factor appeared to measure speed of information processing (see Prifitera, Weiss, & Saklofske, 1998). These results were confirmed with the U.S. standardization sample as well as others (e.g., Canada: Roid & Worrall, 1997).

The WISC-III was published with a supplemental four-factor scoring system that could be obtained if examiners administered two optional subsets (Wechsler, 1991). By including these factor or index scores as an "alternative" system for scoring and interpretation, the research team at The Psychological Corporation proceeded prudently, by introducing the more contemporary scores while leaving the traditional IQs unchanged. Thus the continuity of the scale across revisions could be preserved while ensuring that the test was grounded in current theory, research, and practice needs. The response from the field was positive; the addition of the Symbol Search subtest and the four-factor model were cited as two of the most important changes (see Kaufman, 1994). As well, the diagnostic utility of the WISC-III was now enhanced by the introduction of the attentional and processing speed factors (see Prifitera & Saklofske, 1998; Weiss, Saklofske, & Prifitera, 2003).

GOALS FOR THE WAIS-III REVISION

The many goals for the WAIS-III (Table 1) included those that were substantive, such as a co-norming research design that empirically linked

TABLE 1   Goals of the WAIS-III Revision[a]

Essential

    Goal 1: Updating of norms

Substantive

    Goal 2: Develop four factor scores

    Goal 3: Link/Co-Norm with WMS-III and WIAT

    Goal 4: Extension of age range beyond 74 years

    Goal 5: Apply age corrections at the subtest level

    Goal 6: De-emphasize performance speed on perceptual tasks

    Goal 7: Enhance fluid reasoning

    Goal 8: Improve diagnostic utility of the scales and subtests

Item/subtest improvement

    Goal 9: Improved item content

    Goal 10: Extension of floor and ceiling

    Goal 11: Enhancement of scoring rules

General updating, cosmetic, and designed to ease transition

    Goal 12: Improved stimulus material

    Goal 13: Publish validity studies

---

[a]Adapted from information in Tulsky, Zhu, and Prifitera, 2000.

the WAIS-III and Wechsler Memory Scale—Third edition (WMS-III, Wechsler, 1997b), and the development of the index score structure. Other changes addressed face validity, such as redrawing the Picture Completion items in color, or were intended to assist the clinician by making the test more user-friendly (e.g., producing a crack-back manual that could stand on the table during test administration). The revision goals have been described previously (see The Psychological Corporation, 1997; Tulsky & Ledbetter, 2000; Tulsky, Zhu, & Prifitera, 2000) and will not be repeated in any great detail here.

DECIDING WHAT TO CHANGE

Revising cognitive tests as well established as the WAIS-III and WMS-III pose unique challenges that are quite different from developing a new, untried test. The Wechsler tests have a lengthy history, and any significant structural changes that would make them unrecognizable as Wechsler tests, might make the data collected for the previous editions less relevant. A search of *Psych Info* conducted in January, 2003, using the key words "WAIS, WAIS-R, WAIS-III, Wechsler Adult Intelligence Scale, Wechsler Bellevue Intelligence scale," yielded 6100 citations, making the Wechsler tests one of the most widely researched and cited tests in psychology. Moreover, practitioners and diagnosticians seemed pleased with the scales and their popularity and widespread use has been documented in articles on test usage (see Archer et al., 1991; Butler et al., 1991; Camara et al., 2000; Harrison et al., 1988; Lees-Haley, Smith, Willisams, & Dunn; 1996; Piotrowski & Keller, 1989; and Watkins et al., 1988). These research articles have repeatedly demonstrated that practitioners gravitate toward familiar instruments when using tests for assessment and research purposes, rather than using a new test. So despite any improvements that could be made to the test, from the standpoint of continuity and familiarity, the fewer changes made to the instruments the better, thereby resulting in a more straightforward linkage between the two editions of the scales.

At the same time, the past several decades witnessed some remarkable advances in our theories and assessment models. New research findings from, for example, neuropsychology (DeLuca, Barbieri-Berger, & Johnson, 1994; DeLuca, Gaudino, Diamond, Christodoulou, & Engel, 1998; Salthouse, 1994; Smith et al., 1992), neuroscience (Christodoulou et al., 2001; Hobbs, 1999; Ricker et al., 2001b; Ricker, Hillary, & DeLuca, 2001a), cognitive psychology (Carroll, 1993; Engle, 2001; Kyllonen & Chrystal, 1990), and school psychology (Flanagan, McGrew, & Ortiz, 2000; Das & Naglieri, 2001; Das, Naglieri, & Kirby, 1994) posed some challenges to traditional assessment with the Wechsler scales. Growing evidence also supported alternate ways to conceptualize and measure cognitive functioning. Contemporary theories of the structure of cognitive functioning emphasize multiple factors of intelligence, which, in turn, create different expectations for new tests and assessment instruments (e.g. Carroll, 1993; Das et al., 1994; Flanagan et al., 2000; Horn & Noll, 1997; Salthouse, 1996). From this perspective, significant modifications to the Wechsler instruments would seem to be both needed and expected.

The WAIS-III project development team was responsible for balancing these competing forces. What changes and improvements could be introduced into the WAIS-III so that the test would be more contemporary and relevant in psychological assessment and diagnosis, yet at the same time balance the forces that may resist change? The WAIS-R was widely used and considered by practicing psychologists to be a diagnostically useful measure. If the test changed too radically and too quickly, the WAIS-III might not be seen as continuous with previous editions, and thus it might be rejected by practitioners. Such had been the fate with the Stanford–Binet, fourth edition (Thorndike, Hagen, & Sattler, 1986). Hence, at every turn, the research team questioned whether changes proposed from various quarters might cause the scale to be less recognizable. Would the historical data from previous editions apply to the new test? Would psychologists feel comfortable and confident with this new test? The magnitude of the decisions could not be taken lightly.

To help sort through such decisions, the development teams of the WAIS-III and WMS-III sought assistance from several sources. A scientific advisory panel was formed to guide the development from the beginning stages of the project. Additionally, the team solicited reviews from experts in the field at many stages throughout the process. Initially reviews were obtained from individuals who critically commented on the WAIS-R, and this further helped to set up the goals for revision. Later in the process, reviewers commented on new subtests and items that were included in the tryout and standardization editions. Also, the tryout and standardization examiners, after testing individuals and gaining "hands-on" experience with the materials, filled out questionnaire or were interviewed about issues of usability. Independent of these efforts, other practitioners were interviewed or participated in focus groups conducted by marketing research firms that had been hired to specifically test new ideas. On various occasions, the outcome was a compromise between introducing a new idea and maintaining the historical underpinnings of the scale. The most striking example of this compromise is the retention of the traditional Full-Scale IQ (FSIQ), Verbal IQ (VIQ), and Performance IQ (PIQ) which were given equal weight to the newer and more contemporary Index scores, derived from the factor analyses of the subtests.

CHANGES AND REACTIONS

In the final version, the WAIS-III introduced some important changes, including a four factor model, extended age range, age corrections at the scaled score level, and new subtests for assessing working memory and processing speed. There were other changes that were not made (e.g., such as radical changes to the IQ composite scores, full integration with the WMS-III, removal of subtests that were redundant with other measures and/or did not have sufficient incremental validity). Although the reviews of the WAIS-III have been favorable (e.g., see Kaufman & Lichtenberger,

1999; Sattler & Ryan, 2001), others have criticized the research team for not making more radical changes. For instance, Flanagan, McGrew, and Ortiz wrote

> Although Wechsler's name is still listed as the author of all revisions since his death in 1981, this most likely reflects contractual obligations. The publisher of the Wechsler Scales, as well as members of the work groups organized by the publisher, are more accurately responsible for the slow, incremental changes in the Wechsler Scales. Historical continuity and tradition apparently (have) played a stronger role than theoretical considerations in the revisions of the Wechsler Scales. (Flanagan et al., 2000, p. 10)

Such criticism ignores the key reasons that some degree of continuity must be preserved and is warranted. First, people tend to be resistant to change (Friend & Cook, 1996; Watson, 1969) if change is too radical and too far ahead of the learning curve. It could be argued that smaller incremental steps are warranted or practitioners may abandon a previously often used test because of the dissonance created between the old and new (or simply continue to use the WAIS-R as some still do). This argument is not convincing in itself unless the assumption is that test publishers are only, or mostly, concerned about their market share rather than adhering to the professionally responsible and ethical behaviors expected of test developers. It is also a weak argument in relation to practitioners, one that assumes that practitioners are complacent and more concerned with convenience than in serving the best interests of their clients and society (see American Psychological Association, 1992).

Second, it is important not to dismiss or discard even an imperfect technique that has proven to have broad heuristic value in both the clinical and research spheres. In criticizing the WAIS-III revision, Flanagan and her colleagues may be suggesting that the Wechsler scales should be tied to the theory of crystallized/fluid intelligence (as is the Woodcock Johnson-III) that was originally advanced by Cattell (1963), and further refined over the years by Horn and Cattell (1966) and Horn and Noll (1997). Although such an approach would seem important for a new test that was developed in the context of this larger theoretical model, the Wechsler scales have been important as assessment tools within the context of different theories. In fact, a strength of the Wechsler scales is that they have been robust enough to be used by individuals with different perspectives about intelligence and assessment needs.

Third, the WAIS-III has a rich empirical and clinical history that should not be abandoned but rather built upon. Continued elaboration and refinement will ensure that the Wechsler scales tend to offer a unique perspective while complementing other perspectives and developments related to the assessment of cognitive abilities.

Hence, the ultimate goal for the WAIS-III publication was to provide an instrument that was significantly improved over its predecessors, allowing incremental change to occur. In fact, the changes have been occurring steadily since the WISC-III was published in 1991. The WAIS-III represents a test that deviates more significantly from any other previous revision of any Wechsler test (see The Psychological Corporation, 1997, Tulsky, Zhu, & Prifitera, 2000; for a description of the changes that were made). However, some of the changes that might have been made at the time of publication were not. Other chapters of this book will introduce further key refinements to cognitive assessment with the Wechsler scales that were not advanced in 1997. Most important, the book will cut across the boundaries of the WAIS-III and WMS-III to propose a six-factor model that retains the four WAIS-III factors together with visual and auditory memory factors.

EMPHASIS ON THE FACTOR SCORES

The most significant change in the WAIS-III is the alternative set of summary scores that are organized into more refined domains of cognitive functioning: the Verbal Comprehension (VCI), Perceptual Organization (POI), Working Memory (WMI), and Processing Speed Index (PSI) scores. The composite scoring structure is presented in Table 2.

The WAIS-III certainly went further than the WISC-III in advancing the use of the factor-derived index scores in clinical assessments. In the

TABLE 2   The WAIS-III Subtests Grouped According to Indexes[a]

Verbal Comprehension	Perceptual Organization	Working Memory	Processing Speed
2. Vocabulary	1. Picture Completion	6. Arithmetic	3. Digit Symbol—Coding
4. Similarities	5. Block Design	8. Digit Span	12. Symbol Search
9. Information	7. Matrix Reasoning	13. Letter-Number Sequencing	

[a]From Wechsler, D. (1997a). Copyright © 1997. The Psychological Corporation. Used with permission. All Rights Reserved.

WAIS-III, index scores are given "equivalent weight" to the IQ scores; however, users would administer a different subset of subtests depending upon whether they want index scores or IQ scores (see Figure 1). This permits the examiner to tailor the testing session to the purpose and needs for the assessment. Although it may be thought that the test includes both IQ and index scores, with the decision about which to use left to the psychologist, the index scores are more often being recommended as the most sensitive and useful in clinical assessment (e.g., Hawkins, 1998; Martin, Donders, & Thompson, 2000; Taylor & Heaton, 2001).

The Letter-Number Sequencing and Symbol Search subtests added enough variability to the smaller third and fourth factors, and, as a result, distinct working memory and processing speed factors were supported in several factor analytic studies (The Psychological Corporation, 1997; Saklofske, Hildebrand, & Gorsuch, 2000; Tulsky, Zhu, & Prifitera, 2000; Tulsky & Price, in press). Moreover, the index scores tend to cluster to form

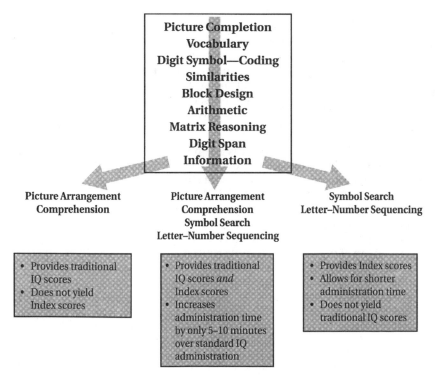

FIGURE 1.   WAIS-III Administration Options. From Wechsler, D. (1997a). Copyright © 1997. The Psychological Corporation. Used with Permission. All Rights Reserved.

different profiles that would appear to facilitate clinical decision making (Donders, Zhu, & Tulsky, 2001). Initial evidence in support of the WAIS-III index scores suggests that these enhance the diagnostic sensitivity and clinical utility of the test battery (Hawkins, 1998; Martin, et al., 2000; The Psychological Corporation, 1997; Taylor & Heaton, 2001). In several clinical samples the VCI tends to be more stable, and the PSI tends to be markedly lower in just about all of the clinical groups (Hawkins, 1998; Martin et al., 2000; The Psychological Corporation, 1997; Taylor & Heaton, 2001).

Given the somewhat lengthy time needed to administer the WAIS-III (Ryan, Lopez, & Werth, 1998; Wechsler, 1997a), two of the more time-consuming subtests (Comprehension and Picture Arrangement) were made optional in the index score structure. This decision was based on findings reported by Tulsky et al., (2000), who demonstrated that these shorter index scores were reliable and similar to the score that would have been obtained if the Comprehension and Picture Arrangement had not been made optional in the standardization sample. By not requiring these two subtests, different subsets of the subtests could be administered to obtain a composite score. As Figure 1 shows, 11 subtests are administered to obtain a FSIQ score. A different subset of the 11 subtests needs to be administered to obtain the four index scores. However, if the user wants both IQ and Index scores, the manual recommends that an examiner administer 13 subtests. The options available to psychologists for administering the WAIS-III give the test a newfound flexibility, which is in keeping with Wechsler's view that such intelligence tests are clinical tools.

It is fair to say that with the publication of the WAIS-III, a compromise was reached. Although the test leaves the option open to psychologists to determine if IQ or index scores are more appropriate to address a referral question, there is a clearer position on the factor-derived scores than was apparent in the WISC-III manual. *The WAIS-III—WMS-III Technical Manual* describes the VCI and POI as "more refined" and "purer" measures of verbal comprehension and fluid reasoning/visual-spatial problem solving than the respective VIQ and PIQ scores (The Psychological Corporation, 1997, p. 186). The VIQ and PIQ instead are more inclusive and broad measures that take longer to administer, in contrast to the index scores, where the emphasis is on the more precise measurement of multiple cognitive abilities. For these reasons, though the VIQ and PIQ scores have been historically interesting, they are now considered less relevant to testing with the Wechsler scales. Alternatives for a general score (e.g., a General Ability Index that is based upon an aggregate of 6 *g* loaded subtests that make up the VCI and POI) make the FSIQ even less important (see Tulsky, Saklofske, Wilkins, & Weiss, 2001).

The co-norming of the WAIS-III and the WMS-III has extended the potential boundaries of cognitive assessment even further. To date, however, much of this potential has gone unrealized. By adding some of the WMS-III subtests to the analyses, a better understanding of the joint cognitive processes and their interrelations can occur. In fact, recent confirmatory factor analytic data (see Tulsky & Price, in press) have demonstrated that the WMS-III subtests add the dimensions of memory to the four-factor model described by the WAIS-III, and the practical application of this research is presented in Tulsky, Ivnik, Price, & Wilkins, (Chapter 4, this volume).

Based upon this research, much of this book elaborates on the premise that a new and more comprehensive model of assessment with the WAIS-III and WMS-III should be based upon six factors of cognitive functioning. Further, these factor scores have more utility and clinical value than traditional IQ (and MQ) scores. An outline of these advances and arguments will be presented in Chapter 4, where the new six-factor model is introduced. At the same time as introducing change, it is important to understand the history of the scales. Therefore, it is important to review the basic structure of the WAIS-III just as it was important to revisit the history (see Tulsky, Saklofske, & Ricker, Chapter 1, this volume) that influenced David Wechsler and the tests he originally designed. A brief description of the events leading up to the publication of the WAIS-III follows. The WAIS-III structure is presented in a historical and contemporary context. Additionally, we include a brief discussion of the changes to the subsequent revisions of the Wechsler Bellevue Form I that Wechsler had hoped to implement (e.g., subtests to measure nonintellective factors). Discussion about the WMS will be presented in Chapter 3 (Tulsky, Chiaravalloti, Palmer, & Chelune, this volume).

EVENTS LEADING UP TO THE WAIS-III

A careful review of the Wechsler scales, in the context of intelligence testing, demonstrate that David Wechsler was largely a "synthesizer" rather than a "creator."[1] His experiences as an examiner in the military, as an employee in a commercial industry with The Psychological Corporation, and as a scholar studying psychometrics at Columbia were, undoubtably, key influences that led him to develop a comprehensively normed intelligence scale.

[1]The authors of this chapter are indebted to John Wasserman, who often shared his views about the origins of the Wechsler scales and recommended key references to the first author during personal communications (January 2001–April 2001).

It is also not surprising that Wechsler would draw items, subtests, and even his views on assessment from these experiences. For example, several subtests and items found in the Wechsler–Bellevue Intelligence Scale, Form I (WB I; Wechsler, 1939a) and later versions were extracted directly from the army testing program (Army Alpha and Beta; Yerkes, 1921), the Binet and Simon (1905/1916a; 1908/1916b; 1911/1916c), Knox's test for immigrants (1914), Pintner and Patterson's (1917) Performance Scale, and Maxfield (1925) and Kohs (1923) Design Blocks test. It was the incorporation and synthesis of these various measures into a battery that included both verbal and visuospatial tasks, the extensiveness of the normative database, and the introduction of the deviation IQ that marked David Wechsler's profound contribution to the mental measurements of that time and to the present day. As Boake (2002) has pointed out, the reviews of the initial WB I were quite positive, and some reviewers even praised Wechsler for using such well-known and accepted clinical procedures. For the curious reader, the full text of the initial reviews of the WB I that were published in the *1940 Mental Measurements Yearbook* (Buros, 1941) have been reprinted in Appendix 2.

Wechsler revised the adult scale three times during his life, and during each of these revisions, he considered adding new subtests. In reality, however, the changes made to the tests in the first 50 years of their existence were relatively slight. Only one major subtest, Vocabulary, was added to the core battery after the original Wechsler Bellevue Scale, Form I had been published. Though Wechsler was convinced that Vocabulary was an important task, he initially left it out of the standardization phase because he originally believed that this subtest was influenced too greatly by cultural forces. Even though empirical findings seemed to change his mind about the utility of a vocabulary subtest, by the time the WB I was to be published, only a subsample of the standardization subjects received Vocabulary, so that he was unable to include it as a core subtest (Wechsler, 1939b). It is unclear if Wechsler initially planned to include Vocabulary in the alternate IQ scale that he developed for the U.S. Army (Wechsler Mental Ability Scale, Form B), as a short form was employed in the Army Special Training Center in World War II due to time constraints (Altus, 1945). Following the war, the Wechsler Mental Ability Scale Form B was repackaged as the Wechsler–Bellevue Intelligence Scale, Form II (WB II), and, in that version, Wechsler did incorporate Vocabulary as a core subtest (Wechsler, 1946). Vocabulary was included in all of the subsequent revisions (WAIS, Wechsler, 1955; WISC-R, Wechsler, 1974; WAIS-R; Wechsler, 1981a). Although, there were several attempts to develop other new cognitive subtests (e.g., Wechsler almost added a version of a colored form board to the WISC-R, but the subtest was dropped after standardization, (Barclay, Yater, & Wechsler, 1972; Hargus & Wasserman, 1994) and nonintellective measures of intelligence, no radical changes were made to the subtests nor to the structure of the Wechsler tests through his lifetime. Before examining each of the subtests on the WAIS-III, including their origins, a few comments will be made regarding Wechsler's attempts at developing tests to tap nonintellective or conative factors.

WECHSLER'S UNREALIZED GOAL: MEASUREMENT OF NONINTELLECTIVE FACTORS

Less well known were Wechsler's attempts to develop a test that measured the conative factors of intelligence (Wechsler, 1950). Wechsler believed that there was a whole dimension of intelligence that was untapped by the Wechsler scales. He argued that functional intelligence must also include nonintellective factors and spent much of his career trying to design such measures. He pilot tested new subtests in the 1955 revision of the WAIS and then again for the WAIS-R in the late 1970s. During this latter revision, Wechsler believed that his attempts to measure the conative factors of intelligence might be realized. During one of his last presentations at the 1979 American Psychological Association's annual conference (Wechsler, 1981b), he raised the question of whether the WAIS-R could be expanded to include

> the four- or five-minute tasks that could be added to an already existing battery of "cognitive" tests, that would correlate sufficiently with the full scale scores, and yet emerge as factorially different? I have been searching for them for the last thirty years. I tried unsuccessfully to find one for the 1955 WAIS. I think I may have been luckier in my latest search, but you will have to wait, like myself, until the results will have been fully worked up. WAIS-R is scheduled for publication in 1980, and perhaps some information about a new test will be included. (p. 85)

The new subtest to which David Wechsler referred was called Level of Aspiration and was included in the WAIS-R standardization kit. The best description of the test is provided by Hargus and Wasserman (1994), who reviewed several documents and books from Wechsler's library. Wechsler used the term and concept previously described by Lewin, Dembo, Festinger, and Sears (1944) based upon the work of two German psychologists

(Dembo, 1931, and Hoppe, 1930). Lewin et al. defined aspiration as goal-striving behaviors that occur within a specified range of difficulty. They believed that a person's level of aspiration can be linked with three factors: the seeking of success, the avoidance of failure, and an individual's cognitive judgments about the probability of his or her success on the task.

In Wechsler's version, the subtest was divided into two parts: Number Squares and Flock of Birds. For the first task, examinees were required to estimate the number of squares that could be drawn 30 min after being informed that the "average person" can draw between 18 and 34 squares (Wechsler, 1976, p. 47) (see Figure 2). Then after drawing the squares, examinees estimated how many squares were actually drawn. This procedure was repeated four times so that the examinee could modify their estimates based on experience. The second part, called Flock of Birds required an examinee to estimate how many birds were present in a picture in two trials of the test (Figure 3). The differences between the examinees' estimates on the trials before and after gaining some experience with the task were believed to be clinically relevant.

Unfortunately, Wechsler's goals went unrealized as poor psychometric properties, design flaws, and problems with the floor of the subtest forced the developers to leave the subtest out of the final WAIS-R publication (Herman, personal communication, August 1995). Hence, the WAIS-R was published without a new subtest and, in essence rather than by design, the consistency of the Wechsler Intelligence Scales was maintained throughout the revisions.

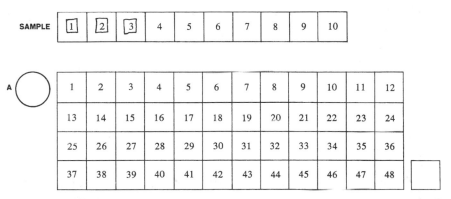

FIGURE 2.   Section of WAIS-R Standardization Record Form (Supplement). Provided courtesy of Eugenia Jaros. Copyright © 1976. The Psychological Corporation. Used with Permission. All Rights Reserved.

FIGURE 3.   Flock of Birds Stimulus Card. Provided courtesy of Eugenia Jaros. Copyright © 1976. The Psychological Corporation. Used with Permission. All Rights Reserved.

DESCRIPTION OF SUBTESTS

In the following section a brief review of the subtests is presented to provide the reader with both a description of the subtests and their origin. With the exception of the new subtests (e.g., Matrix Reasoning, Letter Number Sequencing, and Symbol Search), the subtests have remained relatively intact since their inclusion on the WB I. The literature is filled with other sources that have provided a description for how to administer, score, and interpret specific subtests and profiles of subtest patterns (e.g., Kaplan, Fein, Morris, & Delis, 1991; Kaplan, Fein, Kramer, Delis, & Morris, 1999; Kaufman, 1990; 1994; Kaufman & Lichtenberger, 1999; Sattler & Ryan, 2001), and this information will not be repeated here. As well, this section is not meant to provide an exhaustive review of the subtests, and throughout the book, the interpretation of each subtest will be stressed primarily for what it contributes to an index score level rather than being a "test" in an of its own right.

Vocabulary

The Vocabulary subtest of the WAIS–III is a measure of expressive vocabulary. It has the highest correlation with the Full Scale IQ score as well as high correlations with other subtests (The Psychological Corporation, 1997). It also has the highest factor loadings in exploratory or confirmatory factor analytic studies as well as high correlations with other criterion measures (The Psychological Corporation, 1997; Saklofske et al., 2000; Tulsky & Ledbetter, 2000; Tulsky et al., 2000). For this reason, the subtest is regarded as the best measure of *g*. Research has also demonstrated that this subtest is more resilient to brain dysfunction and aging and, as such, it has often been called a "hold" test (Larrabee, Largen, & Levine, 1985). The subtest also reflects culture and education and is cited as a direct measure of acquired knowledge.

Some of the initial studies of Vocabulary were conducted by E.A. Kirpatrick in the late 1800s and early 1900s (see Colvin, 1923) and Whipple (1908) attributes Kirpatrick as being the first person to develop a vocabulary test. However, the origins of the Vocabulary subtest as we know it date back to the first Binet and Simon scale (1905/1916a). Children were asked, "Do you know what a _____ is?" and then required to define the word. The test was modified and used in the Stanford revision of the Binet scale (Terman, 1916) where 20, 30, 40, or 50 words were administered to a child, starting at age 8, by asking: "What is a _____?" Once again, the child was required to provide a definition in their own words.

Wechsler used the Stanford-Binet test in the army testing program so he would have most definitely administered the Vocabulary test at that time. It appears that Wechsler understood the importance of this subtest from the start. He wrote that "contrary to lay opinion, the size of a man's vocabulary is not only an index of his schooling, but also an excellent measure of his general intelligence (Wechsler, 1939b, p. 100). When the WB-I was first released, however, Wechsler hesitated to include it as a core subtest because he was worried that the subtest would be overly influenced by a person's educational and cultural opportunities (Wechlser, 1939b). Within 2 years after publishing the WB I and the companion book on intelligence testing, he modified his recommendation for the test and suggested that the Vocabulary subtest should always be administered (see Wechsler, 1944). This change wouldn't be made "official" until the WB 2 and the WAIS were published (1946 and 1955 respectively) and Vocabulary was included with the subtests that comprised the VIQ and FSIQ.

The original Vocabulary word list on the WB I was created after Wechsler randomly chose 100 words from the dictionary, tested them in a pilot study, and narrowed the item list by selecting the words that differentiated the two groups. The original Vocabulary subtest on the WB I contained 42 words, and each item was awarded 0, 1, or 1/2 of a point. None of the original words for the WB I were retained in future versions of the adult scale. There is no formal explanation as to why new words were selected and if he used the original methodology of selecting words from the dictionary. In the fourth edition of his book on intelligence, Wechsler (1958) writes that the WAIS vocabulary is (a) about the same difficulty as the WB I, (b) shorter than than the WB I list by 2 items, and (c) contains a larger percentage of action words (verbs). So, the current WAIS-III Vocabulary actually owes more to the WAIS (Wechsler, 1955), as 22 of words were carried over from the WAIS to the WAIS-III along with two additional words that were introduced with the WAIS-R (see Table 3).

For all practical purposes, the administration of the scale has remained the same through the years. When the WAIS was published, Wechsler added a "word card" so that the examiner could point to the word while saying it. Additionally, the scoring system was changed to 0, 1, or 2 points, a change that remains the same through the current kit. In addition to having nine new words, the WAIS-III also has a much more refined scoring criterion based upon extensive scoring studies.

TABLE 3   Items Retained through the Various Versions of the Wechsler Adult Intelligence Scale.

	WBI	WAIS	WAIS-R	New for WAIS-III	WAIS-III total items
Vocabulary	0	22	2	9	33
Information	6	6	6	10	28
Similarities	7	1	3	8	19
Comprehension	6	4	2	6	18
Digit Span	14	0	0	1	15
Arithmetic	7	6	1	6	20
Letter Number Sequencing	0	0	0	7	7
Picture Completion	5	3	3	14	25
Block Design	7[a]	3	0	4	14
Matrix Reasoining	0	0	0	26	26
Picture Arrangement	2	1	2	6	11
Digit Symbol Coding	67	23	3	40	133
Symbol Search	0	0	0	60	60
Object Assembly	3	0	0	2	5

[a]One item on the WAIS-III was originally on the Kohs test, the Wechsler Bellevue I, and the WAIS.

Information

Like the Vocabulary subtest of the WAIS-III, the Information subtest is also a measure of acquired knowledge. This subtest is correlated with the FSIQ score as well as with several other subtests that define the VCI on the WAIS-III (The Psychological Corporation, 1997). This subtest is more of a direct reflection of previous learning. As such, is also relatively resilient against brain dysfunction, and is thought of as a "hold" test (Larrabee et al., 1985). Like Vocabulary, Information is also a reflection of culture and education and is viewed as a direct measure of acquired knowledge.

Frank (1983) attributes the origins of this subtest to Guy Montrose Whipple (1909), who began testing individuals' "range of information" with his own test that required examinees to first rate how capable they believed they were in defining a word and, then to actually define the word after the ratings were made. One hundred test words were chosen based upon their relevance to diverse fields (e.g., American history, knowledge of French, chemistry, golf, social usages, etc.) and required the examinees to have knowledge in a specific area. After World War I, a committee of the National Research Council led by Haggerty, Terman, Thorndike, Whipple, and Yerkes developed a group-administered battery of 22 tests and included information in the test (Pintner, 1923; Whipple, 1921). Several others focused on information as well (e.g., Healy & Fernald, 1911, Knox, 1914); Wells & Martin, 1923). Perhaps, the most important inclusion was in the Army Alpha testing program (Yerkes, 1921; Yoakum & Yerkes, 1920). Questions in the army version appeared in a multiple-choice format so that the test could be administered in a group. Examples of the Army Alpha questions are: "Bombay is a city in . . . China, Egypt, India, Japan," or "A six-sided figure is called a . . . scholium, Parallelogram, hexagon, trapezium," and bear some resemblance to later Wechsler Bellevue Form I items.

Wechsler's version was administered orally where examinees were asked knowledge-based questions directly and had to answer verbally (Wechsler, 1939a). The items included in the WAIS-III were from a variety of sources: of the 28 items on the WAIS-III, 6 items were from the WB I, 6 from the WAIS, 6 from the WAIS-R, and 9 were totally new items developed for the WAIS-III. One additional item was a direct derivative from the WB I, except that the focus of the question was centered on the world rather than on the United States. The largest item-level change in content has traditionally occurred because items were viewed as unsuitable or unfair to various subgroups of the population.

Similarities

The Similarities subtest requires more abstraction than the other verbal subtests, as the individual has to verbally state the relationship between two words. The words are objects or concepts, and as the items increase in difficulty, the relationships between the words become more abstract. At the same time, the Similarities subtest is highly related to the other subtests measuring Verbal Comprehension and FSIQ (The Psychological Corporation, 1997).

The origin of Similarities dates back to the initial Binet-Simon 1905 scale (Binet & Simon, 1905/1916a) and was used in the Stanford revision (Terman, 1916). Similar tasks were included in group-administered tests (Terman & Chamberlain, 1918; Whipple, 1921; Yerkes, 1921). For the Army Alpha, for instance, derivative "analogies" tasks paired words together based upon abstract concepts (Yerkes, 1921).

Once again, Wechsler would have been familiar with the Stanford Binet and the Army Alpha through his work in the military. The core items for the Similarities subtest included in the WAIS-III subtest were developed for the WB I, with some even being extracted directly from the Stanford-Binet and the Terman and Chamberlain tests (1918). Of the 19 items in the WAIS-III, 7 have been taken directly from the WB-I, 1 is a derivative of an item in the initial scale, 1 item comes from the WAIS, and 3 items come from the WAIS-R (see Table 3). The WAIS-III includes eight new items, three of which are at the beginning of the scale to increase the floor and two of which are at the end of the scale to increase the ceiling. A greater emphasis was placed upon developing a clearer basis for scoring the items during the standardization process than had been done in previous editions of the Wechsler adult scales. The WAIS-III has more refined scoring criteria with several more examples to assist the examiner in judging responses and correctly scoring the protocol.

Comprehension

The Comprehension subtest is correlated with the other Verbal Comprehension subtests, overall FSIQ, and also loads on the verbal factor. Though

Wechsler believed that this subtest was a good measure of Verbal ability, he also questioned if it could measure a unique dimension as well (Wechsler, 1939a). He wrote that Comprehension was related to common sense, practical information, and a general ability to evaluate past experience. Several investigators through the years have raised the possibility that this subtest could also be a measure of social judgment or social intelligence (e.g., Kaufman & Lictenberger, 1999). However, such assertions have been difficult to validate. Our own investigation in the normative sample indicate that it is highly correlated with other measures of verbal functioning and, in the majority of cases, provides information that was somewhat redundant to the other verbal measures (see Tulsky et al., 2000). For this reason and because of its administration time relative to the other verbal subtests, the Comprehension subtest was made optional in the index score structure (Wechsler, 1997a).

Like most of the other verbal subtests, Comprehension was initially developed by Binet (Binet & Simon, 1905/1916a) in a subtest called Reply to an Abstract Question. Children were asked questions such as, When one is sleepy, what must one do? or "When one has been struck by a playmate, who did not mean to do it, what must one do?" The subtest was included in the Stanford-Binet (Terman, 1916). The most interesting and likely source for later Comprehension items can be found in Terman and Chaimberlain's (1918) battery. They had no less than three separate subtests with items that resemble modern-day Wechsler items. The Origin of Familiar Things subtests, which was suggested by G. Stanely Hall (Terman's mentor in graduate school), required the examinee to state where things (e.g., eggs, butter, ivory) came from. The Resourcefulness subtest was a direct derivative of the Binet items and contained items like, "What's the thing to do if you are alone in the woods far from home, and a savage bull chases you?" Finally, the Finding Reasons subtest asks the examinee to give all the reasons why something is the way it is (e.g., Why would most people rather have an automobile than a buggy?). This task was included in other tests of the time as well, including the National Intelligence Tests (Pinter, 1923; Whipple, 1921), and in the Army battery of tests. The latter was entitled Practical Judgment and was included in the Army Alpha (Yerkes, 1921; Yoakom & Yerkes, 1920).

The majority of items in the WAIS-III are from previous versions of the scale: Seven of the current items are from the WB I, four are from the WAIS, and two are from the WAIS-R. Some of the items were also extracted directly from the Army Alpha scale (e.g., item 3 on the Army Alpha was "Why is leather used for shoes?" and after just slight rewording, was used as item 5 in the WB I; see Yerkes, 1921; Wechsler, 1939a). Six items on the WAIS-III are new (see Table 3), and two of these were designed specifically to extend the range at the lower end of the scale so that individuals with mental retardation could be better differentiated.

In 1955, the WAIS included unfamiliar proverbs as part of the Comprehension item set. These items are among the most abstract in the subtest and, on the surface, appeared to be a different item type than the other items. For this reason, the research team working on the WAIS-III attempted to separate these item types. Preliminary testing was conducted to determine if the proverbs could be moved into a separate scale of abstract verbal reasoning from the items that seemed more related to practical reasoning. To accomplish this goal, an item set of 35 proverbs from cultures other than America was created and pilot tested in some groups of college students at a local university. From these data, six new proverbs were selected and included in the tryout version of the scale so that a subset of nine proverb items were interspersed among the other items in the Comprehension tryout item set (The Psychological Corporation, 1995). Examples of these items included an unusual Mexican proverb, "Even cats want shoes," that suggests that individuals desire things that they can't use. Included as well was a Chinese proverb, "A one-eyed person is king among the blind," that suggests that strengths and weaknesses vary according to the context in which they are examined.

It was predicted that these unusual proverb items would have a higher correlation with the Similarities subtest than with the total of the "nonproverb" Comprehension items. This was not empirically supported, however, as the proverb items had an equivalent correlation with both the Comprehension and the Similarities tryout total scores (unpublished memo, Tulsky & Zhu, November 7, 1994).[2] Moreover, the sum score of the proverb items had a high to moderate correlation with the sum of the nonproverb Comprehension items, suggesting that the two "types" of items were not that different ($r = 0.64$). Both of these item sets (proverbs and nonproverbs) had equivalent correlations with the other verbal subtest tryout total scores (e.g., in the magnitude of 0.60–0.70; unpublished memo, Tulsky & Zhu, November 7, 1994). These results did not support the premise that the proverb items are fundamentally different from the other "practical reasoning/common sense" types of items. As a result of these data, the idea of removing the proverb items from the final WAIS-III data set was

---

[2]Results based upon WAIS-III tryout data ($N = 450$).

abandoned. This became especially important in light of the observation that two of the proverb items clearly were the most difficult, extending the difficulty level of the entire scale. This result replicated findings that had occurred in the previous editions of the WAIS and WAIS-R. The item total correlations for each age group for these items were within acceptable range, again justifying their inclusion on the subtest. For these reasons, the final form of the WAIS-III comprehension subtest includes two proverbs as the final two (and most difficult) items in the entire items set.

Block Design

In this subtest, the examinee must use blocks with different colored sides (red, white, and half red/white) to construct designs. It is a timed task and the examinee receives extra credit for completing it quickly. It loads on the Perceptual Organization factor and is one of the most sensitive subtests to clinical conditions (see Matarazzo, 1972; Wechsler, 1944) and shows a decline in performance with age (Wechsler, 1930).

Though Samuel Kohs is often given credit for developing the Block Design subtest, its origins can be traced back a few years before that. Healy and Fernald (1911) have been cited as developing the initial task for their battery (as referenced by Frank, 1983) and soon the task was being implemented in several performance-based batteries. The blocks themselves came from children's toys. They were manufactured by the Embossing Company (Hutt, 1925) and sold in toy shops, and by the Milton Bradley Company in boxes of 16 or 36 blocks (Kohs, 1923; Maxfield, 1925; see Figure 4). These blocks were called color cubes and

> were one inch long on the side, each painted in colors in the same manner. Four surfaces of each cube are of solid color—white, blue, red, and yellow, respectively; the other two surfaces are painted in two colors divided diagonally, one side being painted half white and half red, and the other half blue and half yellow. (Maxfield, 1925, p. 98)

Frances N. Maxfield developed a Design Block Test in 1914 and began using it in the Psychological Laboratory and Clinic of the University of Pennsylvania. In Maxfield's version, the examiner constructed a model and then, with the model intact, asked the examinee to construct a similar model with a new set of blocks. There are reports that Maxfield also assessed memory with the blocks by requiring the examinee to construct the pattern after the model was removed (Hutt, 1925; Maxfield, 1925). The test

FIGURE 4.   Photo of variations of "Color Cubes" sold by the Embossing Company at local toy stores. Early versions of the "Design Blocks" test (e.g., Kohs, 1923) were sold without the materials. The Non-embossed blocks virtually identical to these were sold as part of the Wechsler Intelligence scales. Two color "Red" and "White" blocks were introduced in the WAIS in 1955 and the WISC-R in 1974. Color Cubes sets were provided courtesy of Scott Bultman, Uncle Goose Toys; William Meredith, Embossing Company historian, and the author.

(be it called Design Blocks or cube construction) appears to have been popular and several other test authors (e.g., Arthur, 1930; Cornell & Coxe, 1934; Pintner & Patterson, 1917; Yerkes, 1921) incorporated cube construction into their performance batteries. The committee for the army testing program even incorporated a pencil-and-paper version of Cube Construction for the Army Beta Test (Yerkes, 1921; Yoakum & Yerkes, 1920).

The person most responsible for adapting and modifying the task into the version that we know today as Block Design was Samuel C. Kohs (Kohs, 1923). Kohs replaced the three-dimensional models of the designs with printed simulus cards of the designs. Kohs was well trained in testing, having worked with H.H. Goddard at the Vineland Training School and completed his dissertation with Lewis Terman in 1919 (John Wasserman, personal communication, June 2001). The Block Design test had been developed for his dissertation. It is this version of the test that was extracted by Wechsler (1939a, 1939b) for the WB I. Seven of the original 17 Kohs items were included in the WB I, and many are still included in the current version of the test. Kohs used the multicolored blocks that were described by Maxfield above and those same materials were included in the WB I kits. The only small change that Wechsler had made is that only two-color red/white designs are printed on the stimulus card. When the WB I was revised to the WAIS, seven of the original designs were retained, three new items were developed, and special red and white blocks were produced for the kit. Barring a few exceptions, the item set has stayed relatively intact, although for the WAIS-III, four new items were developed.

Wechsler recognized that this was a strong subtest and thought that it was his "best single performance item . . . [as it conformed] to all statistical criteria for a 'good' test" (Wechsler, 1944, p. 94). Block Design correlated with several other measures, indicating that it was highly related to *g*. On the WAIS-III, it is a strong marker variable on the POI. Wechsler also believed that this subtest lent itself to qualitative analysis and thought that the examiner could learn as much about how an individual takes the task through observation and inspection of errors as from the total score.

Picture Completion

The Picture Completion test consists of pictures, each of which has an important part missing. The examinee studies each picture and has to indicate what the missing part is within a 20-second time limit. Picture Completion is thought to measure visual perception and the ability to determine if the missing part is either essential or a function of the object (Wechsler, 1939b).

The subtest's origin comes from the Binet and Simon (1908/1916b) subtest called Unfinished Pictures (or Mutilated Pictures, as translated by Wechsler, 1939b), from which, it was adapted for group testing and incorporated into the Army Beta examination (Yerkes, 1921; Yoakum & Yerkes, 1920) and, independently (as the "Drawing Completion Test") by Rudolph Pintner and Herbert Toops (1918). The name Picture Completion appears to have been derived from the Healy Pictorial Completion Test II (Healy, 1918, 1921) and used in the Army Beta test (Yerkes, 1921; Yoakum & Yerkes, 1920).[3] Wechsler extracted some items from the army mental testing program and others from the Pintner and Toops (1918) test. Figure 5 shows two items that were originally presented in the Army Beta test (Yerkes, 1921;

[3]The Healy Picture Completion Test II was also used as part of the Pitner and Patterson (1917) Performance Scale and the Army Performance Test (Yerkes, 1921; Yoakum & Yerkes, 1920).

from Army Beta   from WB I

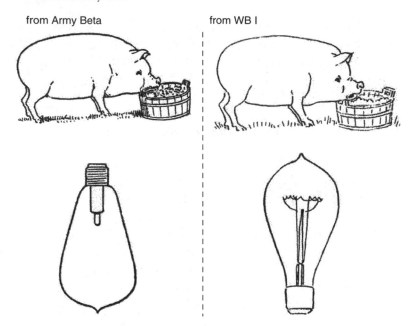

FIGURE 5.   Examples of Picture Completion Items used in the Army Beta and Wechsler Bellevue Form I. Illustrations from the Army Beta from Yerkes, 1921 (in the public domain). Illustrations from the Wechsler Bellevue, Form I copyright © 1939. The Psychological Corporation. Used with Permission. All Rights Reserved.

Yoakum & Yerkes, 1920) and the counterpart on the WB I (Wechsler, 1939a). In the first item, a pig without the tail is shown and the item was redrawn exactly as it had been in the original, without modification. The second item, a light bulb, had been redrawn and modified with a different part missing. However, the similarities between the items are apparent.

The items in the WAIS-III look radically different as they have been redrawn in color and are more contemporary looking. As Table 3 shows, 14 of the items in the WAIS-III are new, and of the existing 11 items, 5 came from the WB I, 3 came from the WAIS, and 3 came from the WAIS-R. The task demands and scoring remains unchanged from the previous versions, however.

Matrix Reasoning

In the WAIS-III, the new Matrix Reasoning subtest replaces Object Assembly as a core subtest that contributes to the PIQ, FSIQ, and POI scores. This subtest was added for several very compelling reasons: it has long been considered to measure "fluid" intelligence, it is a reliable estimate of *g*, it is relatively culture-fair and language-free, it requires no hand manipulation, and has no time limits. An untimed performance measure would also allow for contrasts with other timed nonverbal reasoning tasks, such as Block Design.

The Matrix Reasoning subtest contains 26 items (see Figure 6) and is similar to other items in existing matrix analogy tasks such as Raven's Standard Progressive Matrices (Raven, Raven, & Court, 1998) and Cattell's Culture Fair test (Cattell & Cattell, 1960). The items require the examinee to use reason and problem-solving skills as well as performing various mental manipulations for each item. There are several different types of items, and the examinee has to be capable of approaching novel stimuli to solve the problem.

The reliability coefficients in the standardization sample are quite high across the different age groups (e.g., average $r_{xx} = 0.90$) and the subtest correlates highest with Block Design (.60), and in factor analysis, loads on a factor made up by subtests measuring Perceptual Organization. Preliminary results suggested that the subtest was highly correlated with Raven's Progressive Matrices (The Psychological Corporation, 1997) and with the spatial variables from the Halstead Category Test (Dugbartey et al., 1999). The latter article also replicated the finding in the standardization sample (The Psychological Corporation, 1997) that showed that Matrix

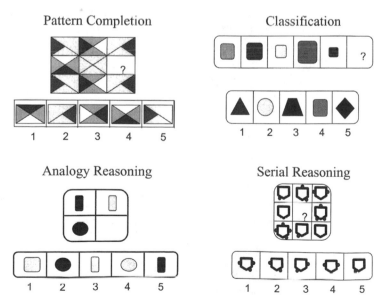

FIGURE 6. Sample Matrix Reasoning Items. Copyright © 1997. The Psychological Corporation. Used with Permission. All Rights Reserved.

Reasoning is highly correlated with several other variables within the WAIS–III including FSIQ, PIQ, and VIQ (Dugbartey et al., 1999).

A more recent report of the criterion-related validity of this scale (see Donders, Tulsky, & Zhu, 2001) has shown that this subtest is not especially sensitive to traumatic brain injury (TBI) as individuals with severe TBI perform well on this task. Even those individuals who have been in a coma for an extended period of time seem to score as well as individuals with less severe TBI or matched control normal functioning subjects. This raised questions such as: Should their scores be intact and how should an examiner interpret performance on this subtest? Is the Matrix Reasoning test a "hold test" that is relatively insensitive to change (Larrabee et al., 1985) or do different groups show differential abilities on the subtest, making it sensitive in some populations and not in others (e.g., evidence of differential validity)? Additional studies of other clinical groups are needed to help answer these questions.

Picture Arrangement

This subtest is made up of a series of pictures that, when arranged in the correct order, tell a little story. The examinee is required to sequence the pictures in the shortest amount of time. This test is purported to measure PIQ; however, previous research studies have demonstrated that the subtest has a large verbal component, as documented by significant correlations with other verbal subtests and split loadings in factor-analytic studies between a verbal- and performance-based factor. This is often interpreted as an indication that individuals verbally mediate as a way of solving the problem. It is also thought of as contributing a unique component of "social judgment" to the Wechsler battery, but data validating its use as a measure of social judgment has not been forthcoming.

Wechsler credits a French psychologist (DeCroly, 1914) as the first person to use this task. It was then tried during the army mental testing program in World War I (Yerkes, 1921). Originally it was developed for the Form Beta (see examples of items in Figure 7), but it was not employed past the item tryout testing. An alternate test entitled the "Foxy Grandpa" series was included in the Army Performance Battery, but Wechsler cites that "it was not used to any great extent." Wechsler would have been exposed to the test during the war, and when this subtest was included in another performance battery (see Cornell & Coxe, 1934), Wechsler elected to follow suit. He incorporated three items from the preliminary testing of the Army Beta (see

FIGURE 7.   Examples of Picture Arrangement Items in the Army Beta Preliminary Form. From Yerkes, 1921. Some items, like these pictured, contained emotionally-laden material. The subtest is often thought to be a measure of "social intelligence."

FIGURE 8.   Examples of Picture Arrangement Items used in the Army Beta Preliminary Form and the Wechsler Bellevue Form I. Illustrations from the Army Beta from Yerkes, 1921. Illustrations from the Wechsler Bellevue, Form I Copyright © 1939. The Psychological Corporation. Used with Permission. All Rights Reserved.

Figure 8) and adapted four items from a "King" cartoon series that appeared in the *New Yorker Magazine* (The cartoonist was Otto Soglow, see Figure 9).

The demands of the task have remained the same through the years, although there has been some evolution of the item content through the revision process. As shown in Table 3, the WAIS-III contains 11 items total, 2 of which were developed for the WB I, 1 from the WAIS, and 2 from the WAIS-R. For the WAIS-III, the artwork was redrawn and placed on sturdier card stock that was purported to facilitate the manipulation of the stimuli (Wechsler, 1997a). Outdated content was modified (e.g., the Little King cartoon drawings, which are unfamiliar to most examinees who take the test to day) have been dropped as well as items that might appear sexist in content. Also, the item difficulty of the test was extended.

Though Picture Arrangement had been a core subtest in previous editions, it was made optional in the computation of the index-based score. This decision was based, in part, on data showing that the subtest measures other constructs in addition to PIQ. Data also indicated that its inclusion did not provide acceptable incremental validity in the normative standardization sample (Tulsky et al., 2000).

Object Assembly

The Object Assembly subtest may be considered a measure of the ability to interpret and organize visually perceived material while working against a time limit (Sattler & Ryan, 2001). Examinees are required to put puzzles together as quickly as they can. Examinees receive points for both accuracy and speed. Pintner and Paterson would write that the examinee must have the "synthetic ability of seeing the parts of a whole and putting these together" (Pintner & Patterson, 1917, p. 56). Wechsler would echo the importance of measuring an individual's ability to determine the whole–part relationship (Wechsler, 1939b), and some contemporary experts continue to cite the importance of measuring this ability (e.g., Kaplan, 1988; Kaplan et al., 1991).

Like most of the Wechsler subtests, Object Assembly has a long, rich history that predates the WB-I. The Profile-like test was originally developed by Knox (1914) for use testing immigrants at Ellis Island to identify those with mental retardation. Pintner and Paterson (1917) adapted the Profile puzzle making it more difficult, and also developed a Manikin test to go along with it. The two puzzles were included in one of the earliest performance batteries of the time (Pintner and Paterson, 1917) and on the

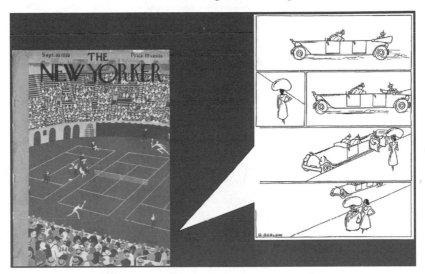

FIGURE 9.   A "Little King" comic strip reproduced from the New Yorker Magazine from September 10, 1932. In the Wechsler Bellevue Scale Form I, 4 New Yorker Magazine comic strips were used as items. This particular item was also included in the WAIS and WAIS-R. Illustration and cover © 2002 The New Yorker collection from cartoonbank.com. Used with Permission. All rights reserved.

army performance measure (Yerkes, 1921). Later, these two puzzles were included both the Cornell–Coxe Performance Ability Scale (Cornell & Coxe, 1934) and Grace Arthur's Point Scale of Performance Tests (Arthur, 1930), which were leading performance scales that had been published before the WB-I. Wechsler used the Profile and Manikin puzzles to test military recruits. He also was determined to include a subtest that required the examinee to construct things and manipulate stimuli, and he found that form boards had ceiling problems when working with adults (Wechsler, 1939b). Hence, he settled on the Object Assembly test, and referred to the puzzles as "separate figure form boards" (Wechsler, 1939b, p. 986) and, as such, it met his goals to include a test requiring construction in the WB I.

At the same time, Wechsler understood the limitations of this subtest. Wechsler wrote that "Object Assembly was included in our battery only after much hesitation" and that this inclusion came after realizing that other form board tests were not difficult enough for use with adults, as they didn't differentiate individuals with high average ability IQ scores or above (Wechsler, 1939, pp. 98–99). In addition to having a restricted range and a ceiling problem, Object Assembly was also plagued by practice effects upon retesting. Wechsler even said that the subtest was almost "useless" for retest purposes (Wechsler, 1939, p. 99). Despite all of these potential limitations, Wechsler believed that the subtest provided clinically relevant information, and it was included in the original WB I and in all revisions since (see Figure 10).

The WBI contained three items (including a slightly modified version of Pintner's Manikin and Profile puzzles), and these three items have been retained in the current WAIS-III. The WAIS-III also includes two new items that are more difficult in an attempt to improve the range of scores. However, a decision was made to make the Object Assembly subtest optional (see Wechsler, 1997a; The Psychological Corporation, 1997), and this decision has received some criticism because it "alters the meaning of the performance IQ, perhaps jeopardizing the continuity of the Performance IQ from the Wechsler Bellevue-I to WAIS to WAIS-R to WAIS-III" (Kaufman & Lichtenberger, 1999, p. 171).

Such criticism is not unexpected, as the summary scores of the WAIS-III differ in structure from its predecessors. Gone from the WAIS-III is is a subtest that requires construction of stimuli, replaced by one that, on the surface, would require different abilities. The developers of the WAIS-III struggled

FIGURE 10.   Kit Assembly of the Object Assembly Subtest for the Wechsler Bellevue. Photo courtesy of the Psychological Corporation.

with the decision (as described earlier in this chapter as well as in Wechsler, 1997a, and Tulsky et al., 2000). However, the limitations of Object Assembly seemed to outweigh the benefits, and the developers began to ask if tradition should be preserved at the expense of overall improvement to the test battery?

Object Assembly is heavily dependent on speed, and individuals who work quickly will obtain higher scores because they receive bonus points. Thirty percent of the possible total points on Object Assembly (e.g., 15 points out of the maximum 52 points) are awarded for bonus points, which confounds the ability that Object Assembly is alleged to measure. Kaufman and Lichtenberger (1999) even point out that the maximum score for a person in the aged 20–34 reference group could be 11 if they obtain a perfect score without receiving bonus points. Especially with the addition of a PSI score, subtests that confound speed and accuracy make the index scores harder to interpret.

In addition to speed, Object Assembly has other flaws. The Object Assembly score has unacceptable error variance, especially at the older age groups, forcing a revision (at least in the older age groups) as the reliability of the score is simply too low to be used effectively. Details of these decisions have been provided in previous publications (e.g., Wechsler, 1997a; The Psychological Corporation, 1997; Tulsky et al., 2000; Tulsky & Ledbetter, 2000) and will not be further reviewed here.

Letter Number Sequencing

This subtest was originally developed by James Gold and his colleagues at the University of Maryland (see Gold, Carpenter, Randolph, Goldberg, & Weinberger, 1997) and incorporated into the WMS-III Standardization Edition with almost no changes for standardization testing. Its strong performance as a working memory task led to its retention in the WMS-III and its incorporation into the WAIS-III. Tulsky and Zhu (2000) have discussed issues about the standardization methodology used with this test, which will not be repeated here.

In this test, subjects were presented with a mixed list of numbers and letters (e.g., R—4—B—9—L—3) and their task is to repeat the list by saying the numbers first in ascending order and then the letters in alphabetical order (e.g., 3—4—9—B—L—R). This subtest is summed with Arithmetic and Digit Span to form the WAIS-III Working Memory Index, and it is summed with the Spatial Span score to form the WMS-III Working

Memory Index. Since it was only administered once in the standardization process, the subtest should only be administered once when both the WAIS-III and WMS-III scales are used (see Tulsky & Zhu, 2000).

Initial support for the subtest indicates that it has a strong working memory component (Crowe, 2000; Gold et al., 1997; Haut, Kuwabara, Leach, & Arias; 2000). For instance, in functional imaging studies, Haut et al. (2000) demonstrated that activation while performing letter–number tasks was consistent with brain activation patterns when performing other working memory tasks. In somewhat different paradigms, Crowe (2000) and the Psychological Corporation (1997) demonstrated that the LNS task is related to Working Memory, especially the Digit Span subtest. These findings also indicated that the letter number sequencing task may not be strictly verbal, as visual spatial components of working memory are activated during performance (Haut et al., 2000) and the task has secondary relationships with visual spatial, information–processing tasks (Crowe, 2000), set shifting, verbal fluency, and attentional tasks (Gold et al., 1997).

There is some evidence that this subtest does discriminate individuals. Donders et al. (2001) have found that the subjects with TBI perform worse on this task than controls matched on key demographic variables. Similarly, schizophrenia patients have impaired performance on this task as well (see Gold et al., 1997).

Digit Span

Wechsler's original description of the "Memory Span for Digits" cited that there was "perhaps no test that has been so universally used in scales of intelligence as that of memory span for digits" (Wechsler, 1939b, p. 85). He cites its use in the Binet scales and several applied settings and points out that its relation to g is among the poorest of all of the scales and that low scores usually indicated that an individual had "attention defects."

In actuality, the origins of the subtest date much further than Binet. Boake (2002) describes the history in more depth as he points out that Ebbinghaus, who is often referenced as the person who first developed a span task with nonsense syllables (e.g., see Frank, 1983). Jacobs (1887) points out that these were difficult for schoolchildren and recommended that digits be used in their place. In collaboration with Galton, they tried out the digit span task with children with mental retardation (see Galton, 1887; Jacobs, 1887).

Bolton (1892) followed this initial study with tests on schoolchildren and by the time Binet and Simon included the task on their battery, it had been cited many times in the literature.

The version of Digit Span in the Wechsler test combined the forwards component and the backwards component into a single test. Wechsler cites two reasons for this decision: (a) the limited range of items that contributed to each of the scores (Forward and Backward) in the original standardization sample, and (b) to prevent memory for spans from having too great an emphasis in the entire battery (e.g., two scores . . . a forward and backward score that were independent; Wechsler, 1944). Wechsler pointed out that only a few items for the forward score and only a few items in the backward score had acceptable variance to differentiate individuals in the standardization sample.

The procedure of combining forward and backward scores has been followed throughout the revision cycles. As Wechsler pointed out, only a few items in the WAIS-III have a wide degree of variance. Frequency values at the item level are provided in Tables 4 and 5. For Digits Forward, the majority of individuals are differentiated based upon a sum of items 4–7; for Digits Backward, the differentiation is based upon a sum of items 2–6. These data support what Wechsler wrote in the early days of the scale: namely that it would be difficult to create a scale when item sets are restricted. Moreover, when ranges are so restricted, the psychometric properties of separate forward and backward scores tend to be low. For all of these reasons, it was decided to retain the Digit Span Total score and not present separate scores for Digits Forward and Backwards.

Such a procedure is not without criticism, however. Edith Kaplan and her colleagues have written that the two scores combine multidimensional constructs and limit the clinical interpretations that can be made when low scores are obtained (Kaplan et al., 1991, 1999). Reynolds (1997) also presented arguments for keeping the scores separate.

The correlation between the Digit Span Forward raw score and Digit Span Backward raw score for the standardization sample is only 0.60, which suggests that there are some differences between the two scores. Moreover, the addition of the construct of working memory on the WAIS-III calls for a review of Digits Backward separately from Digit Span Total. Digits Backward is thought to be a much more demanding working memory task. For this reason, the subtest-scaled, score-normative information is displayed in Table 6. Users should interpret scores in light of the restriction in range that was discussed above.

TABLE 4 Frequency of Item Responses for Digits Forward[a]

Digit Span Forward	Point total	Overall sample	16–17	18–19	20–24	25–29	30–34	35–44	45–54	55–64	65–69	70–74	75–79	80–84	85–89
Item 1	0	0	0	0	0	0	0	0	0	0	0	0	0	0	0
	1	0	0	0	0	0	1	0	1	0	1	1	0	1	1
	2	100	100	100	100	100	100	100	100	100	100	100	100	99	99
Item 2	0	0	0	0	0	0	1	0	1	0	0	0	0	0	0
	1	0	0	0	1	1	1	1	1	1	1	1	1	2	0
	2	99	100	100	100	100	99	100	99	100	100	100	99	98	100
Item 3	0	1	1	1	1	1	1	2	2	2	1	1	1	7	0
	1	3	4	4	5	2	3	2	4	5	2	4	3	2	7
	2	96	96	96	95	97	97	96	95	94	97	95	97	97	93
Item 4	0	6	3	4	4	3	3	5	6	10	7	9	8	13	11
	1	17	13	16	15	9	13	12	13	19	23	21	24	22	26
	2	77	85	81	82	89	85	84	82	72	71	70	69	65	63
Item 5	0	28	24	23	17	21	23	21	21	32	32	38	38	43	46
	1	32	28	30	33	30	38	32	34	28	30	30	38	34	31
	2	40	48	47	51	50	40	48	46	41	39	33	25	23	23
Item 6	0	51	40	43	39	46	46	43	46	54	59	59	67	68	77
	1	27	34	31	32	29	24	32	27	23	22	27	22	22	16
	2	22	26	26	29	26	31	26	28	24	20	15	12	10	7
Item 7	0	77	68	73	67.5	73	76	72	75	76	78	82	87	90	97
	1	15	24	19	21	20	16	21	16	14	15	12	9	5	2
	2	8	9	9	12	8	9	8	9	11	7	7	5	5	1
Item 8	0	94	93	92	93	89	92	96	94	94	94	97	96	97	100
	1	5	6	7	7	9	8	5	6	5	5	3	3	3	0
	2	1	2	2	1	3	1	0	1	2	2	0	2	0	0

[a]Derived from the WAIS-III Standardization Sample (N = 2450). Data Copyright © 2002. The Psychological Corporation. Used with Permission. All Rights Reserved.

TABLE 5   Frequency of Item Responses for Digits Backward[a]

Digit Span Backward	Point total	Overall Sample	16–17	18–19	20–24	25–29	30–34	35–44	45–54	55–64	65–69	70–74	75–79	80–84	85–89
Item 1	0	1	2	1	1	2	1	1	1	2	1	0	0	0	0
	1	1	0	0	1	1	1	1	1	1	2	2	2	4	2
	2	98	99	100	99	98	95	99	99	98	98	98	98	98	98
Item 2	0	3	3	3	2	4	3	4	4	5	4	3	3	2	6
	1	12	6	11	8	10	10	9	9	11	17	18	13	17	21
	2	85	92	87	90	86	88	87	87	85	80	80	85	81	73
Item 3	0	18	14	13	12	15	16	14	14	23	25	22	26	25	24
	1	27	21	25	27	23	25	29	29	27	25	32	35	28	31
	2	55	65	63	62	63	60	58	58	50	51	47	39	47	45
Item 4	0	49	41	36	36	39	44	40	46	56	59	59	62	61	71
	1	30	33	37	33	35	28	39	28	28	39	28	25	23	21
	2	21	27	27	32	27	29	22	27	17	12	14	14	16	8
Item 5	0	75	69	69	67	61	68	73	73	76	79	86	86	89	92
	1	15	18	18	17	21	20	13	16	14	14	7	13	8	6
	2	11	13	14	17	19	12	15	11	10	8	7	2	3	2
Item 6	0	87	86	82	79	79	85	84	88	88	90	93	95	99	97
	1	9	10	12	14	14	13	10	9	8	7	6	3	1	2
	2	4	5	7	7	8	2	7	4	5	4	2	3	0	1
Item 7	0	96	98	94	93	95	97	93	96	95	97	100	100	100	100
	1	3	2	5	5	5	3	7	4	3	2	0	1	0	0
	2	1	1	1	2	1	1	0	1	2	2	0	0	0	0

TABLE 6 Digit Span Backward – Raw to Scaled Score Conversion

Scaled Score	16–17	18–19	20–24	25–29	30–34	35–44	45–54	55–64	65–69	70–74	75–79	80–84	85–89	Scaled Score
1	–	–	–	–	–	–	–	–	–	–	–	–	–	1
2	–	0	0	0	0	0	0	–	–	–	–	–	–	2
3	0–1	1	1	1	1	1	1	0	0	0	0	0	0	3
4	2	2	2	2	2	2	2	1	1	1	1	1	1	4
5	3	3	3	3	3	3	–	2	2	2	2	2	2	5
6	4	4	4	4	4	4	3	3	3	3	3	3	3	6
7	5	5	5	–	–	–	4	4	4	4	4	4	–	7
8	–	–	–	5	5	5	5	–	–	–	–	–	4	8
9	6	6	6	6	6	6	6	5	5	5	5	5	5	9
10	7	7	7	7	7	7	7	6	6	6	–	–	–	10
11	8	8	8	8	–	–	–	7	7	–	6	6	6	11
12	–	–	9	9	8	8	8	8	8	7	7	7	–	12
13	9	9	10	10	9	9	9	9	9	8	8	–	7	13
14	10	10	–	–	10	10	10	10	–	9	–	8	8	14
15	11	11	11	11	11	11	–	–	10	10	9	9	–	15
16	12	12	12	12	12	12	11	11	–	–	10	10	9	16
17	13	13	13	13	13	13	12	12	11	11	11	11	10	17
18	14	14	14	14	14	14	13	13	12	12	12	12	11–12	18
19	–	–	–	–	–	–	14	14	13–14	13–14	13–14	13–14	13–14	19

Arithmetic

In this subtest examinees are read arithmetic problems to which they have to perform the necessary calculations without the use of a pencil and paper. It is a mental arithmetic task, and as such, it is purported to measure "working memory" on the WAIS-III. In reality, however, there is evidence that it measures more than just this simple construct. Traditionally, factor-analytic results have found that the Arithmetic subtest has split loadings on the Verbal and Attention/Working Memory factors (Tulsky & Price, 2002; The Psychological Corporation, 1997) and occasionally, split loadings on the Working Memory and Perceptual Organization factors (Saklofske et al., 2000). Additionally, this subtest has relatively high intercorrelations with other subtests on the Wechsler scale (The Psychological Corporation, 1997) and for that reason, it has a relatively high *g* component.

Wechsler (1939b) realized that Arithmetic had a relatively strong relationship with other subtests measuring ability and felt that it was a "good measure of general intelligence" (p. 84). He cited the long history of using Arithmetic questions when estimating IQ even before the development of psychometric tests and thought that such items had good face validity and would be perceived as "fair" by the examinee (Wechsler, 1944). Arithmetic was a common test at the time, first used by Binet and later in the Healy and Fernald (1911) battery, as screening items by the Public Health Officials at Ellis Island (Mullan, 1917), in Terman-Chamberlain's (1918) group test, in the National Intelligence Tests (see Pintner, 1923; Whipple, 1921), and in the Army Alpha Battery (Yoakum & Yerkes, 1920; Yerkes, 1921). The Army Alpha included Arithmetic questions, but these were relatively easy to develop, and it is unclear if this was the actual source for Wechsler's original subtest. Instead, Wechsler points out that he was more concerned with keeping the subtest short and streamlined so that it wouldn't appear that it was a measure of academic achievement. Over the years, the test has remained relatively consistent, except the objects of the questions and their price have been updated to make the items appear relevant and current. In the WAIS-III, seven items were retained from the Wechsler Bellevue–I, six from the WAIS, and one from the WAIS-R. Also, six new items were added to the scale (see Table 3).

The subtest remains easy to administer and does correlate with many other subtests and index scores. For this reason, it is reasonable to conclude that Arithmetic is multifaceted, requiring verbal, attentional, working memory, and even reasoning skills. For issues of parsimony, it has been included on the WAIS–III working memory index. However, it would appear to measure more than just this ability.

Digit Symbol

The Digit Symbol—Coding subtest has one of the longest histories that has been well documented (Boake, 2002; Whipple, 1915). It was originally developed by Joseph Jastrow of the University of Wisconsin who used letters distributed like those of a typewriter keyboard to be associated to numerals (see Whipple, 1915, pp. 133–134), and in the early 1900s several versions of the test were developed (Healy & Fernald, 1911; Starch, 1911; Woodworth & Wells, 1911). Pintner and Paterson (1917) adapted the Woodworth and Wells task and from their work a version was modified by Arthur Otis and incorporated into the Army Beta examination protocol. Figure 11 depicts

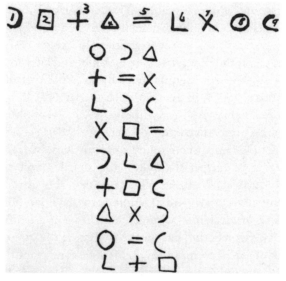

FIGURE 11.   The Association Test developed by Healy & Fernald (1911). In a task designed to "gauge the powers of attention," children had to associate numbers and symbols. Though originally designed as a memory task, it bears strong resemblance to modern day Digit Symbol–Coding tasks, which were developed around the same period. The modern day WISC-III/WISC-IV Coding task can be traced to Woodworth & Wells (1911) association test and the WAIS-III Digit Symbol task can be traced to the Army Beta. The similarity is so great, in fact, that examples from those tests have not be reproduced here to avoid violating test security. *Item reproduced from Healy & Fernald (1911).*

the demonstration that was printed on a blackboard and shown to the recruits who completed the Army Beta test. The version that was included in the Wechsler Bellevue scale was identical to that used in the Army Beta test (Yerkes, 1921; Yoakum & Yerkes, 1920). Slight changes were made in subsequent revisions (e.g., the symbol corresponding to the number "2" was changed in the WAIS revision (Wechsler, 1955); and the number of symbols to be completed has increased). However, for all practical purposes, the subtest has remained the same.

The diagnostic value of this subtest has been demonstrated over the years. Matarazzo (1972) was one of the first to point out that the Digit Symbol subtest is not simply a power test, but is related to "mental" slowing. As such, it is a test in which performance declines over time (Doppelt & Wallace, 1955; Matarazzo, 1972) and is sensitive to a range of clinical conditions (Lezak, 1995). On the WAIS-III, it is combined with Symbol Search to create the Processing Speed Index, which is also very sensitive to clinical conditions (Hawkins, 1998; Martin et al., 2000; The Psychological Corporation, 1997).

One of the reasons that the test is so clinically useful is because there are many reasons for poor performance on the task. Kaplan et al. (1991) have listed various reasons for poor performance on Digit Symbol. Individuals with poor motor coordination, short-term memory deficits, visual perceptual problems, and impaired clerical speed and accuracy will all perform poorly on this task. Some clinicians have employed incidental learning procedures to test for short-term memory deficits (Hart, Kwentus, Wade, & Hamer, 1987; Kaplan et al., 1991). Employing techniques developed for the WAIS-R NI (see Kaplan et al., 1991), the WAIS-III includes optional incidental learning and copy procedures to examine the process and determine what could have caused a poor performance.

The Digit Symbol—Incidental Learning procedures tease out the effects of memory and learning and the Digit Symbol—Copy focuses on perception and graphomotor speed. In the standardization sample, derived mainly from a neuropsychologically normal population, individuals tend to perform well, and it is very rare to score poorly on these tasks (see Table A-11; Wechsler, 1997a). The utility of the Digit Symbol optional procedures (e.g., Digit Symbol Pairing, Digit Symbol Free Recall, and Digit Symbol(Coding) were compared in various clinical populations against control samples matched on key demographic variables (age, sex, ethnicity, and education level). Significantly lower scores in a differential fashion in these clinical groups (see Tulsky, Zhu, Chen, & Kaplan, 1998) suggest that they enhance the specificity of the Digit Symbol subtest.

Symbol Search

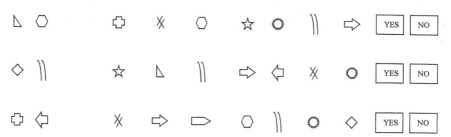

FIGURE 12.   Similated Symbol Search items. Copyright © 1997. The Psychological Corporation. Used with Permission. All Rights Reserved.

Symbol Search

The WAIS-III Symbol Search subtest is designed to measure an individual's speed at processing new information. In this task, the examinee is presented with a series of paired groups, each pair consisting of a target group and a search group (see Figure 12). The examinee's task is to decide whether either of the target symbols is in the search group, a group of five search symbols. The purpose of including this subtest in the WAIS-III is to enhance the measure of processing speed of the instrument and to bring out the four-factor structure that was found on the WISC-III. As mentioned earlier in the chapter, the WISC-III development team settled on the Symbol Search subtest as a way of measuring attention based upon experimental, attentional, and cognitive psychology.

Initial results of this subtest administered to a variety of clinical groups indicate that this is one of the more sensitive measures on the WAIS-III (The Psychological Corporation, 1997; Donders et al., 2001). Moreover, it shares some unique variance with Digit Symbol—Coding, and when the two scores are taken together, define the PSI. The PSI appears to be significantly lower in individuals with a variety of neuropsychological and psychoeducational problems (see Hawkins, 1998; Martin et al., 2000; The Psychological Corporation, 1997).

SUMMARY

This chapter describes some of the problems that have confronted the developers of Wechsler tests when deciding if changes should be made to these established instruments. The WAIS-III had to retain its historical roots, and yet be modified to fit contemporary theory and research findings. The changes made to the WAIS-III represent the most significant set of changes to a series of Wechsler tests. Some have criticized these changes for being too "different," others have criticized the fact that changes were made at all, and some have said that the WAIS-III changes did not go far enough.

What seems clear from empirical studies is that the addition of the new subtests has been positive. The Letter Number Sequencing task has stengthened the measurement of working memory (Crowe, 2000; Haut et al., 2000) and this subtest, together with Symbol Search, have enhanced the clinical utility of the test (Donders, Tulsky, & Zhu, 2001). The largest change, however, would result from placing more emphasis on the index scores, as there is support for such interpretation in clinical settings (e.g., see Martin et al., 2000).

Should we argue that future revisions of the Wechsler tests be built upon the changes introduced here? Areas that will improve the Wechsler scales would be (a) increased emphasis on the factor scores and publication of expanded domains of cognitive functioning (e.g., see Tulsky, Ivnik, Price, & Wilkins, Chapter 4, this volume); (b) revising and strengthening the construct of working memory, (c) constructing subtests that are factorially "purer" and replacing subtests that tend to have loadings on multiple factors. In this book (see Tulsky et al., Chapter 4, this volume), we have incorporated memory into a unified battery of cognitive functioning. The factor-analytic research (see Tulsky & Price, in press) serves as evidence that the memory subtests measure unique factors not captured in the Wechsler tests of intelligence.

Chapter 3 (Tulsky et al., this volume) will critically examine the background and changes that have been made in the WMS-III and reevaluate this test following 5 years of use. The full possibilities of the co-norming project will be discussed in Chapter 4, (Tulsky et al., this volume) and new indices will be developed and used throughout the remainder of the book.

REFERENCES

Altus, W. D. (1945). The differential validity and difficulty of subtests of the Wechsler Mental Ability scale. *Psychological Bulletin, 42,* 238–249.

American Psychological Association (1992). *Ethical standards for psychologists.* Washington, DC: Author.

Archer, R. P., Maruish, M., Imhof, E. A., & Piotrowski, C. (1991). Psychological test usage with adolescent clients: 1990 survey findings. *Professional Psychology: Research and Practice, 22(3)*, 247–252.

Arthur, G. (1930). *A point scale of performance tests*. New York: The Commonwealth Fund.

Barclay, A., Yater, A., & Wechsler, D. (1972). Preliminary investigation of the visuo–motor recall test. *Perceptual and Motor Skills, 34*, 867–872.

Binet, A., & Simon, T. (1916a). New methods for the diagnosis of the intellectual level of subnormals. In *The development of intelligence in children* (E. S. Kite, Trans.). Baltimore: Williams & Wilkins Company. (Original work published 1905)

Binet, A., & Simon, T. (1916b). The development of intelligence in the child. In *The development of intelligence in children*. (E. S. Kite, Trans.). Baltimore: Williams & Wilkins Company. (Original work published 1908)

Binet, A., & Simon, T. (1916c). New investigation upon the measure of the intellectual level among school children. In *The development of intelligence in children*. (E. S. Kite, Trans.). Baltimore: Williams & Wilkins Company. (Original work published 1911)

Boake, C. (2002, February). *From the Binet-Simon to the Wechsler-Bellevue: A century of intelligence testing*. Paper presented at the 20th annual meeting of the International Neuropsychological Society, Toronto.

Bolton, T. L. (1892). The growth of memory in school children. *American Journal of Psychology, 4*, 362–380.

Buros, O. K. (Ed). (1941). *The 1940 mental measurements yearbook*. Highland Park, NJ: Gryphon Press.

Butler, M., Retzlaff, P., & Vanderploeg, R. (1991). Neuropsychological test usage. *Professional Psychology: Research and Practice, 22*, 510–512.

Camara, W. J., Nathan, J. S., & Puente, A, E. (2000). Psychological test usage: Implications in professional psychology. *Professional Psychology: Research and Practice, 31*, 141–154.

Carroll, J. B. (1993). *Human cognitive abilities: A survey of factor analytic studies*. Cambridge, MA: Cambridge University Press.

Cattell, R. B. (1963). Theory of fluid and crystallized intelligence: A critical experiment. *Journal of Educational Psychology, 54*, 1–22.

Cattell, R. B., & Cattell, A. K. S. (1960). *The Culture Fair Intelligence Test*. Champaign, IL: Institute for Personality and Ability Testing.

Christodoulou, C., DeLuca, J., Ricker, J. H., Madigan, N., Bly, B. M., Lange, G., Kalnin, A. J., Liu, W. C., Steffener, J., & Ni, A. C. (2001). Functional magnetic resonance imaging of working memory impairment following traumatic brain injury. *Journal of Neurology, Neurosurgery, and Psychiatry, 71*, 161–168.

Cohen, J. (1952a). Factors underlying Wechsler-Bellevue Performance of three neuropsychiatric groups. *Journal of Abnormal and Social Psychology, 47*, 359–365.

Cohen, J. (1952b). A factor-analytically based rationale for the Wechsler-Bellevue. *Jouirnal of Consulting Psychology, 16*, 272–277.

Cohen, J. (1957). A factor-analytically based rationale for the Wechsler Adult Intelligence Scale. *Jouirnal of Consulting Psychology, 21*, 451–457.

Cohen, J. (1959). The factorial structure of the WISC at ages 7–6, 10–5, and 13–6. *Journal of Consulting Psychology, 23*, 285–299.

Colvin, S. S. (1923). Principles underlying the construction and use of intelligence tests. In G. M. Whipple (Ed.), *The 21st yearbook of the National Society for the Study of Education: Intelligence tests and their use*. Bloomington, IL: Public School Publishing Co.

Cornell, E. L., & Coxe, W. W. (1934). *Cornell–Coxe Performance Ability Scale*. Yonkers-on-Hudson: World Book Company.

Crowe, S. F. (2000). Does the letter number sequencing task measure anything more than digit span? *Assessment, 7(2),* 113–117.

Das, J. P., & Naglieri, J. A. (2001) The Das-Naglieri Cognitive Assessment System in theory and practice. In J. W. Andrews, D. H. Saklofske, & H. Janzen (Eds.), *Handbook of psychoeducational assessment* (pp. 34–63). San Diego: Academic Press.

Das, J. P., Naglieri, J. A., & Kirby, J. R. (1994). *Assessment of cognitive processes: The PASS theory of intelligence*. Needham Heights, MA: Allyn & Bacon.

DeCroly, O. (1914). Epreuve nouvelle pour l'examen mental [New experiments for the mental exam]. *L'Année psychologique, 20,* 140–159.

DeLuca, J., Barbieri-Berger, S., & Johnson, S. (1994). The nature of memory impairments in multiple sclerosis: Acquisition versus retrieval. *Journal of Clinical and Experimental Neuropsychology, 16,* 183–189.

DeLuca, J., Gaudino, E. A., Diamond, B. J., Christodoulou, C., & Engel, R. A. (1998). Acquisition and storage deficits in multiple sclerosis. *Journal of Clinical and Experimental Neuropsychology, 20(3),* 376–390.

Dembo, T. (1931). Der Arger als dynamisches problem [Boredom as a dynamic problem] (Untersuchungen zur handlungs-und affekpsychologie. X. Ed. K. Lewin). *Psychol. Forsch., 15,* 1–144.

Doppelt, J. E., & Wallace, W. L. (1955). Stardardization of the Wechsler Adult Intelligence Scale for older persons. *Journal of Abnormal and Social Psychology, 51,* 312–330.

Donders, J., Tulsky, D. S., & Zhu, J. (2001). Criterion validity of new WAIS-III subtest scores after traumatic brain injury. *Journal of the International Neuropsychological Society, 7,* 892–898,

Donders, J., Zhu, J., & Tulsky, D. S. (2001). Factor index score patterns in the WAIS-III standardization sample. *Assessment, 8,* 193–203.

Dugbartey, A. T., Sanchez, P. N., Rosenbaum, J. G., Mahurin, R. K., Davis, J. M., & Townes, B. D. (1999). WAIS-III Matrix Reasoning test performance in a mixed clinical sample. *The Clinical Neuropsychologist, 13(4),* 396–404.

Engle R. W. (2001). What is working memory capacity? In H. L. Roediger, J. S. Nairne, et al. (Eds), *The nature of remembering: Essays in honor of Robert G. Crowder* (pp. 297–314) Washington, DC: American Psychological Association.

Flanagan, D.P, McGrew, K. S., & Ortiz, S.O (2000). *The Wechsler intelligence scales and Gf-Gc theory: A contemporary approach to interpretation*. Boston: McGraw-Hill.

Flynn, J. R. (1984). The mean IQ of Americans: Massive gains 1932–1978. *Psychological Bulletin, 95,* 29–51.

Flynn, J. R. (1987). Massive IQ gains in 14 nations: What IQ tests really measure. *Psychological Bulletin, 101,* 171–191.

Frank, G. (1983). *The Wechsler Enterprise: An Assessment of the development, structure, and use of the Wechsler Tests of Intelligence*. Oxford: Pergamon Press.

Friend, M., & Cook, L. (1996). *Interactions: Collaborative skills for school professionals, second edition*. White Plains, NY: Longman.

Galton, F. (1887). Supplementary notes on 'prehension' in idiots. *Mind, 12,* 71–82.

Gold, J. M., Carpenter, C., Randolph,C., Goldberg, T. E., & Weinberger, D. R. (1997). Auditory working memory and Wisconsin card sorting test performance in schizophrenia. *Archives of General Psychiatry, 54,* 159–165.

Hargus, M. E., & Wasserman, J. D. (1994). Inside Wechsler's library: Insights, incongruities, and the "lost WAIS items." In *Proceedings of the First Annual International Interdisciplinary Conference on cognitive assessment of children and youth in school and clinical settings* (pp. 199–212). Fort Worth, TX: CyberSpace.

Harrison, P. L., Kaufman, A. S., Hickman, J. A., & Kaufman, N. L. (1988). A survey of tests used for adult assessment. *Journal of Psychoeducational Assessment, 6(3)*, 188–198.

Hart, R. P., Kwentus, J. A., Wade, J. B., & Hamer, R. M. (1987). Digit symbol performance in mild dementia and depression. *Journal of Consulting and Clinical Psychology, 55(2)*, 236–238.

Haut, M. W., Kuwabara, H., Leach, S., & Arias, R. G. (2000). Neural activation during performance of number-letter sequencing. *Applied Neuropsychology, 7(4)*, 237–242.

Hawkins, K. A. (1998). Indicators of brain dysfunction derived from graphic representations of the WAIS-III/WMS-III technical manual samples: A preliminary approach to clinical utility. *The Clinical Neuropsychologist, 12*, 535–551.

Healy, W. (1918). *Manual for Healy Pictorial Completion Test II*. Chicago: C. H. Stoelting Co.

Healy, W. (1921). Pictorial Completion Test II. *Journal of Applied Psychology*, 225–239.

Healy, W., & Fernald, GM (1911). Tests for practical mental classification. *Psychological Monographs, 13 (54)*.

Hobbs, A. (1999). Mapping variation in brain structure and function: Implications for rehabilitation. *Journal of Head Trauma Rehabilitation, 14(6)*, 616–621.

Hoppe, F. (1930). Erfolg und misserfolg [Success and lack of success]. (Untersuchungen zur handlungs-und affekpsychologie. X. Ed. By K. Lewin). *Psychol. Forsch., 14*, 1–62.

Horn, J. L., & Cattell, R.B (1966). Refinement and test of the theory of fluid and crystallized general intelligences. *Journal of Educational Psychology, 57*(5), 253–270.

Horn, J. L., & Noll, J. (1997). Human cognitive capabilities: G_f-G_c theory. In D. P. Flanagan, J. L. Genshart, & P. L. Harrison (Eds.), *Contemporary intellectual assessment: Theories, tests, and issues*. New York: Guilford Press.

Hutt, R. B. W. (1925). Standardization of a color cube test. *Psychological Clinic, 16*, 77–97.

Jacobs, J. (1887). Experiments on "prehension." *Mind, 12*, 75–79.

Jenson, A. R. (1998). *The 'g' factor: The science of mental ability*. Westport, CT: Praeger.

Kaplan, E. (1988). A process approach to neuropsychological assessment. In T. Boll & B. K. Bryant (Eds.), *Clinical neuropsychology and brain function: Research, measurement, and practice* (pp. 125–167). Washington, DC: American Psychological Association.

Kaplan E., Fein, D., Morris, R., & Delis, D. C. (1991). *WAIS-R as a neuropsychological instrument*. San Antonio: The Psychological Corporation.

Kaplan E., Fein, D., Kramer, J., Delis, D., & Morris, R. (1999). *WISC-III PI manual*. San Antonio: The Psychological Corporation.

Kaufman, A. S. (1979). *Intelligent testing with the WISC-R*. New York: Wiley.

Kaufman, A. (1990). *Assessing adolescent and adult intelligence*. New York: Allyn & Bacon.

Kaufman, A. S. (1994). *Intelligence testing with the WISC-III*. New York: Wiley & Sons.

Kaufman A. S., & Lichtenberger, E. O. (1999). *Essentials of WAIS-III Assessment*. New York: John Wiley & Sons, Inc.

Knox, H. A. (1914). A scale based on the work at Ellis Island for estimating mental defect. *Journal of the American Medical Association, 62*, 741–747

Kohs, S. C. (1923). *Intelligence measurement: A psychological and statistical study based upon the block design tests*. New York: Macmillan.

Kyllonen, P. C., & Chrystal, R. E., (1990). Reasoning ability is (little more than) working memory capacity?! *Intelligence, 14*, 389–433.

Larrabee, G. J., Largen, J. W., & Levine, H. S. (1985). Sensitivity of age-decline resistant ("Hold") WAIS subtests to Alzheimer's disease. *Journal of Clinical and Experimental Neuropsychology, 7*, 497–504.

Lees-Haley, P. R., Smith, H.H, Williams, C. W., & Dunn, J. T. (1996). Forensic neuropsychological test usage: An empirical survey. *Archives of Clinical Neuropsychology, 11*, 45–51.

Lewin, K., Dembo, T., Festinger, L., & Sears, P. S. (1944). Level of aspiration. In J. M. Hunt (Ed.), *Personality and the behavior disorders, Volume 1*. New York: The Ronald Press Company.

Lezak, M. D. (1995). *Neuropsychological assessment (3rd ed)*. New York: Oxford University Press.

Martin, T. A., Donders, J., & Thompson, E. (2000). Potential of and problems with new measures of psychometric intelligence after traumatic brain injury. *Rehabilitation Psychology, 45(4)*, 402–408.

Matarazzo, J. D. (1972). *Wechsler's measurement and appraisal of adult intelligence (5th ed)*. Baltimore: Williams & Wilkins. Co.

Maxfield, F. N. (1925). Design blocks: A description of a simple clinical test. *Psychological Clinic, 16*, 98–109.

McAllister, T. W., Saykin, A. J., Flashman, L. A., Sparling, M. B., Johnson, S. C., Guerin, S. J., Mamourian, A. C., Weaver, J. B., Yanofsky, N. (1999). Brain activation during working memory 1 month after mild traumatic brain injury: A functional MRI study. *Neurology, 53*, 1300–1308.

Mullan, E. H. (1917). Mental examination of immigrants: Administration and line inspection at Ellis Island. *Public Health Reports, 32*, (No. 20, May 18, 1917).

Naglieri, J. A., & Das, J. P. (1997). Cognitive assessment system. Itasca, IL: Riverside Publishing.

Neisser, U., Boodoo, G., Bouchard, T. J., Boykin, A. W., Brody, N., Ceci, S. J., Halpern, D. F., Loehlin, J. C., Perloff, R., Sternberg, R. J., & Urbina, S. (1996). Intelligence: Knowns and unknowns. *American Psychologist, 51(2)*, 77–101.

Pintner, R. (1923). The significance of intelligence testing in the elementary school. In G. M. Whipple (Ed.), *The 21st yearbook of the National Society for the Study of Education: Intelligence tests and their use*. Bloomington, IL: Public School Publishing Co.

Pintner, R., & Paterson, D. G. (1917). *Scale of performance tests*. New York: Appleton-Century-Crofts.

Pintner, R., & Toops, H. A. (1918). A drawing completion test. *Journal of Applied Psychology, 2*, 164–173.

Piotrowski, C., & Keller, J. W. (1989). Psychological testing in outpatient mental health facilities: A national study. *Professional Psychology: Research and Practice, 20(6)*, 423–425.

Prifitera, A., & Saklofske, D. H. (1998). *WISC-III clinical use and interpretation*. San Diego: Academic Press.

Prifitera, A., Weiss, L. G., & Saklofske, D. H. (1998). In A. Prifitera & D. H. Saklofske (Eds.), *WISC-III: Clinical use and interpretation*. San Diego: Academic Press.

The Psychological Corporation (1995). *WAIS-III standardization edition*. (Unpublished standardization edition test kit). San Antonio: Author.

The Psychological Corporation. (1997). *WAIS-III—WMS-III technical manual*. San Antonio: Author.

Raven, J., Raven, J. C., & Court, J. H. (1998). *Standard progressive matrices*. Oxford, UK: Oxford Psychologists Press.

Reynolds, C. R. (1997). Forward and backward memory span should not be combined for clinical analysis. *Archives of Clinical Neuropsychology, 12(1)*, 29–40.

Ricker, J. H., Müller, R. A., Zafonte, R. D., Black, K. M., Millis, S. R., & Chugani, H. (2001a). Verbal recall and recognition following traumatic brain injury: A [O-15]-water positron emission tomography study. *Journal of Clinical and Experimental Neuropsychology, 23*, 196–206.

Ricker, J. H., Hillary, F. G., & DeLuca, J. (2001b) Functionally activated brain imaging (O-15 PET and fMRI) in the study of learning and memory after traumatic brain injury. *Journal of Head Trauma Rehabilitation, 16(2)*, 191–205.

Roid, G. H., & Worrall, W. (1997). Replication of the Wechsler Intelligence Scale for Children—Third Edition: Four-factor model in the Canadian normative sample. *Psychological Assessment, 9*, 512–515.

Ryan, J. J., Lopez, S. J., Werth, T. R. (1998). Administration time estimated for WAIS-III subtests, scales, and short forms in a clinical sample. *Journal of Psychoeducational Assessment, 16(4)*, 315–323.

Saklofske, D. H., Hildebrand, D. K., & Gorsuch, R. L. (2000). Replication of the factor structure of the Wechsler Adult Intelligence Scale—Third Edition with a Canadian sample. *Psychological Assessment, 12*, 436–439.

Salthouse, T. A. (1994). The aging of working memory. *Neuropsychology, 8*, 535–543.

Salthouse, T. A. (1996). The processing-speed theory of adult age differences in cognition. *Psychological Review, 103*, 403–428.

Sattler, J. M., & Ryan, J. J. (2001). Wechsler Adult Intelligence Scale—III (WAIS-III): Description. In J. M Sattler (Ed.), *Assessment of children: cognitive applications (4th ed.)* (pp. 375–414). San Diego, CA: Jerome M. Sattler, Inc.

Sattler, J. M., & Ryan, J. J. (2001). WAIS-III subtests and interpreting the WAIS-III. In J. M Sattler (Ed.), *Assessment of children: cognitive applications (4th ed.)* (pp. 415–454). San Diego, CA: Jerome M. Sattler, Inc.

Shiffrin R. M., & Schneider, W. (1977). Controlled and automatic human information processing II. Perceptual learning, automatic attending, and a general theory. *Psyhcological Review, 84 (2)*.

Smith, G. E., Ivnik, R. J., Malec, J. F., Kokmen, E., Tangalos, E. G., & Kurland, L. T. (1992). Mayo's older Americans normative studies (MOANS): Factor structure of a core battery. *Psychological Assessment, 4*, 382–390.

Starch, D. (1911). *Experiments in educational psychology*. New York: MacMillan.

Taylor, M. J., & Heaton, R. K. (2001). Sensitivity and specificity of WAIS-III and WMS-III demographically corrected factor scores in neuropsychological assessment. *Journal of the International Neuropsychological Society, 7*, 867–874.

Terman, L. M. (1916). *The measurement of intelligence*. Boston: Houghton Mifflin.

Terman, L. M. & Chamberlain, M. B. (1918). Twenty-three serial tests of intelligence and their intercorrelations. *Journal of Applied Psychology, 2*, 341–354.

Thorndike, R. L., Hagen, E. P., & Sattler, J. M. (1986). *The Stanford-Binet intelligence scale: Technical manual*. (4th ed.). Chicago: Riverside.

Tulsky, D. S., Chiaravalloti, N. D., Palmer, B. W., & Chelune, G. J. (2003). The Wechsler Memory Scale - third edition: A new perspective. In D. S. Tulsky et al. (Eds). *Clinical Interpretation of the WAIS-III and WMS-III*. (pp. 93–139). San Diego: Academic Press.

Tulsky, D. S., Ivnik, R. J., Price, L. R., & Wilkins, C. (2003). Assessment of cognitive functioning with the WAIS-III and WMS-III: Developement of a 6-Factor model. In D. S. Tulsky et al. (Eds). *Clinical Interpretation of the WAIS-III and WMS-III*. (pp. 145–177). San Diego: Academic Press.

Tulsky, D. S., & Ledbetter, M. (2000). Updating to the WAIS-III and WMS-III: Considerations for Research and Clinical Practice. *Psychological Assessment, 12(3)*, 253–262.

Tulsky, D. S., & Price, L, R. (in press). The Joint WAIS-III and WMS-III factor structure: Development and cross-validation of a 6–factor model of cognitive functioning. *Psychological Assessment*.

Tulsky, D. S., Saklofske, D. H., & Ricker, J. H. (2003). Historical overview of intelligence and memory: Factors influencing the Wechsler scales. In D. S. Tulsky et al. (Eds). *Clinical Interpretation of the WAIS-III and WMS-III*. (pp. 7–41). San Diego: Academic Press.

Tulsky, D. S., Saklofske, D. H., Wilkins, C., & Weiss, L. G. (2001). Development of a general ability index for the WAIS-III. *Psychological Assessment, 13(4)*, 566–571.

Tulsky, D. S., & Zhu, J. (2000). Could test length or order affect scores on the letter number sequencing of the WAIS-III and WMS-III? Ruling out effects of fatigue. *The Clinical Neuropsychologist, 14(4)*, 474–478.

Tulsky, D. S., Zhu, J., Chen, H., & Kaplan, E. (1998). The utility of incidental learning and copy procedures on the WAIS-III, *Journal of the International Neuropsychological Society* (Abstract.)

Tulsky, D. S., Zhu, J., & Prifitera, A. (2000). Assessment of adult intelligence with the WAIS-III. In G Goldstein & M Hersen (Eds.), *Handbook of psychological assessment (3rd ed.)* (pp. 97–129). Amsterdam: Pergamon.

Watkins, C. E., Campbell, V. L., & McGregor, P. (1988). Counseling psychologists' uses of and opinions about psychological tests: A contemporary perspective. *Counseling Psychologist, 16(3)*, 476–486.

Watson, G. (1969). Resistence to change. In W. G. Bennis, K. D., Benne, & R. Chan (Eds). *In the Planning of Change*. New York: Holt, Rinehard & Winston.

Wechsler, D. (1939a). *Wechsler–Bellevue Intelligence Scale*. New York: The Psychological Corporation.

Wechsler, D. (1939b). *Measurement of adult intelligence*. Baltimore: Williams & Wilkins.

Wechsler, D. (1944). *Measurement of Adult Intelligence-Third Edition*. Baltimore: Williams & Wilkins.

Wechsler, D. (1946). *The Wechsler Bellevue Form II*. New York: The Psychological Corporation.

Wechsler, D. (1950). Cognitive, conative, and non-intellective intelligence. *American Psychologist, 5*, 78–83.

Wechsler, D. (1955). *Wechsler Adult Intelligence Scale*. New York: The Psychological Corporation.

Wechsler, D. (1958). *The Measurement and Appraisal of Adult Intelligence-Fourth Edition*. Baltimore: Williams & Wilkins.

Wechsler, D. (1974). *Wechsler Intelligence Scale for Children—Revised.* New York: The Psychological Corporation.

Wechsler, D. (1976). *Wechsler Adult Intelligence Scale: Standardization manual.* Unpublished manual. New York: The Psychological Corporation.

Wechsler, D. (1981a). *Wechsler Adult Intelligence Scale—Revised.* San Antonio, TX: The Psychological Corporation.

Wechsler, D. (1981b). The psychometric tradition: Developing the Wechsler Adult Intelligence Scale. *Contemporary Educational Psychology, 6,* 82–85.

Wechsler, D. (1991). *Wechsler Intelligence Scale for Children—Third Edition.* San Antonio, TX: The Psychological Corporation.

Wechsler, D. (1997a). *WAIS-III administration and scoring manual.* San Antonio, TX: The Psychological Corporation.

Wechsler, D. (1997b). *Wechsler Memory Scale—Third Edition.* San Antonio, TX: The Psychological Corporation.

Weiss, L. Saklofske, D. H., & Prifitera, A. (2003). Clinical interpretation of the WISC-III factor scores. In C. R. Reynolds & R. W. Kamphaus (Eds). *Handbook of Psychological and Educational Assessment of Children: Intelligence and Achievement [2nd Edition].* New York: Guilford Publication.

Wells, F. L., & Martin, H. A. A. (1923). A method of memory examination suitable for psychotic cases. *American Journal of Psychiatry, 3,* 243–257.

Whipple, G. M. (1908). Vocabulary and word-building tests. *Psychological Review, 15,* 94–105.

Whipple, G. M. (1909). A range of information test. *Psychological Review, 16,* 347–351.

Whipple, G. M. (1915). *Manual of mental and physical tests (in two parts). Part II: Complex Processes.* Baltimore: Warwick & York, Inc.

Whipple, G. M. (1921). The National Intelligence Tests. *Journal of Educational Research, 4,* 16–31.

Wielkiewicz, R. M. (1990). Interpreting low scores on the WISC-R third factor: It's more than distractibility. *Psychological Assessment: A Journal of Consulting and Clinical Psychology, 2,* 91–97.

Woodcock, R. W., McGrew, K. S., & Mather, N. (2001). *The Woodcock–Johnson III.* Itasca, IL: Riverside.

Woodworth, R. S., & Wells, F. L. (1911). Association tests: Being a part of the report of the committee of the American Psychological Association on the standardization of procedure in experiemntal tests. *Psychological Monographs, 13,* (whole no. 57).

Yerkes, R. M. (Ed.). (1921). *Memoirs of the National Academy of Sciences Volume XV: Psychological Examining in the United States Army.* Washington, DC: Government Printing Office.

Yoakum, C. S., & Yerkes, R. M. (1920). *Army mental tests.* New York: Henry Holt and Company.

The Wechsler Memory Scale, Third Edition: A New Perspective

David S. Tulsky
Nancy D. Chiaravalloti
Kessler Medical Rehabilitation Research and Education Corporation
University of Medicine and Dentistry of New Jersey
West Orange, New Jersey

Barton W. Palmer
University of California, San Diego
La Jolla, California
and

Gordon J. Chelune
Cleveland Clinic Foundation
Cleveland, Ohio

As is true of the Wechsler Adult Intelligence Scale-Third Edition (WAIS-III, Wechsler, 1997a; Tulsky, Saklofske, & Zhu, Chapter 2, this volume), the Wechsler Memory Scale-III (WMS-III, Wechsler, 1997b) can be simultaneously viewed as a traditional test built on early 20th-century methodology and as a cutting-edge clinical scale reflecting how far memory assessment techniques had evolved as the 20th century drew to a close.

Many of the basic tasks and stimuli in the WMS-III were developed before 1925. For example, Logical Memory and Verbal Paired Associates, which together comprise the primary auditory subtests, and the Visual Reproductions subtest are modifications of tasks developed long before Wechsler first incorporated them into the Wechsler Memory Scale (WMS; Wechsler, 1945). The basic design and many of the stimuli for these subtests have seen little change since they were first normed in the late 1930s to mid-1940s. Indeed, as is true of the subtests in the Wechsler Bellevue Intelligence Scale (Wechsler, 1939) and its subsequent derivatives (i.e., the WAIS, WISC, WAIS-R, WISC-R, WAIS-III, and WISC-III), Wechsler did not, properly speaking, "invent" most of the WMS (1945) subtests. Rather, he adapted them from existing batteries such as the Binet–Simon Scale (Binet & Simon, 1905/1916a, 1908/1916b, 1911/1916c), the Wells and Martin (1923) battery, the Army testing program, and other sources. Even the Word List task, which is new to the WMS-III, can be viewed as a simple modification of Claparede's (1919) word list learning task and its subsequent derivations, (for example, Andre Rey's Auditory Verbal Learning Test, (1964); the California Verbal Learning Test (Delis, Kramer, Kaplan, & Ober, 1987); and the Hopkins Verbal Learning Test (Brandt, 1991).

As was true for the development of Wechsler's scales of intelligence, Wechsler's genius and contribution were not manifested in development of new methods of memory assessment. Rather, Wechsler appreciated a practical need in the field and brought together existing methods with normative data to guide interpretation. It is this advance that provided the basis for applying the tests in clinically useful ways. It is in this respect that the WMS-III follows the tradition set by Wechsler himself. Thus, as will be seen below, decisions about what to retain from the WMS (Wechsler, 1945) and WMS-R (Wechsler, 1987) and what to change, modify, or add in revising the WMS-III, were guided by the desire to provide a familiar and clinically useful battery, yet one that reflects contemporary neuropsychological theories and research findings while meeting contemporary standards for appropriate normative data.

The process of planning and decision making for the new revisions was guided by input from expert panels, focus groups, consultation with practicing psychologists, and senior project directors at The Psychological Corporation (TPC). Before the WAIS-III and WMS-III revision processes had even begun, a Neurogenic Focus Group met at TPC in San Antonio, Texas, in 1990, composed of both psychologists and aphasiologists. At this early meeting, the notion of developing a "family of related tests" was first introduced to TPC, as they were thinking about their future plans for test development eventually leading to the co-norming methodology that was used for the WAIS-III and WMS-III.

The "official" development of the WMS-III started in Fall 1992. Around the time the project began, advisory group meetings were convened during the annual conferences of the American Psychological Association (APA) in Washington, D.C., in 1992 and the National Academy of Neuropsychology (NAN) in Pittsburgh in 1992. The meetings were organized by Mark Ledbetter, who was the WMS-III Project Director, and moderated by Nelson Butters. Butters, a major figure in the field of neuropsychology, was instrumental in the selection of advisory board members. Although the initial panel meeting included a number of leaders in the field of neuro-psychology, it was eventually narrowed to a smaller team consisting of Robert Bornstein, Robert Heaton, Robert Ivnik, and Gordon Chelune, all chosen by Butters for their leadership role in the science and practice of neuropsychology. It was during the November 1992 NAN meeting that it was officially decided to link the WAIS-III and WMS-III projects by co-norming the instruments.

The current chapter will focus on this revision of the WMS within a historical context. It is divided into three sections. We begin with a review of the clinical assessment of memory and how the original WMS helped fill a need in the field. The strengths and weaknesses of the previous editions are then outlined, and we discuss how the shortcomings of the previous editions helped shape the goals and objectives of the current revision. Finally, we review the core index scores and subtests of the WMS-III and describe the origins of the current subtests. In describing the WMS-III revision in the present chapter, we attempt, wherever possible, to provide the reader with an insider's perspective on the rationale for various decisions about what was included, excluded, and modified.

HISTORICAL FACTORS LEADING TO THE DEVELOPMENT OF THE WECHSLER MEMORY SCALE

As outlined in Chapter 1, Binet had a profound impact on the assessment of intelligence and memory (Tulsky, Saklofske, & Ricker, Chapter 1, this volume). In regard to memory, some of the tests incorporated by Wechsler (1945) into the original WMS were taken directly from the Binet–Simon scales (Binet & Simon, 1905/1916a, 1908/1916b, 1911/1916c). It was also because Binet emphatically stated that intelligence and memory were separable constructs (see Binet & Simon, 1905/1916a) that the development of IQ and memory tests took separate paths. Ebbinghaus (1885/1913) began formal experimental studies of learning and memory in the late-19th century. However, few people thought about memory assessment clinically, and fewer still were using formal memory tests in clinical practice. For instance, memory disorders are not even mentioned in a comprehensive 543-page volume on the mental, nervous, and central nervous system disorders seen by the Medical Department of the United States Army during the First World War (Bailey, Williams, & Komora, 1929). Furthermore, although a proliferation of tests and research articles addressed the intelligence assessment (e.g., Boardman, 1917), tests of immediate memory were used in experimental psychopathology paradigms (e.g., Wells, 1913), and theoretical developments in the area of memory (e.g., Hebb, 1961), the clinical application of memory testing was almost nonexistent through much of the early 20th century.

By the early 1920s, only one clinical memory battery had been published (Wells & Martin, 1923). However, the Wells and Martin Memory Examination was not widely used in clinical settings (which may be partially due to an inadequate normative database to facilitate interpretation of the scores, or may simply be due to the lack of attention paid to the clinical evaluation of memory disorders). This lack of attention to the assessment and treatment of memory disorders continued for years. Even when the initial version of the Halstead Neuropsychological Test Battery, the single most widely used fixed neuropsychological test battery, was introduced in 1947, Ward Halstead did not include or mention memory assessment as an integral part of the battery (Halstead, 1947). This omission even persisted through the later expansion and popularization of the battery by Ralph Reitan (Reitan & Davison, 1974). In fact, throughout the 1940s and beyond, memory assessment was rarely performed in clinical settings and remained a secondary area of assessment for decades following, even among the pioneers and leaders in the burgeoning field of clinical neuropsychology.

World Wars I and II catalyzed a general expansion in clinical psychology. Improvements in general medical care led to a greater number of individuals who survived head injuries. Kurt Goldstein, a neurologist who had worked with World War I veterans who sustained head wounds, helped to increase the awareness of the cognitive and memory deficits that result from these injuries (Goldstein, 1942). During World War II clinical psychologists began taking a more active role in diagnosing and treating individuals with cognitive deficits. As military personnel returned from Europe and the Pacific, a new focus within psychology was on those with war-related brain injuries (Phares, 1979; Shaffer & Lazarus, 1952). As a result, the need for a clinical test to detect and evaluate memory disorders was becoming recognized. With Psychologists' increased role in treating casualities during the war and increased focus on the cognitive deficits resulting from injury, the demand for new assessment instruments grew.

Memory assessment, in the decade following World War II, began having a strong practical foundation in aiding clinical assessment (Williams, 1978), as clinicians recognized that deficits in memory often manifest themselves as initial symptoms in certain disease processes (e.g., dementia) before deficits in other areas of functioning presented themselves. Other disorders, such as Korsakoff's syndrome, were marked by severe memory dysfunction within the context of otherwise relatively normal mentation. At times, there were striking cases of memory deficits that might occur in the face of intact verbal comprehension and perceptual organization. For example, the historical case of H.M. who underwent a bilateral temporal lobectomy for the control of temporal lobe epilepsy, demonstrated intact intellectual abilities in the presence of a dense postoperative global amnesia (Scoville & Milner, 1957). A retrograde amnesia was observed, initially, with at least partial clearing over time. However, the anterograde amnesia persisted, with a complete inability to register and recall everyday events. Such cases demonstrate the clinical importance of a detailed assessment of the various components of the memory subsystems identified in the experimental literature. Moreover, given the dearth of clinically relevant memory tests in the field, the WMS represented an important advance in clinical assessment.

THE WECHSLER MEMORY SCALE

David Wechsler, by seeking to develop a standardized memory battery for clinical use in the first half of the 20th century, was well ahead of his time. He himself had become acquainted with experimental memory paradigms early in his career. For his master's thesis in 1917, Wechsler used a test battery to assess verbal memory in patients with Korsakoff's syndrome. This included an unpublished test that was a precursor to the Verbal Paired Associates subtest (Wechsler, 1917a; Wechsler, 1917b). Wechsler also spent a year working at the Boston Psychopathic Hospital with Fred Wells at approximately the time that the Wells and Martin Memory Examination was published (Wells & Martin, 1923; Wells, 1927). It is therefore likely that he became acquainted with the aforementioned Wells and Martin Memory Examination at that time.

Although inspired by the Wells and Martin Memory Examination, the actual development of the WMS did not occur for years. In the 1930s and 1940s Wechsler began development of his Wechsler Bellevue intelligence tests, and progress on the WMS appears to have taken a secondary priority. The development and publication of the WMS did not proceed uninterrupted, but rather appears to have occurred in a series of spurts over several years that were in part interrupted by focus on the two forms of the Wechsler Bellevue Intelligence Examination (Eugenia Jaros, Wechsler's secretary at Bellevue Hospital, personal communication, May 2002), as well as consultation to the military, and other miscellaneous work (e.g., Wechsler published two unrelated articles in 1944 and 1945, which indicated he was working on other projects as well; see the Cornell Selectee Index [Wechsler, Weidner, Mittleman, & Wolfe, 1944] and an experimental study of anxiety [Wechsler & Hartogs, 1945]). At the time of its initial publication, Wechsler (1945), indicated that the WMS had been in use at Bellevue Hospital by 1940 and that the publication of the scale represented the culmination of "10 years of intermittent experimentation" (Wechsler, 1945, p. 87).

Although the Wells and Martin (1923) Memory Examination did not achieve widespread clinical use, its influence on Wechsler and the structure and content of the original WMS is apparent in several respects. Foremost is the fact that Wells and Martin's test involved a variety of different types of memory-related tasks that contributed to a total score, which was then converted to an overall Memory Quotient based on an extremely small sample of individuals with psychosis (e.g., $N = 111$), whose test scores served as normative data. The influence on Wechsler can also be seen in terms of the content of specific test items. Several of the tasks in the WMS (Wechsler, 1945) have direct parallels in the Wells and Martin examination, including items relating to Personal and Current Information, counting backwards and reciting the alphabet, and repeating strings of aurally presented digits forward and backward (i.e., the Digit Span task). The Wells and Martin (1923) Memory Examination also included an associate learning task (otherwise known as Verbal Paired Associates), wherein examinees had to learn and recall a series of unfamiliar town–state associations. It is also interesting to note that the Wells and Martin Memory Examination included several items assessing what today would be labeled semantic (nonepisodic) declarative memory. Although this aspect of memory is assessed in the Wechsler intelligence tests (particularly in the Information subtest), it has never been included in the Wechsler Memory Tests (i.e., the WMS, WMS-R, and WMS-III) which are all primarily measures of episodic declarative memory, (see The Psychological Corporation, 1997).

As stated by Wechsler (1945), the WMS was designed to provide a "rapid, simple, and practical memory examination" (p. 87). The original WMS (1945) included seven subtests: (1) Personal and Current Information, (2) Orientation, (3) Mental Control, (4) Logical Memory, (5) Memory Span (i.e., Digit Span), (6) Visual Reproduction, and (7) Associate Learning (i.e., Verbal Paired Associates). There was an alternate form of the original WMS (i.e., Form II), that allowed test–retest evaluation, but the two versions were not statistically equated.

The WMS approach, like that of the Wells and Martin Memory Examination, was somewhat comparable to that of IQ testing in that a range of diverse memory related tasks were combined to compute an overall Memory Quotient (MQ), which reflected the degree to which an examinee's performance deviated from the normative mean. Note that this approach differed philosophically from an older approach in experimental memory studies, where the focus was simply on the amount of information saved (or the amount of time or additional exposure to relearn material— e.g., Ebbinghaus). Wechsler suggested adding a constant to the total score to correct for age and then provided a table for converting the sum of these scores to an MQ. Wechsler derived these MQ conversions by "plotting the mean [total WMS] scores for different ages against the weighted scores of the Wechsler Bellevue [Intelligence] Scale (age group 20–24 years) and then trying out various constants that would keep the mean MQ for any group equivalent to the mean IQ of that age group" (Wechsler, 1945, p. 90). This was an interesting approach in that, indirectly, Wechsler was asserting that interpretation of memory scores should be partially weighted by general intellectual functioning. Although Wechsler's technique only provided for age-group corrections, the approach seems to anticipate the decision to co-norm the WAIS-III and WMS-III, so that WMS-III results could in part be interpreted in light of examinee's general cognitive functioning. As there were few scales designed to measure memory functioning, the WMS quickly became the state of the art instrument when memory assessment was required, and became extremely popular in the field (see Appendix II Item 8 for initial reactions).

Despite the frequent use of the WMS in research with clinical populations and its sensitivity in detecting deficits in short-term memory, the field of experimental memory research had advanced by the 1960s and 1970s (Baddeley, 1976; Pribram & Broadbent, 1970; Tulving & Donaldson, 1972), and psychologists were growing more critical of the WMS. Perhaps the single most influential critique/response to the original WMS was that by Elbert Russell (1975). Russell was critical of the MQ as he asserted that it seemed to imply a unitary function whose various aspects were additive. He noted that the WMS blurred a potentially important distinction between verbal and figural memory. Moreover, Russell noted that research had suggested a distinction between immediate versus long-term memory, whereas the WMS measured only immediate recall. Fortunately, Russell (1975) went beyond merely criticizing Wechsler's original scale, and his proposed solution was an alternate administration technique for the WMS. The changes advanced in Russell (1975) called for (a) elimination of the

MQ; (b) systematic assessment of verbal versus visual discrepancies; and (c) systematic assessment of immediate versus delayed memory.

The Russell revision called for the comparison of scores from Logical Memory (as a measure of auditory memory) and Visual Reproductions (as a measure of figural memory). He also reintroduced the administration procedure of assessing both immediate and delayed recall for Logical Memory and Visual Reproduction that had been previously used by Rey (1941; see Boake, 2000) in his Word Lists test. The delayed recall was to be administered after a 30-minute interval following the administration of the immediate-recall condition. Although the normative data that Russell provided for these revisions was criticized by some, even Russell (1988) himself, the format changes were readily incorporated by neuropsychologists when administering the WMS, and greatly influenced the structure of the future WMS-R, as well as the future WMS-III.

Russell was not alone in critiquing the model of memory inherent in the WMS scoring. Clinically, western society's introduction to Luria's views regarding neural systems and the functional organization of the brain–behavior relationships (Luria, 1966, 1970, 1973) challenged the concept of memory as a unitary process, and thus the concept of a global MQ was questioned. Furthermore, advances in the clinical study of split brain patients who had undergone hemispherectomy or commissurotomy were influencing the way neuropsychologists viewed memory (see Kinsbourne & Smith, 1974; Nebes, 1974; Sperry, 1968), and a differentiation between verbal and visual memory, as later advocated by Russell (1975), began to develop.

Yet while Russell (1975) advocated separate consideration of verbal versus visual memory, the primary focus of his revisions was still on the detection of brain injury. As neuropsychology began to emerge from what Rourke (1982) described as its *static phase*, with an emphasis on diagnosis, lesion identification, and hemispheric localization, to its *cognitive phase*, that focused more on descriptive brain–behavior relationships, the limitations of the WMS became even more obvious. That is, there was a desire and need to describe more specific memory processes and abilities, not merely derive scores that efficiently discriminated brain-injured from nonbrain-injured patients (or those with left-hemisphere injuries from those with right-hemisphere injuries). The evolution of this new focus is seen in the emphasis on index scores in both the WAIS-III and WMS-III.

Whereas the thrust of Russell's critique had been on the construct validity of the WMS, other critics noted additional psychometric limitations in the 1945 scale. For example, Prigatano (1978) noted several salient weaknesses in the WMS, including (a) the small "standardization sample" consisting only of approximately 200 examinees, divided into two age groups, who were seen at Bellevue Hospital in New York City and who were not suspected of having memory problems,[1] (b) the composite MQ was derived from a sample of only 100 subjects; and (c) there were few reliability studies for the WMS, and those that were reported were conducted in a "varied" and "unsystematic" fashion (p. 820). Like Russell, Prigatano (1978) also expressed concern about the construct validity of the WMS, noting that factor analyses of the WMS had supported more factors than the scale was designed to measure, as purported by Wechsler, and the findings among these studies were generally not consistent. Prigatano also noted that subtests included in the WMS were largely measures of verbal memory, with only the Visual Reproduction subtest measuring visual memory. Prigatano further commented that the exact scores that could be derived from the WMS and, more importantly, exactly what constructs the WMS was measuring, remained to be determined. These latter questions raised uncertainty about the validity of the scale, calling its utility into question for many clinicians and researchers. Additionally, the WMS primarily assessed immediate recall. It did not adequately assess the process of learning (through multiple learning trials), and it contained no assessment of delayed recall and recognition.

While such critiques, and the Russell revision in particular, were highly influential in clinical practice, the first official revision of the WMS was not published until 1987, more than 40 years after Wechsler originally published the scale. Some of the considerations in this revision were similar to those that motivated Russell a decade earlier.

THE PUBLICATION OF THE WMS-R

The revision of the WMS began in the late 1970s, and David Wechsler played a significant role in designing the new subtests for inclusion (Herman, 1988). The project was delayed for a few years following Wechsler's death in 1981 and the relocation of The Psychological Corporation, first to Cleveland, Ohio, and then to San Antonio, Texas, in the mid-1980s. The Wechsler Memory Scale-Revised was published in 1987 (WMS-R, 1987) and attempted to incorporate many of the conceptual changes advocated by

---

[1]Although Wechsler (1945) stated that "The subjects were not hospital patients," (p. 88) it is not clear in the original article how or where they were recruited.

Russell, Prigatano, and others, while also correcting other psychometric problems. The revision featured an improved, though still limited, normative database, and included four new index scores (in addition to a General Memory Index). With the publication of the WMS-R, the comparisons between verbal and visual memory were made at the Index score level as opposed to an individual subtest level that Russell had advanced (e.g., Logical Memory vs. Visual Reproduction) because it increased reliability. The de-emphasis on a single MQ score, the focus on verbal–visual comparisons, and the focus on immediate-delayed comparisons were major improvements in the WMS-R and reflected the dominant thinking in neuropsychology at the time. Yet, despite the improved structure of the WMS-R, several areas of difficulty in the scale were noted.

Probably the most common and immediate criticisms of the WMS-R were limitations related to the normative sample (D'Elia, Satz, & Schretlen, 1989; Loring, 1989). The sample size ($N = 316$) was relatively small com-pared to other well-standardized pychometric scales such as the WAIS-R ($N = 1880$), which had been published a few years earlier. Additionally, Loring (1989) and D'Elia et al. (1989) expressed concerns about the lack of normative data in certain age groups. Beyond concerns with the norma-tive sample, Loring also noted that the visual subtests lacked face validity in their assessment of visual learning and memory and lacked sensitivity to patients with known memory deficits. Moreover, the General Memory Index of the WMS-R reflected immediate recall trials and showed a slight bias toward verbal tests (most likely due to the higher correlations between the verbal subtests and the General Index Composite; see Chelune, Born-stein, & Prifitera, 1990). Additionally, the Delayed Recall Index was not constructed similar to the General Memory Index, making comparisons between immediate and delayed memory difficult.[2]

Indeed, although the sample range, size, and representativeness had in-creased over the WMS standardization sample, the WMS-R standardization sample consisted of only six age groups with approximately 50 individuals within each group (ages 16–17, 20–24, 35–44, 55–64, 65–69, and 70–74). This small sample size increased the probability of measurement error. Furthermore, the normative sample contained age groups for which no data were collected, and the norms for these age groups where computed through interpolation based upon linear regression from adjacent age group

---

[2]Unfortunately, the lack of continuity between immediate and delayed memory was not corrected in the WMS-III, but this is being rectified by Tulsky, Chelune, Price & Millis (2003) who have constructed a new Delayed Memory Index derived from the WMS-III standardization sample.

data. This becomes especially questionable if the changes of memory function across ages are not linear in nature.

The second major criticism of the WMS-R focused on the *novel* visual memory subtests that had been added in this revision. Figural Memory and Visual Paired Associates had been added to the scale with the rationale that the abstract stimuli contained within the subtests would be difficult to encode verbally. However, the field seemed to have had a backlash to such novel tasks. The subtests were not well received and were controversial from the start. Loring (1989) pointed out that the Figural Memory subtest loaded substantially on the Attention/Concentration factor in a group of mixed clinical patients, and he raised questions about what the task was measuring. Moreover, the Figural Memory subtest was a recognition task without a recall component making it different from the other tasks in the battery. The Visual Paired Associates subtest was also criticized. Loring questioned the validity of the subtest as a measure of nonverbal memory because examinees tended to verbally encode the stimuli (Loring, 1989). In addition, Loring pointed out that the validity studies for Visual Paired Associates and Figural Memory in clinical groups were inadequate. Moreover, the new subtests appeared to be limited in their ability to demonstrate differences in functioning of the right and left cerebral hemisphere. Several studies demonstrated that the verbal memory subtests were highly sensitive to left-hemisphere lesions, but performance was relatively preserved in individuals with right-sided lesions (Barr et al., 1997; Chelune & Bornstein, 1988; Naugle, Chelune, Cheek, Lüders, & Awad, 1993; Rausch & Babb, 1993; Saling, Berkovic, O'Shea, et al., 1993). However, the opposite pattern was not observed with the visual subtests, as both right- and left-lesioned groups obtained lower scores than healthy individuals with roughly the same magnitude of impairment.

Loring (1989) also pointed out that the WMS-R did not take sufficient advantage of many of the research findings on memory and learning that had accumulated between the publication of the original WMS and the 1987 revision; that is, the WMS-R reflected earlier concepts of memory rather than newer cutting-edge approaches. Specifically, independent and arguably better tests were developed between 1945 and 1987 for the detailed assessment of specific forms of memory. For example, Buschke (Buschke, 1973; Buschke & Fuld, 1974) developed the Selective Reminding Test in order to examine storage, retention, and other processes distinguished in the experimental verbal learning and cognitive neuropsychological literatures. Similarly, the California Verbal Learning Test (Delis, Kramer, Kaplan, & Ober, 1987), which is administered in a format similar to the Rey Auditory Verbal

Learning Test (Rey, 1941), was also introduced as a memory task that evaluated multiple process components of learning, delayed recall, and delayed recognition. In contrast, the WMS-R remained heavily focused on "immediate memory" with little distinction between learning/encoding, storage, retention, and retrieval.

Finally, the WMS-R (Wechsler, 1987) was also criticized for yielding inadequate recognition memory data (D'Elia et al., 1989; Fastenau, 1996). For example, D'Elia et al. (1989) noted

> There are currently *no* data available regarding recognition testing on delay for any of the original or revised WMS subtests. Without assessing delayed recognition for the material not freely recalled, one is unsure whether the patient has an *encoding* problem or a *retrieval* problem. Until such data become available, the WMS tests should be considered as providing a limited assessment of memory functioning. (p. 565)

Indeed, Fastenau (1996) criticized the WMS-R for these deficiencies and developed recognition procedures for the Logical Memory and Visual Reproduction subtests. Fastenau also added a copy condition to Visual Reproductions to sort out constructional deficits from visual memory deficits.

DEVELOPMENT OF THE WMS-III

The WMS-R had been on the market for only 10 years when the WMS-III was published. This short interval between revisions may be due in part to the opportunity to respond to developments in the field of memory research, the opportunity to co-norm the WMS-III with the WAIS-III, and the perceived problems of the WMS-R that were outlined above. Nevertheless, the time period that elapsed between the publication of the WMS-R and the WMS-III revision saw a significant shift in the popular methods for memory assessment. Four conceptual shifts to the Wechsler model of measuring memory were considered at the start of the WMS-III project.

First, it was believed that a state-of-the-art memory test would address several components of memory and learning (e.g., encoding and learning, storage retention, and retrieval), and the development of core measures that could differentiate among these cognitive processes became one of the central goals of the WMS-III revision. The WMS-III would include index scores reflecting immediate recall, delayed recall, and when possible, recognition following administration of the delayed recall measures. Provision of these index scores was intended to provide greater specificity in distinguishing between clinical disorders.

As had been noted by Fastenau (1996), as well as in the memory literature in general (e.g., Squire, 1986, 1987), there is a clinically important distinction to be made between free recall versus recognition subtests. When the WMS and WMS-R were developed, recognition memory was simply not seen as an important element. However, as conceptual models evolved, the construct of recognition memory had become an important aspect to include in the new memory test. Therefore, the WMS-III places significantly more emphasis upon delayed recognition memory than its predecessors, the WMS or WMS-R. In particular, the WMS-III delayed recognition can be directly compared to a delayed free recall index score.

The second conceptual shift was the inclusion of process scores in the WMS-III revision. In the late 1980s and early 1990s, there was a rise in the process approach to neuropsychological assessment (Kaplan, 1988; Kaplan, Fein, Morris, & Delis, 1991) and to memory assessment (Delis et al., 1987). Therefore, process scores were incorporated into the WMS-III to provide information about the nature of any underlying memory deficits (i.e., giving information about what processes were impaired, beyond the type of information provided about the level of abilities that is the focus of the core index scores). These (optional) process scores are purported to provide additional clinical utility by providing a more in-depth, comprehensive examination of cognition through examination of the process through which the individual reaches his or her response. A major premise in this approach was that the patient's final response is only a piece of the important clinical information; equally important was consideration of the *process* or method the examinee used to get to that response. However, the process scores should be viewed as somewhat more exploratory than the core index scores. Generally, these scores are not normally distributed, have poor reliability, are presented as percentile scores, and there is less clinical and research background presently by which to make firm conclusions about so-called impaired scores.

A third conceptual shift in the WMS-III revision emphasized ecological validity. In the WMS-R, the visual tasks included several figures that were thought to be difficult to verbally encode and were purely visual tasks. However, it is unclear if purely visual tasks exist. In addition, a test made from such material would have little ecological validity and would not be representative of tasks that people encounter on a daily basis in real life. Therefore, in the WMS-III there was a move away from attempting to develop abstract designs purported to be purely visual and not verbally encodable. So, in devising the stimuli for the WMS-III, one consideration was the inclusion of stimuli similar to those that people experience in everyday life—a newscast (Logical Memory Story B), faces of people

(Faces subtest), and pictures of a family engaged in activities (Family Pictures). In developing the tasks, the developers of the WMS-III focused on the mode of presentation of the information (visual, auditory), which can be manipulated experimentally, rather than making assumptions about how the brain is going to process the information. One of the new visual subtests (Family Pictures) even required verbal responses, something that would never have been considered in the WMS-R. In recognition of this focus on the mode of presentation, the verbal material was renamed "auditory" to reflect that it was presented auditorially and the visual information was presented visually.

The fourth shift in the creation of the WMS-III was the reconceptualization of the "traditional" Attention/Concentration factor, by renaming it Working Memory. This factor was thought to parallel the factor on the WAIS-III, thus building a "bridge" between the WMS-III and WAIS-III. There remained one fundamental difference—the WAIS-III Working Memory Index is composed strictly of verbal subtests, whereas the WMS-III Working Memory Index is composed of a verbal and a visual task, with Letter Number Sequencing being the link.

In addition to changes that accompanied the more major conceptual shifts, a major goal of the WMS-III revision was to obtain a larger, more representative and continuous standardization sample, across a broader age range. The sampling plan for the WMS-III was established with 100 individuals per age group and an age range of 16–89 years, which was to be stratified on the following demographic variables: age, education level, ethnicity, and sex. Furthermore, the goal was to obtain an average IQ of 100 at each age level, making it similar to Wechsler's original approach of linking memory with IQ, rather than allowing both procedures to vary independently. However, this later prerequisite proved the most difficult, and a case-weighting procedure (Cochran, 1977) was used to ensure that the sample was "reasonably" representative of the census information for U.S. sample (see Tulsky & Ledbetter, 2000, for the initial report about the case weighting procedure). While case weighting is common in test development and there are strong arguments supporting its use (see Gorsuch, 2001), the technique had not been reported in the published manual (The Psychological Corporation, 1997), an omission that might give the appearance of recruitment problems or, worse, an unrepresentative sample. In actuality, however, the weighting procedure reflects the desire to have a "perfectly balanced" sample with an average IQ of 100 for each age group. Nevertheless, the shear size (weighted $N = 1250$; unweighted $N = 1,032$ Tulsky & Ledbetter, 2000) and age range (16–89) of the WMS-III weighted standardization sample, make it one of the premier normative databases for a memory test.

DESCRIPTION OF WMS-III

The WMS-III incorporated significant changes from the previous edition. As outlined in the *WAIS-III–WMS-III Technical Manual* (The Psychological Corporation, 1997) the WMS-III includes eight primary index scores (three more than had been included in the WMS-R) as well as substantial changes at the subtest level. Notably, the Visual Index scores are composed of new subtests that are unique to a Wechsler scale (e.g., Faces and Family Pictures). These primary indexes, as well as the core subtests from which they are composed, are outlined in Figure 1.

As shown in Figure 1, the WMS-III contains three global composite scores: Immediate Memory Index, General Memory Index (delayed recall),

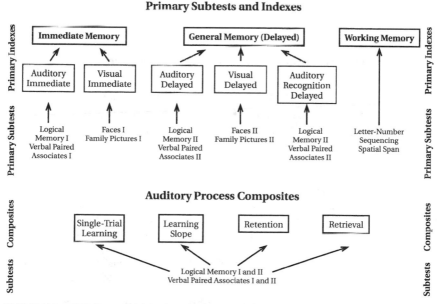

FIGURE 1.   WMS-III Index and Composite Configuration. (Reproduced from Wechsler, 1997. *The WMS-III Administration and Scoring Manual*. San Antonio, TX: The Psychological Corporation. Figure copyright © 1997 The Psychological Corporation. Used with permission. All rights reserved.)

and the Working Memory Index. Within this structure, the WMS-III contains an additional five index scores allowing assessment of auditory and visual immediate memory, auditory and visual delayed memory, and auditory recognition. However, as will be discussed below, confirmatory factor analyses of the original data have not supported some of these indices (and, based upon new analyses, a new structure of cognitive functioning has been proposed by Tulsky, Ivnik, Price, & Wilkins, Chapter 4, this volume). The WMS-III also attempted to develop an Auditory Delayed Recognition Index so that differences between recall and recognition memory could be assessed directly. However, as will be reported below, such comparisons may be difficult to make due to ceiling effects among normals on the Auditory Recognition Index (particularly in terms of the Verbal Paired Associates task). An alternative method for scoring and interpreting recognition scores will be provided later in this chapter. In addition to these primary five index scores, the WMS-III contains numerous process variables, but they are outside the scope of this chapter and will not be reviewed here.

STRUCTURE OF WMS-III INDEX AND SUBTESTS SCORES

The Auditory Immediate and Delayed Index Scores

The subtests contributing to the WMS-III auditory index scores involve the auditory presentations of verbal information. The computation and interpretation of the auditory index scores are described in the *WAIS-III–WMS-III Technical Manual* as

> measures of memory functioning when stimuli are presented in the auditory modality. Low scores, relative to an individual's intellectual and attentional functioning, may suggest a verbal learning or memory problem. A low score on the delayed index, relative to that on the immediate index, may indicate a high rate of forgetting. The assessment of delayed recall should always be made in the context of the immediate condition because delayed recall (i.e., the amount of information available through recall) depends on the amount of information that was initially acquired. (The Psychological Corporation, 1997, p. 191)

The auditory index scores are based upon the sum of scaled scores of the Logical Memory I and the Verbal Paired Associates I subtests. The WMS-III also includes an optional Word Lists subtest that is not factored into the Auditory Index scores. These subtests are reviewed below.

Logical Memory

The Logical Memory subtest of the WMS-III requires the oral presentation of a narrative story to the examinee for immediate recall and subsequent delayed recall and recognition. Logical Memory I and II, on the WMS-III, parallel the traditional WMS and WMS-R subtests. For the immediate version (LM I), the examinee is asked to verbally recall each story immediately after aural presentation; for the delayed version of the stories (LM II), the examinee is asked to recall the stories after a delay interval. Immediately upon finishing the delayed recall portion, the examinee is asked a series of "yes or no" questions in which the examinee has to recognize whether or not each piece of information had been presented in the story. This latter score is a measure of auditory recognition.

The use of a narrative recall to test memory functioning can be traced back to the late 1800s when Binet and Henri (1895, 1896; also see Peterson, 1926, for a review) introduced memory for sentences as they were advancing their work on individual psychology. Their procedure entailed a teacher reading a short prose passage, after which the examinees were to reproduce it in writing. The length of the prose selections ranged from 11 to 86 words, which were divided into component ideas. At the time, Binet and Henri interpreted this test as measuring attention, characterizing the method as a *dynamometer* of attention. It was additionally noted that memory for sentences was approximately 25 times superior than memory for words (Binet & Henri, 1895; and as reviewed by Peterson, 1926).

Wissler (1901) refined this technique when he applied it to students at Columbia University. Students were read a short story and asked to recall as many of the story details as possible. Whipple (1915) later coined the term *logical memory* as the recall of "connected, meaningful material" (p. 205).

This procedure has been used widely in the assessment of intellectual abilities and memory functioning. For example, Healy-Fernald presented the Auditory Verbal Memory Test, which entailed the presentation of prose passages for immediate memory (Healy & Fernald, 1911). In Whipple's Logical Memory Test (which is the first time this term was used), "The Marble Statue" and other stories are read to the examinee, after which the examinee is required to write down everything he or she remembered (Whipple, 1915). Early logical memory stories are presented in Figure 2. Modeled after the Stanford–Binet, the Army Alpha test, which screened United States men for participation in World War I, included the reading of a written narrative, after which individuals were asked to recall as many

Three Houses Burned
(53 words, 19 ideas)
Binet & Simon, 1908

Three | Houses | Burned | Chalons-sur-Marne | September 5th | A very large fire | destroyed | last night | (Three buildings at Chalons), situated in the center of the city. | seventeen families | are without shelter (homes). | The loss will exceed 150,000 francs. | While saving | a child | in it's cradle | a barber's boy | seriously injured | his hands.

Note: in the Binet–Simon version, the children read the stories and then repeated the passage from memory two to three seconds after they had finished reading the passage. The story was modified and adapted to a New York setting by J.E.W. Wallin, (1912).

The Marble Statue
(166 words, 67 ideas)
Reported by Whipple, 1915

A young | man | worked | years | to carve | a white | marble | statue | of a beautiful | girl. | She grew prettier | day by day. | He began to love the statue | so well that | one day | he said to it : | "I would give | everything | in the world | if you would be alive | and be my wife." | Just then | the clock struck | twelve, | and the cold | stone began to grow warm, | the cheeks red, | the hair brown, | the lips to move. | She stepped down, | and he had his wish. | They lived happily | together | for years, | and three beautiful | children were born. | One day | he was very tired, | and grew so angry, | without cause, | that he struck her. | She wept, | kissed | each child | and her husband, | stepped back | upon the pedestal, | and slowly | grew cold, | pale | and stiff, | closed her eyes, | and when the clock | struck | midnight, | she was a statue | of pure | white | marble | as she had been | years before, | and could not hear | the sobs | of her husband | and children.

Test XIII.
Healy & Fernald (1911 Battery)
(82 words, 12 ideas)

If a sailor | on the ocean | is shipwrecked | in a wild country, | he must first look for water to drink, | then he must find a place to sleep | where wild animals can't get at him, | and after that he can take time to look for food, | but he must be careful not to eat poisonous berries or fruit. | Next he had better hunt for other people on the land | and put up a flag | to stop ships which may be going by.

FIGURE 2. Examples of Logical Memory Stories. Three Houses Burned reprinted from Binet & Simon (1908/1916b); The Marble Statue from Whipple (1915); and Test XIII from Healy & Fernald (1911).

details as possible (Yerkes, 1921). As discussed by Tulsky, Saklofske, and Zhu, (Chapter 2, this volume), David Wechsler was very familiar with the World War I test material, and it should not be a surprise that the "Anna Thompson" story that was included in all three versions of the Wechsler Memory Scales was originally developed for the World War I test of mental abilities (Yerkes, 1921).

With the revision from the WMS-R to the WMS-III, a few modifications have been made to the Logical Memory subtest in hopes of improving its evaluative ability. Specifically, the story content was updated. Details contained in the "Anna Thompson" story have been revised to reflect more current societal norms (e.g. "police station," rather than "city hall station" in the WMS-R). Additionally, the former "truck accident" story, which was highly controversial for use with TBI survivors following a motor vehicle accident, was replaced with a more detailed story involving more emotionally neutral content. The third major change in Logical Memory involved the addition of a second presentation of the "Joe Garcia" story, which gives the clinician the opportunity to evaluate prose memory after a repeated exposure as opposed to simply relying on a one-trial presentation. This modification reflects the well-established finding that repeated exposures facilitate learning and retention (e.g., Ebbinghaus, 1895/1913). Moreover, delayed recall will be more informative if the individual has learned more of the information initially. The third major revision in administration of Logical Memory involves the addition of a recognition memory section following the long delay free recall of the stories, as proposed by Fastenau (1996) with the WMS-R Logical Memory subtest. As discussed above, this addition to Logical Memory also reflects current thoughts in the field citing the importance of assessing both recall and recognition abilities, a distinction that can be quite useful in distinguishing individuals suffering from retrieval failure from those with inefficient learning and consolidation (Fastenau, 1996; Squire, 1986).

In addition to modifications in the administration of Logical Memory, the scoring system has been modified to increase the information gained from this subtest. The traditional scoring of the number of details recalled correctly remains. However, the additional scoring of the number of more general thematic *ideas* recalled from the story has been added. This allows the clinician to quantify differences between those individuals who are unable to recall details, but recall the gist of the story, from those who simply cannot retain (or who have difficulty retaining), the information in any form. Interestingly, this thematic *idea* scoring procedure has its origins in the early 1900s, with the originator of Logical Memory, Whipple (1915) noted the "idea score" to be the most popular method for scoring this task, distinguishing between ideas that were "identical" to the narrative from those simply "equivalent" to the narrative. The revised version of the WMS-III also allows the computation of a retention score, which can be compared to retention scores in the normative sample. Once again, Whipple (1915) highlighted the importance of retention, noting that such scores could be computed by examining the percent of information lost between two recollections of the story. In its current usage, this has been applied as a percent retained from immediate recall to delayed recall.

Verbal Paired Associates

The WMS-III Verbal Paired Associates subtest requires the presentation of eight pairs of unrelated words over a series of four trials. Recall of the pairs is assessed after each individual trial and after a 25–35-minute delay. This is done by presenting the examinee with the first word in each pair and asking him or her to provide the second. Recognition memory is also assessed after delayed recall by presenting pairs of words to which examinees have to indicate whether or not they had seen the pair before.

Use of the paired associate procedure in assessing verbal memory dates back to 1917, at which time Wechsler adapted an analogy test by Woodworth & Wells (1911) for use in his master's thesis at Columbia University (Wechsler, 1917a, 1917b). In this original usage, Wechsler administered a series of "preformed associates" or pairs of related words and "new-formed" associates or pairs of unrelated words to individuals with Korsakoff's syndrome (see Figure 3). Wechsler maintained this format of presentation for his original commercially available memory scale, the Wechsler Memory Scale, and for the revised edition of the scale (WMS-R).

Verbal Paired Associates I and II in the WMS-III also parallel the WMS and WMS-R subtests on which they are based. They require examinees to learn pairs of words that are seemingly unrelated. The examinee is asked to repeat the "paired" word over four consecutive administrations to yield the immediate score for Verbal Paired Associates (VPA I). For the delayed portion, the examinee is asked to recall the word that had been paired with the initial word (Verbal Paired Associates II). Following this procedure, recognition memory is tested with the examinee saying "yes" or "no" to whether the pair of words is part of the previously learned set or not.

Although the concept of Paired Associate Learning is maintained in the WMS-III, this revision saw a significant alteration in the test items.

From Woodworth & Wells (1911)

Mixed Relations Test		Mixed Relations Test	
I		*II*	
Eye—see	Ear—	Good—bad	Long—
Monday—Tuesday	April—	Eagle—bird	Shark—
Do—did	See—	Eat—bread	Drink—
+Bird—sings	Dog—	* Fruit—orange	Vegetable—
Hour—minute	Minute—	Sit—chair	Sleep—
Straw—hat	Leather—	Double—two	Triple—
Cloud—rain	Sun—	**England—London	France—
Hammer—tool	Dictionary—	Chew—teeth	Smell—
Uncle—aunt	Brother—	Pen—write	Knife—
Dog—puppy	Cat—	Water—wet	Fire—
Little—less	Much—	He—him	She—
Wash face	Sweep	Boat water	Train
House—room	Book—	Crawl—snake	Swim—
Sky—blue	Grass—	Horse—colt	Cow—
Swim—water	Fly—	Nose—face	Toe—
Once—one	Twice—	Bad—worse	Good—
Cat—fur	Bird—	Hungry—food	Thirsty—
Pan—tin	Table—	Hat—head	Glove—
Buy—sell	Come—	Ship—captain	Army—
Oyster—shell	Banana—	Man —woman	Boy—

From Wechsler (1917b)

Performed		New
Set I	**Set II**	**Set III**
metal—iron	eagle—bird	** crush—dark
** come—go	dog—barks	school—grocery
** baby—cries	insect—fly	cabbage—doll
rose—flower	night—day	in—although
north—south	knife—sharp	jury—eagle
lead—pencil	long—short	obey—inch
up—down	pint—quart	faraway—unlikely
fruit—apple	in—out	necktie—cracker
murder—crime	cabbage—vegetable	sailor—aloud
lock—door	country—France	dig—guilty

FIGURE 3.   Examples of Verbal Paired Associates. Lists reprinted from Woodworth & Wells (1911) and Wechsler, D (1917b). Note: The origins of the Verbal Paired Associates task can be seen in the Woodworth and Wells (1911), where 6–7 items were used as the basis for an early version of Verbal Paired Associates by originally published in Wechsler (1917b). These items would then appear in the Wechsler Memory Tests as nine items (not reprinted here) were included in the original WMS subtest and 10 of other items made up the list of pairs for the alternate form of the WMS (see Stone, Girdner, & Albrecht, 1946).

The eight pairs of words presented are now all unrelated pairs, as these stimuli present the greatest learning challenge to the examinee due to the fact that a pre-formed relationship does not exist in the examinees' memory. In addition, the number of trial repetitions has been changed from a minimum of three trials and maximum of six trials in the WMS-R to a standard four trials in the WMS-III. Recognition memory was also added following delayed recall as the examinee is asked to "recognize" the target words, and this score is a component of the Auditory Recognition Delay Index. However, as will be discussed later in the chapter, this task is extremely easy, with most healthy examinees getting a perfect or near-perfect score.

Word Lists

A significant modification of the WMS-III included the addition of an optional list learning task. The list learning subtest of the WMS-III involves the presentation of a 12-item list of unrelated words over a series of four trials. Word List I is derived from the sum of the four trials. A second list is then presented once for immediate recall, following which the examinee is asked to again recall the first list. Free recall and recognition (yes–no format) of the initial list are later assessed after the delay interval. This procedure allows the assessment of immediate recall, delayed recall, and delayed recognition, as well as the impact of interference on learning and other process-related variables.

Auditory verbal list learning is a widely used paradigm for memory assessment, with its usage dating back to the early 20th century. Boake (2000) described the development of the Auditory Verbal Learning Test, tracing its development back to Edouard Claparede (1919), a Swiss psychologist. This test subsequently underwent modifications, becoming widely known as the Rey Auditory Verbal Learning Test (1941), and continues to be utilized widely.

Despite its very specific and specialized origins, the idea of a verbal list learning task has been conceptualized quite differently over the years, resulting in numerous such tasks available to the 21st-century psychologist. Some of the most popular list-learning tasks include the California Verbal Learning Test (Delis et al., 1987), the Hopkins Verbal Learning Test (Brandt, 1991), and the Selective Reminding Test (Buschke, 1973).

The Visual Immediate and Visual Delayed Index Scores

In the published version of the WMS-III, the Visual Immediate Index is composed of the Faces I and Family Pictures I subtests. The Visual Delayed Index is composed of the Faces II and Family Pictures II subtests. Optional visual memory subtests include Visual Reproduction I and II. However, in this book we have proposed an alternate structure of the visual memory index scores and have developed new normative information for the sums of the Visual Reproduction and Family Pictures scaled scores. For these re-structured visual memory index scores, the Faces subtest is treated as op-tional. These norms and the rationale for replacing the Faces subtest with Visual Reproduction are discussed by Tulsky et al. (Chapter 4, this volume).

Memory for Faces

In Faces I and II on the WMS-III, the examinee is asked to view target faces and distinguish these "target" faces from foils (see Figure 4). For Faces I, the examinee is initially presented photographs of 24 target faces. The examinee is then presented photographs of 48 faces, including the 24 target faces and 24 new faces. The examinee must identify each face, as either a target face or a new one. For Faces II, the examinee is again presented the 24 target faces and 24 different faces and is again asked to identify each face as either a target face or a new one.

Face perception and memory are regarded as special types of visuospatial processing and memory (Farah, Wilson, Drain, & Tanaka, 1998), and the

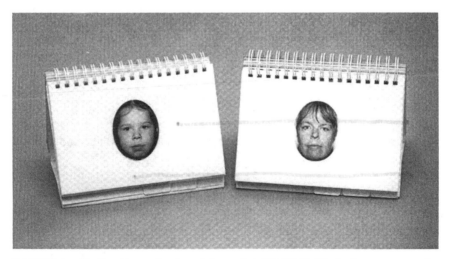

FIGURE 4.   Similated items the Faces Subtest. As in the WMS-III, the faces are cropped so as to show a minimal amount of hair, and the individuals are shown with a neutral expression, not smiling. Half of the faces are of children and half are of adults. The photo has been created by the authors to appear like a WMS-III item. WMS-III faces subtest is a copyright protected by the Psychological Corporation.

ability to encode and remember new, unfamiliar faces has been well studied throughout the past century. McCarthy and Warrington (1990) concluded that "faces are special," and facial recognition appears to be "hardwired" in humans at the earliest ages (pp. 68–69). In fact, the developmental literature shows that even young babies have differential responses to faces as compared to other types of stimuli (Flin & Dziurawiec, 1989; Goren, Sarty, & Wu, 1975).

The earliest accounts in the behavioral neurology literature recognized difficulty in processing facial information (e.g., Charcot, 1883), and later the term *prosopagnosia* was derived to describe individuals who were deficient in the ability to process information about faces. This was described by Bodamer (1947) as "visual category [that is] the most profound and genetically the most primitive in our perception" (see McCarthy & Warrington, 1990, p. 56). Both the clinical and cognitive-perceptual literatures are quite clear and consistent that faces are processed differently by the brain than other visual stimuli.

There is some empirical evidence that some facial recognition tasks may show differential specificity to right-versus left-hemisphere damage (e.g., Milner, Branch, & Raomussen, 1966; Milner, Corkin, & Tenber, 1968; Warrington & James, 1967). Numerous researchers have made use of an idiosyncratic set of faces as stimuli for assessing facial memory (e.g., DeRenzi, Faglioni, & Spinnler, 1966; Milner et al., 1968; Saykin et al., 1992), some of which have been established and validated as facial memory tests, yet have not been widely utilized.

For these reasons, McCarthy and Warrington's (1990) conclusion that "faces are special" seems relevant and leads us to make the following conclusions about using faces as stimuli in a memory test:

1. Faces are encoded differently in the brain. Facial processing appears related to rather specific neuroanatomical substrates (i.e., fusiform gyri).
2. Faces represent a different type of visual stimulus. They cannot be verbally encoded as readily as other stimuli. Faces often possess greater detail (and potentially greater emotional coding—even unfamiliar faces) than nonface visual stimuli.
3. Differential perception and encoding of faces seems to be unique from a developmental perspective as well. Evolutionary theories also emphasize the differences between processing faces and all other visual stimuli.

The idea to include a facial memory subtest in the WMS-III occurred early in the revision process. Nelson Butters, who had established and led the initial advisory panel meetings, had recommended using this special type of stimuli for a visual memory task. Because memory for faces is a common task for all individuals, it was thought that the task would have ecological validity, which is generally lacking in most memory scales and had been one of the criticisms of the WMS-R visual memory subtests.

In addition, a precedent did exist for using faces as stimuli in perceptual tests (Benton, Hamsher, Varney, & Spreen 1983) and memory recognition tests (Benton et al., 1983; Warrington, 1984), and at the time the WMS–III was being developed, facial memory tasks were being included in other neuropsychological tests published by The Psychological Corporation (NEPSY, Korkman, Kirk, & Kemp, 1998; Children's Memory Test, Cohen, 1996). With these precedents in mind, a facial memory subtest seemed like an ideal addition to the WMS–III, and the faces "stimuli" were prepared.

The WMS–III Memory for Faces subtest was modeled after the Recognition Memory Test (Warrington, 1984), a widely used recognition test assessing memory for words and memory for faces. Performance on memory for faces has been shown to be disrupted following damage to the right temporal or right parietal lobes (Warrington, 1984). However, the Recognition Memory Test is thought by some to be limited in that it only requires recognition immediately following presentation. The WMS–III facial memory test in contrast, assesses recognition for the unfamiliar faces both immediately following presentation and after a delay.

Like the majority of the other subtests included on the WAIS–III and WMS–III, the subtests went through many revisions and experimental testing and appeared to be well received by both the standardization examiners and examinees. In the earliest stages of development, the items were pilot tested, cropping the pictures very tightly so that some more easily recognizable features (e.g., hair) would not be showing. In this way, examinees would not have easy cues that might facilitate recognition. Unfortunately, the effect was often frightening to the examinee because the faces did not look "human" with so many normal cues removed (Ledbetter, 1997).

Since the publication of the WMS–III, there have been some reports that questioned the inclusion of the faces subtest on the Visual Memory Index. Factor analyses by Millis, Malina, Bowers, & Ricker (1999) found that the subtest has much lower factor loadings on the WMS–III visual memory factor than Family Pictures, the other Visual subtest. This finding was confirmed by Price, Tulsky, Millis, and Weiss (2002), and replicated by Tulsky and Price (in press). Face recognition seems to be contributing unique variance to the visual memory factor. It is unclear if this result occurs because the Faces subtest is methodologically unique in that it only contains a recognition format without a recall component or if it is because Faces are "special stimuli"). Millis et al. (1999) advised that the Faces subtests should not be combined with the Family Pictures subtests in the construct of "visual memory," and this is one of the reasons why the visual memory factor was reconstituted in this joint factor project. Visual Reproductions did have a higher factor loading, along with Family Pictures, on this visual factor which also aided this decision (see Tulsky et al., Chapter 4, this volume, for a description of how the visual memory factor was reconstituted).

Family Pictures

When individuals present to a clinician with memory complaints, they rarely report that they cannot remember or draw abstract designs or geometric figures (such as in Visual Reproduction). Rather, they tend to report things like forgetting names of people they have met before; they report that they fail to remember things such as where they met someone, where they left their car keys, or where they parked their car. The Family Pictures subtest is a new subtest created for this revision of the WMS, developed in the hope of objectively assessing some of these presenting complaints.

The idea for Family Pictures arose as a result of the search for an ecologically meaningful way of assessing visual-spatial memory, without requiring complex "motor" responding (e.g., drawing). The original idea can be attributed to Robert Ivnik, who conceptualized the task and brought it to the WMS-III team during an advisory panel meeting in San Antonio in 1995. In attendence were Robert Bornstein, Gordon Chelune, Robert Heaton, Robert Ivnik, Mark Ledbetter (WMS-III Project Leader), Aurelio Prifitera, and David Tulsky. The goal was to examine spatial memory for visually presented, meaningful material while still allowing for verbal responding. In essence, most memories are verbally encoded, but often utilize the resources of spatial memory for cuing and accuracy. Even though photographs can be verbally encoded, they convey a great deal of spatial information that we learn and remember automatically. This task was designed to tap into this natural process by assessing spatial memory for visually presented material by asking people to identify spatial interrelationships of the elements in a photograph following examination. This recall is required without the examinee being told that they would have to remember the picture content or how the elements are arranged in relation to one another due to the fact that this is the typical situation in everyday memory.

The WMS-III team then developed and refined what we know today as Family Pictures for both the WMS-III and the Children's Memory Scale (Cohen, 1996). For Family Pictures I, examinees are shown a series of four scenes, all of which involve different characters from the same family. Examinees are told to remember as much as they can about the scene because they will be asked some questions later (Wechsler, 1997b). Each scene is presented for 10 seconds in a sequential fashion. After all the scenes are presented, the examinee is asked to recall which family member was in each scene, what each character was doing, and where the character was located. For Family Pictures II, the examinee recalls the same information without seeing the pictures again.

Tasks similar to family pictures do exist in other test batteries. For example, the Wide Range Assessment of Memory and Learning (WRAML; Adams & Sheslow, 1990) contains a picture memory subtest in which children examine a picture for 10 seconds, after which they see a comparable scene in which items were changed or added. They mark what is different with an "X." This procedure is repeated for four different scenes. Actually, such testing techniques have a long history. In 1911, Healy and Fernald introduced such a test as part of their battery (Healy & Fernald, 1911; Bronner, Healy, Lowe, & Shimberg, 1929), which required free recall of a picture of a butcher shop after a 10-second presentation. Free recall was followed by specific questions about the picture which are asked as "a kind of cross examination, which is calculated to bring out details of the picture which he may have forgotten, as well as his suggestibility" (Healy & Fernald, 1911, p. 22). Similarly, Fred L. Wells (1913) first reported on a test called Picture Postcards, which he later integrated into the Wells and Martin (1923) memory battery. Picture Postcards was a visual recognition test where the examinee is shown 12 "target" postcards depicting natural scenery from regions thought to be unfamiliar to the examinee. Then in a recognition format, the examinee is shown the 12 targets again mixed with 12 foils, and he or she has to indicate whether or not the picture had been seen previously.

Visual Reproduction

The Visual Reproduction subtest of the WMS-III requires individuals to study geometric figures for 10 seconds each and then draw the figures from memory. It was the only visual memory subtest in the original WMS (Wechsler, 1945). The task has a long history in intelligence and memory testing, and nearly all of the designs present in the WMS-III were taken directly from the Binet–Simon scale (Binet & Simon, 1905/1916a) or from the Army Performance Scale.

Binet and Simon (1905/1916a) developed and included their original task in the first edition of their intelligence test as a response to the need to classify school children as mentally retarded or normal. The subtest was entitled "Drawing a Design from Memory," and marked the first time that an examiner would present a stimulus card for 10 seconds and then, upon removal, ask the examinee to draw the design from memory. This administration procedure and the stimuli have been retained over the years (see Figure 5). Currently, we know the task as Visual Reproduction. In the Binet–Simon version, the examinee would be exposed to only one card with the two simple line drawings presented. These two designs still exist in the current WMS-III Visual Reproduction, although they are no longer presented together.

The drawing a design from memory task was utilized consistently throughout the history of mental testing. It was included in the Stanford Revision of the Binet Test (Terman, 1916) and then expanded upon for use in The Army Individual Examination, which tested recruits in World War I (Yerkes, 1921). For the Army tests, four "plates" containing new geographic designs, were actually created by Terman as alternative stimuli for the Stanford–Binet (Yerkes, 1921). Like the original Binet–Simon task, each design was exposed to the examinee for 10 seconds, after which it was removed and the examinee was to draw the design from memory (Yerkes, 1921).

The test that we know today as Visual Reproduction in the Wechsler Scales comes directly from these pioneering efforts, with little modification of the exact stimuli. Two of the four designs on the WMS came from the Design subtest of the Army Individual Performance Battery (Yerkes, 1921) and have continued to be included in the subsequent revisions (WMS-R and WMS-III; they are currently Designs B and C of the WMS-III). A third

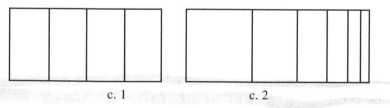

c. 1   c. 2

FIGURE 5.   Item developed for the Army Performance Battery (Yerkes, 1921). In the public domain. Incoporated into Visual Reproduction of the Wechsler Memory Scale, Form II (see Stone, Girdner, & Albrecht, 1946; Stone & Wechsler, 1946).

design in the original WMS and in the subsequent WMS-R (4 circles) was taken directly from the Form Recognition subtest of Army Group Examination Beta (Yerkes, 1921), which was a simple matching to target visuospatial processing task.

Despite the similarity in testing procedures, however, there are significant distinctions between the tests. Notably, the WMS-III has expanded scoring criteria, with quite detailed criteria (Wechsler, 1997). In 1921, the scoring of this task was simple: full credit, half credit, or failure for each item (Yerkes, 1921). The administration procedures have also been expanded since the original WMS was published. Although the WMS included only an immediate recall procedure, and the WMS-R included immediate and delayed recall procedures, the WMS-III has added a series of optional tasks to allow examiners to test recognition memory, constructional praxis, and visual discrimination. Such tasks can be useful in determining the source of deficit observed on the immediate and delayed procedure, particularly for neurological patients who may have significant perceptual and/or visuoconstructional deficits. Finally, changes were made to the subtest items themselves. Specifically, the floor and ceiling levels in Visual Reproduction have been modified through the replacement of the more difficult WMS-R Design B (four circles) with a new item, (the WMS-III Design A), which is a simple line drawing of two "flags" facing opposite directions. The WMS-III subtest includes two new items—Design D, which is made up of two figures each composed of simple geometric shapes that are arranged side by side, and Design E which had been developed and used in the Binet–Simon test battery (Binet & Simon, 1905/1916a) and in the original WMS subtest (Wechsler, 1945).

An additional change in the revision of the WMS-R to the WMS-III is that this subtest is no longer a required component of the standard Visual Memory Index score. In the published form of the WMS-III, it is considered an optional subtest because of the length and multifaceted nature of this subtest. However, as will be presented in Chapter 4 (Tulsky, et al., this volume), this decision has been challenged on psychometric grounds, and the Visual Memory factor has been reconstituted to include Visual Reproduction in the six factor model.

Many other memory scales include Visual Reproduction-like tasks, but include multiple learning trials to help distinguish initial learning difficulties from true memory difficulties, (e.g., Heaton Figure Memory Test (Heaton et al., 1991) and the Brief Visual Spatial Memory Test-Revised (Benedict, Schretlen, Groninger, Dobraski, Shpritz, 1996)). The omission of such learning trials from the WMS-III Visual Reproductions subtests is unfortunate, as the distinction between learning and memory has proven important in the understanding of many neurocognitive conditions, such as schizophrenia (Heaton et al., 1994), multiple sclerosis (DeLuca, Barbieri-Berger, & Johnson, 1994; DeLuca, Gaudino, Diamond, Christodoulou, & Engle, 1998), traumatic brain injury (DeLuca, Schultheis, Madigan, Christodoulou, & Averill, 2000), as well as normal aging (Haaland, Price, & LaRue, 2003).

Another longstanding criticism of Visual Reproductions-like tests has been the confounding of visual-motor and integration difficulties (drawing ability) with visual memory (Barr et al., 1997). Fortunately, the WMS-III procedures include an optional "copy trial" so that this confound can be evaluated. (Note also, this is an example of how the "process" approach has been brought into the mainstream of a standardized test battery.)

Working Memory Index

As reported in the *WAIS-III–WMS-III Technical Manual* (The Psychological Corporation, 1997), this index is thought to measure complex attentional skills that stress the ability to attend to information, to hold and process that information in memory, and to formulate a response based on that information. It is composed of the Letter Number Sequencing scaled score and the Spatial Span scaled score. It shares a subtest, the Letter Number Sequencing subtest, with the WAIS-III (the origins and description of this have been described previously (see Tulsky, Saklofske, and Zhu, Chapter 2, this volume). Digit Span is an optional subtest to this index.

Spatial Span

WMS-III Spatial Span is yet another subtest that has a long history in the assessment literature. The Spatial Span subtest requires the examinee to repeat a number of tapping sequences following demonstration by the examiner, with the spatial sequence getting longer with each trial. Similar to the WAIS-III Digit Span, Spatial Span contains a forward sequence and a backward sequence.

This concept can be traced back to Howard A. Knox (1914) for testing immigrants at Ellis Island. Soon after Knox's intial report on this task was published, the Knox Cube imitation became very popular in performance batteries. Wechsler (1917b) included the original version of the Knox Cube test in his master's thesis as well as an alternate form of the measure that was

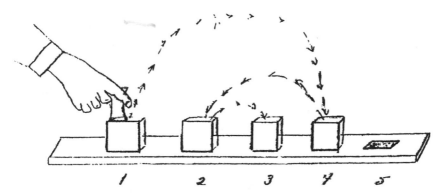

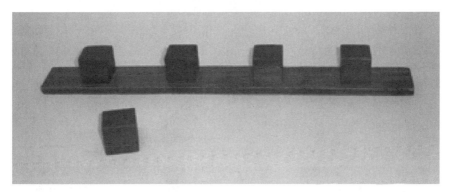

FIGURE 6.   The Knox cube test with an illustration on how to administer an item. (From an unpublished Public Health Service Document [author unknown]. Provided courtesy of Ellis Island collection.) The sequence is from an alternate form of the Knox Cube administration that was provided to Wechsler by E. H. Mullan for use in his Master's thesis (see Wechsler, 1917a, 1917b) and later adapted into the Army Individual Performance Battery. (Photo of the Knox Cube test courtesy of the Ellis Island museum. From the collection of the Archives of the History of American Psychology, Akron, OH.)

developed by members of the Public Health Service working at Ellis Island, and that was shared with him by E.H. Mullan (see Figure 6). It was subsequently adapted by Yerkes (1921) for inclusion in the Army Individual Test Battery as the Knox Cube Imitation subtest. The examinee was presented with a stimulus board consisting of four 1-inch hardwood cubes fastened to a wooden base, numbered 1–4, as well as a fifth cube that was not attached to the wooden base. Using the fifth cube, the examiner would tap a sequence (see Figure 6 for an example) following which, the examinee would repeat the sequence. Each sequence was repeated twice.

In later years, this test was again adapted by Corsi who used it in his doctoral dissertation (Corsi, 1972; Milner, 1971). The Spatial Sequential Learning Task (SSLT: Saykin, et al., 1992) was later developed as yet another adaptation to the task used by Corsi. The SSLT consists of a nine-block board similar to the apparatus presented by Corsi, on which the examinee is asked to reproduce a nine block tapping sequence demonstrated by the examiner (Saykin et al., 1992). The same tapping sequence is repeated until the participant correctly duplicates the entire series on two consecutive trials, or until 15 trails are completed. The number of trials to reach the criterion is the measure of the individual's ability to learn new spatial information. This adaptation of the original Knox (1914) task is designed to assess long-term memory capabilities, as opposed assessing spatial working memory, as in the WMS-III.

The Visual Spatial Span test was initially added to the WMS-R as a visual analog to the Digit Span test. A significant change from the WMS-R to the WMS-III is in the stimuli construction. The WMS-R Spatial Span stimuli consisted of squares printed on a two-dimensional card, whereas those on the WMS-III Spatial Span consist of a three-dimensional array of blocks (see Figure 7) with the block number to be visible only to the examiner. This change was made to facilitate administration and scoring.

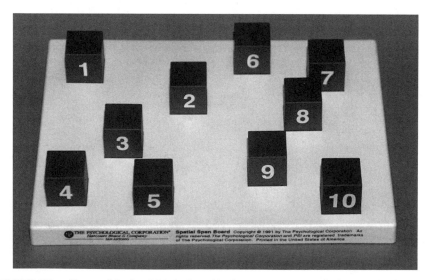

FIGURE 7.   Photo of the Spatial Span board in the WMS-III. (Material copyright © 1991, 1997 The Psychological Corporation. Used with permission. All Rights reserved.)

Note: Photo displays the examiners perspective. The numbers are not visible to the examinee.

Optional Tasks of Basic Processes

Two of the optional WMS-III subtests (Information and Orientation and Mental Control) are primarily of value in providing a context for understanding poor performance on the primary memory indices.

Information and Orientation

The Information and Orientation subtest is an optional component of the WMS-III, and the scores are not incorporated into any of the Index scores. However, difficulties with this subtest would be an important factor to consider in interpreting poor performance on any of the index scores. The subtest represents a merging and expansion of two subtests from the original WMS: that is, in the original WMS Personal and Current Information was a separate subtest from Orientation. Regarding the former, Wechsler (1945) stated that the test discriminated very little (or not at all) between normal or near normal subjects. Instead, the subtest was useful in examining individuals with special defects (e.g., people with aphasia and people with dementia) who tend to score significantly lower on the test (p. 87). He indicated a similar rationale for inclusion of the Orientation subtest. In short, the WMS-III Information and Orientation subtest can be useful in determining whether a patient is oriented to a person, place, time, situation, and the like.

Mental Control

Mental Control is also an optional subtest in the WMS-III, but has appeared in some form on each of the earlier WMS versions. According to the WMS-III manual (Wechsler, 1997b), Mental Control measures the examinee's ability to retrieve overlearned information and to mentally manipulate that information. As formulated in the original WMS (as well as the WMS-R), it consisted of three tasks: (a) counting backwards from 20 to 1, (b) saying the letters of the alphabet, and (c) counting by threes. The latter task was dropped from the WMS-III version, but several additional tasks were added, including counting forwards from 1 to 20, stating the days of the week forward and backward, and stating the months of the year forward and backward. These tasks were added in order to assess an individual's ability to recite and manipulate overlearned information. Wechsler (1945) asserted that the utility of the original Mental Control Subtest was "primarily in cases of organic brain disease that are not too far gone but show deficits which would not be made evident by simple rote memory items" (p. 87–88).

When a patient has poor performance on Mental Control, it suggests that he or she may lack sufficient attentional abilities for adequate performance of the memory tests. That is, whereas impaired memory in the context of intact attention might be interpreted as possibly reflecting impairment in structures or brain systems underlying consolidation of episodic memory (such as the left or right hippocampus), when that same impairment is present in the context of significantly impaired attention, one is much more conservative in their interpretation of the memory findings. Thus, the documented poor performance on memory testing could be attributed to deficient information acquisition due to compromised attentional capacities. In sum, the interpretation of WMS-III performance may be altered significantly depending on the patient's basic attentional skills.

The Auditory Recognition Delayed Index

One of the primary goals of the WMS-III development, when possible, was the administration of a recognition procedure following administration of the delayed recall for Logical Memory, Verbal Paired Associates, Word List, and Visual Reproduction subtests. In the published test, an Auditory Recognition Delayed Index (ARDI) is computed by summing the *raw* recognition scores of Logical Memory and Verbal Paired Associates and then converting this raw total score to a standardized index score. The recognition index is based solely on verbal tasks. The Family Pictures subtest does not lend itself to a recognition procedure, and the Faces subtest is only based upon recognition (there is not a recall procedure for this subtest). Due to these differences in procedures, they were not included in a Recognition index. Moreover, since the Word Lists and Visual Reproduction subtests are optional, they are also not included in the Auditory Recognition Delayed Index, despite having a recognition procedure.

Since the publication of the WMS-III, it has become apparent that most normal individuals perform very well on this index, demonstrating a ceiling effect. Reports have suggested that even patients, some of whom have severe cognitive deficits, often score near perfectly on the measure. To better understand why this occurs, descriptive statistics on the Logical Memory Delayed Recognition Total Score, the Verbal Paired Associates Recognition Total Score, World List Recognition Total Score, and the Auditory Recognition Delayed Total Score have been computed (see Table 1). The distributions of all of these scores are highly skewed in a negative direction with the vast majority of the standardization sample obtaining a perfect score on

TABLE 1　Descriptive Statistics for Auditory Delayed Recognition Total Scores[a]

	Verbal Paired Associates Delayed Recognition total score	Logical Memory Delayed Recognition total score	Word List Delayed Recognition total score	Auditory Delayed Recognition total score
N	Weighted n = 1250 (unweighted n = 1,032)	Weighted n = 1250 (unweighted n = 1,032)	Weighted n = 1250 (unweighted n = 1,032)	Weighted n = 1250 (unweighted n = 1,032)
Minimum	12	13	0	26
Maximum	24	30	24	54
Mean	23.41	24.49	21.93	47.89
Median	24	25	23	49
Mode	24	27	24	51
Std Deviation	1.5	3.5	2.6	4.3

these recognition variables. This results in a restriction in the range of the scores, making it very difficult to scale this index. In fact, in a normal sample, the Verbal Paired Associate Recognition component contributes very little additional variance to the recognition index, as 75% of the WMS-III standardization sample (or 958 out of the weighted N of 1250) obtained a perfect score of 24 points. This indicates that the entire variance of the Auditory Recognition Delayed Index in the standardization sample is made up of the Logical Memory Delayed Recognition score, which is also negatively skewed. However, the Logical Memory Delayed Recognition has more variance than the Verbal Paired Associates Recognition score and validates the argument put forth by clinicians; namely, the subtest and items were too easy and a ceiling effect was present.

Since the recognition scores are so skewed, traditional scaling techniques probably should not have been used to create an index score with a mean of 100 and standard deviation of 15. When nearly all individuals obtain a perfect or near perfect score, conversion to a scaled score metric is deceiving. A more appropriate scaling procedure for the recognition variables would have been a presentation of the percentile data similar to that reported in the WAIS-III Administration and Scoring Manual for the Digit Symbol optional procedures (Table A.11; Wechsler, 1997b). As pointed out in chapter 1 (Tulsky et al., Chapter 2, this volume), these scores can be extremely valuable clinically when deficits are noted. However, because the raw scores were associated with the lowest percentiles, the examiner is clearly using the recognition scores as deficit indices.

Table 2 presents an alternate way to determine if an individual scores as poorly as the lowest performers in the WMS-III standardization sample: Cumulative Percentages for the WMS-III recognition variables. This table shows cumulative percentages for the raw score values and is presented as an option in place of the Auditory Delayed Recognition Index that is described in the WMS-III manual. Even though the majority of normal individuals score quite high on this task, the recognition variables may, in fact, be clinically useful in separating groups. This remains an empirical question. With such skewed distributions, it is rare for someone to miss items. However, when this does occur, it becomes an unusual event, one that should be explored further to determine if the lower score is indicative of a cognitive deficit, or a suboptimal effort (e.g., malingering). Given the skewness of the data, high or average scores are not particularly meaningful. Using the cumulative percentages in Table 2, the recognition variables serve more as "pathonomic" indicators that "flag" potential deficits in recognition that should be explored further. For these reasons, we recommend that the

TABLE 2   Memory Recognition Scores: Cumulative Percentages Associated with Raw Scores[a]

	Cumulative Percentage	16–17	18–19	20–24	25–29	30–34	35–44	45–54	55–64	65–69	70–74	75–79	80–84	85–89
Logical Memory Delayed Recognition	1	20	19	17	17	18	14	19	17	16	16	14	13	14
	2	20	21	17	17	19	15	20	17	17	18	14	14	14
	5	20	21	19	18	20	16	20	18	18	18	15	16	15
	10	22	22	21	19	23	20	21	20	20	19	16	16	16
	25	24	24	24	24	24	24	24	22	22	21	20	19	18
	50	26	26	26	26	26	27	26	25	25	24	23	21	22
Verbal Paired Associates Delayed Recognition	1	23	22	21	18	20	18	20	19	20	18	12	12	12
	2	23	22	22	18	20	19	20	19	20	19	12	13	12
	5	23	23	23	23	22	21	21	21	21	20	15	17	14
	10	24	24	23	24	23	23	22	22	22	21	21	19	18
	25	24	24	24	24	24	24	23	23	23	23	23	22	21
	50	24	24	24	24	24	24	24	24	24	24	24	24	23
Word List Delayed Recognition	1	18	0	17	13	10	15	14	15	11	14	13	10	14
	2	19	18	17	13	16	16	14	17	16	16	13	11	14
	5	21	20	20	18	19	17	17	17	17	16	15	13	15
	10	22	21	20	20	20	18	19	18	18	17	16	15	16
	25	23	23	23	22	22	22	20	21	19	20	20	19	18
	50	24	24	24	23	23	23	23	23	21	22	22	21	20
Auditory Delayed Recognition	1	43	43	40	37	41	36	41	37	37	38	27	26	28
	2	43	45	40	37	42	36	41	40	40	40	27	31	29
	5	44	45	42	41	44	40	43	41	40	40	36	35	33
	10	46	46	45	43	45	44	44	43	42	42	39	37	34
	25	48	48	47	48	48	47	47	45	46	44	43	40	39
	50	50	50	50	50	50	50	49	48	49	47	47	45	45

recognition variables no longer be used in the same manner as the other index scores that are core to the WMS-III.

General and Immediate Memory

The publication of the WMS-III yields two global memory scores: an Immediate Memory Index (IMI) and the General Memory Index (GMI). The technical manual (The Psychological Corporation, 1997) describes the GMI of the WMS-III as "the best overall measure of the types of abilities that are critical to effective memory in day-to-day tasks" (p. 193). To give the most ecologically valid index of "memory," emphasis was placed on delayed memory rather than immediate, and in the WMS-III, unlike the WMS and WMS-R, the GMI is composed of the sum of delayed subtest scaled scores and auditory recognition delayed scores, rather than the immediate subtest scaled scores. Hence, the GMI is similar to the old Delayed Recall Index from the WMS-R.

Continuity between the WMS-R and WMS-III was believed to be preserved by including the Immediate Memory Index, a score that is relatively analogous in composition to the WMS-R General Memory Index (The Psychological Corporation, 1997), and the technical manual reports that the IMI is considered the best global indicator of immediate memory functioning. The technical manual also points out that at least on the surface, there are significant differences at the subtest level that preclude direct comparison between the WMS-III IMI and WMS-R GMI. However, continuity is preserved to the extent that the subtests on the WMS-III assess similar constructs as the Index scores on the WMS-R. In fact, the correlation between the WMS-III IMI and the WMS-R GMI is moderately high ($r = 0.62$; The Psychological Corporation, 1997), which suggests that there is some similarity between the measures, despite their differences.

More relevant to clinicians using the WMS-III is that the IMI and the GMI are NOT directly comparable. The WMS-III IMI is composed of the sum of the scaled scores on the four subtests that compose both the Auditory Immediate Index and the Visual Immediate Index scores. Like the IMI, the WMS-III GMI is composed of the sum of the scaled scores on the four subtests that compose both the Auditory Delayed Index and the Visual Delayed Index. However, the Auditory Recognition Delayed Index score is also included in the WMS-III GMI, which makes direct comparison of immediate and delayed memory less precise. Thus, the GMI is confounded due to the fact that both recall and recognition are included in the score, which is only made more complicated by the previously noted ceiling effects in the Auditory Recognition Delayed Index. To assist examiners with this comparison, Tulsky, Chelune, Price, & Millis (2003) have created a new *Delayed Memory Index* derived from the WMS-III standardization sample using only the auditory and visual delayed recall subtests. This new index includes only the delayed components of the same four subtests found in the IMI.

SUPPORT FOR THE WMS-III STRUCTURE

The initial support for the new WMS-III structure of eight primary index scores was provided in the *WAIS-III–WMS-III Technical Manual* (The Psychological Corporation, 1997). Confirmatory factor analyses (CFA) were used to support the construct validity of this structure by pitting six alternative models against each other and then evaluating the goodness-of-fit statistics. The original report claimed support for a five-factor model consisting of attention/concentration (or working memory), immediate verbal memory, immediate visual memory, delayed verbal memory, and delayed visual memory (see The Psychological Corporation, 1997). Shortly after publication of the WMS-III, Millis et al. (1999) attempted to replicate the factor structure using the covariance matrices that were reported in the *WAIS-III–WMS-III Technical Manual* and were unable to achieve convergence of the five-factor model. Instead, the analyses indicated an inadmissible solution due to a nonpositive definite covariance matrix, and the authors speculated that poor model fit was responsible for the inadmissible solution. Following up on this article, Price, Tulsky, Millis, and Weiss (2002) attempted to replicate the factor structure of the WMS-III using the standardization data set with the goals of (1) re-creating the results that had been obtained and (2) verifying that an error had been made in the original report (The Psychological Corporation, 1977). A warning message on the statistical output that had been accidentally overlooked when the results were first published. Price et al. then replicated their initial results in a restrictive cross-validation study using a sample of extra cases from the standardization sample that had been used in previous analyses by Tulsky and Price (in press). These replication studies confirm that the distinction between immediate and delayed memory cannot be supported, and the construct validity for this model of memory in this test battery has not yet been supported. Based upon these findings, the impact of these results and recommended changes that are advanced by the lead author of this chapter, as well as several of the editors of this volume, are described in Tulsky, et al., Chapter 4, this volume.

CONCLUSIONS

Although the WMS-III includes several new components, some that are unfamiliar and others that might have weaknesses in their design, this revision of the WMS was significant in its attempt to represent the more recent research in the field of memory assessment. Also the WMS-III has one of the largest and most representative standardization databases from which to assess memory and to make optimal clinical recommendations. Furthermore, the value of the powerful database that has been obtained through the co-norming procedure of the WMS-III with the WAIS-III cannot be overstated.

Kate Levine Kogan (1949), in writing the initial review of the Wechsler Memory Scale in the *Third Mental Measurement Yearbook* (reprinted as Item 8 in Appendix 2, this volume), stated that the most important use of the Wechsler Memory Scale is

> in conjunction with the Wechsler-Bellevue intelligence scale, since the memory quotient is designed to be directly comparable to the intelligence quotient. Use of the test permits intra-individual comparison of the patient's memory impairment with his loss in other intellectual functions rather than only a comparison with a general average or norm. (pp. 398–399)

Although the emphasis has moved away from IQ scores to factor scores (see Tulsky et al. chapter 4, this volume) and away from MQ scores to specific memory processes (as described earlier in this chapter), the most significant and meaningful advance in the production of the third editions of the WAIS-III and WMS-III was the use of a conorming methodology. However, during the development phase, the tests were developed in a relatively independent fashion utilizing two distinct project teams that were working on each of the revisions. Although there were attempts to integrate the use of the two tests (e.g., through base rates of discrepancies between these measures), they were still published as unique measures. Some more adventurous goals of combining subtests across the batteries to develop true joint factors of cognitive functioning were not realized in the initial publications, and, in this sense, the continuity of the two separate tests was maintained.

As with every assessment tool, work remains to be accomplished to improve our ability to most effectively apply the tools within the WMS-

III and to interpret the data to its maximal capacity. The WMS-III should therefore be viewed as a work in progress, with ongoing research in the field facilitating improved methodology and means of comparison.

In fact, Chapter 4 (Tulsky et al., this volume) outlines a new structure of subtests that can be given to assess cognitive functioning (a construct that includes both traditional intellectual measures, memory measures, working memory, and processing speed). Moreover, the follow-up chapters discuss new norms and methods of utilizing these tools in a more informed manner.

REFERENCES

Adams, W., & Scheslow, D. (1990). *Wide Range Assessment of Memory and Learning Manual.* Wilmington, DE: Jastak Associates.

Baddeley, A. D. (1976). *The psychology of memory.* New York: Harper & Row, Open University Set Books.

Bailey, P., Williams, F. E., & Komora, P. O. (1929). *The medical department of the United States Army in the World War: Volume X: Neuropsychiatry.* Washington: U.S. Government Printing Office.

Barr, W. B., Chelune, G. J., Hermann, B. P., Loring, D., Perrine, K., Strauss, E., Trenerry, M. R., & Westerneld, M. (1997). The use of figural reproduction tests as measures of nonverbal memory in epilepsy surgery candidates. *Journal of the International Neuropsychological Society, 3,* 435–443.

Benedict, R. H. B., Schretlen, D., Groninger, L., Dobraski, M., & Shpritz, B. (1996). Revision of the Brief Visuospatial Memory Test: Studies of normal performance, reliability, and validity. *Psychological Assessment, 8,* 145–153.

Benton, A. L., Hamsher, K. S., Varney, N. K., & Spreen, O. (1983). *Contribution to neuropsychological assessment.* New York: Oxford University Press.

Benton, A., & Van Allen, M. (1968). Impairment in facial recognition in patients with cerebral disease. *Cortex, 4,* 344–358.

Binet, A., & Henri, V. (1895). La mémoire des phrases, [Sentence memory]. *L'Année Psychologique, 1,* 24–59.

Binet, A., & Henri, V. (1896). La psychologie individuelle, [Individual Psychology]. *L'Année Psychologique, 2,* 411–465.

Binet, A., & Simon, T. (1905/1916a). New methods for the diagnosis of the intellectual level of subnormals. In *The development of intelligence in children* (E. S. Kite, Trans.). Baltimore: Williams & Wilkins Company. (Original work published 1905)

Binet, A., & Simon, T. (1908/1916b). The development of intelligence in the child. In *The development of intelligence in children.* (E. S. Kite, Trans.). Baltimore: Williams & Wilkins Company. (Original work published 1908)

Binet, A., & Simon, T. (1911/1916c). New investigation upon the measure of the intellectual level among school children. In *The development of intelligence in children.* (E. S. Kite, Trans.). Baltimore: Williams & Wilkins Company. (Original work published 1911)

Black, F. W. (1973). Memory and paired associate learning of patients with unilateral brain lesions. *Psychological Reports, 33,* 919–922.

Black, F. W. (1974). The utility of the memory for designs test with patients with penetrating wounds of the brain. *Journal of clinical psychology, 30*, 75–77.

Boake, C. (2000). Historical note: Edouard Claparede and the Auditory Verbal Learning Test. *Journal of Clinical and Experimental Neuropsychology, 22*(2), 286–292.

Boardman, H. (1917). Psychological tests: A bibliography. *Bureau of Educational Experiments, 6.*

Bodamer, J. (1947). Die Prosopagnosia [Prosopagnosia]. *Archiv für Psychiatrie und Zeitschrift für Neurologie, 179*, 6–54.

Bornstein, R., & Chelune, G. (1988). Factor structure of the Wechsler memory scale revised. *The Clinical Neuropsychologist, 2*, 107–115.

Brandt, J. (1991). The Hopkins Verbal Learning Test: Development of a new memory test with six equivalent forms. *The Clinical Neuropsychologist, 5(2)*, 125–142.

Bronner, A. F., Healy, W., Lowe, G. M., & Shimberg, M. E. (1929). *A manual of individual mental tests and testing.* Boston: Little, Brown, and Company.

Buschke, H. (1973). Selective reminding for the analysis of memory and learning. *Journal of Verbal Learning and Verbal Behavior, 12*, 543–550.

Buschke, H., & Fuld, P. A. (1974). Evaluating storage, retention, and retrieval in disordered memory and learning *Neurology, 24*, 1019–1025.

Charcot, J. M. (1883). Un cas de suppression brusque et isolée de la vision mentale de signes et des objets (formes et couleurs). *Progrés Medicale, 11*, 568–571.

Chelune, G. J., & Bornstein, R. A. (1988). WMS-R patterns among patients with unilateral brain lesions. *The Clinical Neuropsychologist, 2*, 121–132.

Chelune, G. J., Bornstein, R. A., & Prifitera, A. (1990). The Wechsler Memory Scale-Revised: Current status and applications. In P. McReynolds & J. C. Rosen, et al. (Eds), *Advances in Psychological Assessment Vol. 7.* (pp. 65–99). New York: Plenum Press.

Claparede, E. (1919). Percentilage de quelques tests d'aptitude. [Percentiles of some aptitude tests] *Archives de Psychologie, 17*, 313–324.

Cochran, W. G. (1977). Sampling techniques (3rd ed.). New York: Wiley.

Cohen, M. J. (1996). *Children's Memory Scale.* San Antonio, TX: The Psychological Corporation.

Corsi, P. M. (1972). *Human memory and the medial temporal region of the brain.* Unpublished doctoral dissertation, McGill University, Montreal, Canada.

D'Elia, L. F., Satz, P., & Schretlen, D. (1989). Wechsler Memory Scale: A critical appraisal of the normative studies. *Journal of Clinical and experimental Neuropsychology, 4*, 551–568.

Delis, D. C., Kramer, J. H., Kaplan, E., & Ober, B. A. (1987). *California Verbal Learning Test—Adult Version.* San Antonio, TX: The Psychological Corporation.

DeLuca, J., Barbieri-Berger, S., Johnson, S. K. (1994). The nature of memory impairments in multiple sclerosis: Acquisition versus retrieval. *Journal of Clinical & Experimental Neuropsychology 16(2)*, 183–189.

DeLuca, J., Gaudino, E. A., Diamond, B. J., Christodoulou, C., & Engel, R. A. (1998). Acquisition and storage deficits in multiple sclerosis. *Journal of Clinical & Experimental Neuropsychology, 20(3)*, 376–90.

DeLuca, J., Schultheis, M. T., Madigan, N., Christodoulou, C., & Averill, A. (2000). Acquisition versus retrieval deficits in traumatic brain injury: Implications for memory rehabilitation. *Archives of Physical Medicine and Rehabilitation, 81*, 1327–1333.

De Renzi, E., Faglioni, P., & Spinnler, H. (1966). The performance of patients with unilateral brain damage on face recognition tasks. *Cortex, 4,* 17–34.

Ebbinghaus, H. 1. (1913). *Memory: A contribution to experimental psychology. (H. A. Ruger & C. E. Bussenius, Trans.)* New York: Teachers College, Columbia University, Bureau of Publications. (Original Work published 1895)

Farah, M. J., Wilson, K. D., Drain, M., & Tanaka, J. N. (1998). What is "special" about face perception? *Psychological Review, 105,* 482–498.

Fastenau, P. S. (1996). An elaborated administration of the Wechsler Memory Scale—Revised. *The Clinical Neuropsychologist, Nov 10(4),* 425–434.

Flin, R., & Dziurawiec, S. (1989). Developmental factors in face processing. In A. W. Young & H. D. Ellis (Eds.), *Handbook of research on face processing.* Amsterdam: North Holland Publishing.

Goldstein, F. (1942). *After-effects of brain injuries in war.* New York: Greene and Stratton.

Goren, C. C., Sarty, M., & Wu, R. W. K. (1975). Visual following and pattern discrimination of face-like stimuli by newborn infants. *Pediatrics, 56,* 544–549.

Gorsuch, R. (2001). Chapter 3. *WAIS-III Canadian Technical Manual.* San Antonio, TX: The Psychological Corporation.

Haaland, K. Y., Price, L., & LaRue, A. (2003). What does the WMS-III tell us about memory changes with normal aging? *Journal of the International Neuropsychological Society, 9,* 89–96.

Halstead, W. C. (1947). *Brain intelligence: A quantitative study of the frontal lobes.* Chicago, IL: University of Chicago Press.

Healy, W., & Fernald, GM (1911). Tests for practical mental classification. *Psychological Monographs, 13 (54).*

Heaton, R. K., Grant, I., & Matthews, C. G. (1991). *Comprehensive norms for an expanded Halstead-Reitan Battery: Demographic corrections, research findings, and clinical applications.* Odessa, FL: Psychological Assessment Resources.

Heaton, R. K., Paulsen, J. S., McAdams, L. A., Kuck, J., Zisook, S., Braff, D., Harris, M. J., & Jeste, D. V. (1994).Neuropsychological deficits in schizophrenia: Relationship to age, chronicity, and dementia. *Archives of General Psychiatry, 51,* 469–476.

Hebb, D. O. (1961). *The organization of behavior: A neuropsychological theory.* New York: Science Editions.

Herman, D. O. (1988) Development of the Wechsler Memory Scale—Revised. *The Clinical Neuropsychologist, 2,* 102–106.

Kaplan, E. (1988). A process approach to neuropsychological assessment. In T. J. Boll & B. K. Bryant (Eds.): Clinical neuropsychology and brain function. Washington: American Psychological Association.

Kaplan, E., Fein, D., Morris, R., & Delis, D. C. (1991). *WAIS—R as a Neuropsychological Instrument.* San Antonio, TX: The Psychological Corporation.

Kinsbourne, M., & Smith, W. L. (Eds.) (1974). *Hemispheric disconnection and cerebral function.* Springfield, IL: Charles C. Thomas.

Knox, H. A. (1914). A scale based on the work at Ellis Island for estimating mental defect. *Journal of the American Medical Association, 62,* 741–747.

Kogan, K. L. (1949). Review of the Wechsler Memory Scale. In O. K. Buros (Ed.), *The third mental measurement yearbook.* (pp. 398–399). New Brunswick: Rutgers University Press. (Reprinted in Appendix 2, this Volume).

Korkman, M., Kirk, U., & Kemp, S. (1998). *NEPSY: A developmental neuropsychological assessment manual.* San Antonio: The Psychological Corporation.

Ledbetter, M. (1997). *An Introduction to the Wechsler Memory Scale, Third Edition.* Video workshop from the Distance Learning Network. San Antonio, TX: The Psychological Corporation.

Loring, D. W. (1989). The Wechsler Memory Scale-Revised, or the Wechsler Memory Scale-Revisited. *The Clinical Neuropsychologist, 3,* 59–69.

Luria, A. R. (1966). *Higher cortical functions in man.* Oxford, England: Basic Books.

Luria, A. R. (1970). The functional organization of the brain. *Scientific American, 222,* 66–78.

Luria, A. R. (1973). *The working brain.* (B. Haigh, Trans.). New York: Basic Books.

McCarthy, R. A., & Warrington, E. K. (1990). *Cognitive neuropsychology.* San Diego: Academic Press.

Millis, S. R., Malina, A.C., Bowers, D. A., & Ricker, J. H. (1999). Confirmatory factor analysis of the Wechsler Memory Scale—III. *Journal of Clinical and Experimental Neuropsychology, 21*(1), 87–93.

Milner, B. (1971). Interhemispheric differences in the localization of psychological processes in man. *British Medical Bulletin, 27,* 272–277.

Milner, B., Branch, C., & Rasmussen, T. (1966). Evidence for bilateral speech representation in some nonrighthanders. *Trans Am Neurol Assoc., 91,* 306–308.

Milner, B., Corkin, S., & Teuber, H. L. (1968). Further analysis of the hippocampal amnesic syndrome: 14 year follow-up study of H. M. *Neuropsychologia, 6,* 215

Naugle, R. L., Chelune, G. J., Cheek, R., Lüders, H., & Awad, I. (1993). Detection of changes in material specific memory following temporal lobectomy using the Wechsler Memory Scale – Revised. *Archives of Clinical Neuropsychology, 7,* 381–395.

Nebes, R. D. (1974). Hemispheric specialization in commissurotomized man. *Psychological Bulletin, 81,* 1–14.

Peterson, J. (1926). *Early conceptions and tests of intelligence.* Yonkers-on-Hudson, NY: World Book Company.

Phares, E. J. (1979). *Clinical psychology: Concepts, methods, and profession.* Homewood, IL: Dorsey Press.

Pribram, K. H., & Broadbent, D. E. (1970). *Biology of memory.* New York: Academic Press.

Price, L. R., Tulsky, D. S., Millis, S. R., & Weiss, L. (2002). Redefining the factor structure of the Wechsler Memory Scale-III: Confirmatory factor analysis with cross-validation. *Journal of Clinical and Experimental Neuropsychology, 24,* 574–585.

Prigatano, G. (1978). Wechsler Memory Scale: A selective review of the literature. *Journal of Clinical Psychology, 34,* 816–832.

The Psychological Corporation. (1997). *WAIS-III–WMS-III Technical Manual.* San Antonio, TX: Author.

Rausch, R., & Babb, T. L. (1993). Hippocampal neuron loss and memory scores before and after temporal lobe surgery for epilepsy. *Archives of Neurology, 50,* 812–817.

Reitan, R. M., & Davison, L. A. (1974). *Clinical neuropsychology: Current status and applications.* New York: V. H. Winston & Sons.

Rey, A. (1941). L'examen psychologique en les cas d'encephalopathie traumatique. [Clinical teats in traumatic encepholopathy]. *Archives de Psychologie, 28,* 286–340.

Rey, A. (1964). *L'examen clinique en psychologie.* [Clinical exams in psychology]. Paris: Presses Universitaries de France.

Rourke, B. P. (1982). Central processing deficiencies in children: Toward a developmental neuropsychological model. *Journal of Clinical Neuropsychology, 4,* 1–18.

Russell, E. (1975). A multiple scoring method for the assessment of complex memory functions. *Journal of Consulting and Clinical Psychology, 43,* 800–809.

Russell, E. (1988). Renorming Russell's version of the Wechsler Memory Scale. *Journal of Clinical and Experimental Neuropsychology, 1,* 235–249.

Saling, M. M., Berkovic, S. F., O'Shea, M. F., & et. al. (1993). Lateralication of verbal memory and unilateral hippocampal sclerosis: Evidence of task specific effects. *Journal of Clinical and Experimental Neuropsychology, 15, 608–618.*

Saykin, A. J., Robinson, L. J., Stafaniak, P., et al. (1992). Neuropsychological changes after anterior temporal lobectomy: Acute effects on memory, language, and music. In T. L. Bennett (ed.), *The neuropsychology of epilepsy.* New York: Plenum Press, 263–290.

Scoville, W. B., & Milner, B. (1957). Loss of recent memory after bilateral hippocampal lesions. *Journal of Neurology, Neurosurgery, and Psychiatry, 20,* 11–21.

Shaffer, G. W., & Lazarus, R. S. (1952). *Fundamental concepts in clinical psychology.* New York: McGraw-Hill.

Sperry, R. W. (1968). Hemisphere deconnection and unity in conscious awareness. *American Psychologist, 23,* 723–733.

Squire, L. R. (1986). Mechanisms of memory. *Science, 232,* 1612–1619.

Squire, L. R. (1987). *Memory and brain* New York: Oxford University Press.

Stone, C. P., Girdner, J., Albrecht, R. (1946). An alternate form of the Wechsler Memory Scale. *Journal of Psychology, 22,* 199–206.

Stone, C. P., & Wechsler, D. (1946). Wechsler Memory Scale form II. New York: The Psychological Corporation.

Terman, L. M. (1916). *The measurement of intelligence.* Boston: Houghton Mifflin.

Tulsky, D. S., Chelune, G. J., Price, L. R., & Millis, S. R. (2003). Development of a new delayed memory index for the WMS-III. Manuscript in preparation.

Tulsky, D. S., & Ledbetter, M. F. (2000). Updating to the WAIS-III and WMS-III: Considerations for research and clinical practice. *Psychological Assessment, 12*(3), 253–262.

Tulsky, D. S., Ivnik, R. J., Price, L. R., & Wilkins, C. (2003). Assessment of cognitive functioning with the WAIS-III and WMS-III: Development of a 6-Factor model. In D. S. Tulsky et al. (Eds). *Clinical Interpretation of the WAIS-III and WMS-III.* (pp. 147–179). San Diego: Academic Press.

Tulsky, D. S., & Price, L. R. (in press). The Joint WAIS-III and WMS-III factor structure: Development and cross-validation of a 6-factor model of cognitive functioning. *Psychological Assessment.*

Tulsky, D. S., Saklofske, D. H., & Ricker, J. H. (2003). Historical overview of intelligence and memory: Factors influencing the Wechsler scales. In D. S. Tulsky et al. (Eds). *Clinical Interpretation of the WAIS-III and WMS-III.* (pp. 7–41). San Diego: Academic Press.

Tulving, E., & Donaldson, W. (1972). *Organization of memory.* New York: Academic Press.

Wallin, J. E. W. (1912). *Experimental Studies of Mental Defectives: A Critique of the Binet-Simon Tests and a Contribution to the Psychology of Epilepsy.* Baltimore: Warwick & York, Inc.

Warrington, E. K. (1984). *Recognition Memory Test Manual.* Windsor: NFER-Nelson.

Warrington, E. K., & James, M. (1967). An experimental investigation of facial recognition in patients with unilateral cerebral lesions. *Cortex, 3,* 317–326.

Wechsler, D. (1945). A standard memory scale for clinical use. *Journal of psychology, 19,* 87–95, 820.

Wechsler, D. (1917a). A study of retention in Korsakoff psychosis. *Psychiatric Bulletin, 2,* 403–451.

Wechsler, D. (1917b). *A study of retention in Korsakoff psychosis.* Unpublished Master's thesis. Columbia University.

Wechsler, D. (1939). *Measurement of Adult Intelligence.* Baltimore: Williams and Wilkins, Co.

Wechsler, D. (1944). The psychologist in the psychiatric hospital. *Journal of consulting psychology, 8,* 281–285.

Wechsler, D. (1945). A standardized memory scale for clinical use. *Journal of Psychology, 19,* 87–95.

Wechsler, D. (1987). *Wechsler Memory Scale—Revised.* San Antonio, TX: The Psychological Corporation.

Wechsler, D. (1997a). *WAIS-III administration and scoring manual.* San Antonio, TX: The Psychological Corporation.

Wechsler, D. (1997b). *WMS-III administration and scoring manual.* San Antonio, TX: The Psychological Corporation.

Wechsler, D. & Hartogs, R. (1945). The clinical measurement of anxiety. *Psychiatric Quarterly, 19,* 618–635.

Wells, F. L (1913). Experimental pathology of the higher mental processes. *Psychological Bulletin, 10(6),* 213–224.

Wells, F. L. (1927). *Mental tests in clinical practice.* Yonkers-on-Hudson, NY: World Book Company .

Wells, F. L., & Martin, H. A. A. (1923). A method of memory evaluation suitable for psychotic cases. *American Journal of Psychiatry, 3,* 243–258.

Whipple, G. M. (1915). *Manual of Mental and physical tests (in two parts) Part II: Complex Processes.* Second Edition. Baltimore: Warwick & York, Inc.

Williams, M. A. (1978). Clinical memory assessment. In P. McReynolds (Ed.), *Advances in psychological assessment, Vol 4.* San Francisco: Jossey-Bass.

Williams, M. A., Rich, M. A., Reed, L. K., Jackson, W. T., LaMarche, J. A., & Boll, T. J. (1998). Visual reproduction subtest of the Wechsler Memory Scale-Revised: Analysis of construct validity. *Journal of Clinical Psychology, 54(7),* 963–971.

Wissler, C. (1901). The correlation of mental and physical tests. *Psychological Review, 3 (Monograph Suppl. 16)*

Woodworth, R. S. & Wells, F. L. (1911). Association Tests. Being a part of the report of the committee of the American Psyhcological Association on the Standardization of procedure in experiemntal tests. *Psychological Monographs, 13* (whole no. 57).

Yerkes, R. M. (1921). *Memoirs of the National Academy of Sciences Volume XV: Psychological Examining in the United States Army.* Washington, D.C.: Government Printing Office.

Ziclinski, J. J. (1993). A comparison of the Wechsler Memory Scale–Revised and the memory assessment scales, administrative, clinical, and interpretive issues. *Professional Psychology: Research and Practice, 24,* 353–359.

Reducing Variance When Interpreting WAIS-III and WMS-III Scores: Introduction to Chapters 4–8

The following set of chapters discuss new research findings with the WAIS-III and WMS-III and present new methods of interpreting WAIS-III and WMS-III scores. These methods are designed to help the clinician reduce, or at least better understand, variance in test performance that is not attributable to the clinical conditions being evaluated. Moreover, these chapters outline more advanced interpretive methods on WAIS-III and WMS-III data, enhancing the clinical utility of these tests.

In Chapter 4, Tulsky, Ivnik, Price, & Wilkins have described a 6 factor structure representing the cognitive constructs measured by the two test batteries. The authors have de-emphasized traditional IQ and general memory scores and, in their place, have delineated a new structure underlying the WAIS-III and WMS-III. New normative information is provided for auditory and visual memory composite scores. In light of the empirical evidence that the Faces subtests are not optimal representatives of the visual memory construct, the recommended memory battery has been reconfigured with Visual Reproduction as core subtests and Faces as optional scores. Most importantly, the model presents more integrated or comprehensive coverage of cognitive functioning rather than maintaining an artificial distinction between intelligence and memory that date back to Binet's work at the end of the 19th/beginning of the 20th century (see Tulsky, Saklofske, & Ricker, Chapter 1).

Chapter 5 presents a view of neurodiagnostic testing that expands current practice. Heaton, Taylor, & Manly observe that, although Wechsler's intelligence and memory tests have corrected for age effects since the original versions of the scales were first published, this correction for age alone does not eliminate large amounts of normal test variance attributable with other demographic factors. The authors show large effects for education, ethnicity, and (on a few measures) gender. They demonstrate that the failure to correct for these other demographic factors can increase error when using the tests for clinical diagnostic purposes. The authors describe how demographic norms for the WAIS-III and WMS-III have been developed. For those practitioners who had been using demographically corrected normative information for the WAIS (Heaton, Grant, & Matthews; 1991) and WAIS-R (Heaton, 1992), and have struggled with the prospect of switching to the new editions without similar demographically adjusted normative information, this chapter is essential reading.

Finally, Heaton, Taylor, & Manly (Chapter 5) provide additional support for the 6 factor WAIS-III and WMS-III factor scores by showing profiles of performance in both normal and clinical groups.

In chapter 6, Hawkins & Tulsky have carefully examined the practice of the clinical interpretation of discrepancies between index scores (e.g., discrepancy analyses). The WAIS-III and WMS-III manuals present base rate data for numerous comparisons as a way for clinicians to detect both statistically significant differences between scores as well as those that are large enough to label them "infrequent" and "unusual." Clinically, it is believed that large discrepancy scores, that are of a magnitude infrequently observed in the standardization population, can be used to infer altered (abnormal) cognitive functioning. However, specific guidelines on how to use these base rate data have been scarce. This chapter provides a detailed explanation of discrepancy analyses, clinically informative trends, conventional profiles and contrasts, and challenges to correct interpretation.

Chapter 7, on "Diagnostic Validity," Smith, Cerhan, & Ivnik introduce methods and tenets common to epidemiology and clinical medicine, to help clinicians consider diagnostic validity with the WAIS-III and WMS-III. The authors carefully review the important terms of evidence based medicine (e.g., sensitivity, specificity, base rates, odds ratios, etc.) and then demonstrate how clinicans can calculate post-tests odds that provide clinically relevant meaning when making a diagnosis on a specific patient. These odds ratios provide quantitative information about a patient that the clinician can use in making diagnostic decisions.

The final chapter in this section, by Lineweaver and Chelune, provides practical information about what procedures that can be applied to the WAIS-III and WMS-III when an individual is tested more than one time and a decision must be made about the possible "change" in functioning from this serial testing. Though clinicians are frequently trying to detect a change in functioning from one period to the next, a straightforward approach to score interpretation can be difficult. When an individual takes either the WAIS-III or the WMS-III twice, the scores on the second testing can be influenced by procedural learning, increased knowledge about the content, and random error variance as well as any changes in functioning. Lineweaver and Chelune provide a systematic way to study this change, and provide new normative information for the interpretation of serial testing scores.

David S. Tulsky

Robert K. Heaton

REFERENCES

Hawkins, K. A., & Tulsky, D. S. (2003). WAIS-III—WMS-III discrepancy analysis: Six-factor model index discrepancy base rates, implications, and a preliminary consideration of utility. In D. S. Tulsky et al. (Eds). *Clinical Interpretation of the WAIS-III and WMS-III.* (pp. 211–272). San Diego: Academic Press.

Heaton, R. K. (1992). *Comprehensive norms for an expanded Halstead-Reitan Battery: A supplement for the WAIS-R.* Odessa, FL: Psychological Assessment Resources.

Heaton, R. K., Grant, I., & Matthews, C. G. (1991). *Comprehensive norms for an expanded Halstead-Reitan Battery: Demographic corrections, research findings, and clinical applications.* Odessa, FL: Psychological Assessment Resources.

Heaton, R. K., Taylor, M. J., & Manly, J. (2003). Demographic effects and the use of demographically corrected norms with the WAIS-III and WMS-III. In D. S. Tulsky et al. (Eds). *Clinical Interpretation of the WAIS-III and WMS-III.* (pp. 181–210). San Diego: Academic Press.

Lineweaver, T. T., & Chelune, G. J. (2003). Use of the WAIS-III and WMS-III in the context of serial assessment: Interpretation reliable and meaningful change. In D. S. Tulsky et al. (Eds). *Clinical Interpret-*

ation of the WAIS-III and WMS-III. (pp. 303–337). San Diego: Academic Press.

Smith, G. E., Cerhan, J. H., & Ivnik, R. J. (2003). Diagnostic validity. In D. S. Tulsky et al. (Eds). *Clinical Interpretation of the WAIS-III and WMS-III.* (pp. 273–301). San Diego: Academic Press.

Tulsky, D. S., Ivnik, R. J., Price, L. R., & Wilkins, C. (2003). Assessment of cognitive functioning with the WAIS-III and WMS-III: Development of a 6-Factor model. In D. S. Tulsky et al. (Eds). *Clinical Interpretation of the WAIS-III and WMS-III.* (pp. 147–179). San Diego: Academic Press.

Tulsky, D. S., Saklofske, D. H., & Ricker, J. H. (2003). Historical overview of intelligence and memory: Factors influencing the Wechsler scales. In D. S. Tulsky et al. (Eds). *Clinical Interpretation of the WAIS-III and WMS-III.* (pp. 7–41). San Diego: Academic Press.

Assessment of Cognitive Functioning with the WAIS-III and WMS-III: Development of a Six-Factor Model

David S. Tulsky
Kessler Medical Rehabilitation Research and Education Corporation
University of Medicine and Dentistry of New Jersey

Robert J. Ivnik
Mayo Foundation

Larry R. Price
Southwest Texas State University
and

Charles Wilkins
The Psychological Corporation

When Tulsky, Saklofske, and Zhu (Chapter 2, this volume) presented the goals of the WAIS-III revision, they acknowledged that a radical revision to the structure of the scale was beyond the scope of the WAIS-III project. Instead, the published WAIS-III maintained the traditional structure of the IQ scores (Full-Scale [FSIQ], Verbal [VIQ], and Performance [PIQ] scores) while it presented (and gave equal weight to) new alternative index scores. Though publication of these new index scores was a step in the right direction, as they enhance the clinical utility and sensitivity of the WAIS-III (Hawkins, 1998; Martin, Donders, & Thompson, 2000), other modifications were not attempted. Modifications, such as dropping the IQ metric or developing and advancing a more comprehensive model of cognitive functioning that incorporated subtests across the WAIS-III and WMS-III, were avoided (see Tulsky, Saklofske, and Zhu, Chapter 2, this volume; and

Tulsky, Chiaravalloti, Palmer, & Chelune, Chapter 3, this volume, for a review of the revision goals). The latter idea of an expanded model of cognitive functioning seemed logical given recent research in the area of cognitive testing.

Over the last 20 years, a few studies have jointly analyzed and integrated subtests across the previous editions of the Wechsler intelligence and Wechsler memory scales. The work has demonstrated additional domains of functioning, and on a few occasions, these research findings have been employed in clinical practice. For example, researchers for the Mayo Older Americans Normative Studies (MOANS; Ivnik et al., 1992; Smith et al., 1992) developed a five-factor integrated model of cognitive functioning based on the concurrent administration of the WAIS-R, WMS-R, and Auditory Verbal Learning Test (AVLT; Schmidt, 1996). These Mayo Cognitive Factor Scores (MCFS; Smith et al., 1994) represent an individual's cognitive functioning in lieu of traditional IQ scores and emphasize the primary cognitive skills evaluated when these tests are given together. MOANS researchers were able to develop the MCFS because the MOANS projects are the first instance in which Wechsler scales (specifically the WAIS-R and WMS-R) have been intentionally "co-normed" (i.e., given together as part of a larger testing "battery") to the same sample of well-defined, cognitively normal people.

The WAIS-III and WMS-III also adopted the co-norming methodology, and an integrated scale that treated the WAIS-III and WMS-III subtests as elements of a single battery could have been easily developed. However, The Psychological Corporation (TPC) elected to emphasize preserving the historical structure of two separate test batteries. As a result, the WAIS-III and WMS-III were treated as separate instruments that measured "different" constructs. The projects' planning, subtest development, and data analyses were conducted separately for each test by independent teams within TPC, even though the new tests had been co-normed. In his review of the WMS-III, Glenn Larrabee cites this failure to identify and most parsimoniously summarize the cognitive abilities that are actually being evaluated when the WAIS-III and the WMS-III are used together as the biggest omission from their most recent revisions (Larrabee, 1999).

In this chapter, we move beyond the traditional Wechsler approach and present a model of cognitive functioning that truly integrates the WAIS-III and WMS-III scales and emphasizes the empirically defined cognitive skills that are evaluated when the tests are used together in place of traditional IQs. Much of this work is based on joint WAIS-III and WMS-III factor analyses described by Tulsky and Price (in press), who found that a six-factor model of cognitive functioning best represents the skills that the WAIS-III and WMS-III examine. This chapter provides new normative information that is necessary for applying the six-factor model to individual assessments. Specifically, new index scores for a composite Auditory Memory, a composite Visual Memory, and new supplementary immediate and delayed Visual Memory Index Scores are presented. A premise of this chapter, and ultimately this volume, is that moving beyond traditional IQ and Memory Quotient Scores to emphasize the more empirical six-factor model will increase clinical sensitivity and specificity.

In saying the above, we are not suggesting that every potentially important cognitive skill is represented in this six-factor model. It is not only possible, but it is highly likely that more than six primary cognitive abilities are important for daily life. However, we are saying that, based on the tasks that comprise the WAIS-III and the WMS-III and our analyses of the data generated by cognitively normal subjects included in TPC's standardization sample, the six-factor model better reflects reality than traditional IQs and, as such, it should be more useful.

CONTEMPORARY MODELS OF COGNITIVE FUNCTIONING

Recent research suggests that a model of cognition should be composed of multiple, somewhat independent cognitive abilities that include both traditional memory and intelligence factors (Carroll, 1993; Horn & Noll, 1997; Smith et al., 1992). The idea of multiple domains of cognitive functioning is not new. Edward Thorndike entered into one of the earliest debates in psychology with Carl Spearman (Thorndike, Lay, & Dean, 1909), proposing that there are multiple abilities. In 1934, L. L. Thurstone wrote that the "multi-dimensionality of mind must be recognized before we can make progress toward the isolation and description of separate abilities" (p. 6). Factor-analytic procedures have guided test development efforts since Thurstone first discussed the principles in his landmark paper, "Vectors of the Mind" (Thurstone, 1934).

In recent years a proliferation of studies have used factor-analytic procedures to specify the domains of cognitive functioning. These efforts have led to new theories about cognitive ability. Recently, for instance, John Carroll (1993) performed extensive factor analyses in a comprehensive meta-analysis and demonstrated the multidimensionality of cognitive functioning. Flannagan, McGrew, and Ortiz, (2000) and Horn and Noll (1997) also have presented theoretical frameworks of cognitive functioning based on empirical analyses. As mentioned above, Smith et al. (1992, 1994) employed factor-analytic techniques to identify the cognitive abilities that are actually being examined when the WAIS-R, WMS-R, and AVLT were administered as a standard test "battery" to a large sample of older adults. Based on this work, the five-factor MCFS (Smith et al., 1994) were created. This information demonstrates that although composite IQ scores are widely used throughout psychology and education, newer factor-based scores provide a representation of cognitive functioning that might be more useful in clinical practice.

FACTOR-ANALYTIC STUDIES OF THE WECHSLER SCALES

The idea of using factor-analytic techniques to explore and verify the dimensions measured by the Wechsler subtests has a long tradition. Though David Wechsler published the initial Wechsler Bellevue (WB) Scale thinking that there were only two domains of functioning, Balinsky (1941) showed in the first factor analytic study that there were three factors underlying the WB Scale. A decade later, Cohen replicated this finding with several studies that reaffirmed the existence of the somewhat less articulated third factor that is distinct from the verbal and performance domains (Cohen, 1952a, 1952b, 1957a, 1957b, 1959). Despite these findings, a formal structure to interpret this third factor was slow in coming. In subsequent updates and alternate forms of the original WB Scale (Wechsler, 1939), [(i.e., the Wechsler–Bellevue Form II (Wechsler, 1946); the WISC (Wechsler, 1949), the WAIS (Wechsler, 1955), the WISC-R (Wechsler, 1974), the WAIS-R (Wechsler, 1981) and the WISC-III (Wechsler, 1991)] all maintained the traditional IQ structure (e.g., VIQ, PIQ, and FSIQ). Little attention was paid to the research that indicated a "third factor" until Alan Kaufman published his interpretive book *Intelligent Testing with the WISC-R* (Kaufman, 1979). In this landmark publication, Kaufman described a format for interpreting Freedom from Distractibility in WISC-R profiles.

The development of the WISC-III marked the first move toward changing, or at lest modifying, the traditional structure of a Wechsler intelligence scale. The developers of the WISC-III sought to develop a new subtest that would help isolate this third factor score. After much work, they developed the Symbol Search subtest based in part on the model of attention advanced by Richard Shiffrin and Walter Schneider (1977: Aurelio

Prifitera, personal communication, October, 1992). Upon completion of the standardization study, factor analyses (Wechsler, 1991) demonstrated that four factors are represented in the scale, rather than the three that had been anticipated. They were labeled Verbal Comprehension, Perceptual Organization, Freedom From Distractibility, and Processing Speed. This structure has been replicated in numerous studies (for example, see Roid, Prifitera, & Weiss, 1993; Roid & Worrall, 1997). Despite this empirical support for the four-factor model, the factor scores were published in the WISC-III as supplemental to "traditional" IQs. Preserving the historical continuity between the editions was a priority. When the WAIS-III was published, the two structures (Index and IQ) were given equal emphasis. Moreover, though expanded domains of functioning were receiving empirical support, TPC maintained the distinction between the WAIS-III and WMS-III as separate tests as if "intelligence" could only be defined by the subtests on intelligence scales. This book challenges that distinction. We believe that David Wechsler always maintained that there were more aspects to "intelligence" than had been measured in the WAIS and WAIS-R, and that the six-factor model for cognitive functioning presented here is, in some ways, more faithful to that tenet. David Wechsler wrote the following:

> Much of the concern about the validity of intelligence tests and the opposition to their use stems from the failure to distinguish sufficiently between what the tests are described as measuring and what they are interpreted as measuring – that is, how one defines intelligence to begin with. Historically, intelligence has been most frequently defined in terms of one or another especially esteemed and unique ability, such as the ability to reason abstractly, to learn, to adapt, and so on. Each of these *abilities* [italics added] broadly characterizes sequences of human behavior which in most instances can be attested to as intelligent in one way or another. But this is not always or exclusively the case. For example, intelligence is multifaceted as well as multidetermined. What it calls for is not always adaptive, nor does it inevitably involve abstract reasoning. Intelligence is not a particular ability but an overall competency or global capacity, which in one way or another enables a sentient individual to comprehend the world and to deal effectively with its challenges. *Intelligence is a function of the personality as a whole and is responsive to other factors besides those included under the concept of cognitive abilities* [italics added]. Intelligence tests inevitably measure these factors as well. (Wechsler, 1981, pp. 7–8).

We acknowledge that this quote can be interpreted several ways. However, we believe that Wechsler intended to subsume *all* cognitive skills under the very broad concept of intelligence, which also includes personality and a variety of non cognitive factors.

When the WAIS-III project began, the development of a four-factor structure for the WAIS-III became an important a priori goal of the revision (as described in Tulsky, Zhu, & Prifitera, 2000; Tulsky, Saklofske, and Zhu, Chapter 2, this volume). The addition of new subtests, Symbol Search and Letter Number Sequencing, had helped solidify the four-factor structure of the WAIS-III (The Psychological Corporation, 1997), and an alternative to IQ scores was presented to users. Expanding the model further than what had been accomplished on the WISC-III was not attempted. Instead, the WAIS-III and WMS-III were treated separately; they were not analyzed together.

Factor analyses of the Wechsler memory scale are present in the literature, although this line of research has not been as productive as factor analyses of the intelligence scales. Early factor-analytic research on the WMS yielded either two factors (general Memory and Attention/Concentration; see Davis & Swenson, 1970), or, more commonly, three factors, (Information/Orientation, General Memory, and Attention/Concentration; see Kear-Colwell & Heller, 1978; Skilbeck & Woods, 1980). When the WMS-R was published, some researchers found that its factor structure was similar to that of the WMS (e.g., a General Memory, an Attention/Concentration factor, and an Information/Orientation factor: Bornstein & Chelune, 1988; Roid, Prifitera, & Ledbetter, 1988) despite the introduction of separate *verbal* and visual memory indices subsumed under the general memory index, that was also distinct from the attention/concentration and delayed indexes. Other researchers claimed that their analyses supported immediate and delayed memory factors as well as an attention factor (Roth, Conboy, Reeder, & Boll, 1990; Burton, Mittenberg, & Burton, 1993; Woodard, 1993) that were distinct from the test's published indexes.

When the WMS-III was published, the *WAIS-III–WMS-III Technical Manual* claimed that five factors could be supported. These included distinct visual and auditory domains, distinct immediate and delayed memory domains, and a working memory domain. Shortly after publication, however, Millis, Malina, Bowers, and Ricker (1999) reported that the factor analyses could not be replicated and questioned the structure underlying the WMS-III. To answer the questions that were raised, Price, Tulsky, Millis, and Weiss (2002) reanalyzed the WMS-III standardization data and determined that the results published in the first edition of the Technical Manual were in error. They presented the accurate fit statistics and then replicated the structure in an independent sample. These analyses support a distinction between the auditory, visual, and working memory factors within the WMS-III. However, the separation of the immediate and delayed memory factors was not supported via factor analyses in the standardization sample.[1]

JOINT WAIS-III/WMS-III FACTOR-ANALYTIC STUDIES

Joint analyses of the WAIS-R and WMS-R are relatively rare, especially in light of the number of studies documenting the factor structure of the WAIS-R and WMS-R separately. The initial joint studies were based on exploratory techniques, and each study indicated that additional cognitive structures are measured when the WMS or WMS-R variables are included in factor analyses with the WAIS or WAIS-R. The first study using both WAIS and WMS variables was performed in 1982, and a six-factor solution made up of Perceptual Organization, Verbal Comprehension, Attention/Concentration, Verbal Learning and Recall, Information and Orientation, and an uninterpretable factor was found (Larrabee, Kane, & Schuck, 1983). Following this work, Ryan, Rosenberg, and Heilbronner (1984), Leonberger, Nicks, Larrabee, and Goldfader (1992), Larrabee and Curtiss (1992; see Larrabee, 2000) also identified five or six-factor solutions when the memory variables are included.

Confirmatory analyses on the WAIS-R and WMS-R also identified additional factors. Smith et al. (1992) used confirmatory techniques to develop a shorter "core" battery based on co-administering the WAIS-R, WMS-R, and AVLT to a sample of cognitively normal adults above age 55. As mentioned above, their analyses supported a five-factor solution that was replicated in a follow-up study. Bowden, Carstairs, and Shores (1999) tested a young adult Australian sample with the WAIS-R and WMS-R and also concluded that five factors fit the data the best.

With the WAIS-III and WMS-III, Tulsky and Price (in press) ran an extensive set of confirmatory factor analyses on the WMS-III standardization sample. They concluded that a six-factor model provided the best fit to

---

[1]The immediate and delayed memory factors could not be extracted due to inadmissible parameter estimates that signaled model specification errors. This result was verified by Price, Tulsky, Millis, and Weiss (2002). Instead, a three-factor model (auditory memory, visual memory, and working memory) is supported by the data The corrected factor analyses is reported by Price et al. (2002).

the data and identified the factors as Verbal Comprehension, Perceptual Organization, Working Memory, Processing Speed, Auditory Memory, and Visual Memory. They also replicated their findings in a large cross-validation sample using highly restrictive model testing. From these analyses, the authors concluded that this six-factor model usefully describes cognitive functioning (see Figure 1).

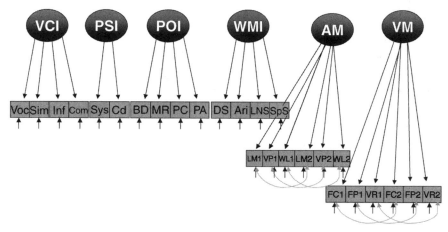

Factors (in Ovals)
VCI – Verbal Comprehension
PSI – Processing Speed
POI – Perceptual Organization
WMI – Working Memory
AMD – Auditory Memory Delayed
VM – Visual Memory

Subtests (in squares)
VOC – Vocabulary
SIM – Similarities
INF – Information
COM- Comprehension
Sys – Symbol Search
Cd – Digit SymbolæCoding
BD – Block Design
MR – Matrix Reasoning

PC – Picture Completion
PA – Picture Arrangement

DS – Digit Span
Ari – Arithmetic
LNS – Letter Number Sequencing
SpS – Spatial Span

LM 1 – Logical Memory Immediate
VP 1 – Verbal Paired Associates Immediate
WL 1 – Word List Immediate
LM 2 – Logical Memory Delayed
VP 2 – Verbal Paired Associates Delayed
WL 2 – Word List Delayed

FC 1 – Faces Immediate
FP 1 – Family Pictures Immediate
VR 1 – Visual Reproduction Immediate
FC 2 – Faces Delayed
FP 2 – Family Pictures Delayed
VR 2 – Visual Reproduction Delayed

FIGURE 1.   The six factor model comprised of Verbal Comprehension, Perceptual Organization, Working Memory, Processing Speed, Auditory Memory, and Visual Memory. The factor analytic studies are described in Tulsky and Price (in press).

THE DEVELOPMENT OF NEW NORMS FOR A SIX-FACTOR MODEL OF COGNITIVE FUNCTIONING

In their factor analyses, Tulsky and Price (in press) included all primary and supplemental subtests from the WAIS-III and WMS-III. The inclusion of so many subtests (26) is neither practical nor necessary, so the first step in preparing the six-factor structure for clinical use requires streamlining the battery. The final number of subtests should be fewer than, or at the very least, the same number as those included on the combined WAIS-III and WMS-III. Selecting the subtests to comprise the Verbal Comprehension, Perceptual Organization, Working Memory, and Processing Speed had already been accomplished for the published WAIS-III and WMS-III tests. For the six-factor model, three factors (Verbal Comprehension, Perceptual Organization, and Processing Speed) were selected from the WAIS-III, and the norms for the sum of scaled scores were obtained from the *WAIS-III Administration and Scoring Manual* (Wechsler, 1997a). The WAIS-III and WMS-III contain slightly different Working Memory Index scores, and the index for the six-factor model could have been taken from either the WAIS-III (composed of Digit Span, Arithmetic, and Letter Number Sequencing) or from the WMS-III (composed of Spatial Span and Letter Number Sequencing). The latter was selected in part for its efficiency (it is composed of only two subtests) and also because it balances verbal and non-verbal response modalities. The norms for the working memory factor can be obtained from the *WMS-III Administration and Scoring Manual* (Wechsler, 1997b).

Specifying the fifth and sixth memory index scores proved to be the greatest challenge. Factor analyses did not support separate immediate and delayed factors, and when such models were specified, significant model specification errors arose. Based on these results alone, it is not appropriate to define separate immediate and delayed memory factors, especially when long-term retention is not a primary question. Hence, composite (i.e., not subdivided into immediate or delayed elements) auditory and visual memory scores were needed.

Development of an auditory memory composite score was straightforward. As discussed by Tulsky, Chiaravalloti, Palmer, and Chelune (Chapter 3, this volume), the subtests that measure auditory memory on the WMS-III (Logical Memory, Verbal Paired Associates, and the optional Word Lists) are all tasks that have a long history of measuring auditory memory. Since the published Auditory Memory Immediate and Delayed index scores on the WMS-III include the combination of Logical Memory and Verbal

Paired Associates, a new sum of scaled scores was computed that combines the immediate and delayed components of Logical Memory and Verbal Paired Associates. The Word Lists remained optional to the Auditory Memory Index.

Developing the Visual Memory Composite score proved to be more difficult. As described in Chapter 3 (this volume), the Faces and Family Pictures subtests on the WMS-III are considered primary, whereas the Visual Reproduction subtest is optional. However, Millis et al. (1999) demonstrated that the Faces subtests have low communality with Family Pictures and, based on this result, point out that Faces does not appear to be related to Visual Memory (at least in the way that Visual Memory is reflected in the other subtests in the WMS-III). This finding also questions the validity of summing Faces with Family Pictures, as is done in the WMS-III. The problem is compounded by the fact that Faces does not have a recall procedure (see Tulsky, Chiaravalloti, Palmer, & Chelune, Chapter 3 this volume). Visual Reproduction, a longstanding visual subtest on the earlier WMS, has a much higher loading on the Visual Memory factor and, as such, appears to be more appropriate for use in an index score. As a result, a new primary Visual composite Index score includes a combination of Family Pictures and Visual Reproduction (and the Faces subtest has been made optional). A complete evaluation of the clinical utility of the Faces subtest cannot be accomplished at this time (in light of a lack of data from clinical samples; see Millis et al., 1999). Therefore, a second composite memory score with the Faces and Family Pictures subtests was also developed, leaving the "final" decision about the most appropriate visual memory factor open until more data are accumulated to more thoroughly examine the validity and clinical utility of the Visual Index Scores.

In developing a six-factor model of cognitive functioning, some potentially useful information about people's ability to hold and retain information in memory after their attention has been directed to other tasks would be lost without including either immediate or delayed factors. The distinction between immediate and delayed recall is considered very valuable. This created a dilemma because immediate and delayed structures have not received empirical support in WMS-III factor studies. Despite this apparent lack of validity data from analyses based on the test performances of *cognitively normal* persons, when clinicians are working with *cognitively compromised* patients, they will still need information relating to immediate and delayed recall capabilities. To meet this need, secondary subfactors are included. In instances where it is diagnostically important to differentitate immediate from delayed memory abilities, separate (but optional) auditory and visual, immediate, and delayed index scores can be calculated. The majority of these index scores are contained in the *WMS-III Administration and Scoring Manual*, but additional immediate visual memory (based on a combination of the Visual Reproduction Immediate and Family Pictures Immediate) and a delayed visual memory index (based on the Visual Reproduction Delayed and Family Pictures Delayed) have been computed.

Figure 2 presents the cognitive model that is represented by the WAIS-III and WMS-III. Table 1 lists the subtests used in the composition of each index score.

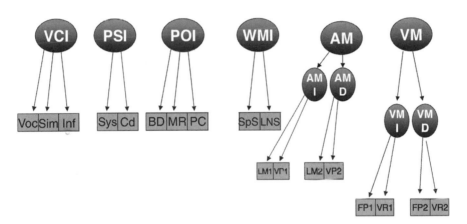

Factors (in Ovals)

VCI – Verbal Comprehension
PSI – Processing Speed
POI – Perceptual Organization
WMI – Working Memory
AM – Auditory Memory
AMI – Auditory Memory Immediate
AMD – Auditory Memory Delayed
VM – Visual Memory
VMI – Visual Memory Immediate
VMD – Visual Memory Delayed

Subtests (in squares)

VOC – Vocabulary
SIM – Similarities
INF – Information
Sys – Symbol Search
Cd – Digit Symbol∾Coding
BD – Block Design
MR – Matrix Reasoning

PC – Picture Completion

LNS – Letter Number Sequencing
SpS – Spatial Span

LM 1 – Logical Memory Immediate
VP 1 – Verbal Paired Associates Immediate
LM 2 – Logical Memory Delayed
VP 2 – Verbal Paired Associates Delayed

FP 1 – Family Pictures Immediate
VR 1 – Visual Reproduction Immediate
FP 2 – Family Pictures Delayed
VR 2 – Visual Reproduction Delayed

FIGURE 2.   The new joint index score structure of WAIS-III and WMS-III. This new structure will be used throughout the remainder of the book.

TABLE 1 Subtests Used in the Composition of the Joint WAIS-III—WMS-III Index Scores

Verbal Comprehension	Perceptual Organization	Working Memory	Processing Speed	Auditory Memory	Visual Memory[a]
Vocabulary	Picture Completion	Spatial Span Letter	Digit Symbol	Logical Memory I	Family Pictures I
Similarities	Block Design	Number	Symbol Search	Logical Memory II	Family Pictures II
Information	Matrix Reasoning	Sequencing		Verbal Paired Associates I	Visual Reproduction I
(Comprehension)	(Picture Arrangement)	(Digit Span)		Verbal Paired Associates II	Visual Reproduction II
		(Arithmetic)		(Word List I)	Faces I
				(Word List II)	Faces II

Scoring and sum of scaled score conversions for the Verbal Comprehension, Perceptual Organization, and Processing Speed Index Scores can be found in the *WAIS-III Administration and Scoring Manual* (Wechsler, 1997a). Scoring and Sum of Scaled score conversions for the Working Memory Index can be found in the *WMS-III Administration and Scoring Manual* (Wechsler, 1997b).

[a]Visual Reproduction has been used as a core subtest in new index scores presented later in this chapter. Depending on which score is used, either Faces or Visual Reproduction will be optional.

To summarize, the following changes have been made related to a joint WAIS-III–WMS-III battery approach to assessment of cognitive functioning:

1. **Index scores are emphasized.** Throughout this volume, index scores are presented in examples, whereas traditional IQ scores, the General Ability Scale (see Tulsky, Saklofske, Wilkins, & Weiss, 2001), the General Memory Index, and the Immediate Memory Index have been downplayed. Moreover, as described in Tulsky, Chiaravalloti, Palmer, and Chelune (Chapter 3, this volume), the recognition index has been removed from the core battery. It is now presented as an optional score.

2. **Only one Working Memory Index is obtained.** Four subtests (i.e., Letter Number Sequencing, Digit Span, Arithmetic, and Spatial Span) are all required to compute two working memory indices for the WAIS-III and WMS-III. For the six-factor structure advanced in this book, only the working memory index from the WMS-III (i.e., Letter Number Sequencing and Spatial Span) is used. This decision was due to efficiency and a desire to have an index score based on both verbal and non-verbal response modalities. There is no evidence that the WMS-III index score has more (or less) utility than the WAIS-III index. However, the two index scores yield redundant information and, from that point of view, administration of all four working memory subtests may be considered undesirable.

3. **Development of Auditory and Visual Memory Scores.** Based on the recent factor-analytic work on the WMS-III (Millis et al., 1999; Price et al., in press) and the joint WAIS-III–WMS-III (Tulsky & Price, in press), composite visual and composite auditory memory indices have been developed. Moreover, the visual memory index has been developed in two ways. First, due to questions relating to the appropriateness of including Faces in the visual index score, a combination of Family Pictures and Visual Reproduction scores define the new index. However, a second (optional) visual memory composite score has been developed that allows users to assess visual memory using the original WMS-III subtest composition.

4. **Optional Assessment of "secondary" immediate and delayed factors.** As reviewed in Tulsky, Chiaravalloti, Palmer, and Chelune (Chapter 3, this volume), immediate and delayed constructs have proven clinical utility. Therefore, in addition to the six-factor model, there are two secondary visual and two secondary auditory factors nested under the primary six factors. If future validity studies support the immediate versus delayed memory distinction, these secondary factors may receive greater weighting.

TABLE 2 Subtest Composition of New Index Scores

Subtest	Auditory composite score	Visual composite score (new)	Visual composite score (original subtest)	Visual immediate (new)	Visual delayed (new)
Logical Memory I	X				
Logical Memory II	X				
Verbal Paired Assoc I	X				
Verbal Paired Assoc II	X				
Family Pictures I		X	X	X	
Family Pictures II		X	X		X
Faces I			X		
Faces II			X		
Visual Reproduction I		X		X	
Visual Reproduction II		X			X

Sum of scaled scores for these new index scores are computed by summing the scaled scores for the subtests listed above. Subtest scaled score conversion tables can be found in the *WMS-III Administration and Scoring Manual* (Wechsler, 1997b). Conversion tables for these sum of scaled scores can be found in tables 4-8 (this chapter).

DEVELOPMENT OF NEW INDEX SCORES

The initial step in meeting our objectives was to develop composite auditory memory and composite visual memory indexes that do not divide memory into immediate and delayed constructs. The new indexes were created in a manner consistent with the development of the original index scores for the WAIS-III and WMS-III (and reported in the technical manual). New sums of scaled scores were formed from each examinee's age-corrected scaled scores on relevant subtests (see Table 2): Logical Memory I + Logical Memory II + Verbal Paired Associates I + Verbal Paired Associates II for the Auditory Composite scale; Visual Reproduction I + Visual Reproduction II + Family Pictures I + Family Pictures II for the Visual Composite scale. As previously discussed, an alternate visual composite score based on the original visual subtests in the WMS-III (Faces I + Faces II + Family Pictures I + and Family Pictures II) was also developed. For each age group, the means and standard deviations of each of these five sums of scaled-score distributions were calculated (see Table 3). There is a high degree of similarity within each of the two composite index scores from age band to age band. Analysis of variance revealed no statistically significant variation by age group in the mean scores for the indices, and Levine tests of homogeneity of variance were also nonsignificant, indicating that the variances of each of these index scores are homogeneous by age. Hence, for each of the new index scores, the distribution of the sums of scaled scores was converted to a scale with a mean of 100 and standard deviation of 15. Successive adjustments were based on computerized smoothing and visual inspection of the distributions. Tables 4–8 list the normative information needed to used these new indexes. These new index scores were then merged with the existing WMS-III standardization and retest data sets so that the following psychometric properties could be obtained.

Psychometric Properties

Reliability coefficients are presented in Table 9 and were calculated with the formula recommended by Guilford (1954) and Nunnally (1978) and used for the WAIS-III and WMS-III index scores as reported in the technical manual (The Psychological Corporation, 1997). The split-half reliability coefficients for the Faces, Family Pictures, Logical Memory, and Verbal Paired Associate subtests were obtained from Table 3.2 of the technical manual. The generalizability/reliability coefficients for the Visual

Descriptive	Statistics	Auditory composite	Visual composite (with new subtests)	Visual composite (with original subtests)	Visual immediate (with new subtests)	Visual delayed (with new subtests)
16–17 years	Mean	39.7	39.7	39.9	19.9	19.9
	Std. deviation	8.3	8.3	9.1	4.5	4.4
18–19 years	Mean	40.0	39.9	39.8	20.1	19.8
	Std. deviation	9.9	9.3	8.9	47.4	5.0
20–24 years	Mean	40.1	40.1	39.9	19.9	20.1
	Std. deviation	9.5	10.5	10.2	5.3	5.6
25–29 years	Mean	39.6	40.3	40.2	20.2	20.0
	Std. deviation	9.9	8.9	8.9	4.8	4.6
30–34 years	Mean	40.6	39.8	40.0	19.9	19.9
	Std. deviation	9.6	9.9	9.2	4.9	5.3
35–44 years	Mean	41.1	40.4	40.5	20.1	20.3
	Std. deviation	9.2	10.1	9.1	5.1	5.4
45–54 years	Mean	40.0	40.1	40.1	19.9	20.2
	Std. deviation	9.9	9.3	9.6	4.8	5.0
55–64 years	Mean	39.9	40.1	40.0	20.1	20.0
	Std. deviation	9.5	9.2	9.4	4.8	4.8
65–69 years	Mean	39.8	40.2	40.1	20.1	20.1
	Std. deviation	10.1	9.3	8.8	5.0	4.8
70–74 years	Mean	40.1	40.1	40.1	20.0	20.1
	Std. deviation	9.1	9.4	9.0	5.0	4.9
75–79 years	Mean	39.9	40.0	39.9	20.0	20.0
	Std. deviation	9.7	9.7	9.5	4.8	5.2
80–84 years	Mean	40.1	40.0	40.1	20.0	20.0
	Std. deviation	9.8	10.6	10.1	5.5	5.5
85–89 years	Mean	40.2	40.0	40.0	20.1	19.9
	Std. deviation	8.8	10.2	9.7	5.6	5.2

Weighted N=1250. Data © 2001, The Psychological Corporation, a Harcourt Assessment Company. All rights reserved.

TABLE 4   Index Score Equivalents of Sums of Scaled Scores: Auditory Memory Index[a]

Sum of scaled scores	Auditory composite	90 % lower	90 % upper	95 % lower	95 % upper
4	45	43	53	42	54
5	46	43	54	42	55
6	47	44	55	43	56
7	48	45	56	44	57
8	49	46	57	45	58
9	51	48	59	47	60
10	53	50	61	49	62
11	55	52	63	51	64
12	57	54	65	53	66
13	59	56	66	55	67
14	61	58	68	57	69
15	63	60	70	59	71
16	65	62	72	60	73
17	66	62	73	61	74
18	68	64	75	63	76
19	70	66	77	65	78
20	71	67	78	66	79
21	73	69	80	68	81
22	74	70	81	69	82
23	76	72	83	71	84
24	77	73	83	72	85
25	79	75	85	74	86
26	80	76	86	75	87
27	81	77	87	76	88
28	83	79	89	78	90
29	84	80	90	78	91
30	85	80	91	79	92
31	87	82	93	81	94
32	88	83	94	82	95
33	90	85	96	84	97
34	91	86	97	85	98
35	92	87	98	86	99
36	94	89	100	88	101
37	95	90	101	89	102
38	97	92	102	91	103
39	98	93	103	92	104
40	99	94	104	93	105

(*continues*)

TABLE 4   (*continued*)

Sum of scaled scores	Auditory composite	90 % lower	90 % upper	95 % lower	95 % upper
41	100	95	105	94	106
42	101	96	106	95	107
43	102	97	107	96	108
44	104	99	109	97	110
45	106	100	111	99	112
46	108	102	113	101	114
47	110	104	115	103	116
48	111	105	116	104	117
49	113	107	118	106	119
50	115	109	120	108	121
51	117	111	121	110	122
52	119	113	123	112	124
53	121	115	125	114	126
54	122	116	126	115	127
55	124	117	128	116	129
56	126	119	130	118	131
57	128	121	132	120	133
58	130	123	134	122	135
59	131	124	135	123	136
60	133	126	137	125	138
61	135	128	138	127	140
62	136	129	139	128	140
63	138	131	141	130	142
64	140	133	143	132	144
65	141	134	144	133	145
66	143	135	146	134	147
67	144	136	147	135	148
68	146	138	149	137	150
69	148	140	151	139	152
70	149	141	152	140	153
71	150	142	153	141	154
72	151	143	154	142	155
73	152	144	155	143	156
74	153	145	156	144	157
75	154	146	157	145	158
76	155	147	157	146	158

TABLE 5   Index Score Equivalents of Sums of Scaled Scores: Visual Memory Index (New Subtest Composition)[a]

Sum of scaled scores	Visual composite (with new subtests)[b]	90% lower	90% upper	95% lower	95% upper	
4	45	43	56	42	57	4
5	46	44	57	43	58	5
6	47	45	58	44	59	6
7	48	46	59	45	60	7
8	49	47	59	45	61	8
9	50	48	60	46	62	9
10	52	49	62	48	63	10
11	54	51	64	50	65	11
12	56	53	66	52	67	12
13	57	54	67	53	68	13
14	59	56	69	55	70	14
15	61	58	70	56	72	15
16	62	59	71	57	73	16
17	64	60	73	59	74	17
18	66	62	75	61	76	18
19	67	63	76	62	77	19
20	69	65	78	64	79	20
21	70	66	79	65	80	21
22	72	68	81	67	82	22
23	73	69	82	68	83	23
24	75	71	83	69	85	24
25	77	72	85	71	86	25
26	78	73	86	72	87	26
27	80	75	88	74	89	27
28	81	76	89	75	90	28
29	83	78	91	77	92	29
30	84	79	92	78	93	30
31	86	81	93	79	95	31
32	87	82	94	80	96	32
33	89	83	96	82	98	33
34	91	85	98	84	99	34
35	92	86	99	85	100	35
36	94	88	101	87	102	36
37	95	89	102	88	103	37
38	97	91	104	90	105	38
39	99	93	105	91	107	39
40	100	94	106	92	108	40

(continues)

TABLE 5   (*continued*)

Sum of scaled scores	Visual composite (with new subtests)[b]	90% lower	90% upper	95% lower	95% upper	
41	101	95	107	93	109	41
42	102	95	108	94	109	42
43	104	97	110	96	111	43
44	105	98	111	97	112	44
45	107	100	113	99	114	45
46	109	102	115	101	116	46
47	111	104	117	102	118	47
48	112	105	117	103	119	48
49	114	107	119	105	121	49
50	116	108	121	107	122	50
51	117	109	122	108	123	51
52	119	111	124	110	125	52
53	121	113	126	112	127	53
54	122	114	127	113	128	54
55	124	116	128	114	130	55
56	126	118	130	116	132	56
57	127	118	131	117	132	57
58	129	120	133	119	134	58
59	131	122	135	121	136	59
60	132	123	136	122	137	60
61	134	125	138	124	139	61
62	135	126	139	125	140	62
63	137	128	140	126	142	63
64	138	129	141	127	143	64
65	140	130	143	129	144	65
66	141	131	144	130	145	66
67	142	132	145	131	146	67
68	144	134	147	133	148	68
69	145	135	148	134	149	69
70	146	136	149	135	150	70
71	148	138	151	137	152	71
72	150	140	152	138	154	72
73	152	141	154	140	155	73
74	153	142	155	141	156	74
75	154	143	156	142	157	75
76	155	144	157	143	158	76

[a]Copyright © 2001, The Psychological Corporation, a Harcourt Assessment Company. All rights reserved.
[b]Comprised of Visual Reproduction and Family Pictures.

TABLE 6   Index Score Equivalents of Sums of Scaled Scores: Visual Memory Index (Original Subtest Composition)

Sum of scaled scores	Visual composite (with original subtests)[b]	90% lower	90% upper	95% lower	95% upper	
4	45	43	57	42	58	4
5	46	44	58	43	59	5
6	47	45	59	44	60	6
7	48	46	60	45	61	7
8	49	47	60	46	62	8
9	50	48	61	46	63	9
10	52	50	63	48	64	10
11	53	51	64	49	65	11
12	55	52	66	51	67	12
13	57	54	68	53	69	13
14	58	55	69	54	70	14
15	60	57	70	56	72	15
16	61	58	71	56	73	16
17	63	60	73	58	74	17
18	64	61	74	59	75	18
19	66	62	76	61	77	19
20	67	63	77	62	78	20
21	69	65	79	64	80	21
22	71	67	80	66	82	22
23	72	68	81	66	83	23
24	74	70	83	68	84	24
25	75	71	84	69	85	25
26	77	72	86	71	87	26
27	79	74	88	73	89	27
28	80	75	89	74	90	28
29	82	77	90	76	92	29
30	84	79	92	77	94	30
31	85	80	93	78	94	31
32	87	81	95	80	96	32
33	89	83	97	82	98	33
34	90	84	98	83	99	34
35	92	86	99	85	101	35
36	94	88	101	86	103	36
37	96	90	103	88	104	37
38	97	91	104	89	105	38
39	99	92	106	91	107	39
40	100	93	107	92	108	40
41	101	94	108	93	109	41

(*continues*)

TABLE 6   (*continued*)

Sum of scaled scores	Visual composite (with original subtests)[b]	90 % lower	90 % upper	95 % lower	95 % upper	
42	103	96	109	95	111	42
43	104	97	110	96	112	43
44	106	99	112	97	114	44
45	108	101	114	99	115	45
46	110	102	116	101	117	46
47	111	103	117	102	118	47
48	113	105	119	104	120	48
49	115	107	120	106	122	49
50	116	108	121	106	123	50
51	118	110	123	108	124	51
52	120	111	125	110	126	52
53	121	112	126	111	127	53
54	123	114	128	113	129	54
55	125	116	129	115	131	55
56	126	117	130	116	132	56
57	128	119	132	117	134	57
58	129	120	133	118	134	58
59	131	121	135	120	136	59
60	132	122	136	121	137	60
61	134	124	138	123	139	61
62	135	125	139	124	140	62
63	137	127	140	126	142	63
64	138	128	141	126	143	64
65	140	130	143	128	144	65
66	141	130	144	129	145	66
67	143	132	146	131	147	67
68	144	133	147	132	148	68
69	146	135	149	134	150	69
70	147	136	149	135	151	70
71	148	137	150	136	152	71
72	150	139	152	137	154	72
73	151	140	153	138	154	73
74	153	141	155	140	156	74
75	154	142	156	141	157	75
76	155	143	157	142	158	76

[b]Comprised of Faces and Family Pictures.

TABLE 7   Index Score Equivalents of Sums of Scaled Scores: Visual Memory Immediate Index (New Subtest Composition)[a]

Sum of scaled scores	Visual immediate (with new subtests)[b]	90 % lower	90 % upper	95 % lower	95 % upper
2	46	46	62	44	64
3	49	48	65	47	66
4	52	51	67	49	69
5	55	54	70	52	71
6	58	56	72	55	74
7	61	59	75	57	76
8	64	61	77	60	79
9	67	64	80	62	82
10	70	66	82	65	84
11	73	69	85	67	87
12	76	71	88	70	89
13	79	74	90	72	92
14	82	77	93	75	94
15	85	79	95	78	97
16	88	82	98	80	99
17	90	83	100	82	101
18	93	86	102	84	104
19	97	89	106	88	107
20	100	92	108	90	110
21	103	94	111	93	112
22	106	97	113	95	115
23	109	100	116	98	117
24	112	102	118	101	120
25	115	105	121	103	122
26	118	107	123	106	125
27	121	110	126	108	128
28	125	113	129	112	131
29	128	116	132	114	133
30	131	118	134	117	136
31	134	121	137	119	139
32	137	123	140	122	141
33	140	126	142	124	144
34	143	129	145	127	146
35	146	131	147	130	149
36	149	134	150	132	151
37	152	136	152	135	154
38	155	139	155	137	157

[a]Copyright © 2001, The Psychological Corporation, a Harcourt Assessment Company. All rights reserved.
[b]Comprised of Visual Reproductions I and Family Pictures I.

TABLE 8   Index Score Equivalents of Sums of Scaled Scores: Visual Memory Delayed Index (New Subtest Composition)[a]

Sum of scaled scores	Visual delayed (with new subtests)[b]	90 % lower	90 % upper	95 % lower	95 % upper
2	45	45	61	43	62
3	48	47	63	46	65
4	51	50	66	48	68
5	54	53	69	51	70
6	58	56	72	54	74
7	61	59	75	57	76
8	64	61	77	60	79
9	67	64	80	62	81
10	71	67	83	66	85
11	74	70	86	68	87
12	77	72	88	71	90
13	79	74	90	72	92
14	82	77	93	75	94
15	85	79	95	78	97
16	88	82	98	80	99
17	91	84	100	83	102
18	94	87	103	85	104
19	97	89	105	88	107
20	99	91	107	90	109
21	102	94	110	92	111
22	106	97	113	96	115
23	109	100	116	98	117
24	112	102	118	101	120
25	115	105	121	103	122
26	118	107	123	106	125
27	121	110	126	108	128
28	124	113	129	111	130
29	127	115	131	114	133
30	130	118	134	116	135
31	133	120	136	119	138
32	136	123	139	121	140
33	139	125	141	124	143
34	142	128	144	126	146
35	145	131	147	129	148
36	148	133	149	132	151
37	151	136	152	134	153
38	154	138	154	137	156

[b]Comprised of Visual Reproduction II and Faces II.

TABLE 9 Reliability of the Index Scores[a]

Index	Age														Average r_{xx}[a]
	16–17	18–19	20–24	25–29	30–34	35–44	45–54	55–64	65–69	70–74	75–79	80–84	85–89	
Auditory Immediate	0.90	0.93	0.92	0.94	0.95	0.93	0.94	0.93	0.94	0.92	0.95	0.95	0.93	0.93
Auditory Delayed	0.76	0.85	0.85	0.88	0.88	0.90	0.87	0.85	0.86	0.87	0.89	0.90	0.85	0.87
Auditory Composite	0.90	0.94	0.94	0.95	0.95	0.96	0.95	0.94	0.95	0.94	0.96	0.96	0.94	0.95
New Visual Immediate	0.79	0.78	0.80	0.84	0.84	0.84	0.83	0.86	0.87	0.87	0.85	0.90	0.89	0.85
New Visual Delayed	0.80	0.78	0.81	0.81	0.84	0.83	0.84	0.86	0.87	0.88	0.86	0.90	0.90	0.85
New Visual Composite	0.89	0.88	0.89	0.91	0.91	0.91	0.91	0.92	0.93	0.93	0.92	0.94	0.94	0.92
Original Visual Immediate	0.82	0.80	0.83	0.84	0.85	0.85	0.86	0.81	0.78	0.79	0.79	0.84	0.84	0.82
Original Visual Delayed	0.79	0.82	0.85	0.82	0.83	0.87	0.87	0.81	0.81	0.80	0.80	0.85	0.86	0.83
Original Visual Composite	0.90	0.90	0.90	0.92	0.92	0.93	0.93	0.89	0.90	0.90	0.88	0.91	0.91	0.91

[a]Some values were reprinted with permission from WAIS-III—WMS-III Technical Manual by The Psychological Corporation, 1997. All other values are copyright © 2001, The Psychological Corporation, a Harcourt Assessment Company. All rights reserved.

[b]"New" refers to the index scores comprised of Faces and Family Pictures. "Original" refers to the index scores comprised of Visual Reproduction and Family Pictures.

Reproduction subtests were obtained from Table 3.3 of the technical manual. The rationale of using split-half versus generalizability coefficients has been explained in the technical manual and is not repeated here. For each age band, the reliability coefficients were calculated across the age groups, and the average coefficient was calculated with the Fisher's z transformation.

Standard errors of measurement were calculated by obtaining the square root of $(1-r_{xx})$ and multiplying this number by the standard deviation. The average SE_M was calculated by averaging the sum of the squared SE_Ms for each age group and obtaining the square root of the result. The 90% and 95% confidence intervals were derived in a manner similar to that used for the other WAIS-III and WMS-III index scores. The estimated true score and the standard error of estimation were obtained according to the formulas listed on page 56 of the *WAIS-III–WMS-III Technical Manual* (The Psychological Corporation, 1997).

The test–retest stability estimates were obtained from the WMS-III sample described in the technical manual. The interval ranged from 2–12 weeks and is based on data obtained from 297 individuals. As in the technical manual, the coefficients were corrected for the variability of the standardization sample (Allen & Yen, 1979).

Reliability Coefficients

Replicating the steps taken for the previously published WAIS-III and WMS-III index scores, reliability coefficients were obtained for the new index scores (see Table 9). The reliability coefficients were calculated with the formula recommended by Guilford (1954) and Nunnally (1978).[2] Table 9 presents the reliability of each of the new index scores by age group, and the average coefficient across all the 13 age groups was calculated with Fisher's z transformation. The table also lists the reliability coefficients for the original Auditory Immediate and Delayed and the original Visual Immediate and Delayed Indexes, so that the coefficients for the new scores could be compared directly to the previously published ones.

As indicated in Table 9, the average reliability for the new WMS-III immediate and delayed index scores are comparable with (even slightly higher [0.85/0.85 vs. 0.82/0.83] than) those indexes published in the WMS-III. The coefficients fluctuate by age, with the original indices having

---

[2]The reliability coefficients for the subtests have been reported previously (The Psychological Corporation, 1997; Tables 3.2 and 3.3) and will not be repeated here.

TABLE 10 Standard Errors of Measurement of the New and Existing WMS-III Index Scores by Age Group[a]

Index	Age													Average SE$_M$[b]
	16–17	18–19	20–24	25–29	30–34	35–44	45–54	55–64	65–69	70–74	75–79	80–84	85–89	
Auditory Immediate	4.74	3.97	4.24	3.67	3.35	3.97	3.67	3.97	3.67	4.24	3.35	3.35	3.97	3.88
Auditory Delayed	7.35	5.81	5.81	5.20	5.20	4.74	5.41	5.81	5.61	5.41	4.97	4.74	5.81	5.57
Auditory Composite	4.68	3.59	3.70	3.23	3.23	3.08	3.27	3.61	3.39	3.56	3.07	3.05	3.59	3.49
New Visual Immediate	6.81	7.01	6.75	5.98	5.99	5.92	6.12	5.70	5.43	5.50	5.78	4.82	5.06	5.95
New Visual Delayed	6.73	7.11	6.47	6.47	5.96	6.10	6.03	5.68	5.34	5.19	5.56	4.71	4.63	5.89
New Visual Composite	5.01	5.25	4.87	4.61	4.40	4.42	4.49	4.20	3.98	3.96	4.20	3.52	3.61	4.38
Original Visual Immediate	6.36	6.71	6.18	6.00	5.81	5.81	5.61	6.54	7.04	6.87	6.87	6.00	6.00	6.31
Original Visual Delayed	6.87	6.36	5.81	6.36	6.18	5.41	5.41	6.54	6.54	6.71	6.71	5.81	5.61	6.20
Original Visual Composite	4.79	4.74	4.64	4.29	4.26	4.06	4.08	4.91	4.82	4.84	5.14	4.59	4.49	4.60

[a]Some values were reprinted with permission from *WAIS-III—WMS-III Technical Manual* by The Psychological Corporation, 1997. All other values are copyright © 2001, The Psychological Corporation, a Harcourt Assessment Company. All rights reserved.

[b]"New" refers to the index scores comprised of Visual Reproduction and Family Pictures; "Original" refers to the index scores comprised of Faces and Family Pictures.

TABLE 11 Stability Coefficients of the New and Existing WMS-III Indexes

Ages 16–54

	First testing		Second testing		Corrected	
	Mean	SD	Mean	SD	r_{12}	r^a
Auditory Immediate	101.7	14.4	111.5	16.3	0.84	0.85
Auditory Delayed	101.9	14.1	110.6	13.9	0.82	0.83
Auditory Composite	102.1	14.5	111.8	15.8	0.86	0.87
New Visual Immediate	102.3	14.1	111.0	13.8	0.75	0.77
New Visual Delayed	102.0	14.1	116.7	14.8	0.73	0.75
New Visual Composite	102.2	14.1	114.5	14.4	0.79	0.80
Original Visual Immediate	102.8	13.7	117.1	16.2	0.74	0.77
Original Visual Delayed	103.0	14.7	117.4	15.7	0.74	0.75
Original Visual Composite	103.4	14.5	118.1	15.5	0.80	0.81

$N = 134$

Ages 55–89

	First testing		Second testing		Average corrected all ages		
	Mean	SD	Mean	SD	r_{12}	r^a	Corrected
Auditory Immediate	97.3	14.8	107.2	17.9	0.85	0.85	0.85
Auditory Delayed	98.5	14.6	108.7	17.1	0.84	0.85	0.84
Auditory Composite	98.1	14.7	108.5	17.8	0.87	0.87	0.87
New Visual Immediate	99.8	15.7	108.1	16.0	0.78	0.78	0.77
New Visual Delayed	101.2	15.1	112.1	16.4	0.80	0.80	0.77
New Visual Composite	100.5	15.5	110.5	16.4	0.83	0.83	0.81
Original Visual Immediate	99.3	16.3	109.6	18.8	0.76	0.73	0.75
Original Visual Delayed	101.1	15.4	111.3	18.9	0.76	0.76	0.76
Original Visual Composite	100.8	15.8	111.3	18.4	0.80	0.80	0.80

$N = 147$

slightly higher values at younger ages and the new index scores having slightly higher reliability values in the older age groups. This is most likely a result of the lower generalizability coefficient for Visual Reproduction in the younger age group (see Table 3.3, The Psychological Corporation, 1997). The reader should also be aware that a different methodology to "split halves" was used for the Visual Reproduction subtests (see The Psychological Corporation, 1997, for the rationale and a description) and that the coefficients reported for Visual Reproduction Immediate and Delayed were used at each age group within the young and old age bands. Overall, however, the coefficients indicate acceptable reliability at the index score level.

More importantly, Table 9 demonstrates that the reliability coefficients are significantly higher for the three new composite scores (auditory composite, visual composite [based on new subtest configuration with Visual Reproduction], and an alternate visual composite [based on the original subtest configuration with Faces]). The average coefficients for these three indexes are: 0.95, 0.92, and 0.91. While this result is not surprising (as the number of subtest scores being included in a reliability coefficient increases, so does the coefficient), it does provide an additional rationale to the interpretation of the WMS-III at this level.

The standard error of measurement (SE_M) provides an estimate of the error inherent in each index score and the lower the SE_M is, the smaller the error there is associated with an index score. Confidence intervals around scores are developed based on the SE_M for a given score. The information has been summarized in *The WAIS-III–WMS-III Technical Manual* and will not be repeated here (The Psychological Corporation, 1997, pp. 53–56). The SE_M's associated with the new index scores are presented in Table 10.

The final index of score error and stability is the Test–Retest stability coefficient. For the WMS-III, 282 individuals completed the scale between 2 and 12 weeks apart. From those data, stability coefficients for the new index scores were computed and are reported in Table 4.11. The Auditory immediate and delayed and the Visual immediate and delayed indexes reported in the WMS-III technical manual have been included in Table 11 to facilitate comparisons across index scores. Overall, the stability of the new immediate and delayed index scores are comparable to the coefficients that had been obtained with the published visual memory indexes. The stability improves when the composite scores are obtained, due to the increased stability after adding the additional subtest scores.

CONCLUSION

This chapter recommends new changes when testing individuals with the WAIS-III and WMS-III. Cognitive assessment is extended to six factors, and new norms have been presented for composite auditory and visual memory scores. Index scores structured around separate immediate and delayed scores are likely useful in clinical practice but have been made secondary based on a lack of validity data to support them. The visual memory indices on the WMS-III have been re-created with the Family Pictures and Visual Reproduction subtests. For these new index scores, the Faces subtests have been made optional. This decision was based in part on factor analytic data that demonstrate that Faces is unrelated to the other subtests on the visual memory factor. Clinically, however, it is unclear if a visual memory score combining with the original subtests (Faces and Family Pictures) would be useful. Throughout the book, collaborators were encouraged to perform their analyses on the six-factor index scores. Chapter 5 (Heaton, Taylor, & Manly, this volume) considers the effects of demographic effects on the new indexes as well as the validity of the demographically corrected six-factor index scores.

REFERENCES

Allen, J. P., & Yen, W. M. (1979). *Introduction to Measurement Theory.* Monterey, CA: Brooks-Cole.

Balinsky, B. (1941). An analysis of the mental factors in various age groups from nine to sixty. *Genetic Psychology Monographs, 23,* 191–234.

Bornstein, R. A., & Chelune, G. J. (1988). Factor structure of the Wechsler Memory Scale—Revised. *The Clinical Neuropsychologist, 2(2),* 107–115.

Bowden, S. C., Carstairs, J. R., & Shores, E. A. (1999). Confirmatory factor analysis of combined Wechsler Adult Intelligence Scale—Revised and Wechsler Memory Scale—Revised scores in a healthy community sample. *Psychological Assessment, 11(3),* 339–344.

Burton, D. B., Mittenberg, W., & Burton, C. A. (1993). Confirmatory factor analysis of the Wechsler Memory Scale–Revised standardization sample. *Archives of Clinical Neuropsychology. 8(6)* 467–475.

Carroll, J. B. (1993). *Human cognitive abilities: A survey of factor analytic studies.* Cambridge, MA: Cambridge University Press.

Cohen, J. (1952a). A factor-analytically based rationale for the Wechsler–Bellevue. *Journal of Abnormal and Social Psychology, 47,* 359–365.

Cohen, J. (1952b). A factor-analytically based rationale for the Wechsler–Bellevue. *Journal of Consulting Psychology, 16,* 272–277.

Cohen, J. (1957a). The factorial structure of the WAIS between early adulthood and old age. *Journal of Consulting Psychology, 21*, 283–290.

Cohen, J. (1957b). A factor-analytically based rationale for the Wechsler Adult Intelligence Scale. *Journal of Consulting Psychology, 21*, 451–457.

Cohen, J. (1959). The factorial structure of the WISC at ages 7–6, 10–16, and 13–6. *Journal of Consulting Psychology, 23*, 285–299.

Davis, L. J., & Swenson, W. M. (1970). Factor analyses of the Wechsler Memory Scale. *Journal of Consulting and Clinical Psychology, 35, 430.*

Flannagan, D.P, McGrew, K. S., & Oritz, S.O (2000). *The Wechsler intelligence scales and Gf–Gc theory: A contemporary approach to interpretation.* Boston: McGraw-Hill.

Guilford, J. P. (1954). *Psychometric methods* (2nd ed.) New York: McGraw-Hill.

Hawkins, K. A. (1998). Indicators of brain dysfunction derived from graphic representations of the WAIS-III/WMS-III technical manual samples: A preliminary approach to clinical utility. *The Clinical Neuropsychologist, 12*, 535–551.

Heaton, R. K., Taylor, M. J., & Manly, J. (2003). Demographic effects and the use of demographically corrected norms with the WAIS-III and WMS-III. In D. S. Tulsky et al. (Eds). *Clinical Interpretation of the WAIS-III and WMS-III.* (pp. 181–210). San Diego: Academic Press.

Horn, J. L., & Noll, J. (1997). Human cognitive capabilities: $G_f - G_c$ Theory. In D. P. Flanagan, J. L. Genshart, & P. L. Harrison (Eds.), *Contemporary intellectual assessment: Theories, tests, and issues.* New York: Guilford Press.

Ivnik, R. J., Malec, J. F., Smith, G. E., Tangalos, E. G., Petersen, R. C., Kokmen, E., & Kurland, L. T. (1992). Mayo's older Americans normative studies: WAIS-R norms for ages 56–97. *The Clinical Neuropsychologist, 6 (suppl.)*, 1–30.

Kaufman, A. S. (1979). *Intelligent testing with the WISC-R.* New York: Wiley.

Kear-Colwell, J. J., & Heller, M. (1978). A normative study of the Wechsler Memory Scale. *Journal of Clinical Psychology. 34(2)*, 437–442.

Larrabee, G. J. (1999). Book and test review: The Wechsler memory scale III. *Archives of Clinical Neurospsychology, 14(5)*, 473–477.

Larrabee, G. J. (2000). Association between IQ and neuropsychological test performance: Commentary on Tremont, Hoffman, Scott, and Adams (1998). *The Clinical Neuropsychologist, 14*, 139–145.

Larrabee, G. J., & Curtiss, G. (1992). Factor validity of various memory testing procedures [Abstract of presentation at the annual convention of The International Neuropsychological Society]. *The Clinical Neuropsychologist, 5*, 261–262.

Larrabee, G. J., Kane, R. L., & Schuck, J. R. (1983). Factor analysis of the WAIS and Wechsler Memory Scale: An analysis of the construct validity of the Wechsler Memory Scale. *Journal of Clinical Neuropsychology, 5*, 159–168.

Leckliter, I. N., Matarazzo, J. D., & Silverstein, A. B. (1986). A literature review of factor analytic studies of the WAIS-R. *Journal of Clinical psychology, 42(2)*, 332–342.

Leonberger, F. T., Nicks, S. D., Larrabee, G. J., & Goldfader, P. R. (1992). Factor structure of the Wechsler Memory Scale–Revised within a comprehensive neuropsychological battery. *Neuropsychology, 6(3)*, 239–249.

Martin, T. A., Donders, J., & Thompson, E. (2000). Potential of and problems with new measures of psychometric intelligence after traumatic brain injury. *Rehabilitation Psychology, 45(4)*, 402–408.

Millis, S. R., Malina, A. C., Bowers, D. A., & Ricker, J. H. (1999). Confirmatory factor analysis of the Wechsler Memory Scale–III. *Journal of Clinical and Experimental Neuropsychology, 21(1)*, 87–93.

Nicks, S. D., Leonberger, F. T., Munz, D. C., & Goldfader, P. R. (1992). Factor analysis of the WMS-R and the WAIS. *Archives of Clinical Neuropsychology, 7*, 387–393.

Nunnally, J. (1978). *Psychometric theory* (2nd ed). New York: McGraw-Hill.

Price, L. R., Tulsky, D. S., Millis, S. R., & Weiss, L. G. (2002). Redefining the Factor Structure of the Wechsler Memory Scale-III: Confirmatory Factor Analysis with Cross-Validation. *Journal of Clinical and Experimental Neuropsychology, 24*, 574–585.

The Psychological Corporation. (1997). *WAIS-III–WMS-III Technical Manual*. San Antonio, TX: Author.

Roid, G. H., Prifitera, A., & Ledbetter, M. (1988). Confirmatory analysis of the factor structure of the Wechsler Memory Scale—Revised. *Clinical Neuropsychologist. 2(2)*, 116–120.

Roid, G. H., Prifitera, A., & Weiss, L. G. (1993). Replication of the WISC-III factor structure in an independent sample [Special issue, Monograph, WISC-III series]. *Journal of Psychoeducational Assessment, 11*, 6–21.

Roid, G. H., & Worrall, W. (1997). Replication of the Wechsler Intelligence Scale for Children—Third Edition: Four-factor model in the Canadian normative sample. *Psychological Assessment, 9*, 512–515.

Roth, D. L., Conboy, T. J., Reeder, K. P., & Boll, T. J. (1990). Confirmatory factor analysis of the Wechsler Memory Scale—Revised in a sample of head-injured patients. *Journal of Clinical and Experimental Neuropsychology, 12(4)*, 834–842.

Ryan, J. J., Rosenberg, S. J., & Heilbronner, R. L. (1984). Comparative relationships of the Wechsler Adult Intelligence Scale—Revised (WAIS-R) and the Wechsler Adult Intelligence Scale (WAIS) to the Wechsler Memory Scale (WMS). *Journal of Behavioral Assessment, 6*, 37–43.

Schmidt, M. (1996). *Rey Auditory and Verbal Learning Test: A handbook*. Los Angeles: Western Psychological Services.

Shiffrin R. M., & Schneider, W. (1977). Controlled and automatic human information processing II. Perceptual learning, automatic attending, and a general theory. *Psychological Review, 84 (2)*.

Skilbeck, C. E., & Woods, R. T. (1980). The factorial structure of the Wechsler Memory Scale: Samples of neurological and psychogeriatric patients. *Journal of Clinical Neuropsychology, 2*, 293–300.

Smith, G. E., Ivnik, R. J., Malec, J. F., Kokmen, E., Tangalos, E. G., & Kurland, L. T. (1992). Mayo's older Americans normative studies (MOANS): Factor structure of a core battery, *Psychological Assessment, 4*, 382–390.

Smith, G. E., Ivnik, R. J., Malec, J. F., Petersen, R. C., Kokmen, E., & Tangalos, E. G. (1994). Mayo Cognitive Factor Scales: Derivation of a short batter and norms for factor scores. *Neuropsychology, 8 (2)*, 194–202.

Thorndike, E. L., Lay, W., & Dean, P. R. (1909). The relation of accuracy in sensory discrimination to general intelligence. *American Journal of Psychology, 20*, 364–369.

Thurstone, L. L. (1934). The vectors of mind. *Psychological Review, 41*, 1–32.

Tulsky, D. S., Chiaravalloti, N. D., Palmer, B. W., & Chelune, G. J. (2003). The Wechsler Memory Scale, Third Edition: A New Perspective. In D. S. Tulsky et al. (Eds). *Clinical Interpretation of the WAIS-III and WMS-III*. (pp. 93–139). San Diego: Academic Press.

Tulsky, D. S., & Price, L. R. (in press). The Joint WAIS-III and WMS-III factor structure: Development and cross-validation of a 6-factor model of cognitive functioning. *Psychological Assessment.*

Tulsky, D. S., Saklofske, D. H., Wilkins, C., & Weiss, L. G. (2001). Development of a general ability index for the WAIS-III. *Psychological Assessment, 13(4),* 566–571.

Tulsky, D. S., Saklofske, D. H., & Zhu, J. (2003). Revising a standard: An evaluation of the origin and development of the WAIS-III. In D. S. Tulsky et al. (Eds). *Clinical Interpretation of the WAIS-III and WMS-III.* (pp. 43–92). San Diego: Academic Press.

Tulsky, D. S., Zhu, J., & Prifitera, A. (2000). Assessment of adult intelligence with the WAIS-III. In G Goldstein & M Hersen (Eds.), *Handbook of Psychological assessment (3rd ed.)* Amsterdam: Pergamon. (pp. 97–129).

Wechsler, D. (1939). *Measurement of adult intelligence.* Baltimore: Williams & Wilkins.

Wechsler, D. (1946). *The Wechsler Bellevue Form II.* New York: The Psychological Corporation.

Wechsler, D. (1949). *The Wechsler Intelligence Scale for Children.* New York: The Psychological Corporation.

Wechsler, D. (1955). *Wechsler Adult Intelligence Scale.* New York: The Psychological Corporation.

Wechsler, D. (1974). *Wechsler Intelligence Scale for Children—Revised.* New York: The Psychological Corporation.

Wechsler, D. (1981). *Wechsler Adult Intelligence Scale—Revised.* San Antonio, TX: The Psychological Corporation.

Wechsler, D. (1991). *Wechsler Intelligence Scale for Children—Third Edition.* San Antonio, TX: The Psychological Corporation.

Wechsler, D. (1997a). *WAIS-III administration and scoring manual.* San Antonio, TX: The Psychological Corporation.

Wechsler, D. (1997b). *Wechsler Memory Scale—Third Edition.* San Antonio, TX: The Psychological Corporation.

Woodard, J. L. (1993). Confirmatory factor analysis of the Wechsler Memory scale–Revised in a mixed clinical population. *Journal of Clinical and Experimental Neuropsychology, 15(6),* 968–973.

Demographic Effects and Use of Demographically Corrected Norms with the WAIS-III and WMS-III

Robert K. Heaton
Michael J. Taylor
University of California, San Diego
and

Jennifer Manly
Columbia University

The joint standardization of the Wechsler Adult Intelligence Scale-III (WAIS-III) and Wechsler Memory Scale-III (WMS-III) provides new opportunities to clarify and refine the cognitive constructs measured by the two test batteries. To this end, recent exploratory and confirmatory factor analyses of the combined batteries have revealed that the WAIS and WMS together measure six cognitive factors: verbal comprehension, perceptual organization, processing speed, working memory, auditory memory, and visual memory (Tulsky & Price, in press, also Tulsky, Ivnik, Price & Wilkins, Chapter 3, this volume). The composition of these six factors is specified in the left column of Table 1.

One interesting finding inherent in these factor definitions is that the auditory and visual memory factors combine immediate and delayed measures from the WMS. The fact that potentially important distinctions between memory encoding and storage are ignored in these definitions has occurred because such distinctions do not appear to account for much variance in the performance of normal adults on the WMS; that is, the immediate and delayed measures are so highly correlated in normals, that creating separate factor scores is not justified. It is unclear whether a different

TABLE 1   Composition of WAIS–WMS Factor Scores

Primary scores	Secondary scores
Verbal Comprehension	Auditory Memory Immediate
Information	Logical Memory I
Vocabulary	Verbal Paired Associates I
Similarities	
	Auditory Memory Delayed
Working Memory	Logical Memory II
Spatial Span	Verbal Paired Associates II
Letter–Number Sequencing	
	Visual Memory Immediate
Perceptual Organization	Family Pictures Recall I
Block Design	Visual Reproductions Recall I
Picture Completion	
Matrix Reasoning	Visual Memory Delayed
	Family Pictures Recall II
Processesing Speed	Visual Reproductions Recall II
Digit Symbol	
Symbol Search	Alternate Visual Memory
	Family Pictures I and II
Auditory Memory	Faces I and II Recognition
Logical Memory I and II	
Verbal Paired Associates I and II	Alternate Visual Memory Immediate
	Family Pictures Recall I
Visual Memory	Faces I Recognition
Family Pictures I and II	
Visual Reproductions I and II	Alternate Visual Memory Delayed
	Family Pictures Recall II
	Faces II Recognition

solution would be obtained if the subject sample included large numbers of patients having disorders that may be distinguished by the presence of memory storage deficits (memory disorders due to mesial temporal or diencephalic pathology; e.g., Alzheimer's disease and Korsakoff's syndrome). Thus, at least for some diagnostic purposes, it may be premature to abandon the distinction between immediate and delayed memory measures. For this reason we recommend retaining separate immediate and

delayed measures as supplemental factor scores, pending further research
with relevant clinical samples. These supplemental scores are defined in the
right column of Table 1.

Another problem associated with the current WAIS–WMS six-factor
model is that the Visual Memory factor includes the Visual Reproduction
subtest, which is listed as an alternate measure in the WMS manual, instead
of the Faces subtest, which contributes scores to the standard WMS
indices. The reason for the choice of Visual Reproduction over Faces is
that the latter test had a lower factor loading than both Family Pictures and
Visual Reproduction; this suggests that Faces may be less representative of
the Visual Memory factor, and inclusion of Faces would also complicate
the desired use of equal weighting of component subtest scores in the
computation of the overall Visual Memory factor score. On the other
hand, the joint WAIS–WMS factor composition forces the examiner to
choose between potentially undesirable alternatives: Either administer the
Visual Reproduction subtest required for the joint WAIS–WMS factor
scores (and forego obtaining the standard WMS indices), or administer
Faces as required for the WMS indices (and forego obtaining the joint
factor scores), or take significantly more time to obtain scores on both
subtests. Ultimately it is an empirical question whether there are problems
associated with substituting Faces for Visual Reproduction in the WAIS–
WMS factor score, or vice versa for the WMS indices. Until the needed
psychometric studies of this issue are completed, we suggest retaining the
WAIS–WMS factor with the former (Faces) substitution as an "Alternate
Visual Memory" score; this too is listed among the "secondary scores"
column of Table 1.

DEMOGRAPHIC INFLUENCES AND
NORMATIVE CORRECTIONS

A second advantage of the joint standardization of the WAIS–WMS is
that co-norming will yield increased precision in analyzing patterns of
factor scores in clinical settings, and particularly for neurodiagnostic purposes. True comparability of the WAIS–WMS factor scores requires that
norms for all the measures were developed with the same, or at least
substantially overlapping, subject sample(s). On the other hand, the simple
fact of co-norming is not enough to achieve optimal precision in detecting
and analyzing patterns of neurocognitive impairment. For these purposes,
standard scores based upon the norms must have the same meanings across

test measures, and for all segments of the normal population (Axelrod & Goldman, 1996).

The purpose of norms in neurodiagnostic applications is to facilitate determining the nature of any difference between the obtained test score and the best estimate of a person's "premorbid" score (i.e., the score he or she would have obtained, absent any neuropsychiatric disorder causing cognitive impairment). Ideally such estimates should take into consideration any aspects of normal people that are known to be significantly associated with (i.e., to predict) test performance. Historically, norms for intelligence and memory tests have been corrected for age only. The standard WAIS norms, for example, require much better performance on tests of processing speed in order to be considered "average" for a 25-year old than for an 85-year-old person.

Although the practice of correcting test norms for age is well established (and necessary to avoid misclassifying older people as having unusually poor test performances), there is now overwhelming evidence that cognitive test performances in normal adults also are associated with other demographic characteristics. Depending upon the test, demographic effects of varying magnitudes have been documented for education level, sex, and ethnicity (Evans et al., 2000; Heaton, Grant, & Avitable, 1996; Norman, Evans, Miller, & Heaton, 2000; Reynolds, Chastain, Kaufmen, & McLean, 1987). Just as failing to adjust norms for age frequently results in misclassifying older adults' cognitive status, failing to consider these other demographic characteristics may result in misclassifying disproportionate numbers of people in other segments of the normal population (Matarazzo & Herman, 1984).

Here we will determine how the demographic variables of age, education, sex, and ethnicity relate to performance of normal adults on the joint WAIS–WMS factors. Also addressed will be a related question that bears on the optimal clinical (especially neurodiagnostic) use of WAIS–WMS factor scores: What are the consequences (in terms of false-positive attribution of "impairment") of ignoring demographic characteristics other than age when interpreting the joint factor scores? Then, using all available data from the WAIS–WMS co-norming project, we statistically remove from the joint factor scores the influence of demographic variables that contribute significantly to prediction of normals' test performance. This provides new standardized scores (T-scores) that simultaneously correct for multiple demographic influences. We will then show how demographically corrected T-scores affect (improve) the rates of misclassifying cognitive impairment in selected segments of the normal population.

SENSITIVITY OF DEMOGRAPHICALLY
CORRECTED WAIS/WMS FACTOR SCORES
TO NEUROCOGNITIVE IMPAIRMENT

First and foremost, test norms influence specificity or the probability of correctly classifying a performance (or person) as normal. As implied above, specificity will ideally be held constant across measures within any test battery and across all segments of the normal population. Normal people should have the same probability of being correctly identified as normal on test A as on test B, regardless of whether they are old or young, male or female, high school or college educated, or Caucasian or African American.

Depending upon the demographic characteristics of clinical patients, use of demographically corrected norms may also affect test sensitivity (i.e., the probability of correctly classifying a person who has a neuropsychiatric illness as being cognitively abnormal). Estimating the *true* sensitivity of a test can be quite complex: Not all patients with most disorders will be impaired on any given cognitive ability (or WAIS–WMS factor), and there may be no independent gold standard of impairment for any individual who has the disorder. Nevertheless, we would argue that the most accurate estimates of test sensitivity within a clinical population will be achieved by measures that minimize diagnostic error caused by demographic influences. Therefore it is of considerable interest to determine how our new, demographically corrected WAIS–WMS factor scores perform in neuropsychiatric populations.

We will begin to explore factor score sensitivity using data originally published in the *WAIS–WMS Technical Manual* (The Psychological Corporation, 1997), from patients with several different neuropsychiatric disorders. Patterns of demographically corrected factor scores and preliminary sensitivity estimates will be presented for the combined clinical sample and for each of eight diagnostic subgroups.

In addition to considering sensitivities of the six WAIS–WMS factors, we will also include results for immediate and delayed components of the memory factors, as well as for the Alternate Visual Memory factor. Of interest is whether any clinical subgroups (especially those with Alzheimer's disease, Korsakoff's syndrome, and temporal lobe epilepsy) show substantially worse delayed than immediate scores, suggesting abnormally rapid forgetting. Questions about Alternate Visual Memory include whether it shows different levels or patterns of results than the standard Visual Memory factor for the total clinical group or individual diagnostic subgroups, and for the immediate and delayed components.

SUBJECT SAMPLES

To answer questions about demographic effects on the various cognitive factors, and to create new demographically corrected factor scores, we used data from all adult (age $\geq$ 20 years) subjects who were administered the WAIS and WMS as part of the test standardization project. Detailed subject-selection criteria are provided in the WAIS/WMS Technical Manual (The Psychological Corporation, 1997). Because we were particularly interested in effects of education and ethnicity, we included the education and ethnicity "oversample" that did not contribute data to the published census-matched norms for these tests. (Note that our purpose is not to establish performance standards for the *general* U.S. adult population, for which census matching is appropriate, but rather to establish standards that are specific to each combination of demographic characteristics; for the latter purpose increased sampling of ethnic minority subjects and subjects with atypically low education levels was needed.) Table 2 describes the total subject samples given the WAIS and the WMS, as well as their respective oversamples; all subjects who were given the WMS, including its oversample, also took the WAIS. It is apparent that the oversamples are younger, have somewhat higher proportions of males and, more importantly, contain more subjects with less than a high school education as well as higher proportions of ethnic minority subjects.

TABLE 2   Descriptions of WAIS–WMS Normal Adult Subject Samples (Ages $\geq$ 20 years).

	Total available sample		Oversample	
	WAIS-III	WMS-III	WAIS-III	WMS-III
N	2312	1073	276	206
Age	51.83	52.05	39.43	40.5
Education	12.23	12.02	10.41	10.71
Gender (% male)	46.5	46.9	49.3	51.5
Ethnicity (%)				
White	75.8	73.6	40.9	46.1
African American	13.0	13.8	30.8	27.2
Hispanic	7.7	8.1	17.0	14.1
Other	3.5	4.5	11.2	12.6

To consider questions about relative sensitivities of the demographically corrected factor scores to cognitive impairments due to neuropsychiatric disorders, we will use WAIS-WMS data from eight diagnostic groups described in the technical manual (pp. 146 to 168, and 311 to 316; The Psychological Corporation, 1997). The demographic characteristics of these diagnostic groups, and of the combined clinical sample ($N = 153$), are summarized in Table 3.

Unfortunately, two of the diagnostic groups (those with left or right temporal lobe epilepsy) were not administered the subtests required for computing the Verbal Comprehension, Perceptual Organization, and Processing Speed factors. These two groups will not be included in the total clinical sample when we consider relative sensitivities of the six WAIS–WMS factors. Despite their missing data on nonmemory factors, the temporal lobe epilepsy groups are the only ones in this available data set that have relatively lateralized brain disorders, which frequently involve structures that subserve memory functions. Thus, their relative findings on the Auditory Memory and Visual Memory (standard and alternate) factors are of particular interest.

DEVELOPING DEMOGRAPHICALLY CORRECTED T-SCORES

Table 2 indicates that a total of 1073 subjects had data needed to compute all six WAIS–WMS factor scores, whereas another 1239 subjects had data only for the three factors derived from the WAIS (Verbal Comprehension, Perceptual Organization, and Processing Speed). We considered it desirable to use all available data to develop demographic corrections for each factor, but only if this would not jeopardize the comparability of the six corrected factor scores. What was needed to allay the latter concern is strong evidence that the subjects with and without WMS data did not differ cognitively, or in terms of the relationships between their demographic characteristics and cognitive functioning. We tested this by developing demographically corrected WAIS factor scores, using data from all subjects, and then comparing the corrected T-scores for subgroups with and without WMS data. Across the three WAIS factors, the two subgroups obtained mean T-scores ranging from 49.7 to 50.1, and SDs ranging from 9.8 to 10.2. Even with the large *n*s, the subgroup differences did not approach statistical significance on any of the factor T-scores. Therefore it was concluded that these two subgroups were indeed comparable, and that it was justified to use all their data to develop these demographic corrections.

TABLE 3 Demographic Characteristics of WAIS–WMS Clinical Samples

	n	Age	Age (SD)	Education	Education (SD)	Male (%)	White (%)
Alzheimer's disease	34	72.0	7.8	14.0	2.7	52.9	88.2
Huntington's disease	14	44.6	12.5	14.1	1.9	28.6	100.0
Korsakoff's syndrome	9	61.7	11.2	11.2	2.7	100.0	100.0
Parkinson's disease	9	74.1	7.3	13.1	1.8	77.8	77.8
Schizophrenia	39	38.0	6.1	13.0	2.2	79.5	61.5
Traumatic brain injury	21	26.8	6.0	13.1	1.5	61.9	100.0
Temporal lobectomy (Left)	15	32.5	7.8	13.8	1.5	26.7	93.3
Temporal lobectomy (Right)	12	30.5	5.7	13.8	1.9	50.0	58.3
Total	153	47.0	19.4	13.4	2.2	60.1	82.4

We have generated regression-based demographic corrections using fractional polynomials to develop formulae that convert uncorrected WAIS–WMS factor scores to T-scores that adjust for the influences of age, education, sex, and certain ethnicities. As can be seen in Table 2, the only ethnic groups sufficiently represented in the subject sample are Anglo (non-Hispanic) Caucasians, African Americans, and Hispanics. Fractional polynomial regression equations were generated separately for the three ethnicity groups, because there were some moderate differences across those groups in the degrees to which the other demographic variables related to (predicted) uncorrected factor scores.

To determine the optimal fractional polynomial regression equations, the method of Royston and Altman (1994) was employed using the statistical package Stata (Stata Corporation, College Station, TX). This approach uses an iterative algorithm for evaluating the influence of combinations of predictors, which have been transformed using a restricted set of predetermined powers (i.e., $-2, -1, -0.5, 0, 0.5, 1, 2, 3$). The algorithm compares all sets of predictors using these transformations to generate the final optimal fit. Royston and Altman's method for selecting optimal fractional polynomials was chosen due to its improved accuracy in curve fitting. More specifically, when simple squares and/or cubes of any of the predictor variables are used, they may overcompensate at the extreme ends of the distribution being predicted. When fractional and negative polynomials are used, however, such overadjustment is reduced by having a more precise fit of the data.

The residuals produced using the optimal fractional polynomial regression equations were then converted to T-scores with a mean of 50 and SD of 10. The resulting distributions did not differ significantly from normal based on Kolmogorov–Smirnoff tests, and were virtually unrelated to the demographic variables being considered here. Furthermore, there were no significant T-score differences across subgroups from the four geographic regions of the U.S. (South, North East, North Central, and West), and T-scores were virtually unrelated to an independent measure of socioeconomic status: the median income of the zip codes of the participants in the WAIS–WMS standardization project (R^2s range from 0–0.01 for the six factors). The raw score to T-score conversions described here are available from The Psychological Corporation in the WAIS–WMS scoring program.

AGE EFFECTS

To some extent age and education are confounded in the WAIS–WMS normative sample (i.e., there is a slight tendency for older subjects to have completed fewer years of education; $r = -.12$). Therefore age effects on the WAIS–WMS factors will be evaluated using education-corrected Z scores. Figure 1 shows that, with the exception of Verbal Comprehension, rather strong and negative linear relationships exist between age (plotted in 5-year intervals) and the various factor scores; that is, performance declines in a linear way between the youngest and oldest age groups. Verbal Comprehension has a more quadratic relationship with age: gradually better scores were obtained across the earlier age levels (20–45), followed by stability during middle age to 65 years, and then some gradual decline for subgroups ranging from 65–89 years old. However, for Verbal Comprehension the age-related performance variability is fairly modest, and the oldest and youngest subgroups performed similarly (mean Z scores of −0.30 and −0.25, respectively). Interestingly, the immediate and delayed components of the Auditory and Visual memory factors show practically identical relationships with age (Figure 1C and D).

Table 4 presents the same information in a different way. Again, Pearson correlations show virtually no linear relationship between age and performance on the Verbal Comprehension factor, yet very significant negative relationships with age exist for the other factors. The strongest of those relationships occur for Processing Speed and Visual Memory (both $rs = -.67$), while more moderate associations with age are seen for Perceptual Organization, Working Memory, and Auditory Memory (rs from −.45 to −.52). Alternate Visual Memory shows somewhat smaller age effects than the standard version. The right side of the table is another way of looking at effect size for age: The mean Z score difference between the highest and lowest age groups. This indicates, for example, a two *SD* difference between the highest performing (youngest) and poorest performing (oldest) age groups on Processing Speed. Clearly, with the possible exception of Verbal Comprehension, all of these age effects on WAIS–WMS factors are clinically very significant.

EDUCATION EFFECTS

Figure 2 and Table 5 provide comparable information about relationships between education level and age-corrected WAIS–WMS factor scores. The

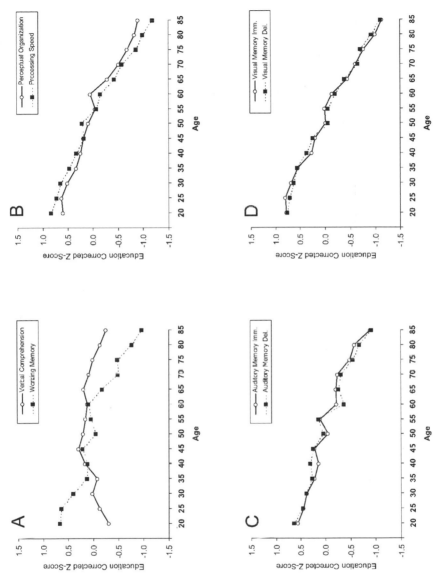

FIGURE 1. Age effects on education-corrected WAIS-III/WMS-III factor scores.
© 1997 The Psychological Corporation. All rights reserved.

largest effects are seen with the three WAIS-based factors of Verbal Comprehension, Perceptual Organization, and Processing Speed. Also, while the figure shows essentially linear education effects for those factors, somewhat different patterns appear for the Working Memory and all memory factors:

TABLE 4 Relationships between Education-Corrected WAIS-III and WMS-III Factor Z-Scores and Age

	R^2	Mean Z-score for lowest performing age group	Mean Z-score for highest performing age group	High–low age group difference
Verbal Comprehension Factor	<0.01	−0.30	0.30	0.60
Perceptual Organization Factor	0.27	−0.90	0.63	1.53
Processing Speed Factor	0.45	−1.18	0.83	2.02
Working Memory Factor	0.24	−0.97	0.68	1.64
Auditory Memory Factor	0.20	−0.92	0.62	1.54
Auditory Immediate Memory Factor	0.17	−0.89	0.56	1.45
Auditory Delayed Memory Factor	0.21	−0.90	0.64	1.54
Visual Memory Factor	0.45	−1.15	0.79	1.94
Visual Immediate Memory Factor	0.45	−1.13	0.80	1.93
Visual Delayed Memory Factor	0.41	−1.11	0.76	1.87
Alternate Visual Memory Factor	0.38	−1.12	0.78	1.90
Alt. Visual Immediate Memory Factor	0.34	−1.01	0.71	1.73
Alt. Visual Delayed Memory Factor	0.38	−1.15	0.81	1.96

TABLE 5   Relationships between Age-Corrected WAIS-III/WMS-III Factor Z-Scores and Education

	R^2	Mean Z-score for lowest performing education group	Mean Z-score for highest performing education group	High–low education group difference
Verbal Comprehension Factor	0.32	−0.82	0.93	1.74
Perceptual Organization Factor	0.18	−0.68	0.61	1.29
Processing Speed Factor	0.17	−0.70	0.56	1.26
Working Memory Factor	0.11	−0.45	0.41	0.87
Auditory Memory Factor	0.09	−0.47	0.46	0.93
Auditory Immediate Memory Factor	0.08	−0.42	0.41	0.83
Auditory Delayed Memory Factor	0.04	−0.34	0.29	0.63
Visual Memory Factor	0.10	−0.47	0.47	0.94
Visual Immediate Memory Factor	0.08	−0.42	0.41	0.83
Visual Delayed Memory Factor	0.07	−0.39	0.37	0.75
Alternate Visual Memory Factor	0.08	−0.44	0.43	0.87
Alt. Visual Immediate Memory Factor	0.04	−0.33	0.28	0.61
Alt. Visual Delayed Memory Factor	0.04	−0.33	0.28	0.61

194   Robert K. Heaton et al.

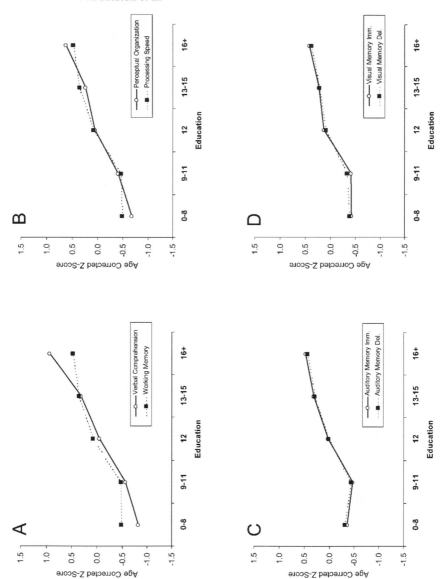

FIGURE 2.   Education effects on age-corrected WAIS-III/WMS-III factor scores.

The two lowest education groups (0–8 and 9–11) show comparably low performance, and a substantial improvement is seen with the high school graduates (12 years); each successive education group after that shows more gradual improvements. Again, both the table and figure show no differences between demographic effects on the immediate and delayed memory measures.

The *r* values in Table 5 are rather modest, particularly for memory-related measures. Although they certainly are statistically significant, are the education effects clinically meaningful? Figure 3 shows the percentages of subjects at five education levels that would be classified as "impaired", using as a criterion scoring at least 1 *SD* below the mean of age-corrected factor scores of the WAIS–WMS standardization sample. Clearly, the classification rates of normals with different educational backgrounds vary quite substantially.

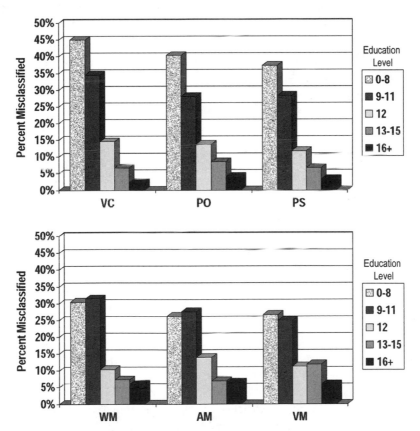

FIGURE 3.   Influence of education level on misclassification rates of age-corrected WAIS-III/WMS-III factor scores in normal adults.
VC=Verbal Comprehension, PO=Perceptual Organization, PS=Processing Speed, WM=Working Memory, AM=Auditory Memory, VM= Visual Memory

For all factors, the likelihood of normal subjects being classified as "impaired" is excessively high (25–45 %) if they have not completed high school. By contrast, almost no subject at the highest education level is similarly classified (2–6 %).

At first glance, with highly educated people the latter finding would not seem to be a problem. These are normals, and almost none are incorrectly classified as "impaired". However, what it means is that highly educated people would need to show a much greater decrement in test performance to be correctly classified as "impaired" using norms that are corrected only for age. That is, when specificity becomes unusually high, a likely consequence is that sensitivity to genuine impairment will drop. This trade off has been demonstrated recently with separate analyses of WAIS–WMS demographically corrected T-scores from the combined clinical sample described above ($N = 174$; Taylor & Heaton, 2001). For all WAIS–WMS factors, adjusting cutoffs to improve specificity beyond about 85 percent (the one SD cutoff used here) traded modest gains in specificity for very substantial losses in sensitivity. For example, by improving the specificity of the Processing Speed factor from 85 to 98 % (using a two *SD* cutoff), estimated impairment rates in the clinical sample drop from 75.4 % to 41.1 %; i.e., a 13 % gain in specificity was traded for a 34 % loss in sensitivity. The data in this study indicate that, for virtually all factor scores of all eight diagnostic samples, the optimal balance between specificity and sensitivity is achieved using a 1 *SD* factor score cutoff to define "impairment".

Perhaps the major point demonstrated by Figure 3 is that specificity (the likelihood of being correctly classified as normal) of factor scores that are only corrected for age varies greatly with education level. This is far from the ideal situation in which specificity is essentially constant within every segment of the normal population.

Sex Effects

Table 6 shows that sex effects on age- and education-corrected WAIS–WMS factor scores are, for the most part, trivial. The largest differences favor women and occur on Processing Speed and the Auditory and Visual Memory factors. However, they translate into specificity differences of only about 5 %. There is not much difference in sex effects on immediate versus delayed memory measures, although females appear to have a somewhat greater advantage on the Alternate Visual Memory factor than on the standard Visual Memory factor. This translates into an arguably nontrivial

TABLE 6 Relationships between Age- and Education-Corrected WAIS-III–WMS-III Factor Z-Scores and Sex[a]

	Proportion of variance explained by sex (η^2)	Male ($N = 503$)	Female ($N = 570$)	Mean difference
Verbal Comprehension Factor	0.01	0.13	−0.11	0.25
Perceptual Organization Factor	0.01	0.09	−0.08	0.17
Processing Speed Factor	0.03	−0.19	0.17	0.36
Working Memory Factor	0.01	0.08	−0.07	0.15
Auditory Memory Factor	0.02	−0.13	0.12	0.25
Auditory Immediate Memory Factor	0.01	−0.11	0.10	0.22
Auditory Delayed Memory Factor	0.02	−0.14	0.13	0.27
Visual Memory Factor	0.01	−0.11	0.10	0.22
Visual Immediate Memory Factor	0.01	−0.10	0.09	0.19
Visual Delayed Memory Factor	0.01	−0.12	0.11	0.23
Alternate Visual Memory Factor	0.04	−0.21	0.19	0.40
Alt. Visual Immediate Memory Factor	0.04	−0.21	0.18	0.39
Alt. Visual Delayed Memory Factor	0.04	−0.20	0.18	0.39

[a]Number of cases for Verbal Comprehension, Perceptual Organization, and Processing Speed are 1075 males and 1237 females.

difference in diagnostic specificity (i.e., 88.4% for females vs. 78.8% for males).

Ethnicity Effects

Table 7 considers ethnicity effects on WAIS–WMS factor scores that are corrected for the three previously considered demographic variables (age, education, and sex). Again, the only ethnicity classifications that are considered here are Caucasian/Anglo (White), African American, and Hispanic. The mean Z-scores for each of these groups are provided in the left side of the table, and η^2 values, on the right, indicate effect sizes for the three ethnicity group pairings. Across all WAIS–WMS factors, the White group scored highest and the African American group the lowest, with the Hispanic group obtaining intermediate scores. Ethnicity effects appear to be reduced for the delayed memory scores compared to the immediate, and for the Alternate compared to the Standard Visual Memory factor.

The effect sizes(η^2) associated with the ethnicity differences in Table 7 appear to be rather modest, accounting for the $\leq 10\%$ of variance in the Z-scores. On the other hand, Figure 4 shows that use of factor scores that are *now* corrected for ethnicity results in major ethnicity group differences in the likelihood of individual subject members being misclassified as impaired. On most factors, African Americans are over three times likelier to be so misclassified than are Whites. Although these differences are somewhat attenuated for the memory factors (especially for Visual Memory), even these show at least a twofold difference in misclassification rates. Clearly, this much ethnicity bias in diagnostic classification rates is not acceptable and requires normative adjustments. As indicated above, this was done by creating age, education, and sex adjustments for each ethnicity group, separately. As expected, with the resulting corrected scores, normal subjects have essentially the same ($\sim 15\%$) likelihood of being misclassified as impaired, regardless of whether they are White, African American, or Hispanic (see Figure 5).

SENSITIVITY OF WAIS–WMS-CORRECTED SCORES TO NEUROPSYCHIATRIC DISORDERS

Table 8 shows the percentages of subjects in the clinical groups who are classified as impaired, using demographically corrected T-scores on

TABLE 7 Mean Z-Scores (Age, Education, and Sex-Corrected) for Three Ethnicity Groups, and Effect Sizes (η^2) for Etnicity Group Comparisons[a]

	White (N = 790)	African American (N = 148)	Hispanic (N = 87)	White vs. Afr. Am. η^2	White vs. Hispanic η^2	Afr. Am. vs. Hispanic η^2
Verbal Comprehension Factor	0.12	−0.57	−0.18	0.06	0.01	0.03
Perceptual Organization Factor	0.14	−0.72	−0.10	0.09	0.01	0.10
Processing Speed Factor	0.10	−0.59	−0.01	0.06	0.00	0.07
Working Memory Factor	0.16	−0.70	−0.25	0.10	0.02	0.04
Auditory Memory Factor	0.12	−0.55	−0.12	0.06	0.00	0.04
Auditory Immediate Memory Factor	0.11	−0.55	−0.08	0.06	0.00	0.05
Auditory Delayed Memory Factor	0.11	−0.51	−0.15	0.05	0.01	0.03
Visual Memory Factor	0.10	−0.47	−0.16	0.04	0.01	0.03
Visual Immediate Memory Factor	0.11	−0.52	−0.17	0.05	0.01	0.03
Visual Delayed Memory Factor	0.08	−0.38	−0.14	0.03	0.00	0.02
Alternate Visual Memory Factor	0.07	−0.41	−0.06	0.03	0.00	0.03
Alt. Visual Immediate Memory Factor	0.07	−0.39	−0.06	0.03	0.00	0.03
Alt. Visual Delayed Memory Factor	0.07	−0.40	−0.05	0.03	0.00	0.03

[a]Sample sizes for Verbal Comprehension, Perceptual Organization, and Processing Speed are White: 1753, African–American: 300, Hispanic: 179.

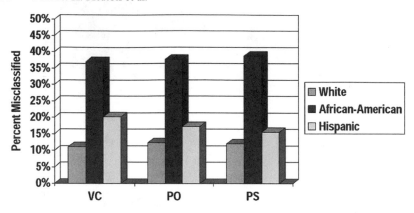

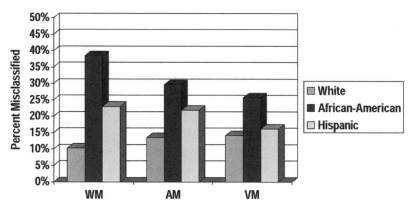

FIGURE 4.   Influence of ethnicity on misclassification rates of age, education, and sex-corrected WAIS-III/WMS-III factor scores in normal adults.
VC=Verbal Comprehension, PO=Perceptual Organization, PS=Processing Speed, WM=Working Memory, AM=Auditory Memory, VM= Visual Memory
© 1997 The Psychological Corporation. All rights reserved.

all standard and supplemental WAIS–WMS factors. This provides truly comparable estimates of sensitivity, because *specificity* of all measures are held constant at about 85%, regardless of the demographic characteristics of the subjects involved.

Using the corrected T-scores in this way, it is apparent that all WAIS–WMS factors show some sensitivity to brain disorders. As expected, however, there is considerable variability in sensitivity estimates across WAIS–WMS measures, and different patterns of impairment are seen across diagnostic groups. Although no firm conclusions are warranted because

TABLE 8 Sensitivity estimates (% impaired) of Demographically Corrected WAIS–WMS Factor Scores with Total Clinical Group and Diagnostic Subgroups[a]

	Total clinical sample (n = 126)	AD (n = 34)	HD (n = 14)	PD (n = 9)	KS (n = 9)	TBI (n = 21)	SZ (n = 39)
Verbal Comprehension	46.0	64.7	42.9	33.3	22.2	57.1	33.3
Perceptual Organization	56.3	79.4	71.4	55.6	22.2	42.9	46.2
Processing Speed	73.6	84.8	100.0	55.6	55.6	90.5	53.8
Working Memory	57.9	79.4	85.7	44.4	11.1	47.6	48.7
Auditory Memory	69.0	97.1	71.4	44.4	100.0	47.6	53.8
Auditory Immediate Memory	69.0	97.1	78.6	44.4	88.9	52.4	51.3
Auditory Delayed Memory	66.7	97.1	71.4	44.4	100.0	42.9	48.7
Visual Memory	82.5	97.1	100.0	66.7	100.0	71.4	69.2
Visual Immediate Memory	78.6	97.1	100.0	55.6	88.9	66.7	64.1
Visual Delayed Memory	80.2	97.1	92.9	55.6	100.0	71.4	66.7
Alternate Visual Memory	83.3	97.1	100.0	55.6	100.0	85.7	66.7
Alt. Visual Immediate Memory	77.0	94.1	92.9	33.3	100.0	85.7	56.4
Alt. Visual Delayed Memory	81.0	97.1	92.9	55.6	100.0	81.0	64.1

[a]AD, Alzheimer's disease; HD, Huntington's disease; PD, Parkinson's disease; KS, Korsakoff's syndrome; TBI, traumatic brain injury; SZ, schizophrenia.

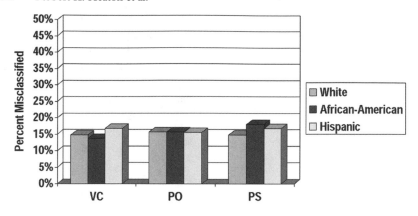

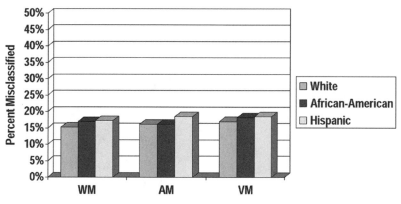

FIGURE 5.   Lack of ethnicity effects on misclassification rates of WAIS-III/WMS-III factor scores with full demographic corrections.
VC=Verbal Comprehension, PO=Perceptual Organization, PS=Processing Speed, WM=Working Memory, AM=Auditory Memory, VM= Visual Memory

of the relatively small *n*s involved (particularly among individual diagnostic groups), some of these differences in sensitivity seem worthy of note. Many of these trends parallel those demonstrated by Hawkins (1998) with standard index scores (i.e., with only age corrections).

Not surprisingly, in view of its component "hold" subtests (Matarazzo, 1972), the Verbal Comprehension factor is generally the least sensitive WAIS/WMS measure to neuropsychiatric disorders. The most notable exception is with Alzheimer's disease (AD), in which reduced performance on this factor probably reflects some breakdown of semantic memory (Butters, Salmon, Heindel, & Granholm, 1988). Also over half of the subjects with traumatic brain injury (TBI) are impaired on this factor, although one wonders whether relatively weak Verbal Comprehension may represent a premorbid characteristic of some subjects with TBI. It should be noted that any clear history of learning disability was listed as an exclusion for TBI patients in this study (The Psychological Corporation, 1997, p. 313).

Although Perceptual Organization and Processing Speed historically have been lumped together within the Wechsler Performance IQ, Table 8 demonstrates that Processing Speed is more often impaired in most neuropsychiatric disorders. Busy clinicians may be particularly interested in the relative sensitivity of the Processing Speed measure because it requires very little time to administer (less than 5 minutes).

The distinction between Working Memory and WMS measures of episodic memory (Auditory and Visual factors) is strikingly apparent in their relative sensitivities to Korsakoff's syndrome (KS). In fact, this group, which is in part defined by its relatively severe impairment of episodic memory, shows *no* impairment of working memory here. As expected, measures of episodic memory also are particularly sensitive to the dementing disorders of AD and Huntington's disease (HD). (Note that the inclusion criteria for the Parkinson's disease (PD) participants in this study did not specify presence of dementia, and in fact restricted the degree of possible cognitive impairment; The Psychological Corporation, 1997, p. 313).

Both the HD and TBI groups showed a pattern of most frequent deficits in Processing Speed and Visual Memory. Although this could reflect relatively greater subcortical involvement in both of these groups, in the case of HD the possibility of upper extremity motor confounds must be considered as well (i.e., upper extremity dyskinesias may be responsible for impaired performances on component tests (especially on Digit Symbol and Visual Reproductions, which require use of a pencil). Arguing against the latter explanation is the fact that the Alternate Visual memory factor does not require upper extremity motor responses, and it shows exactly the same (high) impairment rates in the HD group.

The schizophrenia group demonstrated a rather "flat" profile of impairment on the WAIS–WMS factors, consistent with relatively generalized cognitive dysfunction (Braff et al., 1991). The only slight exceptions might be relative "sparing" of Verbal Comprehension, Perceptual Organization, and Working Memory, all showing less than 50 % impairment rates in this group.

The sensitivity estimates for the standard and alternate Visual Memory measures are equal within the overall clinical group and virtually all of the individual diagnostic groups. The only possible exception is the TBI group, in which three more subjects were impaired on the alternate factor than on the standard one. Clearly, this much difference is not sufficient to justify any conclusions about relative advantages of the two measures.

In view of the heterogeneous nature of the total clinical group, the observed lack of differences between the sensitivities of immediate and delayed memory measures is not surprising. On the other hand, memory storage deficits *would* be expected to differentially affect delayed measures in the AD and KS groups, and there is no apparent evidence of this in the sensitivity figures in Table 8. Such sensitivity figures might not be appropriate for showing differential memory impairments in AD and KS patients, however, because almost all of these patients have at least mild impairment of all memory measures (i.e., impairment rates approach or reach 100 % on all memory measures).

For the purpose of elucidating possible group patterns of memory performance, mean T-scores may be preferable to impairment rates because they are less susceptible to floor effects. Figure 6 shows the patterns of mean memory measures for all six diagnostic subgroups. Panel A reveals relatively equal scores on immediate and delayed memory measures, for the AD group as well as for the HD and PD groups (i.e., for so-called cortical and "subcortical" disorders that might be expected to differ on memory storage abilities). To further investigate the possibility that this is due to floor effects in the AD group (e.g., patients whose very low initial learning precluded identification of tendencies for rapid forgetting), we considered separately those AD patients with at least a 30 T-score on immediate memory measures. Again, no differences between immediate and delayed memory scores were observed.

Panel B of Figure 6 provides the same information for the KS, TBI, and schizophrenia groups. Clearly, the latter two groups show no evidence of excessive forgetting (memory storage problems) on any of the WMS factors. However, the KS group profile does reveal some greater impairment (but less than a 10 T-score difference) on the delayed than on the immediate Auditory and standard Visual Memory measures; no such trend is apparent on the Alternate Visual Memory components. Although these differences may be meaningful, it is unlikely that they are sufficiently robust to be helpful in differential diagnosis. Also, in view of the very small size of this KS group, it is again cautioned that it would be premature to draw any firm conclusions from its results.

Temporal lobe epilepsy (TLE) patients who are postlobectomy also might be expected to evidence memory storage impairments, as well as some material specific impairments depending upon the side of the lesion. Figure 7A shows the mean immediate versus delayed memory T-scores for the two

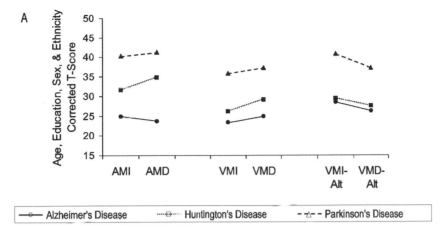

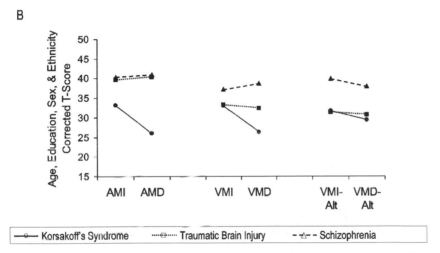

FIGURE 6.   Average demographically corrected T-scores for WAIS-III/WMS-III factor scores of six clinical disorders.

AMI=Auditory Memory Immediate, AMD=Auditory Memory Delayed, VMI=Visual Memory Immediate, VMD=Visual Memory Delayed, VMI-Alt=Visual Memory Immediate-Alternate version, VMD-Alt=Visual Memory Delayed-Alternate version

TLE groups. Neither of these groups had any significant or consistent tendency to perform worse on the delayed memory measures. On the other hand, for both immediate and delayed measures, the left TLE group tended to do worse with auditory than visual memory, whereas the right TLE group evidenced the opposite pattern. This interaction between side of lesion and auditory versus visual memory impairment is more clearly

A

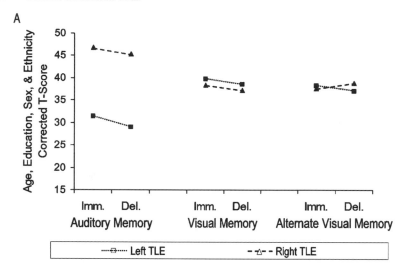

B

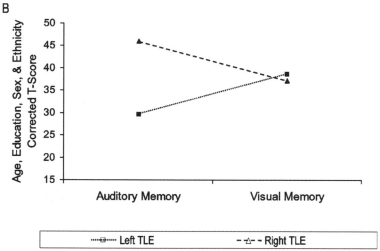

FIGURE 7.   Average demographically corrected T-scores for WMS-III factor scores of epilepsy patients after left (n=15) vs. right (n=12) temporal lobectomy.
AMI=Auditory Memory Immediate, AMD=Auditory Memory Delayed, VMI=Visual Memory Immediate, VMD=Visual Memory Delayed, VMI-Alt=Visual Memory Immediate-Alternate version, VMD-Alt=Visual Memory Delayed-Alternate version
© 1997 The Psychological Corporation. All rights reserved.

demonstrated in Figure 7B, and is confirmed by an analysis of variance (ANOVA) [for Group × Memory Factor Interaction, $F(1, 25) = 20.40$, $p < .001$].

CONCLUSIONS

This presentation of demographic influences on WAIS–WMS performance has focused on two issues of relevance to clinicians, and especially to clinical neuropsychologists. First, we have focused on the six cognitive constructs identified by recent confirmatory factor analyses of the joint WAIS–WMS battery. It is likely that these six factor scores will increasingly be seen as the most useful core data generated by the combined battery, gradually supplanting less precise summary indices (e.g., Verbal and Performance IQs) and subtest scores.

Our second focus has been on the relevance of demographic effects for the development and use of test norms. Particularly when cognitive test scores are used for neurodiagnostic purposes, specificity (the likelihood of correctly classifying a normal person as such) should be as constant as possible across all segments of the normal population. To achieve this goal of equal or constant specificity, it is necessary to adjust test norms for all demographic variables that are found to independently influence test performances of normal adults.

The data from the WAIS–WMS standardization samples indicate that performances on all six cognitive factors were significantly related to education and ethnicity, in addition to age; some (more modest) sex effects were noted as well. These effects have major clinical significance when the WAIS–WMS factor scores are used for neurodiagnostic purposes. That is, when one employs factor scores that are corrected for age alone, as has been standard practice in the past, normal subjects who have lower education levels or are ethnic minorities have substantially increased probabilities of being incorrectly classified as cognitively abnormal or impaired.

It is important to note that these demographic effects are not peculiar to these versions of the WAIS–WMS batteries: Similar findings have been reported for earlier versions of these tests and many other neuropsychological tests (see reviews by Heaton et al., 1996, and Heaton & Marcotte, 2000). To more closely equalize the diagnostic accuracy of cognitive tests across the various segments of the adult population, increasing efforts have been made to develop norms that are adjusted for multiple relevant demographic variables (Diehr, Heaton, Miller, & Grant, 1998; Gladsjo et al., 1999; Heaton, Grant, & Mathews, 1991; Heaton, 1992; Norman et al., 2000).

The large and demographically diverse WAIS–WMS standardization samples make them ideal for the development of norms with the desired, multiple demographic corrections. We have initiated this process for the current presentation, and it is anticipated that The Psychological Corporation has published an expanded version of these norms in its

WAIS–WMS Writer or Scoring Assistant programs. Specifically, the norms will simultaneously correct, as needed, for age, education, sex, and three types of ethnicity (non-Hispanic Caucasian, African American, and Hispanic).

We have proposed a one SD cutoff of demographically corrected WAIS–WMS factor scores (T-scores < 40) to define cognitive impairment. This results in an 85% specificity rate (% of normals correctly called normal) that is constant for the three ethnicity groups, and is not affected by differences in age, education, or sex. Also, because of the co-norming of the WAIS–WMS, T-scores have equivalent meaning across all six cognitive factors. When we applied this criterion of factor score impairment to results of a mixed group of 126 patients who had various neuropsychiatric disorders, the sensitivity estimates ranged from slightly under 50% to approximately 75%. Overall, Verbal Comprehension was the least sensitive factor score, and Processing Speed and Visual Memory were the most sensitive measures. This pattern is identical to that demonstrated by Hawkins (1998) with standard index scores (i.e., with only age corrections).

Sensitivity estimates for the individual neuropsychiatric disorders must be considered quite tentative, in view of the small group sizes ($ns = 9$ to 39). In general, however, the WAIS–WMS findings with these disorders are consistent with previous research using other measures of the same or similar constructs. Virtually all patients with AD were impaired on all measures of episodic memory (both Immediate and Delayed components of Auditory and Visual Memory), and almost all were impaired on Processing Speed and Perceptual Organization as well. All patients with KS evidence similar, marked impairment on testing of episodic memory (both auditory and visual), within the context of generally spared abilities in other cognitive domains; the only exception to the latter is that just over half of the KS patients evidence some impairment of Processing Speed. HD was characterized by universal impairment of Processing Speed and Visual Memory that could not be fully explained on the basis of upper extremity motor confounds. About half of the small group of PD patients were impaired on each of the WAIS–WMS factors, except for Verbal Comprehension.

The TBI group had remarkably consistent impairments of Processing Speed; they also had a high prevalence of Visual Memory impairment, and were less likely to show involvement of other WAIS–WMS factors. Most subjects with schizophrenia evidenced impairments of episodic memory (visual and/or auditory) and Processing Speed, but the pattern of relative strengths and weaknesses was not pronounced in this group.

In the diagnostic groups considered here, there was little evidence of more severe delayed than immediate memory impairments; we found no evidence of consistent memory storage deficits, even in groups that have shown such deficits in previous research (AD and KS; Delis, Massman, Butters, & Salmon, 1991). It is unclear why this is the case, although the groups were small, and at least several of the subjects had such poor immediate memory (learning)scores that it would be difficult to show substantially worse delayed recall. With such patients it may be more helpful to use tests with multiple learning trials, in order to facilitate enough learning to enable meaningful assessment of retention.

The left and right TLE groups also failed to show differences between immediate and delayed memory deficits, despite surgical resections of the hippocampal areas. However, these groups did evidence lateralized, material-specific deficits on the Auditory and Visual Memory factors. Further research would seem warranted to determine the differential sensitivities of these factor scores with focal lesions involving left or right hemisphere memory circuitry.

In conclusion, the findings presented here provide strong, albeit preliminary support for the clinical utility of the WAIS–WMS factor scores. When demographically corrected T-scores were used to ensure relatively high and consistent diagnostic specificity, the scores also showed meaningful patterns of sensitivity to various types of brain disorders. Clearly, however, much more research with these and other disorders is needed to further establish the validity of the WAIS–WMS factor scores in multiple clinical applications.

REFERENCES

Axelrod, B. N., & Goldman, R. S. (1996). Use of demographic corrections in neuropsychological interpretation: How standard are standard scores? *The Clinical Neuropsychologist, 10(2)*, 159–162.

Braff, D. L., Heaton, R., Kuck, J., Cullum, M., Moranville, J., Grant, I., & Zisook, S. (1991). The generalized pattern of neuropsychological deficits in outpatients with chronic schizophrenia with heterogeneous Wisconsin Card Sorting Test results. *Archives of General Psychiatry, 48*, 891–898.

Butters, N., Salmon, D. P., Heindel, W., & Granholm, E. (1988). Episodic, semantic and procedural memory: Some comparisons of Alzheimer and Huntington disease patients. In R. D. Terry (Ed.), *Aging and the brain*. New York: Raven Press.

Delis, D. C., Massman, P. J., Butters, N., & Salmon, D. P. (1991). Profiles of demented and amnesic patients on the California Verbal Learning Test: Implications for the assessment of memory disorders. *Psychological Assessment, 3(1)*, 19–26.

Diehr, M. C., Heaton, R. K., Miller, S. W., & Grant, I. (1998). The Paced Auditory Serial Addition Task (PASAT): Norms for age, education and ethnicity. *Assessment, 5*, 375–387.

Evans, J. D., Miller, S. W., Byrd, D. A., & Heaton, R. K. (2000). Cross cultural applications of the Halstead-Reitan batteries. In E. Fletcher-Janzen, T. L. Strickland, & C. R. Reynolds (Eds.), *The handbook of cultural neuropsychology* (pp. 287–303). New York: Plenum.

210   Robert K. Heaton et al.

Gladsjo, J. A., Schuman, C. C., Evans, J. D., Peavy, G. M., Miller, S. W., & Heaton, R. K. (1999). Norms for letter and category fluency: Demographic corrections for age, education and ethnicity. *Assessment, 6*, 147–160.

Hawkins, K. A. (1998). Indicators of brain dysfunction derived from graphic representations of the WAIS-III/WMS-III teaching manual samples: A preliminary approach to clinical utility. *The Clinical Neuropsychologist, 12*, 535–551.

Hawkins, K., & Tulsky, D. S. (2003). WAIS-III-WMS-III Discrepancy analysis: 6 factor model index discrepancy base rates, implications, and a preliminary consideration of utility. In D. S. Tulsky, D. H. Saklofske, G. J., Chelune, R. K. Heaton, R. J. Ivnik, R. Bornstein, A. Prifitera, & M. Ledbetter. (Eds.). *Clinical Interpretation of the WAIS-III and WMS-III.* San Diego: Academic Press.

Heaton, R. K. (1992). *Comprehensive norms for an expanded Halstead-Reitan Battery: A Supplement for the Wechsler Adult Intelligence Scale-Revised.* Odessa, FL: Psychological Assessment Resources.

Heaton, R. K., Grant, I., & Matthews, C. G. (1991). *Comprehensive norms for an expanded Halstead-Reitan Battery: Demographic Corrections, Research Findings, and Clinical Applications.* Odessa, FL: Psychological Assessment Resources.

Heaton, R. K., & Marcotte, T. D. (2000). Clinical and neuropsychological tests and assessment techniques. In F. Boller, J. Grafman, & G. Rizzolatti (Eds.). *Handbook of Neuropsychology.* Amsterdam: Elsevier Science.

Heaton, R. K., Matthews, C. G., Grant, I., & Avitable, N. (1996). Demographic corrections with comprehensive norms: An overzealous attempt, or a good start? *Journal of Clinical and Experimental Neuropsychology, 18*, 3, 449–458.

Matarazzo, J. D. (1972). *Wechsler's Measurement and Appraisal of Adult Intelligence (5th ed.).* Baltimore: William & Wilkins.

Matarazzo, J. D., & Herman, D. O. (1984). Relationship of education and IQ in the WAIS-R standardization sample. *Journal of Consulting and Clinical psychology, 52*, 631–634.

Norman, M. A., Evans, J. D., Miller, S. W., & Heaton, R. K. (2000). Demographically corrected norms for the California Verbal Learning Test. *Journal of Clinical and Experimental Neuropsychology, 22*, 80–93.

The Psychological Corporation. (1997). *WAIS-III–WMS III technical manual.* San Antonio, TX: Author.

Reynolds, C. R., Chastain, R. L., Kaufman, A. S., & McLean, J. E. (1987). Demographic characteristics and IQ among adults: Analysis of the WAIS-R standardization sample as a function of the stratification variables. *Journal of School Psychology, 25*, 323–342.

Royston, P., & Altman, D. G. (1994). Regression using fractional polynomials of continuous covariates: Parsimonious parametric modelling. *Applied Statistics, 43*, 429–467.

Taylor, M. J., & Heaton, R. K. (2001). Sensitivity and specificity of WAIS-III/WMS III demographically corrected factor scores in neuropsychological assessment. *Journal of the International Neuropsychological Society.*

Tulsky, D.S., Ivnik, R.J., Price, L.R., & Wilkins, C. (2003). Assessment of cognitive functioning with the WAIS-III and WMS-III: Development of a 6-Factor model. In D.S. Tulsky, D.H. Saklofske, G.J. Chelune, R.K. Heaton, R.J. Ivnik, R. Bornstein, A. Prifitera, & M. Ledbetter. (Eds.). *Clinical Interpretation of the WAIS-III and WMS-III.* (pp. 145–177) San Diego: Academic Press.

Tulsky, D.S., & Price, L.R. (In Press). *The Joint WAIS-III and WMS-III Factor Structure: Development and Cross-Validation of a 6-factor model of Cognitive Functioning.* Psychological Assessment.

CHAPTER 6

WAIS-III WMS-III Discrepancy Analysis: Six-Factor Model Index Discrepancy Base Rates, Implications, and a Preliminary Consideration of Utility

Keith A. Hawkins

Yale University School of Medicine

and

David S. Tulsky

Kessler Medical Rehabilitation Research & Education Corporation
Universtiy of Medicine and Dentistry of New Jersey

INTRODUCTION

Although the direct comparison of test scores against norms constitutes the principal form of neuropsychological inference, the limitations of this approach in certain circumstances has led to the development of complementary strategies. The perception that average (or even higher) scores can represent a decline in some individuals, and that low scores do not always reflect impairment in others, has fostered the development of *individual comparison standards* approaches (Crawford, 1996), whereby clinicians tailor their expectations on the basis of the examinee's demographics, or by using current test scores to establish expectations for other scores in the same examination. This latter approach, involving an evaluation of the differences between scores, is called discrepancy analysis (DA). Score comparisons yield hypotheses about relative strengths and weaknesses, which in turn allow for inferences regarding brain integrity.

Prior to the development of the WAIS-III–WMS-III battery, DA with the Wechsler tests was largely restricted to the examination of differentials between verbal and performance IQ scores, or the comparison of summary intellectual and memory scores. The introduction of new WAIS-III and WMS-III indexes makes numerous additional comparisons possible. In addition, the factor analytic source of the index structure, and the co-norming of the tests, places DA with the WAIS-III WMS-III on a firmer psychometric footing.

This chapter begins with consideration of the logic of DA, including the difference between the statistical significance of a difference score and its base rate frequency. Ways in which the discrepancy base rate data provided in this chapter differ from those provided by The Psychological Corporation are detailed, and clinically informative trends apparent within these are explored. With the assistance of the *WAIS-III WMS-III Technical Manual* clinical samples (The Psychological Corporation, 1997), index pairings that are likely to be especially informative are identified. Issues pertaining to the validity of DA are then addressed.

UNDERSTANDING DIFFERENCE SCORES: THE LOGIC OF DISCREPANCY ANALYSIS

Clinical Meaning versus Statistical Significance

Fundamental to DA is an appreciation of the difference between statistical and clinical significance. The difference between two scores may be statistically significantly but clinically meaningless because the discrepancy is common in the normal population. A statistically significant difference is simply one that it is significantly different from zero,[1] indicating that there is a high probability that it would be consistently found with retesting. The superiority of one score over the other is probably real (rather than chance) and represents a reliable characterization of the person's relative strengths and weakness. In contrast, clinical significance depends upon the frequency (base rate) of the difference in the normal population (Matarazzo & Herman, 1984). Comparing the difference score against its frequency in the standardization sample tells us how unusual it is. The greater the rarity, the

---

[1]Actually a simplification, for reasons explored later. More correctly, a statistically significant discrepancy is one that reliably differs from the expected difference between scores.

greater the likelihood of abnormality. A related consideration is whether the difference commonly occurs in clinical populations of interest: a difference score becomes interesting if it occurs rarely in the normal population but frequently in a clinical group that the person might possibly belong to.

Psychometric Foundations

Spearman (Spearman, 1904) argued that most cognitive abilities should be approximately equal and reflect a general cognitive factor or g. In contrast, E. L. Thorndike, Lay, and Dean (1909) argued that "scatter" or ability differences (e.g., subtest-to-subtest or index-to-index) are the norm in healthy individuals. To this day compelling arguments are made for or against g, and analyses of the WAIS-III–WMS-III standardization data support both the existence of several factors and a general ability factor. In recognition of the moderate to high degree of intercorrelation among the WAIS-III subtests, the exploratory factor analyses undertaken with the standardization data during the development process were not restricted to orthogonal rotation (The Psychological Corporation, 1997), and the resulting factors do correlate.[2]

In fact, if the indexes derived from these analyses did not correlate at least moderately, pairwise comparisons as a source of neuropsychological inference would make little sense. The complete absence of a relationship across ability domains would not preclude the description of an individual's relative strengths and weaknesses, but it would preclude using difference scores to infer that the abilities represented by the lower score had failed to develop normally or, later, had been undermined by injury or neuropathological process. However, because the indexes correlate (see Table 1), a score on one can be used to set an expectation for performance on another, subject to various caveats and limitations explored in this chapter.

Descriptive versus Inferential Uses of Discrepancy Data

Although the perspective adopted within this chapter primarily pertains to neuropsychological inference—meaning that the focus is upon DA as a method of drawing inferences about brain integrity—we recognize that discrepancy data may be used in other ways. At the descriptive level,

---

[2]Factor analysis does not alter the existing correlations among test scores—it simply facilitates interpretation.

TABLE 1   WAIS-III WMS-III Index Intercorrelations (Six Factor Model with Alternative Visual Memory Indexes)

	Verbal Comprehension	Perceptual Organization	Processing Speed	WMS-III Working Memory	Auditory Memory	Visual Memory	Visual Memory (Original)
Perceptual Organization	.66*						
Processing Speed	.52*	.58*					
WMS-III Working Memory	.51	.62	.54				
Auditory Memory	.57	.47	.43	.42			
Visual Memory	.46	.54	.50	.45	.57		
Visual Memory (Original)	.33	.35	.38	.31	.44	.76	
Full-Scale IQ	.90*	.86*	.68*	.68	.60	.57	.40
General Memory Index	.55	.49	.48	.45	.85	.74	.76

*Correlation coefficient within the WAIS-III 2450-subject standardization sample. All other correlation coefficients are within the WMS-III weighted 1250 standardization sample.

DA may simply function as an economical way of summarizing the relative strengths and weakness of the individual. Knowledge of these will facilitate an understanding of the examinee's cognitive strengths and vulnerabilities, facilitate educational and vocational planning, and inform rehabilitation planning in relevant circumstances. These and similar uses may be entirely free of inferences about the brain or psychiatric status of the patient.

Clinicians employing DA to draw inferences about brain integrity should recognize that sound clinical practice calls for resistance to any premature pull to pathological inference based upon the presence of notable discrepancies between scores. High index scores should not be automatically viewed as reflecting intact (unaffected) abilities, and lesser scores should not be presumed to reflect impairment (implying loss or decline due to disease process or injury). An Index score can be an Index profile high point yet still represent a decline from prior levels, and low points are not inevitably the product of pathology. Naturally, the likelihood of a pathological cause increases as discrepancies grow; clinicians must then remain mindful that a discrepancy may reflect neurodevelopmental rather than more recent insults. Appropriate use of DA calls for the generation of hypotheses that are either corroborated or refuted by other results, background information, behavioral observations, or additional evaluation.

To recap, the existence of discrete ability factors indicates that within-individual ability discrepancies naturally occur; virtually all normal individuals display relative strengths and weaknesses. The real issue is *the rarity of reliable differences*, and whether a given discrepancy is commonly associated with pathology (or, more particularly, a specific condition of interest).

DISCREPANCY DATA PROVIDED IN THIS CHAPTER

WAIS-III WMS-III Discrepancy Data Provided with the Tests

Considerable WAIS-III and WMS-III discrepancy base-rate data are already available, both via the manuals for these tests and scoring software. Table B.2 in Wechsler (1997a) provides cumulative percentages for differences between WAIS-III Index and IQ scores generated from the total standardization sample, and data for the same comparisons broken down by

IQ score ranges are provided in Appendix D of the *WAIS-III WMS-III Technical Manual* (The Psychological Corporation, 1997). WMS-III Primary Index discrepancy base rates are provided in Table F.2 of Wechsler (1997b, p. 206).

The *WAIS-III WMS-III Technical Manual* provides data for two separate ways of determining the rarity of WAIS-III–WMS-III (intellectual–memory) discrepancies: the simple differences method and the predicted differences method. The *simple differences* method provides base rates for unidirectional discrepancies (i.e., the difference score generated by subtracting the memory score from the intellectual score) between the intelligence quotients (FSIQ, VIQ, PIQ) and the WMS Primary Indexes. These base rates, expressed as cumulative percentages, are derived from the total WMS-III sample and are accessed via Tables C.4 (for FSIQ—Memory Index), C.5 (VIQ—Memory Index), and C.6 (PIQ—Memory Index) within Appendix C of the technical manual (The Psychological Corporation, 1997).

The *predicted differences* method involves the statistical prediction of memory scores based upon the relationship, within the standardization sample, of IQ and WMS-III Index scores. Via Tables B.1 (for predictions based upon FSIQ), B.2 (VIQ), and B.3 (PIQ), the examiner generates predicted memory Index scores. The actually obtained memory Index scores are subtracted from these predicted scores (to determine how far short they fall), and, after checking for statistical significance (Tables B.4, B.5, and B.6), the resulting discrepancies are checked against cumulative percentages of differences between predicted and obtained WMS-III Index scores for data generated by predictions based upon FSIQ (Table B.7), VIQ (B.8), or PIQ (B.9). Tables B.1 through B.9 are in Appendix B of the technical manual (The Psychological Corporation, 1997, pp. 264–273).

Generating Six-Factor Model Index Score Discrepancy Base-Rates

This chapter centers on discrepancy data generated for indexes derived from the six factor model, in keeping with the overall focus of this book. Three are from the WAIS-III: Verbal Comprehension Index (VCI), Perceptual Organization Index (POI), and Processing Speed Index (PSI). The Working Memory Index (WMI) and Auditory Memory Index are from the WMS-III, along with two Visual Memory indexes: one a new combination consisting of Visual Reproductions I and II and Family Pictures I and II;

the other, a combination of the WMS-III original primary visual subtests, Faces I and II and Family Pictures I and II[3] (see Tulsky, Ivnik, Price, & Wilkins, Chapter 4, this volume). Both visual indexes are new in that they combine immediate and delayed recall data into single composites. However, for clarity in distinguishing between the two, we label the "new" combination (which brings Visual Reproductions back into the mainstream) as the Visual Memory Index, and the other as the Visual Memory (Original). Note that the Auditory Memory Index also consists of both immediate and delayed recall data, since it combines Logical Memory I and II with Verbal Paired Associates I and II.

WAIS-III index discrepancy data were generated with the WAIS-III (N=2,450) standardization data set. All WAIS-III–WMS-III, and within WMS-III, data were generated from the weighted WMS-III (N=1,250) data set. The actual generation of discrepancy base rates is a simple process: within the applicable standardization sample, scores for one index are subtracted from another. To keep the resulting frequency data concise, we present discrepancy values only for selected percentile rankings (Tables 6 to 15, end of chapter).

How Do These Base Rate Differ from Those Already Available?

For several six factor model contrasts discrepancy data have not previously been available. Base rate data for comparisons between the WMS-III Working Memory Index and any of the WAIS-III or WMS-III indexes representing the six-factor approach have not, hitherto, existed. The substitution of new Auditory and Visual Memory Indexes for all prior WMS-III primary index scores generates an entirely new set of within-WMS-III and WAIS-III–WMS-III index pairings. The development of demographically adjusted scores (Heaton et al., Chapter 5, this volume) for the six-factor model also calls for new discrepancy data. Finally, the base-rate data provided in this chapter are also novel in that all stem from unidirectional comparisons.

---

[3]We present discrepancy data for this second visual memory index since many clinicians will continue to administer the applicable subtests and may wish to compare the resulting composite score against others.

Unidirectional versus Bidirectional
Discrepancy Base Rates

Existing within-WAIS-III and within-WMS-III, discrepancy data are *bi-directional*, that is, apply regardless of which score is superior. For VCI-POI comparisons, for example, a cumulative percentage listed for a given difference (say 15 points) is listed as 23.1 in Table B.2 of (Wechsler, 1997a), meaning that a difference of this size (or greater) is seen in 23.1% of the standardization sample for differences in either direction, that is VCI > POI plus POI > VCI. However, clinical hypotheses are typically unidirectional. In the case of a patient suspected of suffering a loss of verbal capability, the examiner may wish to compare the *superiority* of the patient's POI (over VCI) against unidirectional base rates, that is, frequency data relevant just to a superiority of POI over VCI. Uncorrected bidirectional data overestimate unidirectional frequency roughly twofold (Tulsky, Rolfhus, & Zhu, 2000). A POI superiority over VCI of 15+ points is seen in no more than 11.2% of standardization cases, rather than in the 23.1% implied by the (bidirectional) data provided in Table B.2.

Tulsky et al. (2000) found that simply halving the frequency provided in Table B.2 of Wechsler (1997a) generally suffices when evaluating a within WAIS-III unidirectional clinical hypothesis, but generated unidirectional tables for clinical reference nonetheless. These tables eliminate the risk of clinicians forgetting to half the frequencies provided in Table B.2 when assessing a unidirectional hypothesis.

The unidirectional data provided by Tulsky et al. (2000) are based upon discrepancy distributions within the entire standardization sample. There is, however, a pressing reason for generating unidirectional base rates *stratified by IQ level*. Halving bidirectional frequencies works for discrepancies generated with the total sample, because the distributions of discrepancy scores for various IQ or Index pairings are evenly distributed around the mean—the distributions approximate symmetrical bell curves. We know, though, that within the WAIS-R standardization sample VIQ-PIQ discrepancy asymmetries were present at the extremes of the IQ spectrum (Matarazzo & Herman, 1985), and similar effects within the distributions of WAIS-III Index discrepancies should be expected. The generation of unidirectional data broken down by FSIQ ranges allows for the simultaneous exploration of the effects of ability level on discrepancy *magnitude* (size) and *direction* (resulting from any asymmetries present in the standardization data). By discrepancy direction, we mean any tendency for one score to be predominately superior to the other within segments of the standardization sample. If, for example, higher IQ subjects tend to have higher VCI than POI scores, applying a single set of bidirectional base rates to the difference scores of high-IQ subjects will result in underestimation of frequency when VCI is the higher score, and overestimation when POI is the higher score. A VCI superiority may be judged to be more unusual than it actually is, and, conversely, a superior POI maybe considered more commonplace than it actually is. We elaborate on this later.

To recap this section, Tulsky et al. (2000) provide unidirectional **WAIS-III** discrepancy frequency data, but these do not control for the effects of IQ level. The frequency data within the *WAIS-III WMS-III Technical Manual* provide control over the effect of IQ level on overall discrepancy magnitudes, but, being bidirectional, fail to control for any effects of IQ level on discrepancy direction. Within this chapter, FSIQ stratified unidirectional base rate data are provided for contrasts between the VCI, POI, and PSI.

Existing frequency data for **WMS-III** discrepancies are bidirectional and based upon total sample data, and so fail to account for the effects of ability level on either discrepancy size or direction. This chapter provides unidirectional discrepancy data, stratified by FSIQ, for contrasts of the new (six-factor model) memory index scores. These data are stratified by FSIQ level and are unidirectional to control for both size and direction effects.

WAIS-III–WMS-III (across test) discrepancy data to date have involved only IQ (rather than WAIS-III Index) data (The Psychological Corporation, 1997; Hawkins & Tulsky, 2001). We complement these data by generating unidirectional base rates for various across-test index contrasts selected on the basis of their probable clinical utility.

UNDERSTANDING DISCREPANCY BASE RATES: CLINICALLY INFORMATIVE TRENDS

Several clinically informative trends emerge from the standardization base rate data.

The Rarity of a Discrepancy Varies across Comparison Pairs

Although it would be clinically convenient if a "one-size-fits-all" rule of thumb applied when assessing discrepancy rarity, the rarity of a given discrepancy (say, 15 points) actually varies considerably depending upon which indexes are compared. The frequency of a discrepancy of any particular size varies in proportion to the correlation between the two indexes in question.

Generally, larger natural discrepancies are seen between indexes yielding small correlation coefficients. Conversely, highly correlated variables yield smaller discrepancies. This relationship is explored within Table 2, where, for example, we note that VCI and POI correlate .66, whereas VCI and the Visual Memory Index consisting of the original WMS-III combination (Family Pictures and Faces) correlate at .31. The stronger VCI–POI correlation results in less spread in the distribution of discrepancy scores (standard deviation = 12.4, compared to 17.5 for the VCI–Visual Memory distribution), and, correspondingly, in lower values at key percentile rankings. A 12-point superiority of VCI over POI exceeds that seen in 85% of standardization cases, whereas an 18-point superiority of VCI over Visual Memory (Original) is required to attain the same degree of infrequency.

Table 2 shows that to be unusual, a discrepancy between weakly correlated index scores must be larger than one between more strongly related variables. As correlations decrease (left to right in Table 2), the standard deviations of the distributions of difference scores increase, and larger discrepancies become more common. The relationship between strength of correlation and distribution of discrepancy scores is also illustrated in Figure 1, which shows that the more moderately correlated set of two sets of index pairs generate a distribution curve with considerably more kurtosis than that observed in the distribution of the less correlated pair. In turn, the discrepancy distribution of the less correlated set is flatter and features more extreme scores.

Discrepancies Vary in Size across Intellectual Levels

Larger discrepancies might be expected at higher ability levels simply because higher scores create more latitude for their emergence. On the other hand, one might imagine that many subjects fall into the lower strata precisely because they have performed especially poorly on one major index or another.

In fact, neither FSIQ nor general memory capacity (i.e., GMI) correlate strongly with discrepancy magnitude. The coefficients are very small (averaging considerably less than .2), and, accordingly, discrepancy size varies only modestly across ability levels for most index pairs. Table 3 contrasts the discrepancy standard deviations for low and high FSIQ groups for numerous index contrasts. As a rule of thumb, weakly correlated indexes tend to show

TABLE 2 Relationship between Index Correlation and Normal Discrepancy Magnitude[a, b]

	VCI – POI	POI – WMI	POI – PSI	VCI – Aud Mem	Aud Mem – Vis Mem	WMI – PSI	PCI – Vis Mem	VCI – PSI	VCI – WMI	POI – Aud Mem	VCI – Vis Mem	WMI – Vis Mem	Aud Mem – Vis Mem (Orig)	WMI – Aud Mem	POI – Vis Mem (Orig)	VCI – Vis Mem (Orig)	WMI – Vis Mem (Orig)
Correlation	.66	.62	.58	.57	.57	.54	.54	.52	.51	.47	.46	.45	.44	.42	.35	.33	.31
Discrepancy standard deviation	12.4	12.8	13.8	13.9	14.1	14.1	14.0	14.7	14.6	15.4	15.5	15.6	16.1	16.2	16.8	17.2	17.5
85th percentile discrepancy	12	12	14	15	14	15	14	15	16	16	16	16	17	17	17	18	18

[a] This table illustrates the relationship between the correlation between a given index pair and the size of the discrepancies observed between scores on these indexes in the total standardization sample. As the correlations decrease (left to right) the standard deviations of the distributions of normal discrepancies increase, reflected in a parallel increase in 85th percentile values in the standardization sample distribution. *Data:* Correlational and discrepancy data involving a WMS-III Index (WMI, Aud Mem, Vis Mem (Orig), Vis Mem) are derived from the WMS-III weighted 1250 sample. All other data are derived from the WAIS-III 2450 sample. The 85th percentile discrepancy values are for undirectional data generated by the subtraction of the second Index score from the first. For example, VCI–POI means VCI minus POI.

[b] *Variables:* VCI, Verbal Comprehension Index; POI, Perceptual Organization Index; PSI, Processing Speed Index; WMI, WMS-III Working Memory; Aud Mem, Auditory Memory Index (composite Logical Memory I & II and Paired Associates I & II); Vis Mem, Visual Memory Index (composite Family Pictures I & II and Visual Reproductions I & II); Vis Mem (Orig) = Visual Memory WMS-III Original (composite Family Pictures I & II and Faces I & II).

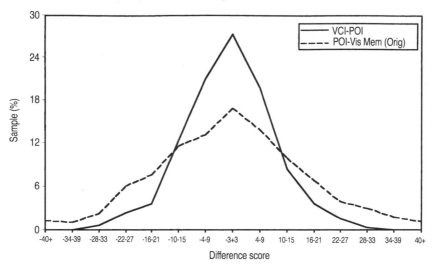

FIGURE 1. Discrepancy distributions vary across pairings: a comparison of a moderately correlated (VCI–POI, .66) and modestly correlated (POI-Visual Memory Original, .35) index pairings. VCI, Verbal Comprehension Index; POI, Perceptual Organization Index.

large discrepancies across the IQ range, with little change in magnitude from low to high IQ. More strongly correlated indexes, especially when one (or each) of the pair correlates strongly with FSIQ (e.g., within-WAIS-III contrasts), show a more pronounced effect of IQ level. The discrepancies of these pairs are smaller at lower IQ levels, but they grow to a proportionately greater extent with rising FSIQ.

Figure 2, a bar histogram, contrasts VCI–POI discrepancy distributions for the low (< 80) and high (> 119) FSIQ segments of the standardization sample, and Figure 3 contrasts the POI–Visual Memory Index distributions for slightly less extreme IQ groups. As can be seen, the low- and high-ability distributions within each index contrast are not noticeably different in breadth, particularly in the POI–Visual Memory case. However, the distributions of lower ability groups tend to show greater kurtosis, and, conversely, a greater proportion of higher ability subjects display extreme discrepancies (just as Matarazzo & Herman, 1985, reported for WAIS-R VIQ–PIQ discrepancies). Table 3 and Figures 2 and 3 therefore could be considered to support either the argument that discrepancies vary surprisingly little in size across the ability levels, or that larger discrepancies are to be expected with rising ability level, depending upon which index pairs, or discrepancy distribution features, one chooses to emphasize.

TABLE 3 IQ Level and Normal Discrepancy Magnitude: Comparisons of Standard Deviations for Low (FSIQ < 85) and High (FSIQ > 115) Standardization Sample Groups[a]

	VCI – POI	VCI – PSI	VCI – WMI	VCI – Aud Mem	VCI – Vis Mem	VCI – Vis Mem (Orig)	POI – PSI	POI – WMI	POI – Aud Mem	POI – Vis Mem	POI – Vis Mem (Orig)	WMI – PSI	WMI – Aud Mem	WMI – Vis Mem	WMI – Vis Mem (Orig)	Aud Mem – Vis Mem	Aud Mem – Vis Mem (Orig)
Discrepancy standard deviation FSIQ < 85 group	9.9	10.7	12.1	11.9	13.5	14.5	9.7	11.0	14.7	13.3	15.4	12.2	15.3	14.6	16.0	12.9	14.1
Discrepancy standard deviation FSIQ > 115 group	14.0	16.0	15.8	14.5	15.7	16.6	14.9	13.1	15.7	14.2	16.6	15.4	16.4	16.1	18.0	15.4	16.5

[a]This table illustrates the relationship between FSIQ level and discrepancy size (reflected in the standard deviations of discrepancy scores) via a comparison of the approximately lowest 15% and highest 15% of the standardization sample. Discrepancy data involving a WMS-III Index (WMI, Aud Mem, Vis Mem (Orig), Vis Mem) are derived from the WMS-III weighted 1250 sample. All other data are derived from the WAIS-III 2450 sample. *Variables:* VCI, Verbal Comprehension Index; POI, Perceptual Organization Index; PSI, Processing Speed Index; WMI, WMS-III Working Memory; Aud Mem, Auditory Memory Index (composite Logical Memory I & II and Paired Associates I & II); Vis Mem, Visual Memory Index (composite Family Pictures I & II and Visual Reproductions I & II); Vis Mem (Orig), Visual Memory WMS-III Original (composite Family Pictures I & II and Faces I & II).

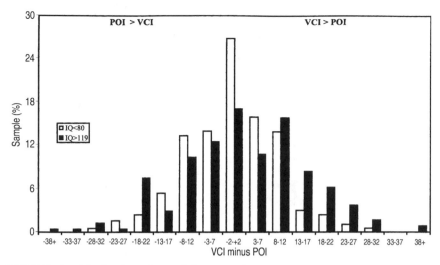

FIGURE 2. Distributions for Verbal Comprehension Index (VCI) minus Perceptual Organization Index (POI) discrepancies for two ability groups: Full–Scale IQ (FSIQ) < 80 and FSIQ 120+.

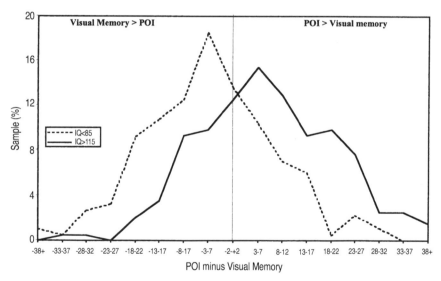

FIGURE 3. Distributions for Perceptual Organization Index (POI) minus Visual Memory discrepancies for two ability groups: Full–Scale IQ (FSIQ) < 85, and FSIQ 116+.

Although similar in breadth, the curves of the low and high-IQ groups in Figure 3 overlap only partially. This illustrates an important feature of discrepancy base rates that we now turn to.

The Direction of Discrepancies Varies with Intelligence Level

Although the effect of IQ on discrepancy magnitude is typically modest, IQ level can exert a profound effect on discrepancy direction. *Direction of discrepancy* refers to the tendency of one index to exceed the other at one end of the ability spectrum, with the situation reversed at the other end. Discrepancy direction is what clinicians ponder when wondering whether high-IQ subjects normally have higher VCI than POI scores, or whether examinees with lower levels of education, or IQ, are likely to do better on the POI.

Factors That Impact Discrepancy Direction

Direction effects are especially prominent among intellectual index–memory index discrepancy base rates, with FSIQ–General Memory Index contrasts providing a striking example. At lower intelligence levels, memory scores typically exceed IQ. At higher IQ levels, the converse is true. Whereas 86.6% of cases with an IQ higher than 119 display higher FSIQ than GMI scores, just 16.1% of IQ < 80 do so. Only 1% of subjects with an IQ below 80, and just 4.5% of IQ 80–89, display an IQ superiority of 15 points or more, whereas over 33% of those with IQ 120+ exhibit such a margin (Hawkins & Tulsky, 2001).

What causes this extreme shift in dominance of one score over the other? Two factors are responsible. First, intellectual and memory scores correlate only moderately within the standardization sample (FSIQ–GMI $r = .60$; The Psychological Corporation, 1997), and second, in the context of this limited relationship, a large directionality effect is guaranteed when the sample is stratified on the basis of one of the contrasted scores (i.e., FSIQ).

To understand the relationship of variable correlation to discrepancy direction, consider a situation where the variables don't correlate at all ($r = 0$). In this case, the best prediction of the mean of a second score (e.g., memory), given knowledge of the first (e.g., IQ), is 100, no matter how bright (or dull) the sample is. A sample with a mean IQ of 125 will show very large IQ–memory discrepancies (averaging 25 points or so), and a group with a mean IQ of 75 will show a similarly large discrepancy but in the opposite direction, with memory considerably higher. The IQ–memory discrepancy magnitude and directionality displayed within the standardization data should represent an intermediate position between this example (no correlation) and the situation that would emerge if IQ and memory scores correlated perfectly (in which case IQ minus GMI in normal subjects would always equal 0, and any discrepancy would be abnormal). While this latter situation is impossible, it is conceptually helpful.

Put in other words, when two indexes don't correlate perfectly you get a regression to the mean type of effect—that is, if someone has a higher than average score on one index, chances are that the second score will be lower as there is more room beneath the first score than above it.[4] If the IQ is 115, one standard deviation above the mean, it follows that 84% of all possible scores on any contrasted index (such as the GMI) are lower, and so chances are that any contrasted score will fall below 115. Conversely, if the first score is lower than average, chances are the second (contrasted) score will be higher.

The second part of the explanation—that a directionality effect is guaranteed by the act of stratifying on the basis of one of the contrasted scores (IQ)—is interwoven with the first (the modest correlation of the indexes). When IQ is one of the contrasted scores, the stratification of discrepancy base rates on the basis of FSIQ means that the IQ score is constrained, i.e., must fall within a restricted range (the applicable IQ stratum), whereas the comparison score (GMI in our example) is free to vary. If the IQ is over 120, and the IQ—GMI discrepancy is compared against IQ-stratified base rates, the IQ score, *ipso facto*, has to be 120 or higher. The GMI score, however, can fall anywhere. Given the moderate correlation between IQ and GMI, it is likely to fall some distance below the IQ score.

Less Extreme Causes of Directionality

We have stressed that direction effects are guaranteed when one of the contrasted scores (e.g., IQ) also serves as a grouping (stratifying) variable in the generation of discrepancy base rates. However, similar directionality effects emerge from intellectual–memory index comparisons when the intellectual variable is not FSIQ. Only 2% of the standardization subsample with FSIQ < 80 feature a superiority of VCI over Auditory Memory of 15

---

[4]The tendency of extreme scores to regress due to error variance explains only to a minor extent the tendency for contrasted scores to be lower than a high predictor score, or to be higher than a low predictor score. Error variance is not primarily responsible for the modest correlation between the indexes. Although regression to the mean commonly refers to movement towards the mean of a score upon retesting (due to the role of chance/error factors in generating the initial extreme value), it is legitimate to use the phrase in the more general manner employed here.

points or more. In contrast, 34 % of FSIQ 120+ cases feature a VCI superiority of 15+ (and over 20 % show discrepancies of 20+ points). The flip side of this picture is a superiority of memory scores at lower IQ levels: over 25 % of the IQ < 80 group show a Auditory Memory Index superiority of 15+ points. The explanation is that the VCI correlates with the stratifying variable, FSIQ, to a far greater extent than does the Auditory Memory Index.

In any pairing, the index that correlates to the greater extent with general ability tends to be the superior score at higher ability levels and the inferior score at lower ability levels. This applies even when neither of the indexes is from the WAIS-III. As is evident in Table 4, paired indexes differing widely in how strongly they correlate with FSIQ show strong discrepancy direction effects, while those that correlate to a similar degree with FSIQ show a minimal direction effect.

Table 4 is more easily interpreted when considered conjointly with Figure 3. The indexes represented in Figure 3, POI and Visual Memory, correlate to different degrees with FSIQ (Table 4), and, accordingly, there is a shift in the distribution of discrepancy scores between low- and high-IQ groups (Figure 3). The mean unidirectional discrepancy for the low-IQ group is a negative value (Table 4; and the curve is shifted to the left, Figure 3), whereas the mean for the high-IQ group is positive and reflected in the shift to the right of the curve. A clear majority of high-IQ cases feature a superiority of POI over visual memory, whereas only a minority of low-IQ cases do so.

Do Direction Effects Matter?

Ability-related intellectual–memory discrepancy direction effects are trivial for the considerable portion of the population whose IQs fall around the mean. Additionally, contrasts not involving base rates stratification on the basis of either index in the pairing typically show an attenuated effect relative to the blatant trends apparent with intellectual–memory pairings. Nonetheless, direction effects should not be dismissed simply as a psychometric oddity. Memory and intellectual abilities do not correlate strongly,[5] and so it is a clinical reality that a true FSIQ of 110, 115, or 120 (or any value much above 100) is more likely than not to be accompanied by a lower true GMI, and a low-IQ score by a higher memory score.

[5]The magnitude of correlation will vary according to memory test administered. A list-learning test consisting of obscure words will likely show a higher correlation with IQ than one consisting of more commonly used words, for example. It would also be less valid for general use.

TABLE 4 Relationship of Differential between Index-Full-Scale IQ Correlations and Direction Effect in IQ-Stratified Discrepancy Base Rates[a]

	Correlation with FSIQ (first index/second index)	Difference in correlation with FSIQ	Mean discrepancy: < 80 FSIQ group	Mean discrepancy: 120+ FSIQ group	Change in discrepancy mean from low to high FSIQ group	Cases with first index > second index, IQ< 80 (%)	Cases with first index > second index, IQ 120+ (%)	Difference from low to high IQ group of cases with first index superior (%)
WMS-III WMI – PSI	.68/.67	.01	-1.2	-0.5	0.7	44	43	-1
Auditory Memory – Vis Mem	.60/.57	.03	2.0	3.2	1.2	60	56	-4
VCI – POI	.90/.86	.04	-0.4	1.9	2.3	46	56	10
WMS-III WMI – Aud Mem	.68/.60	.08	-4.7	0.5	5.2	37	52	15
WMS-III WMI – Vis Mem	.68/.57	.11	-2.7	3.8	6.5	42	57	15
POI – WMS-III WMI	.85/.68	.17	-2.3	4.4	6.7	38	57	19
POI – PSI	.86/.68	.18	-2.0	5.5	7.5	39	59	20
Auditory Memory – Vis Mem (Orig)	.60/.40	.20	-2.7	6.9	9.6	39	64	25
VCI – WMS-III WMI	.89/.68	.21	-1.4	7.1	8.5	47	60	23
VCI – PSI	.90/.68	.22	-2.3	7.4	9.7	44	67	23
POI – Aud Mem	.85/.60	.25	-6.9	5.0	11.9	27	54	27
WMS-III WMI – Vis Mem (Orig)	.68/.40	.28	-7.4	7.4	14.8	31	66	35
POI – Vis Mem	.85/.57	.28	-4.9	8.2	13.1	30	69	39
VCI – Aud Mem	.89/.60	.29	-6.1	7.6	13.7	29	61	32
VCI – Vis Mem	.89/.57	.32	-4.1	10.8	14.9	33	69	36
POI – Vis Mem (Orig)	.85/.40	.45	-9.6	11.8	21.4	24	76	51
VCI – Vis Mem (Orig)	.89/.40	.49	-8.8	14.4	23.2	22	80	58

[a]Some coefficients between WAIS-III indexes and FSIQ differ within this table, and from those in Table 1, because for the purposes of this demonstration the correlation within the WMS-III data is the appropriate comparison when the contrast index is from the WMS-III. All discrepancy data unidirectional (first index minus the second).

Second, whenever there is a disparity in relationship to general ability between contrasted indexes, direction effects will be seen. For example, VCI (or POI) typically exceeds PSI among brighter cases, with the converse true at lower levels of general intelligence. Another example: two thirds of superior IQ subjects display a superiority of WMS-III Working Memory over Visual Memory (Original), and the same proportion of low-IQ subjects show the opposite (Table 4).

Third, the more extreme the predictor score (the one that the target index is discrepant from), the more likely it is that (a) the contrasted score will fall between it and the population mean, and (b) a large discrepancy will exist. Compared to a POI of 115, a POI of 125 is more likely to be accompanied by a lower PSI, and, generally speaking, the POI–PSI discrepancy will have to be larger to attain the same degree of clinical meaning.

Finally, any grouping variable correlated with IQ, such as education, will generate directionality effects similar to those seen with IQ. Highly educated subjects tend to show a superiority of VCI over PSI, with the converse true at lower levels, and so on.[6]

Stratified base rates (or the predicted difference method) take care of direction effects, but clinicians should remain mindful of these few basic facts because they also apply to other neuropsychological test data.

WHICH INDEX CONTRASTS ARE MOST
LIKELY TO BE CLINICALLY USEFUL?

Weakly correlated pairs feature large natural discrepancies, so abnormal differences have to be considerable. It seems logical, but is in fact a simplification, to presume that DA with strongly correlated index pairs will be more informative than DA with indexes showing weaker associations. Indexes that show a sharp differential in sensitivity to pathology, but only a modest association in normals, could prove more informative than more strongly correlated (but less dissociable) indexes.

[6]In fact, direction effects should be seen whenever one index in a pair correlates more highly than the other with any third variable that cases can be ranked upon. Some examples: the VCI correlates more strongly with Auditory than Visual Memory, so high VCI scores are typically accompanied by a superiority of Auditory Memory over Visual Memory; low VCI scores by a superiority of Visual over Auditory Memory. Similarly, high POI scores will typically be accompanied by a superiority of Visual over Auditory Memory score, with the converse true for low POI scores.

Despite the importance of the requirement that the contrasted indexes display a *differential sensitivity* to whatever condition is of interest, clinicians will find only limited data in the literature to guide them. The relative sensitivity of the indexes to diverse conditions will take years to establish. Fortunately, a good start has been provided by the publication within the *WAIS-III–WMS-III Technical Manual* of data for clinical samples selected on the grounds of "their known or presumed susceptibility to disordered learning, cognition, and memory as well as their relative frequency in receiving neuropsychological evaluations" (The Psychological Corporation, 1997, p. 144). Seven conditions—Alzheimer's disease, Huntington's disease, Parkinson's disease, traumatic brain injury (TBI), chronic alcohol abuse, Korsakoff's syndrome, and schizophrenia—constituted the major adult samples for whom both WAIS and WMS-III data were available. These samples provide a preliminary testing ground for WAIS-III–WMS-III discrepancy analysis.

Sensitivity to Brain Dysfunction *per se*

The technical manual samples allow for a preliminary response to the question: Are the new cognitive and memory indexes subjected to a differential degradation by the brain insults or pathologies of these conditions? Are any quasi-generic "red flags" of brain compromise supported—that is, do profile commonalities emerge across these samples?[7] The answer is yes: the PSI and Visual Memory Indexes appear to be highly sensitive to brain dysfunction *per se* (Figures 4, 5, and 6; see also Hawkins, 1998, and Heaton et al., Chapter 5, this volume).

VCI-PSI

PSI was the WAIS III Index profile low point for all seven conditions, being on average 15.4 points lower than the highest index of each sample. In contrast, VCI was the high point for five of the seven conditions (mean VCI–PSI difference = 14.2), and for one exception the VCI was minimally lower than the profile high. Against the 85th percentile VCI–PSI

---

[7]Some neuropsychologists will cringe at any form of the "Is there organicity?" question, but the possible presence of general indications of brain dysfunction/damage is frequently a pertinent and legitimate issue, either in its own right, or as a "first take" on data prior to more nuanced analyses.

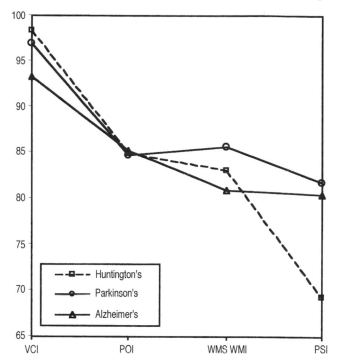

FIGURE 4. Six-factor model index WAIS-III plus WMS-III WMI profiles for the *Technical Manual* Huntington's, Parkinson's, and Alzheimer's samples. VCI, Verbal Comprehension Index; POI, Perceptual Organization Index; WMS WMI, WMS-III Working Memory Index; PSI, Processing Speed Index.

discrepancy applicable per sample FSIQ mean,[8] 100 % of the Huntington's cases would be red-flagged, along with 80 % of the Parkinson's, 68 % of TBI, 66 % of Alzheimer's, 45 % of schizophrenia, 29 % of alcohol abuse, and 10 % of Korsakoff's cases.

These data are encouraging, but beg a critical question: would the PSI alone yield a similar return? Compared to the discrepancy approach, a PSI below 85 actually red-flags more patients with Korsakoff's syndrome (60 vs. 10 % for the VCI–PSI 85th percentile), TBI (91 vs. 68 %), schizophrenia (60 vs. 45 %), and Alzheimer's disease (71 vs. 66 %), but fewer of the Parkinson's, Huntington's, and Alcohol Abuse patients (60 vs. 80 %, 93 vs. 100 %, and

---

[8]For this preliminary exploration, for all but one sample we adopted the expedient of comparing the discrepancies of each patient against the 85th percentile value for the IQ stratum that their sample mean falls into, as opposed to evaluating the discrepancy against base rates for the FSIQ stratum applicable for each patient. The exception is the alcohol abuse sample, which is examined more closely later in this chapter.

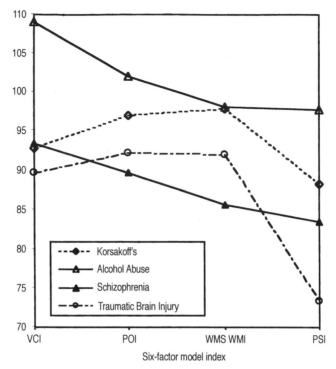

FIGURE 5.   Six-factor model WAIS-III and WMS-III WMI index profiles for the technical manual Korsakoff's, alcohol abuse, schizophrenia and traumatic brain injury samples. VCI, Verbal Comprehension Index; POI, Perceptual Organization Index; WMS WMI, WMS-III Working Memory Index; PSI, Processing Speed Index.

14 vs 29%, respectively). Some of these differences will not be statistically significant, may be specific to the sample rather than the diagnosis, and all stem from just preliminary analyses. Nonetheless, these findings raise interesting questions to be revisited when we consider the fundamental issue of the utility of discrepancy analysis.

The Sensitivity of Visual New Learning

Memory for visuospatial information is more vulnerable to aging than memory for verbal material (Levin & Larrabee, 1983), and Russell (1981) argued that the visual memory test of the original WMS was more sensitive to diffuse organic conditions than its verbal counterpart. The Visual Memory means for 14 clinical samples reported in the WMS-R manual (Wechsler, 1987) were lower than the Verbal Memory means, and a similar pattern emerges from the WMS-III clinical samples data (Hawkins, 1998).

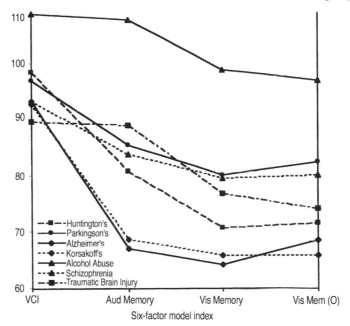

FIGURE 6. Verbal Comprehension Index (VCI)–Memory Index profiles for technical manual clinical samples.

Figure 6 shows that the WMS-III Visual Memory and Visual Memory (Original) means are similar, lower than the Auditory Memory Index means, and considerably lower than the VCI means. Since VCI–Visual Memory Index discrepancies are smaller than VCI–Visual Memory Index (Original) discrepancies in normals, the former will display greater utility.[9] The average difference between the mean VCI and mean Visual Memory Index for the clinical samples is 19.6 (compared to 12.9 for VCI–Auditory Memory), considerably higher than 11, the 85th centile value appropriate for these groups based on current FSIQ (Table 8). The average (19.6) is elevated by the inclusion of groups with pronounced discrepancies (Alzheimer's and

---

[9]Although it seems less suited to DA, wholesale abandonment of the Visual Memory (Original) Index might be ill advised as little is yet known about its properties. Does the index correlate poorly with others because Faces taps an exclusive ability? Will replacement of Faces with Visual Reproductions, a test more vulnerable to verbal mediation, result in a reduction in sensitivity to deficits more purely visual in nature (perhaps secondary to focal right hemisphere damage)? Or is it that Faces taps highly specific processes that are inadequately related to broader visual memory? These issues are further complicated by psychometric considerations (e.g., item difficulty).

Korsakoff's, 29.1 and 26.9 points respectively), but the differences in the remaining groups are all at least moderate (all numbers rounded): 28 (Huntington's); 17 (Parkinson's); 14 (schizophrenia); 13 (TBI); and 10 (alcohol abuse).

Once again, however, the vulnerability of the more impacted index is such that consideration of it alone red-flags a considerable portion of patients. In every sample except one, as many or more patients are red-flagged by the Visual Memory score alone as by the VCI–Visual Memory discrepancy: 100 % vs. 94 % (Alzheimer's), 100 % vs. 90 % (Korsakoff's), 79 % vs. 61 % (schizophrenia), 70 % vs. 60 % (Parkinson's), 93 % vs. 93 % (Huntington's), and 64 % vs. 64 % (TBI). The exception is alcohol abuse: whereas only 21 % display a Visual Memory Index score below 85, 36 % show a VCI–Visual Memory discrepancy that exceeds the 85th percentile.

Brain Dysfunction Markers

Neuropsychologists are often asked whether brain compromise has occurred—or persists—when other evidence is equivocal. Has the patient recovered from the mild head injury sustained 12 months earlier? Has the patient's metabolic condition impaired brain functioning? Regardless of how determined, it is clear that depressed PSI or Visual Memory Index scores are common concomitants of brain disorder (or at least the pathology of several conditions that could be characterized as exerting a rather diffuse, or sometimes primarily subcortical, impact upon the central nervous system). A low PSI or low Visual Memory Index is displayed by around 82 % of the patients comprising these samples. A virtually identical proportion show either a sizable VCI–PSI or VCI–Visual Memory discrepancy (defined here as at the 85th percentile or greater).

Individualizing the discrepancy analysis to bring into play either the VCI or POI (whichever is higher per individual) as the contrast to the PSI or Visual Memory Index would increase the proportion of patients tagged by an abnormal discrepancy, but the false-positive rate among normals would also increase. Similarly, combining the low PSI–low Visual Memory Index method with the VCI–PSI or VCI–Visual Memory discrepancy approach tags over 90 % of the clinical sample patients, but also results in an increased false-positive error rate. Exactly what works best with what conditions, and when, will require more sophisticated analyses than those reported here, followed by cross-validation in several relevant samples. This would rapidly become a complex process; it serves current purposes simply to note that the

PSI and Visual Memory Index are commonly depressed in patients suffering conditions that are commonly in question within a neuropsychological referral. Apart from this "generic" vulnerability, these indexes appear to show some variability in sensitivity across clinical conditions, and on that basis could play a role in differential diagnosis. This possibility will be explored in greater depth later.

CONVENTIONAL CONTRASTS: WITHIN-WAIS-III

The *WAIS-III WMS-III Technical Manual* discusses WAIS Index pairs selected in accord with certain clinical and theoretical assumptions. VCI–POI contrasts represent a refinement of the traditional VIQ–PIQ comparison, while other indexes are paired on an *a priori* basis. Due to a common reliance upon verbal material, there is consideration of the pairing of the VCI and WMI, but not the POI and WMI. Similarly, the PSI is contrasted with the POI, but not the VCI. This selectivity was intended to steer clinicians away from "shotgun" analyses, though it is now recognized that some contrasts not considered in the manual, such as VCI–PSI, are informative and clinically justifiable.

VCI-POI

Despite clinical lore regarding the vulnerability of visuoconstructional abilities and novel problem solving to brain dysfunction, the POI emerges from the clinical samples as less depressed (relative to the other indexes) than might have been anticipated. Along with Digit Symbol, the POI does not include Picture Arrangement (PA), which loads on both the perceptual organizational and verbal factors (The Psychological Corporation, 1997), and is sensitive to damage in either hemisphere (Warrington, James, & Maciejewski, 1986). The inclusion of these tests in the PIQ, but not the POI, muddies the factorial purity of the former and clarifies the latter, but also lessens the sensitivity of the POI to general compromise: the PIQ is lower than POI in all seven clinical samples (Hawkins, 1998). Focal damage may be a different matter, with the differential sensitivity of the POI and VCI to lateral insult (caused by, e.g., stroke, tumor, or contusion) remaining largely undetermined. Since the VCI and POI possess greater factorial purity than the VIQ and PIQ, they may better serve the neuropsychologist in delineating specific intellectual strengths and weaknesses.

VCI–WMI and POI–PSI Comparisons

Both the WMI and PSI are relatively narrow measures of cognitive activity that may provide useful descriptive information, either on their own or via contrasts with other indexes. The Psychological Corporation (1997) stresses that VCI–WMI comparisons can reveal differences between the individual's capacity to hold and process information in working memory and his or her acquired knowledge and verbal reasoning skills. Similarly, the POI–PSI score difference can reveal differences between an individual's visual-spatial and fluid reasoning skills and the ability to process information quickly.

Though the WMI may help the clinician tease out causes of poor performances elsewhere, the clinical samples suggest a limited role with regard to inferential reasoning about brain integrity. The WAIS-III WMI (Digit Span, Arithmetic, Letter–Number Sequencing) appears to occupy something of a "middle ground" of sensitivity to the pathologies represented by the seven conditions (Hawkins, 1998). The six-factor model substitutes the WMS-III WMI (Letter–Number Sequencing, Spatial Span), and, whereas the WAIS-III WMI is heavily verbal, the WMS-III WMI consists of both visual and verbal challenges and may prove somewhat more sensitive to some clinical conditions. In the Alzheimer's disease and alcohol abuse samples the mean WMS-III WMI is considerably lower, but lesser differences between the WAIS-III WMI and WMS-III WMI are observed in the other clinical samples. Though almost as depressed as the PSI in the Alzheimer's and alcohol abuse samples, the WMS-III WMI is not the profile low point for any of the seven conditions, and its potential to facilitate differential diagnosis is unclear. Focal injury is quite another issue and one that awaits data.

CONVENTIONAL CONTRASTS: WITHIN WMS-III

Working Memory versus Memory Indexes

The WMI can be compared to the Auditory and Visual indexes to evaluate possible differences between attention and the acquisition and encoding processes that, in part, depend upon intact attention. A low WMI in the context of low Memory indexes and higher intellectual functioning could indicate that deficits in attention are affecting the examinee's ability to learn new material (The Psychological Corporation, 1997).

Auditory versus Visual Index

Differences between the auditory and visual indexes may indicate lifelong strengths and weaknesses or acquired deficits in new learning and memory processes when information is presented in different modalities. Other abilities (e.g., attention, receptive and expressive language abilities, perceptual organizational abilities, and vocabulary and articulation) may also influence auditory and visual memory scores (The Psychological Corporation, 1997). Along with the possibility of a differential sensitivity to diffuse compromise, an obvious question regarding the WMS-III indexes pertains to sensitivity to lateral insult. Preliminary data from temporal lobe epilepsy patients post lateral surgery show encouraging modality (auditory vs. visual) effects (Hawkins, 1998; The Psychological Corporation, 1997). Patients who had undergone right-hemisphere surgery displayed a lower visual mean index (relative to auditory), whereas the left-hemisphere patients displayed a lower auditory index mean (than visual). Both groups, however, displayed low Visual Index means, supporting the notion that the visual indexes are sensitive to brain damage generally. Since these trends are easier to grasp visually we refer the reader to Hawkins (1998). These small surgical groups were not matched on demographics or premorbid status, and so constitute a bare minimum of data upon which to speculate. More recent findings underscore the complexity of these issues with regard to epilepsy (Wilde, et al., 2001; Heaton et al., chapter 5, this volume), and as yet little other data of relevance have been published.

WAIS-III–WMS-III CONTRASTS

Traditional IQ-Memory Comparisons

Discrepancies between intelligence and memory are sometimes used to evaluate memory (The Psychological Corporation, 1997), based upon the assumption that IQ provides a reasonable estimate of the ability to learn and remember new material. Memory scores that are appreciably lower may suggest an acquired memory impairment (Milner, 1975; Prigatano, 1974; Quadfasel & Pruyser, 1955). Bornstein, Chelune, and Prifitera (1989) found that a discrepancy of 15 points between FSIQ and Delayed Memory Index was obtained by only 10% of the WMS-R standardization sample, but in about 33% of a mixed clinical sample with conditions associated with memory impairment. These data are supportive, but hardly compelling.

Future research should include comparisons of the efficacy of alternative ways of determining whether a given discrepancy is abnormal (i.e., a comparison of the simple and predicted difference methods). We have argued in favor of the predicted-difference method, since it takes into account score reliability, the correlation between the two measures, and corrects for regression to the mean (Hawkins & Tulsky, 2001; The Psychological Corporation, 1997), but the discrepancy base rates provided in this chapter actually approximate a hybrid approach. Strictly speaking, the provision of empirically derived base rates for discrepancies equates to a simple difference approach. Breaking these down by IQ level, however, is similar to the predicted difference method insofar as stratification provides a degree of control over the effects of correlation and regression to the mean.

VCI as "Best Estimate" of Premorbid Status

In the search for evidence of memory impairment, the substitution of the VCI for FSIQ allows for the generation of a discrepancy between a relatively resilient cognitive measure (VCI) and the memory score of interest. In clinical circumstances, discrepancies between the VCI and memory scores will typically be larger than those between the FSIQ (or other intellectual scores) and memory data (see Figures 4, 5, and 6). Since the correlation between the VCI and Auditory Memory in the standardization sample (.57) approximates that between FSIQ and Auditory Memory (.60), the relative resilience of the VCI should usually offset the slightly larger "natural" discrepancies that will exist between it (rather than FSIQ) and Auditory Memory.

Discrepancies between the POI and WMS-III Scores

The Psychological Corporation (1997) suggests that if the difference between an examinee's VIQ and PIQ scores is 10 points or more, the higher of the two could be used (instead of FSIQ) as a best intellectual estimate for the purposes of IQ–memory DA. In a similar vein, the clinician may consider contrasting the POI with memory data when the POI is substantially higher than VCI and, in the clinician's judgment, establishes the best memory performance expectation. Within the overall standardization sample, 85th percentile discrepancies between the POI and the memory indexes are generally comparable to those between the VCI and the memory indexes (Table 2). At least on the basis of "natural" discrepancy size, the POI will function adequately as the intellectual contrast against which memory data are compared when appropriate clinical circumstances prevail.

Index-to-Index Discrepancies

The development of the six factor auditory and visual memory indexes facilitates the exploration of modality-specific impairment. The associations between laterality of surgical intervention and WMS-III modality of presentation observed within the technical manual's temporal lobectomy samples provide preliminary support for the practice of paying attention to memory data generated via the modality of presentation traditionally associated with processing in the hemisphere of interest, especially when considered in the context of a literature supporting this practice (The Psychological Corporation, 1997). An evaluation for right hemisphere mesial temporal lobe dysfunction, for example, could include particular consideration of the discrepancy between the patient's POI and Visual Index scores. To the extent that a selective impact upon intellectual functions is suspected as well (either on clinical/theoretical grounds or because the POI is substantially depressed relative to the VCI), VCI–Visual Memory Index comparisons should also be considered. Obviously, intellectual–memory analyses should be complemented by within-WMS-III (Auditory–Visual) discrepancy analysis.

The suggestion that the VCI could be contrasted against visual memory may seem poorly considered since, theoretically, lesser relationships should pertain between intellectual and memory variables representing different constructs. Analyses along these lines could also be viewed as encouraging discrepancy "fishing expeditions," whereby the clinician scans all possible discrepancy data with a view to developing a post hoc explanation for any that are large. However, carefully considered cross-construct analyses are defensible. Indexes labeled as representing specific constructs do so, in any pure sense, only to a limited extent. The Psychological Corporation (1997, p.17) stresses that "rather than purporting to tap exclusively a hypothetical verbal or visual memory system, the WMS-III distinguishes between auditory and visual memory by the modality of presentation of the subtests." Although stronger relationships exist between construct-related indexes (e.g., the VCI–Auditory Memory correlation at .57 exceeds the VCI–Visual Memory coefficient of .46), these differences in strength of association are not always as large as might have been anticipated (e.g., the correlation between POI and Visual Memory at .54 does not substantially exceed the POI–Auditory Memory correlation of .47; Table 1). The rationale for examining a contrast ultimately resides in demonstrations that large differences are disproportionately seen in clinical states: at heart, the issue is whether an empirical justification exists, no matter how unlikely the pairing.

DOES DISCREPANCY ANALYSIS WORK?

Discrepancy analysis occurs whenever an index or IQ score is evaluated in the context of another. Although this is a widespread practice, there are nonetheless serious grounds for questioning its utility when used to infer brain dysfunction, or in differential diagnosis. We address these concerns as a series of challenges.

Challenge 1: All the Indexes are Depressed by Brain Impairment

In an ideal world, the indexes would correlate strongly and yet display a pronounced differential sensitivity to brain impairment generally, and/or to focal insults or specific clinical conditions. As might be expected on the basis of their origins in factor analysis, the correlations between the indexes are typically modest and large discrepancies exist naturally. Conversely, the factor-analytic foundations are positive with regard to the requirement that the indexes display differential vulnerability, because they should tap relatively distinct universes of functioning.

It was determined earlier that the PSI and Visual Memory indexes do show greater sensitivity than the other indexes in several conditions, but it also seemed to be the case that DA often offers little information beyond that obtained by inspection of single scores alone. One reason is that the indexes typically show *relative*, rather than *absolute*, levels of resilience (or sensitivity) to brain insult. Presumptive evidence is provided by the VCI means: although typically the profile highpoint, the mean VCI is less than the population mean (100) in six of the seven clinical conditions (Figures 4 and 5).

Differential vulnerability actually embodies two intertwined issues, one pertaining to sensitivity to brain compromise *per se*, the second to the issue of differential diagnosis. Is the differential sensitivity of indexes to diffuse insult sufficient to be informative? Are the index profiles sufficiently distinct, from clinical condition to clinical condition, to facilitate differential diagnosis?

Light Shed by Historical Data: VIQ–PIQ Discrepancies

Measures of intellectual ability assess the synthesized products of multiple processes, as opposed to discrete functions, and therefore are vulnerable to a wide range of insults. By this argument, if one intellectual index is depressed, the others will be as well. This runs counter to the traditional practice of inspecting the VIQ and PIQ for a discrepancy, but is nonetheless reasonably supported by data despite Wechsler's (1958) prediction that large differentials between VIQ and PIQ scores would be found more commonly in pathological than normal samples. It is commonly presumed that the PIQ is more sensitive to impairment generally, due to the inclusion of tests placing a greater premium upon novel problem solving (fluid intelligence) and rapid responding. A second presumption is that the PIQ is more sensitive to right-hemisphere pathology, the VIQ to left. These presumptions enjoy empirical support, but at levels that indicate limited diagnostic utility.

VIQ–PIQ comparisons possess at best moderate utility in localizing pathology at the level of the hemisphere. Based on Wechsler-Bellevue (W-B) and WAIS literature, Kaufman (1990) noted a general trend for stroke or tumor to result, on average, in a substantial inferiority of PIQ relative to VIQ in right-hemisphere-lesioned patients. Left-hemisphere lesions result in an inferiority of VIQ relative to PIQ, on average, but the trend is less consistent and the discrepancy is typically smaller (Bornstein, 1983; Bornstein & Matarazzo 1982; Kaufman, 1990). Warrington, James, and Maciejewski (1986) studied 656 patients with unilateral lesions and concluded that although there was only sparse evidence "for a more fine grained selective impairment associated with localization of lesion" (p. 238), there were distinctive WAIS patterns of impairment associated with laterality of lesion. Although high incidences of Performance discrepancies (VIQ > PIQ) in the right-hemisphere lesion group and of Verbal discrepancies (PIQ > VIQ) in the left-hemisphere group were found, the utility of discrepancy scores as an indicator of laterality was weakened by the finding that 50 % of the discrepancies fell within the −10 to +10 range. Worse still, a sizable portion of patients displayed a discrepancy opposite to that expected.

Head trauma provides a reasonable test of the proposition that VIQ–PIQ differences shed light on the presence of a more general brain insult. Though focal lesions may be present, diffuse or widely distributed injuries predominate within TBI. The WAIS-R literature reveals that although the PIQ means of TBI samples are normally somewhat lower than their VIQ means, the differences are typically small and insufficiently consistent to serve as a strong source of inference (Hawkins, Plehn, & Borgaro, 2002). A large prospective study indicates that the VIQ is depressed by head trauma in reasonable proportion to injury severity, and that focal lesions do not account for this (Dikmen, Machamer, Winn, & Temkin, 1995). These findings are buttressed by the WAIS-III technical manual TBI sample. Twenty-two patients with initial Glasgow Coma Scale scores <13 and with loss of consciousness exceeding 60 minutes tested 6 to 18 months postinjury obtained a PIQ mean just 5.1 points lower than their mean VIQ. Small though this difference is, it compares favorably with the difference between the VCI and POI means of −2.5 (i.e., POI is superior).

Narrower Measures of Cognitive Activity: The PSI

Although casting doubt on the value of VIQ–PIQ DA, TBI findings indicate that the introduction of the PSI, a narrower index, should enhance DA because the tendency for the WAIS or WAIS-R PIQ to be lower than VIQ in part reflects the sensitivity of Digit Symbol. For five of six WAIS studies reported by Farr, Greene, and Fisher-White (1986), Digit Symbol featured the lowest subtest mean, and it was second lowest for the sixth study. WAIS-R studies reporting subtest data show the same trend (Crawford, Johnson, Mychalkiw, & Moore, 1997; Guilmette, Dabrowski, Kennedy, & Gnys, 1999; Little, Templer, Persel, & Ashley, 1996; Paniak, Silver, Finlayson, & Tuff, 1992). Confirming this trend, the differences between the VCI and PSI (16.2) and POI–PSI means (18.7) are significantly greater than the VIQ–PIQ difference of 5.1 in the WAIS-III TBI sample (Hawkins, 1998).

The depression of the PSI across the clinical samples combined with the predominance of the VCI as profile high point suggests both a general and more specific diagnostic role for VCI–PSI comparisons. VCI–PSI discrepancies may provide a rough-and-ready guide to the likelihood of compromise, at least when a general condition is suspected (i.e., one featuring reasonably diffuse or widely distributed compromise, or prominent subcortical features). The circumstances under which these discrepancies shed additional light to that gained via inspection of the PSI need to be determined;[10] later in this section we identify one possible such circumstance.

---

[10]The depression of the PSI within the samples is all the more striking when one considers that the true extent of PSI decline is masked by the virtual certainty that the profile highs have also fallen from premorbid levels. Since the VCI itself is not immune to degradation,

The potential for more specific contributions to diagnosis is suggested by the high percentage of cases showing an abnormal discrepancy in conditions where it might be most expected, Huntington's disease (100%), Parkinson's disease (80%), and TBI (68%), and by consideration of the profiles of the AD and KS samples. Whereas both conditions feature poor memory performances, most of the Alzheimer's patients, per their VCI–PSI discrepancies, display a *relative* weakness on the PSI as well. In comparison, only 1 of the 10 Korsakoff's patients do so—a normal rate. Here DA exhibits an advantage over simple consideration of the absolute scores. A significant proportion of each sample scored beneath 85 on the PSI (71% AD and 60% KS), but these low absolute PSI levels are misleading insofar as the KS feature low levels of premorbid functioning (50% had less than 12 years of education, compared to 12% of the Alzheimer's group). In comparison, the relative intactness of the PSI indicated by the lack of sizable VCI–PSI discrepancies is consistent with there being a lesser impact on general cognition in KS.

"Brain-Damaged" versus More Nuanced Judgments

One explanation for the persistence of DA is that, diagnostically, neuropsychological input is often most valued when least verifiable by other means. A patient with obvious symptoms of AD is less likely to be referred than a patient showing equivocal signs. A month-long coma following head injury leaves little doubt that the brain was damaged; mild head injury with questionable loss of consciousness is quite another matter. Similarly, neuropsychological opinion may be considered critical in determining whether the CNS has been affected by a systemic illness, exposure to toxins, or a drug or alcohol habit. In many such circumstances, an absolute score approach will result in high rates of false negative error, because setting the normalcy threshold at one standard deviation below the mean—a liberal level— requires, *ipso facto*, an average fall of one standard deviation from premorbid status (Cohen, 1988). The decline must be even greater for the sizable portion of the population with above-average premorbid abilities, yet the factors responsible for the neuropsychological opinion being highly valued—a lack of compelling evidence from other sources, or because the

---

the gathering of complementary data (pronunciation or word recognition tests, such as the WRAT-R Reading, NART, or Gates MacGinitie Vocabulary) might possibly enhance the utility of the PSI as a potential red flag for compromise. Establishing when such contrasts are justified (as compared to inspection of single scores alone) should be a research priority.

suspected condition is in its very early stages, if present at all—mean that any deficits that exist are probably subtle.

How does this translate into support for DA? Rewording, Is the patient brain damaged? to Are there any indications of a loss of capacity? is helpful, because the question is then more likely to elicit a response that involves more than just the matching of single scores against cutting points. A focus on decline (rather than the more black-or-white brain damage) brings into play the *pattern* of scores (e.g., relevant discrepancies). Whether the pattern bears any similarity to that seen in the condition suspected, regardless of where the scores fall in absolute terms, becomes a focus.

Nonetheless, the real issue remains validity: Is DA in the context of normal range scores empirically supported? Why presume that DA will work any better with subtle states (as compared to, say, relaxing the cutting points employed with absolute scores) when little evidence of a superiority of DA emerged from our initial explorations of the clinical samples?

One factor responsible for the limited efficacy of DA is the tendency for all indexes to decline following insult. Conceivably, in milder states the *differential* sensitivity of the indexes may be greater. Although a severe insult or disease progression may sink all boats, in the mild or early stages the resilient indexes may be, relatively speaking, even more resilient, and the vulnerable, comparatively speaking, even more vulnerable. Whenever this proves true (and it needs to be demonstrated), the relative efficacy of DA should improve.

Additional considerations stem from the realities of everyday practice. Neuropsychologists do not render diagnostic formulations on persons randomly drawn from the street, and typically do not base opinions on test data alone. Patients arrive with a referral and a history, and the test data *per se* often play a supportive, or confirmatory, rather than definitive, diagnostic role. What the examiner *expects* is an obvious influence: Based upon the referral circumstances, what pathology is most likely at play, and what is known about the neuropsychological sequelae of that condition? What are reasonable alternative explanations, and how are they neuropsychologically characterized? When adequate knowledge of the neuropsychological sequalae of relevant conditions exists, DA may well assist in determining whether there has been relevant decline despite the presence of only normal scores. Rather than asking, Does score *x* fall beneath threshold *y*?, the examiner may ask, Does the overall clinical picture support the diagnosis under consideration?, or: Is the neuropsychological profile consistent with the patient's complaints? Consider the following case:

Case One. A 25-year-old high school graduate tested in a vocational context obtained a WMI of 109, VCI of 114, POI of 106, and PSI of 100. The examinee has no history of brain insult or of serious illness, and presents without complaints.

Knowing that a reasonable amount of index scatter occurs commonly, the examiner is likely to view this WAIS-III profile as relatively unremarkable. All the scores are within the normal range and consistent with demographics. Now consider:

Case Two. A 25-year-old high school graduate tested 2 years after a car accident that left her in a coma for 4 days obtained a WMI of 109, VCI of 114, POI of 106, and PSI of 100. Her family describes her as being less patient than she was prior to the accident. She denies being more irritable, but complains of being "not as mentally quick or agile" as she used to be. She does not appear psychologically depressed.

Although the scores are identical in both cases, many examiners will argue that the relative depression of the PSI in Case Two supports the patient's complaint of persisting mental slowing, even though the score, considered alone, is obviously normal. The 14-point VCI–PSI discrepancy is not especially uncommon among average IQ individuals (about one in six display it; Table 10), but may nonetheless be judged to support the examinee's complaints given the context, and the known effects of traumatic brain injury.

Contextual influences do not guarantee accuracy, but they should improve the chances of a correct decision.[11] Diagnostic accuracy rates in mild states will be inferior to those attained with severe pathology, but higher error rates are not necessarily intolerable. Simply exceeding chance may sometimes be acceptable—or at least preferable to no input at all—and an opinion may be little less valuable for want of certainty. A measured rather than definitive opinion may be rendered, as in: "Taken in the context of history and complaints, it is more likely than not that these findings reflect the persisting effects of traumatic brain injury."

A related argument is that clinicians often balance *error risk* against *error cost*. In some situations a false positive error may be preferable to a false

[11]The premise is that identical data can possess different meanings depending upon context. Chest pain may be interpreted differently depending upon whether the patient is 22 or 52 years old; identical blood pressure readings can vary in significance depending upon the broader clinical context, and so on. An opposing argument is that we are promoting a form of "experimenter bias," wherein the clinician's interpretations of data may be unduly influenced by situational expectations.

negative because the costs associated with being wrong are more acceptable. Stating there is no evidence of pathology when it exists could result in the withholding of treatment, or a failure to secure financial or rehabilitative support for a patient who consequently suffers great personal loss. A refusal to consider the possibility of insult or decline simply because no score, considered alone, falls into a range designated abnormal would be irresponsible in many circumstances.

But where does the clinician stop? In the preceding TBI cases, the VCI–PSI discrepancy of 14 falls at the 85th percentile, which could be considered clinically indicative. What if the discrepancy had been 12? A discrepancy of that size is still relatively uncommon, and is more likely to be seen in someone who has sustained TBI than normal persons (Hawkins, 1998; Martin, Donders, & Thompson, 2000). All other things being equal, a person with an 84th percentile discrepancy is virtually as likely as person with an 85th percentile discrepancy to be exhibiting the consequence of an insult, and a subject with an 81st percentile discrepancy is only marginally less likely to be doing so.

In the final analysis, the critical issue is that the clinician does not mislead others about the bases of his or her conclusions, or about the level of confidence that can be placed in those conclusions. The adoption of likelihood ratio approaches (Smith et al., chapter 7, this volume) will liberate the discipline from the yes–no, normal–abnormal decision making constraints tied to absolute cutoffs (whether for single score or discrepancies) that neuropsychologists currently work with. However, the empirical foundations for likelihood methods must first be established via the collection of WAIS-III and WMS-III data on well-characterized clinical samples at various stages of illness progression or injury severity.

Empirical Validation

The case for preserving DA may, so far, appear little more than an attempt to save a method that we are wedded to by habit. Is there any evidence that DA facilitates diagnosis at all? One of the clinical samples—alcohol abuse—actually does illustrate its potential. At first glance the sample looks normal, with solidly average index means. Must we conclude that alcohol has no impact?

The sample index profile suggests otherwise, since, as is often the case when a general condition impacts the brain, the VCI constitutes the highpoint, and the PSI and Visual Memory Index means the lows (Figures 5 and 6). Using the 85th percentile value as the cutting point, by VCI–PSI discrepancy 29 % are identified as having suffered an insult or loss of capacity. Thirty-six percent show an abnormal VCI–Visual Memory Index discrepancy, and 46 % show an abnormal discrepancy in either one, or both, of these contrasts. These are nonspecific indicators, to be sure, and it could be the case that for some subjects these discrepancies predated the alcohol abuse. Regardless, they speak to abnormality. Particularly when the patient exhibits a drop in adaptive functioning, discrepancies such as these could be considered to indicate that alcohol abuse has caused cognitive declines related to brain changes.

DA would appear to be marginally efficacious in this sample were it not for other considerations. DA outperforms the absolute score approach: a normal portion of the sample scored beneath 85 on the PSI (14 %), and 21 % did so on the Visual Memory Index. The portion with a lower than 85 score on either (25 %) is lower than the portion with an abnormal discrepancy from VCI in either index (46 %). This DA detection rate may be better than it appears, as it is conceivable that only some members of the sample have, in fact, suffered insult—in which case the true level of accuracy could be higher.

Challenge 2: Subtest Variability

Just as the meaning of a FSIQ score is called into question when the VIQ and PIQ (or Index scores) are highly discrepant, considerable variability across the subtests making up an index will make comparisons of that index with others less valid or informative. Comparisons of one index against another are easier to justify if the subtests within each respond in a reasonably consistent manner to pathology. Despite their common factorial loading in normal samples, certain subtests may be expected, *a priori*, to differ in sensitivity to insults of various kinds. Visual intellectual challenges requiring rapid responding, for example, could be more sensitive to diffuse insult than untimed tests.

Though pathology-specific within-index dissociations will almost certainly be demonstrated in particular conditions, marked differences in subtest sensitivity are not evident in the clinical samples. Table 5 shows that the mean scores on subtests making up the cognitive indexes are quite similar within each. Digit Symbol and Symbol Search typically fall quite closely together. Picture Completion might seem less taxing of fluid intelligence than other POI subtests, but it does not appear to be any less sensitive in these samples. Matrix Reasoning does not appear less sensitive for not being timed. Similarities tends to be little more depressed than Information or Vocabulary.

TABLE 5 Cognitive Subtest Means for the Technical Manual Clinical Samples[a]

Index[b]	Subtest	AD (n = 35)	TBI (n = 22)	Alcohol (n = 28)	Hunt (n = 15)	KS (n = 10)	Park (n = 10)	SZ (n = 42)	All (n = 162)	Rank (total sample)	Mean Ranking[c]
VCI	Information	8.06	8.41	12.25	10.67	8.60	9.40	9.52	9.57	1	2.7
	Vocabulary	9.63	7.86	11.39	9.73	8.40	9.60	8.21	9.26	2	3.7
	Similarities	8.51	8.18	11.36	8.87	9.00	9.40	8.67	9.12	3	3.1
POI	Matrix Reason	8.03	9.86	10.29	7.47	9.60	8.00	8.36	8.80	4	3.9
	Block Design	7.23	7.73	10.21	7.67	10.20	7.10	9.36	8.58	5	5.1
	Picture Compl	7.23	8.55	10.64	7.40	8.80	7.40	7.24	8.12	6	5.3
WMS WMI	Spatial Span	6.71	9.41	9.04	7.27	10.40	7.20	7.67	8.04	7	5.7
	Letter Number	5.94	7.82	10.50	6.53	8.90	7.70	7.10	7.63	8	6.7
PSI	Symbol Search	5.79	5.27	9.86	4.07	8.60	6.60	6.86	6.77	9	8.7
	Digit Symbol	6.51	4.50	9.39	3.80	6.80	6.60	6.95	6.62	10	9.4

[a]AD, Alzheimer's disease; TBI, traumatic brain injury; Alcohol, chronic alcohol abuse; Hunt, Huntington's Disease; KS, Korsakoff's syndrome; Park, Parkinson's disease; SZ, schizophrenia; All, total clinical sample.

[b]VCI, Verbal Comprehension Index; POI, Perceptual Organization Index; WMS WMI, WMS-III Working Memory Index; PSI, Processing Speed Index.

[c]The mean of ranking within each sample. For example, Vocabulary features the highest subtest mean for AD (rank = 1), but is the sixth highest for TBI (rank = 6).

When ranked by mean score, the subtests fall in a sequence entirely consistent with index composition (i.e., all the VCI subtest means exceed those of the POI, which in turn are higher than the WMS-III WMI and PSI subtest means; Table 5). Pending factor-analytic studies of clinical samples and other empirical approaches to this question, these data suggest that in many clinical circumstances the indexes will hold together quite well.

Challenge 3: Reliability

The reliability of a discrepancy is less than the reliability of either of the scores from which it derives. Discrepancy scores are inherently less reliable than single scores, as the instability of both scores are incorporated into the discrepancy. We have yet to generate comprehensive reliability data to accompany the discrepancy base rates presented in this chapter. This is less of a problem than it appears: as a rule, discrepancies become statistically significant before they become unusual. For example, a 9-point VIQ–PIQ bidirectional difference is statistically significant at the .05 level, but over 37% of the standardization sample display discrepancies of that size or larger (Wechsler, 1997a).

Although a reliable difference is usually thought of as one that differs from 0 to a statistically significant degree, it is preferable to think of differences in terms of whether they differ reliably from the *expected difference*. When whole sample unidirectional differences are considered, the typical discrepancy mean is 0. Subjects displaying larger VCI than POI scores are cancelled out by others with larger POI than VCI scores, and so on. In contrast, unidirectional differences in stratified samples often display a nonzero mean because of the direction effects discussed earlier. Among standardization subjects with a FSIQ lower than 80, the mean unidirectional discrepancy between VCI and the Visual Memory Index (Original) is approximately −8. A discrepancy of just 3 may be both unusual (85th percentile) and statistically significantly different from the expected difference of −8. In other words, the fact that a discrepancy is small does not preclude it from being considered unusual, and reliably so.

**Challenge 4: False Negatives Resulting From
Co-occuring Intellectual–Memory Declines**

A decline in intellectual functioning commonly co-occurs with memory impairment, causing a substantial false negative risk when intellectual–memory discrepancies are examined to evaluate memory. Complicating this issue is the relative dearth of information on how various conditions manifest themselves on the WAIS-III and WMS-III. It is, however, obvious that whenever the impact of a condition upon intellectual and memory abilities is roughly equal, the discrepancy between intellectual and memory scores will average zero. To assume on the basis of the lack of a discrepancy that there has not been a loss of memory capacity would clearly be wrong. DA is but one method of inference: to avoid this error, the clinician draws upon additional data (patient history, medical status, reason for referral, other test data, knowledge of diverse conditions, and so-forth) in order to recognize when an examinee is exhibiting a broad-spectrum decline.

Discrepancy magnitude may conceivably facilitate differential diagnosis. Some conditions, such as KS, feature a relatively isolated effect upon memory, and still others, such as AD, typically exhibit sizable intellectual–memory discrepancies in their early stages. In these conditions, or when the referral question is whether the patient is amnesic, substantial intellectual–memory discrepancies should be seen, with the intellectual indexes largely falling within the normal range (or at levels closer to premorbid estimates).

The application of stratified base rates somewhat offsets the danger that memory decline could be underestimated due to a parallel, but lesser decline, in intellectual functioning. The effect of IQ decline on the size of the discrepancy is offset by a trend within the base-rates towards an ever decreasing superiority of intellectual score over memory as the FSIQ falls towards 100 (and by the rising superiority of memory score over IQ as the IQ strata are descended beneath 100). In short, the masking of a discrepancy that occurs due to a co-existing IQ decline is countered by the fact that a given discrepancy becomes *less* frequent (i.e., more unusual) at lower IQ levels (Hawkins & Tulsky, 2001). However, the circumstances under which discrepancy data are more informative than memory scores alone remain to be demonstrated.

Challenge 5: The Insensitivity of Intellectual–Memory Discrepancy Analysis

Intellectual–Memory DA is too blunt a tool to capture critical aspects of memory dysfunction, a problem that may be exacerbated by the collapsing of immediate and delayed recall data into single scores within the six-factor model. IQ-memory discrepancies cannot be sensitive to all the patterns of memory deficits observed in particular clinical populations (Butters, 1986). A comprehensive assessment of memory involves consideration of data pertaining to attention, learning curves, interference, savings (rate of forgetting), recognition relative to free recall, and so forth.

DA with the six-factor index model may seem especially questionable, because the new visual and auditory indexes collapse immediate and delayed recall data into single scores. Neuropsychologists are typically careful to distinguish between recall immediately following the presentation of material and recall after a reasonable delay. Delayed recall appears more closely akin to lay conceptions of memory, with measures of delayed recall simulating everyday circumstances where a sound memory equates with being able to recall information after a period of time and intervening activity. Delayed recall is also more sensitive to damage to CNS structures, such as the hippocampus, that have been implicated in consolidation. Consolidation is the process whereby the brain absorbs information in a manner that makes retrieval beyond the point of continuous conscious retention (or rehearsal) possible: we learn a fact, move on to other things, and a day later recall it without having thought of it again. These considerations argue against the collapsing of immediate and delayed recall within single scores.

Surprisingly, some support for the single score approach emerges from the clinical samples, since their data indicate that the GMI (delayed index) is no more sensitive than the Immediate Memory Index to impairment. Within 10 distinct samples the Immediate and General Memory Indexes differ little (Hawkins, 1998), and nor do the immediate and delayed visual or auditory indexes, respectively, for these groups.[12] Hawkins (1998) discusses possible reasons for these surprising findings. Regardless of the explanation, the fact that the immediate and delayed scores do not dissociate supports the pooling of immediate and delayed data into single composites, since the resulting Auditory and Visual Memory indexes should possess a distinct advantage in reliability over their components (i.e., immediate and delayed scores).

Note, though, that the development of these new indexes does not preclude separate consideration of immediate and delayed scores, or, for that matter, the learning processes scores generated by the WMS-III. Some subjects do better on delayed trials, presumably because anxiety, or disorganization, undermined their earlier efforts, an observation that may rule out

---

[12]Alzheimer's disease, Huntington's disease, Parkinson's disease, TBI, schizophrenia, alcohol abuse, Korsakoff's syndrome, multiple sclerosis, left-hemisphere lobectomy, and right-hemisphere lobectomy.

the amnesic condition otherwise suggested by the poor immediate recall. DA and learning/recall process analyses are not mutually exclusive; the clinician should not be blind to the wealth of data generated by the WMS-III. A valid assessment of memory functioning often requires consideration of variables such as learning slope, savings scores (forgetting rate), and retrieval and recognition scores.

Challenge 6: Memory Deficit False Positives with High-IQ Subjects

In intellectual–memory DA, the employment of a simple difference approach using a single set of base rates will cause high rates of *false positives* among subjects with higher IQs. Clinicians expecting high IQ scores to be accompanied by equally high memory scores will be vulnerable to false positive error with regard to memory decline. The corrective is simple: use of either the predicted difference method of the Technical Manual, or reference to the IQ stratified base rates provided in this chapter, and in Hawkins and Tulsky (2001).

Challenge 7: Memory Deficit False Negatives with Low-IQ Subjects

In intellectual-memory DA, reference to a single set of base rates when applying the simple difference method will cause high rates of *false negatives* among subjects with low IQs. Since the memory scores of normal low IQ subjects typically exceed their IQ scores, their memory scores must typically decline substantially following an insult before a large intellectual–memory discrepancy will emerge. Again, the corrective appears to be simple: use of either the predicted difference method of the technical manual, or reference to the IQ-stratified base rates provided in this chapter and in Hawkins and Tulsky (2001).

There is, however, a consequence to use of either method that may cause discomfort. In some circumstances these methods result in the interpretation of a small superiority of intellectual score as indicating memory decline, which, on its face, may seem likely to result in high rates of false positive error. Furthering this discomfort is the following conundrum: The same IQ–memory difference score can be either rare, *or common*, depending upon whether you stratify the standardization sample on the basis of IQ score or on the basis of memory score.

Based upon FSIQ-stratified IQ–memory discrepancy base rates, we expect low-IQ examinees to exhibit higher memory scores. A GMI just a few points lower than IQ in an examinee with a low IQ could be considered to herald an acquired memory impairment because the base rates show that most lower IQ subjects exhibit a higher GMI. The 3-point memory inferiority of an examinee with a FSIQ of 79 and GMI of 76 looks uncommon when compared against IQ-stratified base rates: the vast majority of low IQ cases exhibit higher memory scores. Just 13% of standardization sample (IQ < 80) cases feature an IQ superiority of 3 points or larger.

But the converse is also true: Above-average memory scorers should typically display a lower IQ, *and below average memory scorers a higher IQ*. If we look at the GMI of an examinee first, and discover it to be well below average, we should expect the (as yet unexamined) IQ to be higher. Stratifying the standardization sample on the basis of GMI confirms that a low GMI is typically accompanied by a higher FSIQ. The same IQ-GMI 3-point discrepancy that looks uncommon against the IQ-stratified base rates is actually exceeded in 74% of low GMI (< 80) standardization cases. Against the base rates of the low GMI standardization cases, an IQ superiority has to reach 26 points to look as uncommon as the 3-point IQ superiority does against the low-IQ base rates.

The same discrepancy therefore looks either highly suggestive of memory impairment when compared against IQ stratified IQ–GMI base rates, or not at all so when compared against GMI-stratified base rates. Is it really the case that the same discrepancy could be considered normal *or* abnormal simply on the basis of which score (IQ or memory) is examined first? Arguing that it makes more sense to predict memory on the basis of IQ than the other way around provides an out, a practice supported by the provision of one-way (intellectual minus memory) discrepancy base rates in the technical manual, and by the clinical tradition of using IQ score to set an expectation for memory score, rather than vice-versa.

The preceding discussion refers to IQ–GMI discrepancies. Fortunately, the direction effects responsible for the conundrum are less pronounced in the base rates that emerge from six-factor model intellectual–memory contrasts (FSIQ obviously correlates with FSIQ, the stratification basis, to a greater degree than any other intellectual index). Nonetheless, the conundrum remains, and the resolution proposed could seem arbitrary. Empirical data from samples of clinical subjects with known or strongly suspected declines in memory functioning could put this matter to rest: In studies of at-risk individuals, do persons of lower intelligence who exhibit only a small superiority of intellectual over memory performance progress to Alzheimer's disease to the same extent as persons of superior intelligence who display much larger intellectual–memory discrepancies? Similar questions could be asked of other conditions of relevance.

Challenge 8: The Advent of Demographically Adjusted Scores

The development of demographically adjusted scores mitigates a linchpin rationale for discrepancy analysis. A fundamental rationale for DA has been that the application of a single set of norms and cutting scores for the entire population carries substantial false negative error risk for higher ability subjects (Crawford, 1996) and false positive risk for lower ability subjects. DA represents an attempt to counter these risks by using a score, or scores, considered less vulnerable to injury to predict the score of interest (i.e., to estimate where that score fell premorbidly). Heaton et al. (Chapter 5, this volume) developed the alternative strategy of adjusting scores based upon the influence of demographic variables, such as education, on ability level. Other demographics being equal, to appear normal once adjusted, the raw scores of a highly educated individual must be higher than those of a lesser-educated individual. Since such adjustments significantly mitigate the problems associated with use of "one-size-fits-all" norms and single cutting scores, DA may appear no longer necessary or justifiable.

DA and demographically adjusted scores are not, however, mutually exclusive aids: it is conceivable that DA *with demographically adjusted scores* could prove to be a useful complement to a primary reliance on adjusted scores. A critical question is whether DA provides additional inferential leverage over that provided by the simple inspection of demographically corrected scores alone, and, if so, under what circumstances.

Prospects for profile analysis with demographically adjusted data

Demographic adjustment does not eliminate all the difficulties encountered in the neuropsychological analysis of cognitive data. Demographic factors account for significant amounts of variance in ability, but imperfectly estimate the scores of individuals. Hypothetically, using a regression-derived equation, we may estimate that white males with 14 years of education score 106 on the PSI, but if we test any one such individual the chances are that his PSI will actually fall some distance away—consistent with the large error of estimate associated with this methodology. If our individual had a true (but unknown) premorbid PSI of 116 and tested at 101 post insult, neither his adjusted T score (of roughly 47) nor obtained PSI will, considered alone, reveal that he has suffered a significant decline in processing speed.

A critical point is, of course, that the premorbid PSI in the preceding case is unknown; demographic adjustment has been developed precisely because the true premorbid status of patients *is* typically unknown. Nonetheless, knowing the method to be imperfect, clinicians will be tempted to enhance inferential accuracy by considering factors such as whether the patient's level of education seems consistent with other indicators of premorbid intellectual competence, or to interpret the score of interest against the patient's index profile. This latter temptation will be felt most keenly in circumstances where reliance on a cutting score, albeit an adjusted one, carries heightened error risk: false-negative errors will be greater among patients who were, premorbidly, higher than average in ability (for demographic group), and false-positive error rates will be higher among lower ability cases. Consider the following hypothetical case.

A 62-year-old teacher with a master's degree presents with complaints that he has become increasingly forgetful and is referred for assessment to rule out the possibility of early stage Alzheimer's disease. He does not appear clinically depressed, but has suffered recent disappointments at work that could be causing distraction. His demographically adjusted WMS-III T-scores are on the low side — Auditory Memory 43 and Visual Memory 42 — but so too, are his intellectual T-scores: VCI 43; POI 47; WMI 42 and PSI 45.

Since no score of interest falls beneath a T of 40 and there is little scatter to the profile most clinicians would see little in these data that would support a diagnosis of early Alzheimer's disease—or of relative weakness in memory functioning, for that matter. But what if the index profile were different?

A 62-year-old teacher with a master's degree presents with complaints that he has become increasingly forgetful and is referred for assessment to rule out the possibility of early stage Alzheimer's disease. He does not appear clinically depressed, but has suffered recent disappointments at work that could be causing distraction. His demographically adjusted WMS-III T-scores are on the low side (Auditory Memory 43 and Visual Memory 42), but do not fall into the impairment range. His intellectual T-scores are substantially higher: VCI 58; POI 55; WMI 48 and PSI 49.

The scores of primary interest — Auditory Memory and Visual Memory — now appear in quite a different light, despite being exactly the same in both scenarios. The intellectual scores (VCI 58; POI 55; WMI 48 and PSI 49) suggest that these memory scores (43, 42) reflect a meaningful decline in memory functioning. Fewer than 10% of normal cases, for example, will show a differential between VCI and memory T scores as large as those seen in this case (Table 16). When any adjusted score of interest — say the PSI in a case of suspected TBI—falls just above 40 in a profile characterized by higher than average scores, clinicians will be tempted to interpret the score against the profile.

The converse—when a score of interest falls beneath 40, but not at a level appreciably lower than other scores—should prompt clinicians to consider the possibility of a false-positive result.

Base rates for Discrepancies between Demographically Adjusted Scores

In order to determine whether a discrepancy between demographically adjusted T-scores is abnormal, one must still refer to base rates. We have generated a single set from the standardization sample as a whole (Tables 16 and 17), but view this as just a preliminary foray. Adjusted score discrepancies still exhibit direction effects, for example, and these await full exploration. Individuals who perform better on the intellectual indexes (VCI, POI) than is typical for their demographic characteristics will typically show lower PSI, WMI, and memory scores, with the converse being true for those with low intellectual index scores. An example: standardization sample cases with VCI T-scores in excess of 60 display, as a group, substantially lower memory scores, with mean discrepancies of around 8 T scores (i.e., the memory scores are the better part of a standard deviation lower). Whether there are important variations in these trends across education levels, or ethnic groups, remains to be determined.

CONCLUDING COMMENTS

DA with factorially sound composite scores makes more sense than the analysis of differences between less homogenous indices, and in that regard the most recent revisions of the WAIS and WMS have enhanced the potential of DA to contribute to neuropsychological diagnosis. Preliminary explorations of standardization sample unidirectional discrepancy base rates reveal several noteworthy trends, some intuitive, other less so:

- Highly correlated indexes feature smaller natural discrepancies than weakly correlated indexes.

- Although very large discrepancies are more commonly seen at high IQ levels, the discrepancies exhibited by low-IQ subjects are, by and large, little smaller than those observed among subjects with high IQs. Across 17 index contrasts, the mean difference in discrepancy standard deviation from the lowest 15 % in FSIQ of the standardization sample to the highest 15 % is just 2.6 points.

- More important than differences in discrepancy size are the effects of rising IQ (and any strong correlate, such as education) on discrepancy direction, the tendency for one index score to be lower than another at low FSIQ levels, but higher at higher IQ levels. These effects reflect the typical modest correlation between the contrasted indexes, combined with the fact that one of the contrasted pair usually correlates more strongly with FSIQ than the other.

One obvious clinical implication is that clinicians should exercise caution when contrasting a score of interest (e.g., PSI or memory index) against an index that they are using to set an expectation for that score, such as the VCI or POI. When the predictor score is high (e.g., a VCI of 125), a sizable inferiority of the second score is to be expected on psychometric grounds alone. Direction effects vary in strength in relation to the magnitude of correlation between the two scores, and the difference between them in correlation with FSIQ. The score of a high-FSIQ subject on a strong correlate of FSIQ (e.g., VCI) will typically be much higher than his or her score on an index that correlates weakly with both FSIQ and the predictor index.

The converse implication of the stratified base rates is conceptually more problematic. Although clinicians may accept that a high intellectual score (e.g., VCI) is normally accompanied by, say, a lower memory score (so large discrepancies can be interpreted as normal), they may be less comfortable interpreting small memory score decrements in lower IQ individuals as abnormal. Reassuring demonstrations that it is legitimate to do so will require carefully designed studies of relevant conditions.

Although intended to assist clinicians in refining their analyses of differences between WAIS-III–WMS-III index scores, this chapter has also addressed the fundamental issue of the validity of DA. Based upon preliminary explorations of data from diverse clinical samples, it seems that more often than not the analysis of differences between scores adds little to diagnostic accuracy beyond that gained by the simple inspection of the index scores (considered singularly). On the other hand, analyses of data from a sample of chronic alcohol abusers suggests that DA might possibly contribute most when the damage wrought by a condition is relatively mild. Since the opinion of a neuropsychologist may matter most in mild or early stage states, this suggests that DA will continue to play an important role in neuropsychological analysis.

Quite aside from issues pertaining to the utility of DA with regular scores, it is clear that the role of DA has been diminished by the development of demographically adjusted scores. The existence of these scores, however, does not preclude clinicians from examining the demographically adjusted index profiles of their patients (perhaps in a secondary or complementary manner). The appeal of DA will remain greatest when clinicians sense that examinees are "atypical" for their demographics. Patients who are brighter than average for their demographics may still suffer a loss of capacity without the adjusted score(s) of interest falling below a predesignated cutting point, and many lower than average (for their demographic group) subjects will not exceed the cutting score, irrespective of whether they have suffered an insult or not. In either case, clinicians may believe that consideration of the index profile will assist them in assessing the likelihood of a loss in the capacities of interest. Reference to appropriate discrepancy base rate data should be considered critical to any such analyses. That said, the conditions under which clinicians using DA can surpass the diagnostic accuracy afforded by simple consideration of adjusted individual scores remain undetermined.

Finally, the presentation within this chapter of unidirectional discrepancy data is predicated on the presumption that clinicians will be selective in their examination of differences between scores (i.e., that they will refer to the base rates in Tables 6–17 with specific hypotheses in mind). In that regard they are disadvantaged by the limited clinical data yet available. The validation of DA with these instruments calls for the generation of data across a broad range of clinical circumstances and conditions, and there remains much work to be done.

ACKNOWLEDGEMENTS

Data presented in this chapter are drawn from the *Technical Manual of the Wechsler Adult Intelligence Scale/Wechsler Memory Scale: Third Edition,* or are based upon analyses performed by the authors with the WAIS-III WMS-III standardization samples data. Copyright 1997 by the Psychological Corporation. Adapted and reproduced by permission. All rights reserved. We wish to thank Robert Ivnik, Roger Graves, Robert Knight, Robert Heaton, and Gordon Chelune for their helpful comments on this chapter, or on manuscripts that were forerunners to it.

TABLE 6 WAIS-III and WAIS-III–WMS-III Index Discrepancy Base-Rates, FSIQ Less than 80[a]

Percentiles	Discrepancy												
	VCI – POI	VCI – WMI	VCI – PSI	VCI – Aud Mem	VCI – Vis Mem	VCI – Vis Mem (Orig)	POI – VCI	POI – WMI	POI – PSI	POI – Aud Mem	POI – Vis Mem	POI – Vis Mem (Orig)	WMI – PSI
50	0	-1	-1	-5	-5	-8	0	-3	-2	-7	-4	-7	-2
75	6	8	5	2	3	-1	6	4	5	2	3	0	7
85	9	10	9	5	7	3	10	9	8	6	10	4	11
90	11	12	11	8	11	6	12	10	9	11	12	7	13
95	17	17	13	11	15	9	17	15	13	16	14	14	22
98	22	19	17	20	16	25	23	28	22	27	26	19	32

[a]*Variables:* VCI = Verbal Comprehension Index; POI = Perceptual Organization Index; PSI = Processing Speed Index; WMI = WMS-III Working Memory; Aud Mem = Auditory Memory Index (composite Logical Memory I & II and Paired Associates I & II); Vis Mem = Visual Memory Index (composite of Family Pictures I & II and Visual Reproductions I & II); Vis Mem (Orig) = Visual Memory WMS-III Original (composite of Family Pictures I & II and Faces I & II). *Data:* Discrepancy data involving a WMS-III Index (WMI, Aud Mem, Vis Mem (Orig), Vis Mem) are derived from the WMS-III-weighted 1250 sample. All other data are derived from the WAIS-III 2450 sample. WAIS-III and WMS-III data copyright © 1997 by The Psychological Corporation, a Harcourt Assessment Company. Used with permission, all rights reserved.

Percentiles data were generated with SPSS 10 using the default algorithm, "definition 1" (waverage), accessible at www.spss.com/cech/stat/algorithms/freq.pdf, and were then rounded to closest whole number. The percentile values (extreme left column) show where a given discrepancy falls relative to the distribution of discrepancy scores, with higher values reflect increasing rarity. A discrepancy falling at the 85th percentile *exceeds* that seen in 85 % of cases within the sample; a discrepancy at 90th percentile exceeds 90 %, and so on. *All data are directional*, (i.e., they reflect the score generated by subtracting the second index from the first) (e.g., VCI − POI means VCI *minus* POI). Example: in Table 6, a superiority of VCI over POI of 9 falls at the 85th percentile for standardization sub-sample IQ < 80, and an 11-point margin falls at the 90th percentile.

TABLE 7 WMS-III Index Discrepancy Base Rates, FSIQ Less than 80[a]

Percentiles	Discrepancy						
	WMI – Aud Mem	WMI – Vis Mem	WMI – Vis Mem (Orig)	Aud Mem – Vis Mem	Aud Mem – Vis Mem (Orig)	Vis Mem – Aud Mem	Vis Mem (Orig) – Aud Mem
50	−4	−4	−8	3	−3	−3	3
75	6	7	4	11	5	6	12
85	13	12	9	12	11	10	16
90	16	20	14	14	14	15	19
95	23	24	20	20	23	16	23
98	24	31	28	23	24	21	29

[a] *Variables*: VCI = Verbal Comprehension Index; POI = Perceptual Organization Index; PSI = Processing Speed Index; WMI = WMS-III Working Memory; Aud Mem = Auditory Memory Index (composite Logical Memory I & II and Paired Associates I & II); Vis Mem = Visual Memory Index (composite of Family Pictures I & II and Visual Reproductions I & II); Vis Mem (Orig) = Visual Memory WMS-III Original (composite of Family Pictures I & II and Faces I & II). *Data*: Discrepancy data involving a WMS-III Index (WMI, Aud Mem, Vis Mem (Orig), Vis Mem) are derived from the WMS-III-weighted 1250 sample. All other data are derived from the WAIS-III 2450 sample. WAIS-III and WMS-III data copyright © 1997 by The Psychological Corporation, a Harcourt Assessment Company. Used with permission, all rights reserved.

Percentiles data were generated with SPSS 10 using the default algorithm, "definition 1" (waverage), accessible at www.spss.com/tech/stat/algorithms/freq.pdf, and were then rounded to closest whole number. The percentile values (extreme left column) show where a given discrepancy falls relative to the distribution of discrepancy scores, with higher values reflect increasing rarity. A discrepancy falling at the 85th percentile *exceeds* that seen in 85 % of cases within the sample; a discrepancy at 90th percentile exceeds 90 %, and so on. *All data are directional*, (i.e., they reflect the score generated by subtracting the second index from the first) (e.g., VCI − POI means VCI *minus* POI). Example: in Table 6, a superiority of VCI over POI of 9 falls at the 85th percentile for standardization sub-sample IQ <80, and an 11-point margin falls at the 90th percentile.

TABLE 8 WAIS-III and WAIS-III–WMS-III Index Discrepancy Base Rates, FSIQ 80–89[a]

						Discrepancy							
Percentiles	VCI – POI	VCI – WMI	VCI – PSI	VCI – Aud Mem	VCI – Vis Mem	VCI – Vis Mem (Orig)	POI – VCI	POI – WMI	POI – PSI	POI – Aud Mem	POI – Vis Mem	POI – Vis Mem (Orig)	WMI – PSI
50	0	-3	-1	-3	-4	-9	0	-2	-2	-4	-3	-7	0
75	7	6	5	7	6	4	6	5	5	5	4	3	9
85	11	10	9	11	11	9	10	10	8	14	10	7	14
90	14	13	11	14	17	12	12	12	9	19	16	11	17
95	19	18	13	18	24	19	17	18	13	25	20	16	19
98	24	23	17	23	31	25	23	23	22	34	29	30	20

[a]*Variables:* VCI = Verbal Comprehension Index; POI = Perceptual Organization Index; PSI = Processing Speed Index; WMI = WMS-III Working Memory; Aud Mem = Auditory Memory Index (composite Logical Memory I & II and Paired Associates I & II); Vis Mem = Visual Memory Index (composite of Family Pictures I & II and Visual Reproductions I & II); Vis Mem (Orig) = Visual Memory WMS-III Original (composite of Family Pictures I & II and Faces I & II). *Data:* Discrepancy data involving a WMS-III Index (WMI, Aud Mem, Vis Mem (Orig), Vis Mem) are derived from the WMS-III-weighted 1250 sample. All other data are derived from the WAIS-III 2450 sample. WAIS-III and WMS-III data copyright © 1997 by The Psychological Corporation, a Harcourt Assessment Company. Used with permission, all rights reserved.

Percentiles data were generated with SPSS 10 using the default algorithm, "definition 1" (waverage), accessible at www.spss.com/tech/stat/algorithms/freq.pdf, and were then rounded to closest whole number. The percentile values (extreme left column) show where a given discrepancy falls relative to the distribution of discrepancy scores, with higher values reflect increasing rarity. A discrepancy falling at the 85th percentile *exceeds* that seen in 85 % of cases within the sample; a discrepancy at 90th percentile exceeds 90 %, and so on. *All data are directional,* (i.e., they reflect the score generated by subtracting the second index from the first) (e.g., VCI – POI means VCI *minus* POI). Example: in Table 6, a superiority of VCI over POI of 9 falls at the 85th percentile for standardization sub-sample IQ < 80, and an 11-point margin falls at the 90th percentile.

TABLE 9 WMS-III Index Discrepancy Base-Rates, FSIQ 80–89[a]

	Discrepancy						
Percentiles	WMI – Aud Mem	WMI – Vis Mem	WMI – Vis Mem (Orig)	Aud Mem – Vis Mem	Aud Mem – Vis Mem (Orig)	Vis Mem – Aud Mem	Vis Mem (Orig) – Aud Mem
50	−3	−2	−4	−1	−4	1	4
75	10	8	4	9	8	13	19
85	19	13	11	14	12	18	22
90	21	18	16	20	16	21	27
95	27	26	22	24	24	24	30
98	32	34	32	32	28	35	36

[a]*Variables*: VCI = Verbal Comprehension Index; POI = Perceptual Organization Index; PSI = Processing Speed Index; WMI = WMS-III Working Memory; Aud Mem = Auditory Memory Index (composite Logical Memory I & II and Paired Associates I & II); Vis Mem = Visual Memory Index (composite of Family Pictures I & II and Visual Reproductions I & II); Vis Mem (Orig) = Visual Memory WMS-III Original (composite of Family Pictures I & II and Faces I & II). *Data*: Discrepancy data involving a WMS-III Index (WMI, Aud Mem, Vis Mem (Orig), Vis Mem) are derived from the WMS-III-weighted 1250 sample. All other data are derived from the WAIS-III 2450 sample. WAIS-III and WMS-III data copyright © 1997 by The Psychological Corporation, a Harcourt Assessment Company. Used with permission, all rights reserved.

Percentiles data were generated with SPSS 10 using the default algorithm, "definition 1" (waverage), accessible at www.spss.com/tech/stat/algorithms/freq.pdf, and were then rounded to closest whole number. The percentile values (extreme left column) show where a given discrepancy falls relative to the distribution of discrepancy scores, with higher values reflect increasing rarity. A discrepancy falling at the 85th percentile *exceeds* that seen in 85 % of cases within the sample; a discrepancy at 90th percentile exceeds 90 %, and so on. *All data are directional*, (i.e., they reflect the score generated by subtracting the second index from the first) (e.g., VCI – POI means VCI *minus* POI). Example: in Table 6, a superiority of VCI over POI of 9 falls at the 85th percentile for standardization sub-sample IQ < 80, and an 11-point margin falls at the 90th percentile.

TABLE 10   WAIS-III and WAIS-III–WMS-III Index Discrepancy Base Rates, FSIQ 90–109[a]

Percentiles	VCI – POI	VCI – WMI	VCI – PSI	VCI – Aud Mem	VCI – Vis Mem	VCI – Vis Mem (Orig)	POI – VCI	POI – WMI	POI – PSI	POI – Aud Mem	POI – Vis Mem	POI – Vis Mem (Orig)	WMI – PSI
50	0	−1	−1	0	0	0	0	−1	−1	1	−2	−1	0
75	8	8	9	9	8	10	8	7	8	9	8	10	9
85	12	14	14	14	12	16	13	12	13	15	12	15	15
90	15	17	17	17	15	20	16	15	16	18	15	20	18
95	21	22	22	21	22	27	21	18	22	23	20	27	23
98	25	30	26	28	27	32	27	24	26	30	27	30	29

[a]*Variables:* VCI = Verbal Comprehension Index; POI = Perceptual Organization Index; PSI = Processing Speed Index; WMI = WMS-III Working Memory; Aud Mem = Auditory Memory Index (composite Logical Memory I & II and Paired Associates I & II); Vis Mem = Visual Memory Index (composite of Family Pictures I & II and Visual Reproductions I & II); Vis Mem (Orig) = Visual Memory WMS-III Original (composite of Family Pictures I & II and Faces I & II). *Data:* Discrepancy data involving a WMS-III Index (WMI, Aud Mem, Vis Mem (Orig), Vis Mem) are derived from the WMS-III-weighted 1250 sample. All other data are derived from the WAIS-III 2450 sample. WAIS-III and WMS-III data copyright © 1997 by The Psychological Corporation, a Harcourt Assessment Company. Used with permission, all rights reserved.

Percentiles data were generated with SPSS 10 using the default algorithm, "definition 1" (waverage), accessible at www.spss.com/tech/stat/algorithms/freq.pdf, and were then rounded to closest whole number. The percentile values (extreme left column) show where a given discrepancy falls relative to the distribution of discrepancy scores, with higher values reflect increasing rarity. A discrepancy falling at the 85th percentile *exceeds* that seen in 85% of cases within the sample; a discrepancy at 90th percentile exceeds 90%, and so on. *All data are directional,* (i.e., they reflect the score generated by subtracting the second index from the first) (e.g., VCI − POI means VCI *minus* POI). Example: in Table 6, a superiority of VCI over POI of 9 falls at the 85th percentile for standardization sub-sample IQ < 80, and an 11-point margin falls at the 90th percentile.

TABLE 11 WMS-III Index Discrepancy Base Rates, FSIQ 90–109[a]

Percentiles	Discrepancy						
	WMI – Aud Mem	WMI-Vis Mem	WMI – Vis Mem (Orig)	Aud Mem – Vis Mem	Aud Mem – Vis Mem (Orig)	Vis Mem – Aud Mem	Vis Mem (Orig) – Aud Mem
50	1	0	−1	−1	−1	1	1
75	11	10	12	8	11	9	11
85	16	15	18	13	16	14	16
90	23	20	23	16	19	17	20
95	29	25	30	21	25	24	25
98	33	35	35	31	34	30	32

[a]*Variables*: VCI = Verbal Comprehension Index; POI = Perceptual Organization Index; PSI = Processing Speed Index; WMI = WMS-III Working Memory; Aud Mem = Auditory Memory Index (composite Logical Memory I & II and Paired Associates I & II); Vis Mem = Visual Memory Index (composite of Family Pictures I & II and Visual Reproductions I & II); Vis Mem (Orig) = Visual Memory WMS-III Original (composite of Family Pictures I & II and Faces I & II). *Data*: Discrepancy data involving a WMS-III Index (WMI, Aud Mem, Vis Mem (Orig), Vis Mem) are derived from the WMS-III-weighted 1250 sample. All other data are derived from the WAIS-III 2450 sample. WAIS-III and WMS-III data copyright © 1997 by The Psychological Corporation, a Harcourt Assessment Company. Used with permission, all rights reserved.

Percentiles data were generated with SPSS 10 using the default algorithm, "definition 1" (waverage), accessible at www.spss.com/tech/stat/algorithms/freq.pdf, and were then rounded to closest whole number. The percentile values (extreme left column) show where a given discrepancy falls relative to the distribution of discrepancy scores, with higher values reflect increasing rarity. A discrepancy falling at the 85th percentile *exceeds* that seen in 85 % of cases within the sample; a discrepancy at 90th percentile exceeds 90 %, and so on. *All data are directional*, (i.e., they reflect the score generated by subtracting the second index from the first) (e.g., VCI – POI means VCI *minus* POI). Example: in Table 6, a superiority of VCI over POI of 9 falls at the 85th percentile for standardization sub-sample IQ < 80, and an 11-point margin falls at the 90th percentile.

TABLE 12 WAIS-III and WAIS-III—WMS-III Index Discrepancy Base Rates, FSIQ 110–119[a]

Percentiles	VCI – POI	VCI – WMI	VCI – PSI	VCI – Aud Mem	VCI – Vis Mem	VCI – Vis Mem (Orig)	POI – VCI	POI – WMI	POI – PSI	POI – Aud Mem	POI – Vis Mem	POI – Vis Mem (Orig)	WMI – PSI
50	1	5	4	3	4	6	–1	3	4	0	4	6	3
75	9	13	15	13	17	17	8	10	15	13	12	15	10
85	13	20	20	17	21	25	14	16	19	18	18	20	16
90	19	23	24	23	25	29	18	20	23	23	23	26	19
95	23	28	29	25	32	37	23	23	28	26	29	35	23
98	30	37	36	36	40	47	29	31	32	31	34	41	31

[a] *Variables*: VCI = Verbal Comprehension Index; POI = Perceptual Organization Index; PSI = Processing Speed Index; WMI = WMS-III Working Memory; Aud Mem = Auditory Memory Index (composite Logical Memory I & II and Paired Associates I & II); Vis Mem = Visual Memory Index (composite of Family Pictures I & II and Visual Reproductions I & II); Vis Mem (Orig) = Visual Memory WMS-III Original (composite of Family Pictures I & II and Faces I & II). *Data*: Discrepancy data involving a WMS-III Index (WMI, Aud Mem, Vis Mem (Orig), Vis Mem) are derived from the WMS-III-weighted 1250 sample. All other data are derived from the WAIS-III 2450 sample. WAIS-III and WMS-III data copyright © 1997 by The Psychological Corporation, a Harcourt Assessment Company. Used with permission, all rights reserved.

Percentiles data were generated with SPSS 10 using the default algorithm, "definition 1" (waverage), accessible at www.spss.com/tech/stat/algorithms/freq.pdf, and were then rounded to closest whole number. The percentile values (extreme left column) show where a given discrepancy falls relative to the distribution of discrepancy scores, with higher values reflect increasing rarity. A discrepancy falling at the 85th percentile exceeds that seen in 85% of cases within the sample; a discrepancy at 90th percentile exceeds 90%, and so on. *All data are directional*, (i.e., they reflect the score generated by subtracting the second index from the first) (e.g., VCI – POI means VCI *minus* POI). Example: in Table 6, a superiority of VCI over POI of 9 falls at the 85th percentile for standardization sub-sample IQ < 80, and an 11-point margin falls at the 90th percentile.

TABLE 13   WMS-III Index Discrepancy Base Rates, FSIQ 110–119[a]

Percentiles	WMI – Aud Mem	WMI – Vis Mem	WMI – Vis Mem (Orig)	Aud Mem – Vis Mem	Aud Mem – Vis Mem (Orig)	Vis Mem – Aud Mem	Vis Mem (Orig) – Aud Mem
				Discrepancy			
50	–2	1	3	2	3	–2	–3
75	11	11	14	11	13	8	8
85	18	16	20	17	20	14	12
90	23	20	27	20	23	18	18
95	28	27	34	23	32	23	23
98	35	42	44	30	36	30	27

[a]*Variables*: VCI = Verbal Comprehension Index; POI = Perceptual Organization Index; PSI = Processing Speed Index; WMI = WMS-III Working Memory; Aud Mem = Auditory Memory Index (composite Logical Memory I & II and Paired Associates I & II); Vis Mem = Visual Memory Index (composite of Family Pictures I & II and Visual Reproductions I & II); Vis Mem (Orig) = Visual Memory WMS-III Original (composite of Family Pictures I & II and Faces I & II). *Data*: Discrepancy data involving a WMS-III Index (WMI, Aud Mem, Vis Mem (Orig), Vis Mem) are derived from the WMS-III–weighted 1250 sample. All other data are derived from the WAIS-III 2450 sample. WAIS-III and WMS-III data copyright © 1997 by The Psychological Corporation, a Harcourt Assessment Company. Used with permission, all rights reserved.

Percentiles data were generated with SPSS 10 using the default algorithm, "definition 1" (waverage), accessible at www.spss.com/tech/stat/algorithms/freq.pdf, and were then rounded to closest whole number. The percentile values (extreme left column) show where a given discrepancy falls relative to the distribution of discrepancy scores, with higher values reflect increasing rarity. A discrepancy falling at the 85th percentile *exceeds* that seen in 85 % of cases within the sample; a discrepancy at 90th percentile exceeds 90 %, and so on. *All data are directional*, (i.e., they reflect the score generated by subtracting the second index from the first) (e.g., VCI – POI means VCI *minus* POI). Example: in Table 6, a superiority of VCI over POI of 9 falls at the 85th percentile for standardization sub-sample IQ < 80, and an 11-point margin falls at the 90th percentile.

TABLE 14 WAIS-III and WAIS-III–WMS-III Index Discrepancy Base Rates, FSIQ 120+[a]

Percentiles	Discrepancy												
	VCI – POI	VCI – WMI	VCI – PSI	VCI – Aud Mem	VCI – Vis Mem	VCI – Vis Mem (Orig)	POI – VCI	POI – WMI	POI – PSI	POI – Aud Mem	POI – Vis Mem	POI – Vis Mem (Orig)	WMI – PSI
50	2	8	9	4	11	16	−2	4	6	4	7	10	−2
75	11	20	20	18	21	24	7	13	15	16	18	22	7
85	17	23	25	26	28	29	11	18	22	23	20	29	11
90	19	27	27	28	33	39	18	23	25	27	24	33	13
95	24	33	33	32	40	44	20	26	30	33	31	39	22
98	29	37	40	41	50	50	28	36	39	42	36	47	32

[a] *Variables:* VCI = Verbal Comprehension Index; POI = Perceptual Organization Index; PSI = Processing Speed Index; WMI = WMS-III Working Memory; Aud Mem = Auditory Memory Index (composite Logical Memory I & II and Paired Associates I & II); Vis Mem = Visual Memory Index (composite of Family Pictures I & II and Visual Reproductions I & II); Vis Mem (Orig) = Visual Memory WMS-III Original (composite of Family Pictures I & II and Faces I & II). *Data:* Discrepancy data involving a WMS-III Index (WMI, Aud Mem, Vis Mem (Orig), Vis Mem) are derived from the WMS-III-weighted 1250 sample. All other data are derived from the WAIS-III 2450 sample. WAIS-III and WMS-III data copyright © 1997 by The Psychological Corporation, a Harcourt Assessment Company. Used with permission, all rights reserved.

Percentiles data were generated with SPSS 10 using the default algorithm, "definition 1" (waverage), accessible at www.spss.com/tech/stat/algorithms/freq.pdf, and were then rounded to closest whole number. The percentile values (extreme left column) show where a given discrepancy falls relative to the distribution of discrepancy scores, with higher values reflect increasing rarity. A discrepancy falling at the 85th percentile *exceeds* that seen in 85% of cases within the sample; a discrepancy at 90th percentile exceeds 90%, and so on. *All data are directional,* (i.e., they reflect the score generated by subtracting the second index from the first) (e.g., VCI − POI means VCI *minus* POI). Example: in Table 6, a superiority of VCI over POI of 9 falls at the 85th percentile for standardization sub-sample IQ < 80, and an 11-point margin falls at the 90th percentile.

TABLE 15   WMS-III Index Discrepancy Base Rates, FSIQ 120+[a]

				Discrepancy			
Percentiles	WMI − Aud Mem	WMI − Vis Mem	WMI − Vis Mem (Orig)	Aud Mem − Vis Mem	Aud Mem − Vis Mem (Orig)	Vis Mem − Aud Mem	Vis Mem (Orig) − Aud Mem
50	1	3	5	3	8	−3	−8
75	13	15	21	15	18	7	5
85	19	22	27	20	25	13	12
90	23	25	31	22	28	18	18
95	26	30	39	25	41	23	27
98	30	33	45	39	44	29	30

[a]*Variables*: VCI = Verbal Comprehension Index; POI = Perceptual Organization Index; PSI = Processing Speed Index; WMI = WMS-III Working Memory; Aud Mem = Auditory Memory Index (composite Logical Memory I & II and Paired Associates I & II); Vis Mem = Visual Memory Index (composite of Family Pictures I & II and Visual Reproductions I & II); Vis Mem (Orig) = Visual Memory WMS-III Orignal (composite of Family Pictures I & II and Faces I & II). *Data*: Discrepancy data involving a WMS-III Index (WMI, Aud Mem, Vis Mem (Orig), Vis Mem) are derived from the WMS-III–weighted 1250 sample. All other data are derived from the WAIS-III 2450 sample. WAIS-III and WMS-III data copyright © 1997 by The Psychological Corporation, a Harcourt Assessment Company. Used with permission, all rights reserved.

Percentiles data were generated with SPSS 10 using the default algorithm, "definition 1" (waverage), accessible at www.spss.com/tech/stat/algorithms/freq.pdf, and were then rounded to closest whole number. The percentile values (extreme left column) show where a given discrepancy falls relative to the distribution of discrepancy scores, with higher values reflect increasing rarity. A discrepancy falling at the 85th percentile *exceeds* that seen in 85% of cases within the sample; a discrepancy at 90th percentile exceeds 90%, and so on. *All data are directional*, (i.e., they reflect the score generated by subtracting the second index from the first) (e.g., VCI − POI means VCI *minus* POI). Example: in Table 6, a superiority of VCI over POI of 9 falls at the 85th percentile for standardization sub-sample IQ < 80, and an 11-point margin falls at the 90th percentile.

TABLE 16 WAIS-III and WAIS-III–WMS-III Index Discrepancy Base-Rates for Demographically Adjusted T Scores[a]

Percentiles	Discrepancy										
	VCI – POI	VCI – WMI	VCI – PSI	VCI – Aud Mem	VCI – Vis Mem	POI – VCI	POI – WMI	POI – PSI	POI – Aud Mem	POI – Vis Mem	WMI – PSI
50	1	1	1	0	0	−1	0	0	0	0	0
75	7	8	8	7	8	6	6	7	7	6	7
85	10	11	12	11	11	10	10	11	12	10	10
90	13	14	15	14	15	12	12	13	15	13	13
95	17	18	19	19	19	16	16	17	19	17	16
98	21	22	24	22	22	20	20	21	24	22	21

[a]*Variables:* VCI = Verbal Comprehension Index; POI = Perceptual Organization Index; PSI = Processing Speed Index; WMI = WMS-III Working Memory; Aud Mem = Auditory Memory Index (composite Logical Memory I & II and Paired Associates I & II and Visual Reproductions I & II); Vis Mem = Visual Memory Index (composite of Family Pictures I & II and Faces I & II). *Data:* Discrepancy data involving a WMS-III Index (WMI, Aud Mem, Vis Mem (Orig), Vis Mem) are derived from the WMS-III–weighted 1250 sample. All other data are derived from the WAIS-III 2450 sample. WAIS-III and WMS-III data copyright © 1997 by The Psychological Corporation, a Harcourt Assessment Company. Used with permission, all rights reserved.

Percentiles data were generated with SPSS 10 using the default algorithm, "definition 1" (waverage), accessible at www.spss.com/tech/stat/algorithms/freq.pdf, and were then rounded to closest whole number. Values corresponding to a given percentile are rounded. *How to read this table:* The percentile values (extreme left column) show where a given discrepancy falls relative to the distribution of discrepancy scores, with higher values reflect increasing rarity. A discrepancy falling at the 85th percentile *exceeds* that seen in 85% of cases within the sample; a discrepancy at 90th percentile exceeds 90%, and so on. *All data are directional*, i.e. they reflect the score generated by subtracting the second index from the first (e.g., VCI – POI means VCI *minus* POI). Example: in Table 16, a superiority of VCI over POI of 10 falls at the 85th percentile, and a 13 point margin falls at the 90th percentile.

TABLE 17 WMS-III Index Discrepancy Base Rates for Demographically Adjusted T Scores[a]

Percentiles	Discrepancy			
	WMI − Aud Mem	WMI − Vis Mem	Aud Mem − Vis Mem	Vis Mem − Aud Mem
50	0	0	0	0
75	8	7	7	7
85	12	12	10	10
90	15	14	12	13
95	19	18	15	16
98	24	23	21	21

[a]*Variables:* VCI = Verbal Comprehension Index; POI = Perceptual Organization Index; PSI = Processing Speed Index; WMI = WMS-III Working Memory; Aud Mem = Auditory Memory Index (composite Logical Memory I & II and Paired Associates I & II); Vis Mem = Visual Memory Index (composite of Family Pictures I & II and Visual Reproductions I & II); Vis Mem (Orig) = Visual Memory WMS-III Original (composite of Family Pictures I & II and Faces I & II). *Data:* Discrepancy data involving a WMS-III Index (WMI, Aud Mem, Vis Mem (Orig), Vis Mem) are derived from the WMS-III-weighted 1250 sample. All other data are derived from the WAIS-III 2450 sample. WAIS-III and WMS-III data copyright © 1997 by The Psychological Corporation, a Harcourt Assessment Company. Used with permission, all rights reserved.

Percentiles data were generated with SPSS 10 using the default algorithm, "definition 1" (waverage), accessible at www.spss.com/tech/stat/algorithms/freq.pdf, and were then rounded to closest whole number. Values corresponding to a given percentile are rounded. *How to read this table:* The percentile values (extreme left column) show where a given discrepancy falls relative to the distribution of discrepancy scores, with higher values reflect increasing rarity. A discrepancy falling at the 85th percentile *exceeds* that seen in 85 % of cases within the sample; a discrepancy at 90th percentile exceeds 90 %, and so on. *All data are directional*, i.e. they reflect the score generated by subtracting the second index from the first (e.g., VCI−POI means VCI *minus* POI). Example: in Table 16, a superiority of VCI over POI of 10 falls at the 85th percentile, and a 13 point margin falls at the 90th percentile.

REFERENCES

Bornstein, R. A. (1983). Verbal IQ-Performance IQ discrepancies on the Wechsler Adult Intelligence Scale-Revised in patients with unilateral or bilateral cerebral dysfunction. *Journal of Clinical and Consulting Psychology, 51*, 779–780.

Bornstein, R. A., Chelune, G. J., & Prifitera, A. (1989). IQ-Memory discrepancies in normal and clinical samples. *Psychological Assessment, 1*(3), 203–206.

Bornstein, R. A., Matarazzo, J. D. (1982). Wechsler VIQ versus PIQ differences in cerebral dysfunction: A literature review with emphasis on sex differences. *Journal of Clinical Neuropsychology, 4*(4), 319–334.

Cohen, J. (1988). *Statistical power analysis for the behavioral sciences.* Hillsdate, NJ Erlbaum.

Crawford, J. R. (1996). Assessment. In *The Blackwell dictionary of neuropsychology.* (pp. 108–116). London: Blackwell.

Crawford, J. R., Johnson, D. A., Mychalkiw, B., & Moore, J. W. (1997). WAIS–R performance following closed-head injury: A comparison of the clinical utility of summary IQs, factor scores, and subtest scatter indices. *Clinical Neuropsychologist, 11*(4), 345–355.

Dikmen, S. S., Machamer, J. E. Winn, H. R., & Temkin, N. R. (1995). Neuropsychological outcome at 1-year post head injury. *Neuropsychology 9*(1), 80–90.

Guilmette, T. J., Dabrowski, J., Kennedy, M. L., & Gnys, J. (1999). A comparison of nine WAIS–R short forms in individuals with mild to severe traumatic brain injury. *Assessment, 6*(1), 33–41.

Hawkins, K. A. (1998). Indicators of brain dysfunction derived from graphic representations of the WAIS-III/WMS-III Technical Manual clinical samples data: A preliminary approach to clinical utility. *Clinical Neuropsychologist, 12*(4), 535–551.

Hawkins, K. A., Plehn, K., & Borgaro, S. (2002). Verbal IQ–performance IQ differentials in traumatic brain injury samples. *Archives of Clinical Neuropsychology, 17*(1), 49–56.

Hawkins, K. A., & D. S. Tulsky (2001). The influence of IQ stratification on WAIS-III/WMS-III FSIQ-General Memory Index discrepancy base-rates in the standardization sample. *Journal of the International Neuropsychological Society, 7*(7), 875–880.

Heaton, R. K., Taylor, M. J., & Manly, J. (2003). Demographic effects and use of demographically corrected norms with the WAIS-III and WMS-III. In D. S. Tulsky, et al. (Eds). *Clinical Interpretation of the WAIS-III and WMS-III.* San Diego, Academic Press, 181–207.

Kaufman, A. S. (1990). *Assessing adolescent and adult intelligence.* Needham Heights, MA: Allyn & Bacon, Inc.

Levin, H. S., & Larrabee, G. J. (1983). Disproportionate decline in visuospatial memory in human aging. *Society for Neuroscience Abstracts, 9*, 21.

Little, A. J., Templer, D. I., Perel, C. S., & Ashley, M. J. (1996). Feasibility of the neuropsychological spectrum in prediction of outcome following head injury. *Journal of Clinical Psychology, 52*(4).

Martin, T. A., Donders, J., & Thompson, E. (2000). Potential of and problems with new measures of psychometric intelligence after traumatic brain injury. *Rehabilitation Psychology, 45*(4).

Matarazzo, J. D., & Herman, D. O. (1984). Base rate data for the WAIS-R: Test–retest stability and VIQ–PIQ differences. *Journal of Clinical Neuropsychology, 6*(4), 351–366.

Matarazzo, J. D., & Herman, D. O. (1985). Clinical uses of the WAIS-R: Base rates of differences between VIQ and PIQ in the WAIS-R standardization sample. In B. B. Wolman, (Ed.), *Handbook of intelligence: Theories, measurements, and applications.* (pp. 889–932). New York: John Wiley & Sons.

Milner, B. (1975). Psychological aspects of focal epilepsy and its neurosurgical management. *Advances in Neurology, 8,* 299–321.

Paniak, C. E., Silver, K., Finlayson, M. A., & Tuff, L. P. (1992). How useful is the WAIS–R in closed head injury assessment? *Journal of Clinical Psychology, 48*(2).

Prigatano, G. P. (1974). *Memory deficits in head injured patients.* El Paso: Southwestern Psychological Association.

The Psychological Corporation (1997). *WAIS-III WMS-III technical manual.* San Antonio: The Psychological Corporation.

Quadfasel, A. F., & Pruyser, P. W. (1955). Cognitive deficits in patients with psychomotor epilepsy. *Epilepsia, 4,* 80–90.

Russell, E. W. (1981). The pathology and clinical examination of memory. In S. B. Filskov & T. J. Boll. (Eds.), *Handbook of clinical psychology.* (pp. 287–319). New York, Wiley.

Spearman, C. (1904). General intelligence, objectively determined and measured. *American Journal of Psychology, 15*(2), 201–293.

Thorndike, E. L., Lay, W., & Dean, P. R. (1909). The relation of accuracy in sensory discrimination to general intelligence. *American Journal of Psychology, 20*(3), 364–373.

Tulsky, D. S., Ivnik, R. J., Price, L. R., & Wilkins, C. (2003). Assessment of cognitive functioning with the WAIS-III and WMS-III: Development of a 6-factor model. In D. S. Tulsky, et al. (Eds). *Clinical Interpretation of the WAIS-III and WMS-III.* San Diego, Academic Press, 145–177.

Tulsky, D. S., Rolfhus, E. L., & Zhu, J. (2000). Two-tailed versus one-tailed base rates of discrepancy scores in the WAIS-III. *Clinical Neuropsychologist, 14*(4), 451–460.

Warrington, E. K., James, M., & Maciejewski, C. (1986). The WAIS as a lateralizing and localizing diagnostic instrument: A study of 656 patients with unilateral cerebral lesions. *Neuropsychologia, 24*(2), 223–239.

Wechsler, D. (1958). *The measurement and appraisal of adult intelligence.* Baltimore, MD: Williams & Wilkins.

Wechsler, D. (1987). *Manual for the Wechsler Memory Scale—Revised.* San Antonio, TX: The Psychological Corporation.

Wechsler, D. (1997a). *Wechsler Adult Intelligence Scale—Third Edition.* San Antonio, TX: The Psychological Corporation.

Wechlser, D. (1997b). *Wechsler Memory Scale—Third Edition.* San Antonio, TX: The Psychological Corporation.

Wilde, N., Strauss, E., Chelune, G. J., Loring, D. W., Martin, R. C., Hermann, B. P., Sherman, E. M. S., & Hunter, M. (2001). WMS-III performance in patients with temporal lobe epilepsy: Group differences and individual classification. *Journal of the International Neuropsychological Society, 7*(7), 881–891.

CHAPTER 7

Diagnostic Validity

Glenn E. Smith, Jane H. Cerhan, and Robert J. Ivnik,
Department of Psychiatry and Psychology
Mayo Clinic
Rochester, Minnesota

OVERVIEW

The 'diagnostic validity' of a test refers to the test's ability to differentiate persons with and without a specified disorder. It is the most important type of criterion–related validity for clinical psychologists and neuropsychologists selecting tests to inform the diagnostic process. The diagnostic validity of tests has traditionally been evaluated with null–hypothesis significance testing of mean group differences. For example, evidence for the diagnostic validity of the Wechsler Adult Intelligence Scale-Third Edition (WAIS-III) and Wechsler Memory Scale-III (WMS-III) is provided in the technical manual (The Psychological Corporation, 1997) in the form of mean comparisons of normals and selected clinical groups (Alzheimer's disease, traumatic brain injury, temporal lobe epilepsy, etc.).

While these null–hypothesis significance testing analyses provide general information about how groups with various disease entities perform on the WAIS-III and WMS-III, such group comparisons are less useful to the clinician wishing to determine the utility of these measures as aides in diagnosing individual patients (Ivnik et al., 2000). In this chapter, methods more commonly used in epidemiology and clinical medicine will be presented as important alternatives for establishing diagnostic validity of the WAIS-III and WMS-III. First, concepts that are fundamental to this approach to diagnostic validity are discussed, including sensitivity, specificity, odds ratios, base rates, and, positive and negative predictive value. Then, the likelihood ratio is presented as an important and practical statistic for calculating posttest odds that reflect the actual diagnostic meaning of a specific patient's test score.

After reviewing these concepts for the reader, they are applied to data from the clinical Alzheimer's disease (AD) sample collected as part of the WAIS-III–WMS-III standardization. These analyses may not generalize well to the diagnostic utility of the WAIS-III and WMS-III in most clinical settings because of the severity of the dementia in that AD sample. However it is hoped that they are informative for investigators designing future studies of the diagnostic validity of these instruments for a variety of clinical applications.

GROUP VERSUS INDIVIDUAL STATISTICS

Understanding tests' reliability and validity is fundamental to our discipline (Anastasi & Urbina, 1997). Traditionally, group descriptive statistics intended to characterize test reliability and validity, such as test–retest correlation coefficients and convergent validity coefficients, have provided convenient and broadly applicable means of communicating about and comparing test properties. The provision of such statistics is an obligation of test developers (American Education Research Association, 1999) and has been critical to test users' ability to compare and select instruments that meet minimum measurement standards. In other words, group descriptive statistics—such as means, standard deviations, and especially correlation coefficients—have traditionally been used to evaluate tests.

However, as psychological tests have come to be used as an aid to clinical diagnosis, it has been common practice to usurp some of these group statistics to attempt to enhance the utility of our measures. Such application of group statistics to decisions about individuals can be problematic. This is illustrated by the case of discrepancy-analyses with the Wechsler Intelligence scales. Up through the WISC-R (Wechsler, 1974) and WAIS-R (Wechsler, 1981) manuals, the publisher provided data on the degree of discrepancy between subtest scores and summary indices that were statistically significant at the $p < 0.15$ level. These cutoffs were based on standard errors of difference scores, a group statistic. This information tells you if two apparently different scores can really be assumed to be different statistically, or if they could represent the same "underlying" score differing only because of random measurement error.

Perhaps unduly influenced by general factor (g) theories of cognitive function, clinicians have often made the mistake of assuming *statistical* significance implies *clinical* significance. This is only true if one assumes that all cognitively normal people should generate the same level of performance across all of their abilities. Numerous studies have demonstrated that this is not true even for the finite set of abilities measured by the Wechsler instruments (Crawford & Allan, 1996; Ivnik, Smith, Malec, Petersen, & Tangalos, 1995; Matarazzo, Daniel, Prifitera, & Herman, 1988). Normal people display various patterns of cognitive strengths and weaknesses. The third editions of the WISC (Wechsler, 1991) and WAIS (Wechsler, 1997) manuals now emphasize the distinction between statistically significant difference scores and clinically significant difference scores by providing both significance levels for various difference scores *and* the frequency of these difference scores in the general population. For example, WAIS-III Verbal IQ—Performance IQ differences of 9 points or greater are statistically significant at the .05 level, but ~43% of the standardization sample had difference scores in this range. Thus, some statistically significant score differences are relatively common in the general population. Clearly, these score differences do not necessarily indicate an underlying abnormality, as has sometimes been argued by clinicians (Lezak, 1995). This illustrates the perils of applying group-oriented statistics to decisions about individuals.

Group statistics traditionally used to provide evidence for the reliability of a test also have limited utility in interpreting individuals' test results. For example, test–retest correlations are intended to describe how much variability in longitudinal testing might be attributable to measurement error, assuming the underlying psychological construct is stable and that fluctuations must reflect error. The idea that the construct being measured may not be stable is antithetic to reliability theory. Yet, many clinically interesting phenomena are not stable. Aspects of memory change as people age (Albert, 2000), undergo neurosurgery, acute effects of trauma subside, etc. When longitudinal change is anticipated, knowledge of measurement fluctuation resulting from error alone (i.e., test–retest correlations derived from group statistics) is insufficient for clinical inference. Rather, knowledge of typical patterns of individual change in both neurologically "stable" and "unstable" populations is needed. Application of individual statistics such as change-score frequencies may be necessary to identify extraordinary change in a given person. The challenges of repeated testing are described elsewhere in this volume.

Traditional psychometric statistics for establishing a measure's validity also have limited utility in the diagnostic process. The *WAIS-III and WMS-III Technical Manual* (Psychological Corporation, 1997) provides diagnostic validity evidence in the form of group mean comparisons across a variety of diagnostic groups (Alzheimer's disease, Parkinson's disease, Huntington's disease, multiple sclerosis, traumatic brain injury, epilepsy, alcohol disorders, and schizophrenia). These data are reproduced in Table 1. Across all these groups, mean differences were observed according to patterns that fit clinical expectations. However, we (Ivnik et al., 2000) have highlighted the limitations of null hypothesis significance testing involving means comparisons as a validation method for diagnostic applications. Our analyses focused on the Mayo Cognitive Factor Scores (MCFS) (Smith et al., 1994), which are factor-analysis-derived indices based on co-administration of the WAIS-R, WMS-R (Wechsler, 1987), and Rey Auditory Verbal Learning Test (AVLT) (Rey, 1964). We have shown that there were statistically significant, cross-sectional and longitudinal differences between normals and a dementia cohort on all five MCFS measures. Nevertheless, many of these measures were not particularly useful in discriminating between *individuals* in these groups. Analyses using diagnostic validity statistics, to be described below (e.g., odds ratios), revealed only selected MCFS measures to have good diagnostic validity for dementia.

The Ivnik et al. (2000) study highlights the difference between null-hypothesis significance testing analysis, which establishes the impact of brain dysfunction on cognitive tests, and data analysis that focuses on the diagnostic usefulness (e.g., sensitivity, specificity, etc.) of the same measures. Each analytic approach is important for understanding the implications that can be drawn from cognitive data that relate to comparisons of normal and impaired persons. Our results demonstrated that "highly significant" null-hypothesis significance testing differences between groups on cognitive tests cannot be used as evidence for the diagnostic power of the same tests. Although null-hypothesis significance testing and diagnostic validity statistics are complementary approaches to data analysis, the results of one should not be used to support conclusions that are more appropriately based on the findings of the other. All of the MCFS measures in that study were "significant" based on null-hypothesis significance testing analyses, and most would be described as "highly significant." Impressive group and interaction effects were present on the repeated measures analysis of variance, establish-

TABLE 1 WAIS-III and WMS-III Performance of Samples with Neurologic Disorders, Temporal Lobe Epilepsy, and Alcohol-Related Disorders[a]

| | Alzheimer's disease mild mean (SD) | Huntington's disease mean (SD) | Parkinson's disease mean (SD) | Traumatic brain injury mean (SD) | Multiple sclerosis mean (SD) | Temporal Lobe Epilepsy | | Chronic alcohol abuse mean (SD) | Korsakoff's syndrome mean (SD) |
						left lobectomy mean (SD)	right lobectomy mean (SD)		
N	35	15	10	22	25	15	12	28	10
WAIS-III scales/ indexes[b]									
VIQ	92.2(13.1)	90.9(70.0)	94.6(8.3)	89.6(12.4)				108.6(12.7)	94.5(10.3)
PIQ	81.7(13.2)	78.2(8.9)	82.3(12.3)	84.5(13.8)				101.2(14.5)	92.2(17.7)
FSIQ	86.6(13.1)	84.0(8.2)	88.2(10.1)	86.5(10.9)				106.1(13.5)	92.8(13.6)
VCI	93.0(12.0)	98.4(8.9)	96.9(7.3)	89.6(12.7)				109.0(11.4)	92.7(9.3)
POI	84.8(12.4)	84.9(9.3)	84.7(12.1)	92.1(15.0)				102.0(14.0)	96.9(15.4)
WMI	87.2(17.3)	81.7(10.3)	89.6(12.1)	89.8(13.1)				104.6(12.3)	98.4(15.5)
PSI	79.6(14.4)	69.3(7.8)	81.7(10.3)	73.4(10.7)				97.7(12.5)	88.2(19.3)
WMS-III primary indexes									
Auditory Immediate	68.7(11.0)	78.3(13.3)	86.0(17.4)	89.3(19.3)	97.7(14.4)	77.9(16.3)	95.0(11.3)	108.0(15.4)	73.1(7.8)
Visual Immediate	70.6(10.9)	73.5(7.1)	84.7(15.1)	74.9(13.9)	81.5(14.3)	86.5(15.4)	83.5(9.1)	96.0(14.5)	67.8(6.8)
Immediate Memory	62.9(11.4)	70.9(11.0)	82.3(17.8)	78.9(17.7)	88.0(15.9)	78.1(16.2)	87.2(10.7)	102.5(16.5)	64.4(8.2)

(*continues*)

TABLE 1 *(continued)*

| | Alzheimer's disease mild mean (SD) | Huntington's disease mean (SD) | Parkinson's disease mean (SD) | Traumatic brain injury mean (SD) | Multiple sclerosis mean (SD) | Temporal Lobe Epilepsy | | Chronic alcohol abuse mean (SD) | Korsakoff's syndrome mean (SD) |
						left lobectomy mean (SD)	right lobectomy mean (SD)		
N	35	15	10	22	25	15	12	28	10
WAIS-III scales/ indexes[b]									
Auditory Delayed	66.1(9.6)	83.7(12.5)	85.8(17.2)	89.6(21.8)	92.8(19.1)	75.4(14.5)	93.5(11.9)	107.3(15.5)	63.5(5.3)
Visual Delayed	67.5(8.1)	71.2(10.5)	80.9(13.1)	74.3(13.9)	82.2(16.6)	85.3(16.5)	84.3(11.7)	97.9(13.5)	65.4(8.3)
Auditory Recognition Delayed	65.6(8.6)	88.0(9.8)	90.0(14.1)	93.6(16.6)	92.4(14.5)	83.0(18.5)	92.1(15.7)	109.6(13.0)	64.5(8.0)
General Memory	60.4(8.9)	76.4(10.5)	81.8(15.1)	81.9(16.5)	86.7(17.8)	77.3(15.1)	87.6(12.7)	105.2(14.2)	57.8(6.7)
Working Memory	80.4(16.9)	83.1(11.1)	85.6(13.0)	91.9(11.9)	94.8(18.2)	95.4(15.6)	97.8(12.9)	98.0(9.3)	97.8(13.0)

[a]Adapted from The Psychological Corporation (1997). Data copyright © 2002 by the Psychological Corporation. All rights reserved.

[b]VIQ, Verbal IQ; PIQ, Performance IQ; FSIQ, Full-Scale IQ; VCI, Verbal Comprehension Index; PUI, Perceptual Organization Index; WMI, Working Memory Index; PSI, Processing Speed Index.

ing that the dependent measures were sensitive to differences between normal and impaired participants' cognitive changes over clinically relevant time intervals (i.e., one to two years). The exact same data also indicated highly varied levels of diagnostic accuracy for these same measures, some of which barely exceeded chance (Ivnik et al., 2000). In the sections that follow, we will describe measures better suited to addressing a tests' diagnostic validity than null hypothesis significance tests. First, it is important to understand the question being asked when considering a test for use in the diagnostic process.

ASKING THE RIGHT QUESTION

Null-hypothesis significance testing addresses whether groups differ on the measures of interest. Put another way, null-hypothesis significance testing of mean scores queries, Does knowing which group a person comes from help predict his or her test score? Mathematically this question is phrased as

$$\text{expected(Test Score)} = \beta(\text{group membership}) + \text{Constant}. \qquad (1)$$

This may be an important question for establishing knowledge about the test. However, solving equation (1) does not address the diagnostic validity of the test. The diagnostic question, Can we predict a person's group membership (i.e., diagnosis) from his or her test score? is posed in mathematical terms as

$$\text{expected(Group Membership)} = \beta(\text{Test Score}) + \text{Constant}. \qquad (2)$$

This equation represents the appropriate diagnostic validity test because it parallels the diagnostic question facing the clinician in each individual case. Assessing equation (2) is an exercise in nonparametric statistics.

Logistic regression is one nonparametric statistical approach helpful in examining the adequacy of predictor variables in classifying cases. This technique generates cut scores and classification-accuracy statistics. One illustration of this procedure is a clinical validation study of the MCFS (Ivnik et al., 1994). In the MCFS validation study, logistic regression analysis showed four of the five MCFS indices were statistically significant in terms of distinguishing clinical from normal-cognition cohorts. Moreover, this analysis suggested that the Retention index of the MCFS alone was an adequate predictor of clinical status (optimal sensitivity/specificity = .72/.87). This single index was a better predictor of group membership than an index of interfactor variability. That is, absolute as opposed to relative cognitive weakness was a better indicator of clinical status. Addressing equation (1) (with null-hypothesis significance testing) does not easily allow this kind of comparison between various approaches to diagnostic inference. Using categorical statistical techniques, like logistic regression, to address equation (2) directly answers questions of diagnostic validity. This method can be used to identify the best measures for developing the type of diagnostic validity indices described below.

In clinical diagnostic applications, it is a test's ability to make correct individual predictions that establishes its validity. However, psychometric tradition has not emphasized statistical approaches suited to answering the correct diagnostic validity question. In the next section, we present diagnostic validity indices more commonly used in epidemiology and biostatistics, and we propose their direct relevance to establishing the diagnostic validity of psychological tests, including the WAIS-III and WMS-III.

DIAGNOSTIC VALIDITY INDICES

The diagnostic validity of a test can be reflected in indices such as sensitivity, specificity, overall diagnostic accuracy or hit rate, and odds ratios. These statistics are presented as proportions, or probability statements, and describe the diagnostic capabilities of a test in the context of a specific "cut" score. Each is defined relative to the information presented in Figure 1, as follows

Sensitivity (Sn) = The proportion of persons who have the condition that are predicted by the test to have it; or, the probability that the test identifies the presence of the condition

$$= A/(A + C) \qquad (3)$$

Specificity (Sp) = The proportion of persons that do not have the condition who are predicted by the test to not have it; or, the probability that the test identifies the absence of the condition

$$= D/(B + D) \qquad (4)$$

Hit Rate (HR) = The proportion of persons that are accurately classified by the test; or, the probability of a test correctly predicting the condition

$$= (A + D)/(A + B + C + D) \qquad (5)$$

In applying each of these statistics to a specific test, it is important to recognize that factors unrelated to the test will cause these values to vary.

Person Has Condition of Interest

		Yes	No	
Test Predicts	Yes	A	B	A+B
Condition of interest	No	C	D	C+D
		A+C	B+D	

Base rate = A+C/A+B+C+D

FIGURE 1.   Schematic for understanding the diagnostic capabilities of clinical tests.

The sensitivity and specificity of a given test may vary depending on characteristics of the condition being evaluated. For example, the sensitivity and/or specificity of a test might be different for early and mild Alzheimer's disease versus late and severe Alzheimer's disease. As such, two or more tests' sensitivity and specificity parameters can only be meaningfully compared when they are examined relative to an identical condition of interest (COI). At the same time, sensitivity and specificity values for a specific test should be relatively invariant for a precisely defined condition. That is, they should not differ greatly from one setting to another as long as the test is reliable and the condition being examined is comparable in each setting. However, different tests of the same phenomenon (e.g., "memory" as assessed by a story recall test versus a word–list recall test) may not be equally sensitive or specific for a given condition (e.g., Alzheimer's disease), even when that condition's features, such as severity or duration, are identical.

Odds Ratios

Odds ratios (ORs) are a way to express "risk" of a disorder associated with scores on a particular test (Bieliauskas, Fastenau, Lacy, & Roper, 1997; Ivnik et al., 2000). Risk is typically expressed as "odds" and odds are the ratio of two probabilities. The odds associated with a single event are defined as the probability of the event occurring divided by the probability that the event does not occur:

$$\text{Odds} = \frac{\text{Probability of event}}{1 - \text{probability of event}}. \tag{6}$$

For example, if the probability that the team you selected will win a game is set at .75 (or 75 %), then the odds of your winning the bet are .75 / .25, or $3{:}1 = 3.0$. This is a straightforward risk estimate because it depends on the probability of occurrence for a single event. Estimating risk for one event (e.g., being cognitively impaired) based on the results of a related event (e.g., obtaining a specific score on a diagnostic test) is more complex (see Fletcher, Fletcher, & Wagner, 1996; Knapp & Miller, 1992; Sackett, Haynes, Guyatt, & Tugwell, 1991, for detailed discussion).

Odd ratios are the ratio of two risks. They quantify the risk of having a COI for all people who earn a test score that indicates they should have the COI (risk #1) in comparison to the risk of having the COI for all people who earn a test score that indicates they should not have it (risk #2). Relative to Figure 1's framework, the risk of having a COI for all people who earn a test score that indicates they should have the COI = Risk#1:

$$= \frac{\text{Probability of COI when test indicates COI}}{\text{Probability of not having COI when test indicates COI}}$$
$$= \frac{A/(A+B)}{B/(A+B)} = A/B. \tag{7}$$

Also relative to Figure 1, the risk of having a COI for all people who earn a test score that indicates they should not have the COI = Risk#2:

$$= \frac{\text{Probability of COI when test does not indicate COI}}{\text{Probability of not having COI when test does not indicate COI}}$$
$$= \frac{C/(C+D)}{D/(C+D)} = C/D. \tag{8}$$

The odds ratio then is

$$= \frac{\text{Odds of having the COI when test indicates COI}}{\text{Odds of having the COI when test does not indicate COI}} = \frac{Risk\#1}{Risk\#2}$$
$$= \frac{A/B}{C/D} = \frac{AD}{BC}. \tag{9}$$

Odds ratios are useful for assessing (and comparing) the diagnostic validity of a specific test in relation to a designated cut score. In this way, it provides information on the diagnostic utility of the measure. If an odds ratio value is designated as X for a test score Y on test Z, information about odds ratios allows statements of the following general form to be made: "*Persons who score at or below Y on test Z are X times more likely to be cognitively impaired than are persons who score above Y on test Z.*"

DIAGNOSTIC VALIDITY INDICES AND THE WAIS-III AND WMS-III

To examine diagnostic validity indices for WAIS-III and WMS-III measures, the Psychological Corporation was asked to provide data from the 35 individuals with clinically diagnosed, probable Alzheimer's disease described in the technical manual (The Psychological Corporation, 1997). In addition, The Psychological Corporation provided data on normal subjects from the standardization sample who were selected to have comparable age, gender, and education demographics to the Alzheimer's disease patients. One hundred and forty normals were selected to provide an Alzheimer's disease base rate of 0.2 or 20% within the overall cohort:

$$0.2 \text{ or } 20\% = \frac{\text{All AD persons}}{\text{All people in sample}} = \frac{35 \text{ AD persons}}{35 \text{ AD} + 140 \text{ Normal Persons}}. \quad (10)$$

For illustrative purposes, data were provided on two WAIS-III and two WMS-III indices: Verbal Comprehension, Perceptual Organization, Visual Immediate Recall, and Auditory Delayed Recall. Table 2 shows that

TABLE 2   Descriptive Statistics for Alzheimer's Disease Sample and Age- and Gender-Matched Normal Sample[a]

	Alzheimer's disease ($n = 35$)	Normals ($n = 140$)	p
Women (%)	43	43	1.0
Education group (%)			
< 9	3	3	
9–11	8	14	
12	17	19	.8
13–15	23	30	
> 15	49	34	
	Mean (s.d.)		
Age	72.2 (7.8)	70.1 (9.1)	.18
Verbal Comprehension Index	93.0 (12.0)	108.0 (14.6)	.0001
Perceptual Organization Index	84.8 (12.4)	103.8 (15.1)	.0001
Visual Immediate Memory Index	70.6 (10.9)	102.2 (15.5)	.0001
Auditory Delayed Recall Index	66.1 (9.5)	103.4 (15.6)	.0001

[a]Data copyright © 2002 by the Psychological Corporation. All rights reserved. Unpublished data provided by the Psychological Corporation.

Alzheimer's disease patients and the normal controls are comparable in terms of gender and education. There is a trend for the normals to be slightly younger, but this is not statistically significant. Note that the Alzheimer's disease patients' mean Auditory Delayed Recall index is quite low. The Visual Immediate Recall index is also very impaired. Perceptual Organization performance falls in the low average to borderline range, and their mean Verbal Comprehension Index is low average. By most definitions, this profile of cognitive functioning would be associated with moderate dementia. Thus, this Alzheimer's disease group probably includes patients who are more impaired than people who would typically be seen for an initial, diagnostic cognitive evaluation. Some patients in this cohort could probably be correctly classified with simple mental status screening alone. For that reason, the subsequent analysis of the diagnostic validity of the WAIS-III and WMS-III indices may be biased in a favorable direction. As noted earlier in relation to sensitivity and specificity, to establish the diagnostic validity of instruments for specific populations, it is important that persons in the studied groups are representative of those likely to be seen in clinical settings. Thus, the present analyses are provided for illustrative purposes, rather than as a conservative test of the diagnostic validity of WAIS-III and WMS-III indices for Alzheimer's disease.

Figure 2 illustrates the concepts of sensitivity, specificity, and odds ratios in this sample. Figure 2(A), shows Perceptual Organization data assuming a cutoff of ≤ 70. The odds ratio from the Perceptual Organization Index cutoff score of ≤ 70 is $(6^*138)/(2^*29)$ or 14. Figure 2(B) depicts an Auditory Delayed Recall Index cutoff score of ≤ 70. The Auditory Delayed Recall cutoff score has modest sensitivity (.71), and excellent specificity (.99). The odds ratio for an Auditory Delayed Recall index cutoff score of ≤ 70 is $(25^*138)/(2^*10)$ or 172.5. Thus, in this subgroup drawn from the WAIS-III–WMS-III standardization sample, persons scoring ≤ 70 on Perceptual Organization are 14 times more likely to have Alzheimer's disease than persons who do not score below 70, whereas persons scoring below the same cutoff score on the Auditory Delayed Recall Index are 172.5 times more likely to have Alzheimer's disease than persons with scores > 70 on this index.

Again, odds ratios allow for statements about the likelihood that people with scores *equal to or below* a specified cutoff are impaired relative to the likelihood that people with scores above the cutoff are impaired (i.e., how much greater is the chance that people are impaired if they score poorly than if they score well). Clinically, however, we have a need for statements about the likelihood that a single patient is impaired *given their specific score*, relative

A

Person Has Alzheimer's disease

		Yes	No	
Perceptual	<70	6	2	8
Organization Index	>70	29	138	167
		35	140	

Base rate = 35/175=.2 or 20%

Sensitivity=6/35=.17 Specificity=138/140=.99

Positive Predictive Value=6/8=.75   Negative Predictive Value=138/167=.83.

B

Person Has Alzheimer's disease

		Yes	No	
Auditory Delayed	<70	25	2	27
Recall Index	>70	10	138	148
		35	140	

Sensitivity=25/35=.71   Specificity=138/140=.99

Positive Predictive Value=25/27=.93   Negative Predictive Value=138/148=.93.

FIGURE 2. Diagnostic validity statistic for Alzheimer's disease. (A) WAIS-III Perceptual Organization Factor. (B) WMS-III Auditory Delayed Recall Index. (Data copyright © 2002 by the Psychological Corporation. All rights reserved.)

to the likelihood that the same patient is not impaired (i.e., how much greater is the chance that patient with score x is impaired vs. not impaired). This type of statement, which gets at the crux of the clinical use of diagnostic tests, is best evaluated by predictive values (Fletcher, Fletcher, & Wagner, 1996; Sackett et al., 1991). The calculation and use of predictive values are discussed in the next section.

FROM DIAGNOSTIC VALIDITY TO CLINICAL UTILITY

Fortunately, authors in psychology are beginning to utilize the diagnostic validity statistics discussed above with greater frequency (Binder, Rohling, & Larrabee, 1997; Buschke et al., 1999; Grober, Lipton, Hall, & Crystal,

2000). These reports can assist clinicians in test selection. Once this decision is made, and an actual patient's test score is known, somewhat different information is needed. Now, the question relates to the diagnostic meaning of the particular score earned by the particular patient, rather than the diagnostic validity of the test in general. The probability that a patient does, or does not, have the condition of interest based on that patient's specific test score(s) is represented by a test's predictive values.

Relative to Figure 1, predictive values can be defined as follows:

Positive Predictive Value (PPV) = The proportion of persons who are predicted by the test to have the condition that actually have it; or, the probability that a test is correct when it predicts that the condition is present

$$= A/(A + B). \tag{11}$$

Negative Predictive Value (NPV) = The proportion of persons who are predicted by the test to not have the condition that actually do not have it; or, the probability that a test is correct when it predicts that the condition is absent

$$= D/(C + D). \tag{12}$$

PPV and NPVs answer the most important diagnostic question asked by clinicians using tests, What is the probability that my patient has the condition of interest? For example, using the PPV of a test, we can determine how much more (or less) likely it is that a person with score X has condition Z than that the person with score X does not have condition Z. This, along with other information taken into account in the case of an individual patient, is usually the critical information to be gleaned from the diagnostic testing process. The patient in this example must meet inclusion and exclusion criteria applied in the studies in which the predictive values were established. In other words, other diagnoses cannot be ruled out if patients with those diagnoses were excluded from the diagnostic-validity investigations.

It should be recognized that sensitivity and specificity describe the operational characteristics of the distribution of test scores when individual status regarding the condition of interest is known. In this regard, specificity and sensitivity are akin to group means; they do not define the operation of the test when the scores are known but group membership is not. PPV and NPV provide this information. Unlike sensitivity and specificity, however, PPV and NPV are influenced by the base rate (BR) of the condition of interest in the target population. PPV and NPV are mathematically related to sensitivity, specificity, and base rate as follows:

$$PPV = 100^* \frac{BR^*Sn}{(BR^*Sn) + [(1 - BR)^*(1 - Sp)]} \tag{12}$$

and

$$NPV = 100^* \frac{(1 - BR)^*Sp}{[(1 - BR)^*Sp] + [BR^*(1 - Sn)]} \tag{13}$$

These equations reflect the importance of base rate to values of PPV and NPV. Because of this, it is important for clinicians to understand the BR of the condition of interest in the populations in which they intend to employ tests. If the clinician plans to use the test to screen populations where the condition of interest is rare, they will have very different PPV and NPV than if they intend to use the test where the condition is frequent. Because of the importance of BRs, they are given further consideration in the next section.

UNDERSTANDING BASE RATES

In this chapter we have elected to use the term *base rate* to represent the proportion of people in some larger reference sample that have a condition of interest. For example, we noted that there were 35 people with Alzheimer's disease in the total sample of 175 people for whom The Psychological Corporation provided WAIS-III and WMS-III data for this chapter. Thus we pointed out the BR of Alzheimer's disease in that sample was .2 or 20 %. Other terms, including *prevalence* and *pretest probability* can be used to describe the same idea. We elected not to routinely use the term *prevalence* because not all applications described in this chapter meet the rigorous epidemiological definition of prevalence, including our example above (cf. Rothman & Greenland, 1998). Later in the chapter we will begin to use the term *pretest probability* instead of BR. Although in most respects these terms can be used interchangeably, we elected to use *base rate* as a statistic that applies to a group of people and pretest probability as a statistic that applies to an individual case. The pretest probability is generally best estimated by the BR for a given setting. For example, if we draw a person at random from our 175-person WAIS-III–WMS-III sample, what is the pretest probability that person has Alzheimer's disease? It is .2 (i.e., the BR). However, we differentiate BR from pretest probability to continue our emphasis on distinguishing statistics better suited to groups from those that apply to individuals.

Comparison of our findings (Malec, Smith, Ivnik, Petersen, & Tangalos, 1996) and those of Masur (Masur, Sliwinski, Lipton, Blau, & Crystal, 1994) illustrates the importance of BRs to PPV and NPV. In the study by Malec et al. (1996), cluster analysis was used to establish "profiles" of MCFS among cognitively normal people the *first* time they were tested. Four profile types, three of which involved relative memory weakness, were selected a priori as likely to be associated with increased risk for the development of dementia. The cohort of normals on which the cluster analysis was based was followed for 3–4 years. Six percent of this cohort developed cognitive impairment in this interval (i.e., BR = 6%). This is actually twice the cumulative incidence expected for this period (Kokmen, Beard, O'Brien, Offord, & Kurland, 1993). The association of at-risk status (i.e., having one of the four specified profiles) and actual outcome is listed in Figure 3a. From this figure, we can see that membership in an at-risk cluster was associated with increased risk for development of cognitive impairment. Persons from the at-risk clusters were seven times more likely to display cognitive impairment at follow-up, as 21% (10/47) of the members of the at-risk clusters developed cognitive impairment compared to just 3% (6/238) of the members of the nonrisk clusters. In terms of epidemiological numbers, 10 of the 16 persons who displayed cognitive impairment were from the at-risk clusters, so sensitivity was 63%. However, as noted, only 10 of 47 at-risk persons developed

A

Developed Cognitive Impairment

		Yes	No	
In "At-Risk"	Yes	10	37	47
Group	No	6	232	238
		16	269	285

Base rate = 16/285=5.6%

B

Person Developed Dementia

		Yes	No	
Test Predicted	Yes	32	15	47
Dementia	No	32	238	270
		64	253	317

Base rate = 64/317=20.1%

FIGURE 3.   Predicted status and actual cognitive impairment outcome. (A) (Data adapted from Malec et al. (1996). (B) (Data adapted from Masur et al., 1994).

cognitive impairment (i.e., PPV was just .21). These numbers reveal that at-risk profiles were excessively sensitive. Although almost two-thirds of the patients who developed cognitive impairment were captured by at-risk profiles, more than three-fourths of the members of the at-risk cohort did not go on to display cognitive impairment in this interval. This is possible because the overall base rate of incipient dementia was so low at 6%. In contrast, not having at-risk status was associated with very high NPV (323/328 or .97). The low BR enhanced the power of the nonrisk profile as a very strong indication that cognitive impairment would not develop in the interval.

Masur et al. (1994) had previously conducted a similar study. As in the Malec et al. (1996) study, they found that relative weakness on memory tests was a statistically significant predictor of which normals from the Bronx Aging study would convert to cognitive impairment during longitudinal follow-up. Figure 3b presents the association of their test cutoff with outcome. In this study, PPV is .68—over three times that of the Malec study. Is this because they have a better test instrument? Not necessarily. Two key differences between these studies should be noted. First, the Masur et al. (1994) study has a lower NPV (.88). If the cutoff were changed so that the NPV matched the Malec et al. (1996) study, the PPV would drop. Still, at comparable NPVs, the Masur et al. PPV is approximately two times greater than in the Malec et al. study. However, the second key difference between these studies was their cumulative incidence rates (i.e., BR). In the Masur et al. study, cumulative incidence was over three times higher than in the Malec study (20 versus 6%). This alone would account for a significant difference in PPV, even if both studies had used identical tests.

A common error in applying PPV and NPV statistics is to assume that the prevalence of a condition in the general population is the relevant BR in a given research study or clinical application. Among patients being seen in a memory disorders clinic, for example, the BR of dementia is much higher than the prevalence of dementia in the general population. In these settings it may be more challenging for the clinician to identify conditions that do not reflect dementia than it is to identify dementia. In other words, in these settings, NPV may have equal or greater importance than PPV. In contrast, screening for dementia in older adults who come to a primary care practice will identify far fewer new dementia cases. The challenge may be in identifying conditions that are dementia (i.e., PPV is important). In any event, it is important to understand and *determine* the appropriate BR. Sackett et al. (2000) describe methods for generating a reasonable estimate of base rates.

Once BR has been determined or estimated, clinicians can use likelihood ratios, determined in test-validation studies, to calculate predictive values for test scores obtained in their own clinics.

Likelihood Ratios

Likelihood ratios (LR), like odds ratios, are a way to express risk. Although statements that flow from likelihood ratios and odds ratios are similar, they have important and subtle differences. Odds ratios compare the risk of having the condition of interest for people in one group (i.e., those scoring at or below a cutoff score) to the risk of having the condition of interest for people in another group (i.e., those scoring above the same cutoff score). In contrast, the reference group for LRs is persons who have the same score as the patient, so the LR is a more meaningful statistic for quantifying the risk of having a condition of interest after a patient's test score has been obtained. Therefore, odds ratios appear to be better for comparing the overall diagnostic usefulness of a test's selected cutoff score for group analyses. LRs can be calculated for every possible score on a test. Then, the LRs can be used to calculate predictive values and thus the probability of disease in a patient earning a particular score.

The LR is defined as the probability of the obtained test result in the presence of the condition divided by the probability of the obtained test result in the absence of the condition (Fletcher et al., 1996). Relative to the conceptual framework presented in Figure 1, the LR for a test score is:

$$\frac{A/(A+C)}{B/(B+D)} = \frac{\text{Sensitivity}}{1 - \text{Specificity}} \tag{14}$$

LRs are specific to tests, to all of a test's possible scores, and to the application to which the test is applied. Using LRs allows us to take into account the greater predictive power of test scores at the extreme ends of a distribution. We have previously described the use of LRs as a way to translate diagnostic utility statistics into clinically useful data for specific test score ranges in the diagnosis of Alzheimer's disease (Cerhan et al., 2002; Ivnik et al., 2001). Table 3 lists LRs for Category Fluency scores generated by Cerhan et al. (2002). In that study, a person's odds of having Alzheimer's disease increased 22 times if they were found to have a Category Fluency score of 20. However, caution must be used in making such statements, as further information is needed to apply these LRs to diagnostic decisions. It can be similar to saying that a person is 22 times more likely to win a lottery with 22 tickets compared to 1 ticket. Even with 22 tickets the person may still be unlikely to win the lottery if the ratio of tickets to prizes is low. The value of LR tables, such as Table 3, is to aid in calculating the probability of Alzheimer's disease in persons with specific fluency scores generated under demographic conditions and exclusion criteria as defined in the study in which the LRs were established (e.g., other major neurologic disorders were ruled out). In other words, this information can be used to calculate PPVs for real patients as described next.

Recall that LRs express the same information as sensitivity and specificity combined (LR = sensitivity/1-specificity; Fletcher et al., 1996). LRs are therefore relatively unaffected by changes in BR. However, as discussed earlier, the BR of the disease in the population from which the patient is drawn will impact the probability of a particular score indicating disease in a specific patient (PPV). In order to determine the probability that a given patient with a given score has a condition of interest, one can use the LR and the pretest odds (i.e., BR applied to the individual) of the disorder in the population being tested, to calculate posttest odds. Remembering the relationship of odds to probability;

$$\text{Pretest Odds} = \frac{\text{Pretest probability}}{1 - \text{Pretest probability}} \tag{15}$$

TABLE 3   Likelihood Ratios for the Distribution of Category Fluency Scores in Alzheimer's Patients and Normal Controls[a]

Total category fluency score	Subjects in each score range (#)		Likelihood ratio
	Normals N (%)	Alzheimer's patients N (%)	
Below 19	0 (0.0)	19 (47.5)	> 22
19–20	1 (0.5)	4 (10.0)	22
21–22	2 (0.9)	7 (17.5)	19
23–24	6 (2.7)	1 (2.5)	1
25–26	9 (4.1)	2 (5.0)	1
27–28	7 (3.2)	4 (10.0)	1
Above 28	196 (88.7)	3 (7.5)	< 1

[a]Adapted from Cerhan et al., 2002. Data copyright © 2002 by the Mayo Foundation. All rights reserved.

Posttest odds can then be calculated using the formula:

$$\text{Posttest odds} = \text{Pretest odds} * \text{Likelihood ratio} \qquad (16)$$

These posttest odds can then be translated back into more user-friendly posttest probabilities using the inverse formula:

$$\text{Posttest probability} = \frac{\text{Posttest odds}}{1 + \text{Posttest odds}} \qquad (17)$$

Again, the PPV, or the posttest probability, allows for statements such as, "*Based on the patient having earned a score of y on test z, the probability that this patient has the condition of interest is x*" (where *x* is equal to the posttest probability calculated above). This is the statement of greatest clinical relevance in a given diagnostic situation.

An advantage of reporting LRs for a test's scores, rather than PPV is that LRs are portable; PPVs are not. Since LRs are relatively independent of the BR conditions under which they are determined, LRs from one representative sample can be applied to a different cohort with a different BR as long as the condition of interest is the same. Table 4 illustrates of the use of the LRs from Table 3 in two different settings. Columns 2 and 3 provide posttests odds and probabilities, assuming Category Fluency is being used to screen a general population of persons over 65, where the BR of Alzheimer's disease would be expected to be approximately 2.5% (Beard, Kokmen, O'Brien, & Kurland, 1995). Columns 4 and 5 illustrate use of these LRs in a hypothetical memory disorders clinic where the BR of Alzheimer's disease is .66 (based on our clinical experience this may be a conservative estimate of BRs in memory disorders clinics). For example, recall the person mentioned above whose odds for having Alzheimer's disease was increased 22 times, based on having a Category Fluency score of 20. If this person were presenting to a memory disorders clinic with an Alzheimer's disease base rate of .66, Table 4 suggests the probability of Alzheimer's disease in this case is .97. On the other hand, if this person were drawn from the general population even with the Category Fluency score of 20, the probability of Alzheimer's disease is only .36. This example and Table 4 illustrate the relative contributions of BR and test score in determining the actual probability of Alzheimer's disease in a given person. Sackett et al. (2002) provide a useful nomogram for simplifying the calculation of posttest probabilities from LRs.

Clinicians may use LRs or PPVs depending on the context in which they are operating. If they intend to communicate the odds that a patient's test score indicates the COI solely from knowing that test score and without

TABLE 4   Category Fluency Score Likelihood Ratios and Posttest Odds and Probabilities for Alzheimer's Disease in Two settings with Different Base rates[a]

Total category fluency score	Likelihood ratio	General population Prevalance = 2.5% Pretest odds = .0256		Memory disorders clinic Base rate = 66% Pretest odds = 2	
		Posttest odds	Posttest probability (PPV)	Posttest odds	Posttest probability (PPV)
Below 19	> 22	—	—	—	—
19–20	22	.564	.36	44	.98
21–22	19	.486	.32	38	.97
23–24	1	.026	.026	2	.66
25–26	1	.026	.026	2	.66
27–28	1	.026	.026	2	.66
Above 28	0.8	.002	.002	.16	.14

taking into consideration the BR of the specific COI in the sample from which the patient is drawn, then they should quote the LR (which could also be expressed as a "probability"). In this situation, the report should clearly state that the probability only takes into consideration the test score that the patient earned *without regard* to the base rate of the condition in any specific context. If clinicians intend to communicate the probability (which could also be expressed as an "odds" statement) that a patient's test score indicates the COI in the context of having given the test in a setting where it is possible to estimate the base rate of the COI, then they should quote the appropriate predictive value. In this situation, the report should clearly state that the probability takes into consideration both the test score that the patient earned *and* the base rate of the condition in a specified context.

LIKELIHOOD RATIOS AND WAIS-III AND WMS-III INDICES

The concepts and procedures described above can be used to extend the diagnostic validity information provided by the Psychological Corporation in the *WAIS-III and WMS-III Technical Manual* (The Psychological Corporation, 1997) regarding Alzheimer's disease patients. Recall that very large, statistically significant differences between the Alzheimer's disease group and the normal control group on WAIS-III–WMS-III means comparisons were reported in Table 2. As noted elsewhere in the chapter, this type of data has traditionally been used as evidence of the diagnostic validity. In fact, the technical manual (The Psychological Corporation, 1997) presents these means in the section on WAIS-III and WMS-III validity. We have argued that the presentation of such data is insufficient to demonstrate diagnostic validity. Just because group means are statistically different does not indicate that there is sufficient separation of each groups' distribution of test scores to validate the test as useful for making individual diagnostic determinations. Figures 4a–d present the distributions of Verbal Comprehension, Perceptual Organization, Visual Immediate Memory, and Auditory Delayed Recall index scores for the Alzheimer's disease group and the normal group used throughout this chapter. The distributions of scores on the Auditory Delayed Recall index show the least overlap. There is significant overlap for the Verbal Comprehension index.

The inadequacy of simple means comparisons for establishing diagnostic validity can also be seen in the results of logistic regression analysis conducted to determine the relative utility of each measure in predicting group

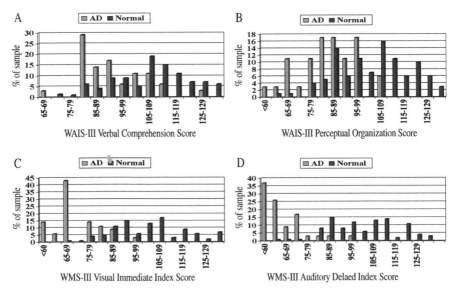

FIGURE 4.   Distribution of WAIS-III/WMS-III index scores for Alzheimer's disease (AD) patients and age, education and gender matched standardization sample normals. (A) Verbal Comprehension. (B) Perceptual Organization. (C) Visual Immediate Memory. (D) Auditory Delayed Memory. (Data copyright © 2002 by the Psychological Corporation. All rights reserved.)

membership (i.e., either Alzheimer's disease or normal control). Verbal Comprehension, Perceptual Organization, Visual Immediate Memory, and Auditory Delayed Recall index scores were entered into the logistic regression model in stepwise fashion. The results of this model are presented in Table 5. In spite of the significant group mean differences on null-hypothesis significance testing, Verbal Comprehension and Perceptual Organization did not enter as significant terms in the logistic regression model. Auditory Delayed Recall entered the logistic model first and was followed by Visual Immediate Memory. This logistic model has substantial diagnostic accuracy (maximal hit rate of 97.1%). The logistic model indicates that Verbal Comprehension and Perceptual Organization do not add to the diagnostic utility in classifying Alzheimer's disease patients versus normals beyond Auditory Delayed Recall and Visual Immediate Memory Indices. The Auditory Delayed Recall index has the greatest utility followed by the Visual Immediate index. This suggests that these latter scores are candidates for developing LRs. The logistic model itself could be used to derive probability scores (p) that are each associated with an LR. The equations for deriving these scores are:

$$\text{Logit}(p) = 20.59 - (0.162^{*}\text{Auditory Delay Index})$$
$$- (.104^{*}\text{Visual Immediate Index})$$

and

$$p = \frac{e^{\text{logit}(p)}}{1 + e^{\text{logit}(p)}} \tag{18}$$

These equations are clinically unwieldy. Ivnik et al. (2001) utilized a more convenient multiple regression methodology to determine LRs for a linear combination of MCFS. However, clinicians may be unwilling to employ

TABLE 5 Stepwise Logistic Regression Analysis for Alzheimer's Disease versus Normal Status[a]

	Step entered	Parameter estimate (SE)	Wald chi-sq	p
INTERCEPT	—	20.59 (4.23)	23.75	0.001
Auditory Delay Index	1	−0.162 (0.0381)	18.12	0.0001
Visual Immediate Index	2	−0.104 (0.039)	6.93	0.009

[a]Data copyright © 2002 by the Psychological Corporation. All rights reserved.

even multiple-regressions calculations in routine clinical practice. So, for purposes of this analysis the simple sum of Auditory Delayed Recall plus Visual Immediate index scores was calculated. A simple–sum approach weights each index equally, which deviates from logistic or linear regression approaches, and may reduce group classification accuracy. Clinicians who choose this approach for its computational ease need to be aware of this trade–off between computational ease and diagnostic precision. LRs for ranges of the summed Auditory Delayed plus Visual Immediate score in predicting the presence of Alzheimer's disease are provided in Table 6. As can be seen from the table, summed index scores less than 150 provide a very high LR. Conversely, summed scores above 170 provide very low LRs, suggesting that the presence of Alzheimer's disease is unlikely in persons with scores above this range. As described in earlier sections, the next step in determining the probability of Alzheimer's disease for a given individual in clinical practice would be to combine the LRs in Table 6 with BR information to determine predictive values.

As an example, imagine a clinician practicing in a memory disorders clinic. A prior survey on final diagnosis of patients presenting to this clinic suggests that 75 % of patients evaluated there received a diagnosis of Alzheimer's disease. It is known from the literature that such clinical diagnosis is about 90 % accurate (National Institute on Aging, 2000). Thus a conservative estimate of the BR of Alzheimer's disease at the memory disorders clinic is $.75^* .9 = .68$. This equates with a pretest odds of 2.125 (.68/1−.68). Now imagine that the following patients are referred for psychometric assessment

TABLE 6   Likelihood Ratios for Alzheimer's Disease: WMS-III Auditory Delay + Visual Immediate Index Score Ranges[a]

Auditory Delay + Visual Immediate score	Patients with test score in this range (#)		Likelihood ratio
	Alzheimer's disease ($n = 35$)	Normals ($n = 140$)	
< 129	15	1	60.4
130–149	12	1	48.3
150–169	6	8	3.0
170–179	1	14	.3
> 180	1	116	.03

and, as part of a larger battery, a clinician obtains the WAIS-III and WMS-III scores listed in Table 7.

Patient 1 is an 86-year-old retired engineer with 16 years of education. In the past year, he has noticed that he has increasing problems with short-term memory. He reports that he does not have a problem recalling events that occurred several years ago. However, he has difficulty remembering events that occurred within one day or within a week. His wife has not accompanied him during this visit, but reported to the referring clinician that her husband has difficulty remembering things such as the day of the week and appointments. Otherwise the patient is active in his day-to-day activities including helping with bookkeeping for their family business. He uses the computer to balance the checkbook. He drives and has not been lost in familiar settings such as his neighborhood. His mother had Parkinson's disease and she died of its complications.

Although his Verbal Comprehension, Perceptual Organization, and Visual Immediate Recall index scores appear normal, his Auditory Delayed Recall index clearly falls in the abnormal range relative to standard norms. The sum of his Visual Immediate Recall and Auditory Delayed Recall scores is 165. Consulting Table 5 reveals this score is associated with a LR of 3.0 for Alzheimer's disease. Thus the posttest odds value (pretest odds * LR = 2.125*3) for Patient #1 is 6.375. If justified by other features of history, examination and test findings, the clinician could report that the posttest probability of Alzheimer's disease for this gentleman is .84 (6.375/1 + 6.375).

Patient #2 is a 77-year-old female with 17 years of education. She is a retired artist. Until five months ago, she lived by herself and functioned well; more recently she reports a noticeable change as far as her memory and her

TABLE 7 Demographics and WAIS-III and WMS-III Index Scores for Two Hypothetical Patients

Patient	1	2
Age	86	77
Gender	Male	Female
Education	16	17
Occupation	Retired mechanical engineer	Retired artist
Verbal Comprehension Index	106	129
Perceptual Organization Index	114	130
Visual Immediate Memory Index	97	132
Auditory Delayed Recall Index	68	102

ability to function are concerned. She is accompanied by a relative who is quite concerned, mostly about the patient's memory. The patient worries that it is time for a change in her living situation, she wonders if she needs assistance since her difficulty remembering her medications and difficulty getting around and keeping her house may worsen. She also acknowledges that she probably is depressed about the possible need for a change in her living circumstance.

Patient #2 displays no scores in the impaired range on the four WAIS-III–WMS-III measures. Her sum of Auditory Delayed Recall and Visual Immediate Recall scores is 234! The LR associated with this score is below .03. This provides a posttest odds value of 0.06375 and a posttest probability of .06. Depending on other performances in the battery, the clinician may be on firm grounds to argue that it is unlikely Alzheimer's disease in causing her memory complaints.

CLINICAL APPLICATION

The scenarios above provide straightforward examples of the use of LRs for illustrative purposes. Recall that the LRs generated from the The Psychological Corporations clinical Alzheimer's disease sample might not be appropriate for use in diagnosing this disease in cases of more subtle decline. It does help establish the validity of these instruments to know that the WAIS-III and WMS-III data can discriminate normal older controls from age- and gender-matched, moderately demented patients. However, the real test of the utility of these measures will come when the instruments are tested in samples more commonly seen in clinical settings, such as patients with mild cognitive impairment (Smith et al., 1996). We also need more validity evidence to consider more complex, and perhaps more common, scenarios in which a patient has concomitant neurologic risk factors (e.g., transient ischemic attacks) and/or the question is of differential diagnosis among subtypes of dementia.

Sackett et al. (2000) provide useful guidelines for designing studies of the diagnostic validity and utility of tests and evaluating studies' applicability to specific cases. They suggest four important questions should be addressed:

- Was there an independent, blind comparison with a "gold" standard diagnosis?
- Was the diagnostic test evaluated in an appropriate spectrum of patients?

- Was the gold standard applied regardless of the diagnostic test result?
- Was the test validated in a cross-validation sample?

Future investigations of psychological tests and reanalysis of past studies, for that matter, using these guidelines will help us build a body of diagnostic-validity evidence needed for our measures (Neuropsychology Assessment Panel, 1996).

In considering the case examples in the last section, it should be noted that we certainly do not mean to suggest that administering the Visual Immediate and Auditory Delay Indices alone is an adequate cognitive evaluation for dementia! Clearly, the clinical decision–making process is complex. For example, there are those who would argue that the second case illustrates the importance of obtaining Verbal Comprehension and Perceptual Organization Scores even though the logistic regression analysis reported earlier in the chapter suggests Verbal Comprehension and Perceptual Organization do not add to diagnostic validity for Alzheimer's disease above and beyond the memory scores. These clinicians would note that the discrepancy between her auditory delayed recall and verbal comprehension score is almost as large as for Patient #1 and would argue that the second patient's auditory delayed recall index score is abnormal for her IQ. Those clinicians might be right that such a discrepancy score is a more useful index than the absolute scores, although our prior findings with the MCFS (Ivnik et al., 2001) do not support this conjecture. However, It is not the goal of this chapter to establish the best algorithm of WAIS-III and WMS-III measures for recognizing Alzheimer's disease. Rather, the goal is to illustrate the need for a method to better establish the diagnostic validity of algorithms that will assist clinical decision making in individual cases. Whether a clinician prefers to use discrepancy scores or absolute scores, he is she is well served to know the LRs for such scores.

It also cannot be overemphasized that the ability to make statements involving posttest probabilities does not replace the need for good clinical judgment. Obviously a person presenting to a memory disorders clinic with Auditory Delay Index Scores of < 70 would not be reported to have a .84 probability of having Alzheimer's disease if his or her history included chronic alcohol abuse, blackouts, and poor nutrition. Nor would any kind of posttest probability statement be appropriate if the test taker was felt to have made poor effort or was subsequently found to have sensory deficits that interfered with valid testing. Rather, the utility of these diagnostic statistics is to provide quantitative evidence the clinician can weigh in the decision-making process. These statistics—like the psychological tests they apply to—must be used in clinically appropriate ways.

REFERENCES

Albert, M. (2000). Neuropsychology and cognitive aging: What have we taught each other? In S. Qualls & N. Abeles (Eds.), *Psychology and the aging revolution: How we adapt to longer life* (pp. 25–42). Washington, DC: American Psychological Association.

American Education Research Association, N. C. o. M. i. E. (1999). *Standards for educational and psychological testing.* Washington, DC: American Psychological Association.

Anastasi, A., & Urbina, S. (1997). *Psychological testing* (7th ed.). Upper Saddle River, NJ: Prentice-Hall, Inc.

Beard, C., Kokmen, E., O'Brien, P., & Kurland, L. (1995). The prevalence of dementia is changing over time in Rochester, Minnesota. *Neurology, 45,* 75–79.

Bieliauskas, L., Fastenau, P., Lacy, M., & Roper, B. (1997). Use of the odds ratio to translate neuropsychological test scores into real-world outcomes: From statistical significance to clinical significance. *Journal of Clinical and Experimental Neuropsychology, 19,* 889–893.

Binder, L., Rohling, M., & Larrabee, G. (1997). Review of mild head trauma: I. Meta-analytic review of neuropsychological studies. *Journal of Clinical and Experimental Neuropsychology, 19*(3), 421–431.

Buschke, H., Kuslansky, G., Katz, M., Stewart, W., Sliwinski, M., Eckholdt, H., & Lipton, R. (1999). Screening for dementia with the Memory Impairment Screen. *Neurology, 52,* 231–238.

Cerhan, J., Ivnik, R., Smith, G., Tangalos, E., Petersen, R., & Boeve, B. (2002). *Comparing the diagnostic utility of Letter Fluency, Category Fluency, and Letter Fluency minus Category Fluency difference scores in Alzheimer's disease.* Manuscript Submitted for publication.

Crawford, J., & Allan, K. (1996). WAIS-R subtest scatter: Base-rate data from a healthy UK sample. *British Journal of Clinical Psychology, 35*(Pt 2), 235–247.

Fletcher, R., Fletcher, S., & Wagner, E. (1996). *Clinical epidemiology: The essentials.* Baltimore, MD: Williams & Wilkins.

Grober, E., Lipton, R., Hall, C., & Crystal, H. (2000). Memory impairment on free and cued selective reminding predicts dementia. *Neurology, 54*(4), 827–832.

Ivnik, R., Smith, G., Cerhan, J., Boeve, B., Tangalos, E., & Petersen, R. (2001). Understanding the diagnostic capabilities of cognitive tests. *The Clinical Neuropsychologist, 15* (1), 114–124

Ivnik, R., Smith, G., Malec, J., Petersen, R., Kokmen, E., & Tangalos, E. (1994). MOANS Cognitive Factor Scales (MCFS): Distinguishing normal and clinical samples by profile variability. *Neuropsychology, 8,* 203–209.

Ivnik, R., Smith, G., Malec, J., Petersen, R., & Tangalos, E. (1995). Long-term stability and inter-correlations of cognitive abilities in older persons. *Psychological Assessment, 7,* 155–161.

Ivnik, R., Smith, G., Petersen, R., Boeve, B., Kokmen, E., & Tangalos, E. (2000). Diagnostic accuracy of four approaches to interpreting neuropsychological test data. *Neuropsychology, 14,* 163–177.

Knapp, R., & Miller, M. (1992). *Clinical epidemiology and biostatistics.* Baltimore, MD: Williams & Wilkins.

Kokmen, E., Beard, C., O'Brien, P., Offord, K., & Kurland, L. (1993). Is the incidence of dementing illness changing? A 25-year time trend study in Rochester, Minnesota (1960–1984). *Neurology, 43*, 1887–1892.

Lezak, M. (1995). *Neuropsychological assessment* (3rd ed.). New York: Oxford University Press.

Malec, J., Smith, G., Ivnik, R., Petersen, R., & Tangalos, E. (1996). Clusters of "impaired" normal elderly do not decline cognitively in 3–5 years. *Neuropsychology, 10*, 66–73.

Masur, D., Sliwinski, M., Lipton, R., Blau, A., & Crystal, H. (1994). Neuropsychological prediction of dementia and the absence of dementia in healthy elderly persons. *Neurology, 44*, 1427–1432.

Matarazzo, J., Daniel, M., Prifitera, A., & Herman, D. (1988). Inter-subtest scatter in the WAIS-R standardization sample. *Journal of Clinical Psychology, 44*, 940–950.

National Institute on Aging. (2000). *Progress report on Alzheimer's disease: Taking the next steps* (NIH Publication No. 00–4859). Silver Spring, MD: National Institutes of Health.

Neuropsychology Assessment Panel. (1996). Assessment: Neuropsychological testing of adults. Considerations for neurologists. *Neurology, 47*, 592–599.

The Psychological Corporation. (1997). *WAIS-III-WMS-III: Technical Manual.* San Antonio, TX: The Psychological Corporation.

Rey, A. (1964). *L'examen clinique en psychologie* [Clinical exams in psychology]. Paris: Presses Universitaires de France.

Rothman, K. J., & Greenland, S. (Eds.). (1998). *Modern epidemiology*, (2 ed.). Philadelphia: Lippencott-Raven.

Sackett, D., Haynes, R., Guyatt, G., & Tugwell, P. (1991). The interpretation of diagnostic data, *Clinical Epidemiology: A Basic Science for Clinical Medicine* (Second ed.). Boston: Little, Brown and Company.

Sackett, D., Straus, S., Richardson, W., Rosenberg, W., & Haynes, R. (2000). Diagnosis and screening. In *Evidence-based medicine: How to practice and teach EBM* (2nd ed., pp. 67–93). Edinburgh: Churchill Livingstone.

Smith, G., Petersen, R., Parisi, J., Ivnik, R., Kokmen, E., Tangalos, E., & Waring, S. (1996). Definition, course, and outcome of mild cognitive impairment. *Aging, Neuropsychology, and Cognition, 3*, 141–147.

Smith, G., Ivnik, R., Malec, J., Petersen, R., Kokmen, E., & Tangalos, E.G. (1994). Mayo Cognitive Factor Scales: Derivation of a short battery and norms for factor scores. *Neuropsychology, 8*, 194–202.

Wechsler, D. (1974). *Wechsler Intelligence Scale for Children—Revised.* New York: The Psychological Corporation.

Wechsler, D. (1981). *Wechsler Adult Intelligence Scale—Revised.* San Antonio, TX: The Psychological Corporation.

Wechsler, D. (1987). *Wechsler Memory Scale—Revised.* New York: The Psychological Corporation.

Wechsler, D. (1991). *Wechsler Intelligence Scale for Children—Third Edition.* San Antonio, TX: The Psychological Corporation.

Wechsler, D. (1997). *Wechsler Adult Intelligence Scale—Third Edition.* San Antonio, TX: The Psychological Corporation.

CHAPTER 8

Use of the WAIS-III and WMS-III in the Context of Serial Assessments: Interpreting Reliable and Meaningful Change

Tara T. Lineweaver and Gordon J. Chelune

The Cleveland Clinic Foundation
Cleveland, Ohio

Broadly defined, *psychology* is the scientific study of behavior. However, behavior is not a static construct, but is rather a dynamic process that is highly variable both between and within individuals. Indeed, it is this variability that has fascinated psychologists for decades. When the editors of this volume first met to discuss their goals for this project, there emerged a common desire to focus on more than simple guidelines for the application and use of the latest revisions of the Wechsler tests. As experienced researchers, clinicians, and test users, we wanted to examine the WAIS-III and WMS-III in terms of those factors that systematically account for variability in observed test performances. It was our belief that through a better understanding of the factors that account for variability among observed scores, clinicians would be in a more informed position to make meaningful interpretations of the new Wechsler tests and the cognitive abilities they are designed to reflect in adults.

Already we have seen how the joint consideration of the WAIS-III and WMS-III subtests leads to a finite number of factors or sources of variability that mirror meaningful cognitive domains (cf. Tulsky, Ivnik, Price, &

Wilkins, Chapter 4, this volume) and how demographic considerations can further account for sizable differences in performance between individuals (cf. Heaton, Taylor, & Manly, Chapter 5, this volume). In this chapter, we take a somewhat different perspective. Rather than looking at factors that account for between-subject variability in performance, we examine the variability or differences in WAIS-III and WMS-III scores when these tests are administered to the same individual on more than one occasion. The focus of this *within-subject* perspective is on the difference or change in performance from test to retest, with the goal of identifying what is a meaningful or reliable change in test performance.

It should be clear from the outset that we see serial assessment as an increasingly important aspect of clinical practice and as one that requires clinicians to understand test–retest change scores as unique cognitive variables with statistical and clinical properties that are different from the test measures from which they are derived. We begin by briefly look-ing at the role of serial assessment in clinical practice and then consider the concepts of "reliable change," factors that affect change scores, and methods that have been used to assess reliable change in the context of serial assess-ments. We next examine the test–retest properties of the WAIS-III and WMS-III and describe the use of standardized regression-based norms for several variables to illustrate how meaningful change can be assessed. We conclude with a discussion of how an understanding of the WAIS-III and WMS-III test–retest properties can impact the interpretation of a patient's retest scores and inferences concerning his or her clinical status.

SERIAL ASSESSMENT AND EVIDENCE-BASED HEALTH CARE

Psychological tests are generally designed only to assess the current state or capacity of an individual. Nonetheless, clinicians have often used psycho-logical instruments in a repeated fashion to monitor patients over time, simply deducing whether there has been a change in the patient's clinical status by comparing current test performances against baseline test data. If test–retest differences are large relative to the scale of the test, a meaningful change is believed to have occurred, whereas if the differences are small, the patient's condition is considered to be stable. Although academic psycholo-gists have long puzzled over the psychometric complexities of measuring change (Cronbach & Furby, 1970), little more than passing attention has been given in clinical practice to such factors as practice effects, measurement error, or regression to the mean until recent years, except perhaps in the context of forensic assessments (Matarazzo, 1987; Putman, Adams, & Schneider, 1992). Fortunately, pressures from evidence-based medicine for outcomes accountability have led to a growing body of data concerning methods of assessing reliable change that can be used in clinical practice at the level of the individual (Chelune, 2002; Maassen, 2000; Murkin, 2001).

The concept of *outcomes management* was introduced by Paul Ellwood as the cornerstone of the health maintenance organization (HMO) movement (Johnson, 1997). This movement grew out of a perception that "a substantial portion of health care expenditure in the United States is wasted on unproven or ineffective tests and treatments" (Horwitz, 1996, p. 30). As originally conceived, the costs of health care could be reduced and care improved if reimbursement was provided for only those procedures and treatments that have value and that can be objectively demonstrated to positively affect or change a patient's condition in a cost-effective manner. The HMO movement therefore proposed a value-driven, evidence-based health care system in which "outcomes accountability and following the outcomes of patients and managing them on the basis of epidemiologic information" (Johnson, 1997, p. 12) is central to clinical practice.

Within a value-driven health care system, psychological and neuropsychological evaluations for the purpose of diagnosis or description are of value only if they can be shown to enhance the management of a patient's condition. Hence, there is a growing emphasis on clinical outcomes research in which test data serve as predictors of individual clinical outcomes (e.g., Chelune & Najm, 2001; Chui & Zhang, 1997; Desmond, Moroney, Bagiella, Sano, & Stern, 1998). Alternatively, cognitive assessments are also being used as outcome endpoints in the evaluation of the efficacy of other procedures such as medications, surgical interventions, medical management, rehabilitation, and so on (Andrew, Baker, Bennetts, Kneebone, & Knight, 2001; Fischer et al., 2000; Foldvary et al., 2001; Kneebone, Andrew, Baker, & Knight, 1998; Martin et al., 1998). In outcomes research, psychological tests are increasingly being given in a serial manner, and neurocognitive change is directly deduced by comparing current test performances against baseline test data. Since the WAIS-III and WMS-III are commonly used in clinical practice and will undoubtedly be utilized as measures of outcomes accountability, it is important for the clinician to be able to determine whether observed test–retest changes at the level of the individual are reliable and meaningful.

CASE EXAMPLES

In addition to the role that serial assessments play in predicting and evaluating outcomes, clinicians often encounter situations involving serial assessments in the context of forensic evaluations. Before proceeding with our discussion of reliable and meaningful change, let us introduce a few case examples using the WAIS-III and WMS-III. Two patients, T and R, are both 56-year-old men referred for forensic evaluations by their respective attorneys. Both men present with complaints of memory problems after sustaining mild closed head injuries with brief losses of consciousness in unrelated motor vehicle accidents.

Patient T grew up in the Midwest and has a high school education. He worked successfully in retail sales until he was involved in the automobile accident. Since that time, he has been unable to work. He is a relatively healthy man who evidences no signs of emotional distress or psychopathology. He is seen for a psychological evaluation about 1 year after his injury and is administered the WAIS-III and the WMS-III. His scores on the newly constructed joint factors of these instruments (cf. Chapter 4) are depicted in Table 1.

Based on his WAIS-III and WMS-III scores, it is apparent that Patient T is a man of Low Average to Average intellectual abilities, with mildly inefficient working memory skills. His test scores reveal relative deficits in his processing speed, auditory memory, and visual memory. Thus, it appears that

TABLE 1   Case Examples: Scores of Two Patients on the Joint Factors of the WAIS-III and WMS-III

Factor score	Patient T	Patient R
Verbal Comprehension	91	87
Perceptual Organization	86	89
Processing Speed	69	79
Working Memory	74	81
Auditory Memory	68	81
Immediate	74	83
Delayed	61	80
Visual Memory	70	86
Immediate	79	85
Delayed	64	88

Patient T may have indeed suffered mild to moderate declines in his memory and processing speed secondary to his closed head injury.

Patient R is similar to Patient T in many ways. He, too, grew up in the Midwest, achieved a high school education, and worked in retail sales. His prior medical history is noncontributory, and he is well adjusted in terms of his emotional and personality functioning. He is tested approximately 18 months after his injury, and his scores on the WAIS-III and WMS-III joint factors are also depicted in Table 1.

A review of this patient's test performances indicates that his intellectual abilities are in the Low Average range, as are his working memory, auditory memory, and visual memory. The only score that falls outside of the Low Average range is his Processing Speed Index, which lies at the high end of the Borderline range. In contrast to the first case presented, none of Patient R's test scores stands out as being particularly impaired. Thus, it would appear that he has recovered relatively well from his closed head injury.

Instead of T and R representing two unrelated cases, suppose these test scores actually reflect the test performances of one individual at two different points in time—at original testing (T) and at retest (R). After being previously evaluated by another professional approximately 1 year after his injury, this patient is now referred by his lawyer for a second assessment 6 months later (i.e., 18 months postinjury). Does knowing that the second set of retest scores are from the same individual 6 months later change our interpretation, or do these scores still suggest that the patient has recovered from the deficits he initially exhibited 1 year after his injury? The following discussion will review the issues that should be considered and will illustrate methods that can be used to guide the process of answering this question.

FACTORS AFFECTING TEST–RETEST PERFORMANCES

In an ideal world and in the absence of any significant intervening events, one's performance on a test should be the same at retest as it was at the time of original administration. However, cognitive tests such as the WAIS-III and WMS-III do not produce scores that are perfectly stable or reliable, and clinicians interested in discerning meaningful change must deal with the residuals of these statistical properties: bias and error. Table 2 outlines some of the common sources of bias and error that need to be considered when evaluating test–retest changes.

TABLE 2   Common Sources of Bias and Error in Test–Retest Situations

---

I. Bias

    A. Intervening Variables

        1. *Events of interest (e.g., surgery, medical intervention, rehabilitation)*

        2. Extraneous events

    B. Practice Effects

        1. Memory for Content

        2. Procedural Learning

        3. Other Factors

            a. Familiarity with Testing Context and Examiner

            b. Performance Anxiety

    C. Demographic considerations

        1. Age (maturational effects and aging)

        2. Education

        3. Gender

        4. Ethnicity

        5. Baseline ability

II. Error

    A. Statistical errors

        1. Measurement Error (SE_M)

        2. Regression to the Mean (SE_{est})

    B. Random or Uncontrolled Events

Bias

Bias simply represents a systematic change in performance. The most important source of bias for clinicians and researchers alike is that which is attributed to the variable of interest. Our ability to detect a meaningful change as the result of an intervention, treatment, or the impact of time on disease progression or recovery of function requires us to separate the effects associated with these factors from those due to other extraneous sources of bias.

Practice Effects

The most common form of extraneous bias on cognitive measures given twice is a positive *practice effect* in which performance is enhanced by previous exposure to test materials or to the testing situation. Where large positive practice effects are expected (e.g., the average retest increment for the WMS-III General Memory Index is 12.15 points; The Psychological Corporation, 1997), the absence of change is relatively rare and may actually reflect a decrement in performance.

Although practice effects are often attributed to explicit memory for the test content, several additional factors may account for improvements in performance at retest. Positive carryover effects due to procedural learning or to the application of previously developed effective strategies for completing tasks may also positively impact scores at retest (Benedict & Zgaljardic, 1998). Likewise, familiarity with the testing process, examiner, or task requirements may place an examinee at increased ease, or, alternatively may heighten anxiety in cases where the initial testing experience was perceived as unpleasant. Another source of systematic bias is aging, with a positive maturational effect expected in children and a negative bias in the elderly. Even though tests such as the WAIS-III and WMS-III make age corrections to the test scores at both time 1 and time 2, this does not necessarily correct for age differences in the ability of patients to benefit from practice and its associated impact on test–retest change. Other demographic factors that commonly impact initial levels of performance such as education, gender, and ethnicity may also systematically influence retest scores, and the amount of test retest change expected on a measure may vary across different levels of baseline performance. For instance, prior research has demonstrated that individuals with higher overall abilities, as indicated by higher WAIS-R Full Scale IQ scores at initial testing, demonstrate greater practice effects across time (Rapport, Axelrod, et al., 1997; Rapport, Brines, Axelrod, & Theisen, 1997).

Because serial assessments are increasingly being performed, publishers are beginning to provide more extensive information concerning test–retest stability. For example, the test–retest sample presented in the manual for the WAIS-R (Wechsler, 1981) consisted of 119 cases, whereas the retest sample for the WAIS-III includes data for 394 cases (The Psychological Corporation, 1997); the WMS-III includes 297 test–retest cases (The Psychological Corporation, 1997). Although stability estimates based on test–retest correlations are generally quite good for the WAIS-III summary IQ scores (range .91 to .96) and for the WMS-III primary Index scores (range .70 to .88), these estimates simply reflect how consistent the relative standings of individuals in the retest sample are across the two assessments. They do not directly assess how similar (or stable) scores are at the *individual level* across the test–retest interval. For example, if the Verbal Comprehension Index score of every individual in the retest sample improved by exactly 3 points at retest, the test–retest correlation would be a perfect 1.0, despite the presence of a 3-point systematic bias impacting retest scores.

Examination of the test–retest means reported in the *WAIS-III–WMS-III Technical Manual* (The Psychological Corporation, 1997) indicates that significant gains are consistently noted in the WAIS-III summary IQ scores and WMS-III primary Index scores earned by individuals over the 2 to 12-week test–retest interval. Similar gains have been reported for the WAIS-III after both 3-month and 6-month retest intervals (Basso et al., 2002), with the magnitude of these gains being comparable regardless of which test–retest interval intervened between the two assessments.

Significant test–retest gains are also evident for the newly derived factor scores described in Chapter 4 (this volume). We calculated the average test and retest scores earned by the 281 individuals in the WAIS-III—WMS-III test–retest sample who had complete data for both test batteries at two assessment points. The basic demographic characteristics of this test–retest sample are displayed in Table 3, and the resulting means, standard deviations, and associated test–retest correlation coefficients for the factors are summarized in Table 4. Although fairly evenly distributed across individuals as reflected by the high test–retest correlations (range = .76 to .93), a careful review of these data indicate that practice effects certainly impact scores on the Wechsler scales. Whereas mean scores on each factor were near 100 at original testing, the retest factor scores ranged from approximately 102 to 113. Repeated-measures analyses of variance indicated that the gains documented across all factors were statistically significant (all $ps < .01$), reflecting the presence of significant practice effects. Further, the amount of bias from practice is not directly related to the test–retest stability (reliability) coefficients, as can be seen by comparing the results for the Working

TABLE 3   Demographic Characteristics of 281 Individuals with Complete Test–Retest Data on the WAIS-III and WMS-III

	Mean (SD)
Age	53.00 (23.04)
Education	12.35 (2.54)
Test–retest interval (days)	35.63 (12.17)
	Percent of sample
Gender (men)	51.6
Ethnicity (white)	79.0

TABLE 4   Test and Retest Means (*SD*) Earned by Individuals in the WAIS-III WMS-III Test–Retest Sample and Associated Test–Retest Correlations

Factor score (subtests)[a]	Time 1	Time 2	F (1, 280)	p	r^2
Verbal Comprehension	100.91	103.56	69.70	<.001	.93
(Vocab, Info, Sim)	(13.80)	(14.53)			
Perceptual Organization	100.61	105.83	105.27	<.001	.84
(PC, BD, MR)	(13.62)	(15.78)			
Processing Speed	100.91	104.54	58.89	<.001	.87
(DSym, SymS)	(14.73)	(16.01)			
Working Memory	100.51	102.17	7.50	<.01	.76
(L-N, SSpan)	(13.81)	(14.96)			
Auditory Memory	100.02	110.04	379.24	<.001	.86
(LM I & II, VPA I & II)	(14.76)	(16.97)			
Visual Memory	101.32	112.52	402.45	<.001	.81
(FP I & II, VR I & II)	(14.81)	(15.52)			

[a]Vocab, Vocabulary; Info, Information; Sim, Similarities; PC, Picture Completion; BD, Block Design; MR, Matrix Reasoning; DSym, Digit Symbol; SymS, Symbol Search; L-N, Letter-Number Sequencing; SSpan, Spatial Span; LM, Logical Memory; VPA, Verbal Paired Associates; FP, Family Pictures; VR, Visual Reproduction.

Memory Factor (WMF) to those for the Auditory Memory Factor (AMF). Although the AMF scores demonstrate much higher test–retest correlations than WMF scores (.86 vs. 76), they also show greater susceptibility to bias from positive practice effects (10 points vs. 2 points on average). Thus, across all of these factors, scores at retest can be expected, on average, to be higher than during original testing, and the amount of improvement expected in scores varies across factors.

There is a common misconception that use of alternative forms of a test may be an effective means of avoiding or minimizing the effects of test familiarity. While carefully constructed alternative forms may dampen the effects of content-specific practice for some measures (Benedict & Zgaljardic, 1998), research suggests that serial use of such instruments still results in a significant practice effect. Goldstein et al. (1990) attempted to use alternate forms in a multicenter study of hypertension in the elderly, and they found significant improvements in test performance at follow-up even if alternate forms were employed. Franzen and colleagues (1996) looked at the reliability of alternate forms of the Trail Making Test among three patient groups using a counter-balanced design. Patients performed better on the second trial of the test regardless of whether the original form or alternate version was given first. Ruff, Light, and Parker (1996) also noted significant improvements in verbal fluency on alternate forms (C-F-L vs. P-R-W) of the Benton Controlled Oral Word Association Test (Benton, Hamsher, & Sivan, 1994) over a 6-month test–retest interval. While alternate forms may control for one source of the effects of practice, namely content, they do not control for procedural learning and other factors that contribute to the overall practice effect. Even worse, rote use of alternate forms may lull the practitioner into ignoring other issues that may impact test–retest change, such as reliability and error. Thus, alternate forms do not necessarily avoid the problems inherent in serial assessments, and the use of two separate instruments may make interpretation of test–retest change scores more difficult.

Error

Measurement Error

In addition to considering the systematic biases present when tests such as the WAIS-III and WMS-III are used in serial assessments, test measures themselves are imperfect and can introduce an element of error to test scores. In the absence of perfect reliability, a person's score on a test will likely vary somewhat across evaluations, even when no true underlying change has occurred. The less reliable a test, the more retest scores are likely to deviate from original scores due to random fluctuations in measurement. This source of error is termed *measurement error* and is reflected by the *standard error of measurement* (SE_M). The SE_M of a test is inversely related to the reliability of the test and pertains to the theoretical distribution of random variations in observed test scores around an individual's true score. Tests with low reliability have a large SE_M surrounding the true score at both baseline and on retest, and large test–retest differences may occur simply due to measurement error. However, even small test–retest differences may be reliable and clinically meaningful for tests with high reliability because they have a small SE_M surrounding the true score. In the context of serial evaluations, simple difference scores are particularly vulnerable to the influence of measurement error. Difference scores, in essence, combine the measurement error associated with scores from each of the two evaluations, and thereby magnify the impact of measurement error on test results. Thus, in order to interpret the clinical significance of change scores, they must be interpreted in light of their measurement errors.

Regression to the Mean

A second source of error that is directly related to the issue of reliability is *regression to the mean*, which describes the susceptibility of retest scores to fall closer to the population mean at retest than during the initial assessment. This happens because, on average, an individual's true score is actually closer to the mean of the population than his or her observed score. Thus, baseline scores that fall above the mean are typically reduced somewhat at retest, whereas those originally below the mean are expected to increase across the test–retest interval. Clinically, this can lead to spurious conclusions. For example, patients in rehabilitation settings who initially obtain test scores below the population mean may appear to get substantially better on retesting (scores closer to the population mean) simply due to the effects of regression to the mean. Conversely, a high-functioning patient undergoing open heart surgery may perform above the population mean prior to surgery, but may appear to deteriorate as a result of surgery if regression to the mean is not taken into account.

The magnitude of test–retest change associated with regression to the mean is a function of two factors. One factor is the reliability of the test measure being used. Scores on highly reliable measures are less vulnerable to the effects of regression to the mean than those earned on less reliable measures. A second factor is the extent to which test scores deviate from the population mean at baseline. As baseline scores become more extreme, they are increasingly likely to regress back toward the population mean at retest. Consider the WAIS-III variable, Performance IQ (PIQ), with a test–retest reliability of .91, and the WMS-III variable, Visual Immediate Memory (VIM), with a test–retest reliability of .75 (cf. The Psychological Corporation, 1997, pp. 61, 63). If an individual obtained a baseline score of 120 on each test variable, estimates of regression to the mean (Glutting, McDermott, & Stanley, 1987) would predict the patient would obtain a PIQ at retest of 118 but a VIM of 115. From this example, it is apparent that baseline scores that deviate substantially from the population mean on test measures with lower test–retest reliability are more likely to show greater test–retest changes due to regression to the mean than scores on more reliable measures, even in the absence of any intervening events.

When practice effects are considered together with the combined effects of measurement error and regression to the mean, interpretation of change scores becomes a complex matter. The effects of bias and error are always present when a test is given twice (whether in the same form or an alternative form), and they can confound and obscure the true impact of an intervention or treatment and make the interpretation of meaningful change difficult. However, if we are to demonstrate that our tests are useful in detecting real change within the context of evidence-based health care, we must find methods that allow us to account for systematic bias and error when interpreting change scores. Once this is accomplished, we can determine whether clinically meaningful change has occurred in an individual case.

METHODS FOR ASSESSING RELIABLE CHANGE

Bias and error are problems only to the degree that they are unknowns and are not taken into account when interpreting change scores. Several methods that are designed to account for these factors have been developed (see review by Chelune, 2002). While a detailed elaboration of these methods is beyond the scope of the present chapter, they can be described as falling into two broad categories. The first approach consists of variations on the *Reliable Change Index*, a method initially proposed by Jacobson and colleagues (Jacobson, Follette, & Revenstorf, 1984; Jacobson & Truax, 1991) for deriving cutoff scores that reflect changes that are rare in the general population. This method is useful for making categorical decisions about whether an individual has shown a meaningful and reliable change and can be derived on the basis of information typically contained in any good test manual (i.e., test–retest means, *SDs*, and reliability coefficients). The second approach is *Standardized Regression-Based (SRB) Change Scores*, which involve regression-based prediction equations that estimate retest scores based on baseline performance (McSweeny, Naugle, Chelune, & Lüders, 1993).

Both Reliable Change Indices and SRB Change Scores are statistical methods designed to take into account the reliability and stability of test measures when attempting to interpret changes in scores from test to retest. As statistical methods, they provide a strong foundation for clinical interpretation and decision making. Like reliable and valid test scores from a single evaluation, the information that emerges from the appropriate application of these procedures must also be considered within the context of historical and behavioral data provided by patients and their families. Because these methods have only recently gained popularity in the psychological assessment literature, their ecological validity is yet to be determined.

That is, change that appears reliable and clinically meaningful based on the application of these statistical procedures may or may not correspond to functional changes in the everyday activities of patients. Future research will be necessary to address this question. What these methods can determine is whether changes in test scores across assessments are reliable (i.e., likely to be documented again were the patient to be retested) and whether the changes occur infrequently enough in the general population to most likely represent an unusual and meaningful clinical result.

Reliable Change Indices

Reliable change methods generally attempt to describe the spread of the distribution of test–retest change scores that would be expected to occur in the absence of true underlying change. Note that the emphasis is on the mean and standard deviation of the *differences between baseline and retest scores*, not the actual test scores at time 1 and time 2. Where the mean and *SD* of the test–retest differences are known, the mean reflects the average practice effect, and the *SD* reflects the distribution of change scores around this mean. If the distribution of change scores is normally distributed, one can use the *SD* of the difference scores to estimate how frequently a given difference would occur in the general population. For example, 90% of scores would be expected to fall within ± 1.64 *SD* from the mean of the differences. Those that exceed +1.64 *SD* or fall below −1.64 *SD* would be expected to occur in less than 10% of the population (5% in each tail of the distribution). Dikmen, Heaton, Grant, and Temkin (1999) and Temkin, Heaton, Grant, and Dikmen (1999) used this approach to examine test–retest scores on the WAIS (Wechsler, 1955) in a large sample of stable individuals tested twice over an average of 11 months. The mean practice effect was 3 points and the *SD* of differences was 4.6. Using these data, one would estimate that 90% (±1.64 *SD*) of retest change scores would fall within the range of ±7.54 points around the average practice effect (mean) of 3 (i.e., range of −4.54 to 10.54).

Unfortunately, direct information concerning the magnitude and distribution of test–retest change scores is not always available. In these situations, it is possible to use "reliable change" methods to estimate the distribution of expected change (Jacobson et al., 1984; Jacobson & Truax, 1991). Jacobson and his colleagues (1984, 1991) developed a method of defining reliable change in terms of the *standard error of differences* (S_{diff}). The S_{diff} is derived from a measure's SE_M, and is given by the formula: $S_{diff} = (2(SE_M)^2)^{1/2}$.

The S_{diff} describes the distribution of expected test–retest difference scores around a mean of 0 (no difference). However, because difference scores imply that a test has been give twice, there is a SE_M at both baseline and at retest. Thus, Jacobson and associates (1984, 1991) simply multiply the SE_M twice in their calculation of S_{diff}. Since S_{diff} represents an area under the normal curve, one can derive Reliable Change Index (RCI) scores that would be expected to encompass a known percentage of the general population.

While the RCI method developed by Jacobson and Truax (1991) for evaluating reliable change attempts to control for measurement error, it does not take into account any systematic bias or practice effect; that is, the practice effect is assumed to be equal to zero. Chelune and colleagues (Chelune, Naugle, Lüders, Sedlak, & Awad, 1993; Sawrie, Chelune, Naugle, & Lüders, 1996) formulated a practice-adjusted RCI method that centers the distribution of expected difference scores around a non-zero constant that reflects the mean practice effect observed in individuals taking the test twice. Iverson (2001) has presented RCI data for the WAIS-III and WMS-III using a modified practice-adjusted method. Rather than simply assuming the SE_M is the same at baseline as at retest and multiplying by two as in the Jacobson and Truax (1991) approach, Iverson calculated the S_{diff} by pooling the actual SE_M data at baseline and at retest. Although these RCI methods treat "practice" as a constant and are open to criticism for their failure to consider regression to the mean (Bruggemans, Van de Vijver, & Huysmans, 1997), they do attempt to take into account both measurement error and practice.

A third reliable change method attempts to account for both measurement error and regression to the mean by using the *standard error of prediction*, although practice effects are still treated as a constant (Basso, Bornstein, & Lang, 1999; Bruggemans et al., 1997; Chelune, 2002). Basically, this approach examines the relationship between test and retest scores as a matter of prediction; that is, it determines the most probable value of a retest score given the specific value of the score at baseline and the degree of association between baseline and retest scores (test–retest reliability coefficient). The calculation of reliable change indices based on the standard error of prediction incorporates the *standard error of estimate* (Garrett, 1958), which provides some control for regression to the mean and measurement error. Calculation of the *standard error of prediction* simply requires knowledge of the test–retest reliability coefficient and the SD of observed retest scores, and is given by the formula: $SE_P = SD_Y * (1 - r_{12}^2)^{1/2}$. The formula provides a close approximation of the theoretical distribution of test–retest difference scores when adjusted for the mean practice effect (cf. Chelune, 2002).

Standardized Regression–Based Change Scores

Another method designed to account for the impact of bias and error on change across assessments and related to the standard error of prediction RCI model is the Standard Regression-Based (SRB) approach. SRB equations for evaluating change scores allow clinicians to determine whether a change observed in an individual's test scores across serial assessments is reliable and meaningful by calculating how much it deviates from expectations in light of the potential influence of bias and error. The bias introduced by demographic factors such as age, educational background, baseline levels of performance, and so on, is taken into account by entering these variables as potential predictors of retest scores in a linear regression analysis. To the extent that they influence retest performance, these variables will emerge as significant predictors of retest scores. Thus, a regression equation can be derived that accounts for potential sources of bias and that estimates retest performances based on the test–retest scores earned by a large sample of individuals in the general population. Substituting an individual patient's baseline score and other relevant characteristics into the regression equation allows an expected retest score for that individual to be determined. Discrepancies between observed and predicted retest scores indicate whether the patient's actual retest performance exceeded or failed to reach expected levels given typical positive practice effects and other sources of bias and error (Hermann et al., 1996; McSweeny et al., 1993; Sawrie et al., 1996).

Knowing that a difference exists between predicted and observed performance provides little information regarding the meaning of this discrepancy. What is of particular interest to clinicians is whether the magnitude of this discrepancy is sufficiently rare in the normal population that it represents a clinically significant change. Large discrepancies between predicted and observed performances may frequently occur in the general population due solely to limitations in measurement at test and at retest and error associated with less than perfect predictability of retest scores. To address the potential impact of error and to determine whether observed discrepancies between predicted and actual retest scores are meaningful, the amount by which a retest score deviates from expectations must be considered relative to the amount of error intrinsic to the prediction process. This error is represented by the *standard error of regression* (*SE*$_{reg}$). By dividing the difference between an actual and a predicted retest score by the standard error of regression, the discrepancy is converted into a *z-score of change*. Z-scores of change are expressed in standard deviation units. Thus, they indicate how discrepant an individual change is relative to expectations and provide information about how frequently a discrepancy of that magnitude would be expected to occur in the general population of stable individuals. For example, z-scores of change exceeding ±1.64 fall outside of a 90% confidence interval (CI) and would be expected to occur less than 5% of the time in normal populations tested twice. Therefore, a change of this magnitude is relatively rare and can be interpreted as reflecting a clinically meaningful individual change in the measured attribute once bias and error have been taken into account. Likewise, a more conservative criterion (change falling outside of the 95% CI; z-score of change exceeding ±1.96) or more liberal criterion (change falling outside of the 80% CI; z-score of change exceeding ±1.28) could be used for defining meaningful change. Regardless of the cutoff selected, z-scores of change allow clinicians to determine whether the change observed in an individual case is rare enough to likely correspond to an underlying meaningful change in the attribute being assessed once sources of bias and error are taken into account. It is important to keep in mind that we are discussing reliable change in terms of a *single* variable. In clinical practice, clinicians and researchers most often look for patterns of change across multiple variables and consider the co-probability of changes. Three scores, each exceeding an 80% RCI, may be much more significant than a single test–retest change exceeding a 95% RCI. However, for the purposes of our current discussion, we will limit our focus to assessing meaningful and reliable change for a given test variable.

MEANINGFUL AND RELIABLE TEST–RETEST CHANGE ON THE WAIS-III AND WMS-III

Recent comparisons of various RCI and SRB approaches (Heaton et al., 2001; Temkin et al., 1999) have found that the various methods of defining reliable change yield similar results. However, our preferred approach is the SRB method, as it allows for a differential consideration of baseline performance and demographic variables. The following data are from normal individuals tested twice over a relatively brief test–retest interval, and they are intended to be illustrative of the SRB approach. Although these data may be ideal for clinical outcome studies that have short test–retest intervals and that assume the patient is "normal" at baseline (e.g., pre– vs. post– cardiac surgery), research has not yet demonstrated whether they can be directly applied to the study of other populations where the patient is known to have a compromised brain and is followed over an extended period of time (e.g., recovery of function in rehabilitation settings).

Using data from the 281 individuals in the test–retest sample with complete data on both revisions of the Wechsler tests (The Psychological Corporation, 1997), we applied SRB methods to understand test–retest change on each of the six WAIS-III and WMS-III factor scores and on the Immediate and Delayed components of the Auditory and Visual Memory factors. Stepwise regression analyses were performed to determine the linear combination of variables that best predicted retest performance. Our predictor variables included baseline performance and several demographic variables, with those variables that accounted for at least 1 % of the variance in retest scores being retained in the final equation. Table 5 summarizes the variables that accounted for significant portions of variance in retest scores on each of the factors, the multiple R, the percentage of variance (R^2) accounted for by the final SRB equation, and the SE_{reg} or degree of dispersion or error around predicted scores.

As seen in Table 5, baseline scores on the factor of interest were consistently the strongest predictor of retest performance. Across the six WAIS-III–WMS-III factors and the four memory subfactors, baseline performances on the measure of interest accounted for 57 % (Working Memory) to 87 % (Verbal Comprehension) of the variance in retest scores. For all of the factors except the Verbal Comprehension Factor, other variables improved the prediction of retest scores above and beyond that which could be accomplished using baseline scores alone.

Because baseline performance was the only significant predictor of test–retest change on the Verbal Comprehension Factor, the simple SRB equation that resulted from this analysis will be used to illustrate how the influence of practice and regression to the mean are taken into account by SRB methodology. The SRB equation for the Verbal Comprehension Factor is as follows:

$$VCF_{predicted} = 4.624 + (.980 * VCF_{baseline}) \qquad (1)$$

The constant in the equation indicates that a general practice effect is expected on the Verbal Comprehension Factor whenever an individual takes the WAIS-III twice. However, the fact that the regression coefficient associated with baseline scores differs from 1.0 suggests that knowing an individual's baseline score can improve the clinician's ability to predict retest

TABLE 5   Standardized Regression-Based Prediction of Test–Retest Change on Each WAIS-III—WMS-III Factor

Retest factor score[a]	Baseline factor score and demographic predictors	Multiple R	R^2	R^2 increment	SE_{reg}
Verbal Comp	Verbal Comp	.931	.867	.867	5.30
Perceptual Organization	Perceptual Organization	.878	.770	.708	7.62
	Processing Speed			.027	
	Age			.025	
	Verbal Comp			.010	
Processing Speed	Processing Speed	.879	.773	.758	7.65
	Age			.015	
Working Memory	Working Memory	.776	.602	.570	9.47
	Perceptual Org			.033	
Auditory Memory	Auditory Memory	.872	.760	.742	8.35
	Full Scale IQ			.018	
Immediate	Auditory Immediate	.854	.729	.712	9.02
	Full Scale IQ			.017	
Delayed	Auditory Delayed	.841	.707	.680	8.56
	Full Scale IQ			.027	
Visual Memory	Visual Memory	.828	.685	.657	8.75
	Full Scale IQ			.017	
	Age			.013	
Immediate	Visual Immediate	.787	.619	.588	9.26
	Full Scale IQ			.021	
Delayed	Visual Delayed	.798	.636	.588	9.56
	Age			.025	
	Full Scale IQ			.023	

[a]Verbal Comp, Verbal Comprehension; Perceptual Org, Perpetual Organization

scores above and beyond a *fixed* practice effect. This coefficient simultaneously takes into account the differential amount of test–retest change expected for individuals at different levels of baseline performance and regression to the mean. As an example, if someone were to earn a score of 80 at initial testing, and his or her score were substituted into the SRB equation, he or she would be expected to earn a score of 83 at retest; that is, he or she would be expected to show a three-point test–retest improvement. However, if another individual were to obtain a score of 120 at initial testing, his or her predicted retest score would be 122, only a two-point gain. This example demonstrates that the combined influence of practice effects and regression to the mean is not constant across differing levels of baseline performance.

Studies investigating practice effects on the WAIS-R, the WMS-R, and other commonly utilized memory tests have found that individuals with higher overall abilities, as indicated by higher WAIS-R Full Scale IQ scores at initial testing, demonstrate greater practice effects across time (Rapport, Axelrod, et al., 1997; Rapport, Brines, et al., 1997). To examine whether this relationship also holds true with regard to the most recent revisions of the Wechsler scales, we included baseline scores on measures other than the primary factor of interest in our SRB analyses. For the Memory factors and subfactors, baseline Full Scale IQ (FSIQ) was used to determine whether general ability level influenced the amount of practice individuals in the test–retest sample demonstrated on memory tests at follow-up assessment. For all remaining factors, baseline scores on the other non-memory factors (Verbal Comprehension, Perceptual Organization, Processing Speed, and Working Memory) were utilized as an indication of general ability independent from the primary ability of interest and were entered as potential predictors of retest factor scores.

As seen in Table 5, baseline FSIQ scores improved the prediction of test–retest change on both of the primary Memory Factors and on all four of the Memory subfactors. In all cases, higher FSIQs at baseline were associated with greater improvements in memory scores secondary to practice effects at retest. With regard to the non-memory factors, the prediction of retest scores on the Verbal Comprehension Factor and the Processing Speed Factor were not significantly improved by considering scores in other domains. However, the SRB equations corresponding to both the Perceptual Organization Factor and the Working Memory Factor were significantly better at predicting retest scores when abilities other than those that were specific to the Factor of interest were included. For example, when combined with baseline Working Memory Factor scores, higher baseline scores on the Perceptual Organization Factor were associated with larger test–retest improvements on the Working Memory Factor. In fact, baseline Perceptual Organization scores accounted for 3% of the variance in Working Memory scores at retest, even after the variance accounted for by baseline Working Memory was taken into account. Thus, our data support the conclusions drawn by Rapport, Brines, et al. (1997) in their work with previous versions of the Wechsler scales; that is, individuals of higher baseline ability tend to demonstrate greater practice effects than those of lower baseline intelligence.

The influences that demographic characteristics (i.e., age, education level, gender, and ethnicity) and the length of test–retest interval might exert on the magnitude of change apparent across WAIS-III and WMS-III factors were also examined by including these variables as potential predictors in the SRB analyses. Including the length of the test–retest interval as a potential predictor of expected change did not significantly improve the fit of any of the regression equations. This finding is consistent with evidence in the literature that the magnitude of observed practice effects is fairly constant regardless of the amount of time (up to at least 6 months) intervening between the initial testing and the follow-up assessment (Basso et al., 2001; Hermann et al., 1996; Sawrie et al., 1996). Likewise, other than age, none of the demographic characteristics emerged as significant predictors of test–retest change on any of the intellectual or memory factors. Age significantly improved the prediction of retest scores on the Perceptual Organization Factor, the Processing Speed Factor, and two of the three Visual Memory measures. Although age only accounted for between 1 and 3 % of the variance in test–retest change, age exerted a statistically significant influence on the magnitude of practice effects observed on these factors, with older adults demonstrating less benefit from previous exposure to test materials than their younger peers. This was true regardless of the fact that the factor scores themselves are age-corrected at both baseline and at retest by virtue of being derived from age-corrected subtest scaled scores.

Based on our analyses of data from the 281 individuals in the WAIS-III—WMS-III test–retest sample, several variables appear to affect the amount by which scores on each of the WAIS-III—WMS-III joint factors would be expected to differ across serial assessments in the absence of any real change in neurocognitive status. Baseline levels of performance are major determinants of retest scores and reflect the overall reliability of the factor of interest. Likewise, an individual's *general* ability level at initial testing can affect the amount of change expected in specific domains. Finally, the age of the individual being tested exerts a statistically significant influence over how much improvement he or she demonstrates across the test–retest interval on some factors. Thus, SRB equations and z-scores of change that take into account these variables are essential tools for clinicians to use when attempting to determine whether the changes observed in an individual case represent clinically meaningful results once potential sources of bias and error are considered.

The SRB equations described above are based on data obtained from neurologically intact individuals. The extent to which the resulting standards will apply to brain-injured populations is not yet known. A recent article by Iverson (2001) reported separate reliable change estimates for WAIS-III and WMS-III Index and subtest scores for patients with Alzheimer's disease, chronic alcohol abuse, and schizophrenia. Results suggested that the expected impact of measurement error on retest scores differed across these three patient populations. Future work designed to further examine the potential influence that neurological injury or neurological disease can exert both on practice effects and on test reliability will be necessary to determine the most appropriate normative standards to use when interpreting test–retest scores in clinical populations. However, until such empirical information becomes available, SRB norms based on the test and retest scores earned by non-clinical populations provide the best methodology for understanding and interpreting test–retest change in both research and clinical settings.

APPLICATION OF THE SRB APPROACH

Table 6 provides a practical example of how the application of the SRB approach can be used to evaluate the significance of change scores derived

TABLE 6   Case Example Revisited: Test and Retest Scores of One Patient on the New WAIS-III and WMS-III Factors

Factor Score	Test	Retest	Difference Score	SRB Predicted Score	SRB z-score
Verbal Comprehension	91	87	−04	94	−1.28
Perceptual Organization	86	89	+03	87	+0.22
Processing Speed	69	79	+10	74	+0.63
Working Memory	74	81	+07	80	+ 0.11
Auditory Memory	68	81	+13	77	+0.44
Immediate	74	83	+09	82	+0.08
Delayed	61	80	+19	74	+0.71
Visual Memory	70	86	+16	85	+0.10
Immediate	79	85	+06	94	−0.92
Delayed	64	88	+24	83	+0.56

Note: Prorated Full Scale IQ score at initial assessment = 79.

from serial assessments. We return to our case example and address the issue of whether knowing that the second set of scores represent retest scores influences our interpretation of the patient's clinical status. Examination of the raw score differences between our hypothetical patient's test (T) and retest (R) performances shows that many of his test scores changed substantially across the test–retest interval. For example, his Auditory Delayed score improved by 19 points and his Visual Delayed score improved by 24 points. However, the SRB predicted scores included in the table demonstrate that a large portion of this improvement is expected solely on the basis of the bias introduced by practice effects and the expected influence of other factors. For example, substituting this 56-year-old patient's baseline score of 64 on the Visual Delayed Memory Factor and his baseline Full Scale IQ of 79, along with other relevant characteristics, into the following SRB equation,

$$\text{Visual Delayed}_{\text{retest}} = 26.5 + (.713 * \text{Visual Delayed}_{\text{baseline}}) \\ +(-.106 * \text{Age}) + (.208 * \text{FSIQ}_{\text{baseline}}) \tag{2}$$

indicates that he would be expected to earn a retest Visual Delayed score of 82.63. When the discrepancy between this predicted retest score and the patient's actual retest score of 88 (+5.37) is divided by the standard error of the regression equation (see Table 5; in this case, 9.56), the corresponding z-score of change falls only about .5 SD above expectation (+.56). Using this z-score to estimate the area under the normal probability curve, one finds that earning a Visual Delayed retest score that is 5 points *above* the predicted retest score would occur in approximately 30% of normal cases, even when no true underlying change intervened. Thus, our patient's 24-point improvement from test to retest no longer appears to represent a clinically rare result. With a SE_{reg} of 9.56, he would have had to earn a score of 98 [82.63 + (1.64 * 9.56)] to show an improvement that falls outside of the 90% CI of expected change.

The SRB z-scores of change in Table 6 indicate that none of this patient's improvements falls even 1 SD away from expected levels once bias and error are taken into account. This finding suggests that the changes in his scores across the test–retest interval could be solely attributable to practice effects and error. In fact, the biggest *real* change in his scores is the relatively small 4-point drop in his Verbal Comprehension Factor score, which falls 1.28 SD below expectations due to a lack of expected practice effects. In addition, the six-point *improvement* in his Visual Immediate memory score across assessments actually represents a nearly 1 SD *decline* relative to expectations once factors known to influence retest performances are taken into account (z-score of change $= -.92$).

The lack of improvements beyond those expected in this patient's scores indicates that the impairments noted at his initial exam may remain problematic for him at retest, even though his actual factor scores from the second assessment are typically in the low average range. Whereas we initially interpreted this second set of scores as representing normal functioning in an individual of low average ability, knowing that they are from a repeat evaluation leads us to conclude that the patient may still have deficits in his processing speed, auditory memory, and visual memory that are being masked by practice effects and regression to the mean. Clinical corroboration and examination of patterns of change across measures (e.g., improvements across multiple measures) may be necessary to clarify whether the changes documented during an evaluation correspond to actual improvements in functioning or merely reflect the influence of bias and error. However, based solely on the test scores themselves, this patient's test results no longer support the inference that his cognitive functioning has recovered during the 6 months intervening between his two evaluations. We may have reached a notably different conclusion had we not considered his test–retest scores within the context of the SRB approach.

Applying SRB techniques in this example transformed what appeared to be rather large test–retest improvements into relatively modest changes across evaluations. However, applying SRB methodology can also allow subtle declines in test scores to be recognized for their potential significance. For example, patients undergoing surgical intervention to treat medically refractory seizure disorders or to place deep brain stimulators to control tremors associated with Parkinson's disease may be evaluated prior to surgery to characterize their baseline abilities and reassessed following surgery to document any changes in their cognitive status. Consider a 53-year-old man who is referred for a cognitive evaluation as part of a comprehensive workup to determine his candidacy for right temporal lobectomy. He earns a Full Scale IQ score of 110 and a Visual Delayed Memory Factor Score of 102. Following his surgery, he is reassessed and earns a Visual Delayed Memory Factor Score of 99, a relatively small 3-point drop in terms of his raw score. However, with the appropriate variables substituted into the following SRB equation,

$$\text{Visual Delayed}_{retest} = 26.5 + (.713 * \text{Visual Delayed}_{baseline}) \\ +(-.106 * \text{Age}) + (.208 * \text{FSIQ}_{baseline}) \quad (3)$$

his predicted Visual Delayed Memory score at retest is found to be 116.49. His actual retest score of 99 is 17.49 points *below* his predicted score and translates into a nearly 2 *SD* decline relative to expectations when divided by the standard error of the regression equation (i.e., 9.56; $-17.49/9.56 = -1.83$ *SD*). A *decline* of this magnitude would be expected to occur in only 3 % of normal individuals tested twice (one-tailed probability) in the absence of any true underlying change. Thus, in this and other similar cases, utilizing SRB methodology may allow clinicians and researchers to more accurately detect declines they may otherwise have attributed solely to random fluctuations across time. From these examples, it should be clear why failure to take into account expected changes secondary to bias, as well as expected fluctuations due to error, could lead clinicians to misinterpret retest scores and possibly reach erroneous conclusions in the context of serial evaluations.

USING DEMOGRAPHICALLY CORRECTED SCORES IN THE CONTEXT OF SERIAL ASSESSMENTS

When conducting psychological assessments, practitioners are typically interested in obtaining the most accurate estimate of an individual's true underlying capacity. Demographic characteristics (e.g., age, education level, gender, and ethnicity) are yet another source of potential bias that can confound test results. Heaton and colleagues (Chapter 5, this volume) outlined the ways in which these variables can influence factor scores on the WAIS-III and WMS-III and proposed the application of demographic corrections to these test scores to improve the sensitivity and specificity of test results.

When using demographically adjusted scores in the context of serial evaluations, the same issues that we have already outlined above must be considered. Sources of bias and error continue to impact test–retest change scores, even when the variance due to demographic characteristics has been accounted for at both time 1 and time 2. Correcting baseline and retest scores for relevant demographic factors does not necessarily remove any effects that these factors might have on test–retest change across time; that is, demographic factors may mediate the magnitude of practice effects and/or introduce other sources of bias.

In the previous discussion of variables that predict retest scores on the WAIS-III and WMS-III joint factors, age emerged as a significant influence in many of the SRB equations for predicting expected test–retest change, even though the factor scores themselves were already age-corrected at both assessment points. To investigate whether the impact of age on factor scores at retest could be attributed to relationships between age and other non-corrected demographic variables, we applied the ethnicity, age, education, and gender corrections proposed by Heaton, Taylor, and Manly (cf. Chapter 5, this volume) to the scores earned by the 281 individuals in the test–retest sample. We then repeated the process of calculating SRB equations for the demographically corrected factors. Interestingly, age demonstrated even stronger relationships with test–retest change (i.e., 1.5 to 4% of the variance in Perceptual Organization, Processing Speed, and Visual Delayed retest scores) once they were demographically corrected at baseline and at retest. Although the actual amount of variance accounted for by age is fairly modest, age does appear to have a direct effect on test–retest changes, at least in some domains, above and beyond the impact it has on the scores themselves at any point in time. Specifically, older individuals typically demonstrate less improvement across the test–retest interval relative to their younger counterparts, and this should be taken into account when interpreting scores from serial assessments, even when demographic corrections are applied. However, other demographic characteristics, such as education and gender appear to exert little influence on test–retest change once their impact on time 1 and time 2 scores have been taken into account.

IMPACT OF SERIAL ASSESSMENTS ON BASE RATES OF DISCREPANCY SCORES

When interpreting test scores, clinicians often rely not only on the absolute value of each score in isolation, but also on the magnitude of discrepancies between scores earned across different domains. For example, in addition to independently looking at the absolute level of performance on measures of intelligence and memory, it is also useful to look at whether the levels of performance in these domains are significantly discrepant from one another. This is often a questionable practice when tests are normed on different populations at different points in time using different sampling techniques. However, one of the primary advantages of the new WAIS-III and WMS-III is the fact that these two Wechsler scales were co-normed. This allows scores both within and between the two tests to be directly compared by calculating the difference between scores of interest. In order for an observed discrepancy to be deemed clinically meaningful, it must be sufficiently rare in the normal population that it most likely represents an abnormal finding. To make this determination, an individual discrepancy is often evaluated relative to its base rate of occurrence in the general population. For example, discrepancy scores that fall outside of the 90 or 95 % CI of those observed in the standardization sample can be considered statistically rare and potentially indicative of a clinically meaningful difference between the two factors being evaluated. Data provided in the respective test manuals and in the *WAIS-III–WMS-III Technical Manual* (The Psychological Corporation, 1997) allow the clinician to determine not only whether an observed discrepancy is statistically reliable, but also how often a given discrepancy is likely to occur in the general population.[1] Hawkins and Tulsky (Chapter 6, this volume) provide a detailed discussion of the appropriate application and interpretation of base rate discrepancy score analysis for the newly derived joint factors of the WAIS-III and WMS-III in the context of a single evaluation.

Just as the meaning of any test score can be altered when it is derived from a repeat evaluation (as illustrated in our earlier case example), the base rates of the differences *between* test scores can also change dramatically from baseline to retest. Differential rates of practice on the individual tests that comprise discrepancy scores can impact not only the magnitude of the discrepancies observed at retest, but also the base rates with which a given discrepancy would be expected to occur in the context of serial assessments. For example, consider a 75-year-old woman who is referred for an evaluation after she presents to her primary care physician with complaints of progressive and gradual decline in her memory. She earns a FSIQ score of 113 and a General Memory Index score of 91 during her initial assessment (FSIQ–GMI discrepancy score = 22). The *WAIS-III–WMS-III Technical Manual* (The Psychological Corporation, 1997) reports that a discrepancy this large (22 points or greater) occurred in only 5 % of the standardization sample. Even though her General Memory Index score remains at the low end of the Average range, it is lower than expected given her level of intellectual functioning, and her test results can be interpreted as being indicative of mild memory decline relative to expectations.

Six months later, the patient is referred for a follow-up assessment to determine whether her memory difficulties have worsened. If no underlying

[1]The *WAIS-III and WMS-III Manuals* (Wechsler, 1997a,b) report cumulative or two-tail base rates, whereas the between-test base rates in the *WAIS-III–WMS-III Technical Manual* (The Psychological Corporation, 1997) reflect directional one-tail discrepancies. The appropriate use and interpretation of these base rate data are discussed by Tulsky, Rolfhus, and Zhu (2000).

change occurred in her IQ or memory abilities during the test–retest interval, and if she showed the average practice effect on both measures (approximately +4 on FSIQ and +12 on GMI), her discrepancy score at retest would only be 14 points. An IQ–Memory discrepancy of this magnitude was observed in nearly 15% of the standardization sample, a much more common finding in the general population than the 22-point discrepancy observed at initial testing. The differential influence of practice on the two scores being compared results in a different IQ–Memory base rate at retest. Due solely to the influence of normal practice effects, this patient's memory score would no longer appear to be significantly discrepant from her intellectual abilities. Thus, in order for a mild memory decline to be detected at a second or subsequent evaluation, a much more profound difference between her IQ and memory score would be required.

As illustrated by this example, differential practice effects can render base rate discrepancy analysis insensitive to true underlying differences between measures in the context of serial assessments. Conversely, discrepancies that appear to be fairly common in the general population on initial testing may become exaggerated by differential practice effects at retest, and may appear to be clinically meaningful incidental only to the bias introduced by previous exposure to test materials. For example, a person with stronger (but not to an unusual degree) nonverbal than verbal abilities at original testing, might show a seemingly clinically significant discrepancy favoring nonverbal abilities at retest due to the greater expected rates of practice on PIQ measures relative to VIQ subtests.

We examined the impact of serial assessments on observed discrepancy scores in the context of the newly derived WAIS-III WMS-III joint factor structure by comparing relevant discrepancy scores at baseline and at retest in our test–retest sample. Whereas the average discrepancies between measures were centered near 0 ($\pm$ 1) at baseline, Table 7 illustrates that differential practice effects and sources of error significantly altered the distributions of discrepancy scores at retest. Average discrepancies at retest systematically shifted in a negative direction (range = -1 to -9), suggesting that the second variable in the discrepancy couplet increased more on retest than the first. The amount of variability inherent in discrepancy scores also increased slightly across evaluations, as reflected in the larger standard deviations at retest than at baseline, indicating that the discrepancy scores are dispersed more widely at retest in the general population. Thus, larger discrepancies will likely be required at retest than at initial testing to be considered abnormal or clinically meaningful.

TABLE 7   Discrepancy Scores at Baseline and at Retest and Corresponding 90% Confidence Intervals Based on Frequencies of Observed Discrepancies in the Test–Retest Sample

Discrepancy score	Baseline mean (SD)	Retest mean (SD)	Baseline 90% CI[a]	Retest 90% CI[a]
Verbal Comprehension –	0.30	−2.28	−20 to +19	−24 to +17
Perceptual Organization	(11.72)	(12.69)		
Verbal Comprehension–	0.00	−0.96	−23 to +23	−26 to +24
Processing Speed	(14.18)	(14.89)		
Verbal Comprehension–	0.62	−6.12	−23 to +26	−30 to +19
Auditory Delayed Memory	(14.48)	(15.22)		
Perceptual Organization–	−0.99	−8.51	−26 to +21	−34 to +15
Visual Delayed Memory	(14.04)	(14.64)		

[a]CI, confidence interval.

The systematic shift in average discrepancy scores and the increased variability in the between-score differences alter the frequency or base rate of their occurrence in the general population. Figure 1 demonstrates the frequency with which discrepancies between intellectual and memory factor scores of varying magnitudes were observed at baseline and at retest in our test–retest sample of 281 individuals. Both the Verbal Comprehension-Auditory Delayed Memory (Fig. 1A) and the Perceptual Organization–Visual Delayed Memory (Fig. 1B) discrepancy scores are centered around 0 at baseline, and approximately half of the 281 individuals earned discrepancy scores in the −9 to +9 range. In addition, the distributions of discrepancy scores from the initial evaluation are fairly symmetrical. However, at retest, the distributions look very different. At the second assessment, it was as common for individuals to earn memory scores that *exceeded* their corresponding intellectual factor scores by 10 to 29 points as it was for them to show little or no difference between measures (i.e., discrepancy scores in the −9 to +9 range). Although negative discrepancies (i.e., Memory scores > IQ scores) of 30 points or more were relatively rare at initial testing (i.e., only 2% of the sample showed discrepancy scores of this magnitude), the frequency of scores in this range increased nearly three-to fourfold at retest (observed in approximately 5–8% of the sample). In contrast, positive discrepancies (IQ scores > Memory score) were much more rare at retest than they were at baseline. Whereas 22–25% of the sample demonstrated positive discrepancy scores of 10 points or more during their baseline assessment,

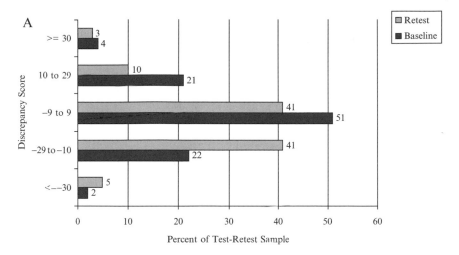

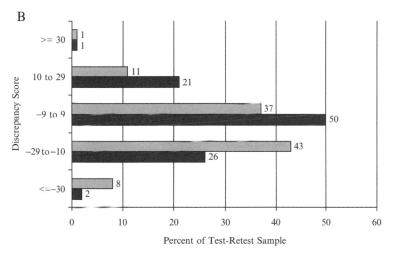

FIGURE 1.   Base rates of discrepancy scores of varying magnitudes earned at baseline and retest. (A) The Verbal Comprehension – Auditory Delayed Memory discrepancy, (B) the Perceptual Organization – Visual Delayed Memory discrepancy.

only half as many individuals (i.e., 12–13% of the sample) earned discrepancy scores in this range at retest.

By this point in the discussion, it should be apparent that clinicians must consider the context of repeat evaluations when interpreting base rates of discrepancies between scores with differential susceptibility to practice effects. Based on the actual frequencies of observed discrepancies in the test–retest sample, Table 7 summarizes discrepancy cutoff scores that define the 90 % CI at baseline and at retest (with 5 % of the sample falling in each tail of the distribution). Although the impact of serial assessments is fairly subtle and has only minor effects on recommended cutoffs for contrasting scores within the WAIS-III, the discrepancy between a WAIS-III score and a WMS-III score required to constitute a "rare" result is more notably influenced by previous examinations. For example, a Verbal Comprehension Factor score must exceed an Auditory Delayed Memory score by 26 points at initial testing to constitute a rare finding (i.e., in this case defined as one expected to occur in less than 5 % of the general population). However, a positive discrepancy of 19 points between these two scores is sufficient at retest to correspond to a 5 % base rate and to suggest the presence of a memory deficit relative to intellectual functioning. Conversely, a score on the Auditory Delayed Memory Factor must exceed that earned on the Verbal Comprehension Factor by 23 points at initial testing but by 30 points at retest for the two scores to be considered significantly discrepant from one another. Thus, serial evaluations can substantially impact the base rates of observed discrepancies between factor scores at retest, and this must be considered when using base rate discrepancy score analysis in the context of repeated assessments.

SUMMARY AND CONCLUSIONS

From our discussion of the WAIS-III and WMS-III test–retest data, it should be clear that one cannot interpret scores from a repeat evaluation in the same manner and with the same meaning as those from an initial evaluation. The systematic bias inherent in retest scores, as well as measurement error, can dramatically alter the magnitude of the scores themselves, rendering them at best questionable and at worst misleading. The meaning of test–retest change can only be elucidated by first taking into account how much change is normally expected across time given the many factors that influence retest scores and then evaluating how commonly or frequently deviations from these expectations occur in the general population. Even patterns of scores across measures and the magnitude of discrepancies between test scores can be profoundly affected by previous experience with the test measures. Although previous exposure to specific test materials and content may constitute one source of systematic bias on retest scores, many other factors also impact test–retest change and must be taken into consideration when serial evaluations are conducted.

With an increasing need for clinicians and researchers to reach conclusions about alterations in the mental state or capacity of individuals across time armed only with psychological tests designed to evaluate functioning at one assessment point, much work remains to be done. The data reviewed in this chapter suggest that both baseline level of ability and age play a role in the amount of test–retest change expected. Although other demographic characteristics did not factor into predicting retest scores in the sample we examined, it is possible that these variables impact test–retest change on other measures. In addition, investigators have only recently begun to examine whether brain compromise mediates the impact of bias and error on test–retest change (Chelune et al., 1993; Ferland, Ramsay, Engeland, & O'Hara, 1998; Hermann et al., 1996; Rawlings & Crewe, 1992; Wilson, Watson, Baddeley, Emslie, & Evans, 2000). For example, it is possible that memory or learning impairments may reduce the amount of practice expected across serial evaluations. If so, these relationships need to be the subject of formal investigation because taking them into consideration along with the other factors discussed in this chapter may be essential to determining whether medical interventions with these individuals alter their clinical outcome. This chapter has outlined a general statistical model for taking into account bias and error when individuals are tested twice. As test–retest data are gathered on neurologically stable brain-injured individuals and patients with neurodegenerative disorders, the same principles can be applied to determine the expected pattern of change over time in these clinical populations. Finally, some studies have offered preliminary data to suggest that the majority of the bias introduced by practice effects may occur between the first and second assessments, with only small improvements expected in test scores across subsequent evaluations (Ivnik et al., 1999; McCaffery, Westervelt, & Haase, 2001; Rapport, Brines, et al., 1997; Theisen, Rapport, Axelrod, & Brines, 1998). Continued research investigating test–retest change in the context of multiple assessments could contribute data essential to understanding and correctly interpreting the types of test scores frequently encountered in forensic settings, in longitudinal research projects, and so on. With only two potential data points to examine, change across time necessarily appears linear in nature, but as additional research documents the character of test–retest changes across more than two evaluations, regression-based models are equipped to examine the possibility that change may follow a nonlinear trajectory.

Within the context of an increasingly value-driven health care environment that emphasizes outcomes management, serial assessment is becoming an important and necessary aspect of clinical practice and research. Whether utilizing test data as predictors of clinical outcomes or as outcome endpoints in the evaluation of the efficacy and safety of medical procedures (e.g., medications, surgical interventions, rehabilitation), psychologists must recognize test–retest change as a unique cognitive variable with its own metric and with its own clinical meaning. In this chapter, we have attempted to review some of the common sources of bias and error that can impact the amount and direction of change expected in retest scores when longitudinal assessments are employed and to introduce clinicians and researchers to methods available for evaluating the reliability and meaning of test–retest change. Although the newly derived joint factors from the WAIS-III and WMS-III were used for illustration purposes, the issues outlined here clearly extend beyond these two instruments and apply to all psychological and neuropsychological instruments used during a comprehensive assessment.

REFERENCES

Andrew, M. J., Baker, R. A., Bennetts, J., Kneebone, A. C., & Knight, J. L. (2001). A comparison of neuropsychologic deficits after extracardiac and intracardiac surgery. *Journal of Cardiothoracic and Vascular Surgery, 15*, 9–14.

Basso, M. R., Bornstein, R. A., & Lang, J. M. (1999). Practice effects on commonly used measures of executive function across twelve months. *The Clinical Neuropsychologist, 13*, 283–292.

Basso, M. R., Carona, F. D., Lowery, N., & Axelrod, B. N. (2002). Practice effects on the WAIS-III across 3- and 6- month intervals. *The Clinical Neuropsychologist, 16*, 57–63.

Benedict, R. H. B., & Zgaljardic, D. J. (1998). Practice effects during repeated administrations of memory tests with and without alternate forms. *Journal of Clinical and Experimental Neuropsychology, 20*, 339–352.

Benton, A. L., Hamsher, K. de S., & Sivan, A. B. (1994). *Multilingual Aphasia Examination*. Iowa City, IA: AJA Associates.

Bruggemans, E. F., Van de Vijver, F. J. R., & Huysmans, H. A. (1997). Assessment of cognitive deterioration in individual patients following cardiac surgery: Correcting for measurement error and practice effects. *Journal of Clinical and Experimental Neuropsychology, 19*, 543–559.

Chelune, G. J. (2002). Assessing reliable neuropsychological change. In R. D. Franklin (Ed.), *Prediction in forensic and neuropsychology: New approaches to psychometrically sound assessment* (pp. 123–147) Mahwah, NJ: Erlbaum.

Chelune, G. J., & Najm, I. (2001). Risk factors associated with postsurgical decrements in memory. In H. O. Lüders & Y. Comair (Eds.), *Epilepsy surgery* (2nd edn, pp. 497–504). Philadelphia: Lippincott-Raven.

Chelune, G. J., Naugle, R. I., Lüders, H., Sedlak, J., & Awad, I. A. (1993). Individual change after epilepsy surgery: Practice effects and base-rate information. *Neuropsychology, 7*, 41–52.

Chui, H., & Zhang, Q. (1997). Evaluation of dementia: A systematic study of the usefulness of the American Academy of Neurology's practice parameters. *Neurology, 49*, 925–935.

Cronbach, L. J., & Furby, L. (1970). How we should measure "change"—or should we? *Psychological Bulletin, 74*, 68–80.

Desmond, D. W., Moroney, J. T., Bagiella, E., Sano, M., & Stern, Y. (1998). Dementia as a predictor of adverse outcomes following stroke: An evaluation of diagnostic methods. *Stroke, 29*, 69–74.

Dikmen, S. S., Heaton, R. K., Grant, I., & Temkin, N. R. (1999). Test–retest reliability and practice effects of Expanded Halstead-Reitan Neuropsychological Test Battery. *Journal of the International Neuropsychological Society, 5*, 346–356.

Ferland, M. B., Ramsay, J., Engeland, C., & O'Hara, P. (1998). Comparison of the performance of normal individuals and survivors of traumatic brain injury on repeat administrations of the Wisconsin Card Sorting Test. *Journal of Clinical and Experimental Neuropsychology, 20*, 473–482.

Fischer, J. S., Priore, R. L., Jacobs L. D., Cookfair, D. L., Rudick, R. A., Herndon, R. M., Richert, J. R., Salazar, A. M., Goodkin, D. E., Granger, C. V., Simon, J. H., Grafman, J. H., Lezak, M. D., O'Reilly Hovey, K. M., Perkins, K. K., Barilla-Clark, D., Schacter, M., Shucard, D. W., Davidson, A. L., Wende, K. E., Bourdette, D. N., & Kooijmans-Coutinho, M. F. (2000). Neuropsychological effects of interferon beta-1a in relapsing multiple sclerosis. Multiple Sclerosis Collaborative Research Group. *Annals of Neurology, 48*, 885–892.

Foldvary, N., Chelune, G., Comair, Y., Bingaman, W., Ruggieri, P., Morris, H., Dinner, D., Geller, E., & Lüders, H. O. (1977). Comparison of neuropsychological and seizure outcome after amygdalohippocampectomy and anterior temporal lobe epilepsy. *Epilepsia, 38 (Suppl. 8)*, 551–552.

Franzen, M. D., Paul, D., & Iverson, G. L. (1996). Reliability of alternate forms of the Trail Making Test. *The Clinical Neuropsychologist, 10*, 125–129.

Garrett, H. E. (1958). *Statistics in psychology and education*. New York: Longmans, Green, & Co.

Glutting, J. J., McDermott, P. A., & Stanley, J. C. (1987). Resolving differences among methods of establishing confidence limits for test scores. *Educational and Psychological Measurement, 47*, 607–614.

Goldstein, G., Materson, B. J., Cushman, W. C., Reda, D. J., Freis, E. D., et al. (1990). Treatment of hypertension in the elderly: II. Cognitive and behavioral function. *Hypertension, 15*, 361–369.

Heaton, R. K., Taylor, M. J., & Manly, J. (2003). Demographic effects and use of demographically corrected norms with the WAIS-III and WMS-III. In D. S. Tulsky et al. (Eds). *Clinical Interpretation of the WAIS-III and WMS-III*. San Diego: Academic Press, pp. 181–210.

Heaton, R. K., Temkin, N., Dikmen, S., Avitable, N., Taylor, M. J., Marcotte, T. D., & Grant, I. (2001). Detecting change: A comparison of three neuropsychological methods using normal and clinical samples. *Archives of Clinical Neuropsychology, 16*, 75–91.

Hermann, B. P., Seidenberg, M., Schoenfeld, J., Peterson, J., Leveroni, C., & Wyler, A. R. (1996). Empirical techniques for determining the reliability, magnitude, and pattern of neuropsychological change following epilepsy surgery. *Epilepsia, 37*, 942–950.

Horwitz, R. I. (1996). The dark side of evidence-based medicine. *Cleveland Clinic Journal of Medicine, 63,* 320–323.

Iverson, G. L. (2001). Interpreting change on the WAIS-III / WMS-III in clinical samples. *Archives of Clinical Neuropsychology, 16,* 183–191.

Ivnik, R. J., Smith, G. E., Lucas, J. A., Petersen, R. C., Boeve, B. F., Kokmen, E., & Tangalos, E. G. (1999). Testing normal older people three or four times at 1-to 2-year intervals: Defining normal variance. *Neuropsychology, 13,* 121–127.

Jacobson, N. S., Follette, W. C., & Revenstorf, D. (1984). Psychotherapy outcome research: Methods for reporting variability and evaluating clinical significance. *Behavior Therapy, 15,* 336–352.

Jacobson, N. S., & Truax P. (1991). Clinical significance: A statistical approach to defining meaningful change in psychotherapy research. *Journal of Consulting and Clinical Psychology, 59,* 12–19.

Johnson, L. A. (1997). Outcomes management a decade out: An interview with Paul Ellwood. *Group Practice Journal, 46,* 12–15.

Kneebone, A. C., Andrew, M. J., Baker, R. A., & Knight, J. L. (1998). Neuropsychologic changes after coronary artery bypass grafting: Use of reliable change indices. *Annals of Thoracic Surgery, 65,* 1320–1325.

Maassen, G. H. (2000). Principles of defining reliable change indices. *Journal of Clinical and Experimental Neuropsychology, 22,* 622–632.

Martin, R. C., Sawrie, S. M., Roth, D. L., Gilliam, F. G., Faught, E., Morawetz, R. B., & Kuzniecky, R. (1998). Individual memory change after anterior temporal lobectomy: A base rate analysis using regression-based outcome methodology. *Epilepsia, 39,* 1075–1082.

Matarazzo, J. D. (1987). Validity of psychological assessment: From the clinic to the courtroom. *The Clinical Neuropsychologist, 1,* 307–314.

McCaffery, R. J., Westervelt, H. J., & Haase, R. F. (2001). Serial neuropsychological assessment with the National Institute of Mental Health (NIMH) AIDS Abbreviated Neuropsychological Battery. *Archives of Clinical Neuropsychology, 16,* 9–18.

McSweeny, A. J., Naugle, R. I., Chelune, G. J., & Lüders, H. (1993). "T-scores for change:" An illustration of a regression approach to depicting change in clinical neuropsychology. *The Clinical Neuropsychologist, 7,* 300–312.

Murkin, J. M. (2001). Editorial. Perioperative neuropsychological testing. *Journal of Cardiothoracic and Vascular Anesthesia, 15,* 1–3.

The Psychological Corporation (1997). *WAIS-III–WMS-III technical manual.* San Antonio, TX: The Psychological Corporation.

Putman, S. H., Adams, K. M., & Schneider, A. M. (1992). One-day test–retest reliability of neuropsychological tests in a personal injury case. *Psychological Assessment, 4,* 312–316.

Rapport, L. J., Axelrod, B. N., Theisen, M. E., Brines, D. B., Kalechstein, A. D., & Ricker, J. H. (1997). Relationship of IQ to verbal learning and memory: Test and retest. *Journal of Clinical and Experimental Neuropsychology, 19,* 655–666.

Rapport, L. J., Brines, D. B., Axelrod, B. N., & Theisen, M. E. (1997). Full Scale IQ as mediator of practice effects: The rich get richer. *The Clinical Neuropsychologist, 11,* 375–380.

Rawlings, D. B., & Crewe, N. M. (1992). Test–retest practice effects and test score changes of the WAIS-R in recovering traumatically brain-injured survivors. *The Clinical Neuropsychologist, 6,* 415–430.

Ruff, R. M., Light, R. H., & Parker, S. B. (1996). Benton Controlled Oral Word Association Test: Reliability and updated norms. *Archives of Clinical Neuropsychology, 11*, 329–338.

Sawrie, S. M., Chelune, G. J., Naugle, R. I., & Lüders, H. O. (1996). Empirical methods for assessing meaningful neuropsychological change following epilepsy surgery. *Journal of the International Neuropsychological Society, 2*, 556–564.

Temkin, N. R., Heaton, R. K., Grant, I., & Dikmen, S. S. (1999). Detecting significant change in neuropsychological test performance: A comparison of four models. *Journal of the International Neuropsychological Society, 5*, 357–369.

Theisen, M. E., Rapport, L. J., Axelrod, B. N., & Brines, D. B. (1998). Effects of practice in repeated administrations of the Wechsler Memory Scale-Revised in normal adults. *Assessment, 5*, 85–92.

Tulsky, D. S., Ivnik, R. J., Price, L. R., & Wilkins, C. (2003). Assessment of cognitive functioning with the WAIS-III and WMS-III: Development of a six-factor model. In D. S. Tulsky et al. (Eds). *Clinical Interpretation of the WAIS-III and WMS-III.* San Diego: Academic Press, pp. 147–179.

Tulsky, D. S., Rolfhus, E. L., & Zhu, J. (2000). Two-tailed versus one-tailed baserates of discrepancy scores in the WAIS-III. *The Clinical Neuropsychologist, 14*, 451–460.

Wechsler, D. (1955). *WAIS manual.* New York: The Psychological Corporation.

Wechsler, D. (1981). *WAIS-R manual.* New York: The Psychological Corporation.

Wechsler, D. (1997a). *WAIS-III test administration and scoring manual.* San Antonio, TX: The Psychological Corporation.

Wechsler, D. (1997b). *WMS-III test administration and scoring manual.* San Antonio, TX: The Psychological Corporation.

Wilson, B. A., Watson, P. C., Baddeley, A. D., Emslie, H., & Evans, J. J. (2000) Improvement or simply practice? The effects of twenty repeated assessments on people with and without brain injury. *Journal of the International Neuropsychological Society, 6*, 469–479.

Dealing with "curveballs" when using the WAIS-III and WMS-III: The interpretation of an unstandardized administration

Occasionally, an examiner is confronted with an unusual situation, one in which the test administration does not or cannot follow the standardized administration protocol. These administrations can present problems as the clinician attempts to interpret the test scores.

Unstandardized administrations serve to increase extraneous variance and can, if the violations to the standardized protocol are significant enough, negate the use of the normative data for scoring and interpretation.

In this section, we present three chapters dealing with the unstandardized administration. In Chapter 9, Harris, Tulsky, & Schultheis, discuss the situation where English is not the first language of the examinee. The chapter presents a thorough review of programs designed to measure intelligence in the non-native English speaker dating back to the early 1900's and demonstrates that these issues have confronted examiners throughtout the history of intellectual assessment. More importantly, Harris et al. present new data on the effect of language preference and acculturation on cognitive scores and provide some guidance to the clinician in situations when testing is needed for an examinee who is less proficient in English.

Chapter 10, by Palmer, Heaton, & Taylor, follows with an equally perplexing situation: What to do when all subtests are not administered. Several situations can result in a subtest not being administered or being "spoiled" due to a non-standardized administration, and in these instances, the examiner must choose between prorating the existing scores to obtain a total score or substituting an optional subtest into the sum of scaled scores before calculating the total score. In Chapter 10, Palmer et al. point out that such situations are not new to examiners. Then, the authors use the standardization data to illustrate how much extraneous variance might be introduced into the normative scores when a subtest is omitted, and they provide crucial information for interpreting scores in such situations. In the chapter, the authors provide empirical evidence suggesting that prorating existing scores tends to be a more accurate practice than substituting the score from an optional subtest to make up for the missing subtest score. Detailed tables are provided that should help examiners adjust their confidence intervals when interpreting such scores.

The final chapter by Jeffrey Braden focuses on a specific instance when a standardized assessment cannot be performed. What happens when the clinician needs to assess the cognitive functioning of an individual with a disability? Do accommodations for hearing, vision, and physical disabilities that a clinician must make cause the results to differ significantly from that which would have been obtained without such accommodations? In Chapter 11, Braden discusses these issues directly and provides a conceptual framework for clinicians to make accommodations decisions for clients with disabilities. Braden draws heavily on the work by Samuel Messick (1995) to argue that accommodations should reduce construct-irrelevant variance, while maintaining adequate construct representation. The chapter ends with a discussion of practices that can guide the examiner when interpreting such scores.

Clearly, the examiner must be aware of how increased variance can affect test scores when situations occur making standandardized assessments impossible. The chapters in this section take an empirical approach to understanding and interpreting scores when such "curveballs" are present.

David S. Tulsky
Donald H. Saklofske

Assessment of the Non-Native English Speaker: Assimilating History and Research Findings to Guide Clinical Practice

Josette G. Harris
University of Colorado School of Medicine
Departments of Psychiatry and Neurology

David S. Tulsky and Maria T. Schultheis
Kessler Rehabilitation Research and Education Corporation
University of Medicine and Dentistry of New Jersey

INTRODUCTION

The diversity of people in America often poses unique challenges to the examiner who is required to perform psychoeducational or neuropsychological testing. Heaton, Taylor, and Manly (Chapter 5, this volume) present data that demonstrate the strong relationship between demographic variables and test performance. They argue that age corrections are insufficient and provide a method for correcting scores for additional demographic variables, such as education level, sex, and ethnicity. Although this approach is an important component of good clinical practice in many settings, there are times when the context of testing will vary from other more typical situations and pose additional variance that cannot easily be identified and corrected. For instance, what happens when an individual has immigrated to the United States and his or her first language is not English?

With increasing frequency, examiners find themselves in the situation of needing to test an individual who is not a native English speaker. Although the Standards for Educational and Psychological Testing (American Education

Research Association, American Psychological Association, and National Council on Measurement in Education, 1999) state that the test generally should be administered in the test taker's most proficient language, too often examiners find themselves in difficult situations without good options. For example, the most proficient language of the examinee may not be the language of the examiner, and another provider or examiner who has proficiency in the language and expertise in the examinee's culture may not be accessible. Examiners may find themselves pressured to conduct the testing, even though the appropriateness of methods and measures to do so are questionable. In other cases, the examinee may appear to speak fluently in English, although not as proficiently as in the native language. The Standards for Educational and Psychological Testing clearly caution test users that the abilities of examinees may be mismeasured by a test given in a language in which they lack proficiency (American Education Research Association et al., 1999). On the other hand, the Standards also address the issue that "fairness of testing in any given context must be judged relative to that of feasible test and nontest alternatives" (p. 73).

The *Guidelines for Providers of Psychological Services to Ethnic, Linguistic, and Culturally Diverse Populations* (American Psychological Association, 1990) state that psychologists should interact in the language requested by the client. While the standards address the issue that dominance or preference may be distinct from proficiency, typically the examiner does not inquire about preference when casual observation suggests the examinee has basic command of the English language. Furthermore, the assessment of language proficiency is not commonly done. Adequate measures are lacking, as are individuals who are skilled in the assessment of language proficiency. So, for persons born outside the United States and who have learned English as a second language, there may be widely differing assessment strategies taken by the examiners who perform the assessments.

The foregoing discussion begs the question of how best to interpret scores when an individual who speaks English as a second language is assessed with English language standardized tests like the WAIS-III and WMS-III. What should the examiner attend to when interpreting such scores and can scores be interpreted at all with the traditional normative samples that accompany the tests? Is there a way the examiner may account for additional variance caused by language use or preference or other acculturation factors? This chapter attempts to address these questions. In the initial part of the chapter, we will review the lengthy history in America of testing individuals from diverse cultural and linguistic backgrounds, which will reveal how early professionals who lacked empirical guidance approached cognitive testing.

We will then examine current trends and opinions about the topic area, and the solutions those in the field have for meeting assessment needs. The third part of the chapter will describe recent research that examines the role of language and acculturation-related factors to determine their utility in interpreting cognitive test performance.

ELLIS ISLAND AND THE ASSESSMENT OF THE IMMIGRANT

The need to develop sound methods for the assessment of individuals from non-native English-speaking backgrounds may seem like a recent challenge, stemming from the rapid growth of ethnic/linguistic and immigrant populations. Actually, the concern dates back to the earliest days of cognitive assessment. In some ways, modern-day psychology as a profession has been inattentive to a challenge that initially presented a century ago. To facilitate our chances of succeeding with this challenge now and in the future, we must first understand the assumptions, motivations, and the mistakes of the past, and then identify new concepts and methodologies for describing cognition and for considering the roles of language and culture in assessment.

America's most famous immigration center, Ellis Island, New York, opened in 1892, and by 1913, three-fourths of all immigrants to this country were coming through the gates of this center (Reed, 1913). Ellis Island opened at a time when the first immigration laws were being passed, barring anyone who would likely become a burden on the state from entering the United States. Immigration laws were passed in 1891, 1903, and 1907, becoming more and more restrictive with each modification. The initial laws excluded "idiots" and "insane persons," and the 1907 law added to the exclusionary list more moderately impaired "imbeciles" and "feeble-minded" individuals. In the earliest years of immigration policy, identification of "mental defectiveness" or "idiocy" (as it was termed in the late 1800s/early 1900s) was not an organized effort. From 1892–1907, only 211 of 9,346,405 immigrants were debarred from entering the United States because of mental deficiency (Annual Report of the Commissioner General of Immigration, 1922). Prior to 1907, the immigration officials had discretion whether to land or to deport an individual certified as feeble-minded, and so there was little investment in identifying these individuals (Williams, 1914). Once the feeble-minded were targeted for exclusion, the pressure increased for better means to screen individuals, and the scope of the problem of assessment became more apparent.

The Inspection Process

Not surprisingly, an elaborate screening system was established by the United States Public Health Service (PHS) at Ellis Island to comply with the 1907 law (Williams, 1914). Different procedures were established for immigrants traveling in the cabin (first or second class) versus those who arrived in steerage. For those passengers traveling in the cabin, the PHS physicians boarded the steamships at the port of New York and made the inspections of the passengers. For those immigrants traveling in steerage, a 2- to 3-hour inspection process by PHS physicians began immediately at Ellis Island, where immigrants were brought by barge after disembarking from the various ships. The "line inspection" was the first step in the process (see Figure 1 and 2) as medical officers and attendants, stationed along lines separated by iron railings, inspected passengers in the reception room of the main building (Mullan, 1917; Williams, 1914). E. H. Mullan (1917), a PHS surgeon, wrote that it was the job of the officers occupying the proximal line position to look for all physical and mental defects in the immigrants passing through the line. He described the initial screening procedures in this manner:

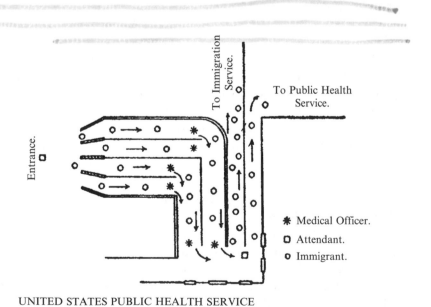

UNITED STATES PUBLIC HEALTH SERVICE

FIGURE 1.   Schemata outlining the inspection of immigrants in the reception room of the Ellis Island main building. (From Mullan, 1917, in the public domain.)

FIGURE 2.   Immigrants waiting in line in the reception room at Ellis Island. (From the Detroit Publishing Company, in the public domain.)

> Many inattentive and stupid-looking aliens are questioned by the medical officer in the various languages as to their age, destination, and nationality. Often simple questions in addition and multiplication are propounded. Should the immigrant appear stupid and inattentive to such an extent that mental defect is suspected, an X is made with chalk on his coat at the anterior aspect of his right shoulder. Should definite signs of mental disease be observed, a circle X would be used instead of the plain X. In like manner, a chalk mark is placed on the anterior aspect of the right shoulder in all cases where physical deformity or disease is suspected. (Mullan, 1917, pp. 735–736).

After passing inspection by the first officer, the immigrant then proceeded in the line to "the eye man" who would look for disease of the eye, and

FIGURE 3.   Immigrants attempting to enter the United States. The mark on the shoulder indicates suspected mental deficiency (Copyright © Culver Pictures, Inc., used with permission. All rights reserved.)

sometimes ask additional questions in an effort to pick up a symptom possibly overlooked by another inspector. If the immigrant passed through the line without a chalk mark, he was deemed to have passed the medical inspection and would enter the upper hall to undergo inspection by the Immigration Service to ascertain whether he might be "an anarchist, bigamist, pauper, criminal or otherwise unfit" (Mullan, 1917, p. 736). According to Williams (1914), two thousand immigrants were screened through the primary inspection in a span of two and one half hours. They passed through four lines at the rate of one every 4.5 seconds, allowing on average 18 seconds for inspection per immigrant.

Approximately 9 of 100 immigrants were set aside in the course of the line inspection to undergo the secondary or "weeding-out" process (Mullan, 1917). Those who were chalk marked with either an X (Figure 3) or circle X (see insert Figure 4) were immediately taken to "the mental room," which consisted of two examining desks and 18 benches. The examiner faced the detained immigrants who sat upon the benches and were called forward one at a time to the inspector who would give them another brief inspection, consisting of counting, addition, and the Cube Test (Figure 4).

FIGURE 4.   Preliminary testing to determine whether full mental examination was warranted. Notice the man (enlarged photo lower left corner) with the "X" mark surrounded by
a circle. This mark was an indication of "definitive signs of mental defect." (Orginally printed
in Mullan, 1917. Photo courtesy of Culver Pictures).

The examiner at that time decided whether to release the individual or to
further detain him overnight for a complete mental examination. Of the nine
immigrants set aside, one or two were so detained, with the circle X cases
sent immediately to the hospital and the X cases detained in detention rooms
of the Immigration Service. The third stage of the examination of the
immigrant began in an examination room where small ethnic groupings
would be sent together for individual brief evaluations by a physician and an
interpreter, in the presence of the other immigrants. This was done so that
individuals had an opportunity to learn from others and thus could be more
readily separated from those who were presumably "subnormal." Those
who were not released following the brief exam would undergo a second
exam by a different physician on a subsequent day, lasting from 20 to 60
minutes. Those further detained underwent yet a third exam at which time
cases of feeble-mindedness would be certified. Immigrants were examined
"by every available test which experience has proved to be useful" and

FIGURE 5.   Surgeon L.L Williams (seated) and the staff of the United States Public Health Service at Ellis Island. Howard A. Knox is pictured on the far left. (Photograph from Knox, 1915. *Scientific American*, January 9, 1915, used with permission.) The original caption reads: "These officers stand guardian to our national health, and the colossal piece of preventive medicine carried on by them saves the country untold millions of dollars each year and helps to maintain the high physical and mental standard of our race."

officers prepared a report of their findings (Figure 5) (Williams, 1914, p. 260). Any discrepancies of opinion between officers always resulted in additional examination, and further examination could also be requested by the Commissioner of Immigration, any medical officer, a relative of the immigrant, or the immigrant's attorney (Williams, 1914). Clearly, the approach by the PHS was to err on the conservative side. "An error which results in unjustly deporting an alien from New York to Eastern Europe is a grievous blunder and is without remedy" (Williams, 1914, p. 265).

H. H. Goddard's Contribution to Early Assessment Challenges

The magnitude of the challenge of inspecting and assessing thousands of immigrants per day was striking. In 1910, Henry H. Goddard (Figure 6) and Edward R. Johnstone from the Vineland Training School in Vineland, New Jersey, were invited to Ellis Island to offer suggestions as to how the PHS could recognize and detain a greater percentage of individuals with mental defectiveness (Goddard, 1912). Goddard summarized the two-day experience in this fashion:

FIGURE 6.   H. H. Goddard from 1906 when he first started at the Vineland Institute. (Courtesy of the Archives of the History of Psychlogy, Akron, OH., used with permission.)

> At the end of the day we both felt ourselves overwhelmed by the size of the problem and the general situation. The physicians seemed to be doing wonderful work in the recognition of physical defect and insanity. The number of immigrants passing thru was so vast; the methods then known of detecting mental deficiency were so slow and cumbersome that it seemed hopeless to make any improvement in the method and while we felt sure that from a statistical standpoint, there must be many defectives who were passing thru, yet we saw no way in which it could be stopped without enormous outlay on the part of the government. (Goddard, 1912, p. 110)

Following his initial visit, Goddard returned to Ellis Island in May of 1912, along with two assistants from the Vineland School "merely for the purpose of seeing the place again" (Goddard, 1912). He reported that to his surprise better facilities had been provided for the physicians and their work, and indeed the whole situation no longer appeared so overwhelming to him. Consequently, he requested permission to conduct an experiment. This experiment consisted of one assistant standing "on the line" during the line inspection and identifying nine "defectives" based upon her experience with the individuals at the Institution at Vineland. In addition, she selected three individuals, presumed to be normal, as control subjects. All selected individuals were sent to the second assistant (blind to presumed mental status) who tested the individuals using the Binet–Simon tests, with the aid of an interpreter. All 12 people, according to Goddard, were correctly diagnosed (Goddard, 1912). In a week-long follow-up study in September 1912, the hit rate of the medical inspectors versus the Vineland workers was evaluated in a second experiment, again using the Binet tests, on 44 individuals. Of 33 cases selected for secondary inspection by the inspectors, 15 were found to be defective using the Binet tests. Of eleven cases selected by the Vineland experts, nine were defective (Goddard, 1912). On the last day of the experiment, Goddard reported that Vineland workers stood in the inspection line and tallied every individual they deemed to be defective by observation. Of 1260 who passed in line, the Vineland workers identified 83 as defective, and the inspectors selected only 18. Goddard assumed that his trained observers were remarkably accurate but that the PHS physicians were making false negative errors. Goddard was not surprised, noting the physicians "do not pretend to be experts on feeblemindedness" and stating that

> . . . persons trained for a year or two in institutions for the feeble-minded . . . can go to Ellis Island or any Immigrant Station and standing by the line as the immigrants pass, pick out with marvelous accuracy every case of mental defect in all those who are above the infant age. (Goddard, 1912, p. 112)

He concluded from these experiments that the Binet tests could be given with the aid of interpreters with "remarkably satisfactory" results. This he concluded, in spite of describing in another publication the reaction of an interpreter during the experiment: "The interpreter said, 'I could not have done that when I came to this country,' and seemed to think the test unfair. We convinced him that the boy was defective" (Goddard, 1913, p. 105).

Perspectives of the Public Health Service Physicians

The PHS physicians at Ellis Island saw significant problems with Goddard's stance and much preferred their own methods devised to meet the onerous responsibility of assessing mental deficiency in the immigrants. They immediately and vociferously rejected Goddard's ideas in public and scientific forums. E. K. Sprague (1914), Public Health Service surgeon, wrote:

> Every legitimate means must be utilized to assist in arriving at a correct decision and even then the alien must be accorded the benefit of the doubt if there is any. For Goddard, who has yet to examine his first alien immigrant, to claim that by means of Binet–Simon tests designed for school children, an accurate and prompt determination can be arrived at as to the mental status of a person who has never attended school and who can not read or write, is as sensible as to claim that with a single instrument any operation in surgery can be successfully performed. (p. 467)

Likewise, Bernard Glueck, another PHS surgeon, saw the use of the Binet tests as an artificial attempt to define feeble-mindedness and he advocated a social definition based upon individuals' abilities to perform their duties as members of society (Glueck, 1913). He wrote:

> Ours is the problem of the immigrant, and since an attempt has been made by some of the followers of Binet to detect feeblemindedness among immigrants by means of their measuring scale of intelligence, we shall have something to say concerning this phase of the problem. Since our immigrants belong to a large number of races, who come to us from practically all parts of the world, and since it was attempted to diagnosticate the feeble-minded from among all these races by means of the Binet–Simon scale, and since further we know that a diagnosis by artificial means of feeblemindedness consists in a comparison of the individual's intelligence with a given standard of average normal intelligence, it may be safely assumed that these investigators considered the Binet–Simon scale of intelligence as the standard of the average normal intelligence of all these various peoples which furnish our immigrants. Is this so? Does the Binet–Simon measuring scale of intelligence or its American modification, evolved as these were from French and American children, represent the average normal intelligence of practically the entire human race? Assuredly not. We are convinced of this both from experience with the immigrant and actual experimental investigation of the subject, and were it considered necessary to adduce facts to prove the fallacy of such a contention, these could easily be gotten from the hundreds of case histories on file at Ellis Island. No such proof, however, is deemed necessary. The Binet–Simon scale was never intended to assume such wide spheres of usefulness and application. (Glueck, 1913, p. 762)

Thus, the PHS officers stayed their own course. The PHS physicians were aware of the challenges before them and the absolute necessity of dealing with the constraints on testing imposed by language, culture, and literacy. They thought it essential to have an evaluative process that would instill confidence in their diagnoses, such that they could "affix their signature" to the certification form and defend their opinions in a court as needed (Sprague, 1914). The physicians voiced a clear preference for brief performance-based tests, which would eliminate reliance upon language, obviate the need for interpreters, and address the serious time constraints facing already burdened inspectors (Glueck, 1913; Knox, 1914; Sprague, 1914). Furthermore, they viewed the use of interpreters as inefficient and impractical, and believed that an interpreter could be eliminated if the examiner had some basic knowledge of a few words and phrases in the examinee's language in order to ask some simple questions (e.g., "Name the days of the week." "How much is 4 away from 10?") (Mullan, 1917; United States Public Health Service, 1918).

Sprague (1914) emphasized the fact that he and his fellow officers continually tried out different methods, retaining those that "experience and ingenuity" dictated were useful. He had introduced in 1912 Seguin's form board, puzzles by Healy and by Fernald, and "complete sets" of the De Sanctis and Binet–Simon tests for possible use as assessment tools (Figures 7 and 8). It was his colleague, Howard A. Knox, a surgeon and ex-military officer, who took the lead in developing a "culturally appropriate" battery, having been appointed in 1912 to oversee the testing of "suspected mental defectives" and to lead a team of PHS physicians (Figure 9).

Knox and his colleagues developed several new performance tests (e.g., Knox's Moron, Imbecile, and Casuist tests, Gwyn's triangle, Kempf's diagonal, the Leaf and Cluster Comparison Test, the Inkblot Imagination Test) and incorporated other frame and puzzle tests such as the geographical or jigsaw test and the Healy and Fernald tests introduced by Sprague (Knox, 1914, 1915) (Figure 10). They supplemented the performance tests with questions involving simple mathematical processes, knowledge based upon the immigrant's previous occupation, and items from Binet's "questionnaire" (Knox, 1914). Some of Knox's tests would be quite influential in the field of assessment and the later Wechsler Battery (e.g., Facial Profile test by Knox and Kempf, and Knox's cube imitation test (See chapters 2 and 3, this volume) (Figure 11).

Knox published the methods he and his colleagues used at Ellis Island in an article entitled, "A Scale for the Estimation of the Degree of Mental Deficiency in Illiterates and Others" (Knox, 1914). The scale consisted of a series of tests and questions established for each year of age from 3 years to 13 years upward, with specific passing criteria for each age. Although the majority of the tests were nonverbal, performance-based measures, verbal items were also included, such as counting from 20 to 1 with no more than two errors (age 8), reciting the days of the week and telling the

FIGURE 7.   An immigrant from Germany takes the Unfinished Pictures subtest from the Binet-Simon scale. In this photo, the stimuli were placed on the wall and the examinee was asked "What is lacking in this picture?" (Photo copyright © Brown Brothers, used with permission. All rights reseved.)

time (age 9), remembering three of five details of a simple story (age 10), and telling the difference between ice and glass (age 11).

Knox believed that the tests were ultimately fair and wrote,

> This entire examination presupposes that the subject has never been taught and that he has only acquired knowledge by the experiences of every-day life. The performance tests especially are not dependent on any previous experience, but the ability to do them is based on the inherent or native power to surmount slight obstacles with which the subject is born and they are applicable to the educated as well as to the illiterate. (Knox, 1914, p. 742)

FIGURE 8.   Photograph from Knox (1915), *Scientific American,* January 9, 1915, in the public domain. The original caption reads: "There is practically nothing in the physiognomy of this immigrant that indicates the gross mental defect that he possesses. The alien is performing, with considerable difficulty, the Seguin formboard, a task which should not require more than 20 seconds in normal adults; this alien required anywhere from 45 seconds to 4 1/2 minutes, and his performances did not improve with practice and repeated trials."

Furthermore, he explained,

> The tests, questions and other details of examination were arrived at as a result of work on persons that were less bright than the average of the various races (illiterates) from which they came. It is evident, therefore, that if this scale errs at all it is on the conservative side and that anyone tested by it receives more than fair treatment. (p. 741)

The Establishment of Assessment Standards and Guidelines

Subsequent to the passage of the Immigration Law of 1907, an additional 3341 immigrants (128 "idiots," 382 "imbeciles," and 2831 "feeble-minded") were denied entry into America between 1908 and 1917 (Annual Report of the Commissioner General of Immigration, 1931). As the screening and testing program advanced, the numbers of immigrants certified as mentally defective increased accordingly (from 19.6 per 100,000 in 1912, to 50.0 per 100,000 in 1913, and to 95 per 100,000 in 1914; Annual Report, Medical Examination of Immigrants, 1914). The PHS continued to

FIGURE 9.   Howard H. Knox and his team of Public Health Inspectors responsible for the mental testing at Ellis Island. From left to right Drs. Knox, Vogel, Glueck, Laughlin, & Gwynn. (Photo courtesy of the National Archives and the Ellis Island Museum, in the public domain.)

struggle for many years with the sheer numbers of immigrants to be inspected, as well as procedural inconsistencies across various ports of entry. Reed (1913), in advocating for procedural standards as well as the initiation of a scientific program of research at Ellis Island, wrote that general opinion dictated that ". . . unsound aliens should be excluded . . . but how to accomplish this most effectively and humanely (was) the central problem" (p. 172). On February 5, 1917, the Immigration Law of 1917 was passed, incorporating the earlier laws, and establishing much needed standards for the inspection and testing procedures and qualifications for examiners. For example, it established new protections for the arriving immigrants by requiring minimum qualifications of the examiners (e.g., that the physical and mental examination of all arriving aliens would be made by medical officers of the PHS who had at least two years' experience in the practice of their profession since obtaining the doctorate of medicine). The act further established that medical officers of the PHS who had special training in the diagnosis of insanity and mental defects would be detailed for duty at all ports of entry designated by the Secretary of Labor. The officers would be provided with "suitable facilities for detention and examination," and the act established that the services of interpreters "shall be provided for such examination" (Figure 12).

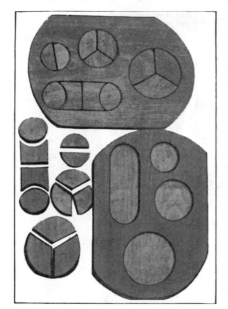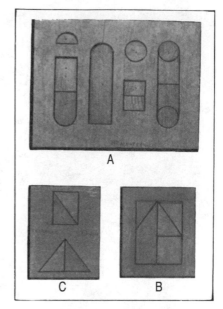

FIGURE 10.   Several Form board puzzles used by (and sometimes created by) the PHS are shown. The puzzle marked "A" is a slightly modified version of the puzzle developed and reported by Healy and Fernald (1911), Construction test B. Puzzle "C" is the triangle test designed by Gwyn of the PHS. Puzzle "B" is the Diagonal test designed by Kempf of the PHS. All of these tests require the examinee to assemble the puzzle as quickly as he/she is able. (Photograph and caption from Knox, 1915, *Scientific American*, January 9, 1915, in the public domain. Note: Caption was labelled incorrectly in the original article. Caption has been corrected.)

Despite the cultural sensitivity and concern for the immigrants displayed by PHS officials, the context of the inspection and testing process was certainly an emotionally demanding and frightfully unfamiliar experience for the immigrants. In describing the physical and emotional duress endured by steerage passengers on a 7 to 10-day transatlantic voyage, Sprague (1914) commented upon the "crowding and sweltering not tolerated today in the worst prison" (p. 466). The experience of then being pulled aside from one's family after a lengthy oceanic voyage, chalk marked as potentially or definitively "defective," and sent to undergo additional evaluation to determine one's fate, must have been extraordinarily stressful.

It is easy to be critical of the early efforts at Ellis Island and to focus on the inadequacy of the assumptions and the methodologies utilized with these linguistic and cultural newcomers to America. By current standards, indeed mental testing at Ellis Island was largely inadequate, of uncertain validity, and ethically questionable. But the extraordinary demands exemplified by the

FIGURE 11   Photograph from Knox (1915), *Scientific American*, January 9, 1915, in the public domain. The original caption reads: "A mentally defective immigrant woman attempting to perform the ... (Knox) ... cube ... (Imitation) ... test, with which she had but little success, having failed in three out of four trails. She was the mother of three children, one of which was defective also, and the other two, while normal intellectually, were, of course, capable of transmitting feeble mindedness and neuropathic tendencies to their offspring." In this picture, the Knox Cube Imitation and the Feature Profile Test Can be seen on the table.

immigration of over one million individuals annually by 1905 (1,285,349 in 1907) (Annual Report of the Commissioner General of Immigration, 1922) suggest that the task facing PHS officers in the earliest years of mental testing in America was staggering. In an interview with PHS physician Grover A. Kempf (September 11,1977), who worked at Ellis Island during this time, he stated, "The mental examinations of immigrants was always haphazard. It couldn't be any other way because of the time given to pass the immigrants along the line" (United States Public Health Service, 1977).

In many ways, these early test pioneers displayed incredible knowledge of and sensitivity to the cultural and linguistic influences on test outcome, in spite of a lack of empirical data to guide them. Acknowledging the limits of their methods, and the influence of environmental and educational advantages on performance, they cautioned about the application of intelligence tests to illiterates who could potentially be miscertified as defective: "Formal tests of ability are therefore poor substitutes for common sense and experience in the mental examination of aliens. ... The deportation of an

FIGURE 12.   Howard A. Knox testing an immigrant with an interpreter present. (Copyright © Brown Brothers, used with permission. All rights reserved).

alien is too serious a matter to depend upon the number of years in intelligence he happens to fall below an arbitrary age standard" (United States Public Health Service, 1918, p. 19). In further addressing the limits of their methods, it was written, "The tests devised for measuring the higher faculties of the mind in the examination room are largely academic and furnish rather unsatisfactory evidence as to the way the subject will use his judgment or reason in solving the problems of everyday life" (United States Public Health Service, 1918, p. 23). At the same time, these early clinicians understandably underestimated the role of experience and learning necessary to succeed on the cognitive tests. Knox believed, for example, that the feature profile puzzle was "eminently fair because everyone has seen a human head" (Knox, 1914, p. 744).

Nevertheless, the PHS physicians strove to do their best and made efforts to document their findings in order to teach others about their methods and to caution others about the limitations of assessment. PHS physicians authored the *Manual of the Mental Examination of Aliens* (United States Public Health Service, 1918), and, among other guidelines, wrote

> Not more than three persons should be present at the examination. The alien should thoroughly understand the interpreter, and the latter should be calm,

patient, and sympathetic. The alien should never be told that he is wrong when he makes a mistake nor discouraged in any way.... The examiner should impress the alien with his good intentions and give an easy test to start with. (p. 15)

It was suggested that "if a timid woman is to be tested and there are other more fearless women present, one of the latter should be taken first" (p. 15) (Figure 13). Other training and guideline publications acknowledged that "racial and other characteristics" were a factor to consider in evaluating the attitude and conduct of individuals and emphasized that the subjects were in completely foreign environments such that "as a result his mental processes are very naturally profoundly disturbed" (United States Public Health Service, 1918, p. 14).

Had test pioneers such as Knox, Sprague, Glueck, Kempf, Gwyn, and Mullan continued their work in the cultural relevance of assessment, indeed the current state of the art and science of evaluating individuals from diverse linguistic and ethnic backgrounds may have come to pause

FIGURE 13.   A female PHS official is shown testing a female immigrant. Photograph courtesy of the National Archives.

at a different place. Instead, however, a new sociopolitical challenge emerged and shifted the focus of testing from immigration to military decision-making.

ASSESSMENT OF MILITARY RECRUITS DURING WORLD WAR I

As discussed in Tulsky, Saklofske, and Ricker (Chapter 1, this volume), mental testing became much more established in the medical and scientific communities as leading psychologists were called upon for the war effort. The subcommittee on methods for the psychological examination of recruits, organized under the American Psychological Association and the Committee for Psychology of the National Research Council, met at the Training School in Vineland, New Jersey to address a series of problems facing the military. The committee, chaired by Robert M. Yerkes and comprised of W. V. Bingham, H. H. Goddard, T. H. Haines, L. M. Terman, F. L. Wells, and G. M. Whipple (see Figure 13, Chapter 1, this volume), proposed to confine their work "to the classification of recruits on the basis of intellectual ability, with special reference to the elimination of the unfit and the identification of exceptionally superior ability" (Yerkes, 1921, p. 299). The committee compiled and constructed a series of tests that they believed measured "native ability rather than the results of school training" (Yerkes, 1921, p. 300).

Although the initial product of the committee's work was the Army Alpha test, which was extensively applied to the testing of educated, literate English-speaking military personnel, the committee also constructed a test for the illiterate, and non-English-speaking recruits, the Army Beta. The Beta included visual and performance tasks, and like the Army Alpha, could be administered in a group format. The premise of the tests was that they would measure native intelligence and would be uninfluenced by "individual differences in language, dialect, schooling, facility and speed in reading and writing, and native linguistic gift" (Yerkes, 1921, p. 231). Over 6,600 foreign-born recruits took the Beta examination, in addition to the 3,619 foreign-born recruits who completed the Army Alpha and the 993 who took other individual intelligence examinations (See Yerkes, 1921). The Beta test was administered using a blackboard with demonstrations at the front of the group examination room (Figures 14 and 15). In describing the testing procedures, Yoakum and Yerkes (1920) wrote: "With the exception of the brief introductory statements and a few orders, instructions are to be given throughout by means of gestures instead

FIGURE 14.   Examiner is in the front of the room demonstrating how to take the Picture Completion subtest using a Beta blackboard. (From Yerkes, 1921, in the public domain.)

FIGURE 15.   Two examiners demonstrating the cube construction subtest of the Beta exam. (From Yerkes, 1921, in the public domain.)

of words. These gestures accompany the samples and demonstrations and should be animated and emphatic" (p. 80).

The army administered additional individual examinations to secure a more accurate measurement of the mental ability of those (recruits) who did not pass the Army Alpha and Beta group tests. Each recruit tested with the Alpha or Beta received a letter grade ranging from *A* to *E*, and those that scored inferior (e.g., a grade of *D* or *E*) were to be administered the individual tests (Yoakum & Yerkes, 1920). Eight hundred two foreign-born recruits received the nonverbal individual performance battery, and, as in the Beta, gestures were suggested as the best means to communicate, although simple words could be used to supplement the gestures for those that might benefit (Yerkes, 1921; Yoakum & Yerkes, 1920).

Literacy tests were explored as a means to segregate recruits who would take the Alpha from those who were illiterate and would require the Beta exam. Numerous difficulties were identified with the existing tests as well as those that were developed at the various camps (e.g., Modified Thorndike, Deven's literacy test). Ultimately, as a general rule recruits were administered the Beta if they reported they could not read newspapers or write letters home (Yerkes, 1921). Additional requirements, such as some formal schooling (e.g., sixth grade), were established at some camps, but the criteria were inconsistently applied and it was felt impossible to develop a uniform standard for assessment decisions (Yerkes, 1921).

The army also explored using measures of language fluency, called linguality tests, to assist in assessing recruits' English language communication skills. The non-English-speaking and illiterate recruits "constituted such a serious clog to military efficiency" that development battalions were organized to teach the recruits to speak, read, and write in English (Yerkes, 1921, p. 355). The psychologist working with the non-English development battalion attempted to develop a measure that would serve to provisionally certify recruits as English- or non–English-speaking. Individual and group linguality tests were developed with both "verbal" and "performance" components (e.g., "What kind of shoes does a soldier wear?" "Put your hat on the table". "Make a cross on the major protuberance of the bludgeon.") The measures were not further developed as the development battalion schools were abandoned following the armistice (Yerkes, 1921).

In Yerkes's eyes, the role of the psychologist was critical to the efficiency of the military during the war effort. Yerkes touted the testing program as highly successful and pointed to the number of individuals who were tested (over 1.7 million), and more importantly to the test scores (generally obtained within 50 minutes), which agreed with officer ratings of personnel, typically obtained only after months of extensive observation. Yerkes promoted the new field well and helped to legitimize psychology as a discipline and a profession. Despite all of the praise, however, there were several negative aspects of the program. Gould (1996) points out the opposing opinion of at least some army officials who became suspicious of Yerkes's intent and conducted independent investigations of the testing program. One, cited by Gould, concluded that the program should be controlled so that "...no theorist may...ride it as a hobby for the purpose of obtaining data for research work and the future benefit of the human race" (quoted in Kevles, 1968, p. 577). Although there is no denying that the army testing program had a profound effect on intelligence testing and psychology in general, critics have questioned its success in actually screening recruits (see Gould, 1996; Kevles, 1968; Reed, 1987; Samelson, 1977).

Perhaps most troublesome was the extensive use of performance tests to measure cognition in those who did not speak English or were illiterate, and the subsequent use of these data. Following the war, published test scores derived from the Army measures were misused as the fodder of racist publications, justification for eugenics, and a rationale for restricting immigration (e.g., Brigham, 1923). The book by Carl Brigham entitled, *A Study of American Intelligence* could be the definitive example of a "race psychology" publication. Brigham grouped individuals by nationality and then rank ordered the groups, concluding that some ethnic groups were superior to others. This was an extremely harmful publication that had an "authoritative" appearance since it was based upon empirical data heavily promoted by Yerkes in his zeal to establish psychology as a legitimate science. Moreover, Yerkes wrote an extremely laudatory foreword to Brigham's book. Yet, Yerkes (1921) himself presented in detail the extensive problems and inconsistencies with the testing program and data collection.

ADVANCES, CURRENT APPROACHES AND OPINIONS

Writers have pointed out that scientists' accounts and interpretations of their data will be influenced, in part, by the sociopolitical forces surrounding the scientist (Kuhn, 1970; Richards, 1997). Richards (1997) wrote: "psychology participates in the collective psychological lives of the societies wherein it is practiced, it does not, and logically 'cannot' simply observe them" (p. xii). Although this does not excuse nor justify any form of racism, it is not surprising to see that intellectual assessment of non-English speakers would both influence and be influenced by the darker sociopolitical forces of the 1920s–1940s in America (e.g., race psychology, eugenics, and Naziism).

In hindsight, there were faulty but logical assumptions made by the early pioneers in testing, including convictions that the tests were true measures of "innate" intelligence and beliefs that nonverbal performance tests could overcome cultural, language, and education barriers. Furthermore, over-interpretation and flawed interpretation of data collected from groups of foreign-born nationals, mixed with ethnocentrism, resulted in beliefs and harmful policies against several cultures and ethnic groups (e.g., discrimin-ation, advancement of restrictive immigration policies, advances in eugenics programs), and helped fuel feelings of mistrust, skepticism of the benefits of testing in general, and a tarnish that overshadows much of the benefits and accomplishments of the Ellis Island and Army testing programs in the earliest years of the previous century.

Advances in the intellectual and cognitive assessment of the non–native English speaker in the ensuing years have been slow. Debates concerning the measurement of intelligence, (e.g., Horn, 1985; Spearman, 1923; Thorn-dike, 1919; Thurstone, 1938), heritable, environmental, and cultural con-tributions to intellectual and cognitive performance (Eysenck & Kamin, 1981; Helms, 1992; Jensen, 1969), and the meaning and utility of IQ and group comparisons (Neisser et al., 1996) have continued. These debates often take place in the context of various sociopolitical and legal challenges (e.g., Lambert, 1981; Sattler, 1981) to the appropriateness of testing ethnic and linguistic minorities with "traditional" standard measures. Samuda (1975) published one of the first books addressing the assessment of Ameri-can minorities and described the influence of language, culture, and socio-economic status on test results, calling for changes in traditional psychometric testing. More recently, there has been insightful commentary on the process of acculturation, the psychological experience of migration, and the implications for assessment and diagnosis (e.g., Arnold, Montgom-ery, Castenada, Longoria, 1994; Comas-Díaz & Grenier, 1998; Dana, 1995). Standards, guidelines, and revisions of the ethics code (American Psycho-logical Association, 1992; 2002) have also been published, suggesting that the field has advanced in its appreciation for the relevant considerations in assessment across cultures and languages. The International Test Commis-sion, for example, has set forth guidelines (Van de Vijver & Hambleton, 1996) for translating and adapting tests into other languages. Test translation and test use is also addressed in the *Standards for Educational and Psychological Testing* (American Education Research Association et al., 1999).

However, there remains a lag in empirical research that could potentially guide examiners faced with assessing individuals who have limited or non-existent English language proficiency. Furthermore, accessibility to measures published and normed in languages other than English for use with non-English speakers living in America is still somewhat limited. Illustrating this point, it was reported that the vast majority of Spanish speakers who receive neuropsychological evaluations in the U.S. are tested with the same tests as their English-speaking counterparts (Echemendia et al., 1994). Commonly, practitioners informally translate the measures themselves, if they speak the language, or utilize an interpreter to administer translated items. In fact, a survey of clinical neuropsychologists revealed that 29% used a personal verbatim Spanish translation of the WAIS-R with monolingual Spanish speakers, 52% used a published Spanish version, and 6% used the published English version. Respondents reported utilizing published Spanish norms, clinical judgment, and, in some cases, published English norms with these cases (Echemendia et al., 1994). This lack of concordance in approaches demonstrates how professionals "fill in the gaps" with their own ideas of what to do when clearly agreed upon techniques or empirical data to guide them are lacking.

Alternatively, several examiners continue to view nonverbal and performance-based tests as the principal tools for evaluating non-English and limited English proficiency examinees. Current measures such as the Beta-III (the third edition of the Army Beta test; Kellogg & Morton, 1999), the General Ability Measure for Adults (Naglieri & Bardos, 1996), Leiter International Performance Scale—Revised (Roid & Miller, 1997), Naglieri Nonverbal Ability Test (Naglieri, 2002), Raven's Progressive Matrices (Raven, 1998), Test of Nonverbal Intelligence—III (Brown, Sherbenou, & Johnsen, 1997), and Universal Nonverbal Intelligence Test (Bracken & McCallum, 1998) serve as examples of the nonverbal "intelligence" tests that are offered by the major test publishers. These are often marketed for the assessment of non-English speakers.

Many in the field maintain assumptions that nonverbal tests are unlikely to reflect the cultural, linguistic, and educational influences seen on verbal measures. Although under some circumstances or with some test stimuli this may be true, there is also evidence to the contrary. For example, Ardila, Rosselli, and Rosas (1989) and Rosselli, Ardila, and Rosas (1990) found that illiterate Colombian adults performed worse than literate adults on all verbal and performance tasks, with the exception of immediate sentence recall. The common assumptions about performance-based tests and their popularity stem from the ~~paucity of verbal test options in other languages,~~ ~~relatively limited empirical research concerning the parameters of their use,~~ ~~and limited second language proficiency of examiners.~~

In many ways, current demands, including legal directives for testing and placement, are similar to those present in the early 1900s. There remains a significant need to conduct assessments of non-English speakers, but few tools, limited expertise, and a dearth of empirical data to guide practitioners and those who must make decisions based upon test outcome. Artiola i Fortuney and Mullaney (1998) have outlined the multiplicity of problems inherent in today's assessment challenge of the non-English speaker and advocate a conservative response, meant to protect the individuals most likely to be harmed in these situations. In fact, these authors have taken the stance that it is unethical to provide services when the language or culture of the examinee is not shared by the examiner. Others maintain that such a stance ignores the current reality that there are not enough providers to match the multitudes of backgrounds, languages, and experiences of the individuals referred for assessment (Harris, Echemendia, Ardila, & Rosselli, 2001) and that a stringent application of current professional ethical standards may impede service provision to a group of individuals needing such assistance, and may, as a result be even more harmful (Harris, 2002).

The current problems and disagreements over the solutions are not unlike the history described earlier in this chapter. The Public Health Service officials at Ellis Island, the military examiners during World War I, and the modern-day clinician have all been faced with situations where the need for testing outstrips the resources. ~~The history provided earlier is a good~~ ~~example of how scientific decisions and clinical practice can be influenced~~ ~~by sociopolitical demands and attitudes, and how leading scientists use their~~ ~~own values and beliefs of the world to fill in gaps when empirical data are not~~ ~~present to guide decisions.~~ How then do we face current challenges when we are faced with gaps in both our methods and our knowledge of cultures that are different from our own? What we can gain from history is an appreciation for the way societal and individual belief structures impact upon the scientific assumptions that are advanced. We must now move beyond the assumptions of the past to develop and test new models and methodologies with regard to the role of culture and language in cognition. It is only then that we can apply new knowledge, avoid a repetition of the mistakes of the past, and move the field of assessment to a new point in history.

THE RELATIONSHIP BETWEEN ACCULTURATION AND COGNITIVE FUNCTIONING

Acculturation, or culture learning (Berry, 1980), is a multifaceted construct representing the process whereby a person adapts to and may become assimilated into another culture. Some people, when orienting to a new culture and surroundings, embrace that new culture, adopting the values, customs, and habits of that culture over time. Others adjust by establishing a surrounding that is filled with customs and habits from their previous culture or society. Acculturation occurs at many levels and involves many aspects of an individual's life. At an elementary level of acculturation, individuals may change (or resist) concrete behaviors such as food consumption or media preferences. At a much deeper and permanent level of acculturation, individuals may shift their value structure and norms (Marin, 1992), embracing the attitudes and values in the new society in which they now live. Use of the language of the new culture may be seen as part of the acculturation process and has been viewed as an intermediate level of acculturation (Marin, 1992; Marin, Sabogal, Marin, Otero-Sabogal, & Perez-Stable, 1987). Language preference is particularly germane to the topic of cognitive assessment, although preference does not necessarily directly correspond with the degree of acculturation of an individual, and both variables (preference and acculturation) should be considered in the assessment process.

The role of culture in the expression of cognitive abilities has received relatively limited attention (e.g., Lecours et al., 1987; Ostrosky, Canseco, Quintanar, Navarro, & Ardila, 1985; Rosselli et al., 1990). Many of the neuropsychological studies that have addressed cultural and linguistic variables have focused on specific populations residing outside the United States, and few have been directed at the study of immigrant populations (Harris & Cullum, 2000; Harris, Cullum, & Puente, 1995). Even fewer have attempted to investigate the specific relationship of acculturation and neuropsychological/cognitive performance (Manly et al., 1998) and never has there been a systematic effort to do so within a major test standardization effort.

One of the more challenging questions today for practitioners concerns the determination of when it is advisable or justifiable to assess a non-native speaker in English, and how to take acculturation into consideration in approaching testing. For example, with regard to language, although English may appear to be the language suitable for the assessment, it does not logically follow that the English language measures selected for assessment are suitable for evaluating an individual. Often there is discontinuity in communicative competence across language modalities (speaking, writing, listening, or reading); additionally, competence may vary across language skills (semantics, syntax, lexicon, phonemes) (MacNamara, 1967; Sandoval & Durán, 1998). Furthermore, an individual educated in the first language may have the academic knowledge in that language rather than the second language in which he or she appears proficient and competent. Even for bilinguals who are balanced and exhibit native fluency in their two languages, a specific complex idea may not be fully accessible for expression when the individual is limited to one language for responding in a test situation (Ardila, 1998; Harris, Echemendia, Ardila, & Rosselli, 2001). And, although fluency and proficiency in the English language are often associated with acculturation or even assimilation into the culture, it is by no means guaranteed. The examinee may share a common language with the normative reference group of the test, but this may be the only variable upon which the individual approximates the reference group. An example of this might be an individual who has been formally schooled in English in his or her Spanish-speaking homeland, and whose educational and other life experiences have all taken place in the homeland and remain quite traditional. Conversely, acceptance of the Anglo-American culture (living and working in the United States) does not guarantee that language or other variables associated with language might not be exerting an influence on testing or the assessment process (Dana, 1995)

We address some of these issues within the context of the WAIS-III and WMS-III in order to understand the impact of language and acculturation on performance on these established tests. To do this we report one study that focused on non-native, but conversationally fluent, English speakers who immigrated to the United States.

THE RELATIONSHIP BETWEEN ACCULTURATION AND WAIS-III AND WMS-III SCORES

For the WAIS-III and WMS-III standardization studies, a demographic questionnaire was created by David Tulsky and J.J. Zhu (unpublished), Project Directors for the WAIS-III revision, and included items designed to assess a host of background variables: (a) socioeconomic status, (b) occupation and education of the examinee and parents, (c) income level, (d) medical status, (e) country of birth and length of time living in the United

States of both the examinee and his or her parents, and (f) language use and preference of the examinee. The questionnaire was administered to 3050 of the examinees who completed the WAIS-III standardization edition. In fact, the vast majority of the individuals who participated in the WAIS-III standardization (i.e., 86% or $N = 2105$ out of 2450) as well as those who participated in the WMS-III standardization (i.e., 86% or weighted $N = 1075$ of the 1250 sample) completed the demographic questionnaire. Several individuals who were not included in the standardization sample, which included the oversamples and additional cases, also completed the demographic questionnaire. Examinees completed the questionnaire in a self-report fashion after having taken the WAIS-III and WMS-III batteries.

For the current study, 151 of the examinees were selected because they reported they were born outside of the United States and that they spoke English as a second language. The individuals represented 37 countries of origin, with the countries of Mexico and Cuba representing two thirds of the sample. All individuals in the sample reported that they were fluent in English, and the standardization test examiner concurred based upon the observation of the examinees' conversation before and during the testing session. The sample included 51% females ($n = 77$) and 49% males ($n = 74$). The mean age of the sample at the time of testing was 39.1 years (range = 16–89) and mean education was 11.12 years (range = 7–17).

For this study, three variables related to acculturation were created from the data obtained on the questionnaire. Whereas traditional analyses of demographic variables have focused on age, education, and gender (Heaton, Grant & Matthews, 1991; Heaton et al., Chapter 5, this volume), these new variables attempt to further contribute to considerations of relevant demographic and language or acculturation-related variables. In the questionnaire, the examinee was asked if he or she was born in the United States, and if not, was asked how many years he or she lived in the United States and at what age immigration occurred. The examinee was also asked about schooling, namely, if he or she had received any schooling outside the United States, and if so, how many years of education were obtained at a U.S. school versus schooling obtained in a different country. Finally, the examinee was asked four questions about language preference.

First, the variable Language Preference was developed to index self-reported language preference for speaking, thinking, reading, and writing. Specifically, responses to four questions, which followed the format, "What language do you prefer to use when (e.g., speaking)," were used to create a single variable of the individual's language preference. To create one variable, responses to each question received a weighting of either 0 (English preference), 0.5 (equal preference for English and the secondary language, e.g., Spanish), or 1 (other language preference). A sum total of the responses to all four questions was calculated for the overall Language Preference variable, where lower values indicate a stronger preference for English and higher values indicate a stronger preference for another language in the identified aspects of communication. As such, the variable provides an index of an examinee's self-reported preference and comfort level in using English versus another language. It is not a measure of language proficiency nor language competence. Second, the variable U.S. Experience was calculated by dividing the number of years residing in the United States by the total age of the examinee. This variable is important as the length of residence in the United States correlates with acculturation (Marin et al., 1987) and in some circumstances may act as a proxy for acculturation. The third variable, U.S. Education was calculated by dividing the number of years educated in the United States by the total number of years of education attained by the examinee. The variable provides a total value for educational experience in the United States, although it is not specific to the academic period of education in the United States (e.g., elementary, high school, or college), which may be an important consideration.

In sum, the three variables created are an attempt to capture elements of language preference and acculturation not previously captured with traditional demographic variables used to correct test scores. Although these constructs may be interrelated and difficult to quantify, preliminary investigation of these constructs may serve to better direct future research and test development efforts in this area. It was predicted that the variables would be related to various measures of cognitive functioning. It was further predicted that these variables would contribute significant unique variance above and beyond the variance accounted for by education level alone.

A series of multiple regression analyses using SPSS Version 10.0 were performed between the new joint WAIS–III—WMS–III factor-scaled scores as the dependent variables and acculturation variables (language preference, U.S. Experience, and U.S. Education) as the independent variables. The joint WAIS–III—WMS–III factor scores are Verbal Comprehension Index (VCI), Perceptual Organization Index (POI), Working Memory Index (WMI), Processing Speed Index (PSI), Auditory Memory Composite, and Visual Memory Composite (with Visual Reproduction) and the Alternate Visual Memory Composite (with Faces). Each of these scores was the dependent variable in one of the analyses (see Tulsky, Ivnik, Price, & Wilkins, Chapter 4, this volume for a description).

TABLE 1   Regression Analysis Summary of Acculturation Variables Predicting WAIS—III and WMS—III Factor Scores

VARIABLE	R^2	U.S. experience			U.S. education			Language preference		
		B	SEB	β	B	SEB	β	B	SEB	β
Verbal Comprehension	.21**	.12	.07	.20	−.13	.05	−.33**	−5.2	1.2	−.48**
Perceptual Organization	.19**	.01	.06	.12	−.13	.04	−.35**	−4.9	1.1	−.49**
Working Memory	.15*	.17	.09	.28	−.15	.07	−.38*	−4.0	1.7	−.34*
Processing Speed	.12**	.01	.07	.13	−.01	.05	−.16	−4.0	1.3	−.35**
Auditory Memory	.15*	.12	.09	.21	−.14	.06	−.35*	−4.2	1.6	−.38**
Visual Memory (with Visual Reproduction)	.08	.00	.08	−.06	−.01	.06	−.19	−3.4	1.5	−.34*
Visual Memory (with Faces)	.07	.00	.09	.03	.00	.07	.07	−2.2	1.7	−.20

* $p < .05$.

** $p < .01$.

WAIS–III and WMS–III standardization data copyright © 1997 by The Psychological Corporation, a Harcourt Assessment Company. All rights reserved. Used with permission.

Table 1 uses the standard regression sums of squares where every independent variable is adjusted for every other independent variable.

Table 1 displays the summary of the analyses with columns displaying the variance accounted for (R^2) in the model, and, for each of the acculturation variables, the unstandardized regression coefficients (B), the standard errors of the coefficient (SEB), and the standardized regression coefficients (β). When the Verbal Comprehension Index or Perceptual Organization Index were used as the dependent measures, the overall model was significant as R^2 for regression was significantly different from zero, $F_{3,\ 99} = 8.52 (p < .001)$ and $F_{3,\ 99} = 7.6 (p < .001)$, respectively for the two analyses. Two of the three independent variables contributed significantly to both the prediction of VCI [Language Preference (p < .001), US Education (p < .01)] and to POI [Language Preference (p < .001), US Education (p < .05)]. When the WMI ($F_{3,\ 60} = 3.50$, p < .05) or Auditory Memory Composite ($F_{3,\ 60} = 3.42$, p < .05) were used as the dependent measures, the pattern of results were similar, with Language Preference and US Education contributing significantly to the prediction of the WMI and to the Auditory Memory Composite, although not as strongly. When the Processing Speed Index (PSI) was the dependent measure, the overall model was significantly different from zero, ($F_{3,\ 99} = 4.58$, p < .01), but only Language Preference (p < .01) was a significant predictor. When the two visual memory composite indices were the dependent measures, the overall models were not significant.

The findings from these initial analyses indicate that language preference and the amount of education received within the US are related to a significant proportion of the variance in several domains of cognitive function as measured by the WAIS–III/WMS–III. Notably, Language Preference was the most predictive. While these initial analyses show a relation between the acculturation–related variables and cognitive function, they do not show the incremental utility of the variables. Namely, do acculturation variables account for variance above and beyond that already captured by more traditional demographic variables (e.g., age, education, ethnicity, gender)?

To answer this question, a second set of analyses were performed using the joint WAIS–III—WMS–III factor scores as the dependent measures and the acculturation variables, along with the education level of the examinee[1] (traditional Education), as the independent variables. Once again, the analyses were conducted using multiple regression. However, the traditional variable Education was entered into the analyses first, followed by the three

[1]The education grouping was described in the technical manual for the WAIS-III–WMS-III. 5 groups were included: 1 is $\leq$ 8; 2 is 9–11; 3 is 12; 4 is 13–15; and 5 is $\geq$ 16.

TABLE 2 Regression Analysis Summary of Acculturation Variables and Education Predicting WAIS—III and WMS—III Factor Scores

VARIABLE	R^2	Education			Language Preference			U.S. Education			U.S. Experience		
		B	SEB	β	B	SEB	β	B	SEB	β	B	SEB	β
Verbal Comprehension	.46**	2.9	.43	.53**	-3.6	1.0	-.33**	-.15	.04	-.39**	.19	.06	.33**
Perceptual Organization	.24**	1.2	.47	.24**	-4.3	1.1	-.42**	-.14	.04	-.38**	.01	.06	.18
Working Memory	.21**	1.7	.77	.27*	-2.9	1.7	-.25	-.16	.07	-.38*	.22	.09	.37*
Processing Speed	.31**	2.6	.51	.46**	-2.6	1.2	-.22*	.01	.05	-.21	.15	.07	.25*
Auditory Memory	.24**	1.9	.72	.32**	-3.0	1.6	-.27	-.14	.06	-.36*	.18	.09	.31*
Visual Memory (with Visual Reproduction)	.09	0.3	.70	.05	-3.2	1.5	-.32*	-.01	.06	-.19	.00	.08	-.05
Visual Memory (with Faces)	.12	1.5	.79	.24	-1.3	1.7	-.12	.00	.07	.07	.01	.10	.11

* $p < .05$
** $p < .01$

WAIS-III and WMS-III standardization data copyright © 1997 by The Psychological Corporation. a Harcourt Assessment Company. All rights reserved. Used with permission.

In Table 2, education was entered into the model in the initial step. Language Preference, U.S. Education, and U.S. Experience were entered in a second step.

acculturation-related variables (Language Preference, US Experience, and US Education). This would allow us to test whether the acculturation-related variables contributed unique variance above and beyond the traditional Education variable. The results of the analyses are reported in Table 2.

Once again, when the VCI or POI were the dependent measures, the overall model was significant, as R^2 for regression was significantly different from zero, $F_{4,\ 98} = 20.5$, (p < .001) and $F_{4,\ 98} = 7.69$, (p < .001), respectively for VCI and POI. In both of these analyses, Education, Language Preference, and US Education were significant predictors of performance (see Table 2). US Experience was a significant predictor of VCI (p < .001), but it was not a significant predictor of POI.

For the regression models that used PSI and WMI as the dependent variables, the overall models were significant, as R^2 for regression was significantly different from zero, $F_{4,\ 98} = 11.0$, (p < .001) and $F_{4,\ 59} = 3.99$, (p < .01), respectively. In both cases, Education (Processing Speed, p < .05 and Working Memory, p < .05), and US Experience (Processing Speed, p < .01 and Working Memory, p < .05), were significant predictors of performance. In the Processing Speed model, Language Preference (p < .05) was also a significant predictor of performance and Education alone accounted for the greatest amount of variance ($r^2 = .22$). In the model that used WMI as the dependent variable, US Education (p < .05) was a significant predictor of performance. Similar findings were observed when Auditory Memory Composite was the dependent measure, where the overall model was significant, $F_{4,\ 59} = 4.6$, (p < .01). Education (p < .01), US Education (p < .05), and US Experience (p < .05) were significant predictors of Auditory Memory Composite performance. Similar to the earlier reported findings, analyses including Visual Memory Composite and the alternate Visual Memory factor score were not significant.

While the second set of analyses provided additional information, it did not provide a clear indication of the incremental benefit of including the new variables. Subsequently, we compared the amount of variance accounted for by Education alone to the amount of variance accounted for by Education in conjunction with the three acculturation-related variables on the WAIS-III/WMS-III factor scaled scores. These findings are summarized in Table 3. Overall, an increase in unique variance accounted for with the addition of these variables was observed for all of the scores. Specifically, the greatest change was seen in Verbal Comprehension Index performance, with 28.3% of the variance accounted for by Education alone, increasing to 45.5% of the variance accounted for with the addition of the acculturation variables. In other words, there was a 17.2% increase in unique variance.

Significant changes in Perceptual Organization Index, Working Memory Index, Processing Speed Index, and Auditory Memory Composite were also observed, with a 16.3% increase in the variance accounted for by the acculturation variables for POI, 14.3% for WMI, 9.2% for PSI, and 12.9% for Auditory Memory Composite. Neither Education nor the acculturation related variables were predictors of the VCI (with and without the original subtests).

These data provide preliminary evidence that language preference and acculturation contribute to some aspects of cognitive performance. Particularly striking is that, with the exception of the Visual Memory Composite, all of our acculturation variables accounted for significant variance above and beyond the more traditional demographic variables of age and education. Our data suggest that when testing someone who is bilingual, it is important to assess acculturation. The examinee's self-reported preferred language is a key variable for planning assessment strategies and other decision making. If the examinee does not indicate a preference for English, then his/her scores may be affected, and, as the individual diverges from the sample upon which the test was developed, the norms may become less meaningful. The examiner should take these factors into account when

TABLE 3   Comparison of Variance Accounted for by Education Alone and Education in Conjunction with Acculturation Variables

	Education	Education and [Lang. Pref., U.S. Educ., U.S. Exp]		
	R^2	R^2	R^2 change	P (of F change)
Verbal Comprehension	.283	.455	.172	.000
Perceptual Organization	.076	.239	.163	.000
Working Memory	.070	.213	.143	.019
Processing Speed	.218	.311	.092	.006
Auditory Memory	.108	.237	.129	.026
Visual Memory	.049	.092	.044	.169
Visual Memory (with original subtests)	.061	.119	.058	.284

deciding how to test the individual and how to interpret scores. Additionally, these considerations should be carefully integrated into the assessment recommendations.

DISCUSSION

Professionals in the field must be willing to advance cognitive and intellectual testing in this new century from its historical beginnings. History has taught us that the practice of cognitive assessment does not occur independently of the sociopolitical context of America or of the world. In much the same way that the medical officers of the 1900s practiced, psychologists today struggle with reconciling the needs of ethnoculturally and linguistically diverse individuals with the reality of limited empirical knowledge, limited professional and technical resources, and sometimes, sadly, limited interest in "special" populations.

We have elsewhere maintained (Harris, 2002) that ethical theories of justice support the argument that ethnicity, culture, and/or language should not exclude an individual from accessing or obtaining an evaluation. Furthermore, the principle of justice may support the argument that those providing assessment services must in fact themselves acquire the training, consultation, and/or supervision to provide services to diverse individuals when an alternative, more suitable provider is not identifiable. It would have been unacceptable for the Public Health Service officers to ignore their charge. But in the case of Ellis Island, the immigration laws *mandated* that immigrants with cognitive impairment be identified, and additionally specifically mandated the personnel and procedures for conducting the evaluations. The ethical dilemma then was more of a moral struggle experienced by those bearing the responsibility for making life-altering decisions of whether to land or to deport an immigrant. Today, as before, practitioners feel pressured, forced, and in some cases are even mandated to provide assessment services to non-English and non-native English speakers. Practitioners experience ethical conflicts about whether or how to provide these assessments. In the absence of data-driven directives for practice, psychologists utilize their own cultural experiences, knowledge, personal morals, professional ethics, and guidelines to assist them in approaching the challenge of assessment and acting responsibly. One's own internal views of race and ethnicity cannot be escaped in the context of these considerations, and this most certainly has a bearing on the decisions ultimately reached by individual practitioners.

Over time, many of the solutions developed within the field to address the assessment of non–native English speakers have been in the form of guidelines and standards for practice, test use, and the training of future practitioners. Culture and language are typically addressed within these documents, and many practitioners intuitively know that these types of factors are valid considerations. What has been lacking though in advancing the field of cognitive testing is the development of strategies and methods based upon empirical research with both verbal and performance–based tests, particularly with regard to the use of popular assessment tools, such as the WAIS–III and WMS–III. Availability of published performance–based tests and historical acceptance of logical, though not necessarily tested assumptions regarding their use give the impression that the field has progressed further than it may indeed have advanced. For example, nonverbal "intelligence" tests are frequently the default method of assessing limited English and non–English language speakers. Yet, the Weschler scales of intelligence, which have been translated and adapted into 18 other languages and in many cases normed (see Table 4), are rarely used in practice in the United States outside of some applications of Spanish WAIS III versions (e.g., *Manual Moderno* and *TEA Ediciónes* published versions).

In the study reported in this chapter, we examined a heterogenous sample of foreign-born individuals who spoke English fluently as a second language. The individuals in this sample are representative of examinees for whom clinicians struggle least with decision making regarding test selection and interpretation. Specifically, they appear to the examiner to be acculturated and proficient in English, and they appear similar to the typical standardization sample for tests developed in the United States. Yet, even after accounting for education, there was additional variance in test scores accounted for by language preference, educational exposure in the United States, and the percentage of time residing in the United States (U.S. Experience). Importantly, these variables contributed differing amounts of variance depending upon the factor analyzed, highlighting the importance of separating education from other cultural and language variables. Because of the small sample size and the heterogencity of languages and cultures represented in the study, however, the results reported here cannot be used to recommend specific adjustments for applied practice. However, these findings should alert the clinician to the importance of exploring these background variables with all examinees prior to cognitive and intellectual assessment. For those individuals who express a clear preference for their native language and for whom U.S. residency has been brief, it may indeed be more appropriate to use a test version developed in the country of origin

TABLE 4

Language	Country / region	Test	Publisher contact information
Chinese	Taiwan	Wechsler Adult Intelligence Scale—Third Edition	Chinese Behavioral Science Corp. 9F-1, 206, Nan-Chuan Road, Sec. 2 Taipei, 100 Taiwan
		Wechsler Intelligence Scale for Children—Third Edition	
Czechoslovakian	Czech/Slovak Republic	Wechsler Adult Intelligence Scale—Third Edition	Psychodiagnostika, Ltd. P.O. Box 44 820 06 Bratislava Slovak Republic
		Wechsler Memory Scale—Third Edition	
		Wechsler Intelligence Scale for Children—Third Edition	
Danish	Denmark	Wechsler Adult Intelligence Scale—Third Edition	Dansk Psykologisk Forlag Hans Knudsens Plads 1A 2100 Kovenhavn 0 Denmark
		Wechsler Adult Intelligence Scale— Revised	
		Wechsler Memory Scale—Third Edition	
		Wechsler Memory Scale—Revised	
		Wechsler Intelligence Scale for Children—Third Edition	
Dutch/Flemish	The Netherlands, Surinam, the Antilles, Flemish provinces of Belgium	Wechsler Adult Intelligence Scale—Third Edition	Swets & Zeitlinger Heereweg 346-b P.O. Box 240 2160 SZ Lisse The Netherlands
		Wechsler Intelligence Scale for Children— Revised	
English	Australian, New Zealand adaptations	Wechsler Adult Intelligence Scale—Revised	The Psychological Corporation Australia 30–52 Smidmore Street Locked Bag 16 Marrickville, N. S. W. 2204 Australia
		Wechsler Intelligence Scale for Children— Third Edition	
		Wechsler Intelligence Scale for Children—Revised	

Language		Test	Publisher
English	Canada	Wechsler Adult Intelligence Scale—Third Edition Wechsler Memory Scale: Third Edition Wechsler Intelligence Scale for Children— Third Edition	The Psychological Corporation Canada 55 Horner Avenue Toronto, Ontario Canada M8Z 4X6
English (Anglicized editions)	Europe	Wechsler Adult Intelligence Scale—Third Edition (WAIS-III UK) Wechsler Adult Intelligence Scale—Revised (WAIS-R UK) Wechsler Memory Scale—Third Edition (WMS-III UK) Wechsler Intelligence Scale for Children—Revised (WISC-R UK)	The Psychological Corporation, Europe Harcourt Place 32 Jamestown Road London NW1 7BY United Kingdom
English	South Africa	Wechsler Adult Intelligence Scale: Third Edition	Human Sciences Research Council 134 Pretorius Street Private Bag X41 Pretoria, South Africa
Finnish	Europe and Scandinavia	Wechsler Adult Intelligence Scale—Third Edition Wechsler Adult Intelligence Scale—Revised Wechsler Memory Scale—Third Edition Wechsler Memory Scale—Revised Wechsler Intelligence Scale for Children—Third Edition Wechsler Intelligence Scale for Children—Revised	Psykologien Kustannus Oy Kolmas Linja 12 00530 Helsinki 53 Finland
French	Canada	Wechsler Intelligence Scale for Children—Third Edition	The Psychological Corporation Canada 55 Horner Avenue Toronto, Ontario Canada M8Z 4X6
French	Europe	Wechsler Adult Intelligence Scale—Third Edition	Les Editions du Centre de Psychologie Appliquée 24, rue de la Plaine 75980 Paris Cedex 20 France

(continues)

TABLE 4 *(continued)*

Language	Country / region	Test	Publisher contact information
		Wechsler Adult Intelligence Scale—Revised	
		Wechsler Memory Scale—Third Edition	
		Wechsler Memory Scale—Revised	
		Wechsler Intelligence Scale for Children—Third Edition	
		Wechsler Intelligence Scale for Children—Revised	
German	Europe, Switzerland Austria	Wechsler Adult Intelligence Scale—Third Edition	Verlag Hans Huber Langgass-Strasse 76 CH - 3000 Bern 9 Switzerland
		Wechsler Adult Intelligence Scale—Revised	
		Wechsler Memory Scale—Revised	
		Wechsler Intelligence Scale for Children—Third Edition	
		Wechsler Intelligence Scale for Children—Revised	
Greek	Europe	Wechsler Adult Intelligence Scale—Third Edition	The University of Athens Department of Psychology Panepistimiopolis Ilissia 15784 Athens, Greece
		Wechsler Intelligence Scale for Children—Third Edition	
Hebrew	Israel	Wechsler Intelligence Scale for Children—Revised	Ministry of Education Psychological & Counseling Services State of Israel 2 Devorah Hanevia Street Jerusalem, 91911 Israel
Hebrew	Israel	Wechsler Intelligence Scale for Children: Third Edition	PsychTech P.O. Box 26250 Jerusalem 91262 Israel
Italian	Europe	Wechsler Adult Intelligence Scale—Revised	Organizzazioni Speciali Via Fra Paolo Sarpi 7/A 50136 F Florence, Italy
		Wechsler Intelligence Scale for Children: Third Edition	

Language	Country	Test	Publisher
Japanese	Japan	Wechsler Intelligence Scale for Children—Revised Wechsler Adult Intelligence Scale—Third Edition Wechsler Adult Intelligence Scale—Revised Wechsler Memory Scale—Revised Wechsler Intelligence Scale for Children—Third Edition Wechsler Intelligence Scale for Children—Revised	Nihon Bunka Kagakusha Co., Ltd. Honkomagome 6-15-17 Bunkyo-ku, Tokyo 113 Japan
Korean	Korea	Wechsler Intelligence Scale for Children—Third Edition Wechsler Intelligence Scale for Children—Revised	Special Education Publishers 697 Sangdo-dong, Dong jak ku, Seoul City 156-030 Korea
Lithuanian		Wechsler Intelligence Scale for Children—Third Edition	Psychological Assessment Ctr. Department of General and Educational Psychology and Laboratory of Special Psychology Vilnius University Vilnius, Lithuania
Polish		Wechsler Adult Intelligence Scale—Revised Wechsler Intelligence Scale for Children—Revised	Polskie Towarzystwo Psychologiczne Zarzard Glowny 00-183 Warsaw ul Stawki 5/7 Poland
Portuguese	Brazil	Wechsler Memory Scale—Revised	Casa do Psicologo Livraria e Editora Ltda. Rua Mourato Coelho 1059, Vila Madalena CEP 05417-011 Sao Paulo, SP Brazil
Portuguese	Europe	Wechsler Intelligence Scale for Children—Third Edition	CEGOC-TEA, Lda Av. Antonio Augusto de Aguiar n 21°-2 andar 1050 012 Lisbon Portugal
Slovenian		Wechsler Intelligence Scale for Children—Third Edition	Center Za Psihdiagnosticna Sredstva Dunajske 106 Sl-1000 Ljubijana Slovenia
Spanish	Argentina	Wechsler Adult Intelligence Scale: Third Edition Wechsler Intelligence Scale for Children—Third Edition	Editorial Paidos, S.A. Defensa 599 1055 Capital Federal Buenos Aires Argentina

(continues)

TABLE 4 (continued)

Language	Country / region	Test	Publisher contact information
Spanish	Mexico exclusive; nonexclusive: Colombia, Ecuador, El Salvador, Peru, Venezuela	Wechsler Adult Intelligence Scale—Third Edition Wechsler Intelligence Scale for Children—Revised	El Manual Moderno Av. Sonora 206 Col. Hipodromo 06100 Mexico, D.F.
Spanish	Europe DAT—Europe exclusively; Nonexclusive: Chile, Argentina, Colombia, Costa Rica, Ecuador, Portugal, Uruguay WAIS-III—Europe exclusively; Nonexclusive: Chile and Uruguay	Wechsler Adult Intelligence Scale—Third Edition Wechsler Intelligence Scale for Children—Revised	TEA Ediciones, S.A. Fray Bernardino Sahagun 24 28036 Madrid Spain
Swedish	Europe and Scandinavia	Wechsler Adult Intelligence Scale—Third Edition Wechsler Intelligence Scale for Children—Third Edition* *Materials translated from U.K. versions of these tests	Psykologi Forlaget AB Box 47054 SE-100 74 Stockholm Sweden

Information provided courtesy of The Psychological Corporation, a Harcourt Assessment Company.

and to use the associated population norms. An examiner or assistant who speaks the language of the examinee and is trained in the basic theory and methods of assessment can be used for this purpose. However, it remains the responsibility of the clinician to ensure that the translation or adaptation has been developed according to established guidelines and standards, and that the normative sample is relevant and representative of the examinee (e.g., International Test Commission, 1993, as reported in Van de Vijver & Hambleton, 1996; Standards for educational and psychological testing; American Educational Research Association et al., 1999). The clinician should not utilize an interpreter to merely translate and present items to the examinee. Aside from issues of validity and reliability, such a procedure is in violation of standard test administration procedures and calls into question the utility and meaning of the scores and their interpretation.

Access to a measure in the examinee's preferred language and availability of an examiner who speaks that language will not always be achievable. Then the question becomes one of what degree of proficiency or linguistic competency on the part of the examinee is necessary to proceed with a test in English? Various issues, including the ethics of pursuing the assessment (Harris, 2002), must be considered, and the possibility of unexplained error variance must be acknowledged. With regard to language fluency, it is important to recognize that individuals may be incongruent in their proficiency or linguistic competence, depending upon the situational demands (e.g., home versus school) and the type of receptive or expressive language skill required for communication in a given situation (e.g., listening versus writing) (MacNamara, 1967; Manuel-Dupont, Ardila, & Rosselli, 1992; Sandoval & Durán, 1998). It is important to try to ascertain whether an individual possesses adequate communication skills in the mode of language expression demanded by the test. Furthermore, it is possible that the examinee will have adequate proficiency for some but not all verbal subtests contained within a test, necessitating adjustments in test administration, scoring, and interpretation. Under such circumstances, clinicians should proceed even more cautiously in utilizing the normative data for interpretation. Published measures of language proficiency have primarily been developed for use in school settings with children and have frequently been criticized as inadequate (e.g., Sandoval & Durán, 1998). In the absence of a suitable measure, and given that the necessary level of proficiency may vary markedly depending upon the task, it is recommended that clinicians directly query examinees about their perceived receptive and expressive competencies, their patterns of language usage, and their comfort level or preference. Furthermore, examiners must directly observe the specific communication skill. Collateral information should also be obtained about language use, preference, and competency. Those who clearly express discomfort and uncertainty about their abilities to respond in English should not be tested in English, unless the potential benefit far outweighs the potential for harm. Those who express a preference for another language, but who claim to have adequate skills and familiarity with the English language, may be assessed in English, although the possibility of underestimation of performance should be noted in the evaluation report.

Once a determination to proceed in English has been made, it is necessary to make accomodations in the test situation and to document the accomodations accordingly. For example, individuals may be allowed to provide a response in either language, and for bilinguals it may be necessary to administer tests, if available, in each language, taking order and practice effects into account (American Educational Research Association et al., 1999). These are important, although not necessarily easily attainable accomodations, in order to minimize the problem of making a cognitive test simply a measure of English language proficiency. This is a particularly important point in the assessment of children, as non-native English students are in the process of acquiring new academic knowledge in English and may have some information or concepts accessible in English and others in Spanish. When an adult has immigrated to the United States following the completion of his or her formal academic schooling, it may be advisable to administer the test in the first language, even though the individual displays adequate conversational skills in English and for all practical purposes appears to function as a bilingual (i.e., equally proficient in the two languages in the relevant communication skill).

The limited response repertoire to date in the assessment of non-English speakers stems from a number of factors. There is a paucity of empirical research, an abundance of English language tests but limited information regarding their cross-cultural and cross-linguistic applications, a dearth of clinical experience with diverse individuals, and limited test options for individuals from other populations. Indeed, the limited availability of data, particularly with the more established tests, and the lack of experience on the part of practitioners may be closely related issues. Perhaps as practitioners come to understand the assumptions and mistakes of the past, other new assumptions and methodologies will be tested and will take the place of outdated approaches, ultimately providing practitioners with a means to gain more experience and become more competent and ethical providers. In the meantime, examiners should know what options are available and what precautions should be exercised in administering and interpreting tests. As one of the Ellis Island PHS officers, E.K. Sprague (1914) first cautioned, "Every legitimate means must be utilized to assist in arriving at a correct decision" (p. 467). Clinicians must ultimately identify the competing ethical issues, weigh the costs and benefits of assessment, and consider the available options in order to successfully meet the challenge of assessing the non-native English speaker.

REFERENCES

American Education Research Association, American Psychological Association, & National Council on Measurement in Education (1999). *Standards for educational and psychological testing*. Washington, DC: American Educational Research Association.

American Psychological Association (2002). Ethical principles and code of conduct. *American Psychologist, 57*(12), 1060–1073.

American Psychological Association (1992). Ethical principles of psychologists and code of conduct. *American Psychologist, 47*, 1597–1611.

American Psychological Association (1990). *Guidelines for providers of psychological services to ethnic, linguistic, and culturally diverse populations*. Washington, DC: Author.

Annual Report of the Commissioner General of Immigration. Washington, D.C. (1922).

Annual Report of the Commissioner General of Immigration. Washington, D.C. (1931).

Annual Report, Medical Examination of Immigrants, Ellis Island, New York Harbor. Fiscal Year ended June 30, 1914.

Ardila, A. (1998). Bilingualism: A neglected and chaotic area. *Aphasiology, 12*, 131–134.

Ardila, A., Rosselli, M., & Rosas, P. (1989). Neuropsychological assessment in illiterates: Visuospatial and memory abilities. *Brain and Cognition, 11*, 147–166.

Arnold, B. R., Montgomery, G. T., Castaneda, I., & Longoria, R. (1994). Acculturation and performance of Hispanics on selected Halstead–Reitan neuropsychological tests. *Assessment, 1*, 239–248.

Artiola i Fortuny, L., & Mullaney, H. A. (1998). Assessing patients whose language you do not know: Can the absurd be ethical? *The Clinical Neuropsychologist, 12*, 113–126.

Berry, J. (1980). Acculturation as varieties of adaptation. In A. M. Padilla (Ed.), *Acculturation: Theory, models, and some new findings*. Boulder, CO: Westview.

Bracken, B. A., & McCallum, S. (1998). *Universal Nonverbal Intelligence Test*. Itasca, IL: Riverside Publishing Co.

Brigham, C. C. (1923). *A study of American intelligence*. Princeton, NJ: Princeton University Press.

Brown, L., Sherbenou, R. J., & Johnsen, S. K. (1997). *Test of Nonverbal Intelligence—Third Edition*. Austin, TX: Pro Ed.

Comas-Díaz, L., & Grenier, J. R. (1998). Migration and acculturation. In J. Sandoval, C. L. Frisby, K. F. Geisinger, J. D. Scheuneman, & J. R. Grenier (Eds.), *Test interpretation and diversity*. Washington, DC: American Psychological Association.

Dana, R. H. (1995). Impact of the use of standard psychological assessment on the diagnosis and teatment of ethnic minorities. In J. F. Aponte, R. Y. Rivers, & J. Wohl (Eds)., *Psychological interventions and cultural diversity*. Boston: Allyn & Bacon.

Echemendia, R. J., Harris, J. G., Congett, S. M., Diaz, M. L., Junco, R., & Puente, A. E. (1994). Neuropsychological assessment and treatment of Spanish-speaking individuals: National survey of neuropsychologists. *The Clinical Neuropsychologist, 8*(3), 351.

Echemendia, R. J., Harris, J. G., Congett, S. M., Diaz, M. L., & Puente, A. E. (1997). Neuropsychological training and practices with Hispanics: A national survey. *The Clinical Neuropsychologist, 11*(3), 229–243.

Eysenck, H. J., & Kamin, L. (1981). *The intelligence controversy*. New York: John Wiley and Sons.

Glueck, B. (1913). The mentally defective immigrant. *New York Medical Journal, 93*, 760–766.

Goddard, H. H. (1912). The feeble minded immigrant. *The Training School, 9*, 109–113.

Goddard, H. H. (1913). The Binet tests in relation to immigration. *Psycho-Asthenics, 18*, 105–107.

Gould, S. (1996). *The mismeasure of man*. New York: W. W. Norton and Co.

Harris, J. G. (2002). Ethical decision making with individuals of diverse ethnic, cultural, and linguistic backgrounds. In S. Bush & M. Drexler (Eds.), *Ethical issues in clinical neuropsychology* (pp. 223–241) Lisse, The Netherlands: Swets & Zeitlinger.

Harris, J. G., & Cullum, C. M. (2000). *Symbol vs. digit substitution task performance in culturally and linguistically diverse populations*. Manuscript submitted for publication.

Harris, J. G., Cullum, C. M., & Puente, A. E. (1995). Effects of bilingualism on verbal learning and memory in Hispanic adults. *Journal of the International Neuropsychological Society, 1*, 10–16.

Harris, J. G., Echemendía, R., Ardila, A., & Rosselli, M. (2001). Cross-cultural cognitive and neuropsychological assessment. In J. J. W. Andrews, H. Janzen, & D. Saklofske (Eds.), *Handbook of Psychoeducational Assessment*. San Diego, CA: Academic Press.

Heaton, R., Grant, I., & Matthews, C. G. (1991). *Comprehensive norms for an expanded Halstead-Reitan Battery: Demographic corrections, research findings, and clinical applications*. Odessa, FL: Psychological Assessment Resources.

Heaton, R. K., Taylor, M. J., and Manly, J. (2003). Demographic effects and use of demographically corrected norms with the WAIS-III and WMS-III. In D. S. Tulsky et al. (Eds). *Clinical Interpretation of the WAIS-III and WMS-III*. (pp. 181–207). San Diego: Academic Press.

Helms, J. E. (1992). Why is there no study of cultural equivalence in standardized cognitive ability testing? *American Psychologist, 47*, 1083–1101.

Horn, J. L. (1985). Remodeling old models of intelligence. In B. Wolman (Ed.), *Handbook of Intelligence: Theories, measurements, and applications* (pp. 267–300). New York: Wiley.

Jensen, A. R. (1969). How much can we boost IQ and scholastic achievement? *Harvard Educational Review, 39*(1), 1–123.

Kellogg, C. E., & Morton, N. W. (1999). *Beta-III*. San Antonio: The Psychological Corporation.

Kevles, D. J. (1968). Testing the Army's intelligence: Psychologists and the military in World War I. *Journal of American History, 55*(3), 565–581.

Knox, H. A. (1914). A scale, based on the work at Ellis Island, for estimating mental defect. *Journal of the American Medical Association, 62*(10), 741–747.

Knox, H. A. (1915). Measuring human intelligence. A progressive series of standardized tests used by the Public Health Service to protect our racial stock. *Scientific American*, January 9, 1915, 52–53, 57–58.

Kuhn, T. S. (1970). *The structure of scientific revolutions*. Chicago: University of Chicago Press.

Lambert, N. M. (1981). Psychological evidence in Larry P. v. Wilson Riles. *American Psychologist, 35*, 937–951.

Lecours, R. L., Mehler, J., Parente, M. A., et al. (1987). Illiteracy and brain damage—I: Aphasia testing in culturally contrasted populations (control subjects). *Neuropsychologia, 25*, 231–245.

Macnamara, J. (1967). The bilingual's linguistic performance: A psychological overview. *Journal of Social Issues, 23*(2), 58–77.

Manly, J. J., Miller, S. W, Heaton, R. K., Byrd, D., Reilly, J., Velasquez, R. J., Saccuzzo, D. P., Grant, I., The HIV Neurobehavioral Research Center Group (1998). The effect of African-American acculturation on neuropsychological test performance in normal and HIV-positive individuals. *Journal of the International Neuropsychological Society, 4(3)*, 291–302.

Manuel-Dupont, S., Ardila, A., & Rosselli, M. (1992). Neuropsychological assessment in bilinguals. In A. E. Puente & R. J. McCaffrey (Eds.), *Handbook of neuropsychological assessment: A biopsychosocial perspective*. New York: Plenum Press.

Marin, G., Sabogal, F., Marin, B., Otero-Sabogal, & Perez-Stable, E. (1987). Development of a short acculturation scale for Hispanics. *Hispanic Journal of Behavioral Sciences, 9*, 183–205.

Marin, G. (1992). Issues in the measurement of acculturation among Hispanics. In K. F. Geisinger (Ed.), *Psychological testing of Hispanics* (pp 235–251). Washington, DC. American Psychological Association.

Mullan, E. H. (1917). *Mental examination of immigrants: Administration and line inspection at Ellis Island*. Public Health Reports 32 (No. 20, May 18, 1917).

Naglieri, J. A. (2002). *Naglieri Nonverbal Ability Test®*–Individual Administration (NNAT®–Individual Administration). San Antonio, TX.: The Psychological Corporation.

Neisser, U., Boodoo, G., Bouchard., T. J., Jr., Boykin, A. W., Brody, N., Ceci, S. J., Halpern, D. F., Loehlin, J. C., Perloff, R., Sternberg, R. J., Urbina, S. (1996). Intelligence: Knowns and unknowns. *American Psychologist, 51*, 77–101.

Ostrosky, F., Canseco, E., Quintanar, L., Navarro, E., Meneses, S., & Ardila, A. (1985). Sociocultural effects in neuropsychological assessment. *International Journal of Neuroscience, 27*, 53–66.

Raven, J. C. (1998). *Raven's Progressive Matrices*. London: Oxford Psychology Press.

Reed, A. C. (1913). The problem of the feeble-minded among immigrants. *Journal of the American Medical Association, 60*, 209–210.

Reed, J. (1987). Robert M. Yerkes and the mental testing movement. In M. M. Sokal (Ed.), Psychological testing and American society 1890–1930 (pp. 75–94). New Brunswick, NJ: Rutgers University Press.

Richards, G. (1997). *'Race', racism and psychology: Towards a reflexive history*. New York: Routledge.

Roid, G. H. & Miller, L. J. (1997). *Leiter International Performance Scale, Revised*. Wood Dale, IL: Stoelting Company

Rosselli, M., Ardila, A., & Rosas, P. (1990). Neuropsychological assessment in illiterates II: Language and praxic abilities. *Brain and Cognition, 12*, 281–296.

Samelson, F. (1977). World War I intelligence testing and the development of psychology. *Journal of the History of the Behavioral Sciences, 13*(3), 274–282.

Samuda, R. (1975). *Psychological testing of American minorities: Issues and consequences.* New York: Harper & Row, Publishers.

Sandoval, J., & Durán, R. P. (1998). *Language.* In J. Sandoval, C. L. Frisby, K. F. Geisinger, J. D. Scheuneman, & J. R. Grenier (Eds.), *Test interpretation and diversity.* Washington, DC: American Psychological Association.

Sattler, J. M. (1981). Intelligence tests on trial: An "interview" with judges Robert F. Peckman and John F. Grady. *The Journal of School Psychology, 19*, 359–369.

Spearman, C. E. (1923). *The nature of intelligence and the principles of cognition.* London: Macmillan.

Sprague, E. K. (1914). Mental examination of immigrants. *The Survey, 31*, 466–468.

Thorndike, E. L. (1927). *The measurement of intelligence.* New York: Bureau of Publications, Teachers College, Columbia University.

Thurstone, L. L. (1938). Primary mental abilities. *Psychometric Monographs* No. 1.

Tulsky, D.S, Ivnik, R. J., Price, L. R., and Wilkins, C. (2003). Assessment of cognitive functioning with the WAIS-III and WMS-III: Development of a six-factor model. In D. S. Tulsky et al. (Eds). *Clinical Interpretation of the WAIS-III and WMS-III* (pp. 147–179). San Diego: Academic Press.

Tulsky, D. S., Ricker, J. H., and Saklofske, D. H. (2003). Historical overview of intelligence and memory: Factors influencing the Wechsler Scales. In D. S. Tulsky et al. (Eds). *Clinical Interpretation of the WAIS-III and WMS-III.* (pp. 7–41). San Diego: Academic Press.

United States Public Health Service (1918). *Manual of the mental examination of aliens.* Miscellaneous Publication No. 18. Washington, DC: Government Printing Office.

Van de Vijver, F., & Hambleton, R. K. (1996). Translating tests: Some practical guidelines. *European Psychologist, 1*, 89–99.

Williams, L. L. (1914). The medical examination of mentally defective aliens: Its scope and limitations. *American Journal of Insanity, 71*, 257–268.

Yerkes, R. (1921). Psychological examining in the United States Army. *National Academy of Sciences, 25*, Washington: Government Printing Office.

Yoakum, C. S., & Yerkes, R. M. (1920). *Army mental tests.* New York: Henry Holt and Company.

ACKNOWLEDGEMENT

The authors wish to thank Ruben Echemendía, Ph.D., Jennifer Manly, Ph.D., Susana Urbina, Ph.D., and Brigida Hernandez, Ph.D., for helpful comments on earlier drafts of this paper. In addition, the authors wish to thank Scott Millis, Ph.D., and Gary O. Zerbe, Ph.D. for assistance with data analysis.

CHAPTER 10

Accuracy of WAIS-III — WMS-III Joint Factor Scores When One or More Subtests Is Omitted or an Alternate Subtest Is Employed

Barton W. Palmer, Michael J. Taylor, and Robert K. Heaton

University of California, San Diego
Department of Psychiatry
La Jolla, California

The factor analytically based structure for joint scoring and interpretation of the Wechsler Adult Intelligence Scale—Third Edition (WAIS-III) (Wechsler, 1997a) and Wechsler Memory Scale—Third Edition (WMS-III) (Wechsler, 1997b) described by Tulsky et al. (Chapter 3, this volume) provides for a broad assessment of cognitive abilities using 14 subtests. Administration of these 14 subtests should take approximately 75 to 90 minutes in cognitively intact examinees, although substantially longer administration times may be required in clinical populations (Axelrod, 2001). As was the case with the IQ and Index scores originally published with the WAIS-III and WMS-III (as well their respective predecessors) examinee or situational factors may yield some instances in which examiners find it is inappropriate or infeasible to administer all of the factor score subtests. In addition, there are conditions in which the examiner may find it necessary or preferable to substitute one of the primary subtests with one of the alternate subtests. In such instances, the test user may need to know whether the factor structure featured in this volume for scoring and interpreting WAIS-III or WMS-III tests can still be applied.

391

Should factor scores be prorated based on available data? If one of the primary subtests is spoiled, can one of the alternate WAIS-III or WMS-III subtests be substituted for the missing subtest? Which approach (prorating or substituting subtests) yields a more accurate estimate of the standard factor scores? Also, for those occasions in which examiners wish to make statements about an examinee's general cognitive ability or memory, how well can the Full Scale IQ or General Memory Index be estimated solely from the subset of WAIS-III or WMS-III subtests needed to calculate the factor scores (i.e., do the additional subtests need to be administered for test results to be valid)? There can be no single answer to these questions that applies to all instances and all contexts under which the WAIS-III and WMS-III tests are used. The goal of the present chapter is to guide test users in answering such questions for themselves by providing normative-based information about the impact of prorating or subtest substitution when using the joint WAIS-III and WMS-III factor scores. The structure of our presentation is as follows: First we present a brief historical overview of prorated summary scores of the Wechsler scales, including attempts to develop abbreviated or "short-form" versions of the Wechsler and similar scales, as well as the use of alternate subtests in prior incarnations of the Wechsler scales. Then, using the data from the WAIS-III and WMS-III standardization and available clinical samples, we examine the accuracy of prorated and alternate subtest-based estimates of the factor scores (as well as the Full Scale IQ [FSIQ] and General Memory Index [GMI]) relative to the standard factor scores as defined in Chapter 3 (Tulsky et al., this volume). We also provide some selected examples wherein we examined the sensitivity and specificity of the factor scores, and of prorated or alternate versions of the factor scores. We conclude with some specific recommendations, as well as caveats about interpreting factor scores when derived from prorating or substitution of missing scores with those from alternate subtests.

BACKGROUND

Standard 5.1 of the *Standards for Educational and Psychological Testing* (American Educational Research Association, 1999) states that "Test administrators should follow carefully the standardized procedures for administering and scoring specified by the test developer, unless the situation or a test taker's disability dictates that an exception should be made" (p. 63). The first half of this statement is an assertion of the general importance of adhering to standardized procedures. However, the latter half of the standard encourages, perhaps even ethically compels, test users to make reasoned deviations from the standardized administration and/or scoring procedures under certain circumstances, such as omitting a particular subtest when that subtest would be inappropriate as a measure of its intended cognitive construct due to a particular examinee's sensory or motor deficits (see Braden, Chapter 11, this volume).

The occasional need to prorate scores when the full battery was not administered, or to make subtest substitutions when calculating an IQ or similar summary score, was recognized and sanctioned, and even used as a marketing tool from the very beginning of the Wechsler scales. The Bellevue Intelligence Examination (also known as the Wechsler–Bellevue Form I) was published by Wechsler in 1939 and consisted of 10 subtests, all familiar to contemporary WAIS-III users: Information, Comprehension, Arithmetical Reasoning, Digit Span, Similarities, Picture Arrangement, Picture Completion, Block Design, Digit Symbol, Object Assembly (Wechsler, 1939).

In the leaflet advertising the original version of the Bellevue Intelligence Scale (reproduced in Appendix II of this volume), the second of four advantages listed for using the scale over other intelligence tests was that the "Scale can be modified in cases of sensory deficit or unusual environment." Further evidence that Wechsler was aware that it was inappropriate to employ some of the subtests in certain instances, and thus that prorating IQ scores from the remaining subtests and/or use of an alternate subtest was occasionally necessary comes from his textbook. When discussing assessment of elderly subjects Wechsler (1939) noted that:

> In the case of older persons it is sometimes necessary to omit one or another of the tests in order to avoid penalizing these subjects for disabilities such as diminished vision or partial deafness. . . . With such subjects a battery of 8 or 9 tests may be substituted for the Full Scale. (p. 147)

Also, although Vocabulary was not part of the standard set of 10 subtests in the original Wechsler–Bellevue scale, it was an alternate subtest, and Wechsler (1939) indicated that "it may be substituted for any of the Verbal items in our scale" (p. 101).

Further evidence of official sanctioning by the Wechsler scales publisher of prorating, when necessary, came during "Great Block Shortage" of the mid-1940s. The Wechsler kits sold during that period included notice indicating that the publisher was unable to obtain an adequate supply of blocks for the Block Design subtest, but advising users that prorating the IQ scores from as few as six or seven subtests might be acceptable (See reproduction and text of the actual notice in Figure 1)

NOTICE
to purchasers of Wechsler Bellevue materials

For almost a year, The Psychological Corporation has been unable to
obtain an adequate supply of satisfactory Kohs blocks for the Block
Design test of the Wechsler Bellevue Intelligence Scale. For the
duration of this shortage, it is fortunate that the scale can be used
with one or more tests omitted--actually as few as six or seven of the
tests may be used in some situations (1). In scoring the scale when
one or more tests are omitted, it is necessary to pro-rate for the
omitted test after the scores obtained have been converted to weighted
scores (2).

While it is possible to omit tests, it is, of course, not desirable to
do so. It now appears likely that the problems attending the manufact-
ure of these cubes will be solved before the fall of 1947. All those
who send their names and addresses with a request to be notified when
blocks are again available will receive announcements as soon as they
are in stock.

(1) Wechsler: The Measurement of Adult Intelligence, Third Edition,
    pages 77 and 145.
(2) ibid., pages 171 and 189.

FIGURE 1.   Notice to purchasers of Wechsler Bellevue Materials.

Provision for the occasional need to prorate or substitute a missing
or spoiled subtest is motivated by recognition of clinical realities that some
subtests may be inappropriate for certain examinees, and that administration
does not always proceed according to plan (e.g., excessive environmental
noise during administration of an attention or memory subtest might invalidate that score). In such instances, the omission or substitution of a particular subtest is usually unplanned, or at least unique to the needs of a
particular examinee, or is an accommodation to the events transpiring in
a particular assessment session. However, a related issue is the attempt to
create and use intentionally abbreviated batteries or "short forms." Although
the rise in managed care added pressure for many test users to employ time-
efficient assessment methods (Sweet, Westergaard, & Moberg, 1995), the
perceived need for abbreviated versions of standard cognitive batteries
predates even the Wechsler–Bellevue scale.

The first formal intelligence scale, the Binet-Simon, was initially published in 1905, and was frequently revised and translated over the subsequent
years (Brody, 2000). Soon afterward, Doll (1917) developed an abbreviated
form of the Binet–Simon scale, noting that each of the standard versions
required "too much time for administration" (p. 197). Also, several of the
subtests eventually incorporated into the Wechsler scales originated in
the Army Alpha and Beta tests (Wechsler, 1939), yet several abbreviated
forms of the Army Alpha were proposed well before the first appearance of
the Wechsler–Bellevue Scale (Atwell & Wells, 1933; Hendrickson, 1931;
Hansen & Ream, 1921). Recent attempts to prospectively develop brief

intelligence measures (rather than retrospectively abbreviating longer measures), such as the Kaufman Brief Intelligence Test (Kaufman & Kaufman, 1990), and the Wechsler Abbreviated Scale of Intelligence (The Psychological Corporation, 1999) also follow in a long tradition (e.g., Kent, 1932, 1942).

In the decade following the 1939 publication of the Wechsler–Bellevue Scale, there was a flurry of publications on proposed abbreviations (S. Cummings, MacPhee, & Wright, 1946; Geil, 1945; Gurvitz, 1945; Hunt, Klebanoff, Mensh, & Williams, 1948; McNemar, 1950; Patterson, 1946, 1948; Rabin, 1943; Springer, 1946). This activity did not stop with the publication of the WAIS (Doppelt, 1956; Levinson, 1957; Satz & Mogel, 1963; Wolfson & Bachelis, 1960; Vincent, 1979), WAIS-R (Evans, 1985; Kaufman, Ishikuma, & Kaufman-Packer, 1991; Reynolds, Wilson, & Clark, 1983; Ryan, Lopez, & Werth, 1999; Silverstein, 1982; Thompson & LoBello, 1994; Ward, 1990) or WAIS-III (e.g., Axelrod, Ryan, & Ward, 2001; Axelrod, Dingell, Ryan, & Ward, 2000; Blyler, Gold, Iannone, & Buchanan, 2000; Pilgrim, Meyers, Bayless, & Whetstone, 1999; Ryan et al., 1999; Ryan & Ward, 1999). Most abbreviation strategies fall into two general categories, those relying on omission of items (e.g., Ryan et al., 1999; Satz & Mogel, 1963; Vincent, 1979; Wolfson & Bachelis, 1960), and those relying on the administration of selected subtests (e.g., Axelrod et al., 2000, 2001; Blyler et al., 2000; Doppelt, 1956; Ward, 1990; Rabin, 1943; Kaufman et al., 1991; Ryan & Ward, 1999; Ward, 1990). A common problem with both approaches is that although the accuracy judged on a group level may seem adequate, individual subjects can show large differences between their estimated and full-version scores (Luszki, Schultz, Laywell, & Dawes, 1970).

Although there have been some attempts to develop short forms of the Wechsler Memory Scale—Revised (WMS-R) (Axelrod, Putnam, Woodard, & Adams, 1996; Woodard & Axelrod, 1995; Woodard, 1993; van den Broek et al., 1998), there has generally been less attention to proposed short forms of the Wechsler Memory Scales (in any of its incarnations) than has been present for various versions of the Wechsler intelligence scales. We suspect, however, the relative lack of publications on short forms of the memory scales does not parallel clinical practice. In our experience, many test users administer and interpret selected subtests rather than the entire WMS-III battery. However, the dangers in drawing conclusions from isolated subtests have been well documented (Heaton, Grant, & Matthews, 1991; Palmer, Boone, Lesser, & Wohl, 1999). Thus, the approach adopted in this volume is to assess more specific memory constructs (such as the verbal versus visual memory factors). However, those more specific constructs are measured with multiple subtests to increase reliability and reduce the influence of nonmemory factors that may impact test performance on any one particular subtest.

The intent of this chapter is not to add to the short form literature (which in the case of the intelligence scales is already enormous) by evaluating, suggesting, or endorsing an intentionally abbreviated battery. However, the information provided here is intended for use in those occasions wherein administration of one or more of the component subtests proves infeasible or inappropriate (i.e., by providing test users with information about "how close" or "how different" various prorated or subtest-substitution-based estimations of the factor scores are likely to be, compared to the standard/full factor scores). By reanalyzing the standardization and clinical sample data that was collected by The Psychological Corporation in norming and validating the WAIS-III and WMS-III, we examined two approaches to estimating the joint factor scores when a subtest is missing: (a) prorating from available tests, and (b) substituting the missing test with an alternate subtest. The accuracy of these estimates was evaluated in terms of the correlations of the estimated version with the full-factor score, the magnitude of discrepancy between the estimates and the full-factor scores, and the proportion of subjects whose estimated score was within a given range of points, or confidence interval (CI) around the full-factor score. We also examined the degree to which FSIQ and GMI could be accurately estimated from those subtests within the factor scores, and the degree to which overall cognitive ability and demographic characteristics influenced the accuracy of prorated estimates of FSIQ. In addition, we examined the sensitivity and specificity of the factor scores, and various methods of estimating those factor scores, in selected subsets of the clinical sample (with demographically matched subsamples from standardization sample) for a subset of the scores. Details of these analyses are provided in the Methods section.

METHOD

Sample

Data presented within this chapter are based on reanalysis of the database for the WAIS-III and WMS-III standardization and clinical samples as described in the *WAIS-III/WMS-III Technical Manual* (The Psychological Corporation, 1997, pp. 19–46 and pp. 311–318). Results for the standardization and combined clinical samples are presented separately. The specific clinical subsamples included in the present analyses were patients with Alzheimer's disease ($n = 37$), Huntington's disease ($n = 15$), Parkinson's disease ($n = 10$), traumatic brain injury ($n = 22$), Korsokoff's syndrome ($n = 10$), and schizophrenia ($n = 42$). (Details of the clinical sample are available in Appendix E of the technical manual, The Psychological Corporation, 1997, pp. 311–318.)

Conversion of Scores to a Common Metric

Each participant's raw score on each subtest was converted to an age-corrected Scaled Score (SS; as provided in Table A.1 within the WAIS-III manual [Wechsler, 1997a; pp. 181–192] and Table D.1 and D.3 from the WMS-III manual [Wechsler, 1997b; pp. 135–147 and pp. 164–189), in which the age-group mean in the normative sample was 10 and the *SD* was 3. We then calculated the mean z-score for each subject within each of the factor score areas; for example, the mean z-score for the Verbal Comprehension factor was the average of the z-scores for the Information, Vocabulary, and Similarities subtests. We then transformed these SSs to a z-score scale, i.e. so that they were expressed on a scale with a mean of 0 and a SD of 1.

Evaluation of Estimation Accuracy

To evaluate the accuracy of prorated estimates of the factor scores, we calculated the correlations between each subtest and its parent factor score for the standardization sample, and separately for the clinical sample. For example, the relationship between the Information subtest and the Verbal Comprehension factor was examined in terms of the correlation between the Information subtest z-score and the mean z-score of all three Verbal Comprehension subtests (Information, Vocabulary, and Similarities) together. We also considered the relationship between subsets of subtests and their parent factor score (e.g., we calculated the correlation between the mean z-score of Information and Vocabulary, combined, to the mean z-score of all three Verbal Comprehension factor subtests together). These part–whole correlations were calculated (and are provided in the Results) in two ways: (a) using the Pearson r formula, and (b) using Silverstein's (1971) part–whole formula. The Silverstein formula corrects for the spuriously high correlations that may arise when a total score is correlated with a part score that is contained in the total score. The standard Pearson *r*s are also provided, however, in order to aid comparisons with those estimations of factor scores that are based on subtest substitutions (for which the Silverstein formula was not applied).

We also calculated the absolute value of the discrepancy between each subject's z-score on the individual subtests (and the mean of combinations of subtests) and the mean z-score of all tests within the parent factor. For example, the absolute value of the Information–Verbal Comprehension factor discrepancy for a subject whose Information z-score was −0.33 (i.e., one-third of a SD below the mean) and whose mean z score for the Verbal Comprehension factor was −0.10 (one-tenth of a SD below the mean) would be 0.23. Expressed on standard score scale (i.e., an IQ-deviation point scale, wherein the mean for normals is 100 and SD is 15), this result would mean that the difference between the subject's true Verbal Comprehension factor score and his or her prorated Verbal Comprehension factor score was 3.45 standard score (~"IQ") points. After the absolute value of each part–whole discrepancy was calculated for each subject, we then calculated the mean of the absolute values of the discrepancies across all subjects in the standardization sample, and again across all subjects in the clinical sample. For the purpose of presentation in the tables and in the Results section below, these results are expressed on a standard score (IQ deviation) scale having a mean of 100 and SD of 15. To illustrate, if the mean absolute discrepancy expressed in z-scores were .67 (two thirds of a SD) this would be expressed on the standard score scale as 10 and could be thought of as a difference equivalent to 10 IQ points.

Correlations and mean discrepancies provide information about how well or how poorly the prorated scores perform in predicting the full ability area scores at a group level. However, it is also important to consider how frequently individual subjects' prorated scores are substantially different from those obtained with the full forms of the ability areas. Because there is no consensus for how much of a discrepancy is "too much," we examined this issue using several different criteria. Many test users are most familiar with thinking about differences in terms of IQ scores, so we calculated the proportions of subjects in the standardization sample, and those within the clinical sample, whose part (or alternative) scores were within ± 5, 10, and 15 standard score (IQ-deviation scale) points of the parent factor score.

As it is also helpful to consider test results in terms of CIs we also examined the proportions of standardization or clinical subjects whose part or alternate scores were within the 95, 90, or 85% CIs around the corresponding full/ parent factor score. It is perhaps worth reminding readers what such CIs represent: If we gave an infinite number of subjects the WAIS-III and calculated their FSIQs, and then determined the 95% CIs for each subject, we would expect that, on average, 95 out of 100 times the range specified by the 95% CIs would encompass the subjects' "true IQ." Note also that an 85% CI is a narrower interval than a 95% interval, because it is expected that 15% of the time the "true score" will fall outside of 85% CIs around observed scores, but only 5% of "true scores" fall outside the 95% CIs.

For example, the average standard error of measurement (SE_M) in the standardization sample for Verbal Comprehension was 3.01. Thus, a subject whose Verbal Comprehension factor score was 110 would have a 95% CI of approximately 104 to 116 (observed score $\pm$ 1.96 SE_M). For the purpose of the present analyses, we determined the CIs using the average SE_Ms for each factor score across the entire age range, rather than calculating separate SE_Ms and CIs for each age group. The CIs for the analyses involving the clinical samples were based on the average SE_Ms for the cognitively normal standardization sample.

Determining the Accuracy of Prorated Estimates of Full Scale IQ and General Memory Index

The rationale for the factor score structure proposed within this volume is, in part, that it is more useful than traditional test groupings (such as in the Verbal or Performance IQs) for examining specific cognitive constructs. Nonetheless, there are occasions in which test users need to make statements about an examinee's overall cognitive abilities or overall memory skills. For such instances, the WAIS-III FSIQ, or WMS-III GMI may still be of interest to some examiners. Of the 11 subtests in the standard WAIS-III FSIQ, 7 are also part of the new factor structure (Vocabulary, Similarities, Information, Picture Completion, Digit Symbol-Coding, Block Design, and Matrix Reasoning). Per the WAIS-III manual (Wechsler, 1997a), Letter–Number Sequencing (which is administered as part of the new factor structure) may be substituted for Digit Span. However, clinicians desiring a standard FSIQ would still need to administer Arithmetic, Comprehension, and Picture Arrangement in addition to the subtests within the new factor structure. As an alternative to increasing the number of tests administered, one may ask: How accurately can the standard WAIS-III FSIQ be estimated from the WAIS-III subtests available from the new factor scores? We considered three ways of estimating FSIQ: (a) a seven-subtest version, using the seven subtests from the standard Full Scale IQ that overlap with those in the joint-factor scores; (b) an eight-subtest version, using the preceding seven subtests plus Letter-Number Sequencing; and (c) a nine-subtest version, using the preceding eight subtests plus Symbol Search. For each of these versions of estimated FSIQ, we computed the average age-corrected score across the component subtests, and converted the result to an IQ Deviation scale wherein the mean among normals is 100 and *SD* is 15. Then, we evaluated the accuracy of each of the FSIQ estimation versions for the standardization sample and for the clinical sample relative to the standard definition of FSIQ in terms of the Pearson correlation between the estimate and actual FSIQ, the mean (and SD) absolute discrepancy between the estimate and actual FSIQ, and the proportions of subjects whose estimated FSIQ was within 5, 10, or 15 points of the standard/actual FSIQ, or within the range specified by a 85, 90, or 95 % CI around their standard FSIQ. Using these same procedures, we also examined the accuracy of a two estimates of the GMI, relative to the standard GMI: (a) a three-subtest version based on the subtest scores within the joint factors that are part of the standard GMI (Logical Memory II recall, Verbal Paired Associates II recall, and Family Pictures II recall), and (b) a four-subtest version based on the preceding three scores plus the recall score from Visual Reproductions II.

Determining the Accuracy of Subtest Substitution-Based Estimates of the Factor Scores

Using the same types of analyses as used for evaluating the accuracy of prorated estimates of the factor scores, we also examined the effects of subtest substitutions (as listed in Tables 7 through 12 in the Results) for several of the factor scores above. For these analyses we used the Pearson correlation formula rather than Silverstein's (1971) part–whole correlation formula because the estimates based on subtest substitution include variance that is not part of the full factor scores that are being estimated.

Impact of Subject Characteristics on The Accuracy of Estimates

To evaluate the degree to which the accuracy of prorated scores might be lower among those examinees with very low or very high levels of cognitive functioning, we also categorized subjects based on their standard WAIS-III FSIQ scores: (a) IQ < 80 ($n = 80$ in the standardization sample, and $n = 41$ in the clinical sample), (b) IQ between 80 and 120 ($n = 856$ in the standardization sample, and $n = 95$ in the clinical sample), or (c) IQ > 120 ($n = 81$ in the standardization sample). (Only the first two groups were examined in the clinical sample because only one person in the clinical sample had a FSIQ above 120.) We then examined the accuracy of the seven-subtest prorated version of FSIQ.

Also, to determine whether the magnitude of the discrepancies might vary as a function of age, education, or gender, we calculated the correlation between each of these variables (in the standardization sample) and the magnitude of the discrepancy between each of the prorated versions of the factor scores and the standard factor score. This was done using Pearson's r for age and education, and eta-squared for gender.

Examining Sensitivity and Specificity

The ability to predict the standard versions of the factor scores is only one type of information that should be considered in evaluating the value of a nonstandard grouping of subtests. Another consideration is the utility of a particular test or group of tests for a specific purpose, such as differentiating brain-injured from nonbrain-injured examinees. For example, if the purpose of the assessment is to determine if the patient has a memory disorder, the test administrator may find it is more important to select the group of tests with the best balance of sensitivity and specificity to such disorders than it is to be able to predict the standard memory factor scores. A full exploration of this issue would go beyond the scope of the present chapter, as the specificity and sensitivity of a given grouping may depend on the specific purpose and population for which the tests are being employed. So, we only explored a few of the possible examples of sensitivity and specificity, and we present these examples for the sake of illustrating the point that clinicians need to be aware of this issue in selecting tests, in addition to considering the ability to predict standard factor scores. The examples we have chosen are the following. Starting with a dementia sample (patients from the mixed clinical sample with Alzheimer's disease ($n = 37$) or Huntington's disease ($n = 15$)), we selected a demographically matched subsample of the standardization sample ($n = 52$). We then examined the sensitivity of the Auditory and Visual Memory factor scores and their respective component scores, as well as subsets of the component scores and/or substitution of one of the component scores with an alternate subtest score. The second set of examples involved schizophrenia patients ($n = 42$) from the clinical sample, and a demographically matched subsample of the standardization sample ($n = 42$), wherein we examined the sensitivity and specificity of the Verbal Comprehension, Perceptual Organization, and Working Memory factor scores, as well as their component subtest scores, subsets of the components, and estimates of the standard factor scores based on substitution of a standard component subtest with an alternate subtest. In each case, sensitivity was defined as the proportion of examinees in the clinical subsample (dementia patients or schizophrenia patients) whose age-corrected scale score (or mean of scale scores) was ≤ 7 (which for an individual score is one *SD* below the mean); specificity was defined as the proportion of examinees in the respective demographically matched standardization subsample whose age-corrected scale score (or mean of scales scores) was > 7.

RESULTS

Organization of the Results Tables and Text

Results are presented in detail in Tables 1 through 16 (tables appear at the end of the chapter), and are organized as follows: Tables 1 through 3 provide results for the standardization sample regarding the effects of prorating the six-factor scores, FSIQ, and GMI when one or more subtest is missing, and Tables 4–6 provide the parallel results for the clinical sample. More specifically, Table 1 (standardization sample) and Table 4 (clinical sample) provide the part–whole correlations and mean (and SD) discrepancies of the prorated estimates of each factor score with the standard (full) factor score. To facilitate ease comparison with results for the subtest substitution versions of the factor scores (Tables 7 and 10, described below), Tables 1 and 4 also provide results in terms of Pearson's *r*. Table 2 (standardization sample) and Table 5 (clinical sample) provide the percent of subjects whose discrepancy between the estimate and full-factor score was within 5, 10, and 15 standard score points. Table 3 (standardization sample) and Table 6 (clinical sample) provide the percent of subjects whose discrepancy between the estimated and full-factor score was within 95, 90, and 85 CIs. Tables 7 through 12 are structured similar to Tables 1 through 6, but these present the impact of subtest substitution within the standardization and clinical samples as means to estimate the factor scores. Specifically, Table 7 (standardization sample) and Table 10 (clinical sample) provide the correlations between selected alternate versions of the factor scores (i.e., with component subtests substituted with an alternate subtest) with the standard factor scores, and also provide information about the mean absolute discrepancy between alternate versus standard factor scores. Table 8 (standardization sample) and Table 11 (clinical sample) describe the proportions of subjects whose alternate version factor scores were within 5, 10, and 15 points of the standard factor scores. Tables 9 (standardization sample) and 12 (clinical sample) list the proportions of subjects whose alternate version factor scores were within 95, 90, and 85 CIs around their standard factor score. Tables 13 (standardization sample) and 14 (clinical sample) provide results for the comparisons of the seven-subtest prorated version of FSIQ to the standard FSIQ grouped in terms of level of FSIQ. Tables 15 and 16 provide information about sensitivity and specificity of selected scores in detecting the cognitive impairment associated with dementias (Table 15) or schizophrenia (Table 16).

We anticipate that in most instances test users employing the factor structure featured in this volume will have test protocols with a maximum of one or two factor scores with missing or substituted subtests. Thus, we have organized the text summary of results in terms of the factor scores so that test users can refer directly to the summary of the results for the factor scores relevant to their particular needs. The one exception is that the results for sensitivity and specificity are summarized in a separate section, below, because only a few of the possible examples of sensitivity and specificity were examined, and those that were conducted are provided for illustrative purposes.

Summary of Results by Factor Score

Verbal Comprehension

The standard Verbal Comprehension factor is composed of three WAIS-III subtests: Information, Vocabulary, and Similarities. Each of the individual Verbal Comprehension factor subtests was strongly correlated with the full Verbal Comprehension factor score in the standardization sample (Table 1), as well as in the clinical sample (Table 4). (Part–whole correlations ranged from .85 for Similarities, to .90 for Vocabulary in each of the two samples.) Moreover, the part–whole correlation of the prorated Verbal Comprehension factor scores using any two of the three subtests with the full Verbal Comprehension factor score was .93 or above in the standardization sample, and .91 or above in the clinical sample.

The mean absolute value of the discrepancies (on an IQ-deviation standard score scale) between the individual Verbal Comprehension subtests and the full Verbal Comprehension factor score ranged from 4.52 ($SD = 3.61$) points for Vocabulary to 5.32 ($SD = 4.13$) points for Similarities in the standardization sample (Table 1), and from 5.23 ($SD = 3.99$) points for Vocabulary to 5.82 ($SD = 4.43$) points for Information in the clinical sample (Table 4). Using any two of the three subtests to prorate Verbal Comprehension, the mean discrepancy with the full Verbal Comprehension factor score was 3.02 points or less with either sample. The best case combination of any two of the three subtests was achieved with Information and Similarities (i.e., omitting Vocabulary), wherein the mean absolute value of the discrepancy with the full Verbal Comprehension factor score was only 2.42 ($SD = 1.96$) IQ-deviation score points in the standardization sample, and 2.85 ($SD = 2.14$) points in the clinical sample.

When Verbal Comprehension was estimated based on any one of the three component subtests, the prorated score was within 15 points of the standard Verbal Comprehension factor score for 97.2 % or more of subjects in the standardization sample (Table 2) and 94.2 % of subjects in the clinical sample (Table 5), but was within a 5-point range for 63.8 % or less of the standardization sample (Table 2) and 56.1 % or less of the clinical sample (Table 5). Similarly, using any one of the three component subtests, the prorated score was within the range specified by a 95 % CI around the full Verbal Comprehension factor score for only 69.1 % or less of the standardization sample (Table 3) and 60.4 % or less of the clinical sample (Table 6).

Use of any two of the three Verbal Comprehension subtests to calculate a prorated estimate of Verbal Comprehension tended to improve the percentage of subjects within any of the specified ranges, over each of the one-subtest prorated estimates. For example, when the combination of Information and Similarities was used to provide a prorated estimate of the full Verbal Comprehension factor, 100 % of subjects (in both the standardization and clinical samples) had prorated scores within a 15-point range of the full-factor score, and 89.8 % of the standardization sample (and 81.3 % of the clinical sample) had prorated scores within five points of the full Verbal Comprehension factor score (Tables 2 and 4). In terms of CIs, prorating Verbal Comprehension using Information and Similarities yielded scores that were within the 85 % CI around the full Verbal Comprehension factor score for 84.6 % of the standardization sample and 74.1 % of the clinical sample (Tables 3 and 6, respectively).

Substituting the Comprehension subtest for any one of the three standard Verbal Comprehension tests did not improve estimation of Verbal Comprehension above the estimates provided by prorating from any two of the standard Verbal Comprehension subtests. For example, in the standardization sample, the three possible combinations of Comprehension with any two of the Verbal Comprehension factor subtests yielded Pearson's r correlations with the standard Verbal Comprehension factor of $r = .96$ to .97 (Table 7); when considered in terms of Pearson's r, the two-subtest combinations were correlated with full Verbal Comprehension factor at .97 or above (Table 1). Similarly, the absolute values of the mean discrepancies with the substituted versions of Verbal Comprehension ranged from 3.30 ($SD = 2.65$) (using Information, Similarities, and Comprehension) to 3.34 (using Information, Vocabulary, and Comprehension), whereas each of the prorated versions using any two-subtest combinations of the standard Verbal Comprehension factor subtests yielded mean discrepancies of 2.75 or less (see Table 1). Also, on the individual subject level, none of the alternate versions of Verbal Comprehension incorporating Comprehension yielded higher rates of subjects within a given point range or CI than did the two-subtest prorated versions. A similar pattern was seen in the clinical sample in comparing the two-subtest prorated versions of Verbal Comprehension (Tables 4 through 6) to each of the possible three-subtest versions incorporating Comprehension in lieu of one of the standard Verbal Comprehension factor subtests (Tables 10 through 12).

Perceptual Organization

The standard Perceptual Organization factor is composed of the Block Design, Picture Completion, and Matrix Reasoning subtests from the WAIS-III. As was the case with Verbal Comprehension, the individual Perceptual Organization subtests all were reasonably strongly correlated with the full Perceptual Organization factor in the standardization sample (part–whole correlations ranged from .74 for Picture Completion to .79 for Block Design and for Matrix Reasoning) (Table 1), as well as in the clinical sample (for whom the part–whole correlations ranged from .73 for Picture Completion to .80 for Block Design) (Table 4). The part–whole correlation of any two Perceptual Organization subtests with the full Perceptual Organization factor was at least $r = .88$ in the standardization as well as in the clinical sample.

The mean absolute value of the discrepancy between the prorated Perceptual Organization factor scores based on any single Perceptual Organization subtest and the full Perceptual Organization factor score ranged from 6.60 ($SD = 4.96$) for Block Design to 7.43 ($SD = 5.71$) with Picture

Completion for the standardization sample (Table 1), and in the clinical sample ranged from 6.97 ($SD = 4.77$) for Block Design to 7.17 ($SD = 5.99$) for Matrix Reasoning (Table 4). Using any two of the three subtests to prorate Perceptual Organization, the highest mean discrepancy (worst case) was found with Block Design and Matrix Reasoning (Mean discrepancy was 4.10 [$SD = 3.11$] for the standardization sample, and 4.44 [$SD = 3.05$] for the clinical sample). The best combination among the subjects in the standardization sample was Picture Completion and Matrix Reasoning (mean discrepancy = 3.66 [$SD = 2.84$]), whereas for the clinical sample the best two-subtest combination was Block Design and Picture Completion (Mean discrepancy = 3.42 [$SD = 2.90$]).

When the Perceptual Organization factor score was estimated based on any one of the three component subtests, the prorated score was within 15 points of the standard Perceptual Organization factor score for 89.7% or more of subjects in the standardization sample (Table 2) and 90.6% of subjects in the clinical sample (Table 5), but was within a five-point range for less than half of either sample. Also, the thusly prorated score was within the range specified by a 95% CI around the full Perceptual Organization factor score for only 69.3% or less of the standardization sample (Table 3) and 77.7% or less of the clinical sample (Table 6).

As was the case with Verbal Comprehension, use of any two of the three Perceptual Organization subtests to prorate Perceptual Organization tended to improve the percentage of subjects within any given specified range over the percentage yielded by single subtest prorated versions. The best two-subtest combination for predicting full Perceptual Organization factor among subjects in the standardization sample was achieved with Picture Completion and Matrix Reasoning (e.g., 73.4% were within a five-point range of the full Perceptual Organization factor score, and 78.6% were within the range specified by a 85% CI around the full Perceptual Organization factor score). The best two-subtest combination for the clinical sample was Block Design and Picture Completion (e.g., 76.3% had a prorated Perceptual Organization within a five-point range of the full Perceptual Organization factor, and 82.0% had a prorated Perceptual Organization within the range specified by an 85% CI around the full Perceptual Organization factor).

Paralleling the findings for subtest substitution in the Verbal Comprehension factor, substituting the Object Assembly or Picture Arrangement subtests for any one of the three standard Perceptual Organization tests did not improve estimation of the full Perceptual Organization factor scores above the estimates provided by prorating from any two of the standard Perceptual

Organization measures. For example, in the standardization sample (Table 7) the three possible combinations of Object Assembly with any two of the Perceptual Organization subtests yielded Pearson correlations with the standard Perceptual Organization factor of $r = .92$ to $.94$ (Table 7), the prorated versions of Perceptual Organization based on any two of the standard Perceptual Organization subtests were correlated with full Perceptual Organization factor at .94 or above when calculated in terms of Pearson's r (Table 1). Also, the absolute values of the mean discrepancies with the substituted versions of Perceptual Organization ranged from 4.15 to 4.86 (Table 7), whereas each of the two-combination prorated versions yielded mean discrepancies of 4.10 or below (Table 1). Furthermore, none of the alternate versions of Perceptual Organization incorporating Object Assembly yielded higher rates of subjects within a given point-range or CI than did the two-subtest prorated versions. A similar pattern was generally seen in the clinical sample in comparing the two-subtest prorated versions of Perceptual Organization (Tables 4 through 6) to each of the possible three-subtest versions incorporating Object Assembly or Picture Arrangement in lieu of one of the standard Perceptual Organization measures (Tables 10 through 12).

Processing Speed

The standard Processing Speed factor is composed of only two subtests: the Digit Symbol-Coding and Symbol Search subtests of the WAIS-III. The part-whole correlation between Digit Symbol and the full Processing Speed factor was .81 in the standardization sample (Table 1) and .85 in the clinical sample (Table 4). The corresponding values for Symbol Search were .78 in the standardization sample (Table 1) and .81 in the clinical sample (Table 4). Prorating Processing Speed based on Digit Symbol alone yielded a mean discrepancy of 4.96 ($SD = 4.14$) points in the standardization sample and 5.04 ($SD = 3.48$) points in the clinical sample. Prorating Processing Speed with just Symbol Search yielded a mean discrepancy of 4.99 ($SD = 4.12$) points in the standardization sample and 4.59 ($SD = 3.30$) points for the clinical sample. Although not listed in the tables, we also reconducted these analyses with the sample restricted to patients with Huntington's disease ($n = 15$), Parkinson's disease ($n = 10$), and traumatic brain injury ($n = 22$), because the latter disorders are commonly associated with psychomotor slowing. Within this small clinical subsample, Digit Symbol and Symbol Search scores were still strongly correlated with the full Processing Speed factor, and the mean absolute value of the discrepancy between the full Processing Speed factor score and the prorated version using Digit Symbol alone was 3.97 ($SD = 2.50$) and using Symbol Search alone was 4.20 ($SD = 3.04$) points.

When Processing Speed was estimated with either one of the two component subtests, over 97% of subjects within the standardization as well as the full clinical sample had estimated Processing Speed factor scores that were within 15 points of their full Processing Speed factor score, although 60% or less of both samples had estimated Processing Speed factor scores within 5 points of their full Processing Speed factor score. Approximately three-fourths of each sample had thusly estimated Processing Speed factor scores that were within the range specified by an 85% CI around the full Processing Speed factor. Again, though not listed in the tables, we reconducted these analyses with clinical subsample restricted to patients with either Huntington's or Parkinson's disease, and found that 100% of this clinical subsample had prorated scores that were within 15-points of the full Processing Speed factor, but 68% or less had prorated scores that were within a 5-point range of the full Processing Speed factor.

No subtest substitutions were evaluated or presented in Tables 7 through 12 for estimating Processing Speed since there was no alternate subtest from the WAIS-III or WMS-III that appeared to be an appropriate measure of this ability.

Working Memory

The Working Memory factor score is composed of Spatial Span (from the WMS-III) and Letter–Number Sequencing (which is part of both the WMS-III and WAIS-III). Note that this definition of the Working Memory factor is identical to the Working Memory Index originally incorporated into the WMS-III, but is different from the Working Memory Index originally published with the WAIS-III (the latter included Arithmetic and Digit Span, as well as Letter–Number Sequencing).

The part–whole correlations of Spatial Span and Letter–Number Sequencing with the full Working Memory factor were $r = .76$ and $r = .79$, respectively, in the standardization sample (Table 1), and $r = .76$ and $r = .79$, respectively, in the clinical sample (Table 4). When each was used alone to prorate the Working Memory factor, the mean absolute discrepancy between the prorated version and the full Working Memory factor was 6.68 ($SD = 5.00$) and 6.32 ($SD = 4.89$) points, respectively, in the standardization sample (Table 1), and 7.00 ($SD = 4.72$) and 5.82 ($SD = 4.14$)

points, respectively, in the clinical sample (Table 4). Using each of the one-subtest prorated versions of Working Memory, approximately 92% of the standardization sample had an estimated score that was within 15 points of the full-factor score (Table 2), and 60–67% were within the range specified by an 85% CI around the full Working Memory factor score (Table 3), but less than 51% of the standardization sample had prorated estimates that were within 5 points of the full-factor score (Table 2). A similar pattern was observed in the clinical sample (Tables 5 and 6).

Regarding estimates of the Working Memory factor, comparison of the values in Tables 7 through 12 to the parallel portions of Tables 1 through 6 reveals that addition of an alternate subtest (Digit Span or Arithmetic), or use of the WAIS-III Working Memory Index (Letter-Number Sequencing, Arithmetic, and Digit Span) did not improve estimation of the full Working Memory factor beyond the estimates achieved by prorating from just one of the standard Working Memory factor component subtests. In the standardization sample, Letter Number Sequencing was itself correlated with the full Working Memory factor at $r = .86$ (i.e., when calculated in terms of Pearson's r), with a mean discrepancy of 6.32 ($SD = 4.89$) (Table 1). With the addition of Digit Span to Letter Number Sequencing, the Pearson correlation with the full Working Memory factor was $r = .82$, and the mean discrepancy was 7.34 ($SD = 5.37$) (Table 7). Similarly, in the clinical sample, the Pearson correlation between Letter Number Sequencing and the full Working Memory factor was $r = .90$, and when used to prorate Working Memory yielded a mean absolute discrepancy of 5.82 ($SD = 4.14$) points (Table 4). When Digit Span was added to Letter Number Sequencing in estimating the Working Memory factor among the clinical sample, the Pearson correlation with the standard Working Memory factor was reduced to $r = .83$, and the mean absolute discrepancy between the estimated Working Memory factor score and actual Working Memory factor score was increased to 7.83 ($SD = 5.86$) points.

Auditory Memory

The Auditory Memory factor is composed of the total recall scores from two WMS-III subtests: Logical Memory I (immediate recall) and II (delayed recall), and Verbal Paired Associates I (immediate recall) and II (delayed recall). The part–whole correlation of each of these four subtest scores with the full Auditory Memory factor was equal to .76 or higher in the standardization sample (Table 1), and .79 or higher in the clinical sample.

Although the best two-score-based estimates of the full Auditory Memory factor score were obtained with a combination of the immediate recall scores from the Logical Memory and Verbal Paired Associates subtests, test users may be more likely to eliminate one of the two Auditory Memory subtests completely (omitting Logical Memory I and II or Verbal Paired Associated I and II), rather than delayed recall portions from both subtests. Using only the Logical Memory I and II scores to prorate the Auditory Memory factor score, the part–whole correlation was .82 in the standardization sample (Table 1) and .85 in the clinical sample (Table 4). When the Auditory Memory factor score was estimated from the combination of Verbal Paired Associates I and II, the part–whole correlation was .83 in the standardization sample and .87 in the clinical sample.

When the Auditory Memory factor was prorated from Logical Memory I alone, the mean absolute value of the discrepancy was 7.12 ($SD = 5.25$) in the standardization sample (Table 1) and 9.00 ($SD = 6.46$) in the clinical sample (Table 4). The corresponding values when Verbal Paired Associates I by itself was 6.57 ($SD = 5.29$) in the standardization sample and 7.55 ($SD = 5.34$) in the clinical sample. When Auditory Memory was estimated based on the immediate and delayed recall scores from any one of the two Auditory Memory factor subtests (i.e., Logical Memory I and II or Verbal Paired Associates I and II), the prorated score was within 15 points of the standard Auditory Memory factor for 95.2% of the standardization sample (Table 2), and 92.6% or more of the clinical sample (Table 5). However, the thusly prorated scores were within 5 points of the full Auditory Memory factor for less than half of the standardization sample (Table 2), and when based Verbal Paired Associates I & II, less than 37% of the clinical sample (Table 5). Similar results were obtained when accuracy was judged in terms of CIs (Tables 3 and 6).

In general, estimation of Auditory Memory by substituting the WMS-III Word List Learning I (immediate recall) II (delayed recall) scores for the parallel scores from either Logical Memory or Verbal Paired Associates (see Tables 7 through 12) did not yield estimates of the full Auditory Memory factor that were much better than those obtained with Logical Memory I and II or Verbal Paired Associates I and II alone. The Pearson correlations between the Word List Learning versions of the Auditory Memory factor and the standard Auditory Memory factor were each $r = .86$ among the standardization sample and $r = .89$ to $r = .92$ in the clinical sample, whereas the prorated version of Auditory Memory based on Logical Memory I and II or Verbal Paired Associates I and II alone yielded Pearson correlations with the full Auditory Memory factor of $r = .87$ for the standardization sample and $r = .91$ for the combined clinical sample. Similar results were obtained when the Word List Learning substituted versions of Auditory Memory were considered in terms of the mean absolute discrepancies with the standard Auditory Memory factor, and the proportions of subjects whose Word List Learning versions of the Auditory Memory factor were within any given point range of the standard Auditory Memory factor.

Visual Memory

The Visual Memory factor consists of the total immediate and delayed recall scores from two visually presented WMS-III subtests: Family Pictures I (immediate recall) and II (delayed recall) and Visual Reproductions I (immediate recall) and II (delayed recall). The part–whole correlation of each of these four subtest scores with the full Visual Memory factor was equal to .66 or higher in the standardization sample (Table 1), and .72 or higher in the clinical sample (Table 4). The best two-score combination in terms of the magnitude of the part–whole correlation was achieved with the immediate recall scores from the two subtests (Family Pictures I and Visual Reproductions I); the part–whole correlation of these two subtests together with Visual Memory factor was .90 in the standardization sample (Table 1), and .89 in the clinical sample (Table 4). However, as with the Auditory Memory factor, test users may be more likely to omit one of the two component subtests altogether, rather than omitting the delayed recall portion from each of the subtests. The Family Pictures immediate and delayed recall scores together had a part–whole correlation with the full Visual Memory factor of .78 in the standardization sample, and .82 in the combined clinical sample. Visual Reproductions immediate and delayed recall scores together had a part–whole correlation with the full Visual Memory factor of .75 in the standardization sample and .97 in the combined clinical sample.

When the Visual Memory factor was prorated from the immediate recall score from any single subtest, the absolute mean discrepancies was 6.87 ($SD = 5.42$) for Family Pictures I and 8.46 ($SD = 6.48$) for Visual Reproductions I in the standardization sample (Table 1), and was 6.91 ($SD = 4.96$) for Family Pictures I and 10.52 ($SD = 7.37$) for Visual Reproductions I in the clinical sample (Table 4). When Visual Memory was estimated based on the immediate and delayed recall scores from any one of the two Visual Memory factor subtests (i.e., Family Pictures I and II or Visual Reproductions I and II), the prorated score was within 15 points of the standard Visual Memory factor for 90.6 % or more of the standardization sample with either combination (Table 2), and 83.0 % of the clinical sample with the combination of Visual Reproductions I and II, and 94.7 % of the clinical sample with the combination of Family Pictures I and II. However, with either the combination of Visual Reproductions I and II or the combination of Family Pictures I and II to estimate the Visual Memory factor, less than 47 % of the standardization sample earned prorated scores within a 5-point range of their full Visual Memory score (Table 2). In the clinical sample, prorating Visual Memory with Family Pictures I and II yielded only 45.2 % of the clinical sample whose prorated scores were within a five-point range of their full Visual Memory score, and when Visual Memory was estimated with Family Pictures I and II, only 25.5 % of the clinical sample earned prorated scores that were within the five-point range of the full Visual Memory factor score (Table 5).

Use of the Faces subtest as an alternate for Visual Reproductions (i.e., using Family Pictures and Faces together rather than Family Pictures and Visual Reproductions together), yielded worse estimates of the standard Visual Memory factor score than did Family Pictures alone. For example, when Visual Memory was estimated by substituting the Faces immediate and delayed recognition scores (Faces I and II, respectively) for the immediate and delayed recall scores from Visual Reproductions I and II, the Pearson correlation between this alternate version of Visual Memory with the standard Visual Memory factor was $r = .76$ in the standardization sample (Table 7), compared to a Pearson's r of .85 for Family Pictures I and II in the standardization sample (Table 1). In the clinical sample, the combination of Family Pictures I & II with Faces I & II had a Pearson's r correlation with the standard Visual Memory factor of $r = .84$ (Table 10) compared to a Pearson's r of .87 for Family Pictures I and II alone (Table 4). The mean (and SD) absolute discrepancy between Visual Memory—Faces and the standard Visual Memory factor was 8.19 ($SD = 6.56$) in the standardization sample (Table 7), and 6.59 ($SD- = 5.46$) in the clinical sample (Table 10). The Visual Memory—Faces score was within 15 standard score points of the standard Visual Memory factor score for 85.4 % of the standardization sample (Table 8), and 89.9 % of the clinical sample (Table 11), but was within 5 points of the standard Visual Memory factor score for only 39.7 % of the standardization sample (Table 8), and less than 49.5 % of the clinical sample (Table 11), and was within the range specified by an 85 % CI around the standard Visual Memory factor for 46.8 % of the standardization sample (Table 9) and 58.0 % of the clinical sample (Table 12).

Predicting Full Scale IQ and General Memory Index from the Subtests within the WAIS-III and WMS-III Factor Scores

Full Scale IQ

As noted above, we examined three ways of estimating FSIQ: (1) using the seven subtests in the joint-factors that overlap with the standard FSIQ (seven-subtest version); (2) using the all seven of the preceding subtests plus Letter-Number Sequencing, which in the WAIS-III manual was sanctioned as an alternate for Digit Span (eight-subtest version); and (3) using all eight of the preceding subtests plus Symbol Search (nine-subtest version). The correlation between each of these versions of estimating FSIQ with the standard FSIQ was very high (all Pearson $rs \geq .97$ in the standardization sample [Table 1] as well as in the clinical sample [Table 4]). The smallest mean discrepancies were found with the seven-subtest version; the mean (and SD) absolute value of the discrepancy for the seven-subtest version was 2.47 (1.89) points in the standardization sample, and 2.48 (1.70) points in the clinical sample, but even with the eight- and nine-subtests versions (which include one or two subtests, respectively, that are not part of the standard FSIQ), the mean absolute value of the discrepancy between each of these estimated IQs and the standard FSIQ were less than 3.86 IQ points in both samples.

The seven-subtest version of estimating FSIQ was also associated with the highest proportion of examinees whose estimated IQ was within five-points of the standard FSIQ (i.e., 89.5 % in the standardization sample [Table 2] and 91.8 % in the clinical sample [Table 5]), but all three methods yielded estimations that were within 10 points of the standard FSIQ for virtually all of the examinees (Tables 2 and 5). A similar pattern of results was observed when considered in terms of the proportions of subjects in the standardization sample or clinical sample whose estimated FSIQ was within a given range specified by 95, 90, or 85 % CIs (Tables 3 and 6, respectively); the seven-subtest version tended to yield slightly higher proportions of examinees whose estimated IQ was within a given CI size around the standard FSIQ.

General Memory Index

As noted above, we also examined two means of estimating the General Memory Index, as originally defined for the WMS-III (Wechsler, 1997b; The Psychological Corporation, 1997) based on the WMS-III subtests available within the WAIS-III and WMS-III joint factors: (a) based on the three scores within the joint-factor scores that are part of the standard GMI (three-subtest version; i.e., Logical Memory II recall, Verbal Paired Associates II recall, and Family Pictures II recall), and (b) based on the preceding three scores plus the recall score from Visual Reproductions II (four-subtest version).

Each of the two methods of estimating the GMI yielded estimates that were strongly correlated with the standard GMI, although the three-subest version was associated with a very slightly higher correlation with the standard GMI than was the four-subtest version in both the standardization sample ($r = .93$ versus .90, Table 1) and the clinical sample ($r = .96$ versus $r = .95$, Table 4). Similarly, the mean absolute discrepancy between the estimated and standard GMI was slightly smaller in the three-subtest version than in the four-subtest version (Tables 1 and 4), and the three-subtest version tended to yield a higher proportion of examinees whose estimates were within various score ranges or CI ranges was compared to the proportions associated with the four-subtest version (Tables 2, 3, 6, and 7).

Impact of the Overall Level of Cognitive Functioning on the Accuracy of Prorated Scores

As shown in Table 13, for those examinees in the standardization sample with IQs below 121, the correlations of the seven-subtest prorated estimate of FSIQ with the standard FSIQ was high ($rs \geq .93$), but among the 81 examinees in the standardization sample with IQs above 120, the part–whole correlation between the prorated estimate and standard Full Scale was only $r = .73$ (Table 13). Comparison of the magnitudes of correlations between the prorated and standard FSIQs among the subjects with midrange IQ scores to those in the low- or high-IQ range revealed no statistically significant differences, but the differences between those with IQs above 120 (part–whole $r = .73$) versus those with midrange IQs (part–whole $r = .93$) did approach significance ($z = 1.69$, $p = .091$). All (100%) of the subjects with IQs above 120 had estimated IQs that were within 10 points of their standard IQ, but only 66.4% had discrepancies that were within the range specified by a 95% CI around the standard FSIQ.

Impact of Age, Education, and Gender on the Magnitude of the Discrepancies between Prorated and Standard Index Scores within the Standardization Sample

There were no significant associations observed between age, education, or gender, and the magnitude of any of the discrepancies between the prorated versions of each factor score and the respective full-factor score (in all instances, the value of r-squared or eta-squared were .01 or below, indicating that these demographic characteristics accounted for none of the variance in the magnitude of discrepancies between prorated versus standard factor score.

Sensitivity and Specificity: Selected Examples

Table 15 provides estimates of the sensitivity and specificity of the Auditory Memory Factor, Visual Memory Factor, and each of the component subtests and prorated or alternate subtest estimates using the dementia group and matched normal comparison group described above. As shown in Table 15, for Auditory Memory, the highest proportion of subjects correctly classified was obtained with the standard forms of the Auditory Memory factor scores (91.4% correct classification, but the difference in the magnitude of these proportions compared with those obtained from prorated or alternate subtests–substitution methods was generally very small, ranging from 82.7% correctly classified (using Verbal Paired Associates II alone or in combination with Verbal Paired Associates I) to 89.5% (using Word List Learning I & II in combination with either Logical Memory I & II or Verbal Paired Associates I & II). It should be noted that the addition of the Word List Learning scores as a substitute for either Logical Memory or Verbal Paired Associates did yield a slightly higher proportion of subjects correctly classified than did either of the prorated versions of the factor scores. For example, Logical Memory I and II alone yielded a correct classification rate of 83.7%, whereas Logical Memory I and II with Word List Learning I and II yielded a correct classification rate of 89.5%.

In terms of Visual Memory (Table 15), the standard Visual Memory factor score yielded a correct classification rate of 91.4%, but this same overall correct classification rate was obtained with Family Picture II alone, and with Family Pictures I & II in combination with Faces I & II. Moreover, slightly higher correct classification rates were observed with Family Pictures I & II alone (92.3% correct) and with Family Pictures I in combination with Visual Reproductions I (93.3% correct. On the other hand, it must also be noted that every method examined yielded relatively high correct classification rates, and all were within a narrow range (i.e., from 80.8% using Visual Reproductions II alone to 93.3% using Family Pictures II in combination with Visual Reproductions II).

The specificity and sensitivity of each of the Verbal Comprehension, Perceptual Organization, and Working Memory Factors, and each of the component subtests and prorated or alternate subtest estimate versions in terms of detecting the memory impairments associated with schizophrenia are provided in Table 16. In all three cases, at least one of the alternate scores yielded a slightly higher proportion of correctly classified examinees than did the standard factor score. For example, for the standard version of the Working Memory factor (Spatial Span in combination with Letter–Number Sequencing), the overall correct classification rate was 72.6%, but Letter–Number Sequencing alone yielded a correct classification rate of 75.0%, as did Arithmetic, and these two tests together yielded a correct classification rate of 78.6%.

DISCUSSION

As illustrated by the above results, and as was expected, none of the estimated versions of the factor scores yields a perfect estimate of the parent factor score, although in a few cases the prorated or alternate versions appeared to have a slightly better balance of sensitivity and specificity to the cognitive impairment associated with select clinical conditions. The tables provided with this chapter are intended to give test users empirical guidance for evaluating the degree of error likely in prorating from a particular subset of the subtests, or using alternate subtests as substitutes for a particular missing subtest. Deciding whether a particular estimate is "close enough" for use in a particular situation is left to the reader's discretion.

Although the pattern of results were generally similar in the standardization and clinical samples, there were occasions when the accuracy of a given estimation method was partially dependent on whether that accuracy is judged in terms of the standardization sample or in terms of the clinical sample. In those settings where most examinees are likely to be from cognitively normal populations, such as vocational assessment, the results from the standardization sample should be given more weight. However, in clinical settings wherein examinees are suspected of belonging to a cognitively impaired population, the results from the clinical sample are apt to be more relevant.

Excluding obvious strategies, such as scheduling a second assessment session to administer the missing subtests, test users with missing subtest data appear to have several options when a subtest score is missing, including (a) to administer an alternate subtest to replace the missing subtest, (b) to estimate the affected factor score(s) by prorating only from the available component subtests, or (c) to disregard the entire ability area represented by the factor score with the missing subtest. In most instances, we suspect options (a) subtest substitution or (b) prorating from available subtests will be the preferable options.

Should missing subtests be substituted with alternate subtests if available, or should the factor scores be estimated based only on the available component subtests? Comparison of the results from prorated estimations (Tables 1 through 6) versus those estimations based on subtest substitution (Tables 7 through 12) indicates that prorating generally yields more accurate estimates of the factor scores than does substitution of missing subtests with alternate subtest scores. This finding is not unexpected, since 100 % of the variance in the prorated estimates of the factor scores is part of the variance within the parent factor scores. In contrast, by adding scores from alternate subtests, additional variance not present in the standard factor score is introduced into the estimate. As our selected examinations of the sensitivity and specificity of various estimates of various combinations of the subtests illustrate, the standard factor scores may not always be superior in terms of detection of cognitive impairment. The decision to prorate or use an alternate subtest as a substitute should in part be based on the purpose of estimating the factor score.

If one's goal is to estimate what a person's standard factor score would have been, then prorating from component subtests generally appears preferable to the use of alternate subtests. However, there are some conditions under which subtest substitution would be preferable to prorating the factor scores. For example, in many research settings the test user needs a stable measure of the underlying construct, but because of the nature of the comparisons being made, the test user is less dependent on knowing that the scores relate in a specifically known way to those of a published normative sample. In such instances, subtest substitution may be a better option than prorating the factor scores. The reliability of a scale or score is, in part, a function of the number of items upon which it is based (Anastasi & Urbina, 1997). Thus, it is likely that the subtest substitution/alternate versions of the factor scores are more reliable than prorated estimates, as the latter are based on fewer subtests. Also, the standard factor scores are not necessarily superior to the alternate versions as measures of the underlying cognitive construct, or as predictors of the presence of neurologic impairment, or level of everyday functioning.

As illustrated by the examples provided in Tables 15 and 16, use of an alternate subtest instead of prorating from the standard component subtests often yields slightly better results in terms of overall proportion of subjects correctly classified. There may also be practical considerations unique to a particular context or setting that may make consistent use of an alternate subtest version of a factor score preferable to the consistent use of a standard or prorated version of that score. For example, consider the Visual Memory factor score (Family Pictures and Visual Reproductions) and its alternate (Family Pictures and Faces). If one were conducting a study in a population where Visual Reproductions was inappropriate as a visual memory measure (e.g., due to its constructional demands), use of the alternate version of the Visual Memory factor score (incorporating the Faces subtest, which has no constructional requirement) may provide a more valid estimate of examinees' Visual Memory abilities than would the standard Visual Memory factor score, and may provide a more reliable estimate of Visual Memory than would an estimation of the Visual Memory factor based on Family Pictures alone. It is an empirical question whether the standard Visual Memory factor or alternate Visual Memory factor is a "better" measure, for example, of right hippocampal functioning, or as a predictor of memory-related task performance in everyday living.

Estimating the factor scores from available component subtests is generally the most appropriate option when test users wish to compare the examinee's scores relative to those of the WAIS-III and WMS-III standardization group, and in some situations (e.g., where time constraints prohibit administration of all subtests) may be more practical than subtest substitution. The current results suggest that, in most instances, test users should strive to administer at least two-subtests for each factor score, i.e., as to be expected, factor score estimates that were based on prorating from combinations of two subtests appeared consistently superior to those based upon single-component subtest scores.

How should the test(s) to be omitted be chosen? Obviously, some of these choices will be dictated by whatever factors motivate subtest omission, such as when one or more subtest is left out because of an examinee's sensory deficits or other disabilities (see Braden, Chapter 11 this volume). Also, certain factor scores may be of more relevance than others to the needs of a particular user, depending upon the purpose of the evaluation, so the relative importance of the factor scores may also dictate which subtests are considered for omission. Another obvious consideration is the time required for administration. For example, among the three subtests within the Verbal Comprehension factor (Information, Vocabulary, and Similarities), the Vocabulary subtest tends to be the most lengthy so would be an obvious candidate for omission when time is an issue. On the other hand, as has been known for nearly a century (Terman, 1918), Vocabulary tends to be among the very best predictors of general intellectual functioning (see The Psychological

Corporation, 1997, Tables A.1. through A.13., pp. 218–230). Such trade-offs need to be considered in retaining or omitting any particular subtest.

In some situations, another consideration regarding which subtest(s) to omit is the relative portability of administration materials. Many of the subtests require no materials beyond the record form (Information, Similarities, Letter–Number Sequencing, Logical Memory, and Verbal Paired Associates), or the record form plus examinee response form (Digit Symbol, Symbol Search). Thus, test users in clinical settings can readily and routinely carry the materials needed for "bedside" administration of these subtests. Other subtests, however, require the presence of a stimulus book or other materials (Vocabulary, Spatial Span, Block Design, Picture Completion, Matrix Reasoning, Family Pictures, and Visual Reproductions), so are somewhat less portable. Beyond the obvious clinical and practical considerations, we offer the following recommendations for choosing among the possible subtest combinations:

Verbal Comprehension

The results described above did not reveal large differences among the various two-subtest combinations in terms of accuracy as estimates of the full Verbal Comprehension factor, but the combination of Information and Similarities (omitting Vocabulary) tended to be among the best in terms of predicting the standard Verbal Comprehension factor score, and as noted above, saves considerable time due to the length of time needed to administer Vocabulary. Thus, all things being equal, this two-subtest combination (i.e., omission of Vocabulary) appears to be an appropriate a priori choice for a prorated version of Verbal Comprehension.

Perceptual Organization

The combination of Picture Completion and Matrix Reasoning appeared to provide the best estimate of Perceptual Organization in the standardization sample. In the clinical sample, the combination of Picture Completion and Block Design in some respects provided a slightly more accurate prediction of the standard Perceptual Organization factor score. Yet, at least within the schizophrenia subsample and the demographically matched standardization subsample, the combination of Picture Completion and Matrix Reasoning yielded the most accurate balance of sensitivity and specificity. In general, the differences between the various combinations of Perceptual Organization component subtests were not large, so the choice of which subtest to omit may be dictated by the specific needs of the testing situation.

Processing Speed

This factor contains only two subtests (Digit Symbol and Symbol Search), and each requires only a few minutes for administration. Thus, there is no clear reason to intentionally omit either subtest if an estimation of an examinee's processing speed skills is of interest. Both function about equally as single-test estimates of the full Processing Speed factor, so if one of the two subtests had to be omitted, the choice should be dictated by other factors. For example, if an examinee were known to have deficits in fine motor coordination, or known injury to his or her preferred writing hand, Digit Symbol might be a better candidate for omission given that it appears to have greater requirements for fine motor coordination.

Working Memory

As with the Processing Speed factor, the Working Memory factor consists of only two subtests, and both appear to be about equivalent as measures of the full Working Memory factor. Thus, choice of which subtest to omit, if either, is thus largely a matter of examiner preference and the demands of the particular testing situation. For example, Letter–Number Sequencing can be administered impromptu at patient bedside, without any additional stimuli or materials, whereas Spatial Span requires the presence of the WMS-III Stimulus Booklet.

Auditory Memory factor

The best two-subtest combination as an estimate of the standard Auditory Memory factor appeared to be the immediate recall scores from Logical Memory and Verbal Paired Associates. However, in most instances, test users may be more likely to omit one of the two component subtests altogether (i.e., omitting Logical Memory I and II, or omitting Verbal Paired Associates I and II), rather than omitting the delayed recall scores from both. In fact, despite the apparently good performance of the estimates based on immediate recall scores, we would encourage test users to always include delayed recall scores. In nonmemory-impaired populations such as the standardization sample, and to some degree even the mixed clinical sample, a very high correlation between the immediate and delayed recall scores is seen due to common method variance. Thus, the immediate and delayed recall scores provide largely redundant information in memory-intact individuals. Although this was not confirmed in the present (small) clinical sample (see Heaton, Taylor, and Manley, this volume), we suspect that such redundancy may not be present within the larger population of amnesic or otherwise memory-impaired examinees, and there could be considerable value garnered from comparing immediate to delayed recall within such memory-impaired examinees. For example, one of the hallmarks of Alzheimer's disease is rapid forgetting, which cannot be fully documented in the absence of a delayed recall trial (Cummings & Benson, 1992; Tröster et al., 1993). Thus, if the examinee's memory is in question, the delayed recall score from at least one (and preferably both) measures should be included. In such instances, it is also important to distinguish retrieval from storage deficits. Thus, even though the recognition scores are not part of the factor scores, administration of the recognition components is recommended for any examinees performing poorly on the free recall sections.

Visual Memory factor

As with Auditory Memory, the best two-score combination for estimating the full Visual Memory factor appeared to be the immediate recall scores from each subtest (Family Pictures and Visual Reproductions). However, the same caveats about the potential value of delayed recall and recognition scores in memory-impaired individuals apply here. The alternate Visual Memory factor (substituting the Faces subtest for Visual Reproductions) did not provide as accurate an estimate of the standard Visual Memory factor as did Family Pictures alone. However, if one's goal is to estimate examinees' visual memory abilities (rather than just to estimate the standard Visual Memory factor score), the alternate version of the Visual Memory factor may be a more appropriate choice than is prorating Visual Memory based on Family Pictures alone. Our exploration of the sensitivity and specificity of the various combinations of the visual memory tests in detecting impairment associated with dementias revealed no difference in the overall correct classification rate associated when Visual Memory was defined by the scores from Family Pictures I and II with Faces I and II, versus when Family

Pictures I and II was combined with Visual Reproductions I and II. Further empirical comparison of the relative sensitivity and specificity of the standard Visual Memory factor versus this alternate Visual Memory definition to relevant external criteria, such as right hippocampal lesions, or memory failures in everyday living is needed in order to definitely state which version provides the "best" measure of visual memory. To our knowledge, that study has not yet been conducted.

Full Scale IQ and General Memory Index

In general, the most accurate prediction of the standard Full Scale IQ was achieved with the seven-subtest version (i.e., by limiting the subtests in the prorated estimate to those seven subtests in the factor scores which were part of the standardized FSIQ) (Vocabulary, Similarities, Information, Picture Completion, Digit Symbol-Coding, Block Design, and Matrix Reasoning). Thus, when one's goal is to estimate what an individual examinee's FSIQ would have been with the standard 11 subtests, addition of Letter–Number Sequencing and Symbol Search to the prorated estimate does not appear warranted. (As discussed below, such estimates may be problematic when used in populations where high IQs are expected.) Similarly, the best estimate of the standard GMI was achieved with the three-subtest estimate (Logical Memory II, Verbal Paired Associates II, and Family Pictures II) (i.e., addition of the Visual Reproductions II recall score did aid prediction of the standard GMI). But again, when one's primary goal is something other than estimation of the standard forms of FSIQ and/or GMI, other considerations (such as sensitivity to cognitive impairment) may yield addition of these alternate subtests to be preferable to the estimates based solely on prorating from the available standard component subtests.

Caveats and Limitations

Several caveats and limitations to the above analyses and recommendations should be noted.

High and Low-Functioning Subjects

As illustrated by our reanalysis of the discrepancies between the prorated FSIQ versus standard IQ score in terms of IQ groups, the accuracy of the prorated versions tended to be best among those subjects with FSIQs below 121. Prorated versions must be used more cautiously, if at all, with individuals known to have high cognitive functioning, or in settings where there is a high likelihood that examinees are in such an extreme ranges. For example, prorated scores would be less useful for determining the IQs of individuals being selected for a "cognitively gifted" program.

Clinical Sample

The WAIS-III and WMS-III standardization sample, used for the analyses within this chapter, was carefully recruited and developed by the test publisher to be large and demographically representative of the general adult population of the United States. However, the clinical sample is relatively small in terms of total size ($n = 136$), particularly within the specific diagnostic conditions (ns ranged from 10 to 42). Because of the quite small sample sizes within diagnostic conditions, we were unable to examine the likely possibility that the accuracy of estimated versions of the factor scores differs depending upon the specific diagnoses. Also, only six diagnostic conditions were considered. Suffice to say, those test users employing the WAIS-III and WMS-III in clinical settings will evaluate examinees from other diagnostic categories that were not represented in the combined clinical sample.

Effects of Reduced Battery Length and Order Effects

The subjects in the WAIS-III and WMS-III standardization and clinical samples completed all the subtests necessary for calculating the six factor scores. There is an implicit assumption in our analyses that the values for prorated versions of the factor scores are the same values that would have been obtained had each subject only completed those selected subtests. This is not necessarily a fully valid assumption. Thompson and colleagues (Thompson, Howard, & Anderson, 1986; Thompson & Plumridge, 1999) found that examinees' scores on a two-subtest WAIS-R short form tended to be elevated relative to the scores that were obtained when those subtests were embedded within the full WAIS-R battery. These investigators suggested that the elevation of scores on the two-subtest short-form may reflect the impact of declining motivation and attention that might occur when subjects are assessed over a lengthier battery. However, this elevation was mostly present only with the two-subtest short forms, not with a four-subtest short form. So, in the context of a larger battery, omission of a few subtests appears unlikely to have a large impact on the level of examinee fatigue or motivation. Consistent with the latter conclusion, Tulsky and Zhu (2000) found no impact of test battery length on Letter Number Sequencing scores (e.g., when the subtest was administered after 5 hours of testing versus when administered after only 90 minutes of testing).

It is also possible that performance of some subtests impacts the examinees' scores on other subtests. For example, performing the Digit Span subtest could conceivably prepare subjects for later performance on the Letter–Number Sequencing task. In that case, omission of Digit Span might decrease scores obtained on the Letter–Number Sequencing subtest. This possibility was partially addressed in another study by Zhu and Tulsky (2000) in which they examined test-order effects in the WMS-III and WAIS-III standardization sample. In this sample, the order of administration was counterbalanced (i.e., 684 subjects completed the WMS-III then the WAIS-III, and 562 subjects completed the WAIS-III then the WMS-III). Yet, in comparing the results from these two subgroups, Zhu and Tulksy (2000) found few significant test-order effects, and even those few were associated with small effect sizes.

CONCLUSIONS

Despite the above limitations, the current results provide test users with a general basis for judging the likelihood of significant error in estimating the factor scores with any particular prorated or subtest substitution method, as well as for estimating FSIQ and the GMI from those subtests available within the six factors featured here. Although none of the estimation procedures yields a perfect prediction of the standard factor scores, FSIQ, or GMI, these standardly defined scores are not themselves perfect estimates of the respective cognitive constructs that they are intended to measure. It is left to the test user to decide how much error in estimating the standard factor score values is acceptable, but the general answers to the questions posed in the Introduction to this chapter appear to be the following: (a) the factor scores can be reasonably estimated from prorated versions; (b) choice of prorating versus subtests substitution depends on the purpose of the assessment (prorating is preferred when one wishes to estimate what the examinee's factor score would have been if all subtests were available, substitution may be preferred when the reliability of the score is more important than the ability to relate the scores specifically to those of the standardization sample, and/or if the substituted version has been shown more sensitive and specific in detecting a targeted condition); and (c) the FSIQ and GMI can be estimated with reasonable accuracy using the relevant scores from subtests within the WAIS-III and WMS-III joint factor structure.

REFERENCES

American Educational Research Association (1999). *Standards for educational and psychological testing*. Washington, DC: Author.

Anastasi, A., & Urbina, S. (1997). *Psychological testing (7th ed.)*. Upper Saddle River, NJ: Prentice Hall.

Atwell, C. R., & Wells, F. L. (1933). Army Alpha revised— short form. *Personnel Journal, 12*, 160–165.

Axelrod, B. N. (2001). Administration duration for the Wechsler Adult Intelligence Scale— III and Wechsler Memory Scale— III. *Archives of Clinical Neuropsychology, 16*, 293–301.

Axelrod, B. N., Dingell, J. D., Ryan, J. J., & Ward, L. C. (2000). Estimation of the Wechsler Adult Intelligence Scale— III Index scores with the 7–subtest short form in a clinical sample. *Assessment, 7*, 157–161.

Axelrod, B. N., Putnam, S. H., Woodard, J. L., & Adams, K. M. (1996). Cross-validation of predicted Wechsler Memory Scale—Revised scores. *Psychological Assessment, 8*, 73–75.

Axelrod, B. N., Ryan, J. J., & Ward, L. C. (2001). Evaluation of seven-subtest short forms of the Wechsler Adult Intelligence Scale-III in a referred sample. *Archives of Clinical Neuropsychology, 16*, 1–8.

Blyler, C. R., Gold, J. M., Iannone, V. N., & Buchanan, R. W. (2000). Short form of the WAIS-III for use with patients with schizophrenia. *Schizophrenia Research, 46*, 209–215.

Brody, N. (2000). History of theories and measurements of intelligence. In R. J. Sternberg (Ed.), *Handbook of intelligence*. New York: Cambridge University Press.

Cummings, J. L., & Benson, D. F. (1992). *Dementia: A clinical approach (2nd ed.)*. Boston: Butterworth-Heinemann.

Cummings, S. B. Jr., Macphee, H. M., & Wright, H. F. (1946). A rapid method of estimating the IQ's of subnormal white adults. *Journal of Psychology, 21*, 81–89.

Doll, E. A. (1917). A brief Binet-Simon scale. *Psychological Clinics, 11*, 197–211, 254, 261.

Doppelt, J. E. (1956). Estimating the full scale score on the Wechsler Adult Intelligence scale from scores on four subtests. *Journal of Clinical Psychology, 20*, 63–66.

Evans, R. G. (1985). Accuracy of the Satz-Mogel procedure in estimating WAIS-R IQs that are in the normal range. *Journal of Clinical Psychology, 41*, 100–103.

Geil, G. A. (1945). A clinically useful abbreviated Wechsler–Bellevue Scale. *Journal of Psychology, 20*, 101–108.

Gurvitz, M. S. (1945). An alternate short form of the Wechsler–Bellevue Test. *American Journal of Orthopsychiatry, 15*, 727–733.

Hansen, C. F., & Ream, M. J. (1921). The predictive value of short intelligence tests. *Journal of Applied Psychology, 5*, 184–186.

Heaton, R. K, Grant, I., & Matthews, C. G. (1991). *Comprehensive norms for expanded Halstead-Reitan battery: Demographic corrections, research findings, and clinical applications*. Odessa, FL: Psychological Assessment Resources, Inc.

Hendrickson, G. (1931). An abbreviation of Army Alpha. *School and Society, 33*, 467–468.

Hunt, W. A., Klebanoff, S. G., Mensh, I. N., & Williams, M. (1948). The validity of some abbreviated individual intelligence scales. *Journal of Consulting Psychology, 12,* 48–52.

Kaufman, A. S., Ishikuma, T., & Kaufman-Packer, J. L. (1991). Amazingly short forms of the WAIS-R. *Journal of Psychoeducational Assessment, 9,* 4–15.

Kaufman, A. S., & Kaufman, N. L. (1990). *Kaufman Brief Intelligence Test (K-BIT). Manual.* Circle Pines, MN: American Guidance Service.

Kent, G. H. (1932). Oral test for emergency use in clinics. *Mental Measurements Monographs,* (Serial No. 9).

Kent, G. H. (1942). Emergency battery of one-minute tests. *The Journal of Psychology, 13,* 141–161.

Levinson, B. M. (1957). Use of the abbreviated WAIS with homeless men. *Psychological Reports, 3,* 287.

Luszki, M. B., Schultz, W., Laywell, H. R., & Dawes, R. M. (1970). Long search for a short WAIS: Stop looking. *Journal of Consulting and Clinical Psychology, 34,* 425–431.

McNemar, Q. (1950). On abbreviated Wechsler–Bellevue scales. *Journal of Consulting Psychology, 14,* 79–81.

Palmer, B. W., Boone, K. B., Lesser, I. M., & Wohl, M. A. (1998). Base rates of "impaired" neuropsychological test performance among healthy older adults. *Archives of Clinical Neuropsychology, 13,* 503–511.

Patterson, C. H. (1946). A comparison of various "short forms" of the Wechsler–Bellevue scale. *Journal of Consulting Psychology, 10,* 260–267.

Patterson, C. H. (1948). A further study of two short forms of the Wechsler–Bellevue Scale. *Journal of Consulting Psychology, 12,* 147–152.

Pilgrim, B. M., Meyers, J. E., Bayless, J., & Whetstone, M. M. (1999). Validity of the Ward seven-subtest WAIS-III short form in a neuropsychological population. *Applied Neuropsychology, 6,* 243–246.

The Psychological Corporation (1997). *WAIS-III/WMS-III technical manual.* San Antonio, TX: Author.

The Psychological Corporation (1999). *Wechsler Abbreviated Scale of Intelligence (WASI).* San Antonio, TX: Author.

Rabin, A. I. (1943). A short form of the Wechsler-Bellevue test. *Journal of Applied Psychology, 27,* 320–324.

Reynolds, C. R., Willson, V. L., & Clark, P. L. (1983). A four-test short form of the WAIS-R for clinical screening. *International Journal of Clinical Neuropsychology, 5,* 111–116.

Ryan, J. J., Lopez, S. J., & Werth, T. R. (1998). Administration time estimated for WAIS-III subtests, scales, and short forms in a clinical sample. *Journal of Psychoeducational Assessment, 16*(4), 315–323.

Ryan, J. J., Lopez, S. J., & Werth, T. R. (1999). Development and preliminary validation of a Satz-Mogel short form of the WAIS-III in a sample of persons with substance abuse disorders. *International Journal of Neuroscience, 98,* 131–140.

Ryan, J. J., & Ward, L. C. (1999). Validity, reliability, and standard errors of measurement for two seven-subtest forms of the Wechsler Adult Intelligence Scale—III. *Psychological Assessment, 11,* 207–211.

Ryan, J. J., Weilage, M. E., & Spaulding, W. D. (1999). Accuracy of the seven subtest WAIS-R short form in chronic schizophrenia. *Schizophrenia Research, 39,* 79–83.

Satz, P., & Mogel, S. (1963). An abbreviation of the WAIS for clinical use. *Journal of Clinical Psychology, 19,* 298–300.

Silverstein, A.B. (1971). A corrected formula for assessing the validity of WAIS, WISC, and WPPSI short forms. *Journal of Clinical Psychology, 27*, 212–213

Silverstein, A. B. (1982). Two- and four-subtest short forms of the Wechsler Adult Intelligence Scale—Revised. *Journal of Consulting and Clinical Psychology, 50*, 415–418.

Springer, N. N. (1946). A short form of the Wechsler-Bellevue Intelligence Test as applied to naval personnel. *American Journal of Orthopsychiatry, 16*, 341–344.

Sweet, J. J., Westergaard, C. K., & Moberg, P. J. (1995). Managed care experiences of clinical neuropsychologists. *The Clinical Neuropsychologist, 9*, 214–218.

Terman, L. M. (1918). The vocabulary test as a measure of intelligence. *Journal of Educational Psychology, 9*(8), 452–466.

Thompson, A. R., Howard, D., & Anderson, J. (1986). 2–subtest and 4–subtest short forms of the WAIS-R—Validity in a psychiatric sample. *Canadian Journal of Behavioural Science, 18*(3), 287–293.

Thompson, A., & Plumridge, S. (1999). Two- and four-subtest short forms of the WAIS-R: A comparative validity study with a normal sample. *Psychological Reports, 84*(2), 371–380.

Thompson, A. P., & LoBello, S. G. (1994). Reliable and abnormal scaled score range estimates for common Wechsler selected subtest short forms. *Journal of Psychological Assessment, 12*, 264–269.

Tröster, A. I., Butters, N., Salmon, D. P., Cullum, C. M., Jacobs, D., Brandt, J., & White, R. F. (1993). The diagnostic utility of savings scores: Differentiating Alzheimer's and Huntington's diseases with logical memory and visual reproduction tests. *Journal of Clinical and Experimental Neuropsychology, 15*, 773–788.

Tulsky, D., & Zhu, J. (2000). Could test length or order affect scores on Letter Number Sequencing of the WAIS-III and WMS-III? Ruling out effects of fatigue. *The Clinical Neuropsychologist, 14*, 474–478.

van den Broek, A., Golden, C. J., Goldstein, D., Loonstra, A., & Ghinglia, K. (1998). Short forms of the Wechsler Memory Scale—Revised: Cross-validation and derivation of a two-subtest form. *Psychological Assessment, 10*, 38–40.

Vincent, K. R. (1979). The modified WAIS: An alternative to short forms. *Journal of Clinical Psychology, 35*, 624–625.

Ward, L. C. (1990). Prediction of verbal, performance, and full scale IQs from seven subtests of the WAIS-R. *Journal of Clinical Psychology, 46*, 436–440.

Wechsler, D. (1939). *The measurement of adult intelligence*. Baltimore: Wilkins & Wilkins Company.

Wechsler, D. (1997a). *Wechsler Adult Intelligence Scale—Third Edition*. San Antonio, TX: The Psychological Corporation.

Wechsler, D. (1997b). *Wechsler Memory Scale—Third Edition (WMS-III)*. San Antonio, TX: The Psychological Corporation.

Wolfson, W., & Bachelis, L. (1960). An abbreviated form of the WAIS verbal scale. *Journal of Clinical Psychology, 16*, 421.

Woodard, J. L. (1993). A prorating system for the Wechsler Memory Scale—Revised. *The Clinical Neuropsychologist, 7*, 219–223.

Woodard, J. L., & Axelrod, B. N. (1995). Parsimonious prediction of Wechsler Memory Scale—Revised memory indices. *Psychological Assessment, 7*, 445–449.

Zhu, J., & Tulsky, D. (2000). Co-norming the WAIS-III and WMS-III: Is there a test-order effect on IQ and memory scores? *The Clinical Neuropsychologist, 14*, 461–467.

TABLE 1   Prorated Estimation of Factor Scores, Full Scale IQ, and General Memory Index: Part–Whole Correlations and Part–Whole Discrepancies for Standardization Sample[a]

Factor or summary score subtest or subtest combination	Pearson's r	Silverstein's part–whole r	Absolute mean discrepancy (SD) between estimated and actual factor score
Verbal Comprehension			
Information	0.90	0.88	5.21 (4.01)
Vocabulary	0.93	0.90	4.52 (3.61)
Similarities	0.90	0.85	5.32 (4.13)
Information & Vocabulary	0.97	0.94	2.75 (2.19)
Information & Similarities	0.98	0.93	2.42 (1.96)
Vocabulary & Similarities	0.97	0.93	2.72 (2.09)
Perceptual Organization			
Block Design	0.85	0.79	6.60 (4.96)
Picture Completion	0.81	0.74	7.43 (5.71)
Matrix Reasoning	0.83	0.79	6.91 (5.20)
Block Design & Picture Completion	0.95	0.88	3.82 (2.87)
Block Design & Matrix Reasoning	0.94	0.89	4.10 (3.11)
Picture Completion & Matrix Reasoning	0.95	0.89	3.66 (2.84)
Processing Speed			
Digit Symbol	0.91	0.81	4.96 (4.14)
Symbol Search	0.91	0.78	4.99 (4.12)
Working Memory			
Spatial Span	0.85	0.76	6.68 (5.00)
Letter–Number Sequencing	0.86	0.79	6.32 (4.89)
Auditory Memory			
Logical Memory I	0.83	0.79	7.12 (5.25)
Logical Memory II	0.85	0.78	6.62 (4.98)
Verbal Paired Associates I	0.84	0.82	6.57 (5.29)
Verbal Paired Associates II	0.81	0.76	7.43 (5.37)
Logical Memory I & Logical Memory II	0.87	0.82	6.20 (4.48)
Verbal Paired Associates I & Verbal Paired Associates II	0.87	0.83	6.09 (4.61)
Logical Memory I & Verbal Paired Associates I	0.97	0.94	2.90 (2.29)
Visual Memory			
Family Pictures Recall I	0.83	0.77	6.87 (5.42)
Family Pictures Recall II	0.84	0.79	6.76 (5.06)

(*continues*)

TABLE 1 (*continued*)

Factor or summary score subtest or subtest combination	Pearson's r	Silverstein's part–whole r	Absolute mean discrepancy (SD) between estimated and actual factor score
Visual Reproductions Recall I	0.75	0.68	8.46 (6.48)
Visual Reproductions Recall II	0.73	0.66	8.72 (6.68)
Family Pictures Recall I & Family Pictures Recall II	0.85	0.78	6.47 (4.89)
Visual Reproductions Recall I & Visual Reproductions Recall II	0.82	0.75	7.13 (5.44)
Family Pictures Recall I & Visual Reproductions Recall I	0.96	0.90	3.55 (2.64)
Full Scale IQ			
7-subtests version[b]	0.98	0.96	2.47 (1.89)
8-subtest version[b]	0.98	n/a[c]	2.64 (2.05)
9-subtests version[b]	0.97	n/a[c]	3.04 (2.31)
General Memory Index			
3-subtest version[b]	0.93	0.90	4.45 (3.35)
4-subtest version[b]	0.90	n/a[c]	5.31 (4.04)

[a]Correlations represent the association between the individual subtests (or mean of combinations of subtests) and their parent factor score, Full Scale IQ, or General Memory Index score within the WAIS III–WMS-III standardization sample, calculated with Pearson's r as well as Silverstein's (1971) part–whole correlation formulae. Mean (and SD) discrepancies are expressed in standard score (~IQ scale) points. WAIS-III and WMS-III Standardization Data, copyright © 2002 by the Psychological Corporation, a Harcourt Assessment Company. All rights reserved.

[b]See text for the component scores included in this estimate.

[c]Silverstein's (1971) formula for part–whole correlations was not applied because the estimated score includes a subtest score that is not part of the score being estimated.

TABLE 2   Prorated Estimation of Factor Scores, Full Scale IQ and General Memory Index: Percent of Standardization Sample within 5, 10, and 15 Standard Score Points[a]

Factor or summary score subtest or subtest combination	Within 5 points (%)	Within 10 points (%)	Within 15 points (%)
Verbal Comprehension			
Information	56.9	86.8	97.6
Vocabulary	63.8	91.4	98.8
Similarities	54.7	86.9	97.2
Information & Vocabulary	85.5	99.2	100.0
Information & Similarities	89.8	99.7	100.0
Vocabulary & Similarities	81.8	99.6	100.0
Perceptual Organization			
Block Design	46.0	76.0	92.8
Picture Completion	40.3	71.1	89.7
Matrix Reasoning	43.6	73.0	91.6
Block Design & Picture Completion	71.6	96.3	99.8
Block Design & Matrix Reasoning	67.6	95.1	99.4
Picture Completion & Matrix Reasoning	73.4	96.4	99.9
Processing Speed			
Digit Symbol	59.6	88.6	97.5
Symbol Search	59.4	88.7	97.4
Working Memory			
Spatial Span	42.0	78.3	92.8
Letter–Number Sequencing	50.7	79.6	93.4
Auditory Memory			
Logical Memory I	42.6	73.4	91.8
Logical Memory II	44.8	78.5	92.4
Verbal Paired Associates I	48.1	78.9	91.8
Verbal Paired Associates II	40.0	72.2	89.8
Logical Memory I & Logical Memory II	46.3	82.5	95.2
Verbal Paired Associates I & Verbal Paired Associates II	48.2	81.2	95.2
Logical Memory I & Verbal Paired Associates I	83.9	99.1	99.8
Visual Memory			
Family Pictures Recall I	45.3	75.0	90.8
Family Pictures Recall II	43.2	75.8	92.8
Visual Reproductions Recall I	37.3	67.0	83.2
Visual Reproductions Recall II	37.8	65.7	82.0
Family Pictures Recall I & Family Pictures Recall II	46.5	77.9	94.5

(*continues*)

TABLE 2 (*continued*)

Factor or summary score subtest or subtest combination	Within 5 points (%)	Within 10 points (%)	Within 15 points (%)
Visual Reproductions Recall I & Visual Reproductions Recall II	43.0	73.5	90.6
Family Pictures Recall I & Visual Reproductions Recall I	74.4	97.6	99.9
Full Scale IQ			
7-subtest version[b]	89.5	99.8	100.0
8-subtest version[b]	86.1	99.5	100.0
9-subtest version[b]	80.8	99.0	100.0
General Memory Index			
3-subtest version[b]	62.6	92.4	99.5
4-subtest version[b]	54.0	86.8	97.4

[a]Numerical values represent the proportions of subjects in the WAIS-III–WMS-III standardization sample whose prorated scores were within 5, 10, or 15 points (on an IQ-deviation score scale) of their respective full-factor score, Full Scale IQ, or General Memory Index score. WAIS-III and WMS-III Standardization Data, copyright © 2002 by the Psychological Corporation, a Harcourt Assessment Company. All rights reserved.

[b]See text for the component scores included in this estimate.

TABLE 3   Prorated Estimation of Factor Scores, Full Scale IQ, and General Memory Index:
Percent of Standardization Sample within 95, 90, and 85 % Confidence Intervals[a]

Factor or Summary Score Subtest or Subtest Combination	Within 95 % CI (%)	Within 90 % CI (%)	Within 85 % CI (%)
Verbal Comprehension			
Information	63.3	55.9	50.1
Vocabulary	69.1	61.8	56.6
Similarities	60.5	58.4	47.7
Information & Vocabulary	91.3	85.0	79.1
Information & Similarities	93.6	89.1	84.6
Vocabulary & Similarities	91.4	86.0	79.7
Perceptual Organization			
Block Design	63.9	56.5	50.6
Picture Completion	69.3	63.8	59.7
Matrix Reasoning	67.9	62.9	58.9
Block Design & Picture Completion	88.6	82.1	76.4
Block Design & Matrix Reasoning	86.4	78.9	72.4
Picture Completion & Matrix Reasoning	90.7	83.7	78.6
Processing Speed			
Digit Symbol	89.2	82.0	77.2
Symbol Search	89.3	82.2	77.0
Working Memory			
Spatial Span	82.2	73.4	65.4
Letter–Number Sequencing	81.9	73.6	68.5
Auditory Memory			
Logical Memory I	52.8	46.7	43.0
Logical Memory II	58.8	49.9	44.5
Verbal Paired Associates I	60.4	52.9	46.1
Verbal Paired Associates II	53.8	44.9	37.8
Logical Memory I & Logical Memory II	60.5	52.4	45.7
Verbal Paired Associates I & Verbal Paired Associates II	62.5	53.5	48.9
Logical Memory I & Verbal Paired Associates I	94.1	88.3	82.7
Visual Memory			
Family Pictures Recall I	67.2	60.5	54.9
Family Pictures Recall II	67.6	59.3	53.1
Visual Reproductions Recall I	58.4	51.5	45.9
Visual Reproductions Recall II	56.9	48.6	44.6
Family Pictures Recall I & Family Pictures Recall II	69.2	61.8	56.3

(*continues*)

TABLE 3   (*continued*)

Factor or Summary Score Subtest or Subtest Combination	Within 95 % CI (%)	Within 90 % CI (%)	Within 85 % CI (%)
Visual Reproductions Recall I & Visual Reproductions Recall II	66.2	57.1	51.2
Family Pictures Recall I & Visual Reproductions Recall I	93.9	89.4	83.4
Full Scale IQ			
7-subtest version[b]	83.3	74.9	68.7
8-subtest version[b]	80.1	72.4	66.3
9-subtest version[b]	73.7	66.4	59.4
General Memory Index			
3-subtest version[b]	88.6	81.6	76.5
4-subtest version[b]	80.5	72.1	65.9

[a]Numerical values represent the proportions of subjects in the WAIS–III/WMS–III standardization sample whose prorated scores were within the range specified by the 95 %, 90 %, or 85 % confidence interval (CI) around their respective full-factor score, Full Scale IQ, or General Memory Index score. WAIS–III and WMS–III Standardization Data, copyright © 2002 by the Psychological Corporation, a Harcourt Assessment Company. All rights reserved.

[b]See text for the component scores included in this estimate.

TABLE 4   Prorated Estimation of Factor Scores, Full Scale IQ, and General Memory Index: Part–whole Correlations and Part–whole Discrepancies for Clinical Sample[a]

Factor or summary score subtest or subtest combination	Pearson's r	Silverstein's Part-Whole r	Absolute Mean Discrepancy (SD) between estimated and actual factor score
Verbal Comprehension			
Information	0.86	0.87	5.82 (4.43)
Vocabulary	0.88	0.90	5.23 (3.99)
Similarities	0.86	0.85	5.52 (4.39)
Information & Vocabulary	0.96	0.93	2.91 (2.24)
Information & Similarities	0.96	0.91	2.85 (2.14)
Vocabulary & Similarities	0.96	0.91	3.02 (2.36)
Perceptual Organization			
Block Design	0.86	0.80	6.97 (4.77)
Picture Completion	0.79	0.73	7.06 (5.76)
Matrix Reasoning	0.82	0.78	7.17 (5.99)
Block Design & Picture Completion	0.96	0.88	3.42 (2.90)
Block Design & Matrix Reasoning	0.94	0.89	4.44 (3.05)
Picture Completion & Matrix Reasoning	0.94	0.89	3.81 (2.98)
Processing Speed			
Digit Symbol	0.93	0.85	5.04 (3.48)
Symbol Search	0.94	0.81	4.59 (3.30)
Working Memory			
Spatial Span	0.88	0.76	7.00 (4.72)
Letter-Number Sequencing	0.90	0.79	5.82 (4.14)
Auditory Memory			
Logical Memory I	0.83	0.79	9.00 (6.46)
Logical Memory II	0.89	0.82	6.81 (5.08)
Verbal Paired Associates I	0.88	0.86	7.55 (5.34)
Verbal Paired Associates II	0.88	0.83	7.94 (5.47)
Logical Memory I & Logical Memory II	0.91	0.85	5.87 (4.98)
Verbal Paired Associates I & Verbal Paired Associates II	0.91	0.87	7.01 (4.52)
Logical Memory I & Verbal Paired Associates I	0.97	0.94	3.88 (3.01)
Visual Memory			
Family Pictures Recall I	0.84	0.79	6.91 (4.96)
Family Pictures Recall II	0.84	0.79	7.02 (4.86)
Visual Reproductions Recall I	0.80	0.72	10.52 (7.37)
Visual Reproductions Recall II	0.82	0.75	10.89 (7.04)

(*continues*)

TABLE 4.   (*continued*)

Factor or summary score subtest or subtest combination	Pearson's r	Silverstein's Part-Whole r	Absolute Mean Discrepancy (SD) between estimated and actual factor score
Family Pictures Recall I			
& Family Pictures Recall II	0.87	0.82	6.44 (4.37)
Visual Reproductions Recall I			
& Visual Reproductions Recall II	0.87	0.79	9.04 (5.34)
Family Pictures Recall I			
& Visual Reproductions Recall I	0.96	0.89	3.57 (2.78)
Full Scale IQ			
7-subtest version[b]	0.97	0.95	2.48 (1.70)
8-subtest version[b]	0.98	n/a[c]	2.74 (2.08)
9-subtest version[b]	0.97	n/a[c]	3.85 (2.66)
General Memory Index			
3-subtest version[b]	0.96	0.92	3.76 (2.92)
4-subtest version[b]	0.95	n/a[c]	4.35 (3.17)

[a]Correlations represent the association between the individual subtests (or mean of combinations of subtests) and their parent factor score, Full Scale IQ, or General Memory Index score within the WAIS-III–WMS-III standardization sample, calculated with Pearson's r as well as Silverstein's (1971) part–whole correlation formulae. Mean (and SD) discrepancies are expressed in standard score (~IQ scale) points. WAIS-III and WMS-III Standardization Data, copyright © 2002 by the Psychological Corporation, a Harcourt Assessment Company. All rights reserved.

[b]See text for the component scores included in this estimate.

[c]Silverstein's (1971) formula for part–whole correlations was not applied because the estimated score includes a subtest score that is not part of the score being estimated.

TABLE 5   Prorated Estimation of Factor Scores, Full Scale IQ, and General Memory Index: Percent of Clinical Sample within 5, 10, and 15 Standard Score Points[a]

Factor or summary score subtest or subtest combination	Within 5 points (%)	Within 10 points (%)	Within 15 points (%)
Verbal Comprehension			
Information	54.0	83.5	95.7
Vocabulary	55.4	87.8	97.8
Similarities	56.1	87.1	94.2
Information & Vocabulary	84.9	97.8	100.0
Information & Similarities	81.3	100.0	100.0
Vocabulary & Similarities	80.6	98.6	100.0
Perceptual Organization			
Block Design	40.3	78.4	94.2
Picture Completion	47.5	70.5	91.4
Matrix Reasoning	46.0	73.4	90.6
Block Design & Picture Completion	76.3	96.4	100.0
Block Design & Matrix Reasoning	60.4	95.7	100.0
Picture Completion & Matrix Reasoning	72.7	96.4	100.0
Processing Speed			
Digit Symbol	55.1	90.6	100.0
Symbol Search	59.4	94.2	99.3
Working Memory			
Spatial Span	37.7	80.2	94.4
Letter–Number Sequencing	51.9	84.0	96.3
Auditory Memory			
Logical Memory I	32.4	62.2	83.0
Logical Memory II	44.1	75.0	100.0
Verbal Paired Associates I	36.2	71.3	89.9
Verbal Paired Associates II	32.4	65.4	87.8
Logical Memory I & Logical Memory II	53.7	81.4	100.0
Verbal Paired Associates I & Verbal Paired Associates II	36.2	76.6	92.6
Logical Memory I & Verbal Paired Associates I	75.5	96.3	98.9
Visual Memory			
Family Pictures Recall I	41.0	78.2	91.0
Family Pictures Recall II	42.6	71.8	92.6
Visual Reproductions Recall I	26.6	54.3	75.0
Visual Reproductions Recall II	23.9	49.5	70.7
Family Pictures Recall I & Family Pictures Recall II	45.2	81.9	94.7

(continues)

TABLE 5   (*continued*)

Factor or summary score subtest or subtest combination	Within 5 points (%)	Within 10 points (%)	Within 15 points (%)
Visual Reproductions Recall I			
& Visual Reproductions Recall II	25.5	57.4	83.0
Family Pictures Recall I & Visual Reproductions Recall I	73.9	96.8	100.0
Full Scale IQ			
7-subtest version[b]	91.8	100.0	100.0
8-subtest version[b]	83.6	100.0	100.0
9-subtest version[b]	63.2	100.0	100.0
General Memory Index			
3-subtest version[b]	70.7	96.8	99.5
4-subtest version[b]	62.8	93.6	100.0

[a]Numerical values represent the proportions of subjects in the WAIS-III–WMS-III combined clinical sample whose prorated scores were within 5, 10, or 15 points (on an IQ-Deviation score scale) of their respective full-factor score, Full Scale IQ, or General Memory Index score. WAIS-III and WMS-III Standardization Data, copyright © 2002 by the Psychological Corporation, a Harcourt Assessment Company. All rights reserved.

[b]See text for the component scores included in this estimate.

TABLE 6   Prorated Estimation of Factor Scores, Full Scale IQ, and General Memory Index: Percent of Clinical Sample within 95, 90, and 85 % Confidence Intervals[a]

Factor or summary score subtest or subtest combination	Within 95 % CI (%)	Within 90 % CI (%)	Within 85 % CI (%)
Verbal Comprehension			
Information	59.0	52.5	46.0
Vocabulary	60.4	54.0	49.6
Similarities	59.7	55.4	46.0
Information & Vocabulary	89.9	82.7	79.9
Information & Similarities	88.5	79.9	74.1
Vocabulary & Similarities	89.2	79.9	74.1
Perceptual Organization			
Block Design	60.4	49.6	40.3
Picture Completion	54.0	49.6	43.9
Matrix Reasoning	77.7	74.1	71.9
Block Design & Picture Completion	91.4	87.8	82.0
Block Design & Matrix Reasoning	85.6	70.5	63.3
Picture Completion & Matrix Reasoning	86.3	79.1	77.0
Processing Speed			
Digit Symbol	89.1	84.8	76.1
Symbol Search	94.9	83.3	76.1
Working Memory			
Spatial Span	94.9	72.8	63.6
Letter–Number Sequencing	82.7	80.2	74.1
Auditory Memory			
Logical Memory I	44.1	34.0	29.8
Logical Memory II	52.7	47.3	42.0
Verbal Paired Associates I	50.0	38.8	34.0
Verbal Paired Associates II	44.1	36.7	31.4
Logical Memory I & Logical Memory II	64.9	55.3	52.1
Verbal Paired Associates I & Verbal Paired Associates II	51.1	38.8	34.6
Logical Memory I & Verbal Paired Associates I	82.4	76.6	68.6
Visual Memory			
Family Pictures Recall I	71.3	58.0	53.7
Family Pictures Recall II	64.4	58.0	55.3
Visual Reproductions Recall I	46.3	38.3	30.3
Visual Reproductions Recall II	38.3	34.0	29.8
Family Pictures Recall I & Family Pictures Recall II	73.9	60.1	56.4

(*continues*)

TABLE 6   (*continued*)

Factor or summary score subtest or subtest combination	Within 95 % CI (%)	Within 90 % CI (%)	Within 85 % CI (%)
Visual Reproductions Recall I & Visual Reproductions Recall II	49.5	41.0	36.7
Family Pictures Recall I & Visual Reproductions Recall I	93.1	87.8	84.6
Full Scale IQ			
7-subtest version[b]	86.6	77.6	69.4
8-subtest version[b]	72.4	64.2	57.5
9-subtest version[b]	57.5	53.4	46.6
General Memory Index			
3-subtest version[b]	92.0	85.1	80.9
4-subtest version[b]	87.8	81.4	75.5

[a]Numerical values represent the proportions of subjects in the WAIS-III–WMS-III combined clinical sample whose prorated scores were within the range specified by the 95 %, 90 %, or 85 % confidence interval (CI) around their respective full-factor score, Full Scale IQ, or General Memory Index score. WAIS-III and WMS-III Standardization Data, Copyright © 2002 by The Psychological Corporation, a Harcourt Assessment Company. All rights reserved.

[b]See text for the component scores included in this estimate.

TABLE 7 Estimation of Factor Scores via Subtest Substitutions: Part–Whole Correlations and Part–Whole Discrepancies for Standardization Sample.[a]

Factor or summary score subtest or subtest combination	Pearson's r[b]	Absolute mean discrepancy (and SD) between estimated and actual factor score
Verbal Comprehension		
Information, Vocabulary, & *Comprehension*	0.96	3.34 (2.63)
Information, Similarities, & *Comprehension*	0.97	3.04 (2.39)
Vocabulary, Similarities, & *Comprehension*	0.96	3.30 (2.65)
Perceptual Organization		
Block Design, Picture Completion, & *Object Assembly*	0.92	4.81 (3.66)
Block Design, Matrix Reasoning, & *Object Assembly*	0.92	4.70 (3.62)
Picture Completion, Matrix Reasoning & *Object Assembly*	0.94	4.15 (3.37)
Block Design, Picture Completion, & *Picture Arrangement*	0.92	4.79 (3.74)
Block Design, Matrix Reasoning, & *Picture Arrangement*	0.91	4.86 (3.92)
Picture Completion, Matrix Reasoning, & *Picture Arrangement*	0.91	4.83 (3.89)
Working Memory		
Spatial Span & *Digit Span*	0.85	6.52 (5.06)
Letter-Number Sequencing & *Digit Span*	0.82	7.34 (5.37)
Spatial Span & *Arithmetic*	0.84	6.56 (5.34)
Letter-Number Sequencing & *Arithmetic*	0.82	7.17 (5.25)
WAIS-III Definition of Working Memory Index (Letter-Number Sequencing, Arithmetic, & *Digit Span*)	0.81	7.40 (5.41)
Auditory Memory		
Logical Memory I & II and *Word List Learning I & II*	0.86	6.36 (4.87)
Verbal Paired Associates I & II and *Word List Learning I & II*	0.86	6.39 (4.85)
Visual Memory		
Family Pictures I & II and *Faces I & II*	0.76	8.19 (6.56)
Visual Reproductions Recall I & II and *Faces I & II*	0.73	5.72 (4.31)

[a]The *r*-values represent the correlations between the specified alternate versions of each factor score (based on substitution of one component subtest with the alternative subtest indicated in italics) and the standard form of the respective factor score for subjects in the WAIS-III/WMS-III standardization sample. Mean (and SD) discrepancies are expressed in standard score (~IQ scale) points. WAIS-III and WMS-III Standardization Data copyright © 2002 by the Psychological Corporation, a Harcourt Assessment Company. All rights reserved.

[b]Silverstein's (1971) formula for part–whole correlations was not applied to the estimates based on subtest substitution because these estimates include variance that is not part of the standard factor score being estimated.

TABLE 8   Estimation of Factor Scores via Subtest Substitutions: Percent of Standardization Sample within 5, 10, and 15 Standard Score Points[a]

Factor or summary score subtest or subtest combination	Within 5 points (%)	Within 10 points (%)	Within 15 points (%)
Verbal Comprehension			
Information, Vocabulary, & *Comprehension*	73.0	98.2	100.0
Information, Similarities, & *Comprehension*	78.1	98.9	100.0
Vocabulary, Similarities, & *Comprehension*	73.0	98.3	100.0
Perceptual Organization			
Block Design, Picture Completion, & *Object Assembly*	60.0	90.2	98.7
Block Design, Matrix Reasoning, & *Object Assembly*	60.1	91.4	98.8
Picture Completion, Matrix Reasoning, & *Object Assembly*	67.2	92.7	99.2
Block Design, Picture Completion, & *Picture Arrangement*	60.4	88.0	98.5
Block Design, Matrix Reasoning, & *Picture Arrangement*	60.6	86.3	98.2
Picture Completion, Matrix Reasoning, & *Picture Arrangement*	60.9	88.2	98.0
Working Memory			
Spatial Span & *Digit Span*	45.7	78.0	92.1
Letter-Number Sequencing & *Digit Span*	36.4	71.9	91.8
Spatial Span & *Arithmetic*	41.9	79.8	94.1
Letter-Number Sequencing & *Arithmetic*	37.9	73.8	92.2
WAIS-III Definition of Working Memory Index (Letter-Number Sequencing, *Arithmetic*, & *Digit Span*)	37.9	73.7	90.5
Auditory Memory			
Logical Memory I & II and *Word List Learning I & II*	49.3	78.4	93.8
Verbal Paired Associates I & II and *Word List Learning I & II*	47.8	78.4	93.5
Visual Memory			
Family Pictures I & II and *Faces I & II*	39.7	67.9	85.4
Visual Reproductions Recall I & II and *Faces I & II*	34.5	65.0	83.1

[a]Numerical values represent the proportions of subjects in the WAIS-III–WMS-III standardization sample whose alternate version factor scores (based on substitution with the alternative subtest indicated in italics) were within 5, 10, or 15 points (on an IQ-Deviation Score scale) of the standard version of the respective factor score. WAIS-III and WMS-III Standardization Data, copyright © 2002 by the Psychological Corporation, a Harcourt Assessment Company. All rights reserved.

TABLE 9   Estimation of Factor Scores via Subtest Substitutions: Percent of Standardization Sample within 95, 90, and 85% Confidence Intervals[a]

Factor or summary score subtest or subtest combination	Within 95% CI (%)	Within 90% CI (%)	Within 85% CI (%)
Verbal Comprehension			
Information, Vocabulary, & *Comprehension*	83.5	74.3	72.9
Information, Similarities, & *Comprehension*	87.4	79.0	76.4
Vocabulary, Similarities, & *Comprehension*	84.3	73.9	72.7
Perceptual Organization			
Block Design, Picture Completion, & *Object Assembly*	78.8	71.2	64.0
Block Design, Matrix Reasoning, & *Object Assembly*	80.5	70.8	64.1
Picture Completion, Matrix Reasoning, & *Object Assembly*	83.7	78.1	70.5
Block Design, Picture Completion, & *Picture Arrangement*	79.8	71.6	63.7
Block Design, Matrix Reasoning, & *Picture Arrangement*	78.7	70.4	63.8
Picture Completion, Matrix Reasoning, & *Picture Arrangement*	79.5	71.3	64.3
Working Memory			
Spatial Span & *Digit Span*	80.1	73.4	67.5
Letter-Number Sequencing & *Digit Span*	74.8	66.3	59.3
Spatial Span & *Arithmetic*	82.4	73.5	66.0
Letter-Number Sequencing & *Arithmetic*	77.7	69.7	61.3
WAIS-III Definition of Working Memory Index (Letter-Number Sequencing, *Arithmetic*, & *Digit Span*)	90.5	86.6	84.0
Auditory Memory			
Logical Memory I & II and *Word List Learning I & II*	60.0	53.3	48.0
Verbal Paired Associates I & II and *Word List Learning I & II*	58.9	51.2	46.1
Visual Memory			
Family Pictures I & II and *Faces I & II*	61.3	52.9	46.8
Visual Reproductions Recall I & II and *Faces I & II*	59.5	52.1	47.7

[a]Numerical values represent the proportions of subjects in the WAIS-III–WMS-III standardization sample whose alternate version factor scores (based on substitution with the alternative subtest indicated in italics) were within the range specified by the 95, 90, or 85% confidence interval (CI) the standard version of the respective factor score. WAIS-III and WMS-III Standardization Data, copyright © 2002 by the Psychological Corporation, a Harcourt Assessment Company. All rights reserved.

TABLE 10   Estimation of Factor Scores via Subtest Substitutions: Part–Whole Correlations and Part–Whole Discrepancies for Clinical Sample[a]

Factor or summary score subtest or subtest combination	Pearson's r [b]	Absolute mean discrepancy (and SD) between estimated and actual factor score
Verbal Comprehension		
Information, Vocabulary, & *Comprehension*	0.95	3.55 (2.66)
Information, Similarities, & *Comprehension*	0.96	3.25 (2.65)
Vocabulary, Similarities, & *Comprehension*	0.92	4.33 (3.53)
Perceptual Organization		
Block Design, Picture Completion, & *Object Assembly*	0.92	4.59 (3.69)
Block Design, Matrix Reasoning, & *Object Assembly*	0.92	4.14 (3.37)
Picture Completion, Matrix Reasoning, & *Object Assembly*	0.93	4.30 (3.33)
Block Design, Picture Completion, & *Picture Arrangement*	0.94	4.57 (3.78)
Block Design, Matrix Reasoning, & *Picture Arrangement*	0.94	3.71 (3.36)
Picture Completion, Matrix Reasoning, & *Picture Arrangement*	0.93	4.52 (3.34)
Working Memory		
Spatial Span & *Digit Span*	0.85	7.48 (6.02)
Letter–Number Sequencing & *Digit Span*	0.83	7.83 (5.56)
Spatial Span & *Arithmetic*	0.89	6.00 (4.42)
Letter–Number Sequencing & *Arithmetic*	0.88	6.29 (4.51)
WAIS-III Definition of Working Memory Index (Letter–Number Sequencing, *Arithmetic*, & *Digit Span*)	0.84	7.26 (5.20)
Auditory Memory		
Logical Memory I & II and *Word List Learning I & II*	0.92	5.37 (4.55)
Verbal Paired Associates I & II and *Word List Learning I & II*	0.89	6.46 (4.52)
Visual Memory		
Family Pictures I & II and *Faces I & II*	0.84	6.59 (5.46)
Visual Reproductions Recall I & II and *Faces I & II*	0.79	7.47 (4.38)

[a]The *r*-values represent the correlations between the specified alternate versions of each factor score (based on substitution of one component subtest with the alternative subtest indicated in italics) and the standard form of the respective factor score for subjects in the WAIS-III–WMS-III combined clinical sample. Mean (and SD) discrepancies are expressed in standard score ($\sim$IQ scale) points. WAIS-III and WMS-III Standardization Data, copyright © 2002 by the Psychological Corporation, a Harcourt Assessment Company. All rights reserved.

[b]Silverstein's (1971) formula for part–whole correlations was not applied to the estimates based on subtest substitution because of these estimates includes variance which is not part of the standard factor score being estimated.

TABLE 11   Estimation of Factor Scores via Subtest Substitutions: Percent of Clinical Sample within 5, 10, and 15 Standard Score Points[a]

Factor or summary score subtest or subtest combination	Within 5 points (%)	Within 10 points (%)	Within 15 points (%)
Verbal Comprehension			
Information, Vocabulary, & *Comprehension*	72.5	97.8	100.0
Information, Similarities, & *Comprehension*	76.1	97.8	100.0
Vocabulary, Similarities, & *Comprehension*	60.1	91.3	99.3
Perceptual Organization			
Block Design, Picture Completion, & *Object Assembly*	65.2	88.4	98.6
Block Design, Matrix Reasoning, & *Object Assembly*	67.4	94.9	99.3
Picture Completion, Matrix Reasoning, & *Object Assembly*	63.8	88.4	100.0
Block Design, Picture Completion, & *Picture Arrangement*	63.0	89.9	99.3
Block Design, Matrix Reasoning, & *Picture Arrangement*	75.4	91.3	100.0
Picture Completion, Matrix Reasoning, & *Picture Arrangement*	65.2	92.0	99.3
Working Memory			
Spatial Span & *Digit Span*	41.4	74.7	88.3
Letter–Number Sequencing & *Digit Span*	30.9	69.1	88.9
Spatial Span & *Arithmetic*	41.7	79.1	96.4
Letter-Number Sequencing & *Arithmetic*	44.6	83.5	96.4
WAIS-III Definition of Working Memory Index (Letter–Number Sequencing, *Arithmetic*, & *Digit Span*)	34.5	77.0	89.9
Auditory Memory			
Logical Memory I & II and *Word List Learning I & II*	57.4	82.4	96.3
Verbal Paired Associates I & II and *Word List Learning I & II*	43.6	78.7	95.7
Visual Memory			
Family Pictures I & II and *Faces I & II*	49.5	76.6	89.9
Visual Reproductions Recall I & II and *Faces I & II*	20.6	43.4	68.4

[a]Numerical values represent the proportions of subjects in the WAIS-III–WMS-III combined clinical sample whose alternate version factor scores (based on substitution with the alternative subtest indicated in italics) were within 5, 10, or 15 points (on an IQ-deviation score scale) of the standard version of the respective factor score. WAIS-III and WMS-III Standardization Data, Copyright © 2002 by the Psychological Corporation, a Harcourt Assessment Company. All rights reserved.

TABLE 12   Estimation of Factor Scores via Subtest Substitutions: Percent of Clinical Sample within 95, 90, and 85% Confidence Intervals[a]

Factor or Summary Score Subtest or Subtest Combination	Within 95% CI (%)	Within 90% CI (%)	Within 85% CI (%)
Verbal Comprehension			
Information, Vocabulary, & *Comprehension*	81.9	72.5	72.5
Information, Similarities, & *Comprehension*	84.1	75.4	69.6
Vocabulary, Similarities, & *Comprehension*	73.9	60.1	60.1
Perceptual Organization			
Block Design, Picture Completion & *Object Assembly*	80.4	73.9	65.2
Block Design, Matrix Reasoning & *Object Assembly*	79.0	73.2	68.1
Picture Completion, Matrix Reasoning & *Object Assembly*	79.0	74.6	65.9
Block Design, Picture Completion & *Picture Arrangement*	79.0	72.5	63.0
Block Design, Matrix Reasoning & *Picture Arrangement*	85.5	79.7	76.8
Picture Completion, Matrix Reasoning & *Picture Arrangement*	80.4	71.0	67.4
Working Memory			
Spatial Span & *Digit Span*	79.6	72.2	65.4
Letter–Number Sequencing & *Digit Span*	74.1	66.7	61.7
Spatial Span & *Arithmetic*	86.3	78.4	67.6
Letter–Number Sequencing & *Arithmetic*	87.8	76.3	69.8
WAIS-III Definition of Working Memory Index (Letter-Number Sequencing, *Arithmetic*, & *Digit Span*)	84.2	76.3	69.8
Auditory Memory			
Logical Memory I & II and *Word List Learning I & II*	69.1	60.1	56.4
Verbal Paired Associates I & II and *Word List Learning I & II*	54.8	47.3	41.0
Visual Memory			
Family Pictures & *Faces*	70.2	64.4	58.0
Visual Reproductions Recall I & II and *Faces I & II*	38.2	29.4	25.0

[a]Numerical values represent the proportions of subjects in the WAIS-III–WMS-III combined clinical sample whose alternate version factor scores (based on substitution with the alternative subtest indicated in italics) were within the range specified by the 95, 90, or 85% confidence interval (CI) the standard version of the respective factor score. WAIS-III and WMS-III Standardization Data, copyright © 2002 by the Psychological Corporation, a Harcourt Assessment Company. All rights reserved.

TABLE 13   Full Scale IQ versus prorated Full Scale IQ for Three IQ categories in the Standardization Sample[a]

	Pearson's r	Silverstein's Part–Whole r	Absolute mean discrepancy (and SD) between estimated and actual factor score
< 80	0.96	0.94	2.12 (1.49)
80–120	0.96	0.93	2.47 (1.89)
> 120	0.78	0.73	2.78 (2.19)
	Within 5 points (%)	Within 10 points (%)	%within 15 points
< 80	96.7	100.0	100.0
80–120	89.3	99.8	100.0
>120	83.0	100.0	100.0
	Within 95% CI (%)	Within 90% CI (%)	% Within 85% CI
< 80	93.7	85.9	82.5
80–120	84.1	76.1	69.7
>120	66.4	54.4	47.3

[a]Sample sizes: IQ < 80, $n = 80$; IQ between 80–120, $n = 856$; IQ > 120, $n = 81$ WAIS-III Standardization Data, copyright © 2002 by the Psychological Corporation, a Harcourt Assessment Company. All rights reserved.

TABLE 14   Full Scale IQ versus prorated (seven subtest version) Full Scale IQ for 3 IQ categories in the Clinical Sample[a]

	Pearson's r	Silverstein's Part–Whole r	Absolute mean discrepancy (and SD) between estimated and actual factor score
< 80	0.88	0.80	2.22 (1.40)
80–120	0.95	0.92	2.60 (1.81)
	within 5 points (%)	within 10 points (%)	within 15 points (%)
< 80	95.1	100.0	100.0
80–120	90.3	100.0	100.0
	Within 95% CI (%)	Within 90% CI (%)	Within 85% CI (%)
< 80	95.1	82.9	78.0
80–120	82.8	75.3	65.6

[a]Only one subject in the clinical sample had an IQ above 120, so results are not provided for this IQ group. Sample sizes: IQ < 80, $n = 41$; IQ between 80–120, $n - 95$. WAIS-III Standardization Data, copyright © 2002 by the Psychological Corporation, a Harcourt Assessment Company. All rights reserved.

TABLE 15   Sensitivity and Specificity of Memory Subtest Substitutions Using Mixed Dementia Group[a]

	Sensitivity[b]	Specificity[c]	% Correctly Classified
Auditory Memory	88.5	94.2	91.4
Logical Memory I	78.8	88.5	83.7
Logical Memory II	76.9	92.3	84.6
Verbal Paired Associates I	86.5	82.7	84.6
Verbal Paired Associates II	90.4	75.0	82.7
Logical Memory I & Logical Memory II	73.1	94.2	83.7
Verbal Paired Associates I & Verbal Paired Associates II	86.5	78.8	82.7
Logical Memory I & Verbal Paired Associates I	84.6	94.2	89.4
Logical Memory I & II and Word List Learning I & II	82.7	96.2	89.5
Verbal Paired Assoc. I & II and Word List Learning I & II	88.5	90.4	89.5
Visual Memory	94.2	88.5	91.4
Family Pictures Recall I	94.2	84.6	89.4
Family Pictures Recall II	94.2	88.5	91.4
Visual Reproductions Recall I	86.5	84.6	85.6
Visual Reproductions Recall II	84.6	76.9	80.8
Family Pictures Recall I & Family Pictures Recall II	94.2	90.4	92.3
Visual Reproductions Recall I & II	86.5	88.5	87.5
Family Pictures Recall I & Visual Reproductions Recall I	96.2	90.4	93.3
Family Pictures Recall I & II and Faces I & II	90.4	92.3	91.4
Visual Reproductions Recall I & II and Faces I & II	84.6	92.3	88.5

[a]Clinical sample participants with Parkinson's disease, Huntington's disease, or probable Alzheimer's disease, and demographically matched subsample of standardization sample. WAIS-III and WMS-III Standardization Data, copyright © 2002 by the Psychological Corporation, a Harcourt Assessment Company. All rights reserved.

[b]Sensitivity = number of examinees in mixed dementia group whose mean scaled score was ≤ 7 / total number of subjects in mixed dementia group.

[c]Specificity = number of normal comparison subjects in demographically matched subsample from the normal standardization sample whose mean scaled score was > 7 / total number of subjects in the demographically matched standardization sample.

TABLE 16   Sensitivity and Specificity of Verbal Comprehension, Perceptual Organization, and Working Memory Subtest Substitutions for people with Schizophrenia and Demographically Matched Controls[a]

	Sensitivity[b]	Specificity[c]	Correctly classified (%)
Verbal Comprehension	26.2	88.1	57.1
Information	19.0	88.1	53.6
Vocabulary	28.6	83.3	56.0
Similarities	23.8	92.9	58.3
Information & Vocabulary	23.8	85.7	54.8
Information & Similarities	26.2	88.1	57.1
Vocabulary & Similarities	28.6	90.5	59.5
Information, Vocabulary, & Comprehension	28.6	88.1	58.3
Information, Similarities, & Comprehension	28.6	90.5	59.5
Vocabulary, Similarities, & Comprehension	31.0	90.5	60.7
Perceptual Organization	35.7	92.9	64.3
Block Design	14.3	90.5	52.4
Picture Completion	45.2	83.3	64.3
Matrix Reasoning	28.6	95.2	61.9
Block Design & Picture Completion	31.0	88.1	59.5
Block Design & Matrix Reasoning	26.2	97.6	61.9
Picture Completion & Matrix Reasoning	42.9	88.1	65.5
Block Design, Picture Completion, & Object Assembly	35.7	85.7	60.7
Block Design, Matrix Reasoning, & Object Assembly	26.2	95.2	60.7
Picture Completion, Matrix Reasoning, & Object Assembly	40.5	90.5	65.5
Block Design, Picture Completion, & Picture Arrangement	35.7	95.2	65.5
Block Design, Matrix Reasoning, & Picture Arrangement	31.0	95.2	63.1
Picture Completion, Matrix Reasoning, & Picture Arrangement	35.7	92.9	64.3
Working Memory	50.0	95.2	72.6
Spatial Span	42.9	83.3	63.1
Letter–Number Sequencing	57.1	92.9	75.0
Digit Span	35.7	92.9	64.3
Arithmetic	69.0	81.0	75.0
Spatial Span & Digit Span	35.7	92.9	64.3
Letter–Number Sequencing & Digit Span	40.5	97.6	69.0

(*continues*)

TABLE 16   (*continued*)

	Sensitivity[b]	Specificity[c]	Correctly classified (%)
Spatial Span & Arithmetic	57.1	88.1	72.6
Letter–Number Sequencing & Arithmetic	61.9	95.2	78.6

[a]WAIS–III and WAIS–III Standardization, Data copyright © 2002 by the Psychological Corporation, a Harcourt Assessment Company. All rights reserved.

[b]Sensitivity = number of examinees in mixed dementia group whose mean scaled score was ≤ 7 / total number of subjects in Schizophrenia group.

Specificity = number of normal comparison subjects in demographically matched subsample from the normal standardization sample whose mean scaled score was > 7 / total number of subjects in the demographically matched standardization sample.

Accommodating Clients with Disabilities on the WAIS-III and WMS

Jeffery P. Braden
University of Wisconsin—Madison

Clinicians who use the Wechsler Adult Intelligence Scale—Third Edition (WAIS-III) (Wechsler, 1997) and the Wechsler Memory Scale (WMS) frequently assess individuals who have disabilities. To assess effectively clients with disabilities, clinicians must decide whether, and how, to adapt the WAIS-III and WMS administration process to accommodate the needs of clients who have disabilities. This chapter provides guidance for making decisions about when and how to accommodate clients with disabilities on the WAIS-III and WMS by reviewing the extant literature on assessment accommodations, especially research using the Wechsler scales.

THE CHALLENGE OF CLIENTS WITH DISABILITIES

Clinicians use the WAIS-III for psychological, educational, vocational, medical, forensic, and other assessment purposes. WAIS-III and WMS scores are often critical to the identification of disabilities. For example, learning disabilities and mental retardation are defined in part by intellectual ability scores (American Psychiatric Association, 2000). Also, WAIS-III and WMS scores are used to "rule out" cognitive disabilities when diagnosing other disorders, such as social emotional problems. Likewise, clients' eligibility for vocational rehabilitation services may depend in part on WAIS-III IQs. Clinicians may make different kinds of recommendations (e.g., whether to support college training for clients) based in part on WAIS-III and WMS results. Medical diagnosis for degenerative neurological conditions, post-morbid trauma, and other conditions with declining intellectual abilities may use WMS and WAIS-III scores as part of the diagnosis. Finally, WAIS-III scores may be used in forensic settings to help decide issues such as whether a defendant has the cognitive ability to participate in his or her own defense, and may be useful in sentencing by providing guidance to the court relating to the clients' cognitive abilities. For example, 13 U.S. states ban capital punishment for convicts with mental retardation.

Although WAIS-III and WMS scores may be useful for clinicians who serve in these different settings, clients with disabilities are vulnerable to misdiagnosis. Some populations or client groups have been underserved or denied effective clinical evaluations. These populations include individuals with sensory disabilities, such as individuals who are hard of hearing or deaf, or those who have visual impairments. Likewise, clients with gross- and fine-motor problems may present assessment challenges, particularly on the Performance Scales. Finally, clinical decisions relating to the collection and use of WAIS-III scores may substantially influence diagnosis of cognitive impairments. In particular, there is controversy regarding the use of Full Scale IQ (FSIQ) when Performance (PIQ) and Verbal IQs (VIQs) differ reliably, or when WAIS-III factor scores differ. Thus, clinicians are challenged to make appropriate decisions when, and when not, to adapt and select parts of the WAIS-III and WMS for administration to clients.

The assessment purpose influences clinicians' decisions regarding whether, when, and how to accommodate clients with disabilities in assessment. For example, if the purpose of the assessment is to provide a formal disability diagnosis, the clinician will want to ensure that the test scores are a valid, norm-referenced reflection of the client's cognitive abilities. In contrast, if the purpose of the assessment is to determine change in cognitive functioning, standardized norm-reference scores may be less relevant to the assessment than qualitative observations of the client's response to items, or the raw score the client achieved on an earlier test administration. If the purpose of an assessment is to determine what a client could accomplish in routine versus ideal conditions, then raw score changes from standard to nonstandard conditions are the most important aspect of the assessment. Each of these purposes constrains or allows a greater range of test accommodations. Therefore, clinicians should consider carefully why they are assessing the client to ensure that the procedures they follow in the assessment are congruent with achieving the purposes of the assessment.

Recent legislation and professional ethics heighten the need for effective assessment of clients with disabilities. Title VI of the Civil Rights Act of 1964, Title IX of the Education Amendments of 1972, Section 504 of the Rehabilitation Act of 1973, and Title II of the Americans with Disabilities Act of 1990 mandate access for individuals with disabilities in a variety of assessment processes and settings (Office of Civil Rights, 2000).

Despite these mandates, there has been little guidance for psychologists regarding the appropriate use of the Wechsler scales for clients with disabilities (Hishinuma, 1995). The WAIS-III and WMS were developed primarily to assess individual differences in the normal population, and to do so using multiple input (e.g., Vocabulary, Block Design) and output (e.g., spoken, pointing, manually manipulated) modalities. For individuals without impairments, the use of multiple modalities is a sound heuristic for ensuring a broad and representative sample of cognition. However, for individuals with one or more disabilities, the likelihood that the mix of input and output modalities will interact with the person's disabilities is great. The guidance provided in the WAIS-III and WMS materials is limited, in part because of the difficulty in anticipating the myriad of disability–test interactions, and in part because test publishers have historically avoided the issues involved. Therefore, there is little direct advice or research to guide clinicians in administration of the WAIS-III and WMS to clients with disabilities.

Fortunately, *The Standards for Educational and Psychological Testing* (hereafter called *Standards*) (American Educational Research Association, American Psychological Association, & National Council on Measurement in Education, 1999) outline specific guidelines for assessing individuals with disabilities (Palmer, Taylor, & Heaton, Chapter 10, this volume). In particular, the *Standards* direct clinicians to consider a range of accommodations and distinguish between accommodations and modifications. Test accommodations are changes to the assessment process that leave the content or construct of the assessment unaffected; in contrast, modifications are changes to the assessment process or content that affect the construct assessed.

The *Standards* go on to identify six ways in which clinicians may alter assessment to serve clients with disabilities (Table 1); however, they do not provide a great deal of guidance with respect to how clinicians should decide when and how to accommodate. The *Standards* recommend that test

TABLE 1   Accommodations and Modifications Recommended in the *Standards* for Clients with Disabilities

Accommodation or modification	Examples
Presentation Format	
Alternate the medium used to present test directions and items.	Use large print or Braille, sign directions in American Sign Language (ASL), provide written directions, read written directions aloud.
Response format	
Change the ways in which individuals respond to test items or directions.	Allow the client to point to select a response, sign, speak, or use a scribe to write or select responses, or use assistive technology.
Modifying timing	
Alter the interval in which tests are usually given.	Extended time, allow more frequent rest breaks, spread assessment over multiple days.
Use portions of a test	
Select portions of a test based on the individual's disability	Use Performance Scale subtests with hearing impaired clients; use Verbal scale subtests with visually impaired clients; eliminate subtests requiring manipulation of material for clients with motor impairments; eliminate specific subtests based on suspected cognitive disabilities.
Test setting	
Alter the setting in which assessment is administered	Use individual instead of group administration; provide accessible furniture for assessment, alter lighting conditions; use quiet, low-distraction setting.
Using substitute tests or alternate assessments	
Replacing a standardized test with a test or alternate assessment specifically designed for individuals with disabilities	Use the Jenkinson (1989) adaptation of the Wechsler with deaf clients; use the Perkins adaptation of the Wechsler with visually impaired clients.

users and test developers use evidence and research to make decisions. However, clinicians must make decisions based on their assessment of the client, and the purposes of assessment. Research cannot completely address the constellation of unique client characteristics, setting demands, and assessment contexts and purposes clinicians confront. The following section will provide a decision-making framework for clinicians to use to make accommodations decisions.

DECISION-MAKING FRAMEWORK FOR ACCOMMODATIONS

The essential purpose of assessment accommodations is to maintain assessment validity by decreasing—and hopefully eliminating—assessment invalidity for clients with disabilities. This premise draws on Messick's (1995) seminal work on assessment invalidity as a framework for making accommodation decisions. Specifically, Messick identified two sources that contribute to assessment invalidity: (a) construct-irrelevant variance, and (b) construct underrepresentation. Understanding each of these sources of invalidity is essential for guiding appropriate decision-making frameworks (see Braden, 1999; Braden, Schroeder, & Buckley, 2001).

Construct-Irrelevant Variance

Clinicians create construct-irrelevant variance when they adopt assessment procedures that capture performance that they do not intend to assess. That is, assessments are intended to measure certain constructs. However, the form or process of the assessment may capture other, unintended, constructs. For example, a reading comprehension test is intended to assess a client's ability to decode and understand text. However, if the client has a visual impairment, and the text is presented in a normal font size, the client may fail the test not because the client cannot decode text, but because the client lacks the visual acuity to decode that specific font. In this example, construct-irrelevant variance was introduced into the assessment because the passage tapped an unintended construct (visual acuity).

Likewise, clinicians who assess clients' intelligence may introduce construct-irrelevant variance into the assessment. Examples include the use of verbal subtests and items with hearing-impaired clients, which confound exposure to English (oral) language with the construct intended to be measured (intelligence). Thus, a low score on a Verbal Scale for a deaf client may reflect low intellectual abilities or it may reflect construct-irrelevant variance of exposure to oral English (Braden, 1994). Likewise, the use of Performance Scales with clients who have visual or physical dexterity impairments may confound the measurement of intellectual abilities with the ability to see or manipulate test items and objects.

Fortunately, clinicians are usually sensitive to sources of construct-irrelevant variance. Later in this chapter, I will review the accommodations that have been recommended for clients with disabilities on the Wechsler scales. Virtually all of these accommodations have the intent, whether stated or implied, to reduce construct-irrelevant variance in assessment. This is an important goal, which clinicians must strive to achieve. However, such accommodations control only one potential source of invalidity (construct-irrelevant variance) while ignoring the other source of invalidity (construct underrepresentation).

Construct Underrepresentation

Clinicians underrepresent the construct of interest when they use methods that fail to capture or adequately represent the intended construct. For example, orally reading a reading comprehension test to a visually impaired client would allow the client access to content of the test. However, it would underrepresent the intended construct—that is, the client's ability to independently decode and understand text. By reading the reading test aloud, the clinician would underrepresent the construct intended (i.e., independent decoding and comprehension of text). Instead, reading the test aloud would change the assessment so that it would represent a different construct—that is, listening comprehension.

How accommodations affect underrepresentation of constructs is not well conceived nor studied in the clinical literature. In fact, some popular accommodations may reduce construct-irrelevant variance—but also increase construct underrepresentation. Construct underrepresentation is a particular problem with respect to the recommendation that clinicians select parts of tests. For example, a popular recommendation for assessing deaf clients' intelligence is to use the Performance Scales of the Wechsler. This recommendation has the effect of decreasing construct-irrelevant variance (i.e., exposure and command of oral English), but may also underrepresent the construct of intelligence. That is, if intelligence is broadly defined as including multiple aspects of cognitive abilities, eliminating language-based reasoning, fund of knowledge, comprehension of social settings, and other language-loaded and culturally based information may underrepresent the construct of intelligence. Accommodations must balance the need to reduce construct-irrelevant variance with the simultaneous goal of maintaining construct representation (or avoiding construct underrepresentation), or they run the risk of invalidating the assessment results.

Representing the Construct of Intelligence

Why has the imperative to retain construct representation received so little attention in the clinical literature? One reason is that psychological constructs are often poorly defined. This is particularly true for intelligence. Intelligence test developers are often vague in their descriptions of the abilities that intelligence tests are intended to measure.

For example, academic achievement tests often use item specification tables detailing the specific domains to be assessed, and further providing the number and types of items used to assess each domain. In contrast, the WAIS-III and WMS manuals do not provide item-specification tables, nor a clearly articulated framework defining the relative processes that compose intelligence, and the relative weight that each process should be given in representing the construct of intelligence.

Vagueness has been fueled in part by the empirical finding that intellectual abilities are indicated in a similar way across a variety of assessment modalities. Charles Spearman first noted this phenomenon and called it the "indifference of the indicator" (Jensen, 1998). Thus, empirical research on intellectual assessment has supported the notion that different kinds of cognitive ability items and subtests may be used interchangeably to estimate general intellectual abilities.

Vagueness is also fueled by the historical lack of consensus regarding the topology or domain of cognitive abilities. Researchers have disagreed, often in fundamental ways, on how to best describe cognitive abilities. Some researchers argued that general intellectual ability was the dominant feature of cognitive abilities, and that subdomains or other abilities mattered little (e.g., Spearman, Burt, Eysenck, Jensen). In contrast, others have proposed cognitive ability taxonomies that eliminate a general intellectual construct when defining cognitive abilities (e.g., Guilford, Thurstone, Gardner, Sternberg).

Fortunately, different lines of research have converged to suggest a common taxonomy of cognitive abilities. The work of Horn and Noll (1997) and Carroll (1993) suggest remarkably similar conceptions of cognitive abilities, both invoking a hierarchical framework with three strata. This three-stratum taxonomy suggests that, at the highest level, cognitive abilities converge to form a general common factor (g) (Jensen, 1998). However, the general factor is in part made up of broad, second-order factors or abilities, which in turn are made up of a multitude of narrow cognitive abilities. Although some researchers still argue for a different taxonomy of cognitive abilities (e.g., Gardner, 1999; Naglieri, 2000), clinicians are increasingly invoking the three-stratum model as a guide to ensuring adequate construct representation in cognitive assessment (e.g., McGrew & Flanagan, 1998).

Some clinicians may perceive the preceding discussion as an academic exercise with little clinical utility. After all, debates on the nature of intelligence have raged, yet clinicians are charged with measuring it (and using highly developed tools for doing so). However, if the discussion is irrelevant, I have failed to achieve my goal of suggesting a framework or taxonomy for identifying construct representation. Clinicians will be unable to minimize construct underrepresentation as a threat to assessment validity if they do not clearly understand the construct to be represented. Consequently, it behooves clinicians to consider the nature and taxonomy of cognitive abilities when deciding on what tests to give, what tests (or subtests) to avoid, and how tests may (or may not) be altered to simultaneously reduce construct-irrelevant variance while retaining construct representation in the assessment. Construct representation is a particularly important issue when clinicians decide to use only parts of a test to assess intellectual abilities.

Deleting Subtests When Estimating Intelligence

Convergence on a common taxonomy of intellectual abilities can guide clinical decisions about when, and when not, to exclude subtests for clients with disabilities. That is, an explicit taxonomy of cognitive abilities, and a hierarchy of the relative importance, allows clinicians to determine whether omitting individual subtests or parts of cognitive batteries is appropriate in the intellectual assessment of an individual.

For example, when assessing an individual with a visual impairment, a clinician might invoke a taxonomy of hierarchical abilities (see McGrew & Flanagan, 1998) to identify key factors to assess in an intellectual assessment. The clinician might invoke Carroll's (1993) work, showing that estimates of fluid and crystallized intellectual abilities are more important for determining general intelligence than estimates of visual processing. Therefore, a clinician might simply omit assessment of visual-processing abilities when estimating the intellectual abilities of a visually impaired client, because the client's visual impairment would introduce construct-irrelevant variance into the assessment of visual processing abilities (i.e., the test intends to measure the construct of visual processing, not visual acuity). Conversely, the clinician might ensure representation of fluid abilities in the assessment by using a vocally administered test of verbal analogies, rather than simply deleting visual, nonverbal tests of fluid abilities (e.g., the Matrix or Block Design subtest). To achieve this goal, the clinician would probably administer the WAIS-III Verbal subtests, and perhaps supplement those tests with a vocally administered test of fluid abilities (e.g., a verbal analogies test) to ensure adequate representation of intellectual abilities in the assessment.

Subtest deletion is not controversial when it is clear that the disabilities that affect test scores are not cognitive in nature. For example, deafness, blindness, and orthopedic disabilities are not cognitive, and therefore most clinicians accept the need to avoid tests that require noncognitive skills (e.g., ability to hear and understand oral language, visual acuity, motor dexterity). The deletion of subtests for individuals with cognitive impairments (e.g., learning disabilities) is a more controversial practice, and will be discussed near the end of this chapter.

A Model for Accommodation Decision Making in Assessment

The clinical decision process that guides this example is illustrated in Figure 1. The figure can guide clinicians to make effective decisions for when to accommodate clients in intellectual assessment. The figure also invites the clinician to ensure that accommodations, to the greatest extent possible, remove construct–irrelevant variance while representing the construct intended to be assessed.

The key to making balanced decisions between changes that reduce construct–irrelevant variance, while still maintaining construct representation, rests on two key points:

- the clinicians' understanding of the constructs that are intended to be assessed, and
- the clinicians' understanding of how an individual's disabilities might introduce task–irrelevant variance into the assessment.

Legal Issues in Accommodations

The distinction between construct underrepresentation and construct-irrelevant variance is similar to the distinction made by Phillips (1993,

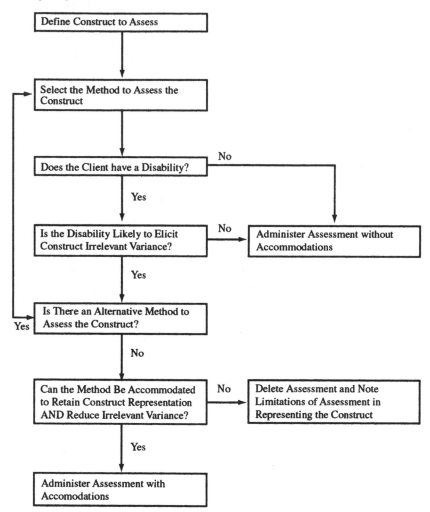

FIGURE 1.   Decision-making process for accommodating clients with disabilities

1994) between access skills and target skills in testing. Phillips argues from a legal perspective that clients with disabilities are entitled to accommodations that reduce the impact of access skills on an assessment outcome, but clients are not entitled to accommodations that alter the target skills intended to be assessed. Phillips defines access skills as the skills needed to access the assessment content and process (e.g., visual acuity, being able to sit at a table when in a wheelchair, understanding the test directions and content).

In contrast, target skills are those skills that the assessment intends to reflect. Target skills might include reading comprehension, intellectual abilities, or the ability to do a particular job or task. With respect to target skills, accommodations would be inappropriate, because accommodations would provide misleading interpretations of the client's abilities—and because other (nondisabled) clients are not entitled to similar assistance. Again, although argued from a legal framework, this distinction between access skills and construct-irrelevant variance is strong, as is the connection between target skills and construct representation. Thus, clinicians would be on strong conceptual and legal grounds when working to reduce construct-irrelevant variance (that is, provide adaptations and accommodations that overcome access skills) while maintaining construct representation (that is, while retaining the features of the assessment for the targeted skills).

To help guide appropriate accommodation decisions, the Office of Civil Rights (2000) in the U.S. Department of Education provided a list of accommodations that states use and/or approve for testing students with disabilities in educational assessment programs. This list is reproduced in Table 2. Although some of these accommodations may be inappropriate for some clinical settings, client populations, or individually administered tests, they nonetheless provide a resource for clinicians to consider possible accommodations.

How Should Accommodations Affect Test Scores?

Phillips (1994, 1996) stated that disabled clients should receive higher scores on tests when receiving accommodations. The phenomenon of improving assessment results for individuals with disabilities, while not improving those for individuals without disabilities, is called "differential boost." That is, individuals with disabilities benefit more from accommodations than individuals without disabilities.

The logic for giving a differential boost is appealing—that is, disabilities prevent an individual from performing well on a test, and so an accommodation will remove that barrier and improve performance. Differential boost is also ethically appealing. For example, large print or wheelchair-accessible furniture are likely to improve the scores of clients with disabilities, but do not improve scores for clients without disabilities. Consequently, accommodations of this type could be offered to any client, but they would only assist clients with disabilities.

TABLE 2   Accommodations for Individuals with Disabilities[a]

Presentation format
    Braille edition
    Large-print editions
    Templates to reduce visual field
    Short-segment testing booklets
    Key words highlighted in directions
    Reordering of items
    Use of spell checker
    Use of word lists/dictionaries
    Translated into sign language

Administration format
    Oral reading of questions
    Use of magnifying glass
    Explanation of directions
    Audiotape directions or test items
    Repeating of directions
    Interpretation of directions
    Videotape in American Sign Language
    Interpreter signs test in front of classroom/student
    Signing of directions
    Amplification equipment
    Enhanced lighting
    Special acoustics
    Alone in study carrel
    Individual administration
    In small groups
    At home with appropriate supervision
    In special education classes separate room
    Off campus
    Interpreter with teacher facing student; student in front of classroom
    Adaptive furniture
    Use place marker
    Hearing aids
    Student wears noise buffers
    Administrator faces student
    Specialized table

(continues)

TABLE 2   (*continued*)

Auditory trainers

Read questions aloud to self

Colored transparency

Assist student in tracking by placing students finger on item

Typewriter device to screen out sounds

Extended testing time

More breaks

Extending sessions over multiple days

Altered time of day that test is administered

Response format

Mark responses in booklet

Use template for recording

Point to response

Lined paper

Use sign language

Use typewriter/computer/ word processor

Use Braille writer

Oral response, use of scribe

Alternative response methods, use of scribe

Answers recorded on audiotape

Administrator checks to ensure that student is placing responses in correct area

Lined paper for large script printing

Communication board

Other

Out-of level testing

[a]Adapted from: Council of Chief State School Officers, Annual Survey: State Student Assessment Programs, Washington D.C., 1999. Reprinted from Appendix C, Table 2, Office of Civil Rights (2000).

However, differential boost presumes the factors affecting client performance work in only one direction—that is, to lower the client's performance. This need not be the case. Some forms of disability-induced construct-irrelevant variance may increase test scores. For example, when the Verbal Scale of the WAIS-III was translated into American Sign Language (ASL) (Kostrubala & Braden, 1997), the initial interpretation of the question "How many are in a dozen?" was signed, "How many are twelve?" The translation was true to ASL, because the sign for "dozen" in ASL is "12." However, although the translation was accurate for the target language, it introduced construct-irrelevant variance that rendered the item easier for deaf clients than for other clients.

Likewise, it is possible that assessment without accommodations elicits construct-irrelevant variance that artificially increases the client's score. For example, individuals with severe mental retardation may score higher on a standard test without accommodations than on an alternative or special test tapping lower levels of ability because the standard test does not have adequate sensitivity to measure the clients' ability levels (i.e., it lacks a sufficient "floor" of easy items, and consequently overestimates cognitive ability). Although it is possible to imagine many more ways in which construct-irrelevant variance would work to lower scores, it is challenging to identify situations in which construct-irrelevant variance might artificially raise scores.

Accommodations might also lower scores by increasing construct representation. For example, an assessment accommodation that substituted silent reading of a passage followed by an interview for a multiple-choice reading test would better approximate the intended construct (e.g., the ability to use text to inform, guide decisions, and influence understanding). However, this accommodation might yield a lower score than the multiple-choice test. The lower score might be a more accurate reflection of the intended construct (reading comprehension), because it better represents the construct than the multiple-choice test. Construct representation and construct-irrelevant variance are reciprocals; increasing one necessarily decreases the other. Generally, assessors have focused on decreasing construct-irrelevant variance, but they could achieve the same goal by increasing construct representation in assessments.

The argument that accommodations are "good" if they induce differential boost is inappropriate from a logical perspective. The assumption that error works in only one direction (to lower scores) is statistically incorrect. Because error is random, it must be normally distributed, which means it works to raise scores as often as it works to lower scores. Also, the assumption that members of different groups should have a similar score means is an example of the *egalitarian fallacy* (see Jensen, 1980, Harris, Tulsky, & Schulthesis, Chapter 9, this volume). In fact, clients with disabilities are often defined by having scores that are different from—and usually lower than—nondisabled peers (e.g., mental retardation). In this scenario, accommodations might (accurately) lower the disabled client's score. The decision of whether an accommodation is appropriate must be made independently of the effect on the client's score, for logical and empirical reasons. For example, Elliott, Kratochwill, and McKevitt (2001) found some students with disabilities performed lower on accommodated tests than they did on nonaccommodated tests.

Furthermore, the presumption that lower IQs are less valid than higher IQs may lead clinicians to overlook important features of the client's condition. For example, individuals whose visual impairment is caused by *toxoplasma gondii* are likely to have lower IQs—and a cumulative deficit in IQ over the developmental span—than individuals whose blindness is caused by other factors (Langset, Midtvedt, & Omland, 1989). Likewise, some neurological conditions (e.g., multiple sclerosis) may confound nonintellectual changes (e.g., loss of motor control) with intellectual declines. Clinicians who accept the concept that accommodations must "boost" scores may inflate estimates of cognitive abilities, and consequently mask important features of the underlying disability in their assessments.

Summary

This section provides conceptual guidelines for clinicians to use for making decisions in accommodations. Again, the dual imperatives to reduce construct-irrelevant variance, while maintaining construct representation, are useful as guidelines. However, successful balancing of these two criteria require substantial background knowledge on the part of the clinician. That is, the clinician must have knowledge about the client's disability, and have a clear understanding of the target skills or construct intended to be represented in the assessment. Although most clinicians would presume to understand the construct as a matter of professional competence (i.e., if psychologists do not understand or are not aware of contemporary theories of intelligence, they ought not to assess it), the requirement to understand disability is one that is less likely to be prevalent among psychologists. Surveys of psychologists (e.g., Bauman & Kropf, 1979; Gibbins, 1989) suggest that most psychologists lack in-depth knowledge of disability, particularly for low-incidence disabilities such as deafness, blindness, or traumatic brain injury. However, psychologists are obligated to get the information they need, either through direct professional training or through consultation with other psychologists who have expertise in the field. Tables 3–6 recommend where psychologists can seek consultation and obtain appropriate information when assessing clients with disabilities.

RESEARCH ON ACCOMMODATIONS

The professional literature contains many recommendations regarding assessment accommodations and adaptations. These recommendations (e.g., Yarnall & Carlton, 1981) stress the need for clinicians to balance the need to maintain standardized assessment conditions with the need to adapt standardized procedures to the unique needs of the client. The *Standards* (section 5.1) echo this approach:

> Test administrators should follow carefully the standardized procedures for administering and scoring specified by the test developer, unless the situation or a test taker's disability dictates that an exception should be made. (p. 63)

Fortunately, a body of literature addresses accommodations using the Wechsler scales with clients who have disabilities that can help guide clinicians on when and how to make exceptions to standardized procedures. Unfortunately for clinicians interested in the WAIS-III and WMS-III, most of this literature focuses on children, or on previous versions of the Wechsler scales. However, I will review the literature on the administration of the Wechsler scales to individuals who are deaf or hard of hearing, who have visual impairments, physical impairments, and other disabilities. In each of these areas, I will briefly summarize the literature and provide a table of the studies investigating Wechsler scale applications to samples of individuals with disabilities. Remember, most of the research has been conducted without a clearly articulated conceptual model to guide accommodations. Consequently, research tends to emphasize adaptations that seek to reduce construct-irrelevant variance, but often ignores or fails to emphasize the concurrent expectation to retain (or increase) construct representation in the assessment. Although investigations frequently show the WAIS/WMS-III measures the same construct structure across individuals with a variety of disabilities (Ryan & Paolo, 2001), this is not equivalent to specifying and using a clearly articulated model for the construct (cognitive ability or memory) to be assessed.

Deafness

The research on the Wechsler scales with deaf and hard-of-hearing clients comprises many assessment accommodations, but repeatedly recommends using the Performance Scale of the Wechsler. Most studies find PIQ to be in the average range for deaf clients with no additional disabilities, but find VIQ to be substantially lower (typically 15 points). Most authors also recommend supplementing Performance Scale directions with written, fingerspelled, or signed communication. Other adaptations include adding additional practice items, using norms based on deaf clients, and eliminating speeded subtests (see Braden, 1992, 1994; Braden & Hannah, 1998; and Jenkinson, 1989, for reviews). Table 3 presents a summary of research regarding the Wechsler scales with individuals who are deaf and hard-of-hearing.

Researchers and clinicians have developed many specialized practices for assessing clients who are deaf and hard-of-hearing. These include the development of specialized instruments, such as the Hiskey-Nebraska Test of Learning Aptitude, the Pintner Nonlanguage Test, and the Snidjers–Ooman Nonverbal Intelligence Test (see Braden, 1994, and Bradley-Johnson & Evans, 1991, for reviews). There have also been efforts to develop separate or special norms for deaf and hard-of-hearing people (Anderson & Sisco, 1977). Many clinicians unfortunately equate the availability of special norms with demonstrated validity and utility of the test (e.g., Gordon, Stump, & Glaser, 1996). However, the availability of special norms is entirely independent of the demonstrated validity and utility of an instrument (e.g., an instrument may be valid without special norms, or may be invalid with special norms), and special norms do not add incremental validity or utility in clinical assessment (Braden, 1994, pp. 85–97; Braden & Hannah, 1998). Efforts to create distinct and special instruments or norms have generally failed to show clinical or practical improvements in assessment beyond reasonable accommodations to established instruments such as the Wechsler scales.

Visual Disabilities

The research on administration of the Wechsler to clients who have visual impairments suggests that the recommendations run essentially the opposite of those recommended for clients with hearing impairments; that is, that clients with visual impairments be given the Verbal scales of the Wechsler. Additionally, recommendations include providing oral directions or reading materials aloud when they are presented in print, and otherwise supplementing the assessment through oral language mediation. Table 4 presents research on accommodations and adjustments to administration.

TABLE 3   Selected Research Using the Wechsler Scales with Samples of Hard-of-Hearing and Deaf Clients

Source	Comments
Alade, E. B. (1992). Determining intelligence quotients of Nigerian deaf children with the Wechsler Intelligence Scale for Children—Revised. *Early Child Development and Care, 80,* 103–107.	Found very low Verbal and Performance IQs using the WISC-R for Nigerian deaf children (95% in the mentally retarded range), suggesting group differences occur within cross-cultural samples of deaf children.
Anderson, R. J., & Sisco, F. H. (1977). *Standardization of the WISC-R Performance Scale for deaf children* (Series T, No. 1., Office of Demographic Studies, Gallaudet College) (Available from ERIC Document No. ED150801). Washington, DC: Gallaudet College.	Provides WISC-R norms based on 1,228 deaf children. However, they are now outdated, and there are no comparable norms available for the WISC-III or WAIS-III.
Braden, J. P. (1994). *Deafness, deprivation, and IQ.* New York: Plenum.	The meta-analysis of research on the intelligence of deaf people finds the distribution of IQ to be similar to normative samples of normal-hearing people, although language-loaded IQs are about one standard deviation lower than language-reduced IQs. The Wechsler scales are the most popular clinical instrument for use with deaf clients.
Braden, J. P., Kostrubala, C. E., & Reed, J. (1994). Why do deaf children score differentially on performance vs. motor-reduced nonverbal intelligence tests? *Journal of Psychoeducational Assessment, 12*(4): 357–363.	Found the manipulative components of Performance tests yield higher estimates of intelligence in deaf clients than motor-free nonverbal tests.
Chovan, W. L., & Benfield, J. R. (1994). Varied sign language systems and their mediating effects on WISC-R Verbal subtests of profoundly deaf students: A replication. *Perceptual and Motor Skills, 78*(1), 61–62.	Found the use of multiple sign systems yielded below average Verbal IQs for deaf clients, contradicting Miller's (1984) findings that such procedures yield average Verbal IQs for deaf clients.
Handy, L. A. (1996). Pantomime administration of the WSIC-III and SB:FE to hearing and otitis prone Native Indian students. *Dissertation Abstracts International, 56*(8), 3058A.	Demonstrates utility of pantomimed administration of WISC-III and Stanford–Binet to Native Indian students in Canada.
Hunt, H. L. (1998). Assessing intelligence in deaf children: Is the Verbal Scale of the WISC-III valid? *Dissertation Abstracts International: Section B: The Sciences and Engineering, 59*(1–B): 0456.	Shows strong correlations between Verbal Scale scores and measures of achievement, but concludes Verbal IQ is inappropriate because it is about 15 points lower than the Performance IQ.
Jenkinson, J. (1989). Use of the WISC-R Performance Scale with hearing-impaired children: A review. *Psychological Test Bulletin, 2*(1), 33–38.	Found the literature generally supported the use of the Wechsler scales with deaf children, and reported an adapted version produced adequate psychometric results.

(continues)

TABLE 3 (*continued*)

Source	Comments
Kostrubala, C. E., & Braden, J. P. (1998). *Administration of the WAIS-III in American Sign Language* [videotape]. San Antonio, TX: The Psychological Corporation.	Provides a formal American Sign Language translation of the WAIS-III. Unpublished data show the translation produces adequate psychometric characteristics in a deaf adult sample.
Maller, S. J., & Ferron, J. (1997). WISC-III factor invariance across deaf and standardization samples. *Educational and Psychological Measurement, 57*(6), 987–994.	The factor structure of the WISC-III is not identical for deaf and hearing children. However, the magnitude of differences is small, and tends to be most pronounced for Verbal subtests.
Meng, X., & Gong, Y. (1995). A comparative study on intelligence between deaf and hearing children. *Chinese Journal of Clinical Psychology, 3*(3), 137–139, 146.	Reports results for deaf clients on the Chinese version of the WISC similar to those reported for North American samples.
Paal, N., Skinner, S., & Reddig, C. (1988). The relationship of non-verbal intelligence measures to academic achievement among deaf adolescents. *Journal of Rehabilitation of the Deaf, 21*(3), 8–11.	Reports that the WAIS-R Performance Scale predicts academic achievement as well as the Hiskey-Nebraska Test of Learning Aptitude in deaf young adults.
Sullivan, P. M. (1982). Administration modifications on the WISC-R Performance Scale with different categories of deaf children. *American Annals of the Deaf, 127*(6), 780–788.	Found deaf students performed better when assessed using signs, either delivered via interpreter or by a signing psychologist, than by written or gestured administration.
Sullivan, P. M., & Montoya, L. A. (1997). Factor analysis of the WISC-III with deaf and hard-of-hearing children. *Psychological Assessment, 9*(3), 317–321.	Found two-factor solution (language comprehension and visual orientation) for WISC-III in deaf children.

As is true for deafness, there have also been efforts to create separate or adapted assessment instruments for individuals with visual impairments. Examples include the Blind Learning Aptitude Test (BLAT) (Newland, 1979), the Stanford-Ohwaki-Kohs Tactile Block Design Intelligence Test For The Blind (Dauterman & Suinn, 1966), tactile forms of matrices tests (Rich & Anderson, 1965), and the Perkins-Binet (Davis, 1980). Generally, these instruments include normative information based on special populations. Although these special norms and specialized procedures (e.g., rendering visual subtests in three-dimensional media to allow haptic responses) promise examiners the ability to measure intelligence in special populations, subsequent research consistently demonstrates that they have no greater utility than standard batteries (such as the Wechsler scales) that

TABLE 4   Selected Research Using the Wechsler Scales with Samples of Clients with Visual Impairments

Source	Comments
Beck, F. W., & Lindsey, J. D. (1986). Visually impaired students' degree of visual acuity and their verbal intelligence quotients. *Educational and Psychological Research*, 6(1), 49–53.	Found no relationship between WISC-R VIQ and degree of visual acuity within 74 children who were blind.
Dekker, R., & Koole, F. D. (1992). Visually impaired children's visual characteristics and intelligence. *Developmental Medicine and Child Neurology, 34*(2), 123–133.	Found near-acuity visual skills are significantly correlated with selected WISC-R subtests, other cognitive tests, and academic achievement; also notes that congenitally blind children have better memory skills but worse spatial skills than adventitiously blind and partially sighted peers.
Groenveld, M., & Jan, J. E. (1992). Intelligence profiles of low vision and blind children. *Journal of Visual Impairment and Blindness, 86*(1), 68–71.	Reports characteristic pattern of cognitive ability scores on the WISC-R and WPPSI-R for blind children, with Verbal Scale scores higher than Performance Scale scores.
Gutterman, J. E., Ward, M, & Genshaft, J. (1985). Correlations of scores of low vision children on the Perkins-Binet Tests of Intelligence for the Blind, the WISC—R and the WRAT. *Journal of Visual Impairment and Blindness, 79*(2), 55–58.	Reports the Verbal Scale of the WISC-R provides better estimates of academic achievement for children with visual impairments than the Perkins–Binet.
Hull, T., & Mason, H. (1995). Performance of blind children on digit-span tests. *Journal of Visual Impairment and Blindness, 89*(2), 166–169.	Reports children who are congenitally blind perform better on the Digit Span subtest of the WISC-R than adventitiously blind and normally seeing peers.
MacCluskie, K. C., Tunick, R. H., Dial, J. G., & Paul, D. S. (1998). The role of vision in the development of abstraction ability. *Journal of Visual Impairment and Blindness, 92*(3), 189–199.	Used the WAIS-R with prelingually and postlingually blind adults and found no difference in their (limited) visual abstraction abilities.
Reid, J. M. V. (1997). Standardized ability testing for vocational rehabilitation in visually impaired adults: A literature review. *Journal of Visual Impairment and Blindness, 91*(6), 546–554.	Reviewed multiple instruments and found the Verbal Scales of the Wechsler to be the most widely accepted. However, clinicians are cautioned not to rely exclusively on verbal measures of cognitive abilities.
Spencer, R. A. (1997). Wechsler Intelligence Scale for Children-third edition Verbal short forms for children with visual impairments. *Dissertation Abstracts International 58*(01), 134A.	Provides evidence that pairs, triads, and quartets of WISC-III Verbal Scale subtests (including Digit Span) yield reliable and accurate estimates of VIQ in samples of children who have partial sight or are legally blind.

(continues)

TABLE 4 (*continued*)

Source	Comments
Vander-Kolk, C. J. (1982). A comparison of intelligence test score patterns between visually impaired subgroups and the sighted. *Rehabilitation Psychology, 27*(2), 115–120.	Reported that a large sample ($N = 597$) of visually impaired adults had WAIS Verbal scale IQs and subtest scores comparable to the normative sample, suggesting no compelling need for alternate norms nor accommodations.
Wyver, S. R, & Markham, R. (1998). Do children with visual impairments demonstrate superior short-term memory, memory strategies, and metamemory? *Journal of Visual Impairment and Blindness, 92*(11), 799–811.	Reports results using Digit Span subtest disputing previous claims that children with visual impairments had better cognitive skills than sighted peers.

have been appropriately accommodated (e.g., Reid, 1997). In many instances, these special instruments produce less accurate estimates of cognitive ability than the modified Wechsler scales (e.g., Gutterman, Ward, & Genshaft, 1985; Streitfeld & Avery, 1968).

Motor Impairments

This section provides a summary of Wechsler scale administration accommodations for individuals who have impairments, particularly those who have impairments in the ability to manipulate objects with their hands. Generally, these recommendations discourage the use of Performance Scale subtests that involve manipulation of objects (e.g., Block Design, Object Assembly), or substituting tests so that clients can respond vocally or by pointing (e.g., Wagner, 1994). However, some alternative tests may yield lower IQs than adapted Wechsler scales (e.g., Craig & Olson, 1991). As is true for the research in other areas, appropriate adaptation of the Wechsler scales is the most widely supported approach for assessing cognitive abilities.

Of course, researchers and clinicians presume that individuals who have physical disabilities requiring the use of wheelchairs or other assistive furniture and devices should have access to the assessment situation. Thus, it is presumed that clinicians would be able to provide assessments using wheelchair–accessible furniture, or other supports, to allow assessment access for individuals who have other types of physical or orthopedic impairments. One subtle issue related to motor ability and assessment is the issue of age-specific subtest norms for developing Weschler subtest scores. Binder (1987) argues that older clients' subtest scores are artificially inflated when clinicians use age-based norms for deriving standard scores, which would result in overestimating abilities (or underidentifying problems). However, it is not clear that this is conceptually defensible, as it is difficult to compare clients to a norm group from which they are not drawn when deriving scores.

Table 5 presents the summary of research addressing the use of the Wechsler scales with individuals who have a range of disabilities, including orthopedic or motor disabilities.

Learning Disabilities

Accommodating individuals who are suspected of having learning or other specific cognitive disabilities is a controversial practice. Some sources (e.g., Sattler, 2001) recommend prorating composite scores by eliminating low subtest scores, or using the higher of two IQs (VIQ or PIQ) when the scale scores differ by 15 points or more. For example, a VIQ that is 15 or more points below the PIQ would cause the examiner to eschew the FSIQ in favor of the higher Performance IQ for determining aptitude–achievement discrepancies in the identification of a learning disability. This practice is questionable on conceptual grounds (see Kamphaus, Petoskey, & Morgan, 1997) because it is a *post-hoc* procedure. That is, most clinicians invoke the decision to use the higher of the two scale scores *after* the assessment. In contrast, most adaptations for visual, hearing, or orthopedic impairments are determined *before* the assessment.

The use of *post-hoc* versus *a priori* decisions is a fundamental point of controversy. That is, many sources argue that clinicians should make decisions regarding adaptations, accommodations, and the use of parts of a battery before the assessment is conducted. This avoids capitalizing on error, and systematically introducing bias into assessment results (i.e., clinicians who always use the higher of two scores are much more likely to overestimate cognitive abilities) in assessments.

TABLE 5   Selected Research Using the Wechsler Scales with Samples of Clients with Orthopedic Disabilities

Source	Comments
Clayton, G. A, Sapp, G. L., O'Sullivan, P., & Hall, L. (1986). Comparative validity of two WAIS—R short forms with vocational rehabilitation clients. *Perceptual and Motor Skills, 63*(3), 1303–1308.	Found two- and four-subtest short forms of the WAIS-R produced unreliable estimates of Full Scale IQs in a heterogeneous sample including individuals with mental retardation, emotional disabilities, and physical/motor impairments.
Hirschenfang, S., Shulman, L., & Benton, J. G. (1968). Psychosocial factors influencing the rehabilitation of the hemiplegic patient. *Diseases of the Nervous System, 29*(6), 373–379.	Found WAIS and WMS scores differed in right versus left hemiplegia clients. Deficits were linked to differential adaptation, with lower scores and right hemiplegia associated with less desirable outcomes.
Kern, R. R., Bordieri, J. E., & Taylor, D. W. (1993). A comparison of Raven's Standard Progressive Matrices with the Wechsler Adult Intelligence Scale—Revised for individuals receiving rehabilitation services. *Vocational Evaluation and Work Adjustment Bulletin, 26*(2), 53–56.	Reported a moderate correlation between the WAIS-R and Ravens for clients who had orthopedic impairments or mental retardation, suggesting the relative independence of these estimators for cognitive abilities.
Ryan, J. J., & Paolo, A. M. (2001). Exploratory factor analysis of the WAIS-III in a mixed patient sample. *Archives of Clinical Neuropsychology, 16*(2), 151–156.	Reported factor structure in a heterogeneous patient sample (neurological/medical, psychiatric, and substance abuse disorders) was comparable to the norm sample for the WAIS-III.
Sattler, J. M. (1972). *Intelligence test modifications on handicapped and nonhandicapped children.* San Diego, CA: San Diego State University Foundation (Available from ERIC Document Reproduction Service No. ED095673).	Found modifications allowing choice/pointing responses were appropriate for some subtests, but not others, for children with cerebral palsy and mental retardation. When adaptations were inappropriate, they inflated (rather than depressed) test scores.

In contrast, the proponents of *post-hoc* decision making argue that clinicians must use the available evidence to determine the validity of scores. In a *post-hoc* decision-making model, clinicians who failed to alter their selection and interpretation of scores based on evidence would be guilty of ignoring information suggesting erroneous or misleading information. For example, using a FSIQ when the PIQ and VIQs differ by more than 15 points would arguably be presenting an estimate of cognitive abilities that is attenuated or lowered. The implicit argument is that if an individual is capable of scoring higher on a set of selected subtests, that the set of other subtests on which the individual scores low misrepresent the individual's intellectual capacity (i.e., How could an individual "score higher than their capacity?").

Interestingly, this argument has two conceptual problems. The first is that it invokes the concept of construct-irrelevant variance, without invoking the concurrent concern over construct representation. That is, clinicians who decide to use the higher of the two composite scores are essentially arguing that construct-irrelevant variance (e.g., deficits in specific cognitive abilities) artificially constrain or lower one of the two composite scores. Therefore, they argue in favor of the higher score, because it presumably carries less construct-irrelevant variance. This argument fails to consider the equally important concept of construct representation. That is, clinicians who make this decision are fundamentally less concerned that the resulting interpretation will be based on a narrower construct, and thus may be subject to invalidity due to the construct underrepresentation.

The second logical problem with the post-hoc decision to use higher scores is the notion of *capacity*. That is, the implicit argument appears to be that an individual's intellectual abilities reflect capability or capacity for performance. In this model, given the choice between a low and a high estimate of capacity, clinicians would be on strong logical grounds to retain the higher of the two estimates. In a mechanical framework, the higher of the two estimates is closer to the capacity of the system; system capacity may be reduced due to many factors, but can never exceed the ideal capacity, and thus higher scores are a more accurate reflection of the ultimate system capacity. Unfortunately, the capacity notion of intellectual abilities is fundamentally flawed (see Jensen, 1998). That is, scores from intelligence and memory tests do not represent capacities, but rather represent probabilistic statements of performance. In a probabilistic framework, the average performance or typical performance is a more valid source of interpretation than peak or extreme performances. Thus, an interpretation based on an extreme score is less valid than an interpretation based on a typical or average score. In this context, the examiner should use the Full Scale IQ, even when the relative components contributing to that composite differ substantially, because the composite better reflects typical performance. Thus, a composite or average performance is a more valid indicator of ability than a peak or extreme score.

However, the practice of post-hoc adjustments of scores to estimate cognitive abilities is still widely practiced. Arguably, examiners who invoke post-hoc decisions to use the higher of two scores, or who would prorate composite scores by eliminating the lowest subtest score(s) contributing to the composite, should be equally likely to eliminate one or two exceptionally high scores when calculating composites, as these isolated scores (or skills) undermine the accurate representation of general cognitive abilities. However, this recommendation is rarely if ever made nor invoked in practice.

Clinicians are often motivated to use the highest possible estimate of cognitive ability because it will increase the chances that a client will become eligible for special services. Learning disability is currently defined by two positive criteria: (a) a difference between aptitude and achievement, and (b) evidence of a disorder in one or more basic psychological processes (Dumont, Willis, & McBride, 2001), and one negative criterion (the absence of other causes for the learning difficulties). Consequently, clinicians increase the probability of diagnosis when they estimate aptitude using the highest possible IQ. Likewise, clinicians are likely to select the lowest composite (or even a single subtest) score from the Wechsler scales to reflect evidence of a basic disorder in psychological processing. Therefore, clinicians often use different rules for estimating intelligence (in which they eliminate low scores from composite calculations, or ignore low composites altogether) than they do for identifying deficits in processing (in which they select the lowest subtest score or composite as evidence of a deficit). Indeed, many professionals (e.g., Slemon & Shafir, 1993) invoke a pattern of low scores on selected subtests (e.g., the Arithmetic, Coding, Information, Digit Symbol/Digit Span, or ACIDS profile) as positive evidence of a learning disability, despite ample evidence that such profiles do not distinguish learning disabled from nondisabled populations (e.g., Maller & McDermott, 1997).

Consequently, accommodating learning-disabled clients on cognitive and memory tests remains a highly controversial practice. Careful examination of other information in this book (see Palmer, Taylor, & Heaton, chapter 10, this volume) shows that prorating subtests at random yields estimates of composite scores that are, on the average, within 4 to 5 points of (and highly correlated with) the full WAIS-III or WMS-III composite. However, clinicians do not omit subtests at random; rather, they tend to omit low subtest scores, or replace them with higher subtest scores. The practice of eliminating low scores systematically inflates composite estimates by approximately 0.33 to 0.60 SDs (or 5–9 points on the typical Wechsler composite metric). The question of whether omission or prorating accurately reflects ability by eliminating construct-irrelevant variance, or whether omission or prorating erodes validity by reducing construct representation, is in large part a conceptual issue. Although reducing construct-irrelevant variance is a worthy goal, it should not lead to construct underrepresentation nor to systematic bias towards higher scores.

Table 6 presents results of research using the Wechsler scales with clients who have learning disabilities. The limited references omit an abundant literature with pre-adult samples. The gist of the literature explores the use of Wechsler Profiles as a tool for diagnosing learning disability; the few studies addressing accommodations are generally limited to studies recommending omission or prorating of composite scores for clients with learning disabilities.

Neuropsychological Assessment and Accommodations

Clinicians interested in neuropsychological assessment often use the Wechsler intelligence and memory scales as tools to assess neurological functioning (e.g., Kaplan, Fein, Morris, & Delis, 1991). The purposes of neuropsycho-

TABLE 6   Selected Research Using the Wechsler Scales with Samples of Clients with Learning Disabilities

Source	Comments
Davis. J. T., Parr, G., & Lan, W. (1997). Differences between learning disability subtypes classified using the revised Woodcock-Johnson Psycho-Educational Battery. *Journal of Learning Disabilities, 30*(3), 346–352.	Shows WISC-III PIQ lower for math disabled than reading disabled students despite matching for FSIQ.
Maller, S. J., & McDermott, P. A. (1997). WAIS-R profile analysis for college students with learning disabilities. *School Psychology Review, 26*(4), 575–585.	Notes more than 90% of WAIS-R profiles for college LD students are comparable to the norm sample, arguing that profile interpretation is a questionable practice.
Morgan, A. W., Sullivan, S. A., Darden, C., & Gregg, N. (1997). Measuring the intelligence of college students with learning disabilities: A comparison of results obtained on the WAIS-R and the KAIT. *Journal of Learning Disabilities, 30*(5), 560–565.	Found the WAIS-R & KAIT to produce similar results for college-aged students with learning disabilities.
Slemon, J. C., & Shafrir, U. (1998, April). *Obtaining efficacy and aptitude measures from the ACID profiles of post-secondary students with and without severe scholastic disabilities.* Paper presented at the Annual Meeting of the American Psychological Association, San Francisco, CA. (Available from ERIC Document Reproduction Service No. ED427457.)	Suggests that college students' expectations of their performance on ACID subtests may be inaccurate, and are less accurate for students with LD. Consequently recommends deletion of Information subtest for LD diagnosis.

logical assessment often differ from those of traditional diagnostic assessment (Caplan & Shechter, 1995). Some of the points of difference include the following:

1. Isolation of specific cognitive functions versus assessment of general cognitive ability
2. The contrast between typical and optimal performance
3. Inference of specific medical or physiological conditions

In some cases, neuropsychologists share the desire to obtain an accurate estimate of the client's general intellectual abilities that is not unduly influenced by the client's disabilities.

Each purpose suggests changes in WAIS-III and WMS administration to accomplish the objectives of the assessment. Recommended changes typically focus on presentation (e.g., written vs. oral directions), response (e.g., pointing or multiple-choice selection vs. oral response), and timing (e.g., allowing extra time to respond, taking more frequent breaks to alleviate fatigue) (Caplan & Shechter, 1995). These changes can allow clients to demonstrate cognitive abilities that might be masked by their other (noncognitive) impairments, and consequently better represent the client's cognitive abilities. At other times, changes in standard assessment procedures are intended to isolate particular cognitive or noncognitive abilities, to contrast performance in one area (e.g., recalling digits presented orally) with those of another (e.g., recalling digits that are printed). Some of the features of the WMS are intended to provide clinicians with opportunities to contrast performance across modality changes. Finally, the use of the Wechsler scales to elicit standard versus optimal performance is a form of dynamic assessment (Grigarenko & Sternberg, 1998), which is typically intended to reveal abilities that may be suppressed or hidden due to various factors. Selected research using adaptations of the Wechsler scales for neuropsychological assessment is presented in Table 7.

However, clinicians should consider carefully their purposes in assessment, and the inferences they draw. Using Wechsler items to elicit responses, and interpret those responses relative to the client (e.g., the client was able to answer the item correctly with support X, but was unable to answer the item correctly under standard administration procedures), may be appropriate for some purposes, but not for others. Some problems of inference are discussed after considering research on clinicians with disabilities.

TABLE 7   Selected Research Using the Wechsler Scales with Samples of Clients with Neuropsychological Disabilities

Source	Comments
Berninger, V., Gans, B. M., St. James, P., & Connors, T. (1988). Modified WAIS-R for patients with speech and/or hand dysfunction. *Archives of Physical Medicine and Rehabilitation, 69*, 250–255.	Describes how changes in presentation, timing, and response improves scores, but not the correlation between standard and accommodated administration, in participants with disabilities compared on nondisabled participants.
Bolla-Wilson, K., Robinson, R., Price, T., & Squires, N. (1984, Feb.). *Visuoconstuctional assembly difficulty: Influence of site of lesion and task.* Paper presented at the 12th annual meeting of the International Neuropsychological Society, Houston, TX.	Used a multiple-choice version of Block Design to assess visualization difficulties in individuals with identified lesions.
Caplan, B., & Caffery, D. (1992). Fractionating Block Design: Development of a test of visuospatial analysis. *Neuropsychology, 6*, 385–394.	Presents a multiple choice version of Block Design (the Block Pattern Analysis Test) to assess visuospatial abilities independent of motor skills in normal and rehabilitation clients in an in-patient setting.
Kaplan, E., Fein, D., Morris, R., & Delis, D. C. (1991). *WAIS-R as a neuropsychological instrument.* San Antonio, TX: The Psychological Corp.	Provides procedures and materials for adaptations to the WAIS-R intended to support neuropsychological assessment (note: no data provided to support validity or reliability of the instrument, although reanalyses of normative data are provided to support identification of unusual score differences).

Research on Clinicians with Disabilities

Clinicians, too, are a diverse group. As individuals with disabilities increasingly move into professions where they have been historically underrepresented or excluded, assessment research must seek to understand how assessment practices can be accommodated for clinicians who have disabilities. Research addressing clinicians with visual impairments (e.g., Keller, 1997; King & Bashey, 1978) suggest that adapted Wechsler administration can provide accurate client assessments. Adaptations emphasizing sign language interpreters have been proposed for clinicians who are deaf and hard of hearing (Kostrubala, 1996; Cited Ford & Braden, 1996). These adaptations generally provide methods for examiners who have disabilities to ensure standardized procedures for administration and scoring of assessment devices, including the Wechsler scales. However, the impact of these accommodations on assessment validity are largely untested in controlled research, and are currently supported by logical analysis and argument (not data).

CONCLUSIONS

Clinicians are bound by two imperatives when they conduct assessments: the need to follow standardized administration practices, and the need to alter standardized practices when assessing individuals with disabilities. Historically, research and recommendations for accommodations have directed clinicians to eliminate construct-irrelevant variance, but failed to invoke the equally important imperative of retaining construct representation in the assessment. The first part of this chapter has focused on the elaboration of these competing imperatives (reducing construct-irrelevant variance while maintaining construct representation), and suggested a decision-making procedure for clinicians to follow when determining whether and how to accommodate clients with disabilities.

The second part of this chapter reviewed research using the Wechsler scales with individuals who have disabilities. This review suggests four general conclusions:

1. The Wechsler scales are consistently the most popular tool for assessing clients who have disabilities related to hearing, vision, orthopedic/motor, neuropsychological, and general and specific cognitive disabilities.
2. Accommodations to the Wechsler scales generally yield estimates of intellectual ability that have psychometric properties equal to or better than instruments with special norms, materials, or procedures developed to meet specific population needs.
3. There is little research using the WMS with disabled populations.
4. Prorating or omitting low scores when estimating the general intellectual ability of clients with specific cognitive disabilities (e.g., learning-disabled clients) is often recommended, yet ignores conceptual arguments against "capacity" notions of intellectual abilities, *post hoc* decisions, and threats to validity created by construct underrepresentation.

Although these conclusions have reasonable support from the research, it is essential to note that there are significant limitations to the strength of these conclusions for guiding clinical practice with the WAIS and WMS-III.

First, all of the research to date employs between-subjects designs for understanding accommodations. This is unfortunate, as most clinicians recognize that the variability within a group (e.g., people who have visual disabilities) is much greater than the variability between groups (e.g., disabled vs. nondisabled groups). Consequently, clinicians must be careful to adapt general principles drawn from research to the specific needs of individual clients.

A second major limitation of the research is the absence of alternate forms of the WAIS–WMS-III Scales to conduct within-person (i.e., within-subject, single case, or $N = 1$) studies of accommodation effects. Ideally, within-person studies would employ multiple alternate forms to study the effects of providing, then withdrawing, various accommodations. The lack of multiple forms is understandable (e.g., the expense of developing and standardizing a single form is well over $1 million), but it is nonetheless unfortunate.

A third limitation lies in the way in which accommodations have been conceptualized and studied. The literature to date tends to describe a single feature of assessment (e.g., using a sign language interpreter, providing a tactile form of the Block Design subtest) in isolation. In practice, most clinicians use accommodation packages, or combinations of individual accommodation practices. For example, clinicians are likely to combine multiple rest intervals, alterations in administration, and substitutions or alterations in test content when assessing an individual, rather than employing only one of these strategies (see Elliott, et al., 2001, for a discussion of this point within educational assessment). Consequently, the variable most often analyzed in research (a single accommodation) is rarely if ever invoked in practice (where clinicians combine multiple accommodations). Future research must employ so-called accommodation packages, or likely combinations of multiple accommodations, when conducting accommodation research.

Despite these limitations, it is clear that there are legal, ethical, and evidence-based imperatives to support the accommodations of individuals with disabilities in assessments. Although clinical assessment will always be guided by science, it must also be guided by the clinical art of accommodating general principles to the specific needs and complexities of an individual client. I conclude this chapter by providing a list of practices to help clinicians accommodate clients with disabilities when using the WAIS/WMS-III.

Practices to Promote

1. Use the decision tree to make appropriate decisions about when to accommodate assessments. In general, accommodations should be avoided, as their value is not clearly supported by research, and their influence on validity is often unknown. Therefore, if clinicians can avoid an accommodation, either because the client's disability will not introduce construct-irrelevant variability in the score, or because a standardized alternative will provide the information needed, they should do so.

2. Consider both construct-irrelevant variance and construct underrepresentation when accommodating a client. Considering both sources of invalidity will be more likely to lead to accommodations that retain validity than consideration of only one source of invalidity.

3. Clarify the "target" versus "access" skills in the assessment. It is appropriate to provide accommodations to eliminate the negative effects of access skills on an assessment, but it is inappropriate to do so to improve target skills.

4. Use accommodations drawn from the client's real-life contexts. Introducing novel accommodations into the assessment may undermine client performance; likewise, using accommodations that the client or others find adaptive is likely to lead to effective accommodations.

5. Use available research to guide accommodation decisions and interpretations. Surprisingly, some research suggests that accommodations may lower client scores, and that unimpaired clients may benefit more from some accommodations than others. Although sparse, the literature can provide some guidance for accommodations decisions.

6. Consider carefully the impact of construct underrepresentation on the validity of pro-rated IQs or other composites developed when subtests are omitted. For example, interpreting PIQ as an index of general intellectual ability for a deaf client may overestimate the client's ability to function in situations in which fund of knowledge, verbal reasoning, or other language-related skills are required.

7. Specify and consider the conditions under which the client obtained scores when interpreting scores. Although it may be true that a client's score increased dramatically when the client was provided a particular accommodation, it behooves the clinician to consider the degree of support (e.g., one-to-one support from a highly educated professional) needed to achieve the score, and the degree to which such supports are likely to be available in other contexts.

8. Replicate findings when possible using alternate forms, independent examiners, or other means to enhance the reliability of the client's performance. The principle of "multiple" (i.e., multiple methods, raters, settings, opportunities) enhances assessment reliability, which is a necessary but not sufficient condition for valid interpretations.

Practices to Avoid

1. Do not report standard scores obtained from invalid accommodations. Some clinicians may choose to alter WAIS and WMS-III procedures in ways that invalidate the intended interpretation of the scores. For example, training, retesting, or other dynamic assessment approaches with the WMS may be useful for medical, neuropsychological, or other purposes. However, procedures that clearly alter the construct represented (e.g., changing the WMS from a memory test to a supported learning test) require the clinician to avoid reporting standard scores (IQs, subtest scale scores), because standard scores from subtests and composites reflect a different construct.

2. Do not confuse distinct frames of reference when interpreting scores. It may be valid to explore how a client's score changes when one tests the limits (i.e., when a clinician provides additional supports following a standard administration to assess score improvement), as long as the changes are reported relative to the client (an individual frame of reference). It is invalid to suggest the improvement of scores reflects a change in a normative frame of reference. Therefore, reporting changes in a qualitative, self-referenced frame (e.g., "when provided with multiple-choice alternatives, the client answered 25% more questions correctly") is preferred to reporting score changes in an IQ format. The latter approach could easily lead to inappropriate inferences (e.g., the client's cognitive ability is similar to individuals obtaining the higher IQ, when in fact those individuals achieved the same score without support, and are therefore much more likely to have higher cognitive abilities than does the client).

3. Do not presume "higher is better" when interpreting scores. Many clinicians erroneously presume that cognition is a phenomenon similar to mechanical potential or capacity, in which score variability only works to depress scores. For example, machines can fall short of or approach their optimal capacity, but never exceed it. Consequently, the higher scores achieved by the machine are probably the best estimate of its capacity. Although tempting, using a similar approach is inappropriate for interpreting cognitive (and other psychological) scores. Instead, scores are reflections

of underlying parameters or latent constructs, which are best estimated by average (not optimal) scores (see Salsberg, 2001, for a discussion of this conceptualization of measurement and how it influenced science generally).

4. Avoid confirmatory bias. Many examiners begin with presuppositions regarding client conditions (e.g., the client's abilities are higher than others suspect, the client's problems in academics or work may be caused by the client's cognitive weaknesses), and then collect data to test these presuppositions. Early data may support the clinician's presuppositions, leading to premature termination of data collection. Clinicians should instead seek data to disconfirm their presuppositions, rather than confirm them, to avoid premature confirmation or diagnosis.

REFERENCES

American Educational Research Association, American Psychological Association, & National Council on Measurement in Education (1999). *Standards for educational and psychological testing* (3rd ed.). Washington, DC: Author.

American Psychiatric Association (2000). *Diagnostic and statistical manual of mental disorders : DSM-IV-TR (4th ed., text revision).* Washington, DC: Author.

Anderson R. J. & Sisco, F. H. (1977). *Standardization of WISC-R Performance Scale for deaf children* (Office of Demographic Studies Publication Series T., No. 1). Washington, DC: Gallaudet University.

Bauman, M. K., & Kropf, C. A. (1979). Psychological tests used with blind and visually handicapped persons. *School Psychology Review, 8*(3), 257–270.

Binder, L. M. (1987). Appropriate reporting of Wechsler IQ and subtest scores in assessments for disability. *Journal of Clinical Psychology, 43*(1), 144–145.

Braden, J. P. (1992). Intellectual assessment of deaf and hard of hearing people: A quantitative and qualitative research synthesis. *School Psychology Review,* 21, 82–94.

Braden, J. P. (1994). *Deafness, deprivation, and IQ.* New York: Plenum Press.

Braden, J. P. (1999). Accommodations in testing: Methods to ensure validity. *Assessment Focus,* (vol. 8, pp. 1–3). San Antonio, TX: The Psychological Corporation. Available on line: at *http://www.psychcorp.com/pdf/assessspr99.pdf*

Braden, J. P., & Hannah, J. M. (1998). Assessment of hearing-impaired and deaf children with the WISC—III. In A. Prifitera & D. H. Saklofske (Eds.), *WISC—III clinical use and interpretation: Scientist–practitioner perspectives* (pp. 175–201). San Diego, CA: Academic Press.

Braden, J. P., Schroeder, J. L., & Buckley, J. A. (2001). *Secondary school reform, inclusion, and authentic assessment* (Research Institute on Secondary Education Reform—Youths with Disabilities Brief No. 3). Madison, WI: Wisconsin Center for Education Research.

Bradley-Johnson, S., & Evans, L. D. (1991). *Psychoeducational assessment of hearing-impaired students: Infancy through high school.* Austin, TX: PRO-ED.

Caplan, B., & Shechter, J. (1995). The role of nonstandard neuropsychological assessment in rehabilitation: History, rationale, and examples. In L. A. Cushman & M. J. Scherer (Eds.), *Psychological assessment in medical rehabilitation: Measurement and instrumentation in psychology* (pp. 359–391). Washington, DC: American Psychological Association.

Carroll, J. B. (1993). *Human cognitive abilities: A survey of factor-analytic studies.* New York: Cambridge University Press.

Craig, R. J., & Olson, R. E. (1991). Relationship between Wechsler scales and Peabody Picture Vocabulary Test—Revised scores among disability applicants. *Journal of Clinical Psychology, 47*(3), 420–429.

Dauterman, W. L., & Suinn, R. M. (1966). *Stanford-Ohwaki-Kohs Tactile Block Design Intelligence Test for the Blind Final Report (Part 1).* Palo Alto, CA: Stanford University School of Medicine (Available from ERIC Document Reproduction Service No. ED012119).

Davis, C. (1980). *Perkins-Binet Tests of Intelligence for the Blind.* Watertown, MA: Perkins School for the Blind.

Dumont, R., Willis, W., & McBride, T. (2001). Yes, Virginia, there is a severe discrepancy clause, but is it too much ado about something? *The School Psychologist, 55*(1), 1, 4–13, 15.

Elliott, S. N, Kratochwill, T. R., & McKevitt, B. C. (2001). Experimental analysis of the effects of testing accommodations on the scores of students with and without disabilities. *Journal of School Psychology, 39*(1), 3–24.

Ford, L., & Braden, J. P. (1996, Aug.). *Equitable psychological assessment for language-minority learners: Theory, research, and practice.* Symposium presented at the Annual Meeting of the American Psychological Association, Toronto, Canada.

Gardner, H. (1999). *Intelligence reframed: Multiple intelligences for the 21st century.* New York: Basic Books.

Gibbins, S. (1989). The provision of school psychological assessment services for the hearing impaired: A national survey. *Volta Review, 91*(2), 95–103.

Gordon, R. P., Stump, K., & Glaser, B. A. (1996). Assessment of individuals with hearing impairments: Equity in testing procedures and accommodations. *Measurement and Evaluation in Counseling and Development, 29*(2), 111–118.

Grigorenko, E. L., & Sternberg, R. J. (1998). Dynamic testing. *Psychological Bulletin, 124*(1), 75–111.

Gutterman, J. E., Ward, M, & Genshaft, J. (1985). Correlations of scores of low vision children on the Perkins-Binet Tests of Intelligence for the Blind, the WISC-R and the WRAT. *Journal of Visual Impairment and Blindness, 79*(2), 55–58.

Harris, J. G., Tulsky, D. S., & Schultheis, M. T. (2003). Assessment of the non-native english speaker: Assimilating history and research findings to guide clinical practice. In Tulsky, D. S. et al. (Eds). *Clinical Interpretation of the WAIS-III and WMS-III.* San Diego: Academic Press, pp. 343–390.

Hishinuma, E. S. (1995). WISC-III accommodations: The need for practitioner guidelines. *Journal of Learning Disabilities, 28*(3), 130–135.

Horn J. L. & Noll, J. (1997). Human cognitive capabilities: Gf-Gc theory. In D. P. Flanagan, J. L. Genshaft, & P. A. Harrison (Eds.). *Contemporary intellectual assessment: Theories, and issues* (pp. 53–91). New York: Guilford.

Jenkinson, J. (1989). Use of the WISC-R Performance Scale with hearing-impaired children: A review. *Psychological Test Bulletin, 2*(1), 33–38.

Jensen, A. R. (1980). *Bias in mental testing.* New York: Free Press.

Jensen, A. R. (1998). *The g factor: The science of mental ability.* Westport, CT: Praeger.

Kamphaus, R. W., Petoskey, M. D., & Morgan, A. W. (1997). A history of intelligence test interpretation. In D. P., Flanagan, J. L. Genshaft, & P. A. Harrison (Eds.), *Contemporary intellectual assessment: Theories, tests, and issues* (pp. 32–47). New York: Guilford.

Kaplan, E., Fein, D., Morris, R., & Delis, D. C. (1991). *WAIS-R as a neuropsychological instrument.* San Antonio, TX: The Psychological Corporation.

Keller, R. M. (1997). *Adaptation of psychological assessment tools for administration by blind and visually impaired psychologists and trainees* (ERIC Document Reproduction Service No. ED428487).

King, D. W., & Bashey, H. I. (1978). Abbreviated WAIS for administration by blind persons: A preliminary study. *Journal of Visual Impairment and Blindness, 72*(3), 94–97.

Kostrubala, C. E., & Braden, J. P. (1998). *Administration of the WAIS-III in American Sign Language* [videotape]. San Antonio, TX: The Psychological Corporation.

Langset, M., Midtvedt, T., & Omland, T. (1989). Toxoplasmosis in blind and partially sighted children and adolescents. *Journal of Visual Impairment and Blindness, 83*(7), 355–358.

Maller, S. J., & McDermott, P. A. (1997). WAIS-R profile analysis for college students with learning disabilities, *School Psychology Review, 26*(4), 575–585.

McGrew, K. S., & Flanagan, D. P. (1998). *The intelligence test desk reference (ITDR): Gf-Gc cross-battery assessment.* Boston: Allyn and Bacon.

Messick, S.A. (1995). Validity of psychological assessment: Validation of inferences from persons' responses and performances as scientific inquiry into score meaning. *American Psychologist, 50*(9): 741–749.

Miller, M. S. (1984) *Experimental use of signed presentations of the Verbal Scale of the WISC-R with profoundly deaf children: A preliminary report of the sign selection process and experimental test procedures.* Paper presented at the International Symposium on Cognition, Education, and Deafness, Washington, DC (ERIC Document Reproduction Service No. ED 170 082).

Naglieri, J. A. (2000). Intelligence testing in the 21st century: A look at the past and suggestion for the future. *Educational and Child Psychology, 17*(3), 6–18.

Office of Civil Rights (2000). *The use of tests as part of high-stakes decision-making for students: A resource guide for educators and policy makers.* Washington, DC: U.S. Department of Education (author). (Available at *http://www.ed.gov/offices/OCR/testing/index1.html*)

Palmer, B. W., Taylor, M. J., & Heaton, R. K. (2003). Accuracy of WAIS-III and WMS-III joint factor scores when one or more subtests is omitted or an alternative subtest is employed. In D. S. Tulsky et al. (Eds). *Clinical Interpretation of the WAIS-III and WMS-III.* San Diego: Academic Press, pp. 391–447.

Phillips, S. E. (1993). Testing condition accommodations for disabled students. *West's Education Law Quarterly, 2*(2), 366–389.

Phillips, S. E. (1994). High-stakes testing accommodations: Validity versus disabled rights. *Applied Measurement in Education, 7*(2), 93–120.

Phillips, S. E. (1996). Legal defensibility of standards: Issues and policy perspectives. *Educational Measurement: Issues and Practice, 15*(2), 5–19.

Reid, J. M. V. (1997). Standardized ability testing for vocational rehabilitation in visually impaired adults: A literature review. *Journal of Visual Impairment and Blindness, 91*(6), 546–554.

Rich, C. C., & Anderson, R. P. (1965). A tactual form of the progressive matrices for use with blind children. *Personnel and Guidance Journal, 43*(9), 912–919.

Ryan, J. J., & Paolo, A. M. (2001). Exploratory factor analysis of the WAIS-III in a mixed patient sample. *Archives of Clinical Neuropsychology, 16*(2), 151–156.

Salsburg, D. (2001). *The lady tasting tea: How statistics revolutionized science in the twentieth century.* New York: W. H. Freeman.

Sattler, J. M. (2001). *Assessment of children: Cognitive applications* (4th ed.). La Mesa, CA: Jerome M. Sattler, Publisher. Newland, T. E. (1979). The Blind Learning Aptitude Test. *Journal of Visual Impairment and Blindness, 73* (4), 134–139.

Slemon, J. C., & Shafrir, U. (1998, April). *Obtaining efficacy and aptitude measures from the ACID profiles of post-secondary students with and without severe scholastic disabilities.* Paper presented at the Annual Meeting of the American Psychological Association, San Francisco, CA. (Available from ERIC Document Reproduction Service No. ED427457.)

Streitfeld, J. W., & Avery, C. D. (1968). The WAIS and HIS tests as predictors of academic achievement in a residential school for the blind. *International Journal for the Education of the Blind, 18*(3), 73–77.

Wagner, P. A. (1994). Adaptations for administering the Peabody Picture Vocabulary Test—Revised to individuals with severe communication and motor dysfunctions. *Mental Retardation, 32*, 107–112.

Wechsler, D. (1997). *Wechsler Adult Intelligence Scale—Third Edition* (WAIS-III). San Antonio, TX: Psychological Corporation.

Yarnall, G. D., & Carlton, G. R. (1981). *Guidelines and manual of tests for educators interested in the assessment of handicapped children* (ERIC Document Reproduction Service Document Number ED209788). Austin, TX: International Research Institute.

Training Others to Administer the WAIS-III and WMS-III: A Guide to Practical Issues

Soon after practitioners began to integrate the WAIS-III and WMS-III into their routine clinical practices, questions began to emerge on various electronic listserves and at professional conferences concerning the nuances of test administration, scoring, and interpretation of these new tests. While considerable attention had been given to developing standardized scoring and administration guidelines during the development of the revised Wechsler tests, use among clinical populations elicited responses and situations that were not anticipated by the publisher. Further, test users began to question the nature of various observed test patterns, the psychometic properties of test variables, and the composition of different subtests. In the spirit of this volume to take the WAIS-III and WMS-III to the next level in terms of clinical use, we felt that it would be fitting to include a chapter that attempts to address 'frequently asked questions' regarding practical matters that are not formally covered in the respective WAIS-III and WMS-III manuals. Since we anticipate that many of the professionals who read this book will be engaged in clinical training and/or supervision of graduate students and interns, we felt that these questions might be most effectively addressed within the context of an instructional or training guide.

To help us achieve our goal, we solicited the assistance of Drs. Laura Lacritz and Munro Cullum to write this chapter. Drs. Lacritz and Cullum not only have considerable expertise in neuropsychological assessment and research, but they also have large clinical practices and work closely with graduate and postgraduate trainees and psychometrists who routinely administer the Wechsler Scales. In preparing their chapter, Drs. Lacritz and Cullum not only discussed test administration and scoring issues with a number of their psychometrists who had extensive experience with the tests, but also solicited feedback from other psychometrists via the National Association of Psychometrists. This helped shape the chapter as a resource for 'frequently asked questions' and also as an instructional guide for training others in test administration and use of the new Wechsler instruments. The resulting chapter provides basic knowledge for graduate students and postdoctoral fellows, which can supplement their reading of the information provided in the respective test manuals and in the other chapters included in this text.

David S. Tulsky

Gordon J. Chelune

CHAPTER 12

The WAIS-III and WMS-III: Practical Issues and Frequently Asked Questions

Laura H. Lacritz, & C. Munro Cullum

University of Texas
Southwestern Medical Center at Dallas

INTRODUCTION

This chapter is designed to address some important practical issues that may not be explicitly covered in the manuals that accompany the WAIS-III (Wechsler, 1997a) and WMS-III (Wechsler, 1997b). The topics covered in this chapter are "must knows" for anyone who uses the WAIS-III and WMS-III, and will be helpful to even seasoned clinicians, as some of the issues raised have important implications for test interpretation. Therefore, this chapter may serve as an adjunct teaching tool for new trainees, a review for veteran examiners, and a quick reference guide for clinicians when questions about the tests arise. The Frequently Asked Questions section at the end of the chapter may be of particular interest to clinicians at various levels of experience, and highlights some of the most current research pertaining to the WAIS-III and WMS-III. Included in this section are suggestions regarding interpretation of some of the new subtests and scores that are available. It is hoped that the information in this chapter will assist readers in becoming more informed and critical users of these tests, and that it will spur others to look for answers when questions regarding these instruments arise. Continued clinical and research experience with these measures in various patient populations will further our understanding of the utility of the WAIS-III and WMS-III components and their interpretation.

WHY USE THE WAIS-III AND WMS-III IF YOU ALREADY HAVE THE WAIS-R AND WMS-R?

The unfamiliarity of new or updated tests can pose barriers to adopting such measures in clinical practice. In addition, when major changes are made in a revised version of an instrument (as with the WMS-III), there is a healthy uncertainty about applying previously formed assumptions and interpretations (based on clinical experience and research findings) of test performance to the new measure. However, there are many reasons why using the WAIS-III and WMS-III makes good clinical sense, even if one is satisfied with previous versions of these tests (see Table 1). Furthermore, the preceding

TABLE 1   Ten Reasons for Switching to the WAIS-III and WMS-III

- Norms reflect greater ethnic diversity
- Larger standardization samples (WAIS-III = 2,450, WMS-III = 1,250 weighted cases) compared with WAIS-R ($n = 1,880$) and WMS-R ($n = 316$)
- Expanded age range norms (up to 89 vs. 74 with the WAIS-R and WMS-R) and more subjects per age band
- WAIS-III and WMS-III co-normed to facilitate more direct comparisons between measures
- Easier to use administration and scoring manuals (e.g., scoring criteria for WAIS-III verbal subtests in same section as administration guidelines)
- Content and artwork of items have been updated and revised to better represent our multicultural society and new subtests were added
- Greater emphasis on age-scaled scores versus reference scaled scores, drawing attention to the impact that certain demographic variables (e.g., age) can have on test performance
- Six-factor model allows for more direct analysis of specific individual strengths and weaknesses and helps guide additional test selection based on referral question
- Greater number of qualitative performance variables (e.g., retention rates, recognition memory subtests, discrepancy tables) available to aid in interpretation
- Less emphasis on timed performance and greater measurement of fluid reasoning on WAIS-III Performance subtests with inclusion of Matrix Reasoning

chapters of this book provide a great deal of detail about the specific changes in the WAIS-III and WMS-III, additional data for new and alternate index scores, rationale for these changes, and utility of the six-factor model when using these tests together that should help readers feel more comfortable with these measures. In addition, global factors such as effects of demo-graphic variables, base rate data, and test–retest issues have been presented to allow for a more sophisticated approach in using these measures and should serve as incentives to upgrade to the WAIS-III and WMS-III. Of course, there are also times when using the former versions of these tests may be indicated, such as when needing to compare results to previous scores obtained from earlier versions of the tests or maintaining consistency in data collection for research purposes. See Tulsky and Ledbetter (2000) for a review of issues driving the need to update these measures and how the revisions impact their use in clinical and research settings.

As results from the 2000 census data (U.S. Department of Commerce, U.S. Census Bureau, 2001) make clear, we are witnessing demographic shifts in our nation, with increasing representation of various ethnic groups and the elderly. Therefore, one advantage to using the WAIS-III and WMS-II is that the standardization samples better reflect demographic changes in our society and are more specifically stratified by ethnic group (e.g., Cauca-sian, African American, Hispanic, other) to be compatible with 1995 census data compared with WAIS-R (Wechsler, 1981) and WMS-R (Wechsler, 1987) standardization samples. Although these efforts clearly represent an improvement compared with the standardization samples from earlier versions of these tests, Heaton et al. (Chapter 5, this volume) cautions users not to underestimate the effects that certain demographic effects may still have on these measures. As a result, the use of demographically corrected norms as interpretive guidelines is advised for the most accurate representa-tion of a person's performance.

The standardization samples for the WAIS-III and WMS-III are larger than previous versions of these tests, particularly for the WMS-III, which is composed of 1,250 weighted cases, compared to only 316 for the WMS-R. In addition, the upper age range has been extended from 74 to 89, which makes these tests particularly attractive for evaluating older individuals. Furthermore, the WMS-III was co-normed with subjects from the WAIS-III standardization sample, which allows for more direct comparisons be-tween performances on these measures. Given that the WAIS-III and WMS-III are significantly correlated, the use of overlapping subjects in the standardization samples of these measures facilitates comparisons of memory and intellectual abilities. To this end, "expected" WMS-III index scores can be derived from WAIS-III scores, and the significance of discrepancies between observed and expected scores can be evaluated. Additional examination of the use of base rates as they pertain to the WAIS-III and WMS-III is presented in Smith et al. (Chapter 7, this volume) to allow for a more critical analysis of score scatter and discrepancies within and across measures. In addition, Lineweaver and Chelune (Chapter 8, this volume) address these concepts in relation to evaluation of retest data and how to detect a meaningful change in performance by taking into account factors such as practice effects, regression to the mean, standard error of measurement, and other forms of bias (e.g., demographic variables).

From a test administration perspective, the WAIS-III and WMS-III are easier to give in some respects, as stimulus books and administration manuals are larger, can be folded to sit upright on the table, and have directions and scoring criteria in the same sections where appropriate. To illustrate, scoring examples and criteria are included in the test administration sections of the WAIS-III manuals for each of the verbal subtests. This is particularly helpful when having to decide whether to query responses or discontinue subtests. Items have been updated to be more culturally diverse, and color has been added to various WAIS-III test stimuli (e.g., Picture Completion, Picture Arrangement), thereby providing a more modern and realistic look to the test. In addition, timing of items, discontinuation criteria, and number of items (e.g., extending the "floor") have been modified on some WAIS-III subtests, and test booklets are more user-friendly (e.g., including start points, larger spaces to record items).

Additional subtests have been included (particularly on the WMS-III), and material-specific index scores can be computed in addition to IQ and subtest scores to provide more qualitative analyses of performance. The six-factor model that has been emphasized in this book highlights a shift away from traditional IQ score analysis of performance to a more qualitative assessment of performance (i.e., incorporating more principles of neuropsychology). As a result, the entire tests do not need to be administered to derive individual index scores. For example, to obtain the Verbal Comprehension and Perceptual Organization index scores, only the Vocabulary, Similarities, Information, Picture Completion, Block Design, and Matrix Reasoning subtests would need to be administered. This is one way that test batteries can be shortened, while still providing meaningful information about global cognitive abilities when IQ scores per se are not needed. More specific details about how subtests were updated and which subtests were added or made optional can be found in Tulsky et al. (Chapter 2, this volume).

ADMINISTRATION

The information provided in this section is based largely on standard administration guidelines as presented in the WAIS-III and WMS-III manuals and may be helpful as an adjunct teaching tool when training new examiners (e.g., graduate students, psychometrists), as common administration pitfalls are highlighted. It should be noted that this is not meant to discourage the use of more qualitative or expanded testing and scoring procedures such as those included in the Wechsler Adult Intelligence Scale-Revised as a Neuropsychological Instrument (WAIS-R NI; Kaplan, Fein, Morris, & Delis, 1991). In addition, we should note that because of test security issues, examples throughout the chapter do not include actual test items and are presented to illustrate particular points that can be extrapolated to items on associated subtests.

Teaching the Basics

In training new examiners, the need to be thoroughly familiar with test stimuli, reverse rules, etc., should be emphasized, particularly when working with impaired or lower functioning patients. It is not uncommon for such individuals to respond to test items and questions in ways that are not in the administration manual, leaving it to the examiner to use his or her clinical judgment and experience to respond appropriately to the situation. Although this may make psychological assessment more intriguing, it can also be anxiety producing for those just starting out, and preparing new examiners for the most common types of "unusual" patient responses is important.

Table 2 provides a basic checklist that could be given to trainees with steps to take in learning to administer the WAIS-III and WMS-III. Whereas one cannot train for every conceivable circumstance, trainees should be encouraged to thoroughly review all test items and instructions as well as practice the tests with someone who responds in atypical, nonstandardized ways. Furthermore, familiarity with practice items, reversal rules, and correct responses (particularly on the Vocabulary, Similarities, Information, and Comprehension subtests of the WAIS-III) is essential to facilitate a smooth and time-efficient administration. In addition to allowing trainees sufficient time to practice tests before administering them to patients, having them score actual protocols during the training process will increase their familiarity with subtest responses and help to better identify when to query and how to score ambiguous answers. A major advantage in the revision of the

TABLE 2   Checklist to Prepare for First Administration of WAIS–III or WMS–III

Take the tests yourself to see what it is like on the other side of the table (scores obviously would not be valid).

Be familiar with all items and correct responses.

Observe one or more test administrations by an experienced examiner.

Practice the tests with others and make sure they make some mistakes. If you practice only with someone who is "normal," you may be thrown off guard when working with an impaired patient.

Practice using the stopwatch and recording accurate times. (A common error for new administrators is to stop tasks prematurely, mistaking 1′20″ on the stop watch for 120″).

Practice scoring real test protocols.

Consider putting tabs in the WAIS–III stimulus book to mark first administration item in order to make page turning more efficient, especially when having to reverse.

The more comfortable you are with these measures, the more comfortable the examinee will be during the testing process.

WAIS–III is the inclusion of the correct responses and scoring examples directly in the administration sections for the Vocabulary, Similarities, and Comprehension subtests. However, this does not reduce the need to be familiar with the correct responses, when to query, and when to move to the next item, as extended study of responses during test administration will prolong the testing process and may bore, fatigue, or irritate patients unnecessarily, potentially compromising rapport and/or subsequent effort. Table 3 includes a list of Do's and Don'ts for WAIS–III and WMS–III administration that could be provided to trainees when first learning these tests.

Introduction of Tests and Establishing and Maintaining Rapport

For many patients, the testing process can be anxiety provoking, and the idea of intellectual and memory testing may evoke fears that they will look or feel "stupid." As a result, some individuals may be hesitant to respond if they are not completely certain of the correctness of their answer. In addition, anxiety can interfere with properly attending to test instructions and items, which could be particularly detrimental to performance on subtests where the standard rules do not provide for repetition of items (e.g., Digit Span, Letter–Number Sequencing, entire WMS–III) or allow for only a single

TABLE 3   Do's and Don'ts of Test Administration

Do's	Don'ts
• Be familiar enough with directions that you can make eye contact with the examinee and easily demonstrate or point to test stimuli when necessary.	• Don't adlib directions.
• Be familiar enough with correct answers to not over- or under-query or give too few/many responses.	• Don't try to score all responses as you go along.
• Note important behavioral observations when appropriate.	• Don't make so many notes that it will be difficult to go back and find the most clinically significant behavioral observations.
• Give breaks when requested and/or if examinee seems overly tired or frustrated.	• Don't take breaks in the middle of subtests or during time-sensitive delay periods if possible.
• Provide encouragement to facilitate examinee's best effort.	• Don't tell examinee whether responses are right or wrong.
• Consider testing the limits to gain additional qualitative information about examinee performance/abilities.	• Don't deviate from the standardized procedures if it will invalidate examinees' scores or corrupt future retest performance.
• Allow examinees to go over time on items (without credit) if you feel it will facilitate rapport and provide qualitative information.	• Don't let examinees continue on items for extended periods of time, as this could cause frustration and ultimate fatigue with the testing process.
• Trust your clinical judgment to deal appropriately when unusual situations occur—there is not always an absolute "right" way to handle unusual examinee responses or questions.	• Don't avoid checking with others to see how they would have handled similar, difficult testing or scoring dilemmas.

Everybody makes mistakes! Try to learn from them and learn from your patients—they are the best teachers!

repetition (e.g., Arithmetic). Making new examiners aware of these potential issues and providing them with scripts to use with patients in how to introduce tests or address common patient fears should help both the examiner and the patient feel more at ease. Using the six-factor model as a framework for memory and intellectual assessment, it can be explained to patients that the assessment process is designed to examine their performance in a number of cognitive domains, some of which can be affected in various medical and psychological disorders. Helping trainees learn to tie the assessment process together with the referral question and the patient's concerns provides for a more sophisticated presentation of the testing process. This is also important when giving patients and referral sources feedback regarding test performance.

> Tip: Help new trainees learn to tailor their testing approach to the individual and be responsive to examinees' needs for information, clarification, reassurance, and support to facilitate the testing process and obtain optimal performance from each individual.

Testing the Impaired Patient

Testing patients who have gross cognitive impairments or sensory deficits (e.g., visual or hearing impairment) can pose a unique set of difficulties (Heaton & Heaton, 1981). Individuals with severe memory problems and/ or impaired comprehension will often need to have test instructions repeated and/or simplified to facilitate their understanding of what is expected of them. This seems to be most problematic on the WAIS-III for the Performance subtests, as well as with the Arithmetic and Letter–Number Sequencing subtests. However, depending upon the level of impairment, problems can arise on any of the subtests. Given that items should not be repeated on Digit Span or Letter–Number Sequencing, it is imperative to determine whether the patient understands the task during the instructions and simplify directions if necessary. Patients with dementia will often ask for Arithmetic items or parts of items to be repeated or request paper and pencil to figure them out. Although paper and pencil cannot be provided, the *entire* question can be repeated one time, *but the time to do so is included in the total time allowed for the item.* Further repetition or simplification of Arithmetic items is not permitted under standard administration procedures. Although reasonable explanation and repetition of instructions is permitted, one must avoid providing the patient with any type of strategy to perform the test, and it must be kept in mind that deviations from standardized test instructions could impact the validity of the results in terms of normative comparisons. This is an area where clinical judgment must be exercised in order to obtain the most useful information. In addition, when working with impaired populations, one should be able to handle the impact of many sensory deficits (e.g., impaired vision or hearing) on test performance. Preparing new examiners to handle these situations will facilitate the testing process with such individuals (see Braden, Chapter 11, this volume for more details).

> ⊙ Warning: Simplification and repetition of instructions is permitted, but avoid providing examinees with ideas about strategies to perform tasks. Keep in mind that deviation from standardized instructions could impact the validity of the results and/or the ability to confidently use the norms to derive standard scores.

Whereas even most impaired patients can tolerate extended neuro-psychological and psychological assessment well, there are instances where this is not the case, and selection of particular subtests for an abbreviated evaluation may be indicated. For instance, some examiners administer only those subtests from the WAIS-III needed to derive the Verbal Comprehension and Perceptual Organization index scores (Vocabulary, Similarities, Information, Picture Completion, Block Design, and Matrix Reasoning). Furthermore, an entire WMS-III can be overly taxing for some patients with severe memory impairment, particularly within the context of generalized cognitive decline such as Alzheimer's disease. Our experience suggests that such individuals seem to be most confused and frustrated by Verbal Paired Associates and Family Pictures, compared to Logical Memory and Faces. Although Visual Reproduction is an optional visual memory subtest, it is very familiar to those who previously used the WMS and WMS-R, and should be considered, particularly in light of the data presented in this book, which suggests Visual Reproduction loads higher on the Visual Memory Factor than does the Faces subtest. Even though Visual Reproduction is more difficult to score than the other visual memory subtests, it is generally understandable for patients with memory impairment. Clarification of some scoring issues associated with the Visual Reproduction subtest will be reviewed later in this chapter.

> Tip: If an examinee cannot tolerate full testing, consider selecting only those subtests needed to calculate the most desirable index scores given the referral question.

Repeating Instructions/Items

When teaching these measures to new trainees, some time should be devoted to how to deal with repetition of items and instructions, as the need to do so commonly arises, particularly with more impaired popula-tions. As stated above, instructions may be repeated or further clarified for each of the subtests as needed, and may be necessary with some patients. On the WAIS-III, it may not be apparent that the patient has misunderstood the task until you actually begin the test. Therefore, a number of subtests allow for some training or have practice items to facilitate understanding. Of the Verbal IQ subtests, only Similarities (item 6), Digit Span backwards (practice items), and Letter–Number Sequencing (practice items) allow for formal demonstration of correct responses, although certain queries are permitted on the other Verbal subtests (i.e., Vocabulary, Information, Comprehension) to give patients an opportunity to clarify their answers where appropriate. Alternatively, all of the Performance IQ subtests have training and/or practice items, including Picture Completion (items 6 and 7), Digit Symbol-Coding (practice items), Block Design (items 5 and 6 and reversal items), Matrix Reasoning (practice items), Picture Arrangement (item1 trial 2), Symbol Search (sample and practice items), and Object Assembly (item 1). If examinees are still unsure of the task after the training and practice items for Digit Symbol-Coding, Matrix Reasoning, and Symbol Search, it is acceptable and warranted to review the items again and/or further explain the task to ensure that examinees understand what they are to do. However, once you have completed the various practice and training items, standard administration rules prohibit the provision of additional help, except to repeat instructions and/or items where allowed. When providing additional clarification or repeating items on timed measures (Arithmetic and all Performance subtests except Matrix Reasoning), timing is not stopped once started. In addition, if a patient resumes working on an item after the timer has been stopped, timing should be restarted and an estimate of how

---

Note: Additional practice/training is permissible on the Digit Symbol-Coding, Matrix Reasoning, and Symbol Search subtests to ensure that examinees understand what is expected prior to commencement of these tasks, but no further assistance can be given once the tests begin.

Note: It is allowable for an examinee to self-correct or continue working on timed measures even after the timer has been stopped (if time remains), but the timer must be restarted and an estimate of how much time has elapsed must be calculated.

much time has passed while the timer was not running should be added to the total time.

On the WMS-III, impaired individuals often have difficulty understanding the instructions for Verbal Paired Associates and Family Pictures. It may be necessary to repeat and simplify directions on Verbal Paired Associates prior to beginning the test in order to ensure that the examinee understands the task. The confusion on Family Pictures often occurs during the recall questions after the scenes have been presented, so it is necessary that the task be as clear as possible to the examinee before beginning the test in order to ensure maximal performance. Therefore, adequate attention is imperative for examinees to perform at their optimal level. This tends to be of particular importance on items that are only presented once, or on tests that require sustained attention to stimuli. For example, the memory testing portion of the Faces and Family Pictures subtests does not begin until all of the items have been presented, so patients must sufficiently attend throughout the presentation period. If they are not paying close enough attention during presentation of the stimuli, they will have trouble being able to recall the information later on. Such a scenario could result in an overinterpretation of poor performance, when in fact the difficulty was the simple result of inadequate attention.

Comprehension of instructions and attention to test stimuli are of equal importance on the Mental Control and Working Memory subtests as well. The Digit Span and Letter–Number Sequencing subtests are identical to those from the WAIS-III and do not need to be readministered on the WMS-III if they have already been given as part of the WAIS-III (and vice versa). In fact, the working memory factor, as presented in the six-factor model, is composed of the Spatial Span and Letter–Number Sequencing subtests from the WMS-III, suggesting that Digit Span and Arithmetic do not necessarily need to be administered. However, the familiarity of these tests, particularly Digit Span, to many examiners may lead to some hesitancy to give up those subtests. Although simple attention and aspects of working memory may remain relatively preserved in some impaired populations (e.g., Alzheimer's disease), portions of the Working Memory subtests may still be challenging for these individuals. Digit Span backwards, Letter Number Sequencing and Spatial Span backwards can be confusing for some patients, and the instructions for these portions of the battery may need to be repeated or clarified, although individual test items should not be repeated. Letter–Number Sequencing can be very frustrating for some patients, and extra encouragement may be necessary to obtain optimal effort.

Tip: Be aware of which subtests are likely to cause the greatest frustration or difficulty for the patient and be prepared to provide extra explanations of tasks, encouragement, and breaks to facilitate performance. Also, let the patient know that many people have trouble with these tests—even patients with reduced awareness of their deficits do not like to feel stupid or inadequate.

When and How to Query

One of the most difficult aspects of administering the WAIS-III for new examiners is knowing when and how much to query ambiguous or incomplete responses on the Vocabulary, Similarities, and Comprehension subtests, as well as some of the Information items. Querying should be done when an examinee provides a partial or incomplete answer that, if elaborated upon, might receive more points. However, you should not query clearly incorrect answers or well-elaborated partial credit responses. For example, a two-point response for an item such as, "Tell me what summer means" includes the notion that summer is a season involving hot weather and/or a season that occurs between spring and fall. A response that included only part of that definition (e.g., "hot weather" or "a season") would be a one-point response that should be queried, while a lower level response (e.g., "When you have to dress cool,") would receive one point and not be queried.

Tip: As a general rule of thumb for verbal subtests, "When in doubt, query."

Examinees will sometimes provide more than one response (e.g., definition for a Vocabulary item) that might include both a two-point and one-point response. In such cases, you should score the best response, unless included in the answer is a fundamental misconception about the item, which would spoil the response and receive a score of zero (e.g., "Summer is a season of the year, it comes between fall and spring"). Whereas the administration manual provides selected items for which querying is necessary, examinees will invariably give answers that are not in the manual, and the examiner must decide if the criteria have been met to properly score the response or if there is a need to elicit further clarification. The best strategy for examiners is, "When in doubt, query." If the query was unnecessary, it can always be excluded from scoring. On the other hand, you do not want to repeatedly query responses unnecessarily due to the potential you might confuse or frustrate the patient, or potentially lead them to spoil their response. All responses should be recorded verbatim to facilitate scoring, help identify if queries were given unnecessarily, and provide maximal data for later qualitative analysis of patients' responses. Table 4 provides some examples of how to respond to various examination responses and situations that may be helpful to provide to new trainees as a quick reference guide. Discussion of frequent querying dilemmas that occur across subtests can be found in the following two sections.

> Note: Verbal responses to the WAIS-III and WMS-III should be recorded verbatim. This allows for optimal scoring accuracy and ready double-checking of responses and is particularly useful in test–retest situations, where qualitative comparison of answers can be highly useful.

> Note: You should not score responses given after an unnecessary query (i.e., when an unambiguous response has already been given), regardless of whether it would improve or spoil the final response.

Testing the Limits

There may be instances when additional informal testing can provide qualitative information about how an individual is able to function that would add to your understanding of that person. However, implementation of such techniques should be hypothesis driven (i.e., you should have a reason for using them). For example, if it is uncertain how time constraints are affecting a patient's scores, allowing the examinee extra time to complete Block Design items could help to ferret that out. To help discriminate the cause of poor Arithmetic performance (attention versus anxiety versus mathematical ability), one might repeat some items giving the patient a pencil and paper. If a patient performs strikingly worse on one subtest compared with the rest of his or her scores, readministering the subtest later in the day could be considered, eliciting any misconceptions about the test before starting (e.g., using too difficult strategies for Picture Completion or Matrix Reasoning; not responding unless 100% certain of answer on Verbal IQ subtests). The impact of "testing the limits" during standardized testing should always be considered when interpreting the results. The WAIS-R NI

TABLE 4   Testing Dilemmas and Suggested Responses

Examinee response	Suggested examiner response
"I don't know."	"Think about it..." "Do you have any idea what _____ means?" "Can you think of any way _____ and _____ are alike?"
Ambiguous or incomplete response (Verbal subtests)	"Explain what you mean." "Tell me more about that."
Uses word in a sentence (Vocabulary)	"But what does _____ *mean*?" "If you were to look up _____ in a dictionary, what would it say?"
Asks for help	"I want to see how well you can do it by yourself."
"I could do this if I had a pencil and paper." (Arithmetic)	"Do the best you can." "Try to work it out."
Names an unessential detail (Picture Completion)	"Yes, but what is the most important part that is missing?" *(can be said only once during course of the subtest)*
Names an object outside of the picture (Picture Completion)	"Something is missing in the picture. What is it that is missing?" *(can be said only once during course of the subtest)*
Describes the picture (Picture Completion)	"Yes, but what's missing?" *(can be said only once during course of the subtest)*
Asks for numbers to be repeated (Digit Span, Letter–Number Sequencing)	"I can't repeat them...do the best you can...see if you can get the next one."
Asks for question to be repeated (Arithmetic)	Repeat problem in its entirety and keep timing.
Pictures appear to be arranged from right to left (Picture Arrangement)	"Tell me where your story starts." Give full credit if cards in correct order but arranged from right to left.
Only gives one correct key concept (Comprehension)	"Tell me another reason why..."
Asks what the pieces make (Object Assembly)	"I can't tell you what it is." "That's what I want you to figure out."
Gives multiple acceptable answers (Verbal subtests)	Score best answer.
Gives incorrect and correct responses	"Now which one is it?" "Which is the *best* answer?"
Examinee describes each item of the pair or says how they are alike (Similarities)	"Yes, but how are they alike...in what way are they the same? *(You should give this prompt only once.)*

has incorporated such qualitative aspects into the test and may be considered as an alternative if more detailed analysis of qualitative performance than can be derived from traditional WAIS subtests is deemed important (e.g., for treatment purposes).

PRACTICAL ISSUES WITH WAIS-III SUBTESTS

This section reviews each of the WAIS-III subtests, first giving the basics of the test and then highlighting issues that can arise when using the WAIS-III with clinical samples. This does not replace the need to carefully study the WAIS-III Administration and Scoring manual before giving the test. An additional teaching resource for training new testers is *The Essentials of WAIS-III Assessment* by Kaufman and Lichtenberger (1999), which reviews many of the technical aspects of basic test administration and interpretation.

Vocabulary

When multiple acceptable two- and one point answers are given, the best response should be scored. If a zero- and one- or two-point response is given, ask which is the preferred answer. If the subject responds with the zero-point answer, then no credit is given for the item. If the examinee provides an ambiguous response, you may query with benign statements, such as, "Tell me more about it," or "Explain what you mean." Queries that could make the individual feel inadequate or defensive (e.g., "I don't understand what you mean") should be avoided. If the individual uses the word in a sentence or has a difficult time generating actual definitions, it is permissible to say something such as, "If you were to look up the word in a dictionary, what would it say?" It is *essential* to write down responses verbatim to facilitate later scoring.

Note: A response is "spoiled" and receives no credit if the examinee's answer includes a fundamental misconception of the item when elaborating in response to a query. For example, if the word was "summer," a response such as "a really cold season" would be considered spoiled.

Tip: With individuals who are stimulus-bound and/or perseverative, it may be helpful to isolate each Vocabulary item in turn (e.g., cover other items with paper) to prevent distraction by the other items.

Aphasic patients often have difficulty with this and other verbal subtests, not because they do not know what the word means, but because they have difficulty expressing themselves. As a result, they may need extra time to compose their answers, require additional queries to clarify their responses, and need some leniency in scoring to measure their true abilities. That is, if their responses convey the essence of the correct answer, some benefit of the doubt may be provided so as not to overly penalize the patient because of their language difficulties. At a minimum, consideration of these qualitative features should be given when interpreting the results. Some frontal patients, particularly those in whom perseveration is a feature of their disorder, may incorporate previous items into their responses for later items or give a variant of the same definition for multiple items. In such cases, it can be helpful to isolate each word in the booklet to reduce exposure to the other words on the page or to redirect the patient to the word they are being asked to define. Another option to test the limits in such cases would be to readminister selective items later in the day. Qualitative examination of responses from psychiatric patients and/or those with psychosis can provide information about the clarity and organization of their thinking. Discriminating if these difficulties are the result of their psychiatric illness or a comorbid neurological process can be challenging, although responses that have a bizarre quality and/or are excessively tangential or disorganized are more characteristic of psychiatric illness unless the patient is also aphasic.

Similarities

It is not uncommon for examinees to state how items are different or to simply describe some feature about each item. For example, if the item was "how are a car and motorcycle alike," an examinee might say, "One has four wheels and the other has two wheels"), which would be an example of a zero-point response. However, if the response is more ambiguous (e.g., "you use both,") you may ask the person to clarify his or her answer with statements such as "Explain what you mean" or "Tell me more about it." If a one- or zero-point response is given for item 6 (starting item), you may provide an example of a two-point response.

In some instances, much qualitative information can be gained from the types of responses (good and bad) that patients make, and proceeding with the test even after the discontinuation criteria have been met (although not including responses in final score) can be considered if it is felt this will add to a better understanding of the individual. Some lower functioning or overly concrete thinkers have great difficulty deviating from the tendency to describe the item or tell how they are different. In such cases, it can be clinically useful to test the limits to see if they can produce a correct response if given additional structure with redirection to the task at hand. For example, you might repeat some items later, saying, "You told me how a car and a motorcycle are different, but now tell me how they are the same; in what way are they alike."

Note: If an examinee responds with "I don't know" to early items, but gets later, more difficult items correct, it is permissible to go back and readminister the earlier items (except on timed measures) and give credit for those responses.

Arithmetic

There is typically little need to query responses on the Arithmetic subtest, although it is acceptable to prompt the examinee for a response if the time limit for the item is about to elapse. If someone appears to have given up or quickly responds with a "don't know" answer, they should be encouraged to continue working by saying something like, "You still have more time, see if you can figure it out." If necessary, you can repeat the item (while timing continues) to draw their attention back to the item. Even though providing examinees with pencil and paper is not allowed, you should not discourage (or encourage) use of their fingers to trace numbers on the table to help solve problems. If the examinee gives you two different responses, without indicating which one is correct, you should ask for clarification (e.g., "Which answer do you want me to write down?").

If you know from the patient's history that math is difficult for the patient or may be particularly anxiety provoking, poor performance on this subtest may be more of a reflection of those issues than of a working memory deficit. In fact, in such cases, you might consider not giving the test at all; instead, relying on the working memory subtests from the WMS-III if a Working Memory index score is desired. Overly impulsive individuals may tend to respond too quickly without allowing adequate time to check the accuracy of their responses. If this is seen, cautions can be given to the patient to slow down, although there is risk that such a directive might negatively impact performance on items where bonus points can be obtained. A testing of the limits approach might be to readminister selective items later in the day, with more direct instructions to be sure of their response before giving it to the examiner.

Information

Responses on the Information subtest are relatively easy to score, as most of the items have straightforward answers. The greatest controversy arises on items 10, 12, 19, 23, and 25, all of which deal with identification of famous individuals. Here again, you can ask examinees to "Explain what you mean," or "Tell me more about that," to help clarify ambiguous responses, but you cannot query incomplete answers (e.g., only two of three essential elements of the answer are provided) or further clarify items for patients (e.g., spelling words or telling the number of required elements).

Although general fund of knowledge, as measured by this subtest, is typically one of the more resistant aspects of cognition to acquired brain damage, individuals with severe memory deficits may ultimately have trouble recalling remote, previously learned information. Indications of this might be variability in performance across items, giving partial responses, or talking around the correct answer so that it may be obvious the person has known this information in the past. In addition, it has been our experience that in some individuals, chronic childhood medical conditions may interfere with initial learning of Information subtest material (e.g., childhood onset of intractable epilepsy or other medical conditions that might result in poor school attendance). As a result, poor performance on this subtest may be more of an artifact of their disorder than a true deficit. This may also be seen in some individuals with limited education (or those with English as a second language, immigrants, etc.) who are actually quite bright, but did not have the opportunity to learn some of the content of the material being tested.

Comprehension

If examinees appear hesitant in responding to Comprehension items, it is acceptable to repeat the question if no response is given within 10–15 seconds. Furthermore, you should repeat the item and encourage a proper response if an argumentative, personal, or social commentary response is given. For example, if the item was "Why should children attend school?" and the examinee responded with, "I don't think that they should," you could respond by saying something like, "But what is the rationale behind why children should attend school," or "Why do most people feel that children should attend school?" This is another one of the Verbal IQ subtests that may "pull" for unusual responses in psychiatric or other patients whose thinking is disorganized. Some examiners may opt not to administer this subtest because it is not included in any of the index scores in the six-factor model, but this subtest may be helpful in cases where assessment of patients' ability to understand their environment and conventional societal viewpoints is desirable.

This is one of the more difficult subtests for new examiners to score, and familiarity with correct responses will greatly improve administration of the test. Responses often need to be clarified for proper scoring, and must be queried on items 5, 6, 7, 10, and 13 (e.g., "Tell me another reason why . . . ") if only one of the general concepts listed is given (two key concepts are required on some items to receive full credit and are marked by an asterisk). However, you may ask for a second response (i.e., concept) only once, unless the initial response is incorrect, in which case you would go to the next item without querying. If the elaboration is incorrect or merely a restatement of the first response, you should move on to the next item. Querying too much on this subtest can result in elevating examinees' scores, and additional responses should not be scored if it is determined that an additional query was unnecessary.

> Note: Comprehension items that require two "key concepts" to receive full credit are marked by an asterisk. If only one of the concepts is given, you may ask for another one (e.g., Tell me another reason why . . . "), but you can give this prompt only once per item.

Digit Span and Letter–Number Sequencing

The primary reason you would need to query or clarify an examinee's response is if their response(s) involved grouping of numbers. For example, if on a Digit Span four digit string (e.g., 5-9-6-2), the examinee said "fifty-nine, sixty-two," you should explain that each number must be repeated

510 Laura H. Lacritz and C. Munro Cullum

singularly and not in groups. Recording responses allows for better analysis of errors. For example, consistent reversal of numbers could be a sign of an auditory processing disorder rather than an attention deficit, if there were other evidence to support this. Variability of performance within the subtests provides further information about inconsistent attention. Therefore, when such variability is present, patients' overall scores may underestimate their attentional capacity, as indicated by the highest digits forward and backwards they are able to repeat. Given that digits forwards is more a measure of primary attention and digits backwards one of working memory, individuals with significant memory deficits may show a larger than expected discrepancy on Digit Span between digits forward and backwards. Patients with Alzheimer's disease, for example, often perform completely normally on digits forward, but have greater difficulty with digits backwards because of the increased complexity of the task and greater reliance on working memory to correctly manipulate the numbers.

Picture Completion

This subtest has an advantage over some others when testing patients with multiple limitations, because it requires minimal verbal or motor response. Although answers are typically given verbally, the examinee may respond by pointing or describing what is missing (if they cannot come up with the exact name of the detail). Therefore, neither motor nor language problems should significantly impact test performance, although slow response latencies may result in poor performance due to the time constraints of the task. If this is thought to be the case, allowing examinees extra time to produce an answer can be considered (although not added to the final score) to test the limits of performance. Examiners should also be cognizant of the possibility of a visual field cut or neglect in cases where responses always pertain to one side of the card and/or include a portion of the picture that is actually depicted. Reorienting the stimuli to the patients "intact" visual field and encouraging them to look at the entire picture before responding should help reduce the impact of these deficits on test performance.

Note: Consider the possibility of a visual field cut or neglect if responses tend to be associated with one side of the stimulus or include parts of the picture that are actually shown.

Digit Symbol-Coding

In an effort to complete this test quickly, some examinees may be careless in their drawing of the symbols. Certain medical conditions (e.g., movement disorders) affect motor control, which can also result in ambiguous responses. It would not make sense to ask the examinee what he or she meant to draw after the test. Furthermore, you do not want to caution them to be *too* careful, as this might slow them down. Instead, you should carefully observe the examinee's performance during the test period to better recognize his or her intention on questionable responses. This will also allow you to quickly catch mistakes, such as skipping items. In contrast to patients who hurry and are careless on this test, others may work meticulously to make precise symbols emphasizing accuracy and ignoring the instructions to work quickly. In such cases, where it is clear that the subject is being overly careful and/or obviously not working quickly, a casual reminder to "Go as quickly as you can" may be in order. Post hoc examination of the designs produced can also be helpful in evaluating the nature of the responses and interpreting the score (e.g., were the symbols drawn in a careless or hurried fashion, or were the symbols meticulously drawn?).

> Note: Subjects should be redirected if completing items out of sequence on Digit Symbol (e.g., "Don't skip around. . . do each item in order"), as those responses are not counted in the final score.

Block Design

This test can be frustrating for some patients, and extra encouragement may be necessary, particularly if a tendency to quit prematurely is seen. Although they may not be able to successfully complete the item, you may derive better qualitative information if they are allowed to work to the end of each item. For example, someone who stops after 30 seconds on Item 11 (the second 9-block design) saying they "cannot do it" does not provide much information. However, if by the end of the time limit, the examinee has completed half of the design correctly, this gives valuable qualitative data to support that the examinee is more slow than impaired compared to someone who still had the blocks scattered or had broken the square configuration of the design in an attempt to reproduce it.

Note: On Block Design and other subtests with bonus points, it is important that examinees know that they should tell you when they are finished, as even a few seconds can make a difference in their score.

Note: Extra encouragement may be needed on Block Design if subjects attempt to quit prematurely. Even if examinees cannot complete the design(s), additional qualitative information may be gained.

A great deal of qualitative information can be gained by closely watching how the patient proceeds with the task. For example, even if the patient ultimately achieves a correct assembly, disorganization in their approach or initial broken configurations may be indications of inefficiencies in this area. Some patients may try to make the task more complicated (e.g., matching the sides of the blocks as well as the tops) and need clarification of the task demands. The revised stimulus booklet for the WMS-III may reduce the possibility of some stimulus-bound behaviors such as stacking blocks on the stimulus cards, although these types of responses can still occur and may be associated with severe impairment and/or frontal dysfunction. Potential effects of motor problems or visual field deficits on performance should be noted when present so as not to overestimate a potential cognitive deficit. Patients with even a mild hemiparesis may tend to not use the affected hand/arm on tasks with a motor component, and such observations should be noted, as this may reduce task efficiency and indicate an area for remediation.

Tip: Use the blank design grids on the answer sheets to replicate incorrect Block Design responses for later qualitative analysis of examinees' performance. Even if an overall score does not change upon retest, patients may show qualitative performance differences. Keep in mind that a given score may be achieved in different ways, and "all failures (or successes) are not alike."

Matrix Reasoning

This is the only Performance subtest that is not timed per instructions, although examinees occasionally assume the test is timed and may respond hastily as a consequence. If this is observed, you can convey to the subject that time is not a factor and encourage them to "look at all of the responses before giving an answer." Alternatively, some examinees may ruminate extensively over each item with little benefit. In such cases, it is acceptable (and may be beneficial) to encourage a response or move the patient along. Remember, however, that examinees should **not** be encouraged to guess randomly. Additional insight into patients' abstract abilities when having trouble on this test may be gained by repeating some items later in the day and having them describe how they derived their answer(s). The use of overly simplistic or complicated strategies may help in understanding patients' difficulty in other areas, particularly if similar patterns are seen across tests.

> Note: Examinees should not be encouraged to guess randomly on Matrix Reasoning, but can be prompted to respond after 30 seconds. See the Frequently Asked Questions for more information on encouraging responding with Matrix Reasoning.

Picture Arrangement

Some examiners may wish to exclude this subtest since it is not included in the six-factor model and can be time consuming. However, when interested in examinees' ability to sequence temporal events and analyze social situations, this subtest should be included. If you notice that the cards have been arranged in an unusual sequence, you may wish to ask the subject after they have finished that item to describe their story. Although this information would have no impact on their score, it may provide useful qualitative information about their performance and perceptual or reasoning abilities. In addition, some psychiatric patients will have difficulty with this subtest, and having them describe their stories may reveal abnormalities in their thinking.

Symbol Search

It is important to make sure examinees understand the task on the sample/practice items before starting the test, which often requires the examiner to emphasize the need for the symbols to be *exactly* the same. If you see someone working too hastily or obstructing some of the stimuli with his or her hand, you can remind them to look at all the items before marking their response. Examinees are not to skip around the page and may need to be reminded to continue on the following page if they finish page 2 with time remaining. Individuals with movement disorders (e.g., Parkinson's disease) often have deficits in processing speed as well as motor functioning, although it may be difficult to separate these deficits on a task with a motor response. These factors should be considered when interpreting test performance, although giving the test may be contraindicated altogether if the motor dysfunction is particularly pronounced.

Object Assembly (optional)

This task can frustrate patients, particularly when they cannot figure out what the pieces should make, or when they recognize the item but are unable to put it together correctly. Interpretively, this distinction may be important, as even if patients are able to assemble some of the pieces, it is of little use to them if they cannot use that information to figure out what the pieces should make. While you cannot tell them what the puzzle depicts or confirm if they are correct, extra encouragement may be necessary. This is especially important since on this test, unlike some of the other Performance subtests, partial credit is given for correct junctures even if the item is not complete.

> Note: In some manuals, the time specified for item 5 (as stated on p. 176 of the administration manual) (120) should actually be 180, as correctly written on page 177 of the manual and in the record form.

PRACTICAL ISSUES WITH THE WMS-III

The response formats for most of the WMS-III subtests are relatively straightforward, as are the types of queries or clarifications needed. This section reviews each of the WMS-III subtests and some of the major clinical issues that arise when using this instrument. It is not meant to be exhaustive and does not replace the need to carefully study the WMS-III Administration and Scoring manual before giving the test.

Logical Memory I and II

After the examinee has repeated what they remember from each story, they should be asked if they remember anything else before moving to the next story or subtest. It is not uncommon for one or more additional details to be recalled when this additional prompt is provided. If the examinee does produce more story details after a prompt, keep prompting for more details until they make it clear they cannot recall anything else. Interpretively, it is interesting to note how much benefit the patient gets from repetition of the second story. A large improvement (> 5 points) with repetition of the story, as well as a large discrepancy between amount learned from each story may indicate that reduced or variable attention is having a negative impact on test performance.

On delayed recall of the stories, examinees will sometimes relate story B when you have asked for story A. There is no need to correct them. Instead, record their response, score with the appropriate story criteria, and then ask for the *other* story you asked them to remember. Large discrepancies between percent retained between the stories (e.g., 10 % from story A, but 90 % from story B) should be interpreted cautiously. Although this might be an indication that repetition of the story B enhanced the patient's retention of the information, the possibility of reduced attention and/or effort should be considered. As a result, the overall percent retention score will not accurately reflect the patient's abilities. In cases where the examinee does not remember *any* details from a story, a specified generic prompt for the story should be given, as indicated in the manual, and then the response is scored normally. However, if only one or two details from a given story are provided, giving the prompt as if the examinee could not recall anything could be considered to test the limits (but not counted in the overall score), as some individuals in this circumstance will recall additional pieces of information when provided with the prompt. For example, patients with Alzheimer's disease will often not benefit or benefit only minimally from being provided with prompts, whereas those with subcortical disorders or some psychiatric illnesses may show significant improvement with prompting.

Tip: Since it is important to log responses verbatim on Logical Memory, consider using a tape recorder with higher functioning or verbose individuals to ensure that responses are recorded precisely, but always write down responses simultaneously as well (in case of equipment failure).

Tip: The use of some sort of short-hand response recording can be very useful on Logical Memory (e.g., "The tall woman from Texas . . ." could initially be recorded, "The T W fr Tx . . . ," although full verbatim responses should be written out as soon as possible.

Verbal Paired Associates I and II

Repetition and clarification of instructions are often necessary on this task, even for "normal" individuals, to ensure accurate understanding. In fact, this test can be overly frustrating for patients with generalized impairment and/ or severe memory deficits. Unlike the other subtests from the WAIS-III and WMS-III, you are *required* to provide feedback about the correctness of the examinee's responses *and* provide the correct answer for each item during the learning trials (but not the delayed recall trial) if the examinee gives the wrong answer or does not respond. In order to keep the test moving, you can provide the correct answer if the examinee has not responded in approximately 5 seconds.

> Note: Even those who do poorly on the recall trials of the Verbal Paired Associates subtest often perform normally on delayed recognition of the word pairs.

Faces I and II

Although somewhat tedious, the examiner is required to present the pictures at a steady rate while saying "Remember this one" to make sure the subject is attending to the task. Examinees should be encouraged to provide a response during the recognition phase even if they are not sure if the face was one presented to them or not. The yes–no recognition response format for this subtest separates it from the other subtests on the WMS-III and may contribute to why the factor loadings on the Visual Memory factor in the six-factor model for these subtests are relatively low.

> Note: The Faces subtest is unique from the other subtests of the WMS-III in that it is really a recognition memory test compared with the others that involve free recall.

Family Pictures I and II

As mentioned previously, this can be a confusing test for some individuals, particularly for those with dementia. Some people confuse the name of the picnic and yard scenes with the *activities* in each scene, and it is permissible to say, "Tell me who was in the Picnic scene. That was the first scene I showed you." While credit is not given if the examinee confuses the names of the scenes by falsely ascribing the activities of one scene to another (e.g., recalls characters and activities from the yard scene when you ask about the picnic scene), this is important qualitative information to have, particularly if scores on this subtest are much below other memory scores. Another point of clarification that is sometimes needed relates to what names the examinee uses for the characters. For example, older patients may call the grandmother the "daughter's mom" or call the girl the grand-daughter. You should clarify characters with the patient if it is unclear whom they are referring to (e.g., "Are you referring to the mother or grand-mother?").

> Note: If an examinee gives a character that is not in the scene, you still have to ask where the character was located and what the character was doing. In addition, if a new character is mentioned in relation to another (e.g., "...the daughter was throwing the ball to the *dog*.") the new character (e.g., the dog) should be queried.

> ⊙ Warning: Refer to the manual when scoring Logical Memory and Family Pictures instead of relying solely on responses in the record book, as there are much more detailed guidelines and examples than provided in the record book.

Digit Span (optional) and **Letter Number sequencing**: see sections above.

Spatial Span

Even though quite simple, this is one of the more challenging tests to administer, and ample administration practice is encouraged to ensure good flow as items become more difficult. Examinees sometimes ask for a sequence to be repeated, which is not permissible, so it is important to make sure they are ready and attending before each item. One of the main challenges, particularly as the number of blocks in the sequence grows, is correctly recording examinees' responses. Although you would not want to ask for them to repeat their sequence, you can ask examinees to slow down to facilitate proper recording of answers.

Word List I and II (optional)

After the examinee has finished spontaneously recalling words after each trial, you should usually ask if he or she can remember any more words. Record perseverations as well as intrusion errors, but use caution in interpreting perseveration errors if they primarily occur after you have queried the examinee for more items. If the examinee questions as to whether a word was on the list or not (e.g., "I can't remember if 'fish' was one of the words,") you should wait a few seconds for them to indicate their response. If no further response is given, you can clarify the intent (e.g., "Would you like me to write that down as an answer?" or "Do you think it was on the list?"). Extra encouragement may be necessary to engage some individuals in the task (e.g., "Do the best you can,"), particularly those with significant memory impairment.

Visual Reproduction I and II (optional)

While the instructions do not include a caution for the examinee to draw the figures carefully, carelessness will have a negative impact on scores. Therefore, if someone seems to be drawing impulsively or carelessly, consider encouraging him or her to slow down or be more careful (e.g., "There's no need to hurry." "Draw it as best you can."). With impulsive patients, you may also have to make sure they attend during the entire 10-second presentation period (e.g., "Keep looking at the picture"), and that they do not attempt to draw the figure during the presentation period. You may need to withhold their pencil in between items if this becomes a problem. Intrusions from other visual memory or copying tests given earlier in the testing session can be seen on delayed recall, and it may be necessary to remind the patient of the task (e.g., "You drew each figure on a different sheet"). Some leniency in scoring should be considered for individuals with movement disorders or when using their nondominant hand (e.g., in case of dominant hand hemiparesis) to perform the task. The detailed scoring involved in this subtest may be a deterrent to administration, although inclusion of Visual Reproduction as part of the six-factor model and the ability to combine this subtest with

Family Pictures to obtain alternate Visual Memory index scores will hopefully make this test more appealing, as we have found it to have greater clinical utility than Faces with some individuals.

Information and Orientation (optional)

Attempts should be made to query any "don't know" responses in order to elicit some type of response. If someone responds to "What year is this?" with "don't know" or "not sure," it is more telling if their eventual response is 1940 versus 2000!

Mental Control (optional)

Typically, these items tend to be relatively easy for people to understand and attempt, although additional explanation may be required for the more difficult items.

FREQUENTLY ASKED QUESTIONS

FAQ Regarding WAIS-III/WMS-III Administration

Does WAIS-III/WMS-III test order affect performance? When administering a lengthy test battery, fatigue can be of concern in relation to subject performance. The issue of fatigue is of particular concern with elderly patients and/or persons with neuromedical problems that can affect stamina and endurance. Therefore, the issue has been raised whether the order in which the WAIS-III and WMS-III are administered during a single evaluation could impact test performance and which subtests may be most susceptible to test-order effects. Zhu and Tulsky (2000) found few significant differences in WAIS-III and WMS-III subtest scaled scores and no differences between Index and IQ scores of subjects in the standardization sample who were given both tests, regardless of which instrument was administered first. Specifically, they found that on the WAIS-III, Digit Span and Coding scaled scores were significantly lower in subjects who were administered the WAIS-III after the WMS-III. For the WMS-III, a statistically (but not clinically) significant order effect was found for Faces II and Logical Memory II scaled scores ($\leq$ .53 scaled score points), but not in a consistent direction. The conclusion was that test order appears to have minimal impact on these two measures.

Do subtests need to be given in the order in which they appear in the test? While it might be ideal to administer the WAIS-III and WMS-III in their entirety from start to finish, this is not always feasible depending on time constraints, patient factors, and referral/research questions. In fact, it is common practice in some settings to administer only selected subtests, or to vary the subtest order depending on the needs of the testing situation (e.g., selected subtests may be used during delay intervals between other memory tests). Tulsky and Zhu (2000) examined the impact of test order and fatigue on Letter–Number Sequencing (LNS) performance by evaluating LNS scores in individuals who were administered the subtest in one of three conditions: (a) those who completed the LNS after approximately 1 1/4 hours of testing as part of the standard WAIS-III battery; (b) individuals who were administered LNS as part of the WMS-III standardization edition; and (c) individuals who were administered LNS as part of the WMS-III standardization edition when it was given after the WAIS-III standardization edition (after approximately 5 hours of testing). The results revealed essentially no differences in LNS test performance or standard error across conditions. Furthermore, there were no age-by-group (i.e., test order) interactions, suggesting that in a normal population the effect of fatigue and order of test administration is insignificant for LNS.

How much time should be allowed for slow responders on Matrix Reasoning? There is no time limit on this subtest, so theoretically, subjects can take as much time as they wish to respond to these items. However, this could result in some individuals, particularly those who may be inhibited or prone to ruminate, taking as long as 45 minutes to complete the subtest, which will prolong the testing session. Individuals in the standardization sample completed 75% of Matrix Reasoning items in 15 seconds or less and more than 90% of items in 30 seconds or less, suggesting that extended response periods were not needed for most subjects. Therefore, Tulsky, Zhu, and Prifitera (2000) have suggested that individuals whose ruminations over items are of little perceived benefit should be encouraged to respond (but not guess randomly) after 30 seconds and move to the next item after 45–60 seconds if no response has been offered. This is supported by the fact that of the 2,450 subjects in the standardization sample, those who took longer than 60 seconds per item to respond were wrong two-thirds of the time. Although timing of this test is not required, this may be a worthwhile variable to explore in future research.

FAQ Regarding WAIS-III and WMS-III Scoring

How should items that are not in the manual be scored? While most items can be easily scored by reviewing common responses in the WAIS-III administration manual, it is not uncommon for examinees to give responses that do not clearly meet stated criteria. For the Vocabulary subtest, you may accept any definition recognized in a standard dictionary and score the response according to the quality of the definition. It is also wise to keep a record of such responses and what score was assigned to the answer to facilitate consistency in scoring at your facility. In fact, many centers (e.g., The University of Texas Southwestern Medical Center at Dallas, Mayo Clinic) have made lists of commonly given answers not in the manual, with associated assigned scores to hasten scoring of difficult or unusual responses.

How do you score responses composed of multiple acceptable answers? Score the best answer. However, if an incorrect response is given with other correct responses, and it is unclear which is the preferred response, you should ask, "Which one is it?" or "What is your *best* answer?"

When is a response "spoiled?" In contrast to a poor elaboration of an acceptable response, an answer is spoiled if the elaboration is obviously wrong, regardless if the initial response to an item would have received some credit. For example, if on the Similarities subtest the examinee responded to, "How are a sweater and a vest alike?" by giving a one-point response followed by, "They both cost money," the answer would be spoiled. Likewise, if the subject initially arranges stimuli correctly on Block Design or Picture Arrangement, but then changes the configuration of the stimuli within the time period, they would not receive credit for the item. From a qualitative perspective, the number of times an examinee "spoils" responses could be important and raises the issue of whether the examiner should intervene with a person who has shown a tendency to spoil responses by going beyond a good answer.

How should the presence of superfluous lines on the Visual Reproduction subtest be scored? The issue of how to score figures with superfluous lines or design elements is not consistently addressed across figures in the WMS-III Administration and Scoring manual. A general rule that can be applied is if the scoring criteria include some statement to indicate a certain number of elements or lines, then superfluous lines would result in a score of zero for that point. For example, the one-point response for item A1 states that "A *single* line is recognizable...," thus, a superfluous line for that figure would be scored as zero. Similarly, criteria for item C2 state that the "rectangle figure is bisected by *one* vertical and *one* horizontal line," and so a superfluous line in that instance would also be scored as zero. However, if not specifically stated, superfluous lines or elements should not prohibit the subject from obtaining maximum points on an item. An example of this situation would be for item D14, if a subject drew more than one figure to the right of the circle segment, they would still get credit for having "a figure to the right of the circle segment."

FAQs Regarding WAIS-III and WMS-III Interpretation

How should WAIS-III IQ/Index discrepancy scores be used? Available WAIS-III discrepancy score tables provide information about how frequently a difference between two IQ scores or index scores was found in the standardization sample. Therefore, base rate data from the standardization sample are available to help identify if a difference between two scores is significantly greater than would be expected or than occurs in the normal sample. However, it should be noted that the discrepancy data provided in Table B.2 of the WAIS-III Administration Manual (Wechsler, 1997a, pp. 206–207) and the associated information that appears in the *Scoring Assistant for Wechsler Scales for Adults* (SAWS-A; 1997[*]) printout represent absolute values and are not directional. For example, a VIQ–PIQ difference score of $+/-10$ points occurred in approximately 37% of the standardization sample, but information has not been provided for directional score differences (i.e., VIQ < PIQ, VIQ > PIQ). This is important to realize so that examiners do not overestimate the frequency with which observed discrepancy scores occur. To address this issue, Tulsky, Rolfhus, and Zhu (2000) examined two different methods for deriving cumulative percentages for directional IQ and Index score differences. They concluded that it is acceptable to divide the cumulative percentages presented in Table B.2 of the *WAIS-III Administration Manual* in half to provide an estimate of directional score differences. Therefore, if 37% of the standardization sample obtains a VIQ–PIQ difference score of $+/-10$ points, then the approximate frequency of obtaining a VIQ > PIQ by 10 or more points would be 18.5%. (For a detailed description of base rates in relation to the WAIS-III and WMS-III, the reader is referred to Smith et al., Chapter 7, this volume, for a more comprehensive discussion of this topic.)

Note: Discrepancies between IQ and Index Scores are more common in individuals with higher FSIQ scores. For example, almost 50% of individuals with a FSIQ of above 120 demonstrate a 10 point or greater discrepancy between PIQ and VIQ compared to 21% of individuals whose FSIQ is below 80.

What options are available for prorating IQ? If it is important to depict a general level of ability through a composite or summary IQ score, several options for the WAIS-III exist. Although many different short forms and suggestions for prorating IQ are available for the WAIS-R, research along these lines is really just beginning in relation to the WAIS-III. Palmer, Taylor, and Heaton address the topic of prorating and estimating IQ and index scores in great detail (Chapter 10, this volume). In addition, two seven-subtest short forms (Information, Digit Span, Arithmetic, Similarities, Picture Completion, Digit-Symbol Coding, and Block Design or Matrix Reasoning) have been proposed by Ryan and Ward (1999), each showing a strong correlation with FSIQ ($r = .96$) using either deviation quotients or proration. Axelrod, Ryan, and Ward (2001) found similar correlations when using these short forms in clinical samples. Regression-based FSIQ estimates using four different two-subtest short forms have additionally been reported (Ringe, Sainc, Lacritz & Cullum, 2002), also showing high correlations with FSIQ ($r = .90$) in a mixed neurological sample. Tulsky, Saklofske, Wilkins, and Weiss (2002) suggest using the General Ability Index (GAI), as originally developed by Weiss, Saklofske Prifitera, Chen and Hildebrand (1999) for the Wechsler Intelligence Scale for Children-Third Edition (WISC-III; Wechsler, 1991). The GAI is derived from the six subtests that comprise the Verbal Comprehension and Perceptual Organization indices and provides a score that reflects global functioning (correlation with FSIQ = .96) when time or other constraints make administering the entire WAIS-III unfeasible. These authors contend that the GAI may actually provide a better indication of global abilities than FSIQ in impaired populations because it does not include the processing speed and working memory subtests that can be most vulnerable to brain damage. Another alternative for deriving IQ estimates is the Wechsler Abbreviated Scale of Intelligence (WASI; Wechsler, 2001), which includes four- or two-subtest formats for estimating FSIQ using alternate Vocabulary, Similarities, Block Design, and Matrix Reasoning subtests composed of different items than those found in the WAIS-III. However, buying a new test when other short forms using actual WAIS-III subtests have similarly high correlations with FSIQ may make using the WASI a less attractive alternative.

Note: When using IQ scores derived from any short form or proration procedure, results should always be qualified as "estimated" scores, and it is often preferable to estimate *ranges* of functioning, avoiding the use of singular IQ scores per se.

Note: It is technically acceptable to *prorate* either VIQ or PIQ if one subtest is missing from each, but prorating Full Scale IQ when more than one subtest is missing is not recommended in the WAIS-III Administration and Technical manuals. However, Axelrod, and Ryan (2000) contend that reliable estimates of FSIQ can be derived when two subtests (i.e., Comprehension and Picture Arrangement) are missing.

Why do the norms for Logical Memory retention rates seem overly forgiving? Given the utility in examining forgetting or retention rates when assessing memory impairment, the WMS-III would appear to represent an improvement from the WMS-R by providing scaled scores for the percent of information retained from each of the memory subtests. However, the scaled score values associated with Logical Memory retention rates tend to be higher than normative studies have reported on like subtests from the WMS-R (e.g., Cullum, Butters, Troster, & Salmon, 1990). Although the range of retention rates on Logical Memory shows a better distribution of scores than some of the other subtests (e.g., Family Pictures), the amount needed to obtain an average score seems lower than one might clinically think should be the case. For example, an 80-year-old who retains only 41% on LM would obtain a scaled score of 8, though recall of less than 50% on most paragraph recall tasks would suggest poor performance. This may be due to the fact that when calculating percent retention, the denominator consists of Story A and the second trial of Story B (usually higher than the first trial of that story), but it is unclear to what degree the repetition of that story enhances later recall. In addition, it must be kept in mind that the scaled scores for percent retention were normed independent of the components of the ratio. Therefore, no distinction was made between a 70-year-old individual who initially recalled only a total of 5 bits of information on LMI and 4 bits of information on LMII (80% retention) and a 70-year-old who recalled 30 bits of information on LMI and 24 bits on LMII (80% retention). Likewise, both examinees would receive the same scaled score for percent retention, although there is obviously a stark contrast in memory abilities between the two cases. Further analysis of retention rates in normal and clinical populations, as well as differential recall of the two stories (to determine the benefit of repeating Story B) may aid in the interpretation of WMS-III retention rate scaled scores.

⊙ Warning: A high retention rate does not necessarily imply good memory if the original amount of information learned was very limited. One-hundred percent retention of one word from Verbal Paired Associates still indicates poor performance on that test.

What impact do floor and ceiling effects have on interpretation of WMS-III retention rates? Review of the range of retention rates and related scaled scores in the WMS-III Administration and Scoring Manual (Wechsler, 1997b) reveals the occurrence of floor and ceiling effects on several subtests. For example, an 80-year-old who recalls none of the word pairs on Verbal Paired Associates still earns a scaled score of 7. Most clinicians would take issue with saying that zero retention of information reflects a low average performance. By the same token, a 50-year-old who retains 100 % of learned word pairs only achieves a scaled score of 12. Therefore, WMS-III retention rates need to be interpreted with caution at the extreme ranges for this subtest. Problems with ceiling effects can also be seen on the Faces and Family Pictures subtests, as examinees must recall 87 % to 99 % of learned information to obtain a scaled score of 10, and the highest scaled score that can be obtained for these scores is 12 for most age ranges. This is in stark contrast to performance on Visual Reproduction, in which retention rates tend to be much lower and are subject to floor effects. The differences between these visual memory tasks and how they are scored may help to explain why such discrepancies can be seen. For example, the Faces subtest is a recognition rather than a free recall task and introduces the possibility of correct guessing on some items. In addition, by the time the patient reaches the delayed recall trial, they have been exposed to the test faces three times, which may also result in raising the "retention" rate on this task. In contrast, the Visual Reproduction subtest is much more detail-oriented than the other visual subtests, and it is easy to lose points on items for even minor deviations from the figures. In addition, given the drawing component, an examinee may perform more poorly on the test for a variety of reasons including motor problems or visuospatial deficits. The Visual Reproduction copy component was designed to help separate out these concepts and can be useful in some cases.

Note: Subjects under age 45 must retain 97 % to 99 % of learned information on Faces and Family Pictures to obtain a median score (i.e., scaled score of 10).

Tip: Since retention rates from immediate to delayed recall tend to be very high for Faces and Family Pictures, performance on the immediate recall trials of these subtests is often of greater clinical utility than delayed recall performance.

Are WMS-III auditory recognition scores inflated? The addition of recognition memory items in the WMS-III for several of the subtests represents a much needed component that was not addressed in the WMS-R. Unfortunately, this is an area that still needs improvement and does not allow for the finer discrimination between free recall and recognition performance that one would want for those subtests to be of maximal benefit. This primarily relates to the fact that the distribution of scores for this index is quite restricted and negatively skewed because most of the standardization sample obtained perfect scores on recognition variables. As a result, the WMS-III Auditory Delayed Recognition Index is more of a deficit than an ability index, in that it is most useful as an indication of deficiency when someone performs poorly (see Tulsky et al., Chapter 3, this volume, more details). Otherwise, normal or even near perfect scores on the Logical Memory and Verbal Paired Associates recognition subtests do not necessarily indicate intact performance in this area. However, there does appear to be a greater range of scores on Logical Memory Recognition than Verbal Paired Associates. (See Tulsky et al., Chapter 3, this volume for a break down of cumulative percentages associated with raw scores for each of the Auditory Recognition Memory variables). Further research is needed in clinical populations to determine how best to use these subtests and of what benefit they can be. Exploration of these scores in suspected malingerers may also be beneficial.

Note: The modal score from the standardization sample for Logical Memory Recognition is 27/30 (mean = 24.5) and for Verbal Paired Associates Recognition is 24/24 (mean = 23.4).

What effects do demographic variables have on the WAIS-III and WMS-III? Heaton (1992) has highlighted the impact of demographic variables on test performance, providing age-, education-, and gender-corrected normative data for the WAIS-R and previously for the WAIS (Heaton, Grant, & Matthews, 1991). Heaton, Taylor, and Manly have also examined the influence of these demographic variables with respect to the WAIS-III and discuss their finding in Chapter 5 of this book. In addition, a preliminary study by Basso and colleagues (Basso, Harrington, Matson, & Lowery, 2000) revealed significant differences between males and females on several variables from the Verbal Paired Associates subtests, including total learning, first trial recall, and percent retained, while no significant differences were found on the Faces subtests.

Which subtests are most affected by age? The shift in emphasis from reference-based to age-corrected scores highlights the importance of considering the effects of age on test results, particularly in relation to the Performance scales of the WAIS-III and the nonverbal memory tests on the WMS-III. In general, the Performance subtests are much more sensitive to effects of normal aging compared with the Verbal subtests, with fewer points needed to obtain a scaled score of 10 beginning at age 45 in comparison to the reference group (age 20–34). More specifically, the Letter–Number Sequencing subtest on the Verbal scales and the Performance subtests that involve speed of information processing (i.e., Digit Symbol and Symbol Search) showed the greatest deviation from the reference group in the older age groups (Ryan, Sattler, & Lopez, 2000).

How similar should IQ and memory index scores be? Since all subjects in the WMS-III standardization sample also took the WAIS-III, direct comparisons between IQ and memory index scores can be made. Given only moderate correlations (.30 to .60) between memory index and IQ scores in the standardization sample, discrepancies between the tests (e.g., lower memory than FSIQ scores) do not necessarily indicate memory impairment. Furthermore, interpreting simple difference scores may be misleading. For example, using FSIQ to estimate memory scores in persons with a large VIQ–PIQ split might underestimate expected memory performance. In addition, because the WAIS-III and WMS-III are only modestly correlated, large differences can be seen even in the normal population, providing another example of how consideration of base rates is important when interpreting test results (Hawkins & Tulsky, 2001, Chapter 6, this volume). Furthermore, as with any neuropsychological measure, scores should not be interpreted in isolation, and it is important to take into consideration personal history, demographic factors, qualitative test characteristics, and results from other neurocognitive tests to make sound interpretations.

How sensitive are the WAIS-III/WMS-III to lateralized brain dysfunction? The addition of the Verbal Comprehension Index and the

Perceptual Organization Index enhances the utility of the WAIS-III in identification of more "pure" verbal or visuospatial deficits than was possible with the WAIS-R. In combined neurological and psychiatric samples from the *WAIS-III/WMS-III Technical Manual* (The Psychological Corporation, 1997b), VCI–POI differences were twice as high as VIQ–PIQ discrepancies (Hawkins, 1998). However, 10- to 15-point differences between these scores are not uncommon in the standardization sample (e.g., 20 % to 40 % for those whose FSIQ is between 90–109; Table D.3 in Technical manual, pp. 304–305), suggesting the need for caution when using discrepancy scores to support a hypothesis of focal brain dysfunction. However, material-specific memory deficits on the WMS-III have been found in epilepsy patients following temporal lobectomy. Left temporal lobectomy patients obtained significantly lower Auditory Index scores than right temporal lobectomy patients, whereas Visual Index scores were similar between the groups. See Hawkins (1998) for a more detailed description of WAIS-III and WMS-III patterns across various clinical samples. Clearly, additional studies of WAIS-III and WMS-III patterns in focal brain disorders are needed to assess the comparability of results to findings using previous versions of these tests.

Which WAIS-III subtests are most sensitive to brain injury? The Processing Speed index appears to be the most sensitive index to brain injury across different neurological groups (Hawkins, 1998). This has been further supported by examination of WAIS-III performance in individuals with mild and moderate to severe traumatic brain injury (TBI) in comparison with a subsample from the standardization sample. Donders et al. (Donders, Tulsky, & Zhu, 2001) found no significant differences between the mild TBI and control groups, whereas the moderate-to-severe TBI group performed significantly worse than the mild group on Letter–Number Sequencing, Picture Completion, Digit Symbol Coding, and Symbol Search.

Miscellaneous FAQ

Why aren't all the WAIS-III subtests included in one of the four index scores? The decision to include only three of the possible four subtests in the Verbal Comprehension index (VCI) and Perceptual Organization index (POI) (i.e., excluding Comprehension from the VCI and Picture Arrangement from the POI) was made for several reasons (Tulsky, Zhu, & Prifitera, 2000). Having a maximum of three subtests in each of the four index scores makes each index more balanced and equally weighted, and the overall VCI and POI scores are essentially the same whether three or four tests are included. Furthermore, excluding the Comprehension and

Picture Arrangement subtests can save a significant amount of administration time.

> Note: Results from WAIS-III factor analysis reveals that the Picture Arrangement subtest loads on both the Verbal Comprehension and Perceptual Organization indexes, making it a less "pure" task of visuos-patial abilities than other Performance subtests (Tulsky et al., 2000).

Is the Faces subtest comparable to the other WMS-III visual memory subtests? The Faces subtest is a recognition memory test and simply requires a yes or no response during the immediate and delayed portion of the test (indicating if the face is one that was originally presented or not). This differs from all of the other memory subtests from the WMS-III, which follow a paradigm of testing immediate and delayed *free* recall of the material. Furthermore, recognition scores are vulnerable to correct guessing (50% chance of choosing the correct answer), which could inflate scores. In addition, a confirmatory factor analysis of the WMS-III revealed that the Faces subtest did not load high on the visual memory factor, with low R^2 values (Millis, Malina, Bowers, & Ricker, 1999). This suggests that the Faces subtest is measuring something different from the other subtests that comprise the visual memory factor (i.e., Family Pictures I and II) or may not be as pure a measure of nonverbal memory as had been hoped. For this reason, an alternative Visual Memory Index has been proposed in this book that includes the Visual Reproduction instead of Faces subtest.

How similar are WAIS-III IQ scores to those from the WAIS-R and why do differences occur? Although correlations between WAIS-III and WAIS-R IQ scores are high (VIQ = .94, PIQ = .86, FSIQ = .93), they are not perfect. WAIS-III VIQ, PIQ, and FSIQ scores are about 1.2, 4.8, and 2.9 points lower than corresponding scores on the WAIS-R, respectively. It is largely accepted that as normative data become outdated on intelligence tests, IQ scores can become inflated, providing a major impetus for periodic updating and re-norming of instruments. Flynn (1987, 1998) has described this phenomenon in detail, positing that the population tends to gain an average of three IQ points over a 10-year period, with greater gains in performance abilities (i.e., PIQ) compared to verbal skills. However, Zhu and Tulsky (1999) suggest that caution should be used in applying Flynn's philosophy to actual patients, as there are many sources of variance unaccounted for by his formulas that could impact an individual's score.

CONCLUSIONS

The new editions of the WAIS and WMS incorporate a number of improvements over previous versions, and this book provides additional interpretive information about these measures that should help those who use them do so with more confidence and expertise. The best way to feel more comfortable with the new tests and how to use them clinically is to use them to develop individual impressions and observations of various populations. This is an exciting opportunity to study the usefulness of these instruments in different settings, with different populations and in comparison to other measures. Certain areas obviously still need improvement, particularly in relation to nonverbal memory assessment and recognition memory. Further investigations of standard scores and discrepancy scores in various populations are also needed to better understand the utility and limitations of the new indices available from these important third-generation assessment tools.

ACKNOWLEDGEMENTS

We would like to extend our gratitude to our excellent team of psychometrists, Christina Darby, Judy Shaw, Dan Eisenman, and Suzanne Pierce, who shared their insights on the WAIS-III and WMS-III. Special thanks to Christina Darby and Judy Shaw for reviewing parts of this chapter to ensure technical accuracy. Thanks also to Tim Nyberg for his assistance with references and proofreading.

REFERENCES

Axelrod, B. N., & Ryan, J. J. (2000). Prorating Wechsler Adult Intelligence Scale-III summary scores. *Journal of Clinical Psychology, 56*, 807–811.
Axelrod, B. N., Ryan, J. J., & Ward, L. C. (2001). Evaluation of seven-subtest short forms of the Wechsler Adult Intelligence Scale-III in a referred sample. *Archives of Clinical Neuropsychology, 16*, 1–8.
Basso, M. R., Harrington, K., Matson, M., & Lowery, N. (2000). Sex differences on the WMS-III: Findings concerning Verbal Paired Associates and Faces. *The Clinical Neuropsychologist, 14*, 231–235.
Cullum, C. M., Butters, N., Troster, A. I., & Salmon, D. P. (1990). Normal aging and forgetting rates on the Wechsler Memory Scale—Revised. *Archives of Clinical Neuropsychology, 5*, 23–30.

Donders, J, Tulsky, D. S., & Zhu, J. (2001). Criterion validity of new WAIS-III subtest scores after traumatic brain injury. *Journal of the Neuropsychological Society, 7*, 892–898.

Flynn, J. (1987). Massive IQ gains in fourteen nations: What IQ really tests. *Psychological Bulletin, 101*, 171–191.

Flynn, J. R. (1998). WAIS-III and WISC-III gains in the United States from 1972 to 1995: How to compensate for obsolete norms. *Perceptual and Motor Skills, 86*, 1231–1239.

Hawkins, K. A. (1998). Indicators of brain dysfunction derived from graphic representations of the WAIS-III/WMS-III technical manual clinical samples data: A preliminary approach to clinical utility. *The Clinical Neuropsychologist, 12*, 535–551.

Hawkins, K. A., & Tulsky, D. S (2001). The influence of IQ stratification on WAIS-III/WMS-III FSIQ-general memory index discrepancy base rates in the standardization sample. *Journal of the International Neuropsychological Society, 7*, 875–880.

Heaton, R. K. (1992). *A Supplement for the Wechsler Adult Intelligence Scale—Revised (WAIS-R).* Odessa, FL: Psychological Assessment Resources, Inc.

Heaton, R. K., Grant, I., & Matthews, C. G. (1991). *Comprehensive norms for an expanded Halstead-Reitan Battery.* Odessa, FL: Psychological Assessment Resources, Inc.

Heaton, S. K., & Heaton, R. K. (1981).Testing the impaired patient. In S. B. Filskor & T. J. Pooll (Eds.). *Handbook of Clinical Neuropsychology* (pp. 526–544). New York: John Wiley & Sons.

Kaplan, E., Fein, D., Morris, R., & Delis, D. C. (1991). *Wechsler Adult Intelligence Scale-Revised as a Neuropsychologial Instrument (WAIS-R NI) manual.* San Antonio, TX: The Psychological Corporation.

Kaufman, A. S., & Lichtenberger, E. O. (1999). *Essentials of WAIS-III assessment.* New York: John Wiley & Sons, Inc.

Millis, S. R., Malina, A. C., Bowers, D. A., & Ricker, J. H. (1999). Confirmatory factor analysis of the Wechsler Memory Scale-III. *Journal of Clinical and Experimental Neuropsychology, 21*, 87–93.

The Psychological Corporation. (1997a). *Scoring Assistant for the Wechsler Scales for Adults.* San Antonio, TX: The Psychological Corporation.

The Psychological Corporation. (1997b). *The WAIS-III – WMS-III technical manual.* San Antonio, TX: The Psychological Corporation.

The Psychological Corporation (2001). *The Wechsler Abbreviated Scale of Intelligence.* San Antonio, TX: The Psychological Corporation.

Ringe, W. K., Saine, K. C., Lacritz, L. H., & Cullum, C. M. (2002). Dyadic short forms of the Wechsler Adult Intelligence Scale–Third Edition. *Assessment, 9*, 254–260.

Ryan, J. J., Sattler, J. M., & Lopez, S. J. (2000). Age effects on Wechsler Adult Intelligence Scale-III subtests. *Archives of Clinical Neuropsychology, 15*, 311–317.

Ryan, J. J., & Ward, L. C. (1999). Validity, reliability, and standard errors of measurement for two seven-subtest short forms of the Wechsler Adult Intelligence Scale—III. *Psychological Assessment, 11*, 207–211.

Scoring Assistant for the Wechsler Adult SAWS-A version 1.1 (computer program) (1997). San Antonio, TX: The Psychological Corporation.

Tulsky, D. S., & Ledbetter, M. F. (2000). Updating to the WAIS-III and WMS-III: considerations for research and clinical practice. *Psychological Assessment, 12*, 253–262.

Tulsky, D. S., Rolfhus, E. L., & Zhu, J. (2000). Two-tailed versus one-tailed base rates of discrepancy scores in the WAIS-III. *The Clinical Neuropsychologist, 14*, 451–460.

Tulsky, D. S., Saklofske, D. H., Wilkins, C., & Weiss, L. G. (2002) *Development of a general ability index for the WAIS-III.* Manuscript submitted for publication.

Tulsky, D. S., & Zhu, J. (2000). Could test length or order affect scores on Letter Number Sequencing of the WAIS-III and WMS-III? Ruling out effects of fatigue. *The Clinical Neuropsychologist, 14,* 474–478.

Tulsky, D. S., Zhu, J., & Prifitera, A. (2000). Assessment of adult intelligence with the WAIS-III. In G. Goldstein, & M. Hersen (Eds.), *Handbook of psychological assessment* (3rd ed., pp. 97–130). New York: Elsevier Science.

U.S. Department of Commerce, U.S. Census Bureau (2001). *Census 2000 block data summary file* [On-line]. Available: www.census.gov/prod/www/abs/decenial.html.

Wechsler, D. (1981). *Manual for the Wechlser Adult Intelligence Scale—Revised (WAIS-R).* San Antonio, TX: The Psychological Corporation.

Wechsler, D. (1987). *Wechsler Memory Scale—Revised.* San Antonio, TX: The Psychological Corporation.

Wechsler, D. (1991). *Wechsler Intelligence Scale for Children-3rd Edition.* San Antonio, TX: The Psychological Corporation.

Wechsler, D. (1997a). *WAIS-III Administration and Scoring Manual.* San Antonio, TX: The Psychological Corporation.

Wechsler, D. (1997b). *Wechsler Memory Scale—Third Edition.* San Antonio, TX: The Psychological Corporation.

Wechsler, D. (2001). *Wechsler Abbreviated Scale of Intelligence.* San Antonio, TX: The Psychological Corporation.

Weiss, L. G., Saklofske, D. H., Prifitera, A., Chen, H. Y., & Hildebrand, D. K. (1999). The calculation of the WISC-III general ability index using Canadian norms. *Canadian Journal of School Psychology, 14,* 1–9.

Zhu, J., & Tulsky, D. S. (1999). Can IQ gain be accurately quantified by a simple difference formula? *Perceptual and Motor Skills, 88,* 1255–1260.

Zhu, J., & Tulsky, D. S. (2000). Co-norming the WAIS-III and WMS-III: Is there a test-order effect on IQ and memory scores? *The Clinical Neuropsychologist,14,* 461–467.

Pioneers in the Assessment of Intelligence and Memory

David S. Tulsky

Nancy D. Chiaravalloti

Kessler Medical Rehabilitation Research Education Corporation
University of Medicine and Dentistry of New Jersey

Tulsky, Saklofske, & Ricker (Chapter 1, this volume) wrote about the history of intellectual assessment focusing on the forces that had more directly influenced Wechsler in the development of his first IQ and memory tests. Included were particular individuals (e.g., Cattell, Binet) and/or major events (e.g., the Army testing program). As stated, the chapter was not meant to be a comprehensive review of all of the individuals responsible for the rapid expansion of intelligence testing at the beginning of the last century. The field is just too rich in history and many of the individuals and events seem to fall outside of the scope of the Wechsler scales and are tangential to this project. However, the influence that men like William Healy, Guy Montrose Whipple, and Louis L. Thustone (to name a few) had made on the field is important to acknowledge. Their work is often overlooked and we believe their contributions should not be forgotten.

Hence, the goal of this appendix is to alert the reader to this rich history by providing thumbnail sketches of some of these pioneers. It should serve as a tribute to many of the researchers and clinicians. So, we attempted to include

Clinical Interpretation of the WAIS-III and WMS-III   **533**

the major figures in testing—those individuals who would have clearly been distinguished as "intelligence testors" in the early to mid 1900's. Due to space constraints, we could not have included everyone who published in this area. Instead, we tried to select those that seem particularly influential.

As history has unfolded itself, some contributions have been remembered in a more favorable light than others. For those individuals whose work has become more controversial, we have included an additional section noting the impact that their work has had on society.

Finally, so that students of psychology and testing could follow-up and read about these figures, we have attempted to list both biographical sources as well as key publications. These should serve as a starting place for those interested in learning more.

The authors would like to acknowledge Corwin Boake, Ph.D. who provided the motivation and encouragement for this Appendix. We would also like to thank the many libraries, academic archives, and publishing companies who provided photographs and permission for their reproduction.

Alfred Binet
1857–1911

Ph.D in Natural Sciences, Académie de Paris (1894)

Self-taught in psychology (earned a "license" from a law school in 1878; undertook some medical studies but did not complete them; became a "reader" or a library psychologist at the Bibliothèque Nationale in France in 1880).

Occupational Milestones:

Salpêtrière Hospital in Paris (studied and worked in Jean Martin Charcot's "laboratory" ~1883–~1890)

Staff, L'Ecole Pratique des Hautes Études, Sorbonne University; Paris, France (1891)

Associate Director, L'Ecole Pratique des Hautes Études, Sorbonne University; Paris, France (1892–1894)

Director, L'Ecole Pratique des Hautes Études, Sorbonne University; Paris, France (1894)

Important Contributions:

* Developer of an innovative approach to assessing intelligence (e.g., the Binet-Simon tests)
* Developer of innovative memory subtests
* Ideas for the measurement of cognitive functioning, developed, in large part, after observing the development of his two daughters
* Founder and editor of the first French psychology journal: *L'Année Psychologique*
* One of the founders of experimental psychology in France
* *Note*: Binet was extremely prolific with diverse publications (includes extensive work on hypnotism and mental illness early in his career. This work was largely unsuccessful)

Hallmark Publications:

Binet, A. & Henri, V. (1896). La psychologie individuelle, *L'Année Psychologique, 2*, 411–465.

Binet, A. (1903). *L'Étude expérimentale de L'intelligence*, Paris: C. Reinwald & Schleicher.

Binet, A. & Simon, T. (1905). Methodes nouvelles pour le diagnostic du niveau intellectuel des anormaux. *L'Annee Psychologique*, 11, 191–244. (English Translation) New methods for the diagnosis of the intellectual level of subnormals. In: *The Development of intelligence in children*. (1916). (E. S. Kite, Translation). Baltimore: Williams & Wilkins Company.

Binet, A. & Simon, T. (1908). Le developpement de l'intelligence chez les enfants. *L'Annee Psychologique*, *14*, 1–94. (English Translation) The Development of intelligence in the child. In: *The Development of intelligence in children*. (1916). (E. S. Kite, Translation). Baltimore: Williams & Wilkins Company.

Binet, A. & Simon, T. (1911). Nouvelles recherches sur la mesure du niveau intellectual chez les enfants d'ecole. *L'Annee Psychologique*, 145–201. (English translation) New investigation upon the measure of the intellectual level among school children. In *The Development of intelligence in children*. (1916). (E. S. Kite, Translation). Baltimore: Williams & Wilkins Company.

Impact on David Wechsler:

Significant Influence:

* David Wechsler had clearly read several of Binet's original papers and books.
* David Wechsler studied with Henri Piéron (who was a colleague and, briefly, a student of Binet). Wechsler would have, almost certainly been exposed to Binet's work at that time (if he had not seen it before).
* David Wechsler extensively used the Stanford Adaptation of Binet-Simon's tests of intelligence.
* Many of the Wechsler tests were taken from the original Binet-Simon and Binet-Henri work.

For More Information:

Wolf, T. H. (1973). *Alfred Binet*. Chicago: University of Chicago Press.

Simon, T. (1912). Alfred Binet. *L'Annee Psychologique*, 18, 1–14.

Larguier des Bancels, J. (1912). L'oeuvre d'Alfred Binet. *L'Annee Psychologique*, 18, 15–32.

Photo Credit:

The photograph appeared along side memorial articles in 1912 of *L'Annee Psychologique*, *18* and in *The Development of Intelligence in Children*. In the public domain.

Cyril L. Burt
1883–1971

B.A., in Classical Languages & Philosophy, Oxford University (1907)

Occupational Milestones:
University of Liverpool, Assistant Lecturer in Experimental Psychology (no higher education in Psychology) (1908–1911 or 1913?)
London County Council, Psychologist (1913–1932)
University College, Chair of Psychology (1932–)

Important Contributions:
* Developed a system for diagnosing mental retardation
* First professional educational psychologist in Great Britain
* Advocated testing children for both high and low ability
* Very interested in juvenile delinquency, which he attributed to environmental causes (unlike the common thought of the time)

Significant (Negative) Impact
* Ran twin studies examining the heritability of intelligence
* Data were called into question in the 1970's; data and results appear to have been fabricated
* Most famous case of suspected scientific misconduct in psychology

Hallmark Publications:
Burt, C. (1925). *Young Delinquent* New York: Appleton-Century-Crofts Company.
Burt, C. (1921). *Mental and Scholastic Tests*. London: London City Council
Burt, C. (1909). Experimental Tests of General Intelligence. *British Journal of Psychology, 3*, 94–177.

Impact on David Wechsler:

Minimal Influence

* Though he was a leading figure in intelligence, his work does not appear to have influenced Wechsler to any great extent.

For More Information:

Hearnshaw, L. S. (1979). *Cyril Burt, Psychologist.* Ithaca, NY: Cornell University Press

Fancher. R. E. (1985). *The Intelligence Men: Makers of the IQ Controversy.* New York: W. W. Norton.

Eysenck, H. J. & Kamin, L. (1981), *The Intelligence Controversy.* New York: John Wiley and Sons.

Photo Credit:

Cyril L. Burt at 49-years-old. Reprinted from Hearnshaw, L. S. (1979). *Cyril Burt, Psychologist.* Plate IX, Ithaca, NY: Cornell University Press, P. 196. Used with permission.

James McKeen Cattell
1860–1944

A.B., Lafayette College (1880)
Ph.D., Institute at Leipzig University (Mentor: Wilhelm Wundt), 1886
Post-Doctoral Fellowship, Cambridge University (Mentor: Sir Francis Galton), 1888

Occupational Milestones:
University of Pennsylvania, Professorship (1889)
Columbia University, Professor of Psychology (1891)
The Psychological Corporation, Founder and CEO (1921)

Important Contributions:
- One of the first American psychologists
- Coined the term "Mental Tests" to describe his program of testing. These tests focused on reaction time, short-term memory, and sensory tasks.
- These "mental tests", and psychometric testing as a whole, were deemed invalid in the early 1900's
- Founder of The Psychological Corporation
- Editor and founder of many leading journals (e.g., Psychological Review; Science, Popular Science Monthly).

Hallmark Publications:
Cattell, J. M. (1890). Mental tests and measurements. *Mind*, *15*, 373–381.
Cattell, J. M. & Farrand, L. (1896). Physical and mental measurements of the students of Columbia University. *Psychological Review*, *3*, 618–648.

Impact on David Wechsler:
Some Influence
- Mentor during graduate school
- Employed by Cattell at The Psychological Corporation where Wechsler served as Secretary (one of his initial jobs)

- However, Wechsler did not incorporate Cattell's tests into his intelligence test nor comment on his influence in his writing.

For More Information:

Sokal, MM (1971) The Unpublished Autobiography of James McKeen Cattell, *American Psychologist, 26*, 626 – 635.

Fancher, R. E. (1985). *The Intelligence Men: Makers of the IQ Controversy.* WW Norton & Company, New York.

Sokal, M. M. (2000). Cattell, James McKeen. Online publication: http://www.and.org/articles/14/14-00101.html; *American National Biography Online.* Copyright 2000 American Council of Learned Societies. New York: Oxford University Press.

Note: the Library of Congress contains an extensive collection of Cattell papers

Photo Credit:

Reprinted from Goodenough, F. L. (1949). *Mental Testing: It's History, Principles, and Applications.* NY: Rinehart & Company Inc.

Edouard Claparède
1873–1940

MD from Geneva (1897); trained as a Neurologist
*Neurologist interested in zoology, animal psychology, and human psychology

Occupational Milestones:
Associate Professor of Psychology at Geneva (1908)

Important Contributions:
- Originater of the list learning tasks for memory assessment – AVLT
- Introduced notions of "implicit" and "explicit" into study of memory
- Described phenomena of "priming effects" and "skill learning"
- Lectured on teaching "abnormal" children
- Studied the association of ideas
- Studied sleep and hysteria (before Kraeplin)
- General Secretary of the 2nd International Congress of Philosophy
- Founded the JJ Rousseau Institute, a school for the sciences of education

Hallmark Publications:
Claparède, E. (1946). *Psychologie de l'enfant et pedagogie experimental Vols. I & II*. Oxford, UK: Delachaux & Niestle.
Claparède, E. (1919). Percentilage de quelques tests d'aptitude. *Archives de Psychologie, 17,* 313–324.

Impact on David Wechsler:
Unknown
- Wechsler probably met, or became familiar with, Claparède's work during his training in Paris.
- However, Claparède's work is not featured prominently in Wechsler's writing nor tests.

For More Information:

Murchison, C. (1932). *History of Psychology in Autobiography.* Clark University Press.

Boake, C. (2000). Historical Note: Edouard Claparède and the Auditory Verbal Learning Test. *Journal of Clinical and Experimental Neuropsychology, 22*, 286–292.

Eustache, F., Desgranges, B., & Messerli, P. (1996). *Review of Neurology, 152*, 602–610.

Photo Credit:

Photograph reproduced from Murchison, C. (1932). *History of Psychology in Autobiography, Vol. II.* Clark University Press. Used with permission.

Hermann Ebbinghaus
1850–1909

University of Bonn, studied history and philosophy (1867 – 1870)
PhD, University of Bonn (1873)

Occupational Milestones:
Taught, traveled and studied in England and France (1875 – 1878)
Founded laboratory at Berlin (1880)
Ausserordentlicher Professor at the Friedrich-Wilhelm University, Berlin (1885)
Full Professor of Philosophy (Breslau) (1894-death)

Important Contributions:
- Spent energy strying to establish Psychology on a quantitative and experimental basis
- Applied Gustave Fechner's psychophysical methods to study higher level mental processes
- One of the leaders in the movement to separate psychology from philosophy
- Attempted to address the "memory problem"
- Originated the use of nonsense syllables in research on memory functions
- Devised a word-completion test to measure intelligence
- Founded the *Journal Zeitschrift fur Psychologie und Physiology der Sinnes Organe* (Journal of Psychology and Physiology of the Sense Organs)

Hallmark Publications:
Ebbinghaus, H.1. (1895). *Memory: A contribution to experimental psychology*. Trans. by H. A. Ruger and C. E. Bussenius, Reprinted in 1913. New York: Teachers College, Columbia University, Bureau of Publications.

Impact on David Wechsler:
Minimal Influence on the Wechsler tests
- Little to no discussion of Ebbinghaus in Wechsler's writing

For More Information:

Shakow, D. (1930). Hermann Ebbinghaus. *The American Journal of Psychology, 42,* 505–518.

Postman, L. (1968). Hermann Ebbinghaus. *American Psychologist, 23,* 149–157.

Photo Credit:

Photograph provided courtesy of the Archives of the History of American Psychology – The University of Akron. Used with permission.

Sir Francis Galton
1822–1911

Apprentice to a surgeon, Birmingham General Hospital (1838)
Instruction, King's College Medical School, London (1839)
Medical education and mathematics, Trinity College, Cambridge, never completed formal education.

Family Background:

- Born into upper class in Great Britain – distinguished family
- Cousin of famous scientist Charles Darwin
- Grandson of famous physician – Erasmus Darwin

Important Contributions:

- One of the founders of psychology and psychological measurement
- Established the first "testing" program: anthropometric laboratory
- Had a profound influence of James McKeen Cattell who studied with him briefly
- Developed the correlation coefficient
- Developed the finger print method of identifying criminals
- Advanced the field of geography

Significant (Negative) Impact on Psychology and "Society at Large":

- Believed in the heiritability of intelligence and other traits
- Founder and leader of the Eugenics movement
- Would influence the practice of eugenics and sterilization programs for individuals with Mental Retardation

Hallmark Publications:

Galton, F. (1869). *Heredity genius: An inquiry into its laws and consequences*. London: McMillan and Co., Ltd.

Galton, F. (1874). *English Men of Science: Their Nature and Narture*. London: McMillan and Co., Ltd.

Galton, F. (1883). *Inquiries into human faculty and its development*. London: McMillan and Co., Ltd.

Galton, F. (1889). *Natural Inheritance*. London: McMillan and Co., Ltd.

Impact on David Wechsler:

Minimal Influence on the Wechsler tests

- Little to no discussion of Galton in Wechsler's writing

For More Information:

Galton, F. (1908). *Memories of My Life*. London: Methuen.

Peason, 1914, 1924, 1930. The Life, Letters, and Labours of Francis Galton. Cambridge University Press.

Harris, J. A. (1911). Francis Galton. Popular Science Monthly, 79. 171–190.

Photo Credit:

Photograph reprinted from Pearson, K. (ed). *The Life, Letters, and Labours of Francis Galton, Volume 2*. Plate II, Cambridge University Press. Used with permission.

Henry Herbert Goddard
1866–1957

B.A., Haverford College, Haverford PA (1887)
M.A., Haverford College, Haverford PA (1889)
Ph.D., Clark University (Mentor: G. Stanely Hall) (1896)

Occupational Milestones:
Professor of Pedagogy and Psychology, State Normal School, West Chester, PA (1899)
Director of Psychological Research, Training School for Feeble-Minded Girls and Boys, Vineland, NJ (1906)

Important Contributions:
- First American psychologist to learn about, and use, the Binet-Simon Scales (around 1908)
- Biggest advocate for the Binet scales. Helped establish mental testing in America
- First psychologist to use intelligence tests in schools to help detect children needing special education services.
- Influenced legislators in NJ to pass a law to mandate that schools provide special classess for children who were deaf, blind, and "feebleminded"
- Adapted the Seguin Formboard for testing "feeble-mindedness"
- Served on the US Government's Committee on Psychological Examination of Recruits (1917–1919)

Significant (Negative) Impact on Psychology and "Society at Large":
- The work for which he is most famous, a book entitled: *The Kalliak Family*, traced the decendents of a feeble-minded girl. This work was used by Goddard and many to follow to demonstrate the "inheritence" of "feeble-mindednessness."
- Leader in the Eugenics movement

- Would influence the practice of eugenics and sterilization programs for individuals with Mental Retardation

Hallmark Publications:

Goddard H. H. (1912). *Kallikak Family: A study in the Heredity of Feeble-Mindedness.* New York: McMillan Company.

Goddard H. H. (1914). *Feeble-Mindedness: Its Causes and Consequences.* New York: McMillan Company.

Goddard H. H. (1915). *The Criminal Imbecile: An Analysis of Three Murder Cases.* New York: McMillan Company.

Impact on David Wechsler:

Minimal Influence on the Wechsler tests

- Little to no discussion of Goddard in Wechsler's writing

For More Information:

Zenderland, L. (1998). *Measuring Minds: Henry Herbert Goddard and the Origins of American Intelligence Testing.* Cambridge, UK: Cambridge University Press.

Fancher, R. (1985). *The Intelligence Men: Makers of the IQ Controversy.* New York: W.W. Norton.

Zenderland, L. (2000). Goddard, Henry Herbert. http://www.anb.org/articles/14/14-00225.html *American National Biography Online* Feb. 2000.

Photo Credit:

Photograph provided courtesy of the Archives of the History of American Psychology – The University of Akron. Used with permission.

Florence L. Goodenough
1886–1959

B.S., Columbia University (1920) (Mentor: R. S. Woodworth, A.T. Poffenberger)
M. A., Columbia University (1921) (Mentor: R. S. Woodworth, E.L. Thorndike)
Ph.D., Stanford University (1924) (Mentor: L. M. Terman)

Occupational Milestones:
Chief Psychologist, Minneapolis Child Guidance Clinic (1924)
Assistant Professor, Institute of Child Welfare, University of Minnesota (1924)
Professor, Institute of Child Welfare, University of Minnesota (1931)

Important Contributions:
- Published the Draw-a-Man Intelligence test (which she had worked on for her Ph.D.)
- Published important text books: Developmental Psychology, Mental Testing, Exceptional Children
- Worked with Terman on his study of gifted children.

Hallmark Publications:
Goodenough, F. L. (1926). *Measurement of Intelligence by Drawings*. Yonkers-on-Hudson, NY: World Book 6.
Goodenough, F. L. (1934). *Developmental Psychology*. NY: D. Appleton-Century Company.
Goodenough, F. L. (1949). *Mental Testing: It's History, Principles, and Application*. New York: Rinehart & Company, Inc.

Impact on David Wechsler:
Minimal Influence on the Wechsler tests.
- Was a contemporary of David Wechsler's.
- However, Wechsler did not incorporate the Draw-a-Man tasks into the Wechsler scales.

Note: Her mentors at Columbia are a little harder to cite. Officially, she was an advisee of Leta Hollingworth but complained to her colleague, Dale B. Harris, that she only saw

Dr. Hollingworth once during her entire year as a Master's student and then for only twenty minutes. She is also said to have worked closely with E. L. Thorndike. However, in a paper by Boring & Boring (1948), she listed R. S. Woodworth and E. L Thorndike as her primary mentors at Columbia. She also studied with L. M. Terman at Stanford University.

For More Information:
University of Minnesota Senate Minutes – June 4, 1959
Lawrence, C. (2000). Goodenough, Florence Laura. http://www.anb.org/articles/14/12-00232. html. American National Biography Online. Feb. 2000.

Photo Credit:
Photograph provided courtesy of the Archives of the University of Minnesota. Used with permission.

William Healy
1869–1963   married Augustus Brunner

MD, University of Chicago (1900)

Occupational Milestones:
Northwestern University
Director of Juvenile Psychopathic Institute (1909)
Summer lecturer, Harvard University (1912–1913)
Director of the Judge Baker Foundation (retired in 1947)

Important Contributions:
* Recognized the need for performance tests to complement the more verbal types of intelligence tests popular at the time
* Developed the Healy-Fernald series of 23 tests, first used in 1911
* Developed the Healy Picture Completion Test and the Healy Puzzle
* Chairman of the Board of Trustees for the Boston Psychopathic Hospital for 25 years
* President of the Boston Society of Neurology and Psychiatry
* Pioneer in the field of juvenile deliquency
* Pioneer in forensic psychiatry/psychology
* First director of the Judge Baker Center in Boston

Hallmark Publications:
Healy, W. & Fernald, GM (1911). Tests for practical mental classification. *Psychological monographs, 13* (54)
Healy, W. (1917). *The Individual Delinquent*. Boston: Little, Brown, and Company
Healy, W. (1921). Pictorial Completion Test II. *Journal of Applied Psychology*, 225–239.

Impact on David Wechsler:
Some Influence
* Wechsler attended conferences and seminars led by Healy and his wife, Augusta Bronner, while training in Boston in the 1920's.
* Wechsler believed in the use of form boards originated by Healy

- Wechsler used the Picture Completion test clinically and in the military and cited the test in his books.
- However, Wechsler acknowledges that he only used the name "Picture Completion" not the task.

For More Information:

Gardner, G. E. (1972). William Healy: 1869–1963. *Journal of the American Academy of Child Psychiatry*, 11, 1–29.

Meltzer, H. 1967 Contributions to the History of Psychology: VI. Dr. William Healy-1869-1963-The Man in his Time. *Psychological Reports. 20*(3, PT. 2) 1028–1030.

Taylor. "Healy, William" http://www. anb.org/articles/12/12-01384.htm
American National Biography Online, Feb. 2000.

Photo Credit:

Photograph courtesy of the Judge Bukes Foundation, Boston, MA. Used with permission.

Howard Andrew Knox
1885–1949

M. D., Dartmouth College, Hanover, NH (1908)
Student Medical Officer, US Army Medical School, Washington DC (1910)

Occupational Milestones:
First Leutenant, Medical Reserve Corps, US Army (1908)
Junior Medical Officer, US Army Medical Corps (1910)
Assistant Surgeon, US Public Health Service (1912)
Acting Clinical Director, State Village for Epileptics, Skillman, NJ (1916)
Private Practice, Bayonne, NJ (1917), Hampton, NJ (1922), and New Hampton, NJ (1924)

Important Contributions:
- Developed a performance battery for testing immigrants for mental retardation at Ellis Island
- Developed the Feature Profile test
- Developed the Knox Cube Imitation test
- Treated and diagnosed early cases of Spanish Influenza

Hallmark Publications:
Knox (1914). A scale based on the work at Ellis Island for estimating mental defect. *Journal of the American Medical Association*, *62*,741–747
Knox, H. A. (1913). Two new tests for the detection of defectives. *New York Medical Journal* for September 13, 1913.
Knox H.A. (1916). *Alien Mental Defective*. Chicago: CH Sterling Company.

Impact on David Wechsler:
Some Influence
- Wechsler was aware of Knox's work.
- Would use the Feature Profile in his Object Assembly test.

- Would use the Knox Cube Imitation test (original and alternate form) for his masters theses research and in the military testing during World War I
- Would adapt the Knox Cube Imitation test and incorporate the task in the WMS-R

For More Information:

Knox, R. (2002). Oral History Interview Archives. Ellis Island Museum.

Richardson, J. T. E. (In Press). Howard Andrew Knox (1885–1949): Neglected Pioneer of Performance Tests. *History of Psychology.*

Richardson, J. T. E. (2001). A Physician with the coast artillery corps: The Military career of Dr. Howard Andreew Knox, Pioneer of Psychological testing. *The Coast Defense Journal,* *15*(4), 88–93.

Photo Credit:

Photograph courtesy of J. T. E. Richardson. From the National Archives. In The Public Domain.

Arthur Sinton Otis
1886–1964

A.B., Stanford University (1910)
M.A., Stanford University (Mentor: L. Terman) (1915)
Ph.D., Stanford University (Mentor: L. Terman) (1920)

Occupational Milestones:

Editor of tests and mathematics at World Book Company (1921–1944)

Important Contributions:

- Developed the first group testing format; adapted the Stanford Binet for group adminis-
  tration
- The group testing format was brought to the committee of Psychologists for the US Army
  in World War I (by Lewis Terman) and was the model for developing the group Beta
  exam.
- Published the Otis Group Intelligence Scale in 1918 (World Book Company) for use in
  schools and educational measurement.
- Also authored numerous books in mathematics (educational text books)
- Published two books on aeronautics following work with the U.S. Navy in WW II
- The Otis-Lennon School Ability Test, Seventh Edition (OLSAT) is currently one of the
  leading group administered tests used in school testing programs.

Hallmark Publications:

Otis, A. S. (1918). An Absolute point scale for the group measurement of intelligence. Part I.
Journal of Educational Psychology, 9, 239–260.

Otis, A. S. (1918). An absolute point scale for the group measurement of intelligence, Part II.
Journal of Educational Psychology, 9(6), 333–348.

Otis, A. S. (1916). Considerations concerning the making of a scale for the measurement of
reading ability. *Pedagogical Seminary, 23*, 528–549.

Otis, A. S. (1917). The derivation of simpler forms of regression equations. *Journal of
Educational Psychology, 8(10)*, 619–621.

Otis, A. S. (1917). A criticism of the Yerkes-Bridgets Point Scale, with alternative sugges-tions. *Journal of Educational Psychology, 8(3)*, 129-150.

Otis, A. S. (1916). Some logical aspects of the Binet Scale. *Psychological Review, 23(3)*, 129–152.

Impact on David Wechsler:

Some Influence

* Otis' criticism of the scaling of IQ and his suggestions influenced Wechsler's creation of the deviation IQ.

For More Information:

Baker, D. B. (2000). Otis, Arthur Sinton. Http://www.anb.org/articles/14/14-00455.html. *American National Biography Online* Oxford University Press.

Siegel, E. J. (1992). *Arthur Sinton Otis and the American mental test movement.* Dissertation Abstracts International, 53(5-A).

Photo Credit:

Photograph obtained from the 1917 Stanford University Year book, Provided courtesy of Stanford University Archives. Used with permission.

Rudolph Pitner
1884–1942

Ph.D., University of Leipzig (1913) (Mentor: W. Wundt)

Occupational Milestones:
University of Toledo (1912–1913)
Ohio State University (1914–1921)
Columbia University, Teacher's College, Professor of Education, (1921–1942)

Important Contributions:
- Determined the application of English scales, such as the Stanford Binet, to non-English individuals to be unfair
- Accomplished a great deal in the assessment of the hard of hearing and physically handicapped populations.
- Concentrated efforts on performance measures, creating one of the earliest performance batteries

Hallmark Publications:
Pitner, R. & Paterson, D. G. (1915) The Binet Scale and the Deaf Child. *Journal of Educational Psychology, Vol. 6*, pp. 201–210.

Pitner, R. & Paterson, D. G. (1917). *Scale of Performance Tests*. New York: Appleton-Century-Crofts.

Pitner, R. (1923). *Intelligence testing: Methods and results*. NY: Henry Holt and Co.

Pitner, R. (1929). *Educational Psychology. An Introductory Text*. New York: Henry Holt and Company, Inc. 1929.

Impact on David Wechsler:
Significant Influence
- Wechsler was aware of Pitner's work.
- Used the Pitner-Paterson Scale extensively in clinical and military testing. Was likely a leading influence on his inclusion of performance tests in his batteries
- Would use the Manikin and Feature Profile in his Object Assembly test.

For More Information:

Symonds, P. M (1942) Rudolph Pitner, 1884–1942. Teachers College Record. 1942 44
204-211.

Hollingworth, H. L. (1943). Rudolph Pitner: 1884–1942. *American Journal of Psychology*,
(1943), *56*, 303-305.

Photo Credit:

Photograph provided courtesy of the archives of Teacher's College-Columbia University.
Used with permission.

Stanley D. Porteus
1883–1972

Occupational Milestones:
University of Melbourne
Director of the Vineland Training Institute
University of Hawaii, Profesosr of Clinical Psychology; Director of Psychology Clinic

Important Contributions:
Developed The Porteus Maze Test

Significant Negative Impact on Psychology and "Society at Large":
- Published research on the "mental capacity" of people from underdeveloped civilizations (e.g., aboriginal tribes in Australia)
- Early Pioneer in "Race Psychology"
- His work on race and intelligence has become so controversial that the University of Hawaii changed the name of "Porteus Hall" to the "Social Sciences Building" following extensive protests against naming a building after someone whose work was so controversial

Hallmark Publications:
Porteus, S. D. (1956). *The Porteus Maze Test and Intelligence.* Palo Alto, CA: Pacific Books.
Porteus, S. D. & Babcock, M. E. (1926). *Temperament and Race.* Boston: Richard Badger.
Porteus, S. D. (1917). Mental Tests with Delinquent and Australian Aboriginal Children, *Psychology Review.*
Porteus, S. D. (1933). *The Maze Test and Mental Differences.* Vineland, NJ: Smith Printing and Publishing House.
Porteus, S. D. (1937). *Primitive Intelligence and Environment.* New York: The McMillan Company.

Impact on David Wechsler:
Some Influence
* Wechsler was aware of Porteus' work.
* Porteus' publications were found in Wechsler's library.
* Wechsler included Porteus' "Maze Test" in the WISC
* Wechsler formally reviewed Porteus' autobiography *A Psychologist of Sorts* and was quite respectful of Porteus' career

For More Information:
Porteus, S. D. (1969). *A Psychologist of Sorts*. Palo Alto, CA: Pacific Books.

Photo Credit:
Photograph reproduced from Porteus, S. D. (1969). *A Psychologist of Sorts: The autobiography and publications of the inventor of the Porteus Maze Tests.* Palo Atto, CA: Pacific Books. Used with permission.

Charles Spearman
1863–1945

Ph.D., University of Leipzig (1904) (Mentor: W. Wundt)

Occupational Milestones:
University College of London, Reader in Experimental Psychology (1907)
University College of London, Chair in General Psychology (1911)
University College of London, Professor of Psychology (1928)

Important Contributions:
* Developed the theory of general intelligence
* Called the theory the "Two-factor theory of intelligence": g=general; s=specific, but it was "g" that caused abilities to be intercorrelated
* Spearman's "rho" correlation coefficient remains a popular non-parametric statistic

Hallmark Publications:
Spearman, C. (1904). "General intelligence," objectively determined and measured. *American Journal of Psychology, 15*, 201–293.
Spearman, C. (1922). *The Nature of Intelligence and the Principles of Cognition.*
Spearman, C. E. (1927). *The abilities of man.* New York: McMillan.

Impact on David Wechsler:
Some Influence
* Wechsler met and studied briefly with Spearman in London.
* Wechsler was influenced by his psychometric rigor and innovativeness.
* Cited Spearman's "g" theory as one of the most significant theories in the book *Measurement of Adult Intelligence.*
* However, Wechsler moved away from Spearman's view, especially later in his life.

For More Information:

Fancher, N. (1985). *The Intelligence Men: Makers of the IQ Controversy*. NY: WW Norton & Co.

Spearman, C. (1930). Autobiography. In C. Murchison (Ed.). *A History of Psychology in Autobiography*, Volume 1. Clark University Press.

Photo Credit:

Photograph reprinted from Fancher, N. (1985). *The Intelligence Men: Makers of the IQ Controversy*. NY: WW Norton & Co. Permission to reprint granted courtesy of the British Psychological Society.

Lewis M. Terman
1877–1956

Ph.D., Clark University (Mentors: G. S. Hall; E. C. Sanford)

Occupational Milestones:
Initially employed as a high school principal following receipt of Ph.D. (1905–1906)
Los Angeles State Normal School, Professor of Child Study and Pedagogy (1906–1910)
Stanford University, Assistant Professor of Education (1910–1917)
Served on the US government's Committee on Psychological Examination of Recruits (1917–1919)
Returned to Stanford in 1919, becoming the executive head of the psychology department in 1923 and retiring in 1942

Important Contributions:
* Produced the first widely used individual measure of intelligence in America: The Stanford-Binet Intelligence Scale (1916)
* Although Terman did not originate the use of the term "IQ", he is responsible for introducing the term to the American vocabulary
* Leader in the military testing movement
* Performed longitudinal study of gifted children

Hallmark Publications:
Terman, L. M. (1911). The Binet-Simon Scale for Measuring Intelligence: Impressions Gained by the Application Upon Four Hundred Non-Selected Children. *Psychological Clinic, 5*; 199–206.
Terman, L. M. (1913). Psychological Principles Underlying the Binet-Simon Scale and Some Practical Considerations for Its Correct Use. *Journal of Psycho-Asthenics, 18*;93–104
Terman, L. M. (1916). *The Measurement of Intelligence*, Boston: Houghton Mifflin Company.
Terman, L. M. (1917). The Mental Powers of Children and the Stanford Revision and Extension of the Binet-Simon Intelligence Scale. *Child, 7*: 287–290.

Terman, L. M. (1917). *The Intelligence of School Children*. Boston: Houghton Mifflin Company.

Terman, L. M. & Merrill, M. A. (1937). *Measuring Intelligence. A Guide to the New Revised Stanford. Binet Test of Intelligence*. Boston: Houghton Mifflin Company:

Impact on David Wechsler:

Significant Influence

* Wechsler used, extensively, the Stanford adaptation of the Binet test.
* Used many of the items and tasks in his batteries.

For More Information:

Minton, H. L. (1988). *Lewis M. Terman: Pioneer in Psychological Testing*. NY: New York University Press.

Terman, L. M. (1932). Autobiography. In: C. Murchison (ed.) *A History of Psychology in Autobiography, Vol II*. Clark University Press.

Henry L. Minton. "Terman, Lewis Madison" http://www.anb.org/articles/14/14-00626. html *American National Biography Online*, Feb. 2000.

Photo Credit:

Photograph provided courtesy of the Stanford University Archives. Used with permission.

Edward Lee Thorndike
1874–1949

Ph.D., Columbia University (1898) (Mentor: J. M. Cattell)

Occupational Milestones:
Teacher of Education, College for Women of Western Reserve University (1898)
Professor of Education, Teacher's College, Columbis University (1901)

Important Contributions:
* Wrote several textbooks. Said that he would write a textbook whenever he was assigned to teach a new course.
* Studied Animal Intelligence and conducted studies of animal learning.
* In humans, he advanced the idea that there are different "kinds" of intelligence rather than a general "g" factor.
* Entered a great debate with Spearman that would span decades about the nature of intelligence.
* Contributed to the growing field of Educational Psychology

Hallmark Publications:
Thorndike, E. L. (1905). *Elements of Psychology.* Syracuse; NY: The Mason-Henry Press.
Thorndike, E. L., Lay, W., & Dean, P. R. (1909). The relation of accuracy in sensory discrimination to general intelligence. *American Journal of Psychology, 20,* 364–369.
Thorndike, E. L., Bregman, E.O.; Cobb, M. V. & Woodyard, E. (1926). *The Measurement of Intelligence.* New York: Bureau of Publications, Teacher's College, Columbia University.
Thorndike, E. L. (1914). *Educational Psychology: Briefer Course.* New York: Bureau of Publications, Teacher's College, Columbia University.

Impact on David Wechsler:
Significant Influence
* Wechsler was a student at Columbia where Thorndike was on faculty.
* Influenced by Thorndike's notion of multiple factors of intelligence.

For More Information:

Thorndike, E. (1932). Autobiography. In C. Murchison (Ed). *History of Psychology in Autobiography, Volume 3*, Clark University Press.

Geraldine Jonçich Clifford. "Thorndike, Edward Lee"; http://www.anb.org/articles/14/14-00632. html; American National Biography Online Feb. 2000.

Photo Credit:

Photograph courtesy of the archives of Teacher's College, Columbia University. Used with permission.

Louis Leon Thurstone
1887–1955

Bachlors of Engineering, Cornell University (1912)
Ph.D., University of Chicago, (1917) ("self-starter in the field")

Occupational Milestones:
Department of Applied Psychology, Carnegie Institute of Technology, (1915) (with Walter Bingham)
Instructor, Engineering, University of Minnesota
Associate Professor of Psychology, University of Chicago (1924)
Professor of Psychology, University of Chicago (1924)

Important Contributions:
* Presented a multifactorial view of intelligence – "Vectors of the Mind"
* Developed scales that measure abstract reasoning
* Believed in multiple factors of intelligence (verbal, spatial orientation, memory)
* Developed a group test of intelligence – called the Primary Mental Abilities
* Significant contributions to measurement theory and practice:
  Redefined factor analyses
  Presented a new view of psychometrics that defined a "psychological continuum"
  Developed the method of "paired comparisons"

Hallmark Publications:
Thurstone, L. L. (1924). *The Nature of Intelligence*. New York: Harcourt, Brace, & Company, Inc.
Thurstone, L. L. (1938). *Primary Mental Abilities*. Chicago: University of Chicago Press.
Thurstone, L. L. (1928). The absolute zero in intelligence measurement. *Psychological Review*, 35, 175–197.
Thurstone, L. L. (1941). Factoral studies of intelligence. *Psychometric monoraphs*, 2, 94.
Thurstone, L. L. (1934). The vectors of the Mind. *Psychological Review*, 41, 1–32

Thurstone, L. L. (1947). *Multiple-Factor Analysis: A Development and expansion of Vectors of the Mind*. Chicago: University of Chicago Press.

Thurstone, L. L. (1927). Psychophysical Analysis. *American Journal of Psychology, 38*, 268–389.

Impact on David Wechsler:

Some Influence

- Though Wechsler didn't cite him as a primary influence, Thurstone's work likely had a profound effect on his views.
- Thurstone's criticism of "mental age" scores and his work on "absolute zero" measurement most likely influenced Wechsler's creation of the deviation IQ score.
- Thurstone's work on multiple factors of intelligence likely caused Wechsler to move away from Spearman's views (especially later in Wechsler's career).

For More Information:

Dale Stout. "Thurstone, Louis Leon" http://www. anb.org/articles/14/14-00635.htm American National Biography Online Feb. 2000.

Photo Credit:

Photograph reproduced from Goodenough, F. L. (1949). *Mental Testing: It's History, Principles, and Applications*. NY: Rinehart & Company, Inc.

David Wechsler
1896–1981

Immigrated from Lespedi, Romania in 1902
B.A., City College of New York (1916)
M.A., Columbia University (1917) (Mentor: R.S. Woodworth)
Ph.D., Columbia University (1925) (Mentor: R.S. Woodworth)

Occupational Milestones:
Enlisted in Sanitary Corps, US Army (1917)
Studied with Charles Spearman & Karl Pearson (1919)
Fellowship with Henri Pieron (1920)
Psychologist, New York Bureau of Child Guidance (1922)
Acting Secretary, The Psychological Corporation (1925–1927)
Psychologist, Brooklyn Jewish Social Service Bureau (1927–1932)
Chief Psychologist, Bellevue Psychiatric Hospital
Faculty member, NYU College of Medicine (1932)

Important Contributions:
- Developed the Wechsler Intelligence scales
- Developed the Wechsler Memory scale
- Wrote leading textbook and numerous articles on intelligence testing

Hallmark Publications:
Wechsler (1939). *The Measurement of Adult Intellence*. Baltimore: Williams and Wilkins.
Wechsler (1935). *Range of Human Capacities*. Baltimore: Williams and Wilkins.
Wechsler (1955). *WAIS Manual*. New York: The Psychological Corporation.
Wechsler (1949). *WISC Manual*. New York: The Psychological Corporation.

For More Information:

Matarazzo, J. D. (1981). David Wechsler (1896–1981) *American Psychologist, 36*, 1542–1542.

Doppelt, J. E. (1981). David Wechsler. Presentation at the 1981 convention of the American Psychological Association. Los Angeles, CA: August, 26, 1981.

Carson, J. Wechsler David. (2000). *American National Biography Online*, Feb. 2000. http://www.anb.org/articles/14/14-00899.html

Photo Credit:

Photograph provided courtesy of Adam Wechsler. Used with permission.

Frederic Lyman Wells
1884–1964

Ph.D., Columbia University in Psychology (1906) (Mentor: J. M. Cattell)

Occupational Milestones:
Columbia University (studied under Cattell)
McLean Hospital, Belmont Mass. (until 1921)
Supervised the selection of tests for the fledgling air service (1917–1918)
One of the 8 psychologists selected by the APA in collaboration with the US military to devise a standardized test that would differentiate the worst and the best recruits in the military
Chief Psychologist, Boston Psychopathic Hospital (1921–1932)
Instructor in experimental psychopathology at Harvard Medical School (1921–1938)
Assistant Professor in experimental psychopathology at Harvard Medical School (1932-)
Staff, Boston City Hospital (1935–1939)
Consultant to the Adjutant General's Office, where he assisted in developing the Army General Classification Test
Psychologist in the Department of Hygiene at Harvard University (1941–1950)
Massachusettes General Hospital (1939–1950)

Important Contributions:
- Became director of Boston Psychopathic Hospital after William Healy left
- Developed "Tests of Association" and the first Digit Symbol task
- Served on the U.S. Government's Committee on Psychological Examination of Recruits (1917-1919)
- Produced the revised Army Alpha in 1932
- Developed the first clinical memory battery

Hallmark Publications:

Woodworth, R. S. & Wells, F. L. (1911). *Association Tests*. Being a part of the report of the committee of the American Psychological Association on the Standardization of procedure in experimental tests. *Psychological Monographs*, *13* (whole no. 57).

Wells, F. L., & Martin, H. A. A. (1923). A method of memory evaluation suitable for psychotic cases. *American Journal of Psychiatry*, *3*, 243–258.

Wells, F. L. (1927). *Mental tests in clinical practice*. Yonkers-on-Hudson, NY: World Book Company.

Impact on David Wechsler:

Significant Influence

*   Wechsler trained for a year with Wells at the Boston Psychopathic Hospital.
*   Wechsler cites Wells as one of the prime influences on the development of the Wechsler Bellevue in the Foreword to The Measurement of Adult Intelligence
*   Wechsler incorporated much of the Wells-Martin Memory Examination into the Wechsler Memory Scale.
*   Wechsler incorporated one of the Woodworth-Wells Association tests into the Wechsler Bellevue Form II (Coding)
*   Wechsler incorporated another Woodworth-Wells Association test into his Masters Thesis and later into the Wechsler Memory Scale (Verbal Paired Associates)

For More Information:

Eugene Taylor. "Wells, Frederic Lyman" http://www.anb.org/articles/14/14-00929.html *American National Biography Online*, Feb. 2000

Photo Credit:

Photograph provided courtesy of the Countway Library and Archives, Harvard University. Used with permission.

Guy Montrose Whipple
1876–1941

A.B., Brown University (1897)
Assistant in psychology, Clark University (1898)
Assistant in psychology, Cornell University (1899)
Ph.D., Cornell University, (1900) (Mentor: E. B. Titchener)

Occupational Milestones:
Assistant Professor, Cornell University (1904)
Assistant Professor, University of Illinois (1914)
Acting Director, Carnegie Institute of Technology (1917)
Professor, Experimental Education, University of Michigan (1919)

Important Contributions:
- Wrote the initial book describing intelligence and physical testing practices in 1910.
- Served on the committee to apply the army testing to civilians and conduct group intelligence testing
- Served on the U.S. Government's Committee on Psychological Examination of Recruits (1917-1919)
- Director of the National Intelligence Test – sponsored by the National Research Council.
- Cofounder of the Journal of Educational Psychology
- Founder of the National Research Counsel on Education
- Began as an experimental psychologist and developed "brass instruments" (e.g., Whipple Disk Tachistoscope")
- Editor for the yearbooks of the National Society for the Study of Education

Hallmark Publication:
Whipple, G. M. (1910). *Manual of Mental and Physical Tests*. Baltimore: Warwick & York, Inc. 1st ed revised and enlarged edition, 2 volumes, 1914 and 1915.

Impact on David Wechsler:

Some Influence

- Wechsler had read Whipple's book and was influenced by some of the tests he reported on.
- For instance, Wechsler was interested in tests of "mirror writing" which is reported in Whipple's book.
- However, there is no indication that Wechsler worked with Whipple in any formal capacity.

For More Information:

Bagley, W. C 1942 Guy Montrose Whipple. *Yearbook of the National Society for the Study of Education. 41*, Part 2 465–469

Ruckmick, C. A. (1942) Guy Montrose Whipple: 1876–1941. *American Journal of Psychology, 55*, 132–134

Samelson, F. "Whipple, Guy Montrose" http://www.anb.org/articles/14/14-00931.html *American National Biography Online*, Feb. 2000.

Photo Credit:

Photograph provided courtesy of the Archives of the History of American Psychology – The University of Akron. Used with permission.

Robert Sessions Woodworth
1869–1962

A.B., Amherst College (1891)

A.B., (1896); M.A (1897) in Psychology (Mentor: William James) & Philosophy, Harvard University

Ph.D. in Psychology, Columbia University (1899) (Mentor: James McKeen Cattell)

Occupational Milestones:

Instructor, Columbia & Bellevue Hospital Medical College (1899–1902)

Researcher and teacher, Edinburgh, Scotland and Liverpool, England (1900–1903) (under physiologist, Sir Charles Sherrington)

Instructorship in Psychology, Columbia University (1903)

Professor of Psychology, Columbia University (1909)

Important Contributions:

* Developed Tests of Association with F. L. Wells (1911) (included subtests of Verbal Paired Associates and Coding)
* Developed a test of emotional stability for World War I recruits which was a forerunner of self-report personality inventories.
* Published extremely influential textbooks that defined psychology. His book *Experimental Psychology* was nicknamed the "Columbia Bible"
* Redefined "experimental" psychology using terms that are standard today (e.g., "independent" and "dependent" variables)
* On initial Board of Directors of The Psychological Corporation; Instrumental in "removing" Cattell from his position as chief operating officer and revamping company in the late 1920's

Hallmark Publications:

Trumbull, G. & Woodworth, R. S. (1938). *Elements of Psychological Psychology*. New York: Scribner.

Woodworth, R. S. (1938). *Experimental Psychology*. New York: Henry Holt and Company.

Woodworth, R. S. (1921). *Psychology*. New York: Henry Holt and Company.
Woodworth, R. S. & Wells, F. L. (1911). Association Tests. *Psychological Monography, 13*, 57.

Impact of David Wechsler:

Significant Influence

* Wechsler trained with Woodworth at Columbia. Woodworth chaired his MA and PhD thesis.
* Wechsler has paid tribute to Woodworth both in writing and in an interview.
* Wechsler incorporated one of the Woodworth-Wells Association tests into the Wechsler Bellevue Form II (Coding)
* Wechsler incorporated another Woodworth-Wells Association test into his Masters thesis and later into the Wechsler Memory Scale (Verbal Paired Associates)

For More Information:

Winston, A. S. (2000). Woodworth, Robert Sessions. http://www.anb.org/articles/14/14-00900.html *American National Biography Online* Feb. 2000

Woodworth, R. S. (1932). Autobiography of Robert Sessions Woodworth. In C. Murchison (ed.). *A History of Psychology in Autobiography*. Clark University Press.

Poffenberger, A. (1962). Robert Sessions Woodworth: 1862–1962. *American Journal of Psychology, 75*, 677–689.

Photo Credit:

Photograph provided courtesy of the Archives of History of American Psychology – The University of Akron. Used with permission.

Robert Mearns Yerkes
1876–1956

A.B., Ursinus Academy and College (1897)
A.B., Harvard University (1898)
M.A., Harvard University, zoology (1899)
Ph.D., Harvard University (Mentors: Charles Davenport, William Castle – genetics; Hugo
Münsterberg – Psychology) (1902)

Note: Boring & Boring (1948) cite Yerkes as being without a primary mentor most likely
because of the diversified training he received from various disciplines.

Occupational Milestones:
Junior faculty appointments, Harvard University (1902–1917)
Director of Division of Psychology; Office of Army Surgeon General; National Research
Council (1917–1919)
Institute of Psychology Yale University (1924–1929)
Professor of Comparative Psychobiology, Yale University (1929–1944)
Director of Yale Laboratories of Primate Biology (1929–1941)

Important Contributions:
- Chaired the Committee on Psychological Examination of Recruits and directed the
Army Psychological Testing Program in World War I
- Prepared a "point scale" adaptation of the Binet-Simon Tests which was published in
1915
- Showed the importance of studying animal behaviors; performed extensive experimen-
tation with mice and primates
- Established the relationship between anxiety and performance: the "Yerkes–Dodson
inverted U-shaped curve"

- Established the "re-writing" of the bylaws of the American Psychological Association which formed the "divisional structure" that exists today
- Chaired the National Research Council Committee for Research in Problems of Sex (1921–1947) which lead to significant advances in sex research.

Hallmark Publications:

Yerkes, R. M.; Dodson, J. D. (1908). The Relation of Strength of Stimulus to Rapidity of Habit Formation. 84 459–482

Yerkes, R. M. (1907). *The Dancing Mouse*. New York: The McMillan Company.

Yerkes, R. M., Bridges, J. W., & Hardwick, R. S. (1915). *A Point Scale for Measuring Mental Ability*. Baltimore: Warwick & York, Inc.

Yerkes, R. M. (1921). *Psychological Examining in the United States Army: Memoirs of the National Academy of Science, Vol 15*. Washington: Government Printing Office.

Yerkes, R. M. & Yerkes, A. (1929). *The Great Apes: A Study of Anthropoid Life*. New Haven: Yale University Press.

Impact on David Wechsler:

Moderate/Some Influence

- Wechsler was extensively influenced by the army testing program.
- Though little is known about Wechsler's interactions with Yerkes during the war, he appeared to work more closely with Boring and Otis than Yerkes himself.
- Later in Yerkes' career, he turned his attention to primate research and had less impact on Wechsler's work

For More Information:

Reed, J. W. (2000). Yerkes, Robert Mearns. http://www.anb.org/articles/14/14-00861.html *American National Biography Online* Feb. 2000

Yerkes, R. M. (1932). Autobiography. In C. Murchison (ed.). *A History of Psychology in Autobiography*. Clark University Press.

Reed, J. (1987). Robert M. Yerkes and the mental testing movement. In M. M. Sokal (ed.) *Psychological testing and american society: 1890–1930*. New Brunswick, NJ: Rutgers University Press. 75–94.

Samelson, F. (1977) World War I Intelligence Testing and the development of psychology. *Journal of the History of the Behavioral Sciences, 13*, 274–282.

Photo Credit:

Photograph reproduced from Goodenough, F. L. (1949). *Mental Testing: Its History, Principles, and Applications*. New York: Rinehart & Company Inc.

Reviews and Promotional Material for the Wechsler–Bellevue and Wechsler Memory Scale

David S. Tulsky

Kessler Medical Research and Education Corporation
University of Medicine and Dentistry of New Jersey

In closing the book, material is presented that will help the user gain additional insight about the state of psychological assessment at the time of the release of the original versions of the Wechsler scales. In this appendix, the reader will find 'odds and ends' dating back to the 1940's including early promotional material, reprints of the reviews of the scales that appeared in the *Mental Measurement Yearbook* series (Buros, 1940, 1949), and a faculty biographical sketch that was completed by David Wechsler, in 1942, shortly after the release of the WB I. Taken together, these materials offer a fascinating glimpse into the field in the 1940's and allow us to further deduce how well the tests were received by the field and how they advanced clinical practice.

The *Wechsler–Bellevue Intelligence Scale, Form I* (WB I) was published in 1939 and within a short time, it enjoyed enormous popularity in the field. The Psychological Corporation published the test material but did not include a users manual in the WB I kit. Instead, the administration instructions for the scale was published separately in a book entitled *The*

Clinical Interpretation of the WAIS-III and WMS-III **579**

Measurement of Adult Intelligence. Users of the WB I had to purchase this book as it contained all of the verbal items and all of the instructions for how to administer the test. Clearly, the book sold far better than expected as the textbook was reprinted (and revised) two times in the first 5 years of its release. In 1944, the third edition of *The Measurement of Adult Intelligence* was published.

The initial items in Appendix 2 are reprints of both the original catalog listing for the WB I (see Item 1) and the original marketing material for the book (see Item 2). These items are particularly interesting as they aid in making inferences regarding the name of the intelligence scale. As can be seen in the Item 2, the new test is referred to as the "New Bellevue Scale." David Wechsler used this terminology and referred to the test kit by that name throughout the text of his book. The first formal use of Wechsler's name appears to have come from The Psychological Corporation as the initial catalog listing advertises the new test kit as the "Wechsler–Bellevue Intelligence Scale." In authoring a book on the Wechsler scales, George Frank referred to the tests as *The Wechsler Enterprise*, because there was no dispute about their clinical, historical, and economic value. With the publication of the third editions, a logo for the "W" was developed and trademarked for the WAIS-III and WMS-III demonstrating how valuable the Wechsler "W" has become. From these materials, we can infer that it was the original marketing team at The Psychological Corporation that recognized the importance of Wechsler's name and helped establish its value.

Items 3–5 consist of reviews of both the WB I and the *Measurement of Adult Intelligence* that have been reprinted in their entirety from the *Mental Measurement Yearbook* (Buros (ed.), 1940). Corwin Boake (2002) has shown how critical reviews of the Wechsler scales can provide insight into why the the Wechsler Scales became so popular and dominant in the field. We have reprinted these key reviews in this Appendix as an effort of making these reviews easily accessible to readers of this book.

From these reviews, we can see that Wechsler's focus of creating a battery to assess intelligence in an adult population served a tremendous need in the field. Though he synthesized familiar instruments into a single battery, there was no scale to date that had combined such a variety of tests measuring diverse mental abilities into a single package. The psychometric and normative data surpassed anything that was available at the time and the large, representative co-normed set of scales were reason enough for clinicians to use the new adult scale. For example, Fred Lyman Wells opens his review (see Item 3) declaring that the WB I is ". . . by a considerable margin the best available procedure for adults in a clinical setting" and Grace Kent in her review (see Item 4) points out that a new scale designed for adults "must strike a responsive cord in every clinical examiner who has had occasion to present the Binet scale to a mature subject of average or superior achievement." Kent seemed to understand the importance of the scale and foreshadowed its popularity. However, her review also reflects the fact that David Wechsler was challenging the field to think differently about intelligence testing and to abandon familiar concepts about scores (e.g., with using the deviation IQ in place of "mental age" normative methods). In discussing Wechsler's redefinition and reconceptualization of the "Intelligence Quotient", Kent writes that "the use of the term, as applied to something entirely different from what we understand by it, is likely to be misleading." She ends her review by criticizing the fact that Wechsler hadn't provided a table of true 'mental age' norms for the ages seven to seventeen and strongly urges him to provide "norms" for each subtest individual by age group as Wechsler had because the Bellevue test did not provide enough normative information to the practicing clinical examiner. Such criticism helps us understand how innovative the test was and demonstrates how resistant to change clinicians tended to be and (as Tulsky, Saklofske, & Zhu, Chapter 2 point out) still are today. In hindsight, the field did come to embrace the Wechsler method and his scaling became the reference point for years to come.

Item 6 contained in this appendix is a reprint of a faculty biographical form that David Wechsler completed by hand in 1942 as part of his appointment to the medical school at New York University. In this biographical sheet, we can also see that Wechsler was experiencing several milestones in his personal life that were occurring at the same time as his professional accomplishments. For instance, Wechsler was married to his second wife in 1939, which is the same year that the WB I was published. Moreover, his first child was born, just one year later, in 1940.

More importantly, we can get a glimpse of Wechsler's professional focus, which appears to be on the development of a parallel form of the WB I called the Wechsler Mental Ability Test. At that time, this new test was developed for use in the military during WW II. The Wechsler Mental Ability Test would later be repackaged and published for civilian use as the Wechsler Bellevue Form II. This would only be repackaged again, a few years later, in 1949, as The Wechsler Intelligence Scale for Children.

Additionally, Wechsler makes frequent reference to his consultation duties with the US military. Together with statements made by two of his colleagues who worked with him at this time (Personal Communication Eugenia Jaros, New York City, June, 2002; Personal Communication, Arthur Weidner, New York City, June, 2002), the references in the biographical sheet provide futher indication that David Wechsler was a patriotic American citizen who was proud of his involvement in the US military. In collaboration with Dr. Weidner (see item 7), Wechsler developed a screening test to determine who was likely to "break down" during military service and he furthered his work on emotionality and psychogalvanic responses (that he had performed earlier for his dissertation). Quite clearly, this was an incredibly active period for David Wechsler.

Item 8, the final piece to be included in this Appendix, is the review of the *Wechsler Memory Scale* that has been reprinted from Oscar Buro's *Third Mental Measurement Yearbook* from 1949. Kate Levine Kogan reviewed the scale and was quite positive by the addition of a measure of memory function "to available clinical techniques." She points out that a strength is that the scale could be used in conjunction with the Wechsler Bellevue and embraces the clinical utility of the new scale. At the same time, it appears that a clinical memory test was a novel idea in the mid-1940's and the extent of the clinical applications were still unknown.

ITEM I–ORIGINAL PRODUCT ANNOUNCEMENT FOR THE WECHSLER BELLEVUE SCALE. REPRINTED FROM THE 1939 PRODUCT CATALOG FROM THE PSYCHOLOGICAL CORPORATION

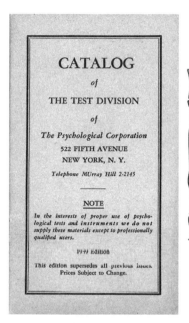

CATALOG

of

THE TEST DIVISION

of

The Psychological Corporation

522 FIFTH AVENUE

NEW YORK, N. Y.

Telephone MUrray Hill 2-2145

NOTE

In the interests of proper use of psychological tests and instruments we do not supply these materials except to professionally qualified users.

1939 Edition

This edition supersedes all previous issues.
Prices Subject to Change.

separately) $2.00. Carrying Case $2.75. Prices for replacement materials on request.

*Wechsler-Bellevue Intelligence Scale (David Wechsler). An individual examination including ten sub-tests at any level. Five verbal: similarities, comprehension, information, arithmetic, and memory for numbers. Five nonverbal: object assembly, block design, picture completion, picture arrangement, and digit-symbol substitution. An alternate test of vocabulary is included. Successes with each type of content are translated into standard score units which are totalled for all scales and converted into I. Q. equivalents by reference to a table. Appeals to mature persons even at lower levels. Well suited for the classification of delinquents, abnormal individuals, and prison inmates. Norms for ages 7-70 years. Test Material $12.50, including 25 record blanks. Record Blanks 75c for 25. Manual: "The Measurement of Adult Intelligence" (order separately) $3.50.

INTERESTS and ATTITUDES

Attitude Scales edited by H. H. Remmers. Scales are now available for measuring attitudes toward high school, teaching, any institution, proposed social action, dis-

Image is from D.S. Tulsky's personal collection, Permission to reproduce was granted by The Psychological Corporation-a Harcourt Assessment Company.

ITEM 2–ORIGINAL PRODUCT
ANNOUNCEMENT BY THE WILLIAMS &
WILKINS COMPANY CIRCA 1939

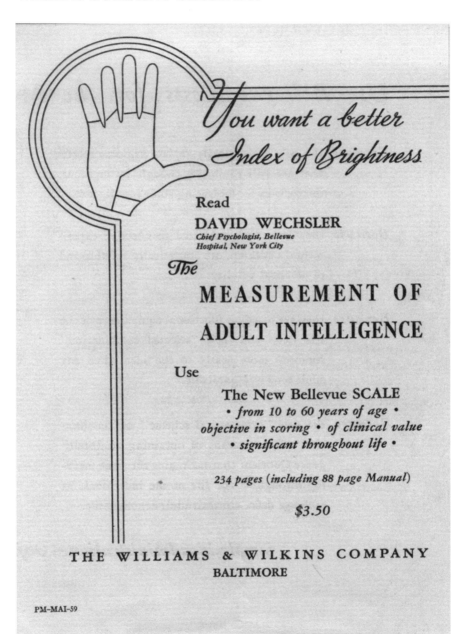

Use Bellevue Tests for the Measurement of Adult Intelligence

Because the new scales finally replace children's tests that are still the main, though incongruous, instruments for measuring adult intelligence.

Because they have been subjected to effective experimental check-up, are statistically reliable and of practical validity.

Because they are based on functional equivalence of the test items and their "selected combination" conforms more nearly to the ideal than any adult tests now available.

Because the new "symmetrical scheme" of classification offers a means of obtaining an Intelligence Quotient that maintains the same meaning throughout the life of the individual, as each age defines its own adult denominator.

Advantage 1: Scale covers a wide range of intellectual abilities; performance as well as verbal. The same types of ability are tested at all levels.

Advantage 2: Scale can be modified in cases of sensory defect or unusual environment. Can aid in diagnosis of psychopathic condition.

Advantage 3: Provides reliable measures of intelligence when evaluated against clinical data, and does so more consistently than any other single scale.

Advantage 4: Is standardized over the age range of seven to seventy years on a selection typical of occupational and educational distribution at every age.

Simple in administration — Objective in scoring — Highly reliable

The Measurement
of Adult Intelligence

The Author: DAVID WECHSLER

*Chief Psychologist, Bellevue Psychiatric Hospital,
Assistant Clinical Professor of Psychiatry, College
of Medicine, New York University. Lecturer,
School of Education, New York University.*

Contents:

**Part I: THE NATURE AND CLASSIFICATION OF INTELLI-
GENCE**

Nature of Intelligence,   Classification of Intelligence,
Need for an Adult Intelligence Scale,   Concept of Mental Deficiency,
Concept of Mental Age and I.Q.,   The Problem of Mental Deterioration.

Part II: THE BELLEVUE INTELLIGENCE SCALES

Selection and Description of Tests,   Standardization and Results,
Population used in Standardizing Tests,   Limitations and Special Merits.

**Part III: MANUAL OF INSTRUCTIONS—THE BELLEVUE INTEL-
LIGENCE TESTS**

TABLES AND APPENDICES

The Tests:

1. An Information Test
2. A General Comprehension Test
3. A Combined Memory Span Test
   for Digits Forwards and Backwards
4. A Similarities Test
5. An Arithmetical Reasoning Test
6. A Picture Arrangement Test
7. A Picture Completion Test
8. A Block Design Test
9. An Object Assembly Test
10. A Digit Symbol Test
Alternate—A Vocabulary Test

Images of the Product Announcement were provided courtesy of the division of archives and special collections of the City College of the City University of New York. Permission to reproduce was granted by the Lippincott, Williams, & Wilkins Company.

ITEM 3–ORIGINAL REVIEWS OF THE WECHSLER–BELLEVUE INTELLIGENCE SCALE

F. L. Wells, Psychologist, Department of Hygiene, Harvard University

This series is by a considerable margin the best available procedure for adults, in a clinical setting. The writer will here discuss it from the standpoint not of general organization, which may be left to reviews of Wechsler's book, but of technical matters having special concern for a workaday user, as the writer has for some time had the good fortune to be. Naturally this involves mention, if not enumeration, of real or fancied flaws in detail. In important features, the scale's status is as above set forth; as it deserves great use, it can also bear minute scrutiny without captiousness.

To begin with, the question of the preceding president will obviously vary in difficulty according to the length of the current incumbency. The "pints" question is an interesting one suggesting that its relative value may have something to do with the misleading association furnished by "quart" (quarter, fourth). The writer does not like the use of the word "obtain"; too high-brow for a question so early in the series. The standard answer to the thermometer question is also of a high level for so early a position, and since the test may be often given in general hospital surroundings, attention should be paid to response in terms of clinical thermometers. "Average height" again seems rather complicated from a vocabulary standpoint for its position in the series. The writer has always favored formulating an information question in the simplest possible terms (e.g., What does rubber come from? About how tall are American women mostly?) even if it involves a recasting of norms. Few things are so disturbing to an examinee's attitude as a question with an unintelligible or even very unfamiliar expression in it. The airplane, North Pole, and United States population questions are specially interesting for their distribution of erroneous answers. The instructions for certain items should make clearer what is the limit of tolerance in the response; as in, e.g., apocrypha, habeas corpus.

In the comprehension subtest the first question would probably benefit by specifying a "new" (uncancelled) stamp. The scoring of the leather question seems needlessly cumbrous. The second alternate involves rather too many variables to be satisfactory from the standpoint of intelligence, whatever might be its significance for an evaluation of personality. Comprehension questions in general give good insights into the examinee's intellectual processes, but it its hard to set up satisfactory scoring criteria for them.

The present questions illustrate dependence on attitude and background; cf. urban and rural background to the "forest" question.

Digit span hardly calls for comment. The most meaningful of the verbal subtests is surely Similarities. The directions are particularly well found. But it is impossible to avoid repeating the criticism that more levels of credit should be recognized, and especially given a wide spread. As to specific items, wood and alcohol make trouble on account of the "wood alcohol" association, and Wechsler must have somehow escaped wrestling with dialect pronunciations of "poem."

Among the arithmetical questions the sugar problem has seemed placed a little late in the series. It is embarrassing to raise invidious questions of commercial ethics, but so much complication has arisen over the prescribed wording of the making change problems, that the word "should" appears preferable to "will." As on other grounds, "get back" is preferable to "receive." (Also in Item 8 of the same, "how much did it cost new" rather than " . . . was it worth new.")

The organization of performance tests always presents greater difficulty than obtains with language content. A more distinctive name than "picture completion" might have been found for the first listed. It is not clear whether there has been a studied inclusion of misleads in such items as the hinge on the door (knobs are hardly move "important" than hinges), the discontinuous cane in the sunset, and the missing antennae of the ship.

Picture arrangement is an excellent testing device, limited by its cumbrousness. (The Bellevue series could have spared itself much of this by printing, as it could easily have done, each one of its pictures on a separate 3 X 5 card.) Cultural difficulties enter, e.g., the taxi outside an urban environment. It has been objected that in the holdup situation the A, B, D, C order is too reasonable to be scored zero, especially since the outmoding of prison "stripes."

The block design series is probably the strongest of the performance subtests. One could wish that more use had been made of the principle, which could well include three-dimensional models. The object-assembly test is cumbrous for what it distinctively contributes, and pencil-and-paper tests, even though nonverbal, seem out of place in a strictly "performance" scale. Fortunately the scale is not a tightly closed system and it is perhaps not too much to hope that the performance scale may be amplified into a manipulative (e.g., block design) and non-manipulative (e.g., digit-symbol) series.

An alternate subtest has been added, a vocabulary test of the Terman type (other words) being taken for the purpose; probably as wise a choice as available. Notation would be easier with double and single credits, as elsewhere, rather than single and half.

That very important and often neglected feature of a test series, the record form, is only moderately well designed. In addition to some rearrangement of material, the writer would prefer to have most of the rulings omitted; they cramp eye movements as well as size of writing, and disregard the consideration that little or nothing may need recording on one item, with a long note on the next.

Special mention should also be made of age norms, tracing the gradual decline of performance after early adult years. In terms of mental age this is some 20 percent between ages 20 and 60 (pp. 56, 196). Although little cited here, perhaps the strongest feature of the scale is its structure, which can serve as a model, in its facility of comparison between records of different well-constructed subtests. For the author of a treatment of Army Alpha from this standpoint, Wechsler lays less stress on this feature than might be anticipated. The chief use of global scores is administrative.

Archives of Neurology and Psychiatry

43, 614, March 1940. *a clear presentation *provides a scale which is simple to give and is reliable.*

Reprinted from: Buros, O. K. (1941). *The 1940 Mental Measurements Yearbook.* Highland Park, NJ: Gryphon Press. Permission to reproduce granted by The Buros Institute of Mental Measurements, Lincoln, NE.

ITEM 4–ORIGINAL REVIEWS OF THE
WECHSLER–BELLEVUE INTELLIGENCE SCALE

Psychology Bulleting 37, 251–4 April 1940.
Grace H. Kent

*The book opens with a ten-page chapter on the nature of intelligence, which is defined as "the aggregate or global capacity of the individual to act purposefully, to think rationally and to deal effectively with his environment." No question is raised by the author concerning the measurability of intelligence as thus defined. The need for a test system intended specifically for study of adult intelligence as opposed to juvenile intelligence is stated in a way which must strike a responsive chord in every clinical examiner who has had occasion to present the Binet scale to a mature subject of average or superior achievement. *In spite of his opposition to the IQ as we know it, the author considers "Intelligence Quotient" too happy a term to be discarded. In his standardization of the Bellevue tests he presents the norms, as determined by standard deviation procedure, in tables by means of which the weighted scores can be converted directly into what he calls the "IQ." This use of the term, as applied to something entirely different from what we understand by it, is likely to be misleading. The strongest feature of the system is the selection of cases for standardization. The norms are based upon scores obtained from 1750 subjects ranging in age from seven to seventy, selected out of 3500 subjects to whom the tests had been presented, the selection being a sampling based upon the occupational distribution of the country's adult white population, as indicated by the 1930 census. The adult subjects were divided into age groups by five-year intervals, the number of cases in a group ranging from 50 subjects in the later fifties to 195 subjects in the later twenties. The collection of such a mass of data is a marvelous achievement. The scale consists of ten test units (plus one alternate), each unit having a wide range of discriminative capacity. Correlations and intercorrelations have been calculated for all possible combinations, and the units are ranked in value according to their correlation with the scale as a whole. The scores have been so weighted as to make the numerical values approximately uniform for the eleven units. Three tables of norms are based upon these weighted scores: one for ten tests, one for five language tests, and one for five performance tests. The student who is not too scrupulous about manipulations of results will be able to obtain approximate ratings from other combinations. Most of the tests are modified forms of tests already in use. The strongest unit of the scale is "Similarities," a series of 12 pairs beginning with *orange–banana* and ending with *fly–tree*. Following Binet, Dr. Wechsler has apparently given more careful attention to criteria for standardization than to criteria for selection of test items. He includes Memory Span for Digits, although acknowledging it to be a weak test as a measure of intelligence. Furthermore, he combines digits forwards and digits backwards under one score, allowing the same credit for five digits forwards as for five digits backwards. He uses also the Symbol-Digit test, observing that the scores show a marked decline with advancing age, but making no mention of visual strain as a possible explanation of this decline. In the tests called "Picture Arrangement" and "Picture Completion," he has used pictures which are too small and too sketchy to be easily understood. It appears that the value of a test, for him, is statistical rather than psychological. The text is carelessly written. "Like" is used as a conjunction, and "where" as a relative pronoun. Throughout the book the author refers to himself as "we," as if the work were a joint product. His irregular use of the "editorial we" is at times misleading, especially when he uses "we" as including (apparently) the small group of students who assisted in making the examinations or the larger group of psychologists who may be expected to use the test in the future. Some of the test materials are contained in six pasteboard boxes, each of which has the name *Bellevue Intelligence Test* blazoned on the cover. Before placing these boxes on the table in full view of the subject, the examiner would do well to cover the offensive labels with something in code. Clinical examiners who are relatively satisfied with some form of the Binet–Simon scale for examination of children will welcome a test which is intrinsically better adapted to adult interests and which is adequately standardized for adults. To this extent, the Bellevue scale will meet a need that has been keenly felt for more than twenty years. It does not, however, show any such advance over the Binet scale as might be expected as a result of our collective experience in the use of tests for a full generation. Students engaged in the development of tests for individual study can learn much from Dr. Wechsler's plan of standardization. The table by means of which a score can be converted directly into the IQ (or its equivalent, preferably under some other name) marks a very important advance over the current method of deriving the IQ. If all tests were thus standardized, the public demand for a one-figure rating could be satisfied honestly and without distortion of results. But the "mental age," although it lends itself to gross abuse, need not be wholly discarded. Many students, with full appreciation of Dr. Wechsler's contribution to higher standards of accuracy in evaluation of test results, will be disappointed because he has made it difficult to derive a satisfactory "mental age" from the scores of his tests. So long as this way of expressing results is so nearly universal, the "mental age" is indispensable as a common denominator. It is a mistake for any author of tests to assume that others will wish to adopt his system as a whole and use it exactly as he himself uses it. Some of us prefer a flexible system to any composite scale. If Dr. Wechsler had included a table of true "mental age" norms for the ages seven to seventeen, not for the three scales, but for each individual unit, the Bellevue tests would be incomparably more useful and would presumably see much wider service. A full-size textbook is too large to be used conveniently as a manual of instructions for test presentation. The third part of this book, containing the instructions and norms, might better have been separated from the reference material in the first two parts. For the convenience of the examiner it is to be hoped that the author will publish additionally a compact booklet or pamphlet containing only what is needed for the daily use of the tests. It is strongly urged that he offer norms (for each unit individually) in the form of simple decile scores for each age group, unweighted and wholly free from mathematical manipulation. He has in his possession much material which would be invaluable to clinical examiners.

Reprinted from Buros, O. K. (1941). *The 1940 Mental Measurements Year book*. Highland Park, NJ: Gryphon Press. Permission to reproduce granted by The Buros Institute of Mental Measurements, Lincoln, NE.

ITEM 5–ORIGINAL REVIEWS OF THE BOOK, THE MEASUREMENT OF ADULT INTELLIGENCE

American Journal of Orthopsychiatry 9, 808–810
O 1939. George Lawton

In this book is described the first attempt to construct an intelligence scale specifically for adults and therefore it is required reading for those interested in mental measurement. Until now, most tests used with adults were not standardized for anyone over 18. This is as true of the new Terman–Merrill Scale as of the old Stanford–Binet. Those rare scales which did include adults in the standardization employed too few to be reliable. Moreover, many of the items in adult examinations had no appeal to mature persons. Too much emphasis is laid on speed as compared with power (accuracy). Credit for correctness of response very often depends upon the invidual's manipulative ability, either of words or of objects, rather than on comprehend of meaning. The Stanford–Binet, for example, is a less successful measure of intelligence at the upper levels where it is overweighted with verbal items. However, to depend solely on performance items in the examination of adults would be equally unsatisfactory, for adults require tests of verbal and performance ability in equal degree. But where the so-called adult examinations are most invalid, as the author justifiably states, is in taking over from psychometric practice with children the concept of M. A. levels and M. A. scores. *Psychologists have not been really getting IQ's with adults at all, since an individual is compared not with others his own age, but with those 14 to 18 years old, the choice of divisor depending on where a given examiner locates the peak of the mental growth curve. *All this shows why the entire approach—both practical and theoretical—to appraising intelligence at maturity has been in urgent need of revision.

a long over-due attempt to deal with the problem as effectively as our psychological statistical knowledge will permit today *Wechsler does not claim originality for individual test items *The discussion of met deterioration is especially important and, incidentally, offers some valuable diagnostic leads to the psychiatrist dealing with seniles. He stresses the concept of "normal mental deterioration," that which occurs after maturity with the natural increase of age. Through the Tables it becomes possible, for the first time, to obtain a reliable estimate of the decrease in mental level of an older subject when compared with others his own age. [The book] describes a fine job of test construction and offers the reader a very satisfying experience.

A great deal of hard work has gone into it, but it is as honest as it is conscientious. Wechsler is not only critical of the shortcomings of other scales but of his own as well. In fact, he devotes an entire chapter entitled "Limitations and Special Merits" to analyzing the result of using the tests with more than 2000 subjects subsequent to standardization. All in all, the Bellevue Scales represent one of the most important pieces of psychometric pioneering to be brought forth in recent years.

*American Journal of Psychiatry 97, 245–6 JI 1940. C. R. Atwell

*may be recommended to any phycisian who is interested in the measurement or the theories of intelligence *The [author's] definition [of intelligence] may be questioned, but it does have the pragmatic value of being a useful concept in developing a test for adult intelligence. The tests fill a long-recognized need by providing material suitable to and standardized for adults. The author's criticism of the concept of mental age as confusing . . . is justified but is probably not so seriously confusing as he indicates. *The author maintains that the average score on the test for the age group should be used in computing the I.Q. for any person of that group. He does, however, give efficiency quotients based on the I.Q.'s of the group from 20–24. For practical purposes, it is quite possible that the efficiency quotients would be more useful, since in considering the adjustment of a patient of 60, we are rather more interested in comparing his performance on a test with adults in general than with 60-year-old adults. *The reviewer has been fortunate to have had the privilege of using these tests for a little more than two years; shortly after they were tried out in this hospital, they were adopted as the basic testing material for our adult patients.

The Bellevue Test may be wholeheartedly recommended for clinical use. The attention paid to the qualitative aspects of the tests both in the author's description of their uses and in his scoring criteria seems a particularly valuable contribution to the clinical worker. *If the statistical material is overlooked the book provides highly enjoyable reading.

B Menninger Clinic 4, 28, January 1940, W. A. V (arvel)

*the Bellevue Adult Scale . . . has been devised with the requirements of the psychiatric clinic in mind and should prove to be a most useful instrument.

The reliability is good, the validity has been checked with reference to clinical data, the test is easy to administer and it has been standardized on adult populations.

Education Abstracts, 4, 390, December, 1939, Wm. Reitz

*an outstanding achievement in the field of intelligence testing. The Bellevue Scales not only furnish reliable and valid IQ's for age ranges 10 to 60 but their validation against clinical case study reports as well as the provision of both "verbal" and "performance" tests makes these scales especially adaptable to the diagnosis of psychopathic conditions and of cases of sensory or verbal defects and unusual conditions of environment. Wechsler's volume merits as important a position in the field of adult intelligence measurements as is held by in regard to the lower age groups.

Journal of the American Medical Association, 114, 683–684 F 24 1940

*All in all, the author presents a new technic which should be of some value to psychiatrists who have bemoaned the lack of the means of evaluating that trait which is so necessary of evaluation but so little understood—general adult intelligence. The present test certainly is a step forward, providing the psychologist working with the psychiatrist another tool in the diagnosis of mental patients.

Journal of Nervous and Mental Disorders 91:548-9 Ap '40. Loyola Ed Digest 15:9 N '39. Austin G. Schmidt

The first part of this work consists of a discussion of the nature and measurement of intelligence. Though brief, the six chapters in this part contain observations and points of view that will be helpful even to the trained psychologist. The second part describes the development and standardization of the Bellevue Intelligence Scales, which are applicable to adults as well as to children. The third part contains the manual for use with the tests, appendices, and norms. The work as a whole is a substantial contribution to the practice and theory of mental testing.

Mental Hygiene (New York) 24, 312–313 April 1940.
Frank K. Shuttleworth

*an outstanding contribution to the measurement of adult intelligence. The tests represent that rare combination of competent execution, from a technical and statistical point of view, and of discriminating attention to a host of practical details, that is so important for effective clinical work. *But while the general procedures are familiar, all but one of the tests are either entirely new or represent considerable adaptations of existing tests. For the most part the individual questions or elements of each test were tried on individuals of known intelligence and hence have been separately validated. While other test-makers have employed some mechanical or statistical rule-of-thumb in the selection of their test elements, Wechsler's selection is notable for the use of statistical procedures plus a high order of horse sense, insight, and discriminating judgment. Chapter 7, on test selection, must be read to be appreciated.

Ohio Journal of Science 40, 51–2 January 1940. Milton
M. Parker

*There has finally been composed a good clinical test of adult intelligence *Without detracting one bit from Dr. Wechsler's accomplishment, it should be said that practically all of the principal concepts employed by him have been described before. His main contribution lies in his combination of these features into a practical and sound measure of adult intelligence. *One of the most interesting of the theoretical sections of the book deals with the problem of mental deterioration. *Wechsler gives adequate proof that the Bellevue scale is reliable as well as valid since it correlates highly with itself and with the Stanford-Binet. *The book is a clear account of that which the author has thought and done, and leaves few questions to be asked.

Personnel Administration 2, 15 March 1940, Walter V.
Clarke

*[the] first 72 pages contain a general discussion of intelligence which is a real contribution to the literature on the subject *his discussion of mental deficiency and mental deterioration are [sicl of particular interest and value. Anyone interested in the problem of intelligence will find in Part

One of this volume a real contribution to present day knowledge and an intense stimulant to thought. *To those interested in the subjects of intelligence or testing, this book is of fundamental value.

Psychiatry, 2, 430–3 April 1939. Isabelle Kendig

It would be premature at this time to attempt an evaluation of the new Bellevue Scale; any judgment of its worth as a measure of adult intelligence must naturally await its thorough try-out by experienced workers throughout the country with groups of every type for whom it is designed. However it is not too early to extend the warmest and most hopeful welcome to such a well-considered and painstaking effort to supply the need for a suitable instrument for testing adults. *The text describing the new scale itself merits careful reading for, besides telling how the tests were selected and standardized, it discusses the nature of intelligence, criticizes our present concepts of mental age and I.Q., and offers new formulations of mental deficiency and mental deterioration. *[The] chapter on deterioration will make everyone over 30 squirm because of the insistence that mental decline sets in at least as early as that. To the present reviewer it is also disappointing because no careful distinction is made between such organic deterioration as Wechsler has chiefly in mind and the purely functional impairment which frequently appears in dementia praecox and as quickly clears up with remission. *It should be noted that the I.Q. employed differs fundamentally from the concept as usually interpreted. *the book [is] worth thoughtful reading quite independently of the new scale for the presentation of which it was written. But the new scale itself may prove to be just that measure of adult intelligence for which psychologists everywhere have been devoutly praying. Certainly we trust that it will prove so and therefore recommend its im-mediate and widespread experimental use.

Reprinted from: Buros, O. K. (1941). *The 1940 Mental Measurements Yearbook*. Highland Park, NJ: Gryphon, Press. Permission to reproduce granted by The Buros Institute of Mental Measurements, Lincoln, NE.

ITEM 6–FACULTY BIOGRAPHICAL FORM COMPLETED BY DAVID WECHSLER

Please fill out & return

FACULTY BIOGRAPHY

For us of
New York University
Bureau of Public Information
Room 63 Press Building
Washington Square   SUMMER 1942

Name *David Wechsler*

College *of Medicine* Department *Psychiatry*

Rank *Asst. Clinical Professor (of Medical Psychology)*

Place of Birth *Roumania*

Date of Birth *Jan. 12, 1896*

Parents' names *Moses, Leah*

Education
Please include dates

Elementary *N.Y.C.   1902–10*

Secondary *De Witt Clinton H.S. 1910–1913*

Colleges (including degrees) *College of City of N.Y. 1913–16, A.B.*
Columbia University 1916–17 M.A.
University of Paris (Sorbonne) 1920–22 Licencié és Sciences
Columbia University 1925 Ph.D.

Honorary degrees (including institution) and other honors received:
American Fellow in French Universities

Prior positions, in other universities or business
Psychologist, Bureau of Children's Guidance N.Y.
and Instructor N.Y. School of Social Work

Positions at New York University *Lecturer, School of Education*

Outside Private and Public Positions now held (including counseling)
Chief Psychologist, Bellevue Hospital, Psychiatric Division

Research work *Emotions, the Psychogalvanic Reflex; Intelligence Tests; tests for Army; Chronaxia*

Principal books and articles *The Measurement of Emotional Reactions*
The Range of Human Capacities (William & Wilkins, 1935)
The Measurement of Adult Intelligence (" " 1942)

Fraternities, professional societies, and clubs. *Am. Psychological Assoc.; A. A. A. S.; Psychometric Society, Amer. Orthopsychiatric Society, etc.*

Church membership... *Jewish; Amer. Zionist Congress*

War Experience. *1918. I. 9., Cpl. Psychological Co., Signal Corps.*
Civilian ~~Defense~~ *War* Activities... *Expert Consultant to Sec. of War*

Married (name, date, place). *to Ruth Halpern, 1939, N. Y. C.*

Children (names and years of birth)... *Adam, born Dec 26, 1940*

Hobbies. *Making Instruments*

Please include below any other data which you feel may be of news value in any announcements by us of promotions, new appointments, speaking engagements, etc.

~~At present~~; Expert Consultant to Sec. of War; Instructor for Adjutant General's School

Author of Wechsler Mental Ability Scale, adopted by the Adjutant General's Dept for use in U. S. Army.

Author of the Wechsler-Bellevue Adult Intelligence Scale

At present engaged in N. R. C., research for development of screening tests for men likely to break down in military service

The Faculty Biographical Form was provided courtesy of New York University archives. Reprinted with permission.

ITEM 7–DR. WECHSLER WITH DR. WEIDNER

Dr. Weschler (left) is pictured with Dr. Arthur Weidner (Right), a fellow Colleague in psychology at Bellevue Hospital, Dr. Weidner worked closely with David Wechsler at Bellevue and on projects consulting to the US military. Photo courtesy of Dr. Arthur Weidner. Used with permission.

ITEM 8–ORIGINAL REVIEW OF THE
WECHSLER MEMORY SCALE

**Kate Levine Kogan, Clinical Psychologist, 154
Chesterfield Road, Pittsburgh 13, Pennsylvania**

This simple, concise measure of memory function has already proved to be a valuable addition to the available clinical techniques. Administration time is brief, directions are clear, and scoring criteria are objective. Perhaps its most important use is in conjunction with the Wechsler-Bellevue intelligence scale, since the memory quotient is designed to be directly comparable to the intelligence quotient. Use of the test permits intra-individual comparison of the patient's memory impairment with his loss in other intellectual functions rather than only a comparison with a general average or norm. Thus, it is possible to distinguish accurately between the kind of memory impairment which is merely one aspect of generalized mental inefficiency and that which represents a specific decrement in memory function. Certain other measures have had a somewhat similar goal. *The Hunt-Minnesota Test for Organic Brain Damage*, for example, is based on the relation between vocabulary level and scores on two types of immediate memory tasks. However, since vocabulary level is commonly accepted as being a better indication of native endowment prior to the onset of illness than it is a measure of functioning level, a different picture is obtained. The *Wechsler Memory Scale*, in conjunction with the intelligence scale, allows for a broader analysis of specific mental interference at the time of examination. Furthermore, allowance is made for memory variations with age.

The test material is sufficiently varied to provide qualitative observations which may have additional value. One can distinguish, for example, cases in which remote memory, data of personal identification, and extremely familiar, well-learned patterns are retained in contrast to faulty performance with the formation of new learning associations; such findings often provide confirmatory evidence of disturbances of attention and concentration. One can compare retention of meaningful material and rote memory. Finally, one can isolate specific disturbance in the area of space-form perception and visual memory. These features make the test findings especially helpful in problems involving differential diagnosis.

The test was designed for use with adults only, and the scoring involves the addition of certain constants to the raw score in order to equate scores at different age levels above twenty years. The test author has stated in a personal communication to the writer several years ago that the test might prove to be useful with adolescents by employing the same age-correction unit established for the 20- to 24-year group. This has not been subjected to experimental verification, but the practice has seemed to yield meaningful and consistent results with adolescents.

Because of its advantages over other similar techniques, this scale is appropriate to a wide variety of research studies. However, the lack of an alternate or parallel form has been felt, especially for those experimental designs which require a "test-retest" method. One group of investigators has recently proposed an alternate form which was designed to provide equivalent material for each of the test items (2). This has been published so recently that there has not been sufficient time for widespread use. However, if it proves to be an accurately equated alternate form it will extend the sphere of usefulness of the Wechsler Memory Scale even further.

Subject Index

A

Acculturation
  cognitive functioning relationship,
    368–370
  Wechsler score relationship, 370–377
AD, *see* Alzheimer's disease
Age effects
  prorated–standard index score
    discrepancies, 430–431
  subtests, 525
  Wechsler test factors, 190
Age norms 19
Alzheimer's disease
  diagnostic validity, 283–285
  likelihood ratios, 290–293, 298–300
  Wechsler factor sensitivities, 202–203
  Wechsler test administration, 497
American Sign Language, Wechsler scale
  accomodations, 461–462
AMF, *see* Auditory Memory Factor
Anthropometric testing 11–16
Aphasic patients, Vocabulary subtest issues,
  504
ARDI, *see* Auditory Recognition Delayed
  Index
Arithmetic subtest
  description and history, 81–82
  impaired patient testing, 496
  practical issues, 505–506
ASL, *see* American Sign Language

Attention/Concentration factor, 106
Auditory Composite Index
  comparison with other index scores,
    238–239
  norm table, 163–164
  prorating and estimating, 423–424
  psychometric properties, 171–175
  rationale and development, 155–156,
    159
  scoring, 160–161
Auditory Delayed Index
  description, 108
  diagnostic validity for Alzheimer's
    patients, 282
  diagnostic validity, likelihood ratios,
    292–297
Auditory Delayed Recognition Index
  description, 114, 126
  new normative information, alternate,
    128–129
  problems associated with index,
    126–128
Auditory Immediate Index
  description, 108
  comparison with visual index, 235
Auditory Verbal Learning Test, 276
Auditory Verbal List Learning, 32, 34, 114,
  274
Auditory Verbal Memory Test, 109
AVLT, *see* Auditory Verbal Learning Test

B
Babcock Test of Mental Efficiency, 33
Base rates
  basic concepts, 287–290
  discrepancy, *see* Discrepancy base rates
  effect on Positive and Negative Predictive
    Values, 286–287
  likelihood ratio application, 290–293
Benton Visual Retention Test, 34
Bessel, Friedrich Wilhelm, 9–10
Bias effects, test–retest performance,
  308–312
Binet, Alfred, 17–18, 31, 535–536
Binet–Simon scales
  background, 394
  children's intelligence, 18–20
  influence on Wechsler scales 59, 62–63,
    67, 76, 81, 95–96
  tests of memory, 32, 95–96
Block Design subtest
  description and history, 65–66
  practical issues, 509–510
Brain dysfunction
  lateralized, Wechsler test sensitivity,
    525–526
  markers, discrepancy analysis, 234–235
  sensitivity, discrepancy analysis usefulness,
    230
Brain impairment, discrepancy analysis
    example
  damage *vs.* nuanced judgments,
    243–246
  empirical validation, 246–247
  overview, 240–241
  PSI, 242–243
  VIQ–PIQ, 241–242
Brain integrity, inferences from discrepancy
    data, 215
BRs, *see* Base rates
Burt, Cyril L., 537–538

C
California Verbal Learning Test
  characteristics, 34
  WMS-R comparison, 103–104

Category Fluency score likelihood ratios,
  290–291
Cattell, James McKeen
  biography, 539–540
  early Psychological Corporation work,
    15–16
  early work at Columbia College, 12–13
  failure of anthropometric tests, 16
  mental test development, 11–12
  questions about testing practices, 13–15
  Wechsler scales of intelligence, 26
Children, intelligence, Binet–Simon scales,
  18–20
Childrens Memory Scale, Family Pictures,
  119
CI, *see* Confidence Interval
Claparède, Edouard, 32, 541–542
Coding subtest, practical issues, 509
Cognitive assessment overview
  acculturation relationship, 368–370
  contemporary models, 149–150
  factor-analytic studies, 150–153
  joint factor-analytic studies, 153–154
  overview, 147–149
  post-war years, 366–367
  six-factor model, 155–157, 160
  Wechsler overview, 147–149
Cognitively compromised person,
    definition, 156
Cognitively normal person, definition,
    156
Conative factors, *see* Non-intellective factors
    of intelligence
COI, *see* Condition of interest
Comprehension subtest
  description and history, 62–65
  practical issues, 506–507
Condition of interest
  likelihood ratios, 292–293
  odds ratios, 282
Confidence Interval
  estimation accuracy evaluation, 398–399
  Full-Scale Intelligence Quotient, 429
Construct-irrelevant variance, Wechsler for
    disabilities, 453–454
Correspondence memory, representation of
    memory, 30–31

Culture Fair test, Matrix Reasoning
similarity, 68
Culture learning, see Acculturation

D
DA, see Discrepancy analysis
Deafness, Wechsler scale accomodations,
464–465
Delayed Memory Index
recommendations for use, 156, 157, 159,
176
WMS-III structure, 108
WMS-R criticisms, 102
Description, discrepancy data, 213–215
Diagnostic validity
definition, 273
extension to clinical utility, 285–287
group vs. individual statistics, 274–279
indices, 283–285
indices overview, 280–281
likelihood ratios, 290–291
odds ratio, 281–282
Difference scores, discrepancy analysis
clinical meaning vs. statistical significance,
212–213
descriptive vs. inferential use of data,
213–215
psychometric foundation, 213
Digit Span subtest
description and history, 75–77
impaired patient testing, 496
new normative tables for WAIS-III,
78–80
practical issues, 507–508
repeating instructions and items, 498–499
Digit Symbol subtest
army beta test, 22–23
coding description, 81
coding repeating instructions and items,
498
copy description, 82
description and history, 81–83
incidental learning description, 83
practical issues, 509
Disabilities, Wechsler scale accomodations

bad practices, 480–481
clinicians with disabilities, 476–477
construct-irrelevant variance, 453–454
construct underrepresentation, 454–455
deafness, 464–465
decision making model, 457
good practices, 479–480
intelligence construct representation,
455–456
learning disabilities, 470–474
legal issues, 457–459
motor impairments, 469–470
neuropsychological assessment, 474–475
overview, 449–453
subtest deletion, 456–457
test score effects, 459–463
visual disabilities, 465–469
Discrepancy analysis
clinical use and utility
co-occurring IQ-memory declines,
249–250
effect of brain dysfunction on index
score, 240–247
case examples, 244–246
insensitivity of global composite scores,
250–252
reliability, 249
subtest variability, 247–249
use of demographically adjusted scores,
254–256
clinical utility of index contrasts
brain dysfunction markers, 234–235
inter-WAIS-III contrasts, 235–236
inter-WMS-III contrasts, 236–237
sensitivity of visual memory, 232–234
VCI-PCI, 230–232
discrepancy-directionality vs.
bidirectional approaches
bidirectional discrepancies, 218–219
discrepancy directions, 225–229
impact of ability level, 220, 223, 224,
252–254
impact of comparison pairs, 219–222
IQ –memory comparisons, 237–240
new base rate tables of WAIS-III–WMS-
III see discrepancy base rates,
216–217, 259–270

Design Memory task, 32, 120–121
Dynamometer, definition, 109

E

Ebbinghaus, Hermann, 36, 95, 99, 543–544
Ecological validity, WMS-III development,
    105–106
Education effects
    prorated–standard index score
        discrepancies, 430–431
    Wechsler factors, 190–196
Ellis Island, immigrant assessment
    Goddard's contribution, 350–352
    inspection process, 346–350
    overview need for assessment, 345
    public health services physicians, 352–362
    immigration law, 397
    testing program, 354–356, 358–359
Error cost, brain damaged *vs.* nuanced
    judgments, 245–246
Error risk, brain damaged *vs.* nuanced
    judgments, 245–246
Ethnicity effects, Wechsler factor scores, 198
Everday memory, associated research, 31
Evidence-based health care, serial
    assessment, 304–305

F

Faces subtest
    practical issues, 514
    WMS-III background and structure,
        115–118
    WMS-III visual memory subtest
        comparability, 527
Factor-analytic studies
    cognitive functioning, 149–150
    joint WMS-III/WMS-III studies,
        153–154
    Wechsler scales, 150–153
    WMS, 152
    WMS-III, 131–132, 152–153
Family Pictures
    practical issues, 514–515

repeating instructions and items, 499
    WMS-III background and structure,
        118–119
Farrand, Livingston, early work with Cattell,
    12–13
Figural Memory Associates, criticisms in
    WMS-R, 103
Finding Reasons subtest, 63
Flock of Birds subtest, 57
"Flynn Effect", 45
Four-factor scoring system, WAIS-III
    structure, 46, 51–53
Fractional polynomial regression equations,
    189
FSIQ, *see* Full-Scale Intelligence Quotient
Full-Scale Intelligence Quotient
    alternatives to a FSIQ, 53
    discrepancy direction causes, 226–227
    discrepancy direction factors, 225–226
    discrepancy direction importance,
        227
    discrepancy size variation, 220–222
    estimation, 428–429
    evaluation, 441–442
    learning disability accomodations,
        470–471
    matrix reasoning contribution, 68–69
    memory index score similarity, 525
    prorated, accuracy, 442
    prorated estimate accuracy, 399–400
    prorated score, cognitive functioning
        effects, 430
    prorated score sensitivity and specificity,
        431–433
    test–retest change, 321
    VCI as premorbid status estimate, 238
    WAIS-III factor score comparison, 53
    Wechsler concept of FSIQ, 27–28

G

g, *see* General cognitive factor
Galton, Sir Francis
    biography, 545
    contributions to assessment, 10–11
Gender effects

prorated–standard index score
    discrepancies, 430–431
Wechsler factor scores, 194–196
General ability index, 53
General cognitive factor, 53, 211
General memory, 102
General Memory Index
    alternatives, 130–131
    discrepancy direction factors, 225–226
    estimation, 429–430
    evaluation, 441–442
    low-IQ subjects, 253
    prorated estimate accuracy, 399–400
    serial assessment effects, 328
    WMS-III structure and criticisms,
        130–131
    WMS-R criticisms, 102
Glueck, Bernard, Goddard criticisms, 353
GMI, see General Memory Index
Goddard, Henry Herbert
    biography, 547–548
    immigrant assessment contributions,
        350–352
    criticisms of Goddard's method, 352–362
    use of the Binet-Simon scale, 19
Goodenough, Florence L., 549–550
Group statistics, diagnostic validity, 274–279

H
Halstead Neuropsychological Test Battery,
    96
Health care, serial assessment, 304–305
Health maintenance organization, 305
Healy, William, 551–552
Hit Rate, diagnostic validity index, 280
HMO, see Health maintenance organization
HR, see Hit Rate

I
Idea scoring, Logical Memory subtest,
    111–112
IMI, see Immediate Memory Index
Immediate Memory Index, 130–131

overview, 130–131
recommendations for use, 156–157, 159,
    176
Immigrants, cognitive assessment see non-
    english speaker (testing)
Individual differences
    Cattell's early work, 11
    contributions from astronomy, 9–10
    scientific study, 7–8
Individual statistics, diagnostic validity,
    274–279
Inference, discrepancy data, 213–215
Information subtest
    description and history, 61–62
    estimation accuracy evaluation, 397–398
Information and orientation subtest, 125
    practical issues, 506, 517
    WMS-III structure, 125
Inspections, Ellis Island, 346–350
Intellectual levels, discrepancy size variation,
    220–222
Intellectual-memory discrepancies
    false negative for declines, 250
    high-IQ subject false positives, 252
    low-IQ subject false negatives, 252–254
    new base rate tables, 258–270
    sensitivity, 250–252
Intelligence level
    discrepancy direction causes, 226–227
    discrepancy direction factors, 225–226
    discrepancy direction importance,
        227–228
    distinction from memory, 32
    research pioneers, 533–559
    Wechsler scales, 26–29
Intelligence Quotient
    discrepancy direction causes, 226–227
    discrepancy direction factors, 225–226
    discrepancy direction importance,
        227–229
    discrepancy false negatives, 252–254
    discrepancy false positives, 252
    discrepancy size variation, 220–222
    index discrepancy score use, 520–521
    introduction of term, 19
    memory index score similarity, 525
    practice effects, 309–310

Intelligence Quotient (*continued*)
  prorating accuracy, 442
  prorating options, 521–522
  retention of intelligence quotient in
      WAIS-III, 44, 47, 148–149
  traditional memory comparisons,
      237–238
  use as a stratification variable in the WMS-
      III, 106–107
  WAIS-III factor score comparison, 52
  WAIS-III *vs.* WAIS-R, 527
  Wechsler's conceptualization, 26–27
Intelligence test history
  Cattell's Columbia College work, 12–13
  Cattell's early work, 11–12
  children, Binet-Simon scales, 18–20
  early Psychological Corporation work,
      15–16
  failure of Cattell's tests, 16
  Galton's early work, 10–11
  military, Yerkes' work, 20–26
  Spearman's two-factor theory, 16–17
  Thorndike's multifactorial theory, 16–17
IQ, *see* Intelligence Quotient

K
Knox, Howard Andrew
  biography, 553–554
  contributions to Ellis Island testing
      program, 354–357, 360
Knox Cube imitation, 122–123

L
Language Preference, acculturation
    relationship, 371–376
Learning disabilities, Wechsler scale
    accomodations, 470–474
Letter–Number Sequencing subtest
  description, 74–75
  impaired patient testing, 496
  practical issues, 507–508
  repeating instructions and items, 498–499
  WAIS-III factor score comparison, 52–53

Level of Aspiration, inclusion in WAIS-R,
    56–57
Likelihood ratios
  category fluency scores, 290–291
  clinical application, 298
  definition, 290
  Wechsler ratios, 293–298
List Learning subtest, 114
Logical Memory subtest
  description and history, 109–112
  practical issues, 512–513
  retention rate norms, 522–523
  score inflation, 524
Logistic regression analysis, basic approach,
    279–280
LR, *see* Likelihood ratios

M
Manikin test, development, 72
Manual of the Mental Examination of Aliens,
    360–361
Matrix Reasoning subtest
  description, 68–69
  practical issues, 510–511
  repeating instructions and items, 498
  slow responder time limits, 518
Mayo Cognitive Factor Scores
  development by MOANS, 146
  likelihood ratio clinical application,
      299
  logistic regression analysis, 279
  overview, 276
Mayo Older Americans Normative Studies,
    146
MCFS, *see* Mayo Cognitive Factor Scores
Measurement error, test–retest performance,
    312
Measurement of Adult Intelligence, 561–562,
    568, 575–579
Memory assessment, historical factors,
    95–97
Memory concepts
  basic concept, 30–31
  clinical assessment, 31–35
  definition, 30

Memory Examination, contributions to
WMS-III development, 95–104
Memory Index
IQ score similarity, 525
Working Memory comparison, 236
Memory Quotient, computation, 99
Memory scores, traditional IQ comparisons,
237–238
Mental age
introduction of concept, 19
IQ determination, 19
Mental Control subtest
practical issues, 517
WMS-III description, 125–126
Mental illness, 9
Mentality, early laboratories, 10–11
Mental Measurement Yearbook, 561–562,
564
Mental retardation, 9
Mental test, development by Cattell,
11–12
Methode medico-pedagogique, 8
Military, intelligence tests, Yerkes' work,
20–26, 362–365
MOANS, *see* Mayo Older Americans
Normative Studies
Models
cognitive functioning, 155–157, 160
discrepancy analysis base-rate data
generation, 216–217
discrepancy analysis sensitivity, 251
Wechsler scale accomodation of
disabilities, 457
Motor impairments, Wechsler scale
accomodations, 469–470
MQ, *see* Memory Quotient
Multifactorial theory, E. L. Thorndike,
16–17

N
NAN, *see* National Academy of
Neuropsychology
Narrative recall, 109
Negative Predictive Value
base rate role, 287–289

definition, 286
diagnostic validity, 286–287
Neurocognitive impairment sensitivity, 185
Neuropsychiatric disorders, sensitivity of
Wechsler-corrected scores, 198–206
Neuropsychology
static to cognitive phase, 100
Wechsler scale accomodations,
474–475
Non-English speaker (testing),
post world war one testing, 366–368
recommendations for practice, 385–387
translated versions of the Wechser tests,
379–384
world war one testing, 21–23, 362–365
Nonintellective factors
contributions to intelligence, 29
flock of birds subtest, 57–58
level of aspiration subtest, 56
measurement, 56–58
Number squares subtest, 57
NPV, *see* Negative Predictive Value
Nuanced judgments, brain damage
comparison, 243–246
Null-hypothesis significance testing
diagnostic usefulness data analysis
comparison, 276, 279
mathematical terms, 279
Number Squares subtest, 57

O
Object Assembly subtest
description and history, 71–74
practical issues, 512
replacement by Matrix Reasoning, 68
Odds ratios
diagnostic validity for Alzheimer's patient,
284–285
overview, 281–282
Oral Word Association Test, 312
Origin of Familiar Things subtest, 63
ORs, *see* Odds ratios
Otis, Arthur Sinton, 555
Outcomes management, concept
introduction, 305

P
PA, *see* Picture Arrangement
Paired Associates Learning, 112–114
Perceptual Organization Index
    acculturation relationship, 372–374
    brain damaged *vs.* nuanced judgments,
        245
    brain dysfunction markers, 234
    diagnostic validity for Alzheimer's patient,
        284
    discrepancy base rate rarity variation, 220
    discrepancy base rates, 218–219
    discrepancy direction importance, 229
    discrepancy size variation, 222
    estimation results, 421–423
    evaluation, 439
    impaired patient testing, 497
    index-to-index discrepancies, 239–240
    likelihood ratios, 294–295, 297, 299
    neuropsychiatric disorders, 203
    PSI contrast, 236
    reliability, 249
    serial assessment effects, 330–332
    test–retest change, 321
    VCI contrast, 235
    WAIS-III factor score comparison, 53
    WMS-III score discrepancies, 238–239
Performance Intelligence Quotient
    discrepancies, brain impairment example,
        241–242
    learning disability accomodations,
        470–471
    Matrix Reasoning contribution, 68–69
    memory index score similarity, 525
    Picture Arrangement contribution,
        70–71
    regression to the mean, 313
    repeating instructions and items, 498
    serial assessment effects, 329
    WAIS-III factor score comparison, 53
Performance Scale, Yerkes' intelligence tests
    in military, 23
PHS, *see* Public Health Service
Pictorial Completion Test II, 67
Picture Arrangement
    description and history, 70–71
    practical issues, 511

Picture Completion test
    army beta test, 22
    description and history, 67–68
    practical issues, 508
Pintner, Rudolph, 557–558
PIQ, *see* Performance Intelligence Quotient
POI, *see* Perceptual Organization Index
Porteus, Stanley D., 559–560
Positive Predictive Value
    base rate role, 287–289
    definition, 286
    diagnostic validity, 286–287
Positive Protective Value, likelihood ratios,
    291–292
PPV, *see* Positive Predictive Value
Practice effects, test–retest performance,
    308–309
Predicted differences method, discrepancy
    analysis base-rate data, 216
Premorbid status, VCI as best estimate, 238
Procedural learning, practice effects, 309
Processing Speed Index
    brain damaged *vs.* nuanced judgments,
        245
    brain dysfunction markers, 234–235
    brain impairment example, 246–247
    discrepancies, brain impairment example,
        242–243
    discrepancy analysis usefulness, 230–232
    discrepancy direction importance, 229
    estimation results, 423–424
    evaluation, 439
    neuropsychiatric disorders, 203
    POI contrast, 236
    test–retest change, 321
Profile puzzle, 72
Prosopagnosia, 116
PSI, *see* Processing Speed Index
Psychology, definition, 303
Psychometrics
    diagnostic validity statistics, 276
    foundation of discrepancy analysis, 213
    Wechsler index score development, 161,
        172
Public Health Service
    Ellis Island inspection service, 346
    official Goddard criticisms, 352–362

R

Raven's Standard Progressive Matrices, 68

RCI, *see* Reliable Change Index

Recognition Memory Test
    data inadequacy in WMS-R, 104
    modeling after Memory for Faces, 117
    WMS-III structure, 114

Regression to the mean, test–retest
    performance, 313–314

Reliability coefficients
    psychometric properties, 161, 172
    Wechsler index score development,
        172–173

Reliable Change Index
    characteristics, 316–317
    definition, 314–315

Reply to an Abstract Question, 63

Russell, Elbert, WMS-III revisions, 99–100

S

S_{diff}, *see* Standard error of differences

Schizophrenia, Wechsler factor sensitivities,
    203

SE_M, *see* Standard error of measurement

Sensitivity
    diagnostic validity index, 280
    discrepancy analysis, 250–252
    discrepancy analysis in brain dysfunction,
        230
    Full-Scale IQ *vs.* prorated FSIQ, 431–433
    intellectual–memory discrepancies,
        250–252
    Visual New Learning Discrepancy
        analysis, 232–234
    Wechsler-corrected scores in
        neuropsychiatric disorders, 198–206
    Wechsler joint factor scores, 401–402
    Wechsler test in lateralized brain
        dysfunction, 525–526

Serial assessments
    case examples, 306–307
    demographically corrected scores,
        326–327
    effect on discrepancy score base rates,
        327–332

evidence-based health care, 304–305
    practice effects, 309–310

Sex effects, *see* Gender effects

Similarities subtest
    description and history, 62
    practical issues, 504–505
    repeating instructions and items, 498

Simple differences method, 216

Six-factor model
    cognitive functioning, 155–157, 160
    discrepancy analysis base-rate data
        generation, 216–217
    discrepancy analysis sensitivity, 251

Sn, *see* Sensitivity

Sp, *see* Specificity

Spatial Sequential Learning Task, 124

Spatial Span
    practical issues, 515–516
    WMS-III description and history,
        122–124

Spearman, Charles
    biography, 561–562
    two-factor theory of intelligence, 16–17
    Wechsler scales of intelligence, 26–28

Specificity
    diagnostic validity index, 280
    Full-Scale IQ *vs.* prorated FSIQ,
        431–433
    WAIS-III/WMS-III joint factor scores,
        401–402

Sprague, E. K., 353–354

SRB Change Scores, *see* Standardized
    Regression-Based Change Scores

SSLT, *see* Spatial Sequential Learning Task

Standard error of differences, 315–316

Standard error of estimate, 316

Standard error of measurement
    definition, 173
    test–retest performance, 312

Standard error of prediction, 316

Standardized Regression-Based Change
    Scores
    application, 323–326
    characteristics, 317–318
    definition, 314
    demographically corrected factors, 327
    Wechsler test–retest change, 318–323

Standards for Educational and Psychological Testing, 366, 392
Statistical significance
    diagnostic validity, 275
    discrepancy analysis, overview, 212–213
Storehouse memory, 30–31
A Study of American Intelligence, 365
Symbol Search subtest
    description, 89
    practical issues, 511–512
    repeating instructions and items, 498
    WAIS-III factor score comparison, 52–53

T
TBI, *see* Traumatic brain injury
Temporal lobe epilepsy, Wechsler factors, 204–205
Terman, Lewis M.,
    biography, 563–564
    committee on psychological examination of recruits, 20, 35
    Stanford adaptations of the Binet-Simon scales, 19
Test–Retest performance
    bias effects, 308–312
    meaningful and reliable change, 318–323
    measurement error, 312
    regression to the mean, 313–314
Test-Retest stability coefficient
    WMS-III index scores, 172–173
    working *vs.* auditory memory factors, 310–311
The Psychological Corporation
    Cattell's early testing, 15–16
    events preceding WAIS-III development, 54
    index-to-index discrepancies, 239
    likelihood ratio clinical application, 298
    likelihood ratios and WAIS-II and WMS-III indices, 293
    POI and WMS-III score discrepancies, 238–239
    WAIS-III revised test structure, 46
    Wechsler diagnostic validity indices, 283
    Wechsler distinction, 146, 151

WMS-III input, 94
WMS-R publication delays, 101–102
Thorndike, Edward Lee
    biography, 565–566
    multifactorial theory of intelligence, 16–17
    Wechsler scales of intelligence, 26–27
Thurstone, Louis Leon, 567–568
TLE, *see* Temporal lobe epilepsy
TPC, *see* The Psychological Corporation
Trail Making Test, practice effects, 311
Traumatic brain injury
    Matrix Reasoning susceptibility, 69
    WAIS-III subtest sensitivity, 526
    Wechsler factor sensitivities, 202–203
T-scores
    demographic corrections, 187–189
    demographic effects and corrections, 184
    Wechsler-corrected scores sensitivities, 200
Two-factor theory, Charles Spearman, 16–17

U
United States Army
    Alpha and Beta test for WWI non-English speaker, 362–366
    Alpha test Arithmetic subtest, 79
    intelligence tests, Yerkes' work, 20–26

V
Value-driven health care, serial assessment, 305
Variance, Wechsler tests for disabilities, 453–454
VCI, *see* Verbal Comprehension Index
Verbal Comprehension Index
    acculturation relationship, 372–374
    brain damaged *vs.* nuanced judgments, 245
    brain dysfunction markers, 234
    brain impairment example, 246–247

diagnostic validity for Alzheimer's patient, 284
discrepancy analysis usefulness, 230–232
discrepancy base rate rarity variation, 220
discrepancy base rates, 218–219
discrepancy direction, 226–227
discrepancy direction importance, 229
discrepancy size variation, 222
estimation accuracy, 397–399
estimation results, 419–421
evaluation, 439
impaired patient testing, 497
index-to-index discrepancies, 239
likelihood ratio clincial application, 299
likelihood ratios, 294–295, 297
POI conventional contrast, 235
premorbid status estimate, 238
reliability, 249
serial assessment effects, 330–332
SRB application, 324
test–retest change, 319, 321
WAIS-III factor score comparison, 53
WMI conventional contrast, 236
Verbal Intelligence Quotient
  discrepancies, brain impairment example, 241–242
  learning disability accomodations, 470–471
  memory index score similarity, 525
  repeating instructions and items, 498
  serial assessment effects, 329
  WAIS-III factor score comparison, 53
Verbal Paired Associates
  practical issues, 514
  repeating instructions and items, 499
  score inflation, 524
  WMS-III description and history, 112–114
Verbal subtests, WMS-R criticisms, 102
VIQ, see Verbal Intelligence Quotient
Visual Delayed Memory
  serial assessment effects, 330–332
  SRB application, 324–326
  WMS-III structure, 114–115

Visual disabilities, Wechsler scale accomodations, 465–469
Visual Immediate Memory
  likelihood ratios, 294–300
  SRB application, 324
  WMS-III structure, 114–115
Visual Immediate Recall, 284
Visual Memory Composite score, 156
Visual Memory Index
  Auditory Index comparison, 237
  brain dysfunction markers, 234–235
  brain impairment example, 246–247
  criticisms in WMS-R, 103
  discrepancy analysis, 232–234
  estimation results, 427–428
  evaluation, 441
  Faces subtest, 117–118, 527
  index-to-index discrepancies, 239
  neuropsychiatric disorders, 203
  POI distributions, 222
  sensitivities, 185
  Wechsler approach, 160
Visual Memory (Original), discrepancy analysis, 233
Visual New Learning, sensitivity in discrepancy analysis, 232–234
Visual Paired Associates, criticisms in WMS-R, 103
Visual Reproduction subtest
  estimation results, 427–428
  impaired patient testing, 497
  practical issues, 516–517
  superfluous line scoring, 519–520
  WMS-III description and history, 119–122
Visual Spatial Span test, addition to WMS-R, 124
Vocabulary subtest
  description and history, 59–61
  practical issues, 503–504
VPA, see Verbal Paired Associates

W
WAIS-III, see Wechsler Adult Intelligence Scale III

WAIS-III–WMS-III Technical Manual
  auditory immediate and delayed index
    scores, 108
  basic WMS-III test description, 107–108
  conventional index contrasts, 235–236
  data analysis specifications, 396
  diagnostic validity evidence, 276
  discrepancy rarity data, 216
  factor scores in neurocognitive disorders,
    185
  five factor model, 152–153
  likelihood ratios, 293
  serial assessment effects on discrepancy
    base rates, 328
  subject samples, 186
  test–retest, 310
  useful discrepancy analysis index contrast,
    230–235
  WMS-III structure support, 131–132
  Working Memory Index, 122–126
WAIS-R, *see* Wechsler Adult Intelligence
    Scale, Revised
WB I, *see* Wechsler–Bellevue Intelligence
    Scale, Form I
WB II, *see* Wechsler–Bellevue Intelligence
    Scale, Form II
Wechsler, David
  biography, 569–570
  development of intelligence scales, 26–29
Wechsler Adult Intelligence Scale, Revised
  nonintellective factors, 56–58
  reasons to switch to WAIS-III, 490–491
  test score norms, 45
  WAIS-III IQ score similarities, 527
  WAIS-III revision necessity, 44–45
Wechsler Adult Intelligence Scale III
    administration
  administration options, 52
  frequently asked questions, 517–518
  goals of the revision, 44–47
  impaired patient testing, 496–497
  patient rapport, 494–496
  query place and methods, 500–501
  repeating instructions and items, 497–500
  teaching basics, 493–494
  testing limits, 501–503
  test introduction, 494–496

Wechsler Adult Intelligence Scale III
    advantages
  additional subtests, 492
  clinical reasons, 490–491
  standardization samples, 491–492
  test administration reasons, 492
Wechsler Adult Intelligence Scale III clinical
    issues
  arithmetic subtest, 505–506
  block design, 509–510
  coding subtest, 509
  comprehension subtest, 506–507
  digit span subtest, 507–508
  digit–symbol subtest, 509
  disability accomodation
    bad practices, 480–481
    basic challenges, 449–453
    clinicians with disabilities, 476–477
    construct-irrelevant variance, 453–454
    construct underrepresentation,
      454–455
    deafness, 464–465
    decision making model, 457
    good practices, 479–480
    intelligence construct representation,
      455–456
    learning disabilities, 470–474
    legal issues, 457–459
    motor impairments, 469–470
    neuropsychological assessment,
      474–475
    subtest deletion, 456–457
    test score effects, 459–463
    visual disabilities, 465–469
  information subtest, 506
  letter–number sequencing, 507–508
  matrix reasoning subtest, 510–511
  object assembly, 512
  picture arrangement, 511
  picture completion, 508
  similarities subtest, 504–505
  symbol search, 511–512
  vocabulary subtest, 503–504
Wechsler Adult Intelligence Scale III
    development
  arithmetic description, 79–81
  block design description, 65–66

change decision, 47–49
comprehension subtest description, 63–65
criticisms to changes, 49–51
digit span description, 75–79
digit symbol description, 81–83
factor score emphasis, 51–54
frequently asked questions, 519–520
goals of revision, 46–47
information subtest description, 61–62
letter number sequencing description, 74–75
matrix reasoning description, 68–69
necessity of revision, 44–45
object assembly description, 71–74
overview, 43
picture arrangement description, 70–71
picture completion description, 67–68
POI–PSI contrasts, 234
preceding events, 54–56
psychometric properties, 161, 172
reliability coefficients, 172–173
similarities subtest description, 62
subtest description overview, 58
symbol search description, 83
test score norms, 45
VCI–POI contrasts, 235
VCI–WMI contrasts, 236
vocabulary subtest description, 59–61
WISC-III contributions, 46
Wechsler Adult Intelligence Scale III factor scores
acculturation relationship, 370–377
age effects, 190
background, 392–396
clinical sample, 442–443
corrected T-scores, 187–189
data samples, 396–397
demographic effects and normative corrections, 183–184
diagnostic validity, 283–285
education effects, 190–196
estimation accuracy evaluation, 397–399
estimation results, 402–419
ethnicity effects, 198
full-scale IQ estimation, 428–429
general memory index estimation, 429–430
metric conversion of scores, 397
order effects, 443–444
overview, 181–183, 391–392
perceptual organization estimation, 421–423
processing speed estimation, 423–424
prorated estimate accuracy, 399–400
reduced battery length effects, 443–444
sensitivities, 185, 198–206
sensitivity and specificity, 401–402
sex effects, 196–198
subject characteristic effects, 400–401
subject samples, 186–187
subtest substitution-based estimate accuracy, 400
verbal comprehension estimation, 419–421
working memory factor, 424–425
Wechsler Adult Intelligence Scale III interpretation
age effects, 525
demographic variable effects, 524–525
IQ/index discrepancy score use, 520–521
IQ/memory index score similarities, 525
IQ prorating options, 521–522
IQ scores, WAIS-R similarities, 527
lateralized brain dysfunction sensitivity, 525–526
subtest inclusion in four index scores, 526–527
subtest sensitivity to brain injury, 526
Wechsler Adult Intelligence Scale III serial assessment
case examples, 306–307
demographically corrected scores, 326–327
effect on discrepancy score base rates, 327–332
Wechsler Adult Intelligence Scale III test–retest performance
bias effects, 308–312
meaningful and reliable change, 318–323
measurement error, 312
regression to the mean, 313–314

Wechsler Adult Intelligence Scale
III–Wechsler Memory Scale III Index
contrasts
  index-to-index discrepancies, 239–240
  POI–WMS-III score discrepancies,
    238–239
  traditional IQ–Memory comparisons,
    237–238
  VCI as premorbid status estimate, 238
Wechsler–Bellevue Intelligence Scale
  factor-analytic studies, 150
  memory scale comparison, 33
Wechsler–Bellevue Intelligence Scale, Form
I
  Block Design description, 66
  development, 27–28
  events preceding WAIS-III development,
    55
  Information subtest description, 61–62
  Object Assembly description, 72–73
  publication, reviews, promotional
    material, 561–563, 565–567,
    569–574
  Similarities subtest description, 62
  subtest background, 393–395
  Vocabulary subtest description, 59–60
Wechsler–Bellevue Intelligence Scale, Form
II, 55–56
Wechsler Intelligence Scale for Children,
  Revised, 44–45
Wechsler Intelligence Scale for Children III
  contributions to WAIS-III, 46
  factor-analytic studies, 150–151
  symbol search description, 83
  WAIS-III factor score comparison, 51, 53
Wechsler Memory scale, 98–101
  russell modifications, 99–100
Wechsler Memory Scale, Revised criticisms,
  102–104
  initial revision, 34
  logical memory subtest, 109
  overview and history, 101–104
  practice effects, 307
  reasons to switch to WMS-III, 490–491
  visual reproduction subtest, 121
  visual spatial Span test addition, 124
Wechsler Memory Scale III administration

frequency asked questions, 517–518
impaired patient testing, 497
patient rapport, 494–496
query place and methods, 501
repeating instructions and items, 497–500
teaching basics, 493–494
testing limits, 501–503
test introduction, 494–496
Wechsler Memory Scale III advantages
  additional subtests, 492
  clinical reasons, 490–491
  standardization samples, 491–492
  test administration reasons, 492
Wechsler Memory Scale III clinical issues
  disability accomodation
    bad practices, 480–481
    basic challenges, 450–453
    clinicians with disabilities, 476–477
    construct-irrelevant variance, 453–454
    construct underrepresentation,
      454–455
    deafness, 464–465
    decision making model, 457
    good practices, 479–480
    intelligence construct representation,
      455–456
    learning disabilities, 470–474
    legal issues, 457–459
    motor impairments, 469–470
    neuropsychological assessment,
      474–475
    subtest deletion, 456–457
    test score effects, 459–463
    visual disabilities, 465–469
  faces I and II, 514
  family pictures I and II, 514–515
  information and orientation, 517
  logical memory I and II, 512–513
  mental control, 517
  spatial span, 515–516
  verbal paired associates I and II, 514
  visual reproduction I and II, 516–517
  word list I and II, 516
Wechsler Memory Scale III development
  attention/concentration factor, 106
  auditory immediate and delayed index,
    108

basic tasks and stimuli, 93–94
basic test, 107–108
change decisions, 47, 49
co-norming with WAIS III, 54
contributing historical factors, 95–97
criticisms to changes, 49, 51
description and structure, 167–181
goals and conception of revision, 104–106
index and composite configuration, 107
initiation, 94–95
input from The Psychological
    Corporation, 94
limitations and weaknesses, 100–101
memory quotient computation, 99
original subtests, 98
psychometric properties, 161, 172
reliability coefficients, 172–173
standardization sample, 106–107
Wells and Martin memory examination
    contributions, 97–98
Wechsler memory scale III factor scores
acculturation relationship, 370–377
age effects, 190
auditory memory estimation, 425–426
background, 392–396
clinical sample, 442–443
corrected T-scores, 187–189
data samples, 396–397
demographic effects and normative
    corrections, 183–184
diagnostic validity, 283–285
education effects, 190–196
estimation accuracy evaluation, 397–399
estimation results, 402–419
ethnicity effects, 198
general memory index estimation,
    429–430
metric conversion of scores, 397
order effects, 443–444
overview, 181–183, 391–392
prorated estimate accuracy, 399–400
reduced battery length effects, 443–444
scoring, 519–520
sensitivities, 185, 198–206, 401–402
sex effects, 196–198
specificity, 401–402
subject characteristic effects, 400–401

subject samples, 186–187
subtest substitution-based estimate
    accuracy, 400
visual memory estimation, 427–428
working memory factor, 424–425
Wechsler Memory Scale III index contrasts
auditory vs. visual Index, 237
working memory vs. memory indexes,
    236
Wechsler Memory Scale III interpretation
age effects, 525
auditory recognition scores, 524
demographic variable effects, 524–525
floor and ceiling effects, 523–524
IQ/memory index score similarities, 525
lateralized brain dysfunction sensitivity,
    525–526
logical memory retention rate norms,
    522–523
visual memory subtest–faces subtest
    comparability, 527
Wechsler Memory Scale III serial assessment
case examples, 306–307
demographically corrected scores,
    326–327
effect on discrepancy score base rates,
    327–332
Wechsler Memory Scale III Standardization
    edition, letter number sequencing
    subtest, 74–75
Wechsler Memory Scale III structure
auditory immediate index scores, 108
auditory recognition delayed index,
    126–130
basic process optional tasks, 125
delayed index scores, 108–112
family pictures, 118–119
general and immediate memory indexes,
    130–131
information and orientation subtest,
    125
logical memory 109–112
memory for faces, 115–118
mental control subtest, 125–126
spatial span, 122–124
support, 131–132
verbal paired associates, 112–114

Wechsler Memory Scale III structure
 (*continued*)
 visual immediate and visual delayed
  Index, 114–115
 visual reproduction subtest, 119–122
 word lists, 114
Wechsler Memory Scale III test–retest
  performance
 bias effects, 308–312
 meaningful and reliable change, 318–323
 measurement error, 312
 regression to the mean, 313–314
Wechsler Scale overview
 development of intelligence scales, 26–29
 early discrepancy analysis, 211–212
 publication, 33–34, 564, 583–584
Wells, Frederic Lyman, 571–572
Whipple, Guy Montrose, 573–574
Wide Range Assessment of Memory and
  Learning, 119
Williams Scale for the Measurement of
  Memory, 34
WISC-III, *see* Wechsler Intelligence Scale
  for Children III
WISC-R, *see* Wechsler Intelligence Scale for
  Children, Revised
WMF, *see* Working Memory Factor
WMI, *see* Working Memory Index
WMS-III, *see* Wechsler Memory Scale III
WMS-III Administration and Scoring Manual,
  157
Woodworth, Robert Session, 575–576
Word Lists
 practical issues, 516
 WMS-III structure, 114
Working Memory factor
 acculturation relationship, 376

 auditory memory factor comparison,
  310–311
 estimation results, 424–425
 evaluation, 440
 memory index comparison, 236
 neuropsychiatric disorders, 203
 test–retest change, 321
Working Memory Index
 VCI conventional contrast, 236
 Wechsler approach, 160
 WMS-III spatial span, 122–124
World War I, non-english speaker testing,
  362–366
World War II, memory assessment after,
  96–97
WRAML, *see* Wide Range Assessment of
  Memory and Learning
Wundt, Wilhelm
 early laboratories, 10
 individual difference study initiation, 7–8
 psychological science contributions, 8–9

Y
Yerkes, Robert Mearns
 biography, 577–578
 intelligence tests in military, 20–26
 non-English speaker testing in World War
  I, 362–364

Z
Z-scores, Standard Regression-Based
 change scores, 318